http://www.fashion.tripnet.se The Fashion Directory.
http://www.firstview.com first VIEW Collections Online.
http://www.headbooks.com Headbooks Online.
http://www.hsn.com Home Shopping Network.
http://www.igedo.com Igedo trade show.
http://www.kidsshow.com International Kids Fashion Sho...
http://www.lectra.com Lectra Systems.
http://www.londonfashionweek.co.uk London Fashion We...
http://www.magiconline.com MAGIC trade show.
http://www.metmuseum.org The Metropolitan Museum of Art.
http://www.mimm.com Miami Trade Mart.
http://www.montrealfashionmart.com Montreal Fashion Mart.
http://www.premierevision.fr Premiere Vision Trade Show (France).
http://www.pretaporter.com Prêt-à-Porter.
http://www.textileshow.com Textile Show.
http://www.textrade.com Global Textiles Network.
http://www.thehome.com Home Fashion Information Network.
http://www.tsnn.com Trade Show News Network.
http://www.virtualrags.com/links.htm Virtual Rags. Various fashion links.
http://www.visualstore.com Visual Store On-line resource for Visual Merchandisers.
http://www.woolmark.com The Wool Bureau.
http://www.worldfashioncentre.nl World Fashion Centre (The Netherlands).
http://www.worldmedia.fr/fashion Fashion Live. Fashion coverage of Paris shows.
http://www1.interstoff.de/intst_brand Interstoff Trade Show (Germany).

Online Sellers

http://barnesandnoble.com Barnes and Noble
http://store.yahoo.com The Yahoo Store. For setting up an e-commerce site.
http://www.amazon.com Amazon.com.
http://www.bloomingdales.com Bloomingdales.
http://www.bluefly.com Bluefly.
http://www.bonton.com Bon-Ton Stores.
http://www.carrefour.fr Carrefour (France).
http://www.catalogcity.com Catalog City. Links to various direct response catalogs.
http://www.dillards.com Dillards Department Stores.
http://www.eatons.com Eaton's (Canada).
http://www.dhc.com Dayton Hudson Corporation. Homepage for Dayton Hudson,
    Marshall Field's, Target, and Mervyn's California.
http://www.federated-fds.com Federated Department Stores.
http://www.galerieslafayette.com/gb/home/sommaire.html Galeries Lafayette. French
    department store.
http://www.gap.com Gap.
http://www.gotts.com Gottschalks.
http://www.jcpenney.com J.C. Penney.
http://www.kmart.com Kmart.
http://www.landsend.com Land's End.
http://www.llbean.com L.L. Bean.
http://www.macys.com Macy's.
http://www.marks-and-spencer.com Marks & Spencer (UK).
http://www.maycompany.com May Company.
http://www.mercstores.com Mercantile Stores.
http://www.modacad.com/home/home_frame.html Modacad Inc. E-commerce and
    e-merchandising firm.
http://www.neimanmarcus.com Neiman Marcus.
http://www.nordstrom.com Nordstrom.
http://www.saksincorporated.com Saks Incorporated. Homepage for Proffitt's, McRae's,
    Younkers, Herberger's, Carson Pirie Scott, and Saks Fifth Avenue.
http://www.scars.com Sears, Roebuck.

(cont'd. on inside backcover)

PROMOTION IN THE MERCHANDISING ENVIRONMENT

PROMOTION IN THE MERCHANDISING ENVIRONMENT

Kristen K. Swanson

NORTHERN ARIZONA UNIVERSITY

Judith C. Everett

NORTHERN ARIZONA UNIVERSITY

FAIRCHILD PUBLICATIONS

New York

Executive Editor: Olga Kontzias
Assistant Editor: Beth Applebome
Production Editor: Sylvia L. Weber
Copy Editor: Donna Frassetto
Art Director: Mary Siener
Production Manager: Priscilla Taguer

Cover Design: Eva Ruutopõld
Cover Photo: Stephane Feugere

Library of Congress Catalog Card Number: 98-074602

ISBN: 1-56367-105-0

GST R 133004424

Printed in the United States of America

CONTENTS

v

PART THREE   PROMOTION MIX

7   ADVERTISING AND THE CREATIVE PROCESS   178

8   PRINT MEDIA 216

PREFACE

Promotion is everywhere. We see it. We hear it. Sometimes we welcome it into our homes and businesses, and at other times it invades our world without our permission. Promotion is exciting and creative, entertaining and informative, and influences us every day on a conscious and subconscious level. We cannot dismiss promotion. The purpose of *Promotion in the Merchandising Environment* is to explain the process of promotion and to describe the promotion mix tools available for creating successful campaigns. This book focuses on the comprehensive nature of promotion in the merchandising environment of fashion and related goods and emphasizes the changing nature of promotion in a global marketplace.

Several themes are evident throughout this text. The first theme is the concept of integrated marketing communications (IMC). In an IMC environment, all promotion elements are thought of as a single communication system with each element supporting the objectives of every other element. Advertising, direct marketing, sales promotion, publicity and public relations, personal selling, special events, fashion shows, and visual merchandising work together to communicate the same message about the product, brand, or organization to the end user. Integrated marketing communications also present a consistent message to the public, including suppliers, competitors, members of the firm or other sponsoring organization, and the media. IMC is reinforced in each chapter with industry examples.

A second theme is the global nature of promotion. In today's society, promotion is undeniably global. With advanced communication and transportation technologies, companies have the ability to locate nearly anywhere in the world. While much promotion is still at the local or national level, manufacturers, designers, and retailers must be able to communicate in the global economic system. Examples of international promotions are included throughout this text.

Changes in technology are driving communications and promotion, the third theme of this book. Technological changes include the rapid increase in the use of computers and the transfer of data by the industry and consumers. Promotion strategies that once were limited to live performances, print, or broadcast formats, must now consider the computer as a means of communication. Additionally, communication technologies are revolutionizing the way we send and receive promotional information. Promotion tools now include satellite, cable, fiber optics, and electronic devices. To address the rapidly changing technology in promotion, we feature a future trends segment at the conclusion of each chapter.

This book focuses on the merchandising environment. We consider merchandising to include forecasting what customers want to buy, investigating where to find that merchandise in the marketplace, determining the price the customer is willing to pay, and making it available through the retail store or other merchandising outlets where the customer is willing to buy the merchandise. Promotion is a key element at each step of the process. In the merchandising environment, promotion is twofold. It is an essential information source for end users to keep abreast of the global marketplace. It is also a fundamental strategy to fulfill the merchandising task for manufacturers, designers, and retailers. This text features examples from distribution channels at all levels to explain the role of promotion in the merchandising field.

The authors believe that fashion is evident in many product categories beyond clothing and accessories, and therefore, while the majority of examples in this text are from clothing and closely related categories, we have included appropriate examples to broaden students' thinking about promotion. Promotion extends to fields beyond fashion. This text is written to teach techniques that can be used in a fashion environment or transferred to other product categories.

The skills necessary to become a promotion practitioner are stressed throughout this text. Photographs, illustrations, checklists, tables, and real-world examples are part of every chapter to encourage creativity in those readers who will eventually produce promotion campaigns. To engage the reader in thinking beyond the boundaries of the text, each chapter features two readings on the topic that provide perspective. The readings range from how-to discussions to case studies to interviews with professionals in the industry.

Other features of the text include chapter objectives and summaries; highlighted key terms, questions for discussion, and additional resources for each chapter; and a comprehensive glossary. An Instructor's Guide has also been developed to assist instructors with suggestions for activities, field trips, and guest speakers to enrich the course.

This text is written to give a logical and informative order to promotion, from basic concepts to specific activities. As teachers and authors, we realize that course curriculums are not always prepared according to a text. It has been our goal, in writing this book, to provide the instructor who teaches all promotion mix aspects in one course with enough information to cover each subject adequately. We also realize that some instructors pull out certain topics, such as forecasting, fashion shows, or visual merchandising, and teach those as independent courses with textbooks specific to the course topic. Therefore, this book is written with the understanding that the chapters may be used independently or collectively to introduce part of the promotion industry or to provide a comprehensive view.

Promotion is fun, exciting, and changing daily. When we first started writing this text, electronic retailing and other technologies were only ideas. As we finished, e-commerce was commonplace. We can only guess what new technologies will emerge in the future. We hope you will find promotion as exciting as we do. We watch television, listen to the radio, read fashion magazines and newspapers, and surf the Net, always finding new and creative promotions.

We would like to thank the following individuals for their assistance with this text: Rebecca Pierson of Union Bay, a former student and now a successful professional in the industry; Carmela Carratie and David Wolfe of the Doneger Group; Katherine Flintoff of Mervyn's; Christine Walker of Walker Media; Helen Atkins of Pretty Polly; and Pam Esser of Esser Designs.

Reviewers selected by the publisher were also very helpful. They include Cindi Baker, Berkeley College; Barbara Frazier, Western Michigan University; Ruth Glock, Iowa State University; Michele Granger, Southwest Missouri State University; Shelley Harp, Texas Tech University; Patricia Huddeston, Michigan State University; Frances Huey, ICM School of Business; Kim K.P. Johnson, University of Minnesota; Gloria Johnston, Fashion Institute of Design and Merchandising; Jamie Kridler, East Tennessee University; Suzanne Marshall, California State University—Long Beach; Barbara Oliver, Colorado State University; Lynda Gamans Poloian, New Hampshire College; Carolyn Predmore, Manhattan College; William Rogers, University of Arizona; Tom Sands, Nassau Community College; Nancy Stanforth, Oklahoma State University; and Carol Tuntland, California State University—Los Angeles.

During the writing of this book, there was a popular television advertisement for a packaging service. It went something like this, "Up on the top floor, the marketing guru is giving a lecture on *thinking outside the box*. Meanwhile, you are down in shipping concerned with *what's in the box.*" We hope this book gives you a good foundation for *working within the box* and at the same time causes you to think *outside the box*.

Kristen K. Swanson
Judith C. Everett

Role of Promotion

Figure 1.1

Citizen watch company captures the international market with its slogan, "How the world tells time."

chapter 1

PROMOTION: A GLOBAL PERSPECTIVE

"*Citizen. How the World Tells Time,*" is the global promotional theme of this watch manufacturer's advertising campaign, begun in 1993. The campaign translated easily from one country to another and remained successful for well over 5 years. Citizen grew to number one in market share for the over-$50 watch category in the United States from 1993 to 1998. The firm capitalized on its global slogan without losing sight of cultural differences among its customers. According to Citizen president Laurence Grunstein, "I think the world is getting smaller, the Internet is helping that, and in time this diversity in advertising may change" (Parr, 1998). The magazine advertisement from the campaign is shown in Figure 1.1.

After you have read this chapter, you should be able to:

Explain the roles of promotion and its function in a global society.

Distinguish promotion from marketing and merchandising.

Recognize the significance of communication in making consumers aware of products and services.

Identify the essential components of the promotion mix within the merchandising environment.

Define integrated marketing communications (IMC) and explain why it is becoming increasingly important in planning and implementing a coordinated promotional mix.

As it is used in this book, **promotion** is a comprehensive term for all of the communication activities initiated by the seller to inform, persuade, and remind the consumer about products, services, and/or ideas offered for sale. The goal of the seller is to have consumers respond by purchasing what is offered. Although some authors feel that promotion involves only nonpersonal approaches to influencing consumers to buy products, this book looks at both personal methods, such as personal selling, and nonpersonal techniques, such as advertising or public relations, to achieve the goals of promotional communication.

Messages created by sellers are intended to attract, inform, and urge buyers to action. Domestic and foreign firms have generated billions of dollars worth of expenditures on various promotional activities. These messages are extremely significant to a firm's complete marketing and merchandising communications program, proof of which may be demonstrated by the dollars spent on advertising and by predictions for its continued growth. In 1980, the expenditures for advertising were $53 billion (Coen, 1994). By 1997, these figures had grown to $187.5, a gain of 7 percent over $175.2 billion in 1996 (Elliot, 1998c).

Ad spending is closely watched because it is believed to be a reliable indicator of the general health of the economy. For example, advertising as a percentage of gross domestic product (GDP) peaked in 1987 and 1988 at 2.35 percent as the economy boomed. When the recession took hold in 1992, the rate for advertising bottomed out at 2.12 percent of GDP. By 1998, Robert Coen, senior vice president and forecasting director at the McCann-Erickson USA unit of McCann-Erickson Worldwide Advertising, predicted that advertising as a percentage of GDP would "match or pass" the preview peak of 2.35, reflecting a strong economy at the end of the 20th century (Elliot, 1998c).

In the fashion field, advertising experts anticipated individual companies would need budgets of between $5 million and $10 million to compete in the 1990s (Lockwood, 1996a). In this highly competitive market, brands such as Tommy Hilfiger, Ralph Lauren, Guess, and Liz Claiborne spent in excess of $20 million to advertise and/or launch their sportswear businesses. These sums seem small, however, when compared to the advertising expenditures of other apparel and beauty businesses. According to Competitive Media Reporting, a New York research company that tracks how much advertisers spend just for placing an advertisement in the media, Nike topped all fashion and beauty competitors by spending over $211.2 million on advertising in 1997. Calvin Klein, Ralph Lauren, and Tommy Hilfiger were the top spenders in the American designer category, while European firms, such as Versace, Gucci, Prada, and Chanel, made the list of top 100 spenders (Lockwood, 1996a). These expenses represent just the costs for media placement and do not take into consideration the costs for producing the commercials or ads. The top 15 "big spenders" for media placement in 1997 are shown in Table 1.1.

This chapter serves as the foundation for studying promotion by defining essential terms used in both academic and professional worlds. Because promotion means different things to different people, the chapter begins by comparing the role of promotion in today's domestic and global society. The global perspective of promotion is a key theme that starts here and is carried throughout the text, for so many firms are crossing international borders. Next, the fundamental terms *marketing, merchandising,* and *communi-*

Table 1.1   **The Top 15 Big Media Spenders in 1997**

Rank	Brand Name	1997 U.S. Media Expenditures (In Dollars)
1	Nike	211,232,200
2	L'Oreal	160,000,000
3	Levi's	100,130,700
4	Revlon	95,901,800
5	Cover Girl	91,351,300
6	Oil of Olay	84,275,500
7	Maybelline	83,489,200
8	Estée Lauder[a]	71,051,900
9	Neutrogena	67,677,300
10	De Beers Diamonds	60,492,900
11	Coty	56,274,400
12	Ralph Lauren/Polo[b]	55,849,500
13	Calvin Klein[c]	52,693,900
14	Wrangler Jeans	39,273,600
15	Tommy Hilfiger[d]	39,090,200

[a]Media spending for the Estée Lauder brand only

[b]Media spending for all Ralph Lauren, Polo, and Polo Sport collections, as well as licensed products such as footwear, home furnishings, Chaps, and Lauren.

[c]Media spending for all Calvin Klein company and licensed lines.

[d]Tommy Hilfiger fragrances are included with the brand total.

Adapted from: Top 100 fashion and beauty advertisers: The big spenders. (1998, May 15). *Women's Wear Daily* (Section II, p. 8).

cation are considered. The chapter then briefly defines the individual tools of promotion used to disseminate messages—advertising, direct marketing, sales promotion, publicity and public relations, personal selling, special events, fashion shows, and visual merchandising—before introducing the concept of integrated marketing communication. Chapter 1 concludes with a discussion about future trends in global promotion.

THE ROLES OF PROMOTION

Promotion means different things to different people. To some people promotion is strictly a business activity. Individuals or firms involved in both public and private sectors use promotional messages to communicate with their target markets. Advertising agencies create promotional situations, and retail stores use promotion to create interest in their products and sales environment. These communications are critical to the success of a company. Messages can be presented in the form of advertisements or transmitted through other promotional methods such as direct mail or fashion show productions.

To other people promotion may be thought of as a social phenomenon. Nearly everyone in the contemporary world is affected by various forms of promotion. This force can be found in social, legal, and ethical environments. Advertising and other promotional activities may be used to promote various causes. Retailers might encourage high school art students to participate in a poster design contest, demonstrating a safety concern, prevention of illegal activities, or ways to protect the environment. By displaying their works of art, the retailer may gain recognition as a responsible citizen of the community and may attract new customers. Political candidates use the public media to promote their economic, environmental, social, or political points of view.

To still others, promotion is a basic element of a free enterprise system. It helps manufacturers and merchandisers make consumers aware of the products and services that are available. Billions of dollars are spent annually to inform customers of the opening of a new store or the specifications of a new and better computer software application or hardware design.

Various techniques or strategies of promotion may be viewed as a positive force accelerating change or as an unnecessary expense influencing people to purchase unwanted products. No matter how these activities are viewed, promotion remains an important element in the global marketplace.

GLOBAL NATURE OF PROMOTION

The term *global* is used when referring to something with worldwide implications. In business, **globalization** is the integration of international trade and foreign investment. As the 21st century begins, the world's economies are roughly as intertwined as they were in 1913 (Uchitelle, 1998b). Despite two world wars and the Great Depression that attempted to dismantle global integration during the 20th century, advanced communication and transportation technologies have created multiple worldwide consumer markets and sources for producing or acquiring merchandise. Today, companies are able to locate almost anywhere in the world, aided by information technology that vastly increases the speed of transactions across borders. Multinational firms, such as IBM, Royal Dutch/Shell, and Imperial Chemical Industries, have led the way for other firms by integrating revenues, research, finances, stockholders, and management over many countries.

While a borderless global economy has been the goal of some individuals and companies, others have disagreed with this movement. Despite interest in overseas sales and investment, nationality binds firms to their home countries. "What we have is United States, European, and Japanese corporations trying to dress in global clothing," according to William W. Keller, executive director of the Center for International Studies at the Massachusetts Institute of Technology (Uchitelle, 1998a).

Despite differences of opinions about the strengths and weaknesses of international trade, we are moving quickly in the direction of a global economy. In 1997 the total U.S. merchandise trade of exports plus imports topped $1.55 trillion, a 10 percent increase over 1996 ("Tracking U.S. Trade," 1998). With no slowdown in international trade anticipated, understanding world cultures and economies will be essential tools for individuals doing business and providing communication and promotional messages to consumers in the 21st century.

Reasons for the Transition to a Global Perspective

Promotional activities—along with other aspects of marketing—are becoming global in their reach, as demonstrated at the beginning of the chapter by the Citizen watch advertising campaign. Several important factors have contributed to the trend toward internationalization. Kitty Dickerson, professor and chair of the Department of Textile and Apparel Management at The University of Missouri-Columbia, identified five reasons for the shifts to a global perspective in the textile and apparel industries. The following have been among the most influential developments of the 20th century causing this change:

1. **Economic growth.** Sustained growth of global economies after World War II resulted in increased international trade. Although there have been economic fluctuations, trade has increased because (a) consumers have had the means to purchase products from various parts of the world, (b) companies have been able to add capacity under the assumption that foreign consumers would be able to sustain demand, and (c) fewer restrictions have typically been applied to imports when the economy has been flourishing.
2. **Improved economic status of developing countries.** In recent years, developing nations have been exporting manufactured products such as apparel rather than exporting agricultural products and minerals. Thus, these developing nations have taken steps toward more economic and industrial expansion, especially in the fields of textiles and apparel.
3. **Increased global communication.** Communication technologies such as satellite transmissions and fiber optics have been introduced in the 20th century, reducing time and distance for international trade. These advances in communication technologies allow importers (individuals or companies that bring merchandise into a country) and exporters (individuals or companies that send merchandise to another country) to conduct business more quickly than ever before. Videoconferencing has been used by such firms as J. C. Penney to broadcast buyers' meetings showing new fashion lines and informing branch managers about promotional activities. Additionally, worldwide communication efforts have stimulated demand for products in various parts of the globe where demand never existed before.

    Demonstrating the impact of increased international communication, a visit to The Gap Internet home page offers viewers from anywhere in the world product information, news, advertising updates, company information, and a store locator service (Fig. 1.2). This firm enables a potential customer to find the nearest international store location or purchase products via the website.

4. **Improved transportation systems.** Transportation systems including airplanes, ships, and trains have made it easier for buyers to access areas almost anywhere in the world. Transportation systems permit individuals to travel farther and faster today than they did even a decade or two ago, contributing to a shrinking world.

5. **Institutional arrangements by business and government.** Various institutional innovations have been implemented to facilitate the exchange of goods and services and the transfer of funds for the payment of those goods and services (Dickerson, 1995).

Passage of various trade agreements, including the North American Free Trade Agreement (NAFTA) in 1994 and World Trade Organization (WTO) in 1995, has broken down traditional trade barriers and led to the global expansion of traditional U.S. retail stores. Despite economic uncertainty in both Mexico and Canada in 1994, by the end of the decade the outlook was more optimistic. In 1997, Mexico surpassed Japan as the United States' second largest export destination with exports to Mexico totaling $71.4 billion compared to $65.7 to Japan ("Tracking U.S. Trade," 1998).

As we have seen so far, breaking down trade barriers and increased interest in foreign products are just a couple of the reasons why retailers have entered into global arrangements. English firms such as Laura Ashley and Burberry's have had a presence in the United States for many years. Americans visiting London or Paris are just as likely to see a Gap store, or find Clinique or Revlon at the British or French department stores. Although Gap stores originated in San Francisco, branches of the retail giant can be found throughout the United States, as well as in the United Kingdom, France, Germany, and Japan. Highlighting this trend, a special report, compiled by Deloitte & Touche, on the "Global Powers of Retailing" was presented as a supplement to *Stores* magazine. Table 1.2 describes the top ten global retailers. With retailers, manufacturers, and designers taking a more global approach, the field of promotion must look beyond any national border.

Figure 1.2

The Gap Internet site offers viewers an opportunity to locate stores near their homes or make virtual visits to stores in the United States, Canada, the United Kingdom, France, Germany, or Japan.

In major U.S. retail organizations such as Sears, J. C. Penney, and Wal-Mart, the international reach of promotional activities is the norm. Brands such as Revlon and Maybelline are no longer simply domestic products; international product usage demands global product awareness. The article in Box 1.1 demonstrates how Zeller's, a Canadian retailer, included promotional strategies as part of the plan to protect itself from the expansion of Wal-Mart into Canada.

Thinking Globally, Acting Locally

Merchandise brands and retail store identities have become international. Today, a consumer can purchase a "Big Mac" in Moscow or a "Maharaja Mac" in New Delhi, or a "Chanel suit" in Paris, San Francisco, or Tokyo. McDonald's has recognized the need to practice **glocalization.** The term, coined by Hans Hijlkema, former president and founder of the European Marketing Confederation, refers to a combination of global branding practices and localized marketing (Miller, 1996b). McDonald's acted locally by customizing the traditional burger to a culture like the one in India that does not eat beef. Since the residents of New Delhi consider cows sacred, McDonald's introduced a two-mutton patty sandwich with special sauce, lettuce, cheese, pickles, and onions on a sesame seed bun (Miller, 1996b).

Table 1.2   **The Top 10 Global Retailers**

Rank	Country of Origin	Name of Company	Retail Format	1997 Retail Revenue ($Mil)	Countries of Operation
1	US	Wal-Mart	Discount, Warehouse	117,958	Argentina, Brazil, Canada, China, Germany, Mexico, Puerto Rico, US
2	US	Sears	Department, Specialty	41,296	US
3	France	Carrefour	Discount, Hypermarket	32,901	Argentina, Brazil, China, France, Italy, Malaysia, Mexico, Poland, Portugal, South Korea, Spain, Taiwan, Thailand, Turkey
4	Germany	METRO AG Gruppe	DIY^a, Mail Order, Specialty, Supermarket, Warehouse	32,304	Austria, Belgium, China, Denmark, France, Germany, Greece, Hungary, Italy, Luxembourg, Netherlands, Poland, Romania, Spain, Switzerland, Turkey, UK, US
5	US	Kmart	Discount	32,183	Canada, Guam, Mexico, Puerto Rico, Virgin Islands, US
6	US	JCPenney	Department, Drug, Mail Order	29,618	Chile, Mexico, US
7	US	Dayton Hudson	Department, Discount	27,757	US
8	Germany	Tengelmann	Drug, Specialty, Supermarket	27,535	Austria, Canada, Czech Republic, France, Germany, Hungary, Italy, Netherlands, Spain, US
9	UK	Tesco	Supermarket	27,001	Czech Republic, France, Hungary, Poland, Slovakia, UK
10	US	Kroger	Convenience, Supermarket	26,567	US

^{a} DIY = do-it-yourself.

Adapted from: Global Powers of Retailing (1999, February). *Stores,* Section II.

BOX 1.1

How Zeller's of Canada Safeguarded Itself from Wal-Mart

Wal-Mart's size, growth rate, and legendary operating efficiencies tend to strike fear into the hearts of future competitors in markets the company is about to enter. When Wal-Mart announced its purchase of over 100 former Woolco stores in Canada in early 1994, its largest future Canadian retail competitor displayed a different set of emotions—resolution, defiance, and quiet confidence. Wal-Mart was taking on, among its other competition, Zeller's, a capable discount department store chain and its venerable parent, Hudson's Bay Company, whose 325 years of trading make it a pillar in the Canadian society and a symbol of longevity, being North America's oldest surviving business corporation.

The Hudson's Bay Company had revenues of more than $5.8 billion in 1994, with roughly $3.4 billion generated by Zeller's. Now competing with Wal-Mart in most of its important markets, Zeller's felt the effect of its new competitor, but by differentiating itself through price points, merchandise categories, and marketing, Zeller's appears to have significantly insulated itself and successfully retained a distinct customer base.

For several years before Wal-Mart's entry into Canada, Zeller's President Paul Walters implemented new strategies to organize the company's merchandise and operating policies to go head-to-head against Wal-Mart. The decision was made knowing that at some point in the future Wal-Mart would eventually enter the Canadian market and Zeller's would have to be prepared. Investing heavily in logistics and systems and limiting fixed costs wherever possible, Zeller's goal was to attain the equivalent of Wal-Mart's lean standards of operating efficiency.

By the time Wal-Mart actually arrived north of the U.S. border, Zeller's prudent anticipatory work proved to be invaluable in the competitive struggle that ensued. Not enough, however, was Zeller's ability to actually increase its market share as it did in the first year of Wal-Mart's invasion. Zeller's embraced many other tactics that solidified its presence as a shopping destination a majority of Canadians relied upon. Among these were the following promotional mix policies:

- **Advertising**—maintaining an aggressive advertising program in print media, radio, and television. Zeller's also initiated the heavy use of promotional flyers, contrasting with Wal-Mart's sparing use of promotional devices.
- **Sales promotion**—capitalizing on Club Z, a customer loyalty program. Club Z rewarded users with accumulated points for merchandise and discounts. Nearly half of the Canadian household were believed to participate in the popular program.
- **Personal selling**—guiding employees to use customer service as an important selling tool.
- **Visual merchandising**—accelerating store renovations and pressing forward with its expansion program. As a result, 62 stores were renovated and 12 new stores were opened in 1994. In 1998, Zeller's acquired Kmart Canada, reopening 36 of the former Kmart stores as boldly designed Zeller stores. By 1998, Zeller's had more than 340 locations in Canada.

While Zeller's response to the Wall-Mart invasion did not come without considerable cost in operating profits, as a result of these efforts Zeller's was able to maintain its position as Canada's most successful discount store.

Sources: Zeller's: How Canada's Hudson Bay Co. Shielded Itself from the Wal-Mart invasion. (1995, Fall). NRF Global Retail Report, *1–2.*
Zeller's celebrates reopening of 21 locations acquired in Kmart merger. (1998, June 1). Canadian Corporate News *[On-line]. Available:* 192.139.81.46/scripts/ccn-release.pl?1998/06/01?0601hbcl? cp=hbce.

In the sports apparel industry, Nike tailored its ads to fit the interests of specific geographic target markets. Nike, a big sponsor of soccer events, did not want to offend its European consumers by featuring the top soccer players from only one or two countries. Instead, the sponsor selected highly rated players from several European teams for its European television commercials based on the premise of a soccer match against the devil. Thus, Nike did not offend any particular nationality. At the same time these soccer commercials were running in Europe, Nike featured American basketball stars in ads produced for the audience in the United States. Sports stars wearing Nike products were the common international theme, but the firm chose to present them in a manner that would be understood by the local consumer.

Customers of the future will be more well educated, quality oriented, and budget conscious. They will require sophisticated promotional strategies to meet their ever-growing demands. To better understand the nature of the promotional process and to have a common frame of reference, it is helpful to define the basic terms of the industry and their relationships.

MARKETING

The marketing process represents how a product is conceived and moved through various channels from producer to consumer. Marketing holds various expectations within American culture. Many individuals use the terms *marketing* and *sales* synonymously. Some professionals believe marketing is simply the process of selling. Others take marketing a step further to include the elements of business, such as product research and development, pricing, and advertising. Marketing involves all of these operations and many more. To prevent confusion, the American Marketing Association approved the following definition of **marketing** in 1985: "the process of planning and executing the conception, pricing, promotion, and distribution of ideas, goods, and services to create exchanges that satisfy individual and organizational objectives" ("AMA Board," 1985).

Marketing activities involve product design and development, distribution of products through marketing channels, pricing, and promotion. The entire marketing process must recognize the interdependence of the marketing activities. Firms that are marketing oriented plan operations around satisfaction of consumer wants and needs.

The **marketing mix** involves the coordination of the four P's—product, price, place, and promotion. Analysts look at the needs of consumers and determine the demand for the product. The price must meet the expectations for quality and value. By offering the needed product at a particular and convenient location, the manufacturer will want to inform the consumer where to find the product. The fundamental challenge for marketing is to synthesize these four elements into a program that will lead to exchange in the marketplace.

Marketing Spotlights Exchange

Exchange is a concept fundamental to marketing. For exchange to occur, there must be two or more participants with something of value to each other. The participants must have the ambition and interest to give up something in exchange for something else. This goes beyond simple communication. Promotion enables one party to inform another about a product or service and to persuade the party that the item will satisfy his or her wants or needs.

Not all marketing transactions involve exchange of tangible goods or services for money; some may also involve intangible feelings of philanthropy and altruism. Nonprofit firms often look to charitable donations to provide services. Goodwill Industries International is an example of a nonprofit organization that offers training and employment services to the disabled and disadvantaged populations. In order to achieve these goals, Goodwill retail stores accept used goods as donations. These items are resold and "profits" are used for training and development. Nonprofit organizations also look to people to provide cash donations. Although many people donate cash or used clothing and household items to such organizations, individuals may not see any tangible gains. The benefits come from the sense of social and psychological fulfillment that humanitarianism and charity produce.

Global Marketing

Marketing activities, once strictly aimed at domestic markets, are evident in virtually every corner of the world. The purpose of domestic and **global marketing** is the same; the difference between the two is created by the external conditions faced by an international or multinational firm. Differences from one country to another can be attributed to culture, language, buying power, education, geography, politics, government regulations, and religion, to mention just a few variables. These factors influence what is acceptable or inappropriate in terms of marketing activities. The article in Box 1.2 supports the benefits of a standardized approach to establishing a global presence.

American designers, manufacturers, and retailers have used marketing and advertising to make their names known throughout the world. Calvin Klein, Ralph Lauren, Donna Karan, and Tommy Hilfiger have become well known in Europe, Asia, and Mexico because of their huge advertising and marketing campaigns.

Additional evidence of the influence of global marketing is shown by increased participation of foreign press and buyers at the New York Collections. Representatives from Milan, Paris, London, Tokyo, Mexico City, and Berlin attend the semiannual events to introduce new American fashion designs. London retailers have praised American designers for their regular deliveries and savvy marketing strategies, including designer visits, which are rare in the United Kingdom. Personal appearances by designers such as Michael Kors at Dickens & Jones have sparked strong sales ("Powerful Marketing," 1996).

MERCHANDISING

Similar to marketing and promotion, the term *merchandising* means different things to different people. There are as many definitions of merchandising in print as there are in common practice. To some people merchandising refers simply to retail selling. Others see merchandising as a product planning and retail distribution process. Academics and practitioners have struggled to develop a functional definition of merchandising for years. The classic definition of merchandising for the retail industry was originally developed by Paul Mazur as: "the planning involved in marketing the right merchandise at the right place at the right time in the right quantities at the right price" (1927).

Merchandising has evolved to take into consideration practices in both retail and manufacturing sectors. Recognizing the need to look at this changing nature of the industry, Kean (1987) proposed the following definition: "merchandising is the analysis and response to the changes (transformations) and processes (advances) which occur in the planning, negotiation, acquisition, and selling of products/services from their inception to their reception and use by the target customer" (pp. 10–11). Kean viewed merchandising as just one part of the marketing continuum.

Grace Kunz proposed the Behavioral Theory of the Apparel Firm (BTAF) in 1995. BTAF identifies marketing and merchandising as two of the five constituencies necessary to operate an apparel firm. Rather than seeing merchandising as a subset of marketing,

BOX 1.2

Standardized Approach Works Well in Establishing a Global Presence

Marketing products and services to international customers can be challenging. How can a company introduce and sell its products in foreign markets? Is there a market for the products in foreign countries?

These are difficult questions that marketing professionals must come to grips with before venturing into uncharted sales territory. To complicate matters further, selling abroad requires an understanding of how the political, legal, cultural, and business environments differ and ultimately influence the ability to generate sales.

Academics have long debated using a standard versus adaptive approach to selling abroad. Ted Levitt's article in a 1983 issue of *Harvard Business Review* endorsed standardized marketing. Both marketing professionals and scholars have committed resources and valuable time to gauge what elements of the marketing mix might be amenable to standardization, when a standardized approach could be used, and in which markets.

Companies have considered standardizing the product, pricing strategy, distribution, and product positioning. Additional criteria that need to be examined are the size of the foreign market, the type of market (consumer vs. industrial), the degree of similarity or difference between foreign and home market, and the level of technology that meets the needs of the final consumer.

The subject of technology plays an important role in the sales process. Since the 1980s, the rate of technological change has increased dramatically. Product development times are shorter as computerized tools facilitate movement through each stage of the process. Consequently, product life cycles have become shorter as improvements and enhancements have become easier. In essence, business environments characterized by rapid technology shifts are more amenable to standardized marketing approaches because the cost of adaptation becomes too high. The computer hardware and software industries illustrate this. Both have standardized products that are sold globally with modifications made for language.

Two ways that businesses are leveraging technology in their favor are through pan-regional advertising and the World Wide Web. In both instances, with just one advertisement, companies can get their message out to consumers in many countries. Pan-regional advertising is especially popular with cable TV broadcasters and is being used to target the largely untapped Latin American consumer market.

The Web epitomizes standardized marketing. Millions of consumers with access to computers, modems, and service providers now have the ability to shop for products and services worldwide.

Today's organizations are striving to develop global brands with global packaging and a central, global advertising strategy. Coca Cola is a prime example. The product is sold throughout the world, yet branding and advertising mirror a common, global theme.

Marketing Lesson

- Companies assessing sales potential for their products in international markets should begin by screening the markets. Group countries together based on characteristics similar to the home market such as language, income distribution, and age demographics.
- Eliminate countries whose markets do not fit with the selected criteria, and concentrate on consumer behavior and business practices in countries where sales are likely.
- Develop region-specific marketing plans to produce an integrated and globally standardized positioning of the product.

Source: Ericson, D. A. (1996, October 7). Standardized approach works well in establishing global presence. Marketing News, 30, 9.

Kunz saw merchandising and marketing as interactive yet equivalent functions. Glock and Kunz (1990) developed the following definition of merchandising, reflecting behavioral theory: "the planning, development, and presentation of product line(s) for identified target markets(s) with regard to prices, assortments, styling and timing" (p. 63).

This text takes the position that merchandising should be considered in the broad context. Thus, **merchandising** involves forecasting what customers want to buy, investigating where to find that merchandise in the marketplace, determining the price the customer is willing to pay, and making it available through the retail store or other merchandising outlets where the customer is willing to buy the merchandise. This practice involves market research, preparing buying plans, selecting specific products, promoting those products to the consumer, and selling the products or services at a profit.

Fashion and Basic Merchandise

Products generally fall into two categories, fashion or basic. **Fashion** refers to the prevailing style or expression that is popular at any given period of time. There are a number of texts and academic courses that cover the fundamental theories of fashion. It is not the intention of this text to cover that material in depth. The following information is offered as an overview to assist in the discussion of promoting fashion and basic merchandise.

Fashion merchandise includes aesthetically appealing products that change frequently and are generally considered nonnecessities. Although fashion merchandise is frequently associated with women's apparel and accessories, it includes much more. Fashion is present in such products as men's, women's, and children's apparel and accessories; cosmetics; and home furnishings. Food; entertainment; durable goods such as home appliances, electronic equipment, and automobiles; and virtually every other aspect of our global culture also have fashion appeals. Fashion merchandise presents unique problems for manufacturers and retailers because consumer demand for these products is constantly changing. The perception that fashion goods are not necessary creates additional problems for firms promoting fashion.

Basic merchandise is at the opposite end of the product spectrum. Basic merchandise includes functional goods that change infrequently and are generally considered necessities. Apparel basics, such as white T-shirts or nude panty hose, are purchased as replacements when the old product wears out, in contrast to fashion purchases, for which the desire for novelty or change takes priority. Basic products also present promotional challenges for the manufacturer or retailer. Have you ever heard a consumer say, "What a great looking white T-shirt. I think I'll buy it"?

The Merchandising Environment

The application of marketing processes frequently involves a wide range of products and services. Marketing executives and academics use all types of products as a part of their practices and studies. It would be just as common to analyze and develop strategies for automobile and beer manufacturers as it would be to do the same for a telephone company or a soap detergent producer.

The **merchandising environment** typically incorporates all of the products and services relating to personal and home surroundings. These products are often considered to be the soft good lines, such as apparel for the entire family, home furnishings, cosmetics, and related merchandise that enhances personal attractiveness. Many individuals consider these products to be the rapidly changing lines rather than hard product lines like appliances or automobiles. Consumers wait to buy expensive hard goods until they need a replacement, as they do for basic soft goods. However, fashion features influence the selection of the new purchase.

This book emphasizes the products and services associated with the merchandising environment. It covers the promotional strategies utilized in the fashion manufacturing and retailing sectors of the global enterprise system. Knowledge of the basic terms of business, including marketing and merchandising, is necessary to make promotional activities in this environment successful. An understanding of the role of communication, our next topic, is also necessary.

COMMUNICATION

By definition, **communication** is a transmission or exchange of information and/or messages. A basic knowledge of communication and communication theory is a necessity for anyone involved in promotion. For communication to occur, there must be some common thinking between the message sender and the message receiver. An understanding of information passed from one person or group to another establishes that common bond. Reaching this common bond is not easy; many attempts to communicate are thwarted by obstacles.

The Communication Process

A model of the communication process will help to explain the difficulties. In this model (Fig. 1.3), the communication process basically involves a sender encoding a message and sending that information to a receiver, who decodes the message and provides a response through feedback.

Communication begins with the sender or the source of the information. This may be an individual or an organization with a message to transmit to other individuals or organizations. This individual may be a salesperson, spokesperson, celebrity, or an organization such as a retailing, manufacturing, or advertising firm. The sender selects a combination of words or symbols to be presented orally or in written/visual form. This arrangement of the words and/or symbols is termed **encoding**. A major challenge to promotion experts is to develop messages and images that are easily understood by all target audiences.

The encoded message is conveyed to the receiver through various **channels**, the methods by which the message is translated. Personal selling channels include direct or face-to-face communication. This may also be called **word-of-mouth** communication. The opposite channel, nonpersonal selling, is often referred to as **mass communication**. The message is sent to many people at once through widely viewed broadcast or print media. Broadcast media consist of television, radio, and some forms of electronic

Figure 1.3

Communication process model.

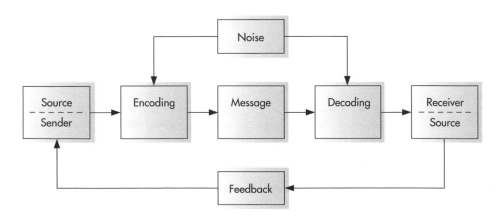

technology. Print media include newspapers, magazines, direct mail, billboards, or any other two-dimensional print designs.

Once the message has been sent, the receiver must **decode** the message or transform it back into thought. This step forces the receiver to interpret what he or she believes the sender wanted the receiver to know and is dependent upon the receiver's frame of reference, or past experiences. Attitudes, values, perceptions, and cultural background are among the characteristics that help the receiver understand or misinterpret the message.

Noise refers to any outside factors that may interfere with the reception of the information or lead to some distortion of the message. Distortion may occur as the information is encoded or during the transmission or interpretation of the message. One way of thinking about noise is as if it were some technical difficulty experienced while broadcasting a television program. Part of the message may be eliminated or changed through signal distortion. Lack of common experiences could lead to similar problems in communication. Miscommunication may take place because of failure to understand the symbols presented in advertisements. The message sent by the advertiser for a popcorn popper could be misunderstood if the receiver views the salt box, used as a prop, as the main product being promoted.

When the receiver sends back some type of response or **feedback**, the sender will know if the intent of the message has been understood. Response may come in many forms, from simple recognition in a face-to-face interaction to the purchase of a product through a toll-free number advertised in a magazine or a sudden increase in sales after a billboard sign is put up. Feedback can close the loop of communication, letting the source know whether or not the message has been accurately sent, decoded, and acted upon.

Communication in the Global Marketplace

The communication process in the global marketplace has challenges beyond normal communication problems. Cultural experiences and language differences contribute to these uncertainties. To be successful, promotional efforts must take into consideration local customs, historical perspectives, and language. Consider the following examples.

A cosmetic firm attempted to sell its products to Japanese consumers by presenting a television commercial that featured a statue of the ancient Roman emperor Nero coming to life as a pretty woman wearing the firm's lipstick walked by. Unfortunately, the product introduction was not accepted because the Japanese women resented the hard sell approach and had no idea who Nero was. In this case, if the firm had wanted to use a historical figure, it should have selected a figure known within the local culture (Ricks, 1993).

The display of certain body parts is considered offensive to some ethnic groups. A U.S. shoe manufacturer showed bare feet in an ad. Although this would not be an indignity to many people, the promotion took place in Southeast Asia where exposure of the foot is considered an insult (Ricks, 1993).

Careless translations, words that have multiple meanings, and the use of idioms have led to many humorous or unintentional interpretations. A Mexican magazine ran an ad for a U.S. shirt manufacturer that had the opposite effect from the one planned. The advertisement read, "Until I used this shirt, I felt good," rather than the intended, "When I used this shirt, I felt good" (Ricks, 1993).

In the global marketplace, English has been prescribed as the common language (Kameda, 1992). In the business world, many nonnative speakers use English to communicate with other nonnative users—for example, Japanese with Koreans, Koreans with Germans, Germans with Indonesians, Indonesians with Greeks, Greeks with Portuguese, and so forth. Although English is the common denominator, misunderstandings are still common.

Promotional blunders in the global marketplace can be avoided by taking several important steps.

1. Conduct research about the intended consumers, especially in foreign markets, taking into consideration customs and culture in addition to language.
2. Select a good translator. It is not enough that the translator use grammatically correct language; he or she must also be intimately familiar with the second language to understand its nuances, colloquialisms, slang, and idioms.
3. Solicit feedback through retranslating and local input.

These steps will help prevent mistakes and misunderstandings.

PROMOTION MIX

The basic tools used for achieving a firm's communication and marketing goals are referred to as the **promotion mix.** In the merchandising environment these promotion mix categories include advertising, direct marketing, sales promotion, publicity and public relations, personal selling, special events, fashion shows, and visual merchandising (Fig. 1.4). These elements may take on various forms and have specific advantages and disadvantages. Each of the promotion mix elements is discussed in a separate chapter in Part III of this text.

Figure 1.4

Promotion mix categories used in the merchandising environment.

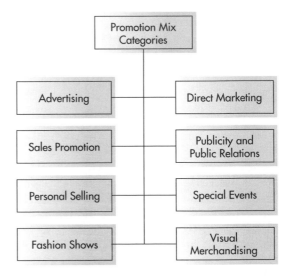

Advertising

Advertising is any nonpersonal information paid for and controlled by the sponsoring organization. This communication contains information about the organization, product, service, or idea created by the sponsoring firm to influence sales. The information is normally featured in public media such as newspapers, magazines, radio, television, direct mail, or any other similar vehicle. Figure 1.5 shows a Norwegian magazine advertisement for a Danish-made product.

The *paid* concept of advertising indicates that the sponsoring agency must purchase either space in the print media or time in the electronic media. The *non-personal* element of advertising requires the message to be transmitted through the mass media. Television, radio, newspapers, or magazines are typical mass media through which an advertising message may be sent to a large group of people. Because of the nonpersonal nature of the communication channel, the ability of the sender to assess the effectiveness of the message is limited. There is no chance to obtain immediate feedback. Before developing and sending an advertising message, the sender must consider how the public will comprehend and react to the message.

Advertising is considered to be one of the most effective methods of distributing information to a large audience at an effective cost. It remains a primary element of the promotion mix. The general topic of advertising is discussed more fully in Chapter 7,

Figure 1.5

Danish-produced Ecco shoes are advertised in a Norwegian magazine.

while print media is the subject of Chapter 8 and broadcast media is the topic of Chapter 9. The creative elements of advertising are covered in Chapters 8 and 9, too.

Direct Marketing

Direct marketing describes the marketing process by which organizations communicate directly with target customers to generate a response or transaction. This communication normally uses a set of **direct-response media** such as mail, telephone, magazines, the Internet, radio, or television with messages aimed directly to the target consumer.

The significance of direct marketing to the promotion mix cannot be underestimated. A study conducted for the Direct Marketing Association reported that more than half (57 percent) of all advertising expenditures in 1995 included some form of direct response. It was estimated that $234.5 billion was spent on advertising that year. Nearly $134 billion of that total was spent on ads designed to prompt consumers to make a direct purchase, ask for more information about a product, or visit a store to make a specific purchase ("Telemarketing," 1996). The Direct Marketing Association predicts that catalog purchases will continue to grow into the 21st century. The organization anticipates sales of $64.6 billion in 2002, up from $48.3 billion in 1997 (Topolnicki, 1998).

Direct marketing has not always been considered a part of the traditional promotion mix. Direct marketing may have started with direct mail and mail-order catalogs, but today it has expanded to include many other areas. Growth and popularity of the Internet have led to direct marketing opportunities unheard of in the past.

Direct marketing techniques range from the simple postcard or sales letter to elaborate sales presentations on videotape. These materials may be developed and distributed via traditional distribution channels and electronic media, or through a personal sales force hired by the marketer. Direct marketing is the theme of Chapter 10.

Sales Promotion

Sales promotion refers to those activities that provide extra value or incentives to the sales force, distributors, or ultimate consumer. It is a set of paid marketing endeavors, other than advertising and personal sales, taken on to immediately stimulate sales. Some professionals refer to the entire promotion industry as sales promotion, which may lead to confusion in the advertising and promotion business. This book uses the term *promotion* as the broader umbrella term that encompasses *all* of the elements of the promotion mix, not just sales promotion. As previously defined, promotion is the element of the marketing mix used by firms to communicate with their potential customers.

Sales promotion may be consumer or trade oriented. The ultimate consumer or product user is the target of consumer-oriented sales promotion. These activities include: contests, coupons, gift-with-purchase, purchase-with-purchase, point-of-sale displays, refunds, rebates, sweepstakes, and sampling among others. Such activities encourage prompt purchase of products and can improve short-term sales. The gift with purchase ad shown in Figure 1.6 is an example of a consumer-oriented sales promotion.

Trade-oriented sales promotion is directed to the distribution intermediaries such as wholesalers, distributors, and retailers. Activities aimed at the trade include promotional and merchandising allowances, price deals, sales contests, special counter displays or sales fixtures, and trade show discounts among others. The topic of sales promotion is explored in Chapter 11.

**BUY 2 KORET® WOOL OR POLYWOOL GARMENTS
TO RECEIVE YOUR GIFT WITH PURCHASE**

Name

Address

City   State   Zip

Send the UPC symbols as proof of purchase, a copy of your
sales receipt, this completed form and your check payable to
Koret of California for $4.95 shipping and handling to:

**Koret Mail Center
Attn: Carol Canning
P.O. Box 496055
Redding, Ca. 96049-6055**

Do not send cash. Allow 6-8 weeks for delivery.
Void where prohibited, restricted or taxed. Offer good in USA only.
Only one (1) umbrella per person. Offer good while supplies last.
Incorrect or photocopied proofs of purchase will not be honored.
Not responsible for late, lost, misdirected or postage due mail.
This offer expires January 30, 1999.

Figure 1.6

The popular gift-with-purchase is an example of a consumer-oriented sales promotion.

Publicity and Public Relations

Although many people use the terms *advertising, publicity,* and *public relations* inter-changeably, there is a distinction between them. Advertising depends upon paid sponsorship in the media, while publicity and public relations do not require payment for space or time. This text adopts the terminology most commonly used within the promotion industry.

Publicity involves nonpaid, unsponsored information delivered through the media and initiated by a party seeking to tell others about a product, service, idea, or event. The message is normally communicated through the use of the press release and/or press kit. The most common result of the press kit or press release is the publication of a feature story in a newspaper or magazine. It may also become a feature story on a television or radio news broadcast. In a manner similar to advertising, publicity involves nonpersonal communication transmitted through the mass media. Unlike advertising, the sponsoring agency does not pay for the placement of the message.

Because the sponsoring agency is not paying for the story about the product, service, or cause, there is a perception of increased credibility. Consumers tend to rely on the mass media to provide unbiased information and may be less skeptical toward favorable information provided through a feature story than they would be toward an advertisement. Another advantage of publicity is its low cost in comparison to advertising. Although there are costs associated with producing news releases and press kits, the sponsoring organization does not pay for space or time.

One limitation of publicity is the lack of control by the sponsoring organization. The story is under the authority of the medium presenting the story. The newspaper, magazine, television station, or radio station may also provide misleading or negative information. Negative stories may prove damaging to the company and its products.

Public relations (PR) involves the interrelationship between service providers and the public to project a positive image of the organization through all levels of communication. Public relations goes beyond the strategies of publicity, attempting to plan and distribute information that will control and manage the nature of the publicity a firm receives. The general objective of public relations is broader than the more limited purpose of publicity.

Part of the confusion about the relationship between public relations and publicity may be due to the fact that public relations uses publicity and a variety of other tools to achieve its goals. Some of the other tools that public relations specialists use to manage a company's image include creating special publications, participating in community activities, fund raising, sponsoring special events, and taking part in public affairs activities.

Although publicity and public relations have not been traditional elements of the promotion mix, these communication tools are frequently included in the operations of the advertising division or agency. Many firms make these functions an integral part of the promotion mix and integrated marketing communication package. Publicity and public relations are discussed in Chapter 12.

Personal Selling

Personal selling is the direct interaction between the customer and the seller for the purpose of making a sale. This interpersonal communication enables the seller to assist or influence the buyer to purchase a product or service or act upon an idea.

Most people think of personal sales taking place only in the retail environment, but personal sales can also take place as part of business-to-business communication. This promotion mix method allows the seller to see or hear the potential buyer's reaction. This feedback allows the seller to adapt the message to meet the needs of the client. Personal selling allows more direct and accurate feedback about the sales message than any other promotion mix technique. A more complete look at personal selling may be found in Chapter 13.

Special Events

Special events are planned activities intended to cause individuals or groups to gather at a specific time and place because of a shared interest. These are specific activities sponsored to attract customers while creating goodwill. Such attractions may include activities like celebrity appearances, product demonstrations or sampling, museum displays, gallery exhibitions, and musical, theatrical, or sports performances.

Although some practitioners may not view special events as an element of the promotion mix, special events are frequently used to build interest and increase traffic in retail stores. Special events can be as simple as product sampling or as complex as a merchandising event cosponsored by a fashion magazine and retail store. It is easy to think of examples of product sampling at a grocery store. Samples of food items are offered as an incentive to purchasing that product. This practice is also common in department and specialty store environments. "Fragrance models" walk through the store offering samples of perfumes or other cosmetics. Magazines such as *Glamour, Seventeen,* or *Vogue* may provide an editor of the magazine as the commentator for a fashion show or beauty makeover, for an audience of retail store customers.

Museum or store exhibits of historical apparel are also considered special events. This type of event would not be possible without the support of a promotional underwriter. A retrospective of apparel designs was featured in an exhibit entitled *"A New*

Look at Christian Dior" at the Metropolitan Museum of Art on the 50th anniversary of the opening of the House of Dior (Fig. 1.7). The exhibit, sponsored by Christian Dior and LVMH/Moët Hennessy Louis Vuitton, featured more than 80 pieces as a tribute to one of the significant fashion designers of the 20th century. A more thorough examination of special events is found in Chapter 14.

Fashion Shows

A **fashion show** is the presentation of apparel, accessories, and other products to enhance personal attractiveness on live models to an audience. This form of promotional communication transmits the message about fashionable attire through physical images as an informal show, formal runway show, production show, or as a video production. The target audience may consist of consumers or trade professionals. Although some individuals may not view the fashion show as a traditional promotion mix element, this book looks at fashion shows as a promotional tool commonly used within the merchandising environment.

The popularity of fashion shows as a promotional activity increases or decreases at various times. In the 1990s fashion shows became hot news items, covered by the en-

Figure 1.7

The exhibit held at the Metropolitan Museum of Art to celebrate the 50th anniversary of the House of Dior was sponsored by Christian Dior and LVMH/Moët Hennessy. An opening reception at the museum provided an opportunity for additional publicity about the exhibition and the sponsors.

tertainment media as well as the traditional fashion media such as magazines and news-papers. Interest in the personalities of the designers, models, and production teams seems almost as great as the interest in the fashions being featured. Fashion shows are the topic of Chapter 15.

Visual Merchandising

Visual merchandising is the physical presentation of products in a nonpersonal ap-proach. Typically products are presented in window displays, store interior merchandise presentations, or remote displays. Figure 1.8 shows the new store design for Urban Out-fitters in London. Store design and merchandise presentation were used as a part of the promotional strategy in the British expansion of this hip American retailer of women's and men's wear and home furnishings aimed at the 18- to 30-year-old fashion customer.

The merchandising environment encourages the creative use of merchandise pre-sentation to generate interest and sales of fashion products. Small "mom-and-pop" re-tailers may rely on window displays and interior merchandise presentation as their only component of promotion. However, an attractive physical space with interesting mer-chandise presentation is an inexpensive promotional technique, especially popular with retailers that have limited promotional budgets. A more complete discussion about vi-sual merchandising is the focus of Chapter 16.

Figure 1.8

Store layout and design are part of the promotional strategy for Urban Outfitters. The interior of the London store is featured here.

INTEGRATED MARKETING COMMUNICATIONS

In the 1990s, marketing and merchandising executives began to realize that the wide range of promotional activities could be more effective when the various elements of the promotional mix were coordinated. The American Association of Advertising Agencies recognized that agencies and practitioners needed to become more active in developing skills beyond those traditionally used in marketing communications in the 1980s. Promotional mix tools were coordinated in an attempt to more successfully communicate to target customers by presenting a consistent image. Many companies started moving toward an integrated marketing communications concept, which involved coordination of the various promotional elements with other marketing activities that communicate to the firm's customers and stakeholders, or interested third parties, such as critics, designers, and members of the press.

The American Association of Advertising Agencies defines **integrated marketing communications (IMC)** as: "a concept of marketing communications planning that recognized the added value of a comprehensive plan that evaluates the strategic roles of a variety of communication disciplines—for example, general advertising, direct response, sales promotion and public relations—and combines these disciplines to provide clarity, consistency, and maximum communications impact" (Schultz, 1993).

IMC requires an umbrella or big-picture approach to planning promotion. It also dictates coordination of the various communications, marketing, and promotion functions. True integration occurs when all aspects of the product, from product development, package design, and brand name creation to price and type of sales location are coordinated. IMC attempts to project a consistent impression about the product in the marketplace. Figure 1.9 shows the IMC planning model.

An IMC approach was used as an efficient way to introduce Rouge Idole, indelible lip-color products. Consumers indicated they wanted a lipstick that would not wear off too quickly, so Lancôme created a product to stay on the lips for an extended period of time. The firm took product design, packaging, brand name, advertising message, and the image of the stores where the product would be sold into consideration as it developed a communication program to introduce the product. The promotional mix tools included advertising, direct marketing, sales promotion, and public relations. Figure 1.10 shows how the product was advertised for the target audiences in both the United States and France. Color Plate 1 shows another effective IMC promotion, this one by Victoria's Secret.

The Estée Lauder Company also uses an IMC approach. The company aggressively advertises its fragrance and cosmetic products in fashion magazines and newspapers. The company then is able to negotiate for store selling space in the prime traffic aisles. The themes used in advertising are repeated in promotional displays, gift-with-purchase, and purchase-with-purchase sales promotions.

FUTURE TRENDS FOR GLOBAL PROMOTION

Robert Coen of McCann-Erickson has been tracking advertising and media trends since 1948 and making predictions twice yearly. Coen predicted continued growth for global promotion through the last decade of the 20th century and anticipated growth well into the 21st.

At the time this book went to print, conditions for international advertising spending were uncertain, primarily because of an economic downturn in Asia. Despite the

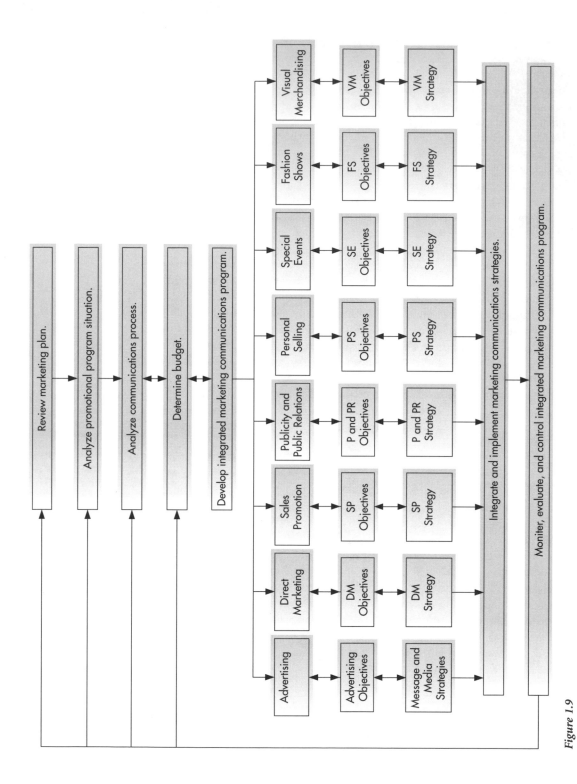

Figure 1.9

Integrated marketing communications model.

Adapted from Belch, G. E. and Belch, M. A. (1998) Advertising and Promotion (4th ed.). Burr Ridge, Ill.: Irwin/McGraw-Hill. p. 23.

Figure 1.10

There are strong similarities between the ads for Lancôme's lipstick in French and American magazines, reflecting a global promotional approach.

economic problems in Indonesia, Malaysia, and South Korea, ad spending was anticipated to grow in countries such as Brazil, Britain, and Mexico. Coen believed the strong U.S. economy with low inflation and unemployment would combine with momentum for the millennium, creating an upsurge in spending similar to the rise in spending in 1976 for the United States bicentennial celebration. Coen predicted that ad spending at the millennium could be "hitting half a trillion dollars" (Elliot, 1998c).

With the easing of commercial restrictions of the Internet and the development of the World Wide Web in the 1980s and 1990s, the stage has been set for the globalization of promotional communication through e-commerce. **E-commerce** is defined as business transactions based on the electronic transmission of data over communication networks such as the Internet (Dryden, 1998). In 1998, 16.8 million American Internet users made at least one purchase on-line. U.S. on-line shoppers are estimated to swell to 64 million by the year 2002 ("E-Commerce retail shopping report," 1998). Although Internet sales in the United States are projected to grow tremendously, worldwide consumer on-line shopping revenues are expected to rise even faster. International sales are predicted to increase from $1.7 billion in 1997 to more than $35 billion in 2002 ("E-Commerce retail shopping report," 1998). As more countries gain access to the Internet, it is anticipated the shopping experience and the promotion of goods and services will become even more global in nature.

Futurist and author Alvin Toffler told members of the National Retail Federation that information is the most precious resource available to them. Information will assist retailers in directing the most appropriate promotional messages to their ultimate consumer. With all of the technological changes taking place, Toffler prophesied that consumers will be able to watch a television program, punch a bar code into their 'smart' television, and order a sweater they saw an actor wearing on the show (Seckler, 1997). As we will explore more fully in Chapter 12, manufacturers have already mastered product placement in television and movies, making this just the next step in bringing global products to individual consumers. The types of promotional activities available to retailers and manufacturers in the future are limited only by their lack of understanding about the changes taking place in an economy driven by knowledge.

This chapter provides basic definitions for promotion, marketing, merchandising, and communication and introduces the promotion mix methods, the techniques used by professionals to distribute information about products and services to individuals and groups throughout the world. Integrated marketing communications, the process that enables senders to expose consumers or other interested parties to their message, brings a variety of these promotional methods together into a coordinated effort. These terms and concepts, which are fundamental to the field of promotion, are explored in depth throughout the book.

SUMMARY

- Promotion is a comprehensive term for all of the activities initiated by the seller or sponsor to inform, persuade, and remind the consumer about goods and services available.
- Billions of dollars are spent yearly, domestically and internationally, to promote products, services, or societal causes. The expenditures for promotional activities are anticipated to continue to grow in the 21st century.
- Marketing involves the research and development, distribution and sales, and promotion of products and ideas to fulfill consumer demand of all types of products.

Exchange is an essential component of marketing. Participants must have the desire and ability to substitute something of value for something else.

- Merchandising involves forecasting what customers want to buy, investigating where to find that merchandise in the marketplace, determining the price the customer is willing to pay, and making it available through the retail store or other merchandising outlets where the customer is willing to buy the merchandise. Fashion merchandising focuses on styles and products that are popular at a given period of time.

- The merchandising environment emphasizes goods that are considered fashion or soft lines, characteristically apparel, home furnishings and decor, and other merchandise to improve an individual's appearance or well-being.

- Communication involves the transmission or exchange of information. Communication theory assists marketing and merchandising executives in accomplishing their professional goals.

- The promotion mix defines the various activities used by the seller to achieve its goals. Promotion mix elements in the merchandising environment include: advertising, direct marketing, sales promotion, publicity and public relations, personal selling, special events, fashion shows, and visual merchandising.

- Integrated marketing communications (IMC) involves the coordination of the various promotional techniques with other marketing activities.

KEY TERMS

advertising
channels
communication
decode
direct marketing
direct-response media
e-commerce
encoding
exchange
fashion
fashion show
feedback

global marketing
globalization
glocalization
integrated marketing
   communications
marketing
marketing mix
mass communication
merchandising
merchandising
   environment

noise
personal selling
promotion
promotion mix
public relations
publicity
sales promotion
special events
visual merchandising
word-of-mouth

QUESTIONS FOR DISCUSSION

1. What is the importance of a global society to the distribution and promotion of products in the merchandising environment?
2. What is the role of communication in the promotional process?
3. How do the elements of the promotional mix relate?
4. What is the role of integrated marketing communications? Why is it important to promotion?

ADDITIONAL RESOURCES

Global powers of retailing. (1998, January). *Stores* (Suppl. 1).
Puffer, S. M. (1996). *Management across cultures: Insights from fiction and practice.* Cambridge, MA: Blackwell.
Ogden, J. R. (1998). *Developing a creative and innovative integrated marketing communication plan: A working model.* Upper Saddle River, NJ: Prentice-Hall.
Sirgy, M. J. (1998). *Integrated marketing communications: A systems approach.* Upper Saddle River, NJ: Prentice-Hall.
Sternquist, B. (1998). *International retailing.* New York: Fairchild.

Figure 2.1

Athletic shoes are available in a seemingly endless variety of styles to meet consumers' footwear needs.

Source: John Cole/Stock Boston/PNI

chapter 2

CONSUMER BEHAVIOR

A re all consumers the same? Not anymore! That's why Coke, Classic Coke, Diet Coke, Diet Classic Coke, Caffeine-Free Coke, Caffeine-Free Diet Coke, not to mention Pepsi, RC Cola, British-based Virgin Cola, and many other house brand cola products are available to us at the store. Look at another example—athletic footwear. Years ago everyone wore "tennis shoes". Although the shoes were called tennis shoes, the same rubber-soled canvas shoe was worn for all athletic needs. Today, upon entering Foot Locker, the consumer is overwhelmed by the variety of athletic shoes, each designed for a specific activity (Fig. 2.1). You can buy walking shoes, running shoes, or hiking shoes, shoes specifically designed for aerobics, cross-training, basketball, golf, or "tennis" along with other individualized sporting shoes, each differentiated to meet the needs of a specific target market, and each with its own sophisticated promotional strategy. Are the choices likely to diminish? Not as long as manufacturers and marketers have the desire and ability to offer products perceived by the buying public to be uniquely different and therefore necessary.

In this chapter we explore the role of consumer behavior as it applies to promotional programs. The chapter begins with a discussion about the consumption process consumers typically follow to purchase new or replacement items or services. Acquisition of a fashion item is illustrated using the product life cycle. Next, the chapter focuses on the consumer and the importance of segmenting consumers into target markets. Various demographic, behavioristic, and psychographic bases for segmentation are reviewed. We then describe the emergence of the global consumer. Once a business has defined its customer through market segmentation, it is important for that business to position its products, brands, and image as the firm most likely to meet the specific needs of the targeted customer. This chapter concludes with a discussion of product positioning.

THE ROLE OF CONSUMER BEHAVIOR IN PROMOTION

The development of a successful promotional plan relies on a clear understanding of who consumers are. How do consumers behave? What will ultimately shift them toward a specific product? Marketers are obliged to familiarize themselves with the

After you have read this chapter, you should be able to:

Describe the role of the consumer in merchandise promotion.

Understand the concept of market segmentation and the importance of target markets.

Identify and describe demographic, behavioristic, and psychographic bases for segmentation of a population.

Explain behavior characteristics of global consumers.

Discuss the concept of product positioning.

behavior of consumers—how they think, what motivates them, and the environment in which they live. Understanding the consumer is complicated by the fact that consumer behaviors are constantly changing. Just when a marketer has figured out a pattern of behavior on which to build a promotion plan, a new piece of information is introduced to consumers and their behavior changes. Complicating matters further is the fact that consumers and marketers perceive promotion in very different ways.

As we pointed out in Chapter 1, nearly everyone in the contemporary world is affected by promotion. While promotion specialists spend considerable time analyzing the best promotional technique to communicate with the consumer, the consumer does not differentiate among techniques. To a consumer, everything an organization does to promote itself is considered advertising, whether or not it was paid for by the sponsoring organization (Schultz and Barnes, 1995). Every time consumers come in contact with a brand, they are exposed to promotion. Exposure may be planned, such as store signage, event sponsorship, or paid advertising, or unplanned, such as seeing shopping bags in the hands of customers at a mall, hearing word-of-mouth experiences from friends, viewing a news story on television, or seeing litter in the street with the identifiable brand. Because consumers associate every contact they make with a brand to be "advertising," it is important that the marketing team coordinate promotion functions using the integrated marketing communications (IMC) approach introduced in Chapter 1. All aspects of the product: brand image, packaging, advertising, sales promotion, and the like, should project a consistent message to the consumer. Understanding the behaviors of consumers can assist marketers in planning promotions from the viewpoint of the consumer.

Consumer behavior is the study of consumers' decision making processes, as they acquire, consume, and dispose of goods and services. Consumers are individuals or households who purchase goods or services for personal use. The consumer may be an individual making a particular purchase, a couple buying an item together, or a group making a collective decision about a purchase. Sales to the consumer may be generated by retail transactions of goods or services or by wholesale transactions made directly to the consumer without benefit of the reseller. **Trade customers** are organizational markets composed of governments, industrial firms, or resellers representing the intermediate stage between manufacturers of raw materials and the ultimate consumer. Retailers are the customer of a trade market.

Consumer behavior is increasingly important to service providers. Services are the biggest and broadest business category in the United States. During the last decade of the 20th century more than one-third of U.S. jobs were in the service industries (Du, Merhagen, and Lee, 1995). While resellers and manufacturers struggle to grow, service businesses are expanding in sales, employment, and number of establishments. Consumers often use the same basic decision making processes to choose a bank, dry cleaner, dentist, or restaurant as they do new outfits or home furnishings; therefore, service providers must pay close attention to the behavior of their potential customers.

Consumption

Consumption is the process of acquiring, using, and discarding products. Figure 2.2 is a flow chart that illustrates consumer acquisition, use, and disposal of products and services. All products, fashion and basic, follow the same consumption process. The process begins with product acquisition, moves through product use, and finishes with prod-

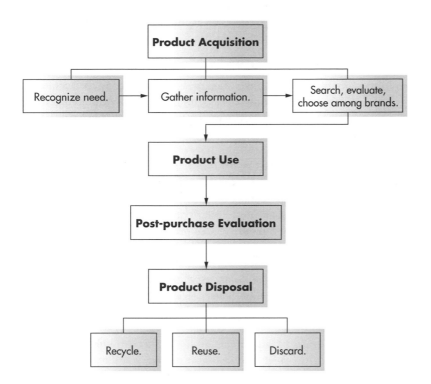

Figure 2.2

A flow chart illustrating the consumption cycle: acquisition, use, and disposal of consumer products and services.

uct disposal. Our discussion concentrates on product acquisition; however, the acquisition of services follows the same procedure.

Acquisition

Before most purchases are made, consumers become aware of the need for a new or replacement product. We may read a fashion magazine and become aware of a new trend, or through use, realize that we need to replace a basic good. Upon recognition of the need we begin to search for information about the product. Product acquisition is the process of searching, evaluating, and choosing among alternative items. Information is gathered (through advertisements, promotion materials, the Internet, personal references, and other means) and alternatives are evaluated for benefits and limitations.

Impulse buying occurs when no previous need recognition has taken place before the purchase is made. Many goods are purchased as impulse buys as a result of the feeling gained by the purchase rather than the utilitarian purpose of the good. Point-of-purchase displays for magazines, candy, and personal care products make impulse buying effortless for the consumer.

Use

Using the information we have gathered, we evaluate the alternatives and make a purchase decision. The product is then put into service for its useful life. The useful life of a product may be once, as with picnic supplies; over a season, as with fashion trend items; or extended over many years, as with a home appliance. Just because we make a purchase does not mean we stop evaluating alternatives. During product use, we make post-purchase evaluations. We may question whether we made the right decision based on the information and the alternatives available at the time. Continual evaluation after the purchase hopefully reinforces that our purchase was the correct decision.

Disposal

At some point during the use of an item, we come to the conclusion that we no longer need or want it. It may be worn out, a replacement product with a new feature may have become available in the marketplace, or the fashion trend may have passed. Product disposal is the decision by the consumer to discard the product once use of the product is complete. Consumers are becoming very concerned with how a product can be disposed of as landfills and other refuse areas are filling up. The practice of reusing and/or recycling both goods and the packaging they come in is becoming standard practice among many consumers and retailers. Origins, a maker of environmentally friendly cosmetics, offers to refill previously used Origins containers if they are brought back to the store. North Face, an outdoor manufacturer, promotes apparel products made from recycled milk containers.

Promotion is used at each stage of the consumption cycle. Promotion is used to plant the seed in consumers' minds to buy a new item. Promotion educates consumers about various products and reinforces their choice after the purchase. Finally, promotion convinces consumers of when and how to dispose of products.

The fashion industry depends on consumers to acquire, use, and dispose of fashion merchandise each season. Fashion merchandise moves through a life cycle based on consumer acceptance. In the next section, we illustrate how acquisition of a fashion item reflects the product life cycle.

The Product Life Cycle

The product life cycle describes the process of acceptance of a trend or fashion item (Greenwood and Murphy, 1978). When the cycle is graphed, it appears as a bell-shaped curve (Fig. 2.3). The product life cycle has three major stages: introduction, acceptance, and regression. Each stage is represented by two groups of consumers: earlier adopters and later adopters.

Introduction

The first stage in the product life cycle—introduction—is marked by two phases, innovation and rise. Early adopters, called **fashion innovators** during this stage will adopt a trend at the very earliest opportunity. Fashion innovators represent only 2 percent of the buying public. They desire distinction and high fashion and are the very first consumers to identify a trend. **Fashion specialists**, later adopters, in the introduction stage will accept the trend as it begins to rise in popularity. Fashion specialists, who represent 14 percent of consumers, purchase sophisticated items and appreciate what is new and in good taste.

Fashion innovators and fashion specialists purchase goods within the introduction stage only through designers or very exclusive stores, paying high prices to own exclusive and novel items. Retail buyers for stores that market to these consumers purchase limited quantities, simultaneously testing many styles and new trends.

At the introduction stage, retail selling precedes actual consumer use. Promotion and advertising campaigns consist of informational, institutional, or prestige ads. Visual merchandise presentations appear at the front of a store or in window displays to introduce the very latest trends. Figure 2.4 is a prestige ad targeted to fashion innovators and fashion specialists during the introduction stage.

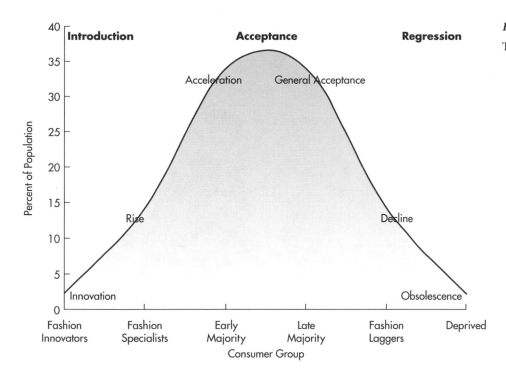

Figure 2.3

The fashion life cycle.

Acceptance

The second stage of the product life cycle—acceptance—comprises the two phases of acceleration and general acceptance. The majority of consumers—slightly more than two-thirds—adopt a product during the acceptance stage. These consumers purchase items in season for immediate use. Consumers who are in the **early majority** purchase during acceleration of the fashion trend. The early majority accounts for 34 percent of consumers, and they purchase fashionable items used as wardrobe builders. These consumers are very receptive to change and generally make purchases at department and specialty stores.

The **late majority** of consumers, also 34 percent of the population, purchase items during the general acceptance phase of a trend. The late majority have a desire to look fashionable but realize that practicality and durability are also important. They purchase goods at all types of stores.

Retail buyers who represent stores that target acceptance stage consumers purchase maximum stocks and complete assortments. During acceleration, they are inclined to reorder "hot" items. Promotions are persuasive, informing consumers of regular price lines and special limited offers. Product ads are abundant, and displays are centered at high traffic areas within the middle of the store.

Regression

The final stage in the product life cycle—regression—is divided between decline and obsolescence phases. The earlier adopters within this stage are called **fashion laggers** and represent 14 percent of consumers. As a fashion declines, consumers are motivated to purchase strictly by economic values. They make purchases at discount houses, chain stores, or at special sales. Later adopters in this stage, representing 2 percent of the population, make purchases when a fashion has reached obsolescence. These financially

Figure 2.4

A prestige ad targeted to fashion innovators and fashion specialists. This cooperative advertisement promotes the designer Giorgio Armani and retailer Bergdorf Goodman.

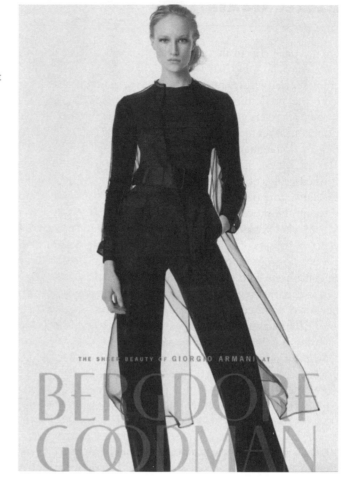

THE SHEER BEAUTY OF GIORGIO ARMANI AT

BERGDORF GOODMAN

deprived consumers are truly value-oriented and only purchase items at clearance and close-out outlets. Fashion laggers are acquiring merchandise at the same time fashion innovators are disposing of the same styles.

Buyers do not purchase items for the regression stage; rather, they reduce stock with markdowns or purchase special quantity items from other vendors. Advertising is produced as clearance reminders. Promotions state reduced prices, clearance, or close-out merchandise. Visual merchandising is very limited, promoting price reduction. Displays change from artistic presentations to sized distributions on sale tables.

An understanding of where consumers fall within the product life cycle allows promotion specialists to create the right marketing mix, matching the needs of the consumer with the sales objectives of the business. Using the product life cycle stages is one way businesses can differentiate consumers into relatively homogeneous groups. It is by no means the only way that consumers can be grouped. In the next section, we discuss market segmentation, the different ways in which consumers can be grouped to identify current and potential customers. A business that can correctly identify its intended target market can tailor the promotion mix in a very effective manner.

MARKET SEGMENTATION

On a typical trip to the mall, are you likely to visit one store or many stores to complete your shopping list? If you are like many present-day consumers you will shop at many specialty stores rather than one department store. Department stores, which once were the predominant store type in apparel retailing, are decreasing in ownership through mergers and acquisitions, while the number of specialty stores in the marketplace continues to increase. In the last decade of the 20th century, specialty stores ranked first in dollar market share nationally, while department stores ranked third ("New Trends," 1995). Specialty stores gained popularity because they catered to a narrowly defined group of consumers with a single or limited number of product categories. A specialty store decides to cater to a narrowly defined group of consumers determined through the process of market segmentation.

Market segmentation is the subdivision of the marketplace into relatively homogeneous subsets of consumers, called target markets or market segments. A **mass market** is a large group of consumers with similar needs. A **niche market** is a small group of consumers with characteristics noticeably different from the mass market. Retailers can use market segmentation to better understand the attitudes, characteristics, or behaviors of their customers and to identify the specific target market they wish to serve.

Ideal market segments possess characteristics that a retailer can identify and access in order to generate sufficient sales. Consumer behavior provides a number of bases for segmenting the marketplace including, among others, age, sex, education, and income; usage patterns; and lifestyle patterns. The bases by which a population can be segmented are endless, limited only by the creativity of marketing analysts. We can only touch the surface of market segmentation bases in this text.

BASES FOR MARKET SEGMENTATION

Consumers identified by similar needs or wants can be grouped as a market segment. For consumer goods, a segment may be composed of individual consumers. For manufactured goods, segments may be a group of retailers with similar, specific needs. Market segments may also be defined as primary or secondary. The **primary market segment** is the essential target group identified for communication. A **secondary market segment** is an auxiliary target group with potential value to the message sponsor. The primary market for children's clothing may be parents, while grandparents may constitute the secondary market with different purchase criteria for the same item. When looking at a target market, it is important to identify not only how many customers a retailer has today, but how different the target market will be in 1, 5, or 10 years. Populations are not static, and their needs and wants change over time.

The factors used to describe a segment are considered bases for segmentation. Bases for segmentation may be demographic, behavioristic, or psychographic.

Demographic Segmentation

Demographics are the statistics used to study a population. These statistics provide an easy tool for comparison and are available for every city block and zip code in the country. Demographic segmentation allow marketers to conceptualize their target market using readily available statistics and review the target market over time to determine patterns of change. The common demographic characteristics used to describe an individual include age, gender, education, income, occupation, race and ethnicity, family size and structure, and disability status. The combination of these individual characteristics creates a composite of relatively homogeneous market segments within the population.

Age

According to Gail Sheehy, author of *New Passages* (1995), a revolution in the life cycle is taking place based on the aging of the population. Individuals are leaving childhood sooner, taking longer to grow up, and living much longer. Adolescence may not be complete until a person is in his or her mid to late twenties, and true adulthood does not begin until age 30. Middle age is being pushed into the fifties, and experiences for individuals in their sixties, seventies, and eighties are changing so rapidly that life for older adults is nothing like that experienced by previous generations. All of these changes cause the purchasing behavior of each market segment to change.

Echo Boomers.   The youngest consumer market has been defined as **echo boomers**— teenagers aged 12 to 19 years. In the mid 1990s, the U.S. Census counted 29 million teenagers. The teen population is growing twice as fast as the total population and is expected to reach 35 million by year 2010 ("Wired," 1998). Echo boomers, also called "generation Y," have been raised in a decade of global access and knowledge unavailable to any generation before them, using media and the computer as their playground.

In order to effectively reach this youngest generation, who have never known a world without digital media, including personal computers, the Internet, CD-ROMs, video games, and cellular phones, Saatchi and Saatchi researched the population to see how media had affected their lives (Levere, 1999). In the study, child psychologists interviewed a sample of 84 people ages 6–20 years across the United States. In addition, cultural anthropologists observed 10 familes at home for 50 hours each.

The study concluded that the media serves several functions for echo boomers. For the very young, it serves as a toy that provides developmental challenges. For the generation Y family, the digital media has become the "virtual hearth" at home. The digital media is generally set up in a public room, and consequently, a number of digital activities are shared by the family, making these media the center of family life (Levere, 1999). The media also serves as a library for generaiton Y, giving them tremendous access to information. The use of digital media has caused generation Y to be more visually and verbally sophisticated than generations before them.

To respond to generation Y, Saatchi and Saatchi recommended that promotion specialists deliver smarter, more sophisticated messages and build brands *with* this youngest generation rather than *for* them (Levere, 1999). Marketers need to "advertise up," by pitching more adult messages. This generation will tune out promotions that sound too young, according to Anne Adriance of Saatchi and Saatchi. Additionally, professionals need to build brands that go beyond the product and empower the youth. An example is Nickelodeon's Big Help volunteer program, which validates kids and does not speak down to them.

Many echo boomers have grown up in two-income households and are accustomed to having many materialistic things. These teenagers have sufficient income to spend on themselves. In fact, income among teenagers rose 29 percent to $111 billion dollars in 1997 ("Wired," 1998). With this added income, teenagers are buying clothing, entertainment, food, personal care items, and sporting goods among other items.

Direct-mail catalogs and teen magazines have found that the ambiance of their promotional campaigns will make or break fashion acceptance by echo boomers ("Wired," 1998). Marketing campaigns most likely to attract teenagers feature real teens in real situations, such as in classrooms or at home preparing for dates. Retailers are using music and entertainment as interactive retailing methods to attract teenagers into stores. For example, Unionbay Sportswear draws teenagers into its stores by offering Sony play stations for compact discs, Internet access, and two movie screens continuously showing images that create a place where kids want to hang out. Figure 2.5 is an advertisement for JNCO, placed in magazines for 12- to 19-year old echo boomers, its target market.

Generation X.   The twentysomething generation, aged 20 to 35 years, has been dubbed **generation X** by marketers. The last census of the 20th century counted 28 percent of the population as these young adults. The consumer behavior of generation X has been shaped by divorce, diversity, and declining incomes (Ritchie, 1995). Generation Xers, most likely children of working parents, have been responsible for household chores, maintenance, and shopping at an earlier age. They are remaining in the household longer, living at home, and keeping close ties to their family as compared to previous generations. They have redefined the extended family to include close friends, stepparents, adopted and half-siblings, live-in lovers, and other diverse relations.

Generation Xers have been designated the family decision maker by many of their parents and relatives. Their parents work and the young adults have been responsible

Figure 2.5
JNCO advertises in magazines with a teenage readership to reach its target market.

for household shopping. These young adults are more familiar with household products than the adults they live with, and they have expertise in items such as electronic equipment, computers, and automobiles. Generation Xers have a major influence on the products and brands purchased for their homes. Additionally, this buying influence is spread to more than one household, since a higher percentage of generation Xers come from divorced families.

As young adults enter the workforce and start families, they continue to spend money on items that express a balance between career and home, including leisure activities and family entertainment, economical and functional clothing, and quality day care and home offices. Items that allow the generation X consumer to keep in touch with others will continue to be considered necessities—not luxuries—and remain popular. These items include car phones, beepers, pagers, and answering and fax machines (Ritchie, 1995).

Generation Xers have grown up on commercials and dislike advertisements that are stupid, misleading, offensive, or boring. Like many of us, they do not want to be disturbed at home by a salesperson on the telephone. They have grown up in a decade in which diversity is accepted, and they are attracted to promotional campaigns that avoid negative stereotypes and offensiveness. According to Ritchie (1995), the diversity of this generation will remain a formidable challenge. Rather than defining targets in terms of primary, secondary, or tertiary levels, targets will be defined as conglomerates of equally important but diverse segments. Message sponsors will need to vary product design, distribution, cost, and promotion according to the prospective group they wish to attract.

Baby Boomers.   The **baby boomer** generation are those people born between the years 1946 and 1964. At the end of the 20th century, the oldest baby boomers were 54; the youngest, 36 years old. Seventy-six million consumers are baby boomers, four out of every ten American adults (Reda, 1998). As baby boomers age, they are causing changes in product and service offerings. Within specific product categories, baby boomers have caused sales to grow and then decline in a predictable pattern as they move through the life cycle.

Younger baby boomers are changing the demand for housing as they choose to remain single longer or live in childless, single parent, or one-child households. This group desires smaller multipurpose appliances, do-it-yourself products, and durable household furnishings. Individuals in this group are more likely to borrow money for purchases because they measure progress in life by the possession of things. Baby boomers are not likely to go without, and this spending pattern is being passed to their children, the echo boomers (Ritchie, 1995).

Older baby boomers, those near 50 years old, are typically characterized as higher income, free-spending individuals whose purchase motives are directed at quality, durability, and variety. This group has already purchased most necessary items and is becoming less materialistic than in earlier years. Investment and retirement planning is becoming important to older baby boomers as well as shopping for others instead of themselves. Within this market segment there is also a population that feels financially burdened because they are raising children (their own or their grandchildren) and at the same time taking care of elderly parents who are living longer than in past generations.

Adult consumers see themselves as 10 to 15 years younger than their chronological age. Consequently, age-based communication strategies that promote messages to the *psychological age* of consumers have a greater opportunity for acceptance by the targeted market. Successful promotions for baby boomers appeal to their age-defying lifestyle. Products and services that do not refer to "mature" or "graying" customers have a stronger chance at acceptance in this group. If a product conjures up an image of old age, it will be instantly rejected by the baby boomer (Reda, 1998).

Silver Streakers. **Silver streakers** are the 50-plus market. By the year 2010, this market will include one out of every three consumers (Lewison, 1997). This market is rapidly changing as the life span beyond retirement increases. This group includes a large number of empty-nesters who feel free to spend money on themselves instead of leaving an estate to their children. These consumers are spending money on entertainment, travel, recreation, adult education, and other convenience- and experience-oriented goods and services. Advertisements that portray senior consumers as attractive, active, healthy, and affluent have had the best results with this market (Reda, 1998).

Gender

Second only to age, gender is a popular statistic to use in segmenting populations. Gender is the sexual identity of an individual. Traditionally, marketers have made a distinction between female- and male-dominated purchases and created campaigns to attract the identified gender. Female-dominated purchases included food, clothing, and household items; male-dominated purchases included investments and insurance. But these distinctions are diminishing as women become equal to men in the workplace and men are assuming equally significant roles in home and family life (Lewison, 1997). Women are making nontraditional purchases, such as banking services, retirement packages, and investments. Now, more than ever, both male and female members of the household are sharing equally in purchasing goods for the home. Retailers need to use the promotion mix to appeal to both members of the household as a team.

Homosexuals are a large market that is beginning to emerge as a mainstream consumer group (Ritchie, 1995). Gays and lesbians have been relatively invisible in the baby boom and silver streak markets but have developed a broad acceptance within generation X. Approximately 6 percent of the population identify themselves as gay or lesbian (Wells, Burnett, and Moriarty 1998). Statistics about homosexuals as an emerging consumer group are limited. However, it is generally acknowledged that upscale well-educated gay and lesbian professionals represent a potentially large market. Campaigns targeted to this population should instill trust, self-understanding, emotional and physical security, and independence (Wells et al., 1998). Heterosexual or homosexual, well-educated individuals provide another base by which to segment consumers.

Education

Today, eight of every ten Americans have high school diplomas. One in four adults over age 24 has a college degree, and an additional 23 percent have attended college ("Educational," 1997). In general, younger people are more likely to have completed higher educational levels than older people because of the opportunities afforded them to attend school and the expectation by society in recent years that one should go to college. The number of college-educated Americans is expected to increase with continued educational opportunities.

Professional, college-educated individuals are a profitable market, but they are hard to keep. They have greater financial ability, which allows them to take greater purchase risks and causes them to be less brand loyal. Promotional strategies aimed at this target group should involve emerging technologies and innovations because this group reads more, watches less television, and requests more information about products and services than target groups with less education. In today's society, educational attainment is correlated with a higher income.

Income

Businesses often look at household incomes to make statistical generalizations about members of the household. An individual's personal income is comprised of **disposable income**, money available after taxes; and **discretionary income**, money available after taxes and necessities such as food and housing have been paid for. A household income of $50,000 will reflect quite different spending probabilities for a single female with no children, versus a married couple with two children.

Income can be reported as mean or median income. **Mean income** is the average value of all incomes within the sample. Mean income will include very small and very large incomes, distorting a true picture of the market segment. For an accurate picture, businesses look at the **median income** of their potential target segment. This is the middle value in the income distribution with an equal number of incomes above and below the midpoint. Pricing strategies that look only at mean incomes may miss the target market to whom the promotion is aimed.

Members of society positioned socioeconomically between the lower working class and the wealthy are considered the **middle class**. Middle class is determined on the basis of annual household after tax income and is the portion of the population grouped around the national average. The middle class may be proportionally smaller today than it was two decades ago, but it has not disappeared. Forty percent of the U.S. population—or more than 100 million people—live in households earning $35,000 to $75,000 a year (Leonhardt, 1997). The middle class, which in the past included nearly everyone, is no longer growing in terms of population or purchasing power but instead, swelling at the top and bottom ends (Leonhardt, 1997). Census data has revealed that since 1980, the wealthiest fifth of the population has seen its income grow by 21 percent, while wages for the bottom 60 percent of consumers have stagnated or even dipped. Mid-decade figures revealed that the highest fifth of the population controlled 49.1 percent of total income (Youmans, 1997). The shrinking of the middle class has caused marketers to adopt a new strategy that encourages companies to tailor their products and promotions to two different target markets divided along economic, educational, and technological lines. This strategy is called two-tier marketing and is described in Box 2.1.

Occupation

The occupation of an individual will influence his or her income. Occupation is the vocation that serves as one's regular source of income. Occupational trends that began in the 1970s continue to have an impact at the turn of the century. Information-based occupations, such as lawyers, doctors, and engineers, have replaced the industrial occupations of farming and private household workers. Record numbers of women have entered the job market. Blue-collar occupations have been progressively replaced with white-collar occupations (Lewison, 1997).

Changing occupational trends have influenced the content and media choice of promotional campaigns. For example, advertisements provide a higher degree of technical information to the consumer than in past decades. In addition to the information presented as part of the campaign, it is common practice to broadcast or print a web site address to direct the consumer to more information about the product or service. Characters within promotion campaigns are nearly always white-collar professionals and increasingly female (Wells et al., 1998).

BOX 2.1
Two-tier Marketing

He was the little tan bear millions of kids grew up with. He tagged along with Christopher Robin, stuck his hand in the honey pot, and figured out new ways to cause harmless mischief. And no matter where children came from or what their parents did for a living, the name Winnie-the-Pooh conjured up a single image gleaned from the classic books by A. A. Milne.

Today's kids, however, will not have that common touchstone. These days, their image of Pooh depends a lot on where they live and how much their parents make. That's because the Walt Disney Co., which owns the rights to Milne's make-believe menagerie, is carefully marketing two distinct Poohs. The original line-drawn figure appears on fine china, pewter spoons, and pricey kids' stationary found in upscale specialty and department stores such as Nordstrom and Bloomingdale's. The plump, cartoonlike Pooh, clad in a red T-shirt and a goofy smile, adorns plastic key chains, polyester bedsheets, and animated videos. It sells in Wal-Mart stores and five-and-dime shops. Except for at Disney's own stores, the two Poohs do not share the same retail shelf.

"Tiffany/Wal-Mart"

It is a strategy that more of America's biggest marketers are adopting—and for good reason. The middle class, which once seemed to include almost everyone, is no longer growing in terms of numbers or purchasing power. Instead, it is the top and bottom ends that are swelling.

While politicians and social critics squabble over why this has happened and what, if anything, should be done about it, marketers are taking action. Saatchi & Saatchi Advertising Worldwide warns of "a continuing erosion of our traditional mass market—the middle class." PaineWebber Inc. has advised investors to follow a "Tiffany/Wal-Mart" strategy and "avoid companies that serve the 'middle' of the consumer market." And Roper Starch Worldwide, the New York-based polling firm, has presented clients with a report called *Two Americas,* suggesting ways to sell to a society divided along economic, educational, and technological lines.

Think of the restaurant business as a metaphor for the economy, says Lester C. Thurow, an economist and former Management dean at MIT. "The $4 meal is doing all right, and the $50 meal is doing all right. The $20 meal is in trouble."

That implies a dramatic shift in the way consumer goods are designed, advertised, and sold. From the dawn of the modern ad agency early in the century through the golden age of mass-marketing in the 1950s and 1960s—when returning GIs bought truckloads of near-identical toys and TV sets for their baby boom offspring—markets have set their sights squarely on that metaphorical $20 meal. America's most venerable brand names, from Levi's jeans to Ivory soap, were built on the premise that a reasonably good product, properly packaged and hyped, could be sold to almost anyone.

Even through the me-generation of the 1970s and the acquisitive 1980s, which brought a host of specialized retailers geared to more individualized tastes, most brands kept their focus squarely on the middle. That time-tested strategy no longer assures success. Indeed, from Detroit to Fifth Avenue, from Silicon Valley to Main Street, Corporate America is rethinking the way it markets its goods and services. In industry after industry, the market is bifurcating.

Class Matters

This new dual world affects far more than just the way goods are sold. Back in the days when everyone gathered around the TV to watch *The Ed Sullivan Show* and then trooped out to buy its sponsors' brands, mass marketing was a unifying force. Now "certain brands become the brands of certain classes, and it helps put people in their uniforms," says Seth M. Siegel, co-chairman at Beanstalk Group, a New York licensing firm. That's true whether it's Prada's hot-selling $450 black vinyl backpack or the Kathie Lee line of clothing at Wal-Mart.

Of course, neither the mass market nor the middle class has evaporated. Coke, Tide, and an array of powerhouse brands still sell to virtually everybody. And the middle class, though less inclusive, is still a powerful force. But the economic trends of the past 30 years have altered its spending habits as well as its composition.

Nowhere have those changes wreaked more havoc than in retailing, where even consumers with a solidly middle-class income—such as Gil Pastore—have become inveterate bargain hunters.

Grabbing Bargains

Gil Pastore pulls his Jeep Cherokee into the Wal-Mart parking lot, buys a small pack of batteries, a big bag of dog food, and 20 minutes later is on his way. The 35-year-old owner of a computer-service business figures Wal-Mart saved him $5 off supermarket prices. Gil follows a distinctly 1990s compulsion of the middle class: he shops discount. Increasingly, the middle class, a group that once expected to pay roughly the same price for the same goods no matter where they bought them is splitting its budget between bargain stores that provide savings and purveyors of affordable luxuries that provide a taste of the good life.

The rules that govern their spending have changed for the middle-class. Stretched budgets have provided middle-class shoppers with plenty of reasons to look for savings, while the sale-filled recession of the early 1990s trained them to expect markdowns. Meanwhile, increasingly hectic work schedules have directed people toward small indulgences such as a $2 cup of coffee, a $10 six-pack of beer, or gourmet take-out dinners. The result: even those with middle-class incomes are contributing to a bifurcation of the mass market. "Status has been redefined, so that it's not just the brand you have but also the deal you got," says Carl Steidtmann, director of research at Management Horizons, the retail consulting division of Price Waterhouse LLP. "People are proud of buying discount."

Just look at Wal-Mart Stores, Inc., where annual sales have more than doubled in the past 5 years, to $93.6 billion. The discounter's legendary efficiency allows it to offer name-brand goods at substantially lower process—an enticing proposition no matter what your income bracket. Indeed, a tour of a typical Wal-Mart parking lot shows shiny new luxury sedans and 4 × 4s alongside aging subcompacts in need of a paint job.

Consumers in all brackets continue to crave a little luxury in their lives. Savvy marketers are figuring out ways to provide it—or at least a close facsimile—for a reasonable price. "If before we were buying ourselves a new car every three years or going on a cruise every two years," says Mark Barden, founding partner at the San Francisco ad agency Black Rocket, "now we're buying ourselves a really, really good cup of coffee."

Indeed, Starbucks Corporation and other upscale coffee houses have proliferated in the last 5 years. Meanwhile, brands from Jeep to Gucci have begun to license their logos for use on items from boom boxes to perfume, appealing to people who like a luxury image but not a luxury price. As marketers from Wal-Mart to Starbucks have discovered, convincing consumers that you offer either a great bargain or a great treat can prove irresistible.

Millionaire's World

By 2005, millionaires will control 60 percent of the country's dollars. The rest will be controlled by middle-class and poorer people stretched thinner than ever. More families can no longer afford things that were once seen as the birthright of the middle class—the occasional new car, the new clothes, and the annual vacation. Many have cut back in the areas their counterparts would not have considered skimping on in decades past.

Ironically, however, the shift has created a lucrative opportunity for marketers who can provide low-end goods and services that are palatable to a straitened consumer with middle-class aspirations. Marketers have come to realize that as a group, low-wage earners control a powerful amount of disposable income. As a result, that swelling demographic has gone from an underserved minority to a group with clout and choice.

One example is happening in retail. Second-hand clothing, once the sole province of thrift shops and winter coat drives, has gone upscale. Sales of clothing and other used goods have doubled since 1987; since 1994 they have grown at almost triple the pace of retail as a whole. "Our pricing is really excellent for struggling young parents, people who grew up understanding what good brands are but who can't afford them now," says Walter F. Hamilton Jr., president of Children's Orchard, a fast-growing children's resale chain. To make those young parents feel O.K. about buying used overalls, Children's Orchard repackages many of its items in shrink-wrap—just like they were new.

But even as some companies aim at either the top or the bottom of the market, there are plenty such as Disney, with its upstairs and downstairs Poohs, hoping to land customers on both sides of the divide. Gap Inc. is remodeling its Banana Republic stores to make them more upscale and has increased the size of the chain by almost 50 percent—or 68 units—in the past 5 years. At the same time, it has headed off some of the competition from the likes of Wal-Mart by creating a hip lower-end chain called Old Navy. Since 1993, the San Francisco company has opened 193 Old Navy outlets, compared with just 21 new Gap stores.

The media that once carried mass advertising have splintered along the same divide. When executives at V.F. Corporation in Wyomissing, PA decided to target Wrangler jeans more narrowly to the $50,000-a-year-and-under market, they reexamined exactly where their TV commercials aired and culled down the audience from shows that appealed to the more affluent consumers, to shows that appealed to the middle-class consumer. The advertising campaign has succeeded: while V.F. as a whole has floundered, Wrangler has been growing at 10 percent a year for the past decade.

How many other brands will be singing a similar song a decade from now? That will depend to a great extent on how well they navigate the new marketplace. It is a through-the-looking-glass world, with the spoils likely to go to those companies that are best able to scale back the mass in mass marketing. Those that persist in trying to reach the most people possible may find instead that they reach no one at all.

Adapted from: Leonhardt, D. (1997, March 17). Two-tier marketing. Business Week, 82–87, 90.

Race & Ethnicity

Race is the biological heritage of an individual. Black and Caucasian are examples of races. Ethnicity is the description of a group bound together by ties of cultural homogeneity and is often based around national origins. "Hispanic" is an ethnicity, not a race. The term refers to people whose ancestry is from Spanish-speaking countries of South and Central America. A Hispanic person will also be designated as a member of the Caucasian, Black, American Indian, or other racial designation.

Ethnic diversity is changing the market segments of the United States. Population estimates indicate that between 1990 and 2040, the percentage of Black people will increase from 12.4 percent of the population to 15.3 percent. The percentage of Asians, Pacific Islanders, and American Indians will increase from 3.5 percent to 7.8 percent, while the percentage of Caucasian people including Hispanics will decrease from 84.1 percent to 76.9 percent (Wells et al., 1998).

Retailers who understand the ethnic differences among potential customers are offering product lines that compliment the appropriate target market. Merchandise selection and promotion activities are influenced by the ethnic mix of the primary and secondary target markets. The race of a potential target group may determine merchandise selection; for instance cosmetic and beauty products that meet the needs of nonwhite consumers (Fig. 2.6). The physical build of the ethnic group that predominates among a store's customers may influence its merchandise assortment. For example, Asian-American females are typically smaller in build than members of some other

Figure 2.6

A skincare advertisement targeted to an ethnic consumer through specific placement in *Ebony* magazine.

ethnic groups. Retailers targeting this market segment should have a larger selection of petite and small sizes. Grocers look at the ethnic mix of potential customers to determine the specific food offerings to be sold at different branches and promote these grocery offerings in media appropriate to the target market. Box 2.2 highlights the importance of ethnic groups to the U.S. economy and focuses on some of the multicultural advertising campaigns that have worked with these populations.

BOX 2.2

Are You Selling to Me?

The current boom in multicultural marketing has changed the face of ethnic advertising, but only after a long record of embarrassing missteps.

In a memorable McDonald's commercial, a father prods his baby to say, "Daddy." Nothing works until the resourceful dad shakes a bag of McDonald's fries before the happy toddler, who obliges by cheerfully uttering, "Papa." Americans liked the spot. Hispanics got it: In Spanish, the word for *dad* and *fries* is the same.

Either way, the ad was a hit. Anglos "responded to the magic of the relationship," says Luis Messianu, chief creative officer at del Rivero Messianu Advertising in Coral Gables, Florida, which created the spot. "Hispanics can tell it was conceived by one of their own." The McDonald's ad and others like it, including the hot "¡ Yo quiero Taco Bell!" campaign, featuring a Spanish-speaking chihuahua, are part of a new wave in multicultural marketing. They develop a strong connection with ethnic consumers by their use of familiar words and images.

Time was, if you were a marketer looking to grab a piece of the ethnic pie, you more than likely tried to reach minority consumers simply by translating English-language commercials verbatim or by substituting African-American, Hispanic, or Asian actors for whites in mainstream scripts. Sometimes the method worked, but it also produced some spectacular flops. Perhaps the marketers of the Chevrolet Nova committed the most famous foreign-language gaffe—the car's name literally means, "doesn't go" in Spanish. More recently, when translated into Chinese, Pepsi's "Come alive" ads declared, "Wake up your dead ancestors."

Money Talks

Marketers are much more careful these days about avoiding embarrassing slip-ups. The incentive has been a flurry of new data. Demographics alone point to the perils of ignoring ethnic markets. According to Census Bureau data released in the fall of 1998, there are 34.5 million African-Americans, who represent 12.7 percent of the U.S. popu-

lation, and 30.7 million Hispanics, who represent 11.3 percent. By 2005, the bureau predicts, those numbers will mushroom to more than 36 million in each group. Add in Asian-Americans, and the ethnic trio currently makes up more than a quarter of the U.S. population.

It is estimated that minorities will grow to nearly one-third of the population by 2010 and almost one-half by 2050, says Vanguard Communications, a New York-based agency that specializes in multicultural marketing. In key markets such as New York, Miami, and Los Angeles, they're already more than half. A study by ad agency Stedman Graham & Partners pegs the buying power of the African-American market at $450 billion and the Latino market at $380 billion. With statistics like these, mainstream marketers are falling all over themselves to reach ethnic consumers.

Fewer Faux Pas

Advertisers are showing their multicultural marketing know-how in different ways. While some are taking the cross-cultural route, with ads that appeal to both ethnic groups and mainstream consumers (the McDonald's "papa" ad is a good example), others are hypertargeting ethnic markets. Instead of treating the Latino audience as one homogeneous group, for example, advertisers are dexterously slicing the market into niches based on differences in languages, sex, religion, age, and country of origin. In 1997, various TV commercials for Budweiser featured a Spaniard, a Puerto Rican, an Argentinean, a Cuban, and a Mexican.

Some ads are reaching out to certain groups by reflecting cultural norms. For Asians, *family* connotes not just parents and children but also grandparents, aunts, and uncles. So ads aimed at this group often teem with multiple generations, says Bill Imada, chief executive officer of Imada Wong Communications Group, an ethnic marketing firm based in Los Angeles.

Marketers are also reaching out with campaigns that put products directly into the hands of targeted customers. Revlon distributes free baskets of hair products at gospel conventions and is a major sponsor of the Stellar Awards, the Grammys of black gospel. Coors Brewing Co. has sponsored a concert tour and sweepstakes in honor of Black Music Month.

Minorities can't always be reached via mainstream media. Doug Alligood, senior vice president of special markets at BBDO Worldwide, has tracked black TV viewing habits for 11 years and found that, when it comes to TV, American blacks and whites may as well be living on separate planets. "None of the top 10 network shows among black households overlap with the top 10 among total U.S. households this year," says Alligood. "The most popular shows for blacks weren't even among the 90 most popular shows for households." This split continues an 11-year trend.

Fortunately, finding multicultural media outlets has never been easier. There has been a virtual explosion in minority media, from cable TV channels to ethnic Yellow Pages.

To respond to this marketing juggernaut, the American Association of Advertising Agencies launched the Hispanic Advertising committee in 1997 and recently kicked off the first O'Toole Multicultural Advertising Award competition. The Association of National Advertisers created the Multicultural Marketing Committee, and the Advertising Research Foundatioin formed the Ethnic Research Council. Individual ad agencies are homing in on multicultural consumers by setting up special units or strategic alliances with minority-owned firms.

"The decade of multicultural marketing was predicted to be the '80s, but it turned out to be the '90s," says Esther Novak, Peruvian-born president of Vanguard Communications. "There were misperceptions about the markets. But that barrier has finally broken down."

Adapted from: Kanner, B. (1999, March). Are you selling to me? Working Woman, *62–65. Reprinted with the permission of Mac-Donald Communications Corporation. Copyright ©1999 by Mac-Donald Communications Corporation.*

Ethnic groups will continue to grow in number and purchasing power. Promotion specialists need to pay close attention to creating advertising that is ethnically targeted. Rabin (1994) articulated several ideas to assist sponsors in communicating with racial and ethnic groups in a multicultural society. The ideas are still relevant and include understanding:

- Social values, methods of communication, and common interests that cross cultural boundaries.
- How religion may shape the way an ethnic group thinks and communicates.
- The existence of bilingual communication among minority populations who work and live among white populations, allowing these populations to speak and understand messages in both cultures.
- The distinct tastes in media that exist among cultural groups.

Rabin suggested creating advertising and promotional messages that consist of universal messages addressing the commonalties and differences within target markets. Use a mix of broadcast and print media to present messages blending words and pictures that have strong oral and strong written communication traditions to attract both cultures. He also suggested seeking permission from community leaders before attempting to open communication channels within ethnic target groups. The most important element in designing a promotion campaign targeted to ethnic groups is to avoid reinforcing racial and ethnic stereotypes.

Family Size and Structure

Another demographic statistic useful in determining target markets is family size and structure. The perception of the household as "parents with children" is no longer realistic. Table 2.1 describes the composition of households by type prior to the year 2000. Of the over 101 million households within the United States, married couples without children represented 28.2 percent and people who live alone represented 25.1 percent. Households with parents and children ranked third proportionally.

Table 2.1   Household by Type

Type of Household	Numbers (in thousands)	Percent[a]
Total households	101,018	100.0
Married couples with children	25,083	24.8
Married couples without children	28,521	28.2
Other families with children	9,583	9.5
Other families without children	7,054	7.0
People living alone	25,402	25.1
Other nonfamily households	5,375	5.3

[a]Does not equal 100 percent due to rounding.

Source: March 1997 Current Population Survey, U.S. Census Bureau.

Certain age groups reflect certain types of households. The majority of single men who live alone are under age 45, while the largest number of single women who live alone are over age 65. Additionally, young people are more likely than older adults to live in a cohabitating or unrelated roommate household.

Contemporary households are composed of few children and are unlikely to involve a member of the extended family. Single-parent households and empty nesters also make up a larger number of households than in the past. Whereas in the past, large economy sizes were the trend in packaging many hard-line goods such as food, manufacturers are now bringing back smaller sized containers to accommodate smaller households in smaller spaces.

Disability Status

Americans who are disabled are another large market that is beginning to emerge as a consumer group. On July 26, 1990 the Americans with Disabilities Act (ADA) was signed into law. The ADA prohibits discrimination on the basis of disability in employment, programs, services, and communication ("Americans," 1998). With the passage of the ADA, businesses have become aware of the 43 million disabled consumers who are a potential target market (Burnett and Paul, 1996). Pursuing disabled consumers enables a company to find new customer groups at a time when population growth is slowing.

Disabled status is a less manageable characteristic to identify and measure than the other demographics characteristics listed above. As with other target markets, submarkets exist within the physically challenged market including those who are mobility disabled, hearing or sight impaired, and have other limitations. In order to advertise and promote effectively to the physically challenged market, marketers must develop data-gathering techniques that will categorize the segment correctly and meaningfully (Burnett and Paul, 1996). Past research has depended on secondary information sources such as employment records, memberships in organizations, and subscriptions to publications targeting the disabled. Disabled consumers want to use media to make their lives easier. Anything that enables them to be just like other consumers will be rewarded with favorable response and loyalty. Advertising that shows an awareness for the needs and wants of the disabled and offers the same insights as their personal sources of information will be well received by disabled consumers (Fig. 2.7).

Figure 2.7

Nordstrom has been a leader in featuring people with disabilities in advertisements.

Behavioristic Segmentation

While demographic characteristics provide a researcher with basic statistical information to determine target groups, this information does not address the behavioral patterns of consumers, which may tell us more about them than their age, income, or ethnic identity. Consumers in the marketplace can also be segmented based on their behavior.

Think about an item you recently purchased. Was it a fashion item or a basic item? How often do you buy this item? Did you wait until you needed to replace it, or did you buy it to have it on hand? When you replaced it, did you buy the same brand or an alternative brand? Do you always purchase this item at the same store, or do you purchase it wherever you happen to be? Were you influenced by sales promotions surrounding the item? All of these questions relate to your behavior as a consumer.

Behavioristic segmentation is a method of segmenting markets based on consumer usage, loyalty, or buying responses to a product or service. Researchers who use behavior segmentation look at what consumers actually do in the marketplace as opposed to what consumers say they do in the marketplace.

Behavioristic segmentation includes the degree of use a consumer exhibits toward a product. Consumer usage patterns define users as regular users, first-time users, prospective users, ex-users, or nonusers. Consumer usage patterns also define consumers as light users, moderate users, or heavy users. Promotions are designed with the type of user in mind. Advertisers may direct promotions to consumers who are very familiar with, and intend to buy the product, as well as to consumers who are completely unfamiliar with the product and have no information on which to base a decision. A new product may be promoted to attract the prospective user. Promotions may be created to convince the light user to become a moderate user, or moderate users to become heavy users. Food producers saturate the media with reminders to purchase specialty food items popular over the holiday season. Holiday liqueurs, baking chocolate, and party mix among other items are crowded in front of the consumer to increase their buying during this time period. The Gap developed a khaki trousers promotion to target all degrees of users by focusing on good, basic khakis. The theme introduced the idea of owning a pair of khakis to nonusers and potential users and, through the same ad, reinforced regular users to update the khakis currently in their wardrobe (Fig. 2.8).

Behavioristic segmentation may be used to determine consumer segments based on brand loyalty. Consumers may insist on certain brands or reject certain brands. Recognition of a specific brand or nonrecognition of all brands may influence buying behavior. Brand familiarity may influence a regular or potential user's intention to buy. Many sales promotion techniques are designed to reinforce brand loyalty to consumers. Behaviors such as buying activity and store preference may also be used to determine segmentation bases. Are consumers most likely to purchase the product at a convenience store, a department store, or a specialty shop? Do consumers comparison shop at several stores before making the purchase or do they purchase the product randomly wherever they happen to be? Behavior segmentation plays an important role in analyzing effective sales promotion techniques, as will be discussed in Chapter 11.

Figure 2.8

The Gap introduced a campaign to promote khaki trousers that targeted all consumer usage patterns.

Psychographic Segmentation

Have you ever filled out the consumer questionnaire included in the packaging of a consumer good? If you have, you have participated in psychographic segmentation by that particular manufacturer. Demographic and behavioristic information does not always provide adequate information to target a specific market. Although demographics give a retailer a basic description of its customers, a better predictor of consumer behavior may be found in the lifestyle profile of the consumer through psychographics. **Psychographic segmentation** is an attempt to profile the lifestyle of consumers based upon activities, interests, and opinions.

Obtaining information on activities, interests, and opinions is more complex than collecting demographic information. While demographic information is exact, psychographic information is subjective and indirect in meaning. There are no commonly accepted definitions for terms frequently used in psychographic questions such as "satisfaction" with a product, or how the product makes you "feel." As a result, psychographic information is more difficult to compare.

Lifestyle information is usually gained through a questionnaire asking consumers what they do, how they spend their time, what they buy, and why they buy it. Interests are obtained by asking about hobbies, travel, and leisure time. Consumers are also asked their views on social issues, world events, economic situations, and values to determine their opinions. Based upon the profile, advertisers develop themes for promotions and select the appropriate media in which to transmit the promotions. For example, very specific questions about activities, interests, and opinions help an advertiser determine the effectiveness of using one magazine over another when placing an ad.

Questionnaires distributed to a random sample of households is a common method used to obtain psychographic information. However, the wording of the question, no matter how carefully presented, may influence the type of answer received. Opinion surveys administered over the phone may be less accurate than mailed surveys because the consumer may not be willing to be entirely truthful with the caller. Mailed surveys may be limited in usefulness because the respondents give short answers without explanations, not revealing attitudes or opinions. Also consumers, while saying one thing, may do something else. Many consumers surveyed have shown widespread interest in recycling, for example, but this interest is not reflected in the purchase of products made from recycled materials.

Psychographic segmentation has become popular as a consumer research tool since the **Values and Lifestyles System (VALS)**, was developed by the Stanford Research Institute (SRI). Many companies have subsequently used VALS to segment markets for advertising purposes. The **VALS** program was developed from the work of motivational and developmental psychologists, particularly that of Abraham Maslow, and his theory of a hierarchy of needs. **Maslow's Hierarchy of Needs** is a motivation theory based on five levels of needs, represented by a pyramid (Fig. 2.9). An individual can pass from one level of the pyramid to the next level only upon attainment of the need at the prior level. At the base level, an individual's basic physiological needs of food, water, and shelter must be met. After these basic needs have been satisfied, the individual next desires safety. Once a level of safety has been gained, the individual seeks love and belonging. As the pyramid narrows, fewer individuals are able to attempt to fulfill the needs of esteem and progress to the top. The top of the pyramid represents self-actualization, in which the individual has achieved his or her full potential and has fulfilled all needs.

Figure 2.9

Maslow's hierarchy of needs.

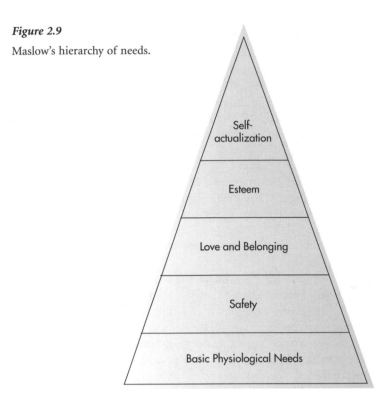

As with Maslow's hierarchy, the VALS program assumes individuals must rise from a base, moving through levels to achieve self-fulfillment (Fig. 2.10). VALS consists of four consumer groups: need-driven, outer-driven, inner-driven, and integrated.

Need-driven consumers are the base of the hierarchy, segmented into survivors and sustainers.

- Indicators used to describe survivors include poverty, old age, poor health, and poor education.
- Sustainers feel angry, rebellious and left out and, as with survivors, reside at poverty level. Sustainers are generally younger than survivors, often of minority heritage, self-confident, expect change in the future, and have not given up hope.

Outer-driven consumers are at the next level in the hierarchy, one of two different tracks based on social, financial, or psychological factors. Neither outer-driven nor inner-driven consumers are considered better off in the hierarchy. Outer-driven consumers are directed by what others think of them and are materialistic by nature. They are segmented as belongers, emulators, or achievers.

- Belongers are defined as America's middle-class, mostly white, with middle-class incomes, older in nature, with strong value systems based on family, church, and country.
- Emulators strive to get ahead by imitating the actions of those whom they consider rich and successful while not necessarily understanding the value system of those they imitate. Consequently, emulators are typically in debt.
- Achievers are most likely to be successful professionals with high incomes, and often hold conservative political views.

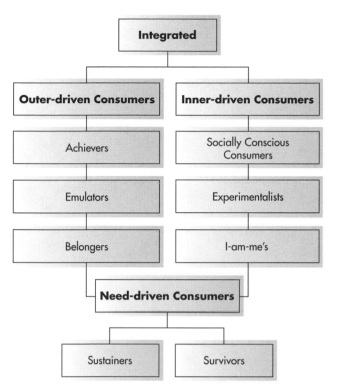

Figure 2.10

Values and lifestyles system
(VALS) diagram.

Inner-driven consumers base opinions on what they think, not what others think. They are also grouped into three segments, the I-am-me's, experimenters, and socially conscious.

- The I-am-me's try to separate themselves from the views of their parents and find their own way. The young adult leaving high school and entering college is typically an I-am-me individual. Most individuals pass through the I-am-me stage quickly.
- Experimentalists generally have reached moderate earning potential and are seeking experiences. They become personably involved in issues that they find important, and are more independent and self-reliant, not depending on others for their success or failure.
- Socially conscious consumers represent individuals concerned with societal issues and trends. Generally more mature, successful, and influential professionals with high incomes, these consumers tend to align themselves with liberal perspectives and are often advocates.

Integrated consumers, or integrates, 2 percent of consumers, represent self-actualized individuals at the top of the VALS hierarchy. They have the highest income and are a combination of socially conscious and achiever consumers.

Using information gained through this research, advertising and promotion planners should be able to determine the consumer group they are seeking to target. Need-driven consumers are the most difficult group to attract with a message because they have a very minimal income to spend on essentials and, therefore, do not pay attention to advertising messages that promote products or services beyond their grasp. Transit media is effective for need-driven consumers because it is free for them. Consumers do not have to buy a publication, view a broadcast or make a purchase to obtain the message.

Promotional messages directed to outer-driven consumers and inner-driven consumers will be quite different. Belongers are attracted to advertising that is value oriented. Emulators are attracted to appeals that allow them to "keep up with the Joneses." Achievers will be attracted to advertising that implies security and future well being. Advertising that promotes "the ability to make your own choice" attracts I-am-me's. The experimental consumer will respond to advertising that reflects self-reliance, such as "do-it-yourself" programming. Advertisements reflecting social values will attract the socially conscious. Integrates are proving to be a difficult market to target because so many of their needs and wants have already been met, and they are not viewers or readers of traditional media outlets. Advertisers who can gain the attention of integrates will find they are a potentially lucrative market of the future.

VALS is only one of many psychographic segmentation tools available to market researchers. Each lifestyle system developed and marketed has the potential to segment consumers in a new and creative way. Any list of systems provided in this textbook would be out of date as soon as the list was written. However, it is very easy for students and promotion planners to find psychographic lifestyle systems over the Internet and determine the system with the most potential to analyze consumers and retailers for promotion effectiveness.

The Global Consumer

As the population increases, businesses and researchers are becoming more concerned with broadening consumer research beyond the traditional considerations of demographic and psychographic bases of segmentation and targeting their customer at a deeper, more emotional level. They are taking a more global view of consumer understanding and finding that consumers around the world are not that different. In the first study of its kind to describe the global consumer, Roger Starch Worldwide, a New York based research firm, interviewed 35,000 consumers in 35 countries to identify shared values that cross national borders. The purpose of the study according to Tom Miller, group senior vice president and director for international operations, "was to put into place a globally comparable system of gathering consumer intelligence and predicting consumer trends around the world" (Elliott, 1998d).

The study identified six distinct global value groups based on belief systems that define worldwide adult consumers long term (Elliott, 1998d). The six groups are strivers, devouts, altruists, intimates, fun seekers, and creatives.

- *Strivers* represent 23 percent of the population and consider material things extremely important. They value wealth, status, ambition, and power. Strivers are more likely to be middle-aged males from developed or developing nations like Japan and the Philippines, and will use the newspaper as their primary media source.
- *Devouts* are adults with more traditional values like faith, duty, obedience, and respect for elders. Devouts represent 22 percent of the population and are concentrated in Africa, Asia, and the Mideast. This group is the least involved with the media and least likely to want Western brands.
- *Altruists* are very outer-focused and interested in social issues and causes. They are generally well-educated females and represent 18 percent of the population. Altruists are often found in Latin America and Russia.
- *Intimates* are worldwide adult consumers who are "people-people," focusing on re-

lationships very close to home such as spouses, family, colleagues, and friends. They make up 15 percent of the population and are frequently found in Britain, Hungary, the Netherlands, and the United States. Intimates are heavy users of media that can be shared to create a common bond with others, such as television, movies, and radio, which people watch or listen to and discuss with others the next day.

- *Fun seekers* are the youngest group of consumers and prize values such as pleasure, excitement, adventure, and looking good. They represent 15 percent of the population and are high users of electronic media.
- *Creatives* are the smallest group at 10 percent, but the highest consumers of media including books, magazines, and newspapers. Creatives value knowledge and technology and are considered global trendsetters in owning a PC or surfing the Web.

Businesses willing to use this information to identify appropriate promotion campaigns will be able to attract the global customer worldwide.

There are two equally important but seemingly opposite points of view that should direct advertising and promotion aimed at the global consumer. On the one hand, communication is readily available around the world with the use of computers, satellite communications, and other technologies; therefore, it should be assumed that consumers from many countries will see the message. On the other hand, messages aimed at the global consumer should be customized to the customer profile of the intended audience. More and more viewers are perceiving mass media messages as noise, not intended for them, and are ignoring the message. According to Schultz and Barnes (1995), "advertising is moving from a focus on efficiency . . . to a focus on effectiveness." Promotion planning should target the best customers worldwide instead of the most customers. Identification of the best customers is achieved only through very sophisticated market segmentation and development of an IMC strategy that is focused on the best customers.

Once market segments are identified, marketers attempt to gain access to the specific consumer segment through communication using the promotion mix. Retailers will react to specific target markets by adjusting the depth and breadth of product lines, regulating price points of selected products, determining the quantity and location of display space devoted to specific product lines, and choosing the amount and type of promotional and advertising support. In doing so, sellers are positioning their product in the minds of the consumer.

PRODUCT POSITIONING

The action a firm takes based on the market segmentation analysis of its current or potential customer base is called **product positioning**. It is the use of the promotion mix to cause consumers to perceive a particular company's product as completely different from other brands of the same product or competing products. Using the correct mix, the right product will be distributed at the right place, for the right price to satisfy consumer acquisition. Positioning is extremely critical in a promotional strategy because it defines the perception the consumer will have of the product or service.

Positioning strategies developed by manufacturers focus on the trade consumer; positioning strategies developed by retailers focus on final consumers; and both focus on the competition. In most cases multiple offerings of similar products exist, causing the consumer to decide between products. Promotion specialists will concentrate on designing campaigns that focus on the benefits a consumer will gain in purchasing a particular firm's product or service. Benefits may include general or specific product features and may fulfill such needs as quality, service, or economical appropriateness. Sea & Ski has positioned its sunblock as the best at providing consumers with benefits such as being oil free, nongreasy, allergy tested, and never animal tested, to appeal to a wide range of consumers (Fig. 2.11). Timex has positioned its watches as tough and dependable using the slogan *"takes a licking and keeps on ticking."* Better service, better performance, or more features are often highlighted in advertisements as benefits to justify a product's price.

Promotion planners may also create positioning strategies that focus on the competition, comparing the advantages of their product over their rivals' products. Positioning a product by use or application can assist in differentiating the product from the competition. Artificial sweeteners have positioned themselves against sugar, competing across product classes. Snapple has boldly positioned itself against the competition by stating it is number three in the soft drink market (behind Pepsi and Coke). Minivans have been newly designed to have a sliding door on both sides. The benefit

Figure 2.11

Sea & Ski has positioned its sunblock as the best with numerous benefits listed for the reader to consider in selecting this product for use.

of two doors versus one door has been demonstrated in television advertisements showing the doors on both sides of the vehicle opening and closing for children and dogs while an announcer states *"the benefits outshine the competition."*

There are several steps involved in developing a competitive positioning strategy:

1. **Identify all relevant competitors**, including competition within and outside the product category. Pepsi and Coke compete not only against other soft drinks but also against beer, bottled water, wine coolers, and fruit juices as beverage alternatives. Stores also compete directly within the same mall and indirectly with, e-commerce, catalog sales, and outlet malls.
2. **Identify how the competition is perceived by consumers.** This requires market research. Attributes of the competition that consumers find appealing may be the overwhelming criteria in their decision to purchase a product. The firm should determine its position in the marketplace with regard to the competition.
3. **Evaluate the perceived needs of the consumer and select a desired position to meet those needs.** A promotional strategy should be implemented that will be most effective in establishing the desired position. Consumers change constantly—demographically, behaviorally, and psychographically—and therefore their tastes and preferences change too. Competitors also continue to change, repositioning themselves within the market, introducing new products and eliminating poor performers. A firm must continually monitor the perception of consumers toward the promotional strategy to see if the position has created desired results.

A business must decide how many target markets to enter and position products for each target market based on the potential for success of each segment. There are three approaches a marketer can take to position merchandise to one or many target groups: (1) undifferentiated marketing, (2) differentiated marketing, or (3) concentrated marketing. The choice of which alternative to use is based on an estimate of revenues generated by the selected target versus the additional promotion costs that will be incurred to market only to the selected market segment.

Undifferentiated marketing is the most cost-saving approach to promote merchandise, but it is also the most risk-oriented strategy. In an undifferentiated marketing strategy, the same promotional mix is offered to the entire population without regard to market segments. History provides an example of an undifferentiated marketing strategy. In the late 1970s the word "generic" was coined for a marketing strategy. Every product sold using this marketing strategy was packaged in plain white paper with bold black lettering spelling out G-E-N-E-R-I-C. The breadth of products was wide, with variety limited to one option, priced below the market standard. Products were diverse and ranged from socks and underwear, to dish soap, food products, dog food, and beer. The same message was presented to every consumer.

The risk in undifferentiated marketing is apparent if consumers are not persuaded to buy the product after promotional tools have been developed and distributed. For this reason, undifferentiated marketing is used less frequently than the other two marketing methods. This strategy is successful only if a company has one product without variations which it chooses to market. Companies may choose a *modified* undifferentiated marketing strategy by selecting the largest target market within a population and marketing to that segment. However, most competitors are also marketing to the largest target market, so one segment is over targeted while all other segments are ignored.

In a **differentiated marketing** approach, a company will provide a different promotion mix to two or more select target markets. Marketers hope that sales will be increased through advertisements tailored to specific groups based on distinctive needs; however, implementing a differentiated strategy can be quite difficult. Increased production costs for two or more campaigns create a disadvantage for this marketing method and the segment characteristics may be difficult to articulate.

National advertisers use differentiated marketing to position themselves to regional target markets using **geographic segmentation**. Typical geographic breakdowns include regions, metropolitan statistical area (MSA) size, density of population, and climate. Regional zip codes are a common geographic segmentation tool based on the first digit or first three digits of the zip code. Metropolitan statistical areas have a population over 250,000 people. Urban, suburban, or rural populations may be geographic targets or differentiation may be based on climate. The geographic unit may be large, encompassing several states, or small, limited to streets within a neighborhood.

National fashion magazines use distinctive advertisements to promote regional trends and styles and highlight the availability of the trend at regional stores. In each case, marketers determine the benefit of boosting local market shares with the additional costs needed for production of the regional issue. *Vogue* used the cover of its magazine to emphasize a differentiated marketing approach when it distributed the same issue under three separate covers, featuring New York, Texas, or Los Angeles (Fig. 2.12).

Concentrated marketing is used by marketers who want to position to one segment of the population regardless of other segments. The targeted segment may not be the largest segment, but it will have the greatest potential for successful sales because of some other factor, such as ethnicity or age.

Figure 2.12

The cover of *Vogue* magazine illustrates a differentiated marketing approach.

FUTURE TRENDS IN CONSUMER BEHAVIOR

The increasing sophistication of psychographic lifestyle analysis systems and statistical analysis of data identified by analysis systems will drive the future of consumer behavior as marketers continue to refine target populations. The factors available to segment populations will continue to expand to include religious attitudes, financial behavior, and emerging lifestyle trends, among others. The analysis of neighborhoods will continue to grow including location of specialized goods, product consumption, service usage, and psychographic profiles. Already identified target segments, such as echo boomers and baby boomers, will continue to be analyzed for further refinement.

A project that focuses on the attitudes, preferences, and behaviors of online service and Internet users, called i VALS, is being tested in sample markets (Wells et al., 1998). Creators of this testing tool are using knowledge, instead of income, to determine basic distinctions between target groups. Increased understanding of the Internet user will continue to be a trend in target market research.

Increased statistical analysis of consumer data will also guide future marketing decisions. Data mining technology is a new form of analysis, still in the infancy stage at the beginning of the 21st century, that can be used to reveal relationships that were not previously evident between pieces of data (Zimmerman, 1998a). For example, Airshop, a junior girls' apparel catalog retailer based in New York, has employed data mining technology to determine characteristics of customers who request a catalog compared to customers who are sent a catalog from a rented or purchased list. Airshop wants to use the data analysis to develop different catalogs for different demographic groups and enhance the strategic layout of the catalog. Data mining technology will continue to expand in the future as a powerful database marketing tool.

Because an accurate promotion mix does not just happen, marketers must combine all elements into a marketing program that will encourage positive exchange between consumers and the reseller using consumer research and information. Although product, price, and place are important, manufacturers and retailers can have the greatest influence on consumers by coordinating a promotion plan that communicates the marketing strategy of the company to the consumer. This communication can only be effective if all parts of the promotional effort—including advertising, direct marketing, personal sales, public relations, and others—work together in an integrated marketing communication strategy.

SUMMARY

- Consumer behavior is the study of the decision making processes involved in acquiring, using, and disposing of goods and services.
- Consumption consists of need recognition, information search, alternative evaluation, postpurchase evaluation, and disposal evaluation.
- Impulse buying occurs when no formal need recognition is identified before the purchase is made.
- The product life cycle describes the process of acceptance of a fashion item or trend through introduction, acceptance, and regression.
- Market segmentation is the subdivision of the marketplace into relatively homogeneous subsets of consumers, called target markets or market segments.

- Demographics such as age, gender, education, income, occupation, race and ethnicity, family size and structure, and disability status can be used to segment markets.
- Behavioristic segmentation is a method of segmenting markets based on consumer usage, loyalty, or buying responses to a product or service.
- Psychographic segmentation examines consumer activities, interests, and opinions.
- Global consumers can be segmented into six distinct global value groups including: strivers, devouts, altruists, intimates, fun seekers, and creatives.
- Product positioning is the use of the promotion mix to cause consumers to perceive a product as a completely different from the competition's products or brands.
- A promotion specialist can choose to use undifferentiated marketing, differentiated marketing, or concentrated marketing approaches to position products to target groups.

KEY TERMS

baby boomer
behavioristic segmentation
concentrated marketing
consumer behavior
consumption
demographics
differentiated marketing
discretionary income
disposable income
early majority
echo boomers
fashion innovators
fashion laggers

fashion specialists
generation X
geographic segmentation
impulse buying
inner-driven consumers
integrated consumers
late majority
market segmentation
Maslow's Hierarchy of Needs
mass market
mean income
median income
middle class

need-driven consumers
niche market
outer-driven consumers
primary market segment
product positioning
psychographic segmentation
secondary market segment
silver streakers
trade customer
undifferentiated marketing
Values and Lifestyle System
   (VALS)

QUESTIONS FOR DISCUSSION

1. What are the similarities of and differences between service providers and product providers, in terms of the consumption process?
2. How do market segmentation and product positioning work hand in hand in creating promotion strategies?
3. How are global consumers different from and similar to one another?
4. Discuss particular demographic aspects of your community with regard to age, income levels, family structure, and cultural diversity. What promotional strategies are most likely to be effective in your community?
5. What bases of segmentation other than those listed in this chapter might help to describe a population?

ADDITIONAL RESOURCES

East, R. (1997). *Consumer behaviour: Advances and applications in marketing.* Upper Saddle River, NJ: Prentice-Hall.

Engle, J., Blackwell, R., and Miniard, P. (1994). *Consumer behavior.* Fort Worth, TX: Dryden Press.

Feather, F. (1997). *The future consumer.* Los Angeles: Warwick Publishing.

Reddy, A. (Ed.). (1997). *The emerging high-tech consumer: A market profile and marketing strategy implications.* Westport, CT: Greenwood Publishing.

Roberts, S. (1998). *Harness the future: The 9 keys to emerging consumer behaviour.* New York: Wiley.

Solomon, M. (1995). *Consumer behavior: Buying, having, and being.* Upper Saddle River, NJ: Prentice-Hall.

Sutherland. M. (1994). *Advertising and the mind of the consumer: What works, what doesn't and why.* Boston: Allen & Unwin.

Underhill, P. (1999). *Why we buy: The science of shopping.* New York: Simon & Schuster.

Promotion Structure

Figure 3.1

Levi's ads, playing the name game, were displayed on out-of-home ads such as these in New York City.

Source: Photos courtesy of Levi Strauss & Co.

PROMOTION ORGANIZATIONS

"*C*alvin wore them." "*Tommy wore them.*" "*Ralph wore them.*" (Figure 3.1). These slogans were featured with the Levi's Red Tab logo on more than 20,000 white billboards in the United States (Socha, 1998). The promotion, created by advertising agency TBWA Chiat/Day, was the first campaign produced by the agency selected by Levi's Jeans to replace Foote, Cone & Belding. Levi's Jeans had just ended a 67-year association with its long-time ad agency. Why does a firm such as Levi's use an outside advertising agency rather than an in-house promotion department to create its corporate image or message? How are advertising agencies organized? Why does a firm decide to change from one agency to another?

The purpose of this chapter is to analyze the organizational structure of the promotion, advertising, and related industries. First, we discuss the role and functions of personnel involved in promotion. Next, the organizational formats for retailing and manufacturing firms are presented. In-house promotion departments of retail or manufacturing firms are considered in relationship to other functional areas. Then, the operating divisions of advertising agencies are taken into account. Methods of evaluating performance, reasons why agencies are dismissed, and how agencies attract new clients are also analyzed. This chapter concludes with a discussion about future trends in promotion organization.

After you have read this chapter, you should be able to:

Explain the roles and functional responsibilities of various people involved in merchandise promotion.

Distinguish the organizational relationships of the promotion division of retail stores, manufacturers, advertising agencies, and specialized services.

Decide whether to use an in-house division or outside agency for promotion assistance.

Determine how to evaluate an advertising agency or promotion department.

PROMOTION PERSONNEL

Four basic categories of personnel are involved in promotion: clients, promotion division or agency employees, media representatives, and suppliers. All four groups are necessary for promotional activities to progress.

Clients are persons seeking recognition for their products or services. They may also be identified as advertisers, sponsors, or marketers. Designers such as Ralph Lauren, manufacturing companies such as Martex, and retailing firms such as Robinson-May are examples of clients or advertisers seeking consumer acceptance for their products. Designers and manufacturing firms may also seek trade acceptance by promoting to each other and by promoting to retailers or the media.

Organizations that assist clients in achieving promotional goals are in-house **promotion divisions** or outside **advertising agencies**. The in-house promotion division includes personnel employed by the designer, manufacturer, or retailer. A large corporation may actually set up an advertising agency that is owned and operated as an independent division of the corporation. Alternatively, the client may choose to plan, create, and implement a promotional strategy by hiring an outside or autonomous advertising agency specializing in these activities.

The third category of personnel are **media representatives** for print and/or electronic communication sources. Print representatives sell space in newspapers, magazines, or out-of-home media, while electronic media representatives sell time on television and radio or space on the Internet to carry the advertiser's broadcast message to the consumer. **Media organizations**, such as the *San Francisco Examiner, CNN,* and *Time* magazine, are major participants in the advertising and promotions process, functioning primarily as providers of information or entertainment to their subscribers, viewers, or readers. These media organizations provide the mechanism for communication and advertising messages to be distributed to large audiences.

The last category of promotion personnel is the **suppliers**. Suppliers assist clients and advertising departments or agencies in preparing promotional materials. Activities of suppliers contribute creatively to the finished advertisement or commercial. These suppliers include photographers, graphic designers, audio and/or video production personnel, typesetters, printers, and other similar personnel. Photographers capture visual images through still photography or video. Graphic designers use their artistic skills to work on layout and design, while typesetters and printers transfer the image to paper. Suppliers may be specialists or generalists who provide support to the clients, agencies or departments, and media representatives.

The size, type of personnel involved, and structure of promotion organizations are as varied as there are different clients with individual needs. A small firm may be run by one individual with responsibility for all aspects of promotion. The promotion division of a huge corporation or a large advertising agency could be a multiperson operation with specialists in every area of research, planning, creating, and evaluating the effectiveness of the promotional effort. The significance given promotion depends upon the size of the company, the type of products or services it produces, competitive and current economic environments, and the commitment of the owner or top management.

Fundamental Tasks of Promotion Personnel

Certain basic functions are necessary for the successful operation of a promotion department or advertising agency. These functions encompass administration, planning, budgeting, coordination, and creation. Administration is the management of the personnel and programs based upon the company's marketing plans and budgets. This management requires analysis of the current situation, evaluation of current promotional activities and personnel, and direction of people and procedures.

Planning is a continual process of defining, refining, and explaining promotional goals and objectives. A formal planning process typically takes place once or twice each year in large companies. This task provides significant input to the success of any promotion and is discussed in detail in Chapter 4 on planning. This preparation leads to budgeting, determining how much to spend on promotional activities in relationship to anticipated income, the topic of Chapter 5.

Coordination, balancing all activities and personnel, is necessary to make sure that functional areas of the firm are working toward the same goals and objectives. The buyer for a retail store must have purchased the shoes that are to be advertised in the newspaper. While the copywriter, who is responsible for verbal content, and the graphic designer, who is responsible for the visual component, create the advertisement, warehouse personnel must have the items ticketed and out on the sales floor. As the media buyer places the ad in the newspaper, the visual merchandisers create displays for customers to locate the merchandise. Coordination is needed between merchandising and promotion personnel in order for this promotion to be successful.

The most obvious task for the promotion division is the creative process, development and implementation of the unique and inventive promotional program. This is the fundamental task that is necessary to produce advertisements, present special events or fashion shows, and lead the way in establishing a positive and fashionable image for the firm.

There are numerous people involved in promotion. All members of the team bring individual abilities and skills that contribute to the overall success of promotional activities. Personal attributes of promotion personnel are the focus of the next section.

Characteristics of Successful Promotion Personnel

Successful people in the promotion industry have many similar personal and professional characteristics. Such people are good planners with the ability to follow through in a prompt and timely manner. They do not leave details until the last minute, and they consider contingencies as a normal function of their jobs. What if there is a big snowstorm in New York and the celebrity commentator is stranded at the airport unable to arrive at the store in Chicago for a personal appearance? The promotion professional prepares for the unexpected and finds a substitute. A positive attitude and sense of humor are helpful when the unforeseen occurs.

Creativity is another attribute of successful promotion professionals. An artistic eye and a flair for the unusual are beneficial. Customers are inspired to make a purchase by an artistic visual merchandise presentation or an inventive advertisement. Successful promotion personnel take the initiative to plan and organize the project in an enterprising manner, bringing all of the elements together.

Successful promotion personnel are able to work under pressure with long or erratic hours to meet very short or unanticipated deadlines. If a client's competition offers a significant price break, how will the client want to respond? It may be necessary to develop a complete new advertisement or commercial to be broadcast within 24 to 48 hours.

Despite being a challenging, competitive, and stressful career, the appeal of working in such a dynamic part of the business world pulls many individuals into careers in the promotion industry. Figure 3.2 provides samples of help wanted ads, seeking employees for various jobs within the promotion industry. Next, we look at the structure of various organizations that employ promotion personnel.

HOW RETAILERS ARE ORGANIZED

Regardless of the size or category of the firm, retailers have specific business functions that are necessary for the business to perform. Merchandise must be purchased and delivered to the store before it is priced, ticketed, and placed on the sales floor where cus-

Figure 3.2

Help wanted advertisements for promotion-related employees in *Women's Wear Daily.*

tomers are able to purchase it. The products must be visually presented or promoted in some manner so that customers know what it is and where it is available. Stores must keep records of what has come into the inventory and what has sold. Information must be collected and distributed to the company owners as well as state and federal agencies. Employees need to be hired, trained, paid, and fired, if necessary. Store security and comfort must be maintained. All of these functions are required for successful retailing operations. A clearly defined organizational structure will designate the appropriate division for handling these responsibilities most efficiently. An **organization chart** is a visible blueprint of the structure of a firm. It shows how responsibilities and authority are delegated within a firm. The organizational structure may vary broadly depending on the size of the firm.

Responsibility gives an individual the obligation to perform certain duties and tasks. In order to assure that responsibilities are carried through, the individual must also be given the authority or power to use physical and human resources to accomplish the duties and tasks. The organization chart clearly demonstrates the person in charge of the responsibilities and the chain of command, or lines of authority, within a company.

The most commonly used retail organizational plan was developed by Paul Mazur (1927). Mazur was commissioned by the National Retail Dry Goods Association, now known as the National Retail Federation, to develop a model for retail organizational structure. His plan consisted of four major functional divisions: merchandising, financial control, operations, and promotion.

Although this model was created decades ago, the organization chart developed by Mazur still remains at the core of modern retailing. The growth of multibranch or chain retailers and the development of computer technology have stimulated expansion of the model to include two additional functional divisions: branch operations and information systems. The **branch operations division** supervises the multi-store operations in various regions or districts. The area managing technology and computer applications is the **information systems division.** The functional areas of a contemporary large retailing organization are shown in Figure 3.3.

Merchandising Division

The **merchandising division** of the retail store is responsible for locating, buying, and reselling products. Buyers are given the primary authority for these activities. This division supervises and administers sales associates, department managers, assistant buyers, buyers, divisional merchandise managers, and general merchandise managers. The head of the merchandise division is the vice president of merchandising.

Operations Division

The branch of the store responsible for sales support functions such as facilities management, security, customer service, merchandise processing, and warehousing is called the **operations division**. The head of the division is the vice-president of operations.

Human Resources Division

In Mazur's original plan, personnel responsibilities were part of the operations division. Personnel, which was renamed **human resources**, has become so significant it is now a separate functional division. The human resources division is responsible for hiring, training, monitoring legal issues and, if necessary, firing personnel. The executive responsible for the management of this division is the vice president of human resources.

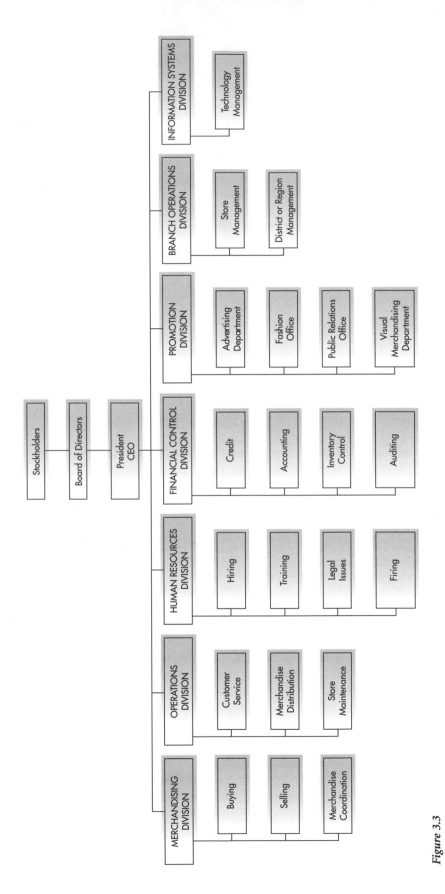

Figure 3.3

Organization Chart: Contemporary Retailing Organization

Financial Control Division

The **financial control division** has the responsibility for administering the budget in addition to handling all of the financial functions, such as payroll, accounts receivable, accounts payable, and inventory control. Auditing is used to check and verify that information is accurate. The head of this division is the vice president of finance or corporate controller.

Promotion Division

Originally, Mazur named the division responsible for stimulating sales through advertising, fashion coordination, and display, the sales promotion division. Since sales promotion has evolved to imply a type of promotion mix activity, one that encourages sales by means of coupons or point-of-sale displays, the use of the term has changed. In modern retailing this division may be called the promotion, advertising, marketing, or public relations division, led by a vice president. Next, we look at the organizational structure of a manufacturing company.

HOW MANUFACTURERS ARE ORGANIZED

The garment and home furnishing industries are characterized by both small and large manufacturing organizations. Cosmetic companies are more typically organized as large corporations. In this section, we profile the organizational structure of a large apparel manufacturing firm as a model for the manufacturing sector. Manufacturing firms, with a well-known designer as the head, are typically organized in a manner similar to this model. The major divisions in an apparel firm are design, production, sales, finance, and promotion (Fig. 3.4). Traditional manufacturers maintain all fundamental divisions as in-house operations, but some manufacturers contract production and promotion activities to outside agencies.

Design Division

The **design division**, headed by a designer, is responsible for designing and producing a minimum of four collections or lines of garments each year. After garments are created, the design department produces samples or prototypes. These samples are used by the sales and/or promotion divisions to sell products to retail buyers and to make the media aware of the new lines of merchandise. A nonapparel manufacturing firm may call this activity new product development.

Production Division

The **production division** is responsible for mass-producing merchandise and filling orders placed by retailers. Production in an apparel company consists of pattern-making, cutting, bundling, sewing, finishing, and maintaining quality control. Although some traditional garment manufacturers produce their own merchandise, many other firms hire outside companies to perform specific or a range of manufacturing processes. This system of hiring outside firms to assemble goods is known as contracting. To take advantage of lower production costs, much of the actual garment construction has moved to foreign countries. This practice is called offshore production.

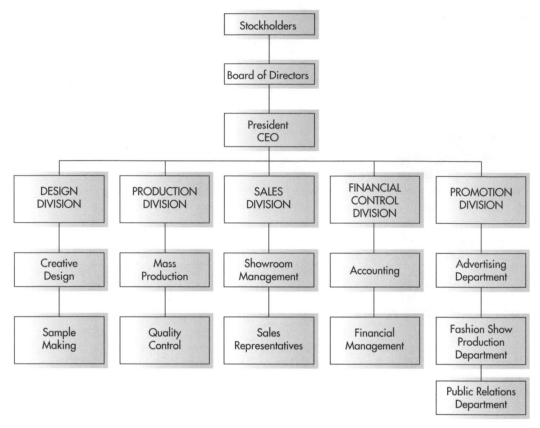

Figure 3.4

Organization Chart: Apparel Manufacturing Organization

Sales Division

The **sales division** has the responsibility of selling the line or collection of merchandise. Sales may take place in a showroom, a sales facility located in a major market center, or through personal sales at the retail buyer's office. Sales personnel are known as representatives or sales reps.

Financial Control Division

The financial control division in the manufacturing environment has similar responsibilities for financial management as it does in retailing. One additional consideration in garment manufacturing is the role of the factor, a finance company that buys a manufacturer's accounts receivables. These receivables consist of retailers' orders that have not yet been paid for and delivered. The finance company takes a commission as a percentage of the total dollar payment and gives the manufacturer the balance of the money. This type of transaction gives the manufacturer cash necessary to operate while the garments are being made and shipped. Sometimes the factor will take over the billing and financial management of the manufacturing firm.

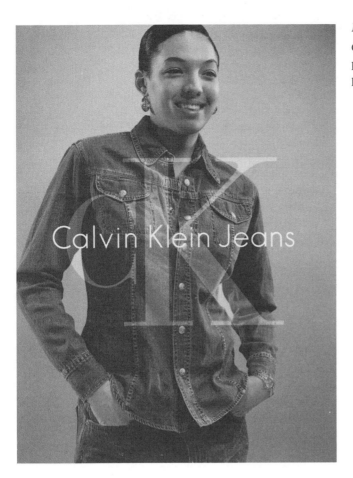

Figure 3.5
Calvin Klein ads are produced by an in-house promotion division.

Promotion Division

Although most manufacturing firms hire outside agencies to handle promotional activities, several apparel producers including Calvin Klein and Benetton maintain an in-house promotion division. The promotion division of a manufacturer or fashion design firm plans and implements a range of services that might include direct-marketing materials, merchandise catalogs, advertisements, fashion show production, and special event sponsorship coordination. An ad from Calvin Klein's in-house advertising department is shown in Figure 3.5. If a manufacturing or retailing company maintains promotion in-house, it is managed as a separate division of the corporation. Next, we consider the organization of an in-house promotion division.

HOW IN-HOUSE PROMOTION DIVISIONS ARE ORGANIZED

The promotion division of a large retailing or manufacturing corporation is managed by a top executive with the title of vice president of promotion. This person may also be known as the vice president of marketing, fashion, or advertising, depending upon how the firm identifies this division. Although the titles of the functional division, as well as management designations, are not consistent from one firm to another, this vice-president has the ultimate authority for any activities used by the company to stimulate the sale of products or services.

Typical promotion mix activities used by retail stores include advertising, fashion shows, special events, publicity and public relations, and visual merchandising. The promotion division communicates information about the store, its fashion image, and the products and/or services available to the public. The intent is to create awareness and interest so potential customers will come into the store.

The promotion division of a retail store is generally divided into four departments: advertising, fashion, public relations, and visual merchandising (Fig. 3.6). The **advertising department** is responsible for planning, creating, placing the advertising in the media, and evaluating the effectiveness of ads. Depending upon the size of the retail firm, some or all of the creative aspects of advertising may be handled by store personnel. If the company is small or desires specialized work, the retail store may hire an advertising agency or media specialist. Most large retail corporations handle their own print ads. A discussion about advantages of staying in-house versus hiring an outside agency follows later in this chapter.

The **fashion department** is involved in developing the fashion image for the company. The manager in charge of this department may have the title of fashion director or special events coordinator. Again, the titles may differ from one retail company to another. The job may differ slightly, but this individual and his or her staff cover all of the designer line openings and analyze the important trends for a season. General trends are interpreted to meet the needs of the store's target customer. The color purple may translate to *aubergine* at a high fashion specialty retailer, *eggplant* at the moderate-price store, and *violet* at the mass merchandiser. The *long and lean* dress could be made from cashmere, wool melton, or acrylic knit, targeted to the appropriate consumer segment. The fashion director helps the buyers select the significant lines and trends for these customers.

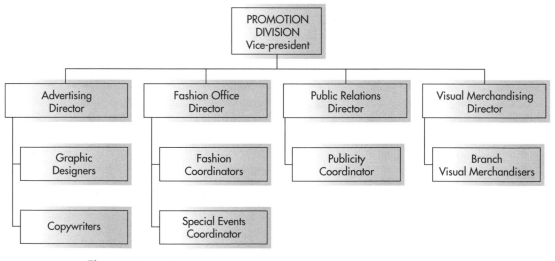

Figure 3.6

Organization Chart: Promotion Division of a Retail Store

Once the trends are identified and purchased, the employees are informed about the trends and trained to sell them by members of the fashion office. These activities may be accomplished through training bulletins, in-store fashion shows featuring store employees, or video productions. Fashion shows and special events are then developed by the fashion staff to disseminate the current fashion message to potential consumers.

The **public relations department** has the responsibility for developing broad-range policies and programs to create a favorable public opinion of the firm. The public relations director uses publicity as one of the tools to create a positive public image. News releases are sent to the media to report community involvement. Working with a local charity to raise money for breast cancer research, by hosting a celebrity performance or using merchandising and design students for an annual fashion show, helps generate a favorable public image. The public relations office works on these types of projects.

Visual presentation of the store image and its merchandise is the primary function of the **visual merchandising department**. This department is involved in creating window and interior displays, developing signs and visual identity by presenting merchandise presentation in a particular style, and selecting merchandise fixtures and showcases. The responsibilities for store planning, layout, and design are also assigned to this department. The director of visual merchandising heads the visual merchandising department.

The breakdown of the promotion division as outlined above is typical for a large retail corporation. In smaller, family-owned specialty stores, all of the promotional functions as well as the other retail functions may be handled by the owner or manager. The size and complexity of the firm will demand versatility or require specialization of the personnel involved.

Promotion mix activities used by manufacturers also typically include advertising, direct marketing, fashion shows, special events, and public relations. The organization of the promotion division of a large manufacturing organization would be similar to the organization of a large retailing firm with the exception of visual merchandising. That function is the responsibility of the showroom staff as part of the sales division.

Advantages of an In-house Promotion Division

There any many reasons why retailing, manufacturing, or design companies maintain in-house promotion departments. One of the primary reasons is to maintain control over the creative message. It is the feeling within some companies that no outside firm can understand product or retail characteristics as well as the company producing or selling them.

Containing costs associated with promotional activities also contributes to the decision to maintain in-house divisions. Firms with large advertising expenditures pay large media commissions to outside agencies. With internal control, the commissions go to the in-house department or agency.

Cost savings or maintaining creative control are not the only reasons that retailers and manufacturers use in-house agencies. In-house agencies are able to focus on the specific market with greater clarity because of their familiarity with the company mission as well as its day-to-day operations. Promotion personnel are not distracted by working on advertising and promotion for another client's product. In addition, there are time savings, assured with tight control over the various processes.

Bad experiences with outside agencies in the past are another reason for maintaining in-house control. Problems may have occurred because of negligence or lack of proper follow through. Other negative perceptions may have resulted after promotions planned by outside agencies did not live up to expectations. Whatever the reason for a bad experience, it may be impossible to overcome a negative opinion.

Cost savings, time savings, greater control, and coordination are all reasons firms cite for maintaining an in-house staff. Some companies simply believe that they are capable of doing a better job than an outside agency.

Advantages of an Outside Agency

Critics of the in-house system say that the promotion department cannot give the client an objective opinion of the promotional process and may not be able to provide the scope of services available from an outside agency. Agencies may have highly talented experts. They can provide a varied viewpoint with greater flexibility. In-house staff may become stale, working on the same products and services. Since the agency has a staff with a variety of backgrounds, it is able to create fresh and original approaches. Also, the outside agency can be terminated if the firm is not satisfied.

After weighing the pros and cons, the retailing or manufacturing firm may choose to use the services of an outside agency rather than maintaining an in-house promotion staff. In that case, the firm would hire an advertising agency to handle the creative development and placement of advertising. It may also choose to hire a specialized marketing communications services firm, such as a professional fashion show production crew or public relations firm, to take care of those particular promotional needs. Next, we discuss the organization of advertising agencies and other types of specialized services available to clients.

HOW ADVERTISING AGENCIES ARE ORGANIZED

Advertising agencies are extremely varied in size and in the range of services provided. Some agencies are small one-person businesses, offering specific assistance. Other advertising agencies are huge companies with thousands of employees in several cities. This section looks at various types of agencies, types of services offered, and how they are organized. A full discussion of how agencies are compensated is in Chapter 5. The world's top 20 advertising organizations are featured in Table 3.1.

Full-Service Agencies

A firm that offers a full range of marketing, communications, and promotion services is known as a **full-service agency**. This type of agency is involved in planning, creating and producing advertising; selecting and buying media time or space; and evaluating advertising effectiveness. In addition to these primary advertising activities, the full-service agency is capable of handling such services as long-term strategic planning; production of sales promotion materials; sales personnel training; and design of packaging, trade show and exhibit space, and materials. Developing a public relations program and publicity materials can also be accomplished by this type of organization.

A full-service agency is made up of various departments that focus on the needs of the client. Most full service agencies are organized around five basic functions: management and finance, creative services, media, research, and account management. Each functional division reports to the agency owner, president, or board of directors. A high

Table 3.1 **The Top 20 Worldwide Advertising Organizations**

Rank 1996	Rank 1995	Organization	Headquarters	Worldwide Gross Income 1995	Worldwide Gross Income 1996	% Change 1996–1995
1	1	WPP Group	London	$3,419.9	$3,125.5	9.4
2	2	Omnicom Group	New York	3,035.5	2,708.5	12.1
3	3	Interpublic Group of Cos.	New York	2,751.2	2,465.8	11.5
4	4	Dentsu	Tokyo	1,929.9	1,999.1	−3.5
5	6	Young & Rubicam	New York	1,356.4	1,197.5	13.3
6	5	Cordiant	London	1,169.3	1,203.1	−2.8
7	9	Grey Advertising	New York	987.8	896.6	10.2
8	8	Havas	Levallois-Perret, France	974.3	924.4	5.4
9	7	Hakuhodo	Tokyo	897.7	958.6	−6.3
10	10	True North Communications	Chicago	889.5	805.9	10.4
11	11	Leo Burnett	Chicago	866.3	805.9	7.5
12	12	MacManus Group	New York	754.2	713.9	5.6
13	13	Publicis Communication	Paris	676.8	624.8	8.3
14	14	Bozell, Jacobs, Kenyon & Eckhardt	New York	473.1	404.5	17.0
15	15	GGT/BBBP Group	London	398.1	380.6	4.6
16	16	Daiko Advertising	Osaka, Japan	256.7	263.6	−2.6
17	17	Asatsu Inc.	Tokyo	242.0	254.2	−4.8
18	19	Carlson Marketing Group	Minneapolis	222.0	189.0	17.5
19	18	Tokyu Agency	Tokyo	214.0	231.1	−7.4
20	20	TMP Worldwide	New York	194.6	177.4	9.7

Adapted from: World's top 50 advertising organizations (1997, April 21). Advertising Age [On-line]. Available: www.adage.com/dataplace /archives/dp097.html.

degree of coordination among the functional areas is necessary for an agency to be successful, since many of the operations are interdependent. An example of an organization chart for a full-service advertising agency is provided in Figure 3.7.

Management and Finance Division

The **management and finance division** handles commercial operations similar to the responsibilities of the operations, finance, and control divisions of a retail store. This division deals with the internal business affairs including managing the office, billing clients, making payments to the various media, and controlling personnel issues. In addition to the basic administrative functions, the management and finance division is involved in generating new business by soliciting new clients.

Creative Services Division

The **creative services division** is the heart of a full-service agency. It is responsible for the creation and execution of the advertisements. Creating advertisements may involve many different people with very specific skills. In large full-service agencies with a number of clients, it takes a great deal of coordination to put together the creative services. The creative services division is managed by the creative director, who sets the creative

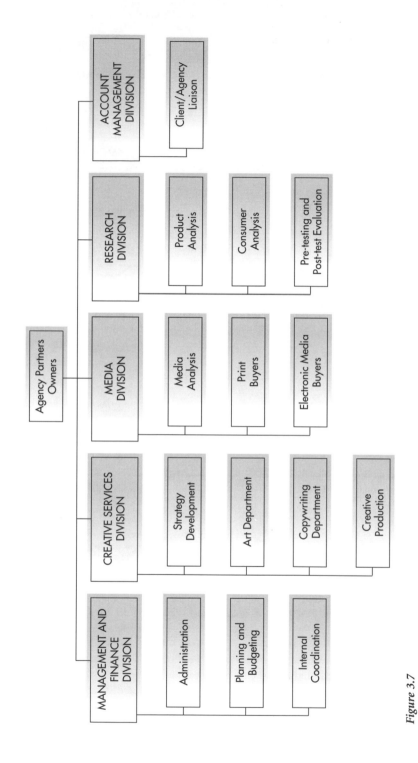

Figure 3.7

Organization Chart: Full-service Advertising Agency

philosophy of the firm. He or she is directly involved in the creation of ads for the agency's most important clients.

The creative services area is generally divided into two functional areas: verbal and visual. Copywriters are the personnel responsible for the verbal communication message. They are involved in envisioning the message and writing the headlines, subheads, and body copy. The art department is responsible for the way the advertisement looks; this is the visual part of the ad. The art director supervises the graphic designers or artists in the development of the layouts. Layouts are drawings that visually represent what the advertisement will look like. For broadcast commercials, a storyboard is the equivalent of the layout, a series of frames or boxes similar to a comic strip that represents the commercial in still form. Artists and writers work together to develop ads to meet the creative strategy for a client.

Once the copy and layout have been completed and approved by the creative director and client, the ad is turned over to the production department. The production department works with photographers, typographers, printers, and other specialists to produce finished ads. These suppliers may work for the agency or they may work on a freelance basis as independent contractors. If the advertisement is a broadcast commercial, a video production crew, actors, and stage set must be coordinated.

In very large advertising agencies where there are many clients and types of projects, coordination may be difficult. These firms may have a **traffic department**, to organize all phases of production, making sure that the deadlines for creative services and media placement are met. The traffic department may be a part of the creative services, media, or account management division. Because the creative services division provides the core function for advertising agencies, it is not surprising that many agencies began as the vision of their creative director. The article in Box 3.1 points out six steps for people interesting in opening their own advertising agency.

BOX 3.1

Starting Your Own Ad Agency, or "Mr. Della Femina, There's a Call for You from President Clinton."

There is a story, perhaps apocryphal, that when one of America's most successful advertising agencies first opened for business and was expecting a prospective client, it hired temporary employees and put them on borrowed, disconnected telephones with instructions to "talk as though you're talking to an important account."

This merry ruse, a variation on the call actors would arrange from "Mr. DeMille" while lounging beside the pool at the Beverly Hills Hotel, illustrates one of the more important requirements for a start-up ad agency, namely, imaginative chutzpah. For new advertising, design, and other communication firms to succeed, the principals must have a certain daring imagination, a willingness to flaunt their creative skill. Who and what you are will be more important to a possible client than what you say you are.

Consider the following examples: One of Northern California's more successful new ad agencies is located in a building and office space that reeks of unconventional imagination. Its office is the message. The principal of another successful start-up sails San Francisco Bay in his boat, a boat he and his partner have painted to look like a black and white cow. This invites conversation, and conversations lead to new clients.

Clients—or at least prospective clients—are of course essential if a new ad agency or other communications firm is to succeed. But there are other elements and requirements to consider when deciding to become an entrepreneur. These considerations, ranging from personal introspection to finding a good bank, will serve as a useful checklist for those planning an escape from The Big Bad Employer.

1. Develop a Business Plan

It is critically important, first, to have a clear idea of what you want to be. Everybody who starts an advertising, design, or other communication firm has a good idea of what they want to do, but all too often they don't know what they want their new firm to be.

Montagine said writing is thinking, and the best way to think critically and systematically about what you want your venture to be is to write a business plan; indeed, force yourself to write a business plan. A business plan has certain general requirements that compel careful thought about what you propose to do and how you plan to do it. When you have answered those questions, you will have a good understanding of goals and purpose. Your business plan need not be lengthy or complex, but it should deal with the major issues facing a new venture. Two good guides to writing a plan are *Growing a Business* by Paul Hawkin, and *Entrepreneuring* by Steven Brandt. They're both available in paperback.

2. Consult with a Financial Advisor

There is a need for a business plan because it is a business, albeit a business that may, like advertising, operate at the intersection of art and commerce. As a business, some attention to finances is important, and this in turn leads to the second recommendation: consultation with a knowledgeable financial advisor. "Knowledgeable" in this case means someone who has extensive experience working with firms in the same service industry.

A knowledgeable financial advisor will know, for example, capital requirements, a reasonable range for expenses, realistic profit percentages, and how to structure fixed-fee compensation. As such, a financial advisor can assist in the preparation of a business plan, and more to the main point, help you decide if you are crazy.

3. Hire a Local Accountant

Since most of the experienced financial advisors to the communications industry are based in New York, you will also need a local accountant to prepare financial statements and tax returns.

4. Decide How to Sell Your Services

Preparing a business plan will lead to the question, "How will this new business generate income?" That, in turn, compels attention to a basic question, namely, "Who's go-ing to sell the services offered?" To succeed, someone with an important stake in the new venture must be able and willing to sell the venture's wares. Breakthrough designers or brilliant copywriters need opportunities to be successful, and those opportunities will largely depend on the sale of their services.

5. Foster a Good Banking Relationship

It is also important to have a good banking relationship. Here again, it is important to have a banker on call who is familiar with your particular service. If you are thinking of creating a new corporate identity firm, find out, for example where Frankfurt Balkind or CKS Partners do their banking, and then see if that bank will meet your needs.

6. Determine Your Role in the Communications Revolution

Finally, consider carefully what role you expect your new venture to play in the extraordinarily complicated communications revolution. No one knows, of course, just where that revolution will lead, but it is not so important to be right about the future as it is to think critically about how, where, and why the new venture might have a role. To illustrate, here are some questions to consider:

- Is it true that he who has the most technology wins?
- When there are 100 or more television channels available, will more people spend more time watching television?
- Where is the line between direct response marketing consultants and an ad agency that specializes in direct response services?
- What are the implications-creative, financial, structural-of ads on public television?

The possible answers to those questions and many, many more are not nearly so important to a new communications venture as an ability and willingness to keep asking questions about the new venture's place in the hubbub of constant change.

Adapted from: Anderson, J. M. (1997). Starting your own ad agency or "Mr. Della Femina, there's a call for you from President Clinton" [On-line]. Available: http://www.clioawards.com/b/bda/htm.
John M. Anderson is a lawyer at Heller Ehrman White & McAuliffe of San Francisco.

Media Division

The **media division** analyzes, selects, and contracts for space or time in the media, delivering the client's message. In order to meet the client's desire to reach a target market, the media department is expected to develop an appropriate media plan. Media specialists research the media to determine the audience attracted and the rates. They review information on demographics, newspaper or magazine readership, radio listenership, or television audience. Knowing this information enables the media specialist to match the client with the suitable media. This division may also have the responsibility to pretest advertising effectiveness and measure overall effectiveness.

The media buyer purchases space in print media or time on broadcast media for the client. A high percentage of the client's advertising budget is spent buying time or space. It is necessary to justify a plan that communicates the message in the right media in a cost-effective manner.

Research Division

The function of the **research division** is to gather, analyze, and interpret information that will be used to develop promotional activities. This information may be gathered through primary research or secondary sources. Primary research involves original research geared to the client's needs. A study is devised, implemented, and deciphered by the research department. Secondary research resources include information previously presented or published.

Account Management Division

The **account management division** provides the link between the client and the agency. The account executive is the agency representative who works with the client, interpreting the client's needs to agency personnel. He or she coordinates agency activities and presents the agency's ideas to the client. Once the client approves the plan, the agency puts that plan into action.

Other Types of Specialized Services

Not every potential advertiser wants or can afford a full-service advertising agency. Many small agencies specialize in specific services. Alternatives to full-service agencies are as varied as the imaginations of the personnel involved.

Creative Boutiques

A **creative boutique** is an agency that provides only creative services, such as innovative layout, logo, or graphic design. A business that has an in-house promotion department may seek the spark of creative inspiration from an outside source. Sometimes a full-service agency may contract a creative services boutique to supplement its own departments when they are extremely busy. A creative boutique can be used on a fee-for-service basis, saving the agency, retailer, or manufacturer the cost of hiring additional temporary personnel.

Direct Marketing Agencies

Direct marketing, one of the fastest growing areas in integrated marketing communications (IMC) promotions, is communication by firms with their target audience through telemarketing, direct mail, or other forms of direct-response promotion. As the interest in this form of promotion has grown, direct marketing agencies have been created to meet the advertiser's needs. **Direct marketing agencies** furnish an assortment of services including research, database management, creative assistance, direct mail, media services, and production capabilities. Database development and administration is one of the most significant roles for a direct marketing firm. Database marketing enables a firm to identify new customers and develop loyalty with existing customers. In addition to these services, some of the direct marketing agencies have expanded into production of infomercials.

The typical direct marketing agency consists of three divisions: account management, creative services, and media services. In some of the firms a fourth division focuses on database management. Similar to a full-service agency, the account management division works with clients to develop a direct-response program. The creative division is responsible for creating the direct-response message through its creative personnel, including copywriters, artists, and other members of the production team. The media division is in charge of media placement.

Direct marketing agencies are similar to full-service advertising agencies. They must seek new clients and provide satisfactory completion of projects. These agencies may be paid on a fee-for-service basis or by a commission.

Fashion Show Production Agencies

Fashion show production agencies provide the services necessary to present fashion shows. Organizations or retail stores may wish to utilize these services when they determine that it is not beneficial to maintain an in-house staff to complete these tasks. Frequently a modeling agency or modeling school has a division for fashion show production. Services may include any or all of the following: selecting and supervising models; reserving the show location; setting up the stage; hiring the lighting, music, and backstage personnel; and hiring the caterers. Services are normally paid on a contract basis.

The Ground Crew, founded by Audrey Smaltz in 1977, is a New York–based company that organizes fashion shows internationally ("The Ground Crew," 1997). Producing 350 to 400 shows each year, the company oversees everything from backstage production to dressing the models. This firm has found a niche as a specific creative specialized service, putting on fashion shows for fashion designers, department stores, and specialty stores in Japan, Milan, and New York.

Market Research Companies

While some advertisers maintain their own research departments, many do not. In that case they hire **market research companies** to help them understand the client's target customers. The research firm will gather objective information that will enable the advertiser to plan and evaluate its advertising and promotion programs.

Some firms with their own research divisions may actually hire a marketing research firm. The in-house staff may not have appropriate expertise to complete the analysis, or the advertiser may wish to have an outside opinion. Market research firms use such data gathering techniques as in-depth interviews, focus groups, and market surveys. Figure 3.8 is an advertisement for a global market research firm.

Media Buying Services

Media buying services are independent firms that exclusively handle purchasing media time, primarily for radio and television. The nature of television has changed dramatically in the past few years. Not only does an advertiser need to consider local sta-

Figure 3.8

A market research firm advertises its global perspective to potential clients.

tions and major national networks, it must also consider the large number of independent networks and cable channels. Media buying services have found a niche, analyzing and purchasing media to meet the needs of their clients. Both full-service agencies and independent advertisers use media buying agencies. Because media buying services purchase large blocks of time and space, they are able to receive discounts. These price reductions can save small agencies or advertisers money on media purchases. Media buying services are paid a fee or commission on their work.

Public Relations Firms

In addition to the services of an advertising agency, a client may seek the services of a public relations firm. It is the responsibility of a **public relations firm** to manage the client's public image, the client's relationships with consumers, and any other services related to publicity. The task of the public relations firm is to evaluate the relationship between the client and the relevant publics, which might include some or all of the following: stockholders, suppliers, employees, government, labor groups, and the general public. Once the public relations firm has evaluated the appropriate constituents, it is able to determine how the client's operation impacts the public, develop public relations strategies and approaches, put these programs into action, and evaluate their effectiveness.

Typical tools and activities of a public relations firm involve conducting research, generating publicity, participating in community events, lobbying public affairs, preparing news releases and other communication information, designing and managing special events, handling crisis management, and supervising all areas of communication. As advertisers move to an IMC model, public relations is combined into the marketing communications mix. This helps to increase message credibility and save media costs. Public relations firms are frequently paid on a contract basis.

Sales Promotion Agencies

Sales promotion agencies specialize in developing and managing sales promotion programs, such as contests, refunds or rebates, premium or incentive offers, sweepstakes, or sampling programs. Although some large full-service advertising agencies have created their own sales promotion divisions, many independent sales promotion agencies serve the needs of their clients.

Sales promotion agencies will work with a client's advertising or direct marketing firm to coordinate sales promotion efforts with the advertising and/or direct marketing efforts. Services provided by a sales promotion agency might include research, planning, creative services, tie-in coordination, premium design and management, catalog development, and contest or sweepstakes management. Sales promotion agencies are generally compensated on a fee-for-service basis.

INTEGRATED MARKETING COMMUNICATIONS SERVICES

Because clients can choose from an in-house department, a full-line agency, or a variety of specialized services to assist with planning, developing, and implementing a promotion program, an IMC approach has become more popular. Some full-line advertising agencies, including Leo Burnett and Lintas: U.S.A., have become IMC superagencies. These agencies expanded their IMC services to include public relations, sales promotion, and direct-response activities, handling communication tools ranging from Yellow Pages to telemarketing, in addition to advertising. Clients need to decide if they want to hire one superagency, or if they want to manage their own IMC programs by hiring separate firms to meet specific needs.

HOW TO EVALUATE AN AGENCY

Because so much money is spent on promotion annually, the client is constantly evaluating the performance of its agency. Regular reviews of the agency's performance are necessary to prove accountability for the expenditures.

Unfortunately agency evaluation is often done on a subjective or informal basis. When sales go down or fail to meet expectations, it is easy to say it is the fault of the advertising agency. The next step is to fire the agency without consideration of the manufacturer's distribution problems or of prices that are out of line with the competition. A formal assessment system can help firms justify that their money is being spent efficiently and effectively.

A formal assessment system may simply look at the planning goals and objectives and how well these were met. However, market share or sales goals may not be the only criteria on which a firm is evaluated. Creative development, market research and ideas, cost controls, or effectiveness of a partnership relationship may also be tools to measure the agency/client relationship. As financial controls tighten and clients require more accountability, firms will require formal evaluation procedures. Figure 3.9 is a sample

STRICTLY CONFIDENTIAL

Agency: _____ Evaluator: _____ Date: _____

1. CLIENT SERVICING
1.1 Agency Management Group

	Better Than Expected	As Expected	Below Expectations
Interest and knowledge of account			
Strategic output			
Response to issues			

Comments _____

1.2 Account Group
Strategic involvement

	Better Than Expected	As Expected	Below Expectations
Knowledge of market, competition			
Ability to interpret data			
Ability to provide sound recommendations			
Ability to communicate effectively			
Open-mindedness, objectivity			
Initiative, proactivity			
Quality of contributions from both cultures			

Comments _____

Operational involvement

	Better Than Expected	As Expected	Below Expectations
Coordination of Account Management teams			
Availability			
Promptness, accuracy in ongoing reports			
Effective, punctual meetings			
Efficient management of hours reports			
Sensitivity to budgets			

Comments _____

2. CREATIVE
2.1 Senior Management

	Better Than Expected	As Expected	Below Expectations
Establish structure to facilitate cultural synergy			
Interest, knowledge of account			
Strategic input			

Comments _____

Figure 3.9

A sample agency performance review based on a model from the Institute of Canadian Advertising. Source: [On-line] http://www.ica-ad.com/remuneration/ExhibitII.html. *(continued on next page)*

2.2 Assigned Personnel
Creative development

	Better Than Expected	As Expected	Below Expectations
Working proactively within strategy			
Knowledge of market, competition			
Cultural team synergy in creative development			
Providing practical, expandable plans			
Ability to capitalize on research			
Well-organized presentation			
Quality of work:			
Copy			
Art			
Production			
Clearly defined lines of authority			
Accepting ideas, feedback in positive fashion			

Comments _____

3. MEDIA
3.1 Senior Management

	Better Than Expected	As Expected	Below Expectations
Interest, knowledge of account			
Strategic input			
Responses to issues, requests			

Comments _____

3.2 Assigned Personnel
Strategic involvement

	Better Than Expected	As Expected	Below Expectations
Knowledge of market, audiences, products/services, objectives			
Use of media research			
Strategic input			
Providing innovative, imaginative media plans			
Keeping advertiser up to date on media trends, developments			

Comments _____

4. OVERALL ASSESSMENT OF AGENCY

	Better Than Expected	As Expected	Below Expectations

Agency's major strengths:

_____

Areas that require improvement:

_____

Figure 3.9 (cont.)

agency performance review based on a model from the Institute of Canadian Advertisers. Only after a client has conducted an objective evaluation of its promotion division or advertising agency should the decision to eliminate the division or fire the agency be considered. Understanding the reasons why advertisers switch or fire advertising agencies can help agencies avoid potential problems. Some of the most commonly cited reasons include:

- **Poor performance.** The client becomes unhappy with the caliber of the advertisement and/or the quality of service rendered.
- **Poor communication.** The account executive responsible for communication from the agency to the client does not work at supporting a positive working relationship hard enough.
- **Personnel changes.** The client hires a new manager who wants to work with an advertising firm that he or she has worked with in the past, or an account executive leaves an agency, taking the client along.
- **Interpersonal conflict.** Rapport between the account executive and client is insufficient for them to continue working together. Personality differences and dissimilar work styles have led to friction.
- **Conflicts of interest.** As many industries including corporate retailing undergo significant changes in ownership due to mergers and acquisitions, accounts are lost due to a conflict of interests.
- **Declining sales.** Perhaps the most common reason for leaving an agency is static or weakening sales. Advertising and promotion are blamed for the problems and a new agency is hired to bring in a new approach.

The agency should be looking for signs in a changing marketplace and be able to adjust plans to meet current conditions and demands. Some of the conditions may be avoidable; others may be beyond the control of the agency. Those conditions that can be controlled require attention by the agency; however, sometimes a change may become necessary. The agency or the client may discontinue the associations, leaving both companies to seek new affiliations. The article in Box 3.2 illustrates how Leo Burnett Company, the giant full-service advertising agency, reorganized to meet changing market conditions.

BOX 3.2

Not So Jolly Now, a Giant Agency Retools

Chicago—No advertising agency has ever had a culture or tradition quite like that of Leo Burnett Co., the sculptor of a Mount Rushmore of American brand icons since the 1930s.

This is the shop that unleashed the booming "ho-ho-ho" of the Jolly Green Giant, the pudgy charm of the Pillsbury doughboy, the steely eyed confidence of the Marlboro Man. It launched United Airlines into "the friendly skies," gave Tony the Tiger his growling "Grrreat!" and invited beer drinkers to debate the chief merit of Miller Lite—whether it "tastes great" or is "less filling."

Famed for its deft grasp of Middle American sensibilities, Burnett enjoyed client loyalty like that of nobody else in the business, nurturing cozy relationships with advertisers that went back decades. And its profits, like its glitzy headquarters in downtown Chicago, soared into the clouds in the 1990s, riding a winning streak that Burnett presumed would never end.

Until it did.

Burnett was knocked back on its haunches when United Airlines switched to a rival agency in 1996. United executives were said to have scoffed at the "friendly skies" slogan as anachronistic—even insulting, especially to harried business travelers who know the combat of air travel.

Next came rebuffs from McDonald's, which snatched away a big chunk of its business as Burnett's final, "My McDonald's," campaign sputtered, and from Miller Lite, which pulled its creative account.

For a long time, Burnett had seen itself as special, holding confidently to the status quo even as the advertising world was changing around it. One of the last big, privately held agencies, it was slow to play by the new rules. When competition forced other shops to work on a fee-for-service basis, for example, Burnett was still demanding the traditional 15 percent commission.

But Burnett turned out not to be so special, after all. In an industry focused on the hot, the new, and the edgy, Burnett's strongest suits—a courtly attention to clients and a safe, sensible, middle-of-the-road creative voice—were decidedly short on dazzle.

Some analysts say Burnett, grown insular and smug, was simply caught flat-footed. Executives at the 63-year-old company, meanwhile, say the agency had come to pay more attention to counting money than making ads—a violation of one of the strictest dictums from the founder himself.

"It was all about how much more we can make, rather than how good our ads can be," acknowledged Richard B. Fizdale, who began a second go-round as Burnett's chairman and chief executive in 1997, when the board dumped its former leader, William T. Lynch, and the chief operating officer, James M. Jenness.

In fact, the sources of the problems confronting Burnett and other big ad agencies are a lot more complicated. No one at Burnett can do much about a corporate world that shuttles chief executives in and out like managers on a George Steinbrenner team and that has an attention span that focuses on nothing older than the last earnings report. It is not easy to build client loyalty in such a culture, as many other shops can attest. Giant advertisers like Levi Strauss, Delta Air Lines, and Kodak all have recently dismissed agencies with which they had had decades-long relationships.

But after stumbling on this new terrain, Burnett has embarked on a mission to remake itself. Aiming to be quicker and smarter, the agency is transforming itself into seven smaller business units, or mini-agencies. And inside the Burnett building, a 50-story granite fortress, some walls have come tumbling down.

A redrawn map has sent more than half of the roughly 2,000 workers in Chicago to new offices, grouping creative and business people together according to brand. Like Dorothy's farmhouse after the twister, nothing is quite where it used to be. Indeed, the Burnett building no longer is, really; the tower was sold last year, and the agency is now a tenant, although it still occupies most of the building.

People in the image industry say it is much too early to tell whether Burnett's overhaul will succeed. Much of what the agency is undertaking merely tracks moves by competitors, who have a head start. And many of those who are in charge, including Fizdale, are closely associated with the recent, sour past.

Still, Burnett ranks tenth in the global ad business in both billings ($5.96 billion in 1996) and gross income ($885.9 million), according to the trade publication *Advertising Age*. And many analysts say the agency seems to be on the right course.

"They've taken some pretty drastic measures," said Linda Fidelman, president of Advice and Advisors in New York, a consultant for companies hiring ad agencies. "But can you successfully introduce change this dramatic in a place so big? That remains to be seen. It's like trying to turn the QE2 around in the middle of the sea."

In what Burnett news releases called "a series of non-traditional initiatives to change its approach," the agency has started to look outside its walls for some answers.

In December 1997, it bought a 49 percent stake in the hot British ad shop Bartle Bogle Hegarty, which is known for an offbeat style typified by a recent campaign for Levi's jeans. One ad focused on the small coin pocket on a pair of Levi's—with a condom tucked inside.

Burnett also established Vigilante, a New York agency that specializes in marketing to what it calls "urban culture." Danny Robinson, Vigilante's chief creative officer, scarcely sounds like an old-guard Burnett man when he says that its daring style will "make our clients' palms sweat, at least a little." Vigilante's ads are appearing in publications like *Vibe*, *Stress*, and *XXL*.

Bowing to clients' demands for specialization, Burnett spun off its media department (which buys commercial time and ad placements for clients) as a separate division, Starcom Media Services. In 1997, Starcom made $2.8 billion in media buys, making it the largest media buyer in the nation.

The agency has also turned to outsiders like Red Spider, a creative advertising consulting group from Britain, and Joe McCarthy, a former ad director for Nike, to push Burnett staff members to think in ways that challenge prevailing notions. Besides sharing their perspectives and criticisms about the agency's creative work, the consultants have led Burnett employees through improvisational acting exercises.

No More One-Stop Shopping

For decades before the 1990s, advertisers typically chose a single, full-service agency to do everything involved in putting their brand before customers' eyes—from positioning the product in the marketplace to creating ads and placing them on radio and television and in newspapers and magazines. That was a world that suited Leo Burnett perfectly. No one can accuse Burnett of shortcomings in research, or business acumen, or meeting the needs of clients.

"You call someone up at Burnett who works, say, on Procter & Gamble, and they'll know P&G inside and out," said Jeff Hicks, a former Burnett executive who is now president of Crispin Porter & Bogusky, an agency in Miami.

But the industry has become much more specialized, with advertisers going to one company for media buying, say, and to another company for marketing. These days, the one thing that clients need from an ad agency is the ad itself. And Burnett's problem, in that regard, is that "they were not doing breakthrough creative work," Hicks said.

While Burnett had a reputation for its homespun touch, many advertisers were looking for ads that meshed better with the times—fast, smart, skeptical. It was Fallon McElligott, a Minneapolis agency that had won a reputation for hipness—with ads like one for Jim Beam picturing a woman smoking a cigar, with the tag line "Get in touch with your masculine side"—that snatched away United Airlines and Miller Lite.

Cheryl Berman, the head of creative services for Burnett in the United States, agreed that her department must play a key role in restoring the agency's luster. "We need to get simpler—ideas that aren't laden with copy, upping the quality," Ms. Berman said. She recalled that Fizdale, the chief executive, had complained about Burnett's tendency to use too many words—what he has described as "verbherrhea."

"The old way of thinking was, 'If you've got 30 seconds, then talk for 30 seconds,'" Ms. Berman said. "But what really catches on are simple, graphic, visual, true ideas. The focus should be: What is the single most important thing we have to say, not the five most important things."

Burnett's central-office style of management, heavy on meetings and process and bureaucracy, had a tendency to stifle creativity, some agency officials acknowledged.

"We'd sit for days and days in meetings," said Michael Conrad, the head of creative services for Burnett's international side. "An idea is something very fragile. Sometimes, I feel within a second I know what to do. But the more I discuss it, the farther away from it I get." The new mini-agency approach, Conrad added, "if we do it right, should cut down on bureaucracy."

For decades, Leo Burnett himself would approve each line of copy before an ad was presented to a client. Later, it was a forbidding Strategy Review Committee that put its stamp of approval on creative work. As one employee described the process, a team would distribute copies of 50-page documents describing a campaign and the top brass would check their watches. Then, as if defending a master's thesis, the team had 45 minutes to show that it either worked or didn't.

In the new order, the client will be much more involved in creating ads—"a member of the team," Ms. Bishop said, and sometimes the coach.

"The old days of being a closed black box where you're off in private doing your work—that just isn't fast enough," she said. She added, however, that even in the old system, some on the creative side always found ways to work closely with clients. "This doesn't mean the client is writing the work," she added. "But the idea of using them as a team member, that's just common sense."

Relax! Think! Have Some Fun!

In what staff members call the Zen conference room on the 26th floor of Burnett's headquarters—a room intended to promote deep thinking—creative and business-side workers sit on the floor, some cross-legged, some leaning on oversize pillows, as they talk about a new campaign for Hallmark Cards. A collection of greeting cards is spread across a coffee table.

"We live and eat and breathe together," said Joan Klug, the account director.

It was not always this way. Before the shake-up, the team working on the Hallmark account, or any other brand, would have been scattered around the Burnett tower. Jeff Chapman, an account supervisor, said: "It used to be, if I had a thought on any subject, I knew it was a 7-minute trip to get to somebody. Now I just holler, 'Hey Tim, hey Joan—what do you think?'"

While offices were being shuffled in December, a few eyebrows were raised about the new notions of togetherness. Some on the creative side, in particular, were not so sure about working elbow-to-elbow with the suit-and-tie number-crunchers. But Burnett people say that tossing together employees from different disciplines has worked.

Adapted from: Johnson, D. (1998, March 22). Not so jolly now, a giant agency retools. New York Times on the Web *[On-line]. Available: http://www.nytimes.com/yr/mo/day/news/financial/burnett-ad-agency.html.*

HOW AGENCIES GAIN NEW CLIENTS

A business relationship between a client and an agency may be initiated by either party. An advertiser may wish to change to a new agency for any of the reasons listed earlier. An agency seeks new clients through the following methods:

- **Referrals.** Many agencies obtain new clients by recommendations from existing clients, media representatives, suppliers, or other agencies unable to handle additional business. By providing good service to the various people involved in promotion, an agency gains recognition and new clients.
- **Solicitations.** Agencies directly request the business of a new client. The head of the agency or a new business development group within an agency searches for and establishes contact with potential clients using solicitation letters, making cold calls, and following up on leads. Solicitations may be conducted through advertising in trade publications. Figure 3.10 is an example of an ad for a communication company seeking new clients in the Fashion Group International Membership Directory.
- **Presentations.** A potential client invites an agency to make a speculative presentation. This allows the agency to present information about its experience, personnel, capabilities, operating procedures, and previous work. In this formal presenta-

Figure 3.10

Trade advertisement for Ampersand Creative, a communications supplier offering services in computer graphics, design, consulting, photography, and film/video editing.

tion, the agency proposes a tentative communication program after investigating the client's current situation. Because these types of presentations are expensive in terms of time and preparation, without any guarantee of obtaining any new business, agencies are not fond of competing for clients in this manner. Nevertheless, many agencies participate in this form of appeal for new business by choice or competitive necessity.

- **Public relations.** Agencies provide pro bono (at cost or free) services to civic, social, or charitable organizations to gain respect within the community. Participation in these activities can lead to new business contacts.
- **Image and reputation.** Agencies that create successful campaigns are respected and are often approached by potential clients because of this reputation. Entering contests and winning awards are other methods of gaining recognition and enhancing the image of the agency.

FUTURE TRENDS IN PROMOTION ORGANIZATIONS

As we enter the 21st century, we are viewing several trends that will influence the future of promotion organizations. First, in the area of promotional organization, agencies are getting larger by merging or acquiring domestic competition. Firms such as TBWA Chiat/Day and DDB Needham that were once independent companies have merged or been acquired to form giant advertising agencies. By bringing former competitors together, research, systems, and back-office duties are streamlined and shared to save money.

Advertising agencies are also getting bigger by becoming global, a trend we first introduced in Chapter 1. Citing strong united global offices linked by common culture, forceful international creative strategies, and tremendous balance, *Advertising Age* selected DDB Needham Worldwide as its top international advertising agency, the 1997 Global Network of the Year (Petrecca, 1998).

Agencies continued to grow through global mergers and acquisitions. BBDO Worldwide acquired Japan's I. & S. Corporation ("BBDO Acquires Stake," 1998). The acquisition of I. & S. expanded BBDO Worldwide's presence in Japan and in the Asia Pacific market. The London-based media network Optimedia International formed an alliance with Prakit Publicis in Thailand, to form a media buying joint venture ("Optimedia, Prakit Publicis Form Joint Venture," 1998). Think New Ideas, based in New York, acquired Red Dot Interactive, San Francisco, and NetComs, London, creating a global interactive strategic and electronic commerce consulting firm ("Think New Ideas Goes Global," 1998). Growth by combining firms or expanding internationally is anticipated to continue well into the 21st century.

As we have learned, clients such as Levi's have been free to leave an agency if they are dissatisfied or want alternative services. To counteract the trend of losing long-term clients, giant advertising agencies have expanded their services beyond traditional advertising. Advertising agencies hope they will be able to retain clients under one roof by offering a variety of promotion products. In 1998, Ammirati Puris Lintas, the giant advertising agency with annual billings estimated at $4.4 billion, formed an in-house interactive marketing group named APL Digital (Elliot, 1998a). The formation of APL Digital is just one example of the growing interest among traditional agencies to stake a claim in cyberspace. Grey Advertising owns a marketing firm, J. Brown/LMC Group, in addition to its divisions for health-care marketing, on-line services, design, promotions, and technology marketing (Seo, 1998). The trend toward offering diverse services does not end there. Saatchi & Saatchi expanded beyond its signature specialty advertising into direct marketing, strategic planning, interactive communications, public relations, and even corporate logo design (Seo, 1998). Diversification and offering wider ranges of promotional products are also anticipated to continue into the 21st century.

In addition to trends toward agency growth and diversification, agencies will be facing extra scrutiny from clients demanding accountability. Agencies will continue to defend their communication plans as more effective than the plans of the competition. Clients will continue to ask for proof that the program accomplished its objectives, making evaluation significant. For example, Visa International called for a review of its creative services by Saatchi & Saatchi, London. The account worth $40 million targeted countries in the European Union ("Visa Europe Account in Review," 1998). Evaluation of promotional effectiveness is the topic of Chapter 17.

Whether a firm chooses to handle promotion tasks in-house or to hire an outside advertising or specialty agency, understanding how these divisions are organized will help that company get its promotion job done properly. Every organization, including retailers, manufacturers, fashion designer firms, and advertising agencies, must be arranged to handle the firm's administration, operation, production, financial, creative, and human resource requirements. In this chapter, we have looked at the organizational structure of the various types of firms involved in promotion, discussed methods of evaluating performance, looked at how agencies attract new clients, and viewed some of the future trends in promotional organization.

SUMMARY

- Clients, promotion department or agency employees, media representatives, and suppliers are the personnel involved in promotion. Clients, persons, or organizations seeking recognition for their products or services create in-house promotion departments or hire outside agencies to assist in achieving promotional goals.
- The basic tasks necessary for successful promotion and advertising are administration, planning, budgeting, coordination, and creation. Specialists or generalists with an overview of the client's needs may accomplish these tasks.
- Retail stores are basically organized in a manner first established by Paul Mazur. Each store must be able to accomplish the essential jobs of merchandising, operations, financial control, and promotion.
- The promotion division might also be called the advertising, marketing, or public relations division, depending upon the retail firm. In addition to the responsibility for promotion, this division is in charge of advertising, fashion image, public relations, special events, and visual merchandising.
- A full-service advertising agency is organized around five basic functions: management and finance, creative services, media, research, and account management.
- Firms offering specialized services may be used to meet the specific needs of the client. These firms include creative boutiques, direct marketing agencies, fashion show production agencies, market research companies, media buying services, public relations firms, and sales promotion agencies.
- Evaluating an agency's performance should involve a regular and formal process. If

expectations have not been met, the client and agency relationship may be dissolved by either group.

- An advertising agency seeks new clients by referrals, solicitations, presentations, public relations, or maintaining a positive image and reputation.
- Future trends in promotional organization include growth due to expansion into the global marketplace, diversification of advertising agencies into nontraditional services, and increased assessment of agency effectiveness.

KEY TERMS

account management division
advertising agencies
advertising department
branch operations division
clients
creative boutique
creative services division
design division
direct marketing agencies
fashion department
fashion show production
   agencies
financial control division

full-service agency
human resources division
information systems division
management and finance
   division
market research companies
media buying services
media division
media organizations
media representatives
merchandising division
operations division
organization chart

production division
promotion division
public relations department
public relations firm
research division
sales division
sales promotion agencies
suppliers
traffic department
visual merchandising
   department

QUESTIONS FOR DISCUSSION

1. What are the fundamental tasks of promotion personnel and the personal characteristics needed for success?
2. How is a retail store typically organized?
3. How does a promotion division function within a retail environment?
4. Why would a company seek an outside advertising agency to handle its promotional activities?
5. How is a full-service advertising agency typically organized?
6. What are specialized agencies, and when are they used?
7 Why does a client fire or leave an agency or specialized service?

ADDITIONAL RESOURCES

Association of National Advertisers, Inc. (1989). *Agency compensation: a guidebook.* New York: Author.

Goldman, K. (1997). *Conflicting accounts: The creation and crash of the Saatchi & Saatchi advertising empire.* Upper Saddle River, NJ: Simon & Schuster.

Hameroff, E. J., and Gardner, H. S. (1997). *The advertising agency business: The complete manual for management and operation.* Lincolnwood, IL: NTC Business.

James, G., Jeffries, A., and McPherson, C. (Eds.). (1997). *Madison Avenue handbook: The image makers source* (35th ed.). New York: Peter Glen.

Krieff, A. (1992). *How to start and run your own advertising agency.* New York: McGraw-Hill.

Figure 4.1

Saatchi & Saatchi web page

chapter 4

PLANNING

M any advertising agencies are planning for their own future in addition
to providing planning services for their clients. Aiming to expand its
business activities beyond its expertise in providing traditional advertising direction, Saatchi & Saatchi, acquired GMG Marketing Services and redefined
its mission to become an *idea company* and *communication specialist.* "We
want to be revered as a hot house for creative ideas," said Bob Seelert, chief
executive of the advertising superagency (Seo, 1998). Increasingly, agencies
such as Grey Advertising, Young & Rubicam, and Foote, Cone & Belding, in
addition to Saatchi & Saatchi, have aggressively recast their efforts into areas
such as direct marketing, strategic planning, interactive communications, co-
marketing, public relations, corporate logo design, technology marketing, and
more. The Saatchi & Saatchi business communication home page (Fig. 4.1)
has links that show the firm's philosophy (mission), clients, work, and integration of divisions.

**After you have read this
chapter, should be able to:**

Discuss reasons why planning is
essential to the success of promotional
activities.

Define the meaning and use of
mission statements.

Identify components of a promotion
plan.

Differentiate various market levels in
the distribution channel.

Compare the diverse categories of
promotion calendars and know when
to use them.

Successful promotional endeavors result from activities that are well planned and well
implemented. Working out the infinite details, from defining goals and objectives to developing strategies to achieve the mission of promotion, and selecting the appropriate
management team to carry out various responsibilities, are all part of the planning
process. Giant textile producers, leading apparel designers, manufacturers, corporate retail conglomerates, and advertising superagencies, such as Saatchi & Saatchi, all have
developed highly sophisticated procedures for promotional planning. Within large
firms, formalized and structured planning is essential. Only a few small businesses participate in promotion planning, but all firms would benefit from this process.

This chapter provides a map for promotion planning. We begin by analyzing the
reasons why planning is so significant. Then, we look at the process of planning from
strategic analysis to the development of promotional goals and objectives. Next, the various levels of the distribution channels used in promotion planning are distinguished.
This is followed by discussion about the various promotion calendars. The chapter concludes with a look at future trends in promotion planning.

PROMOTION PLAN

Promotion planning involves the development of strategies and methods for accomplishing all of the activities necessary to carry out promotional projects. The first step is to define the role of promotion for the company, by carrying out a strategic analysis. From this evaluation of historical circumstances and current market conditions, the company's next step is to interpret its mission. This leads to establishing promotional goals and objectives. Budgetary requirements are also derived from this investigation. The success or failure of various activities are evaluated as the last step in the process before starting the planning process for the next project or time period. Planning and evaluation are ongoing activities.

Without promotion planning unexpected problems may occur. For example, the owner of a sports apparel store plans an appearance by Michael Jordan, makes arrangements for the basketball legend to visit, and plans newspaper advertising with the date and time of the event. What could go wrong? Jordan could miss his flight; a blizzard could keep customers away from the store; the newspaper advertisement might have the wrong day or time; or, the prearranged hotel could be overbooked. Any of these or many other unforeseen problems could occur. Critical or stressful situations may be avoided by anticipating needs, maintaining an organized yet flexible schedule, and planning for contingencies.

Communication is an integral element of planning. The person responsible for picking up merchandise prior to a photo shoot needs to be aware of this obligation. If he or she is not informed, the model and photographer could needlessly waste time while they are waiting for the merchandise to arrive. Lines of communication between members of the promotional team, company management, clients, and consumers must be well defined and functional to avoid problems as the plan is implemented.

Planning enables the organization to forecast how to proceed, with little or no wasted energy, creating order before chaos can result. How far into the future should a company plan? In the next section, we consider the time frame for advance planning.

Planning Time Frame

Most plans fall into one of two time frames: short term or long term. The **short-term plan** may be for a period of 6 months to 1 year. Most retail firms focus on short-term planning by focusing on 6-month merchandise plans. These retail firms are accustomed to planning sales, stock, markdowns, and purchases for the two 6-month periods that constitute the fall season, from August to January, and the spring season, from February to July. It follows that the promotional plans will fall in line with the sales and stock plans created every 6 months. Retail firms normally prepare these merchandise plans approximately 90 days before the start of the season. Promotional plans and budgets closely follow after merchandise plans are established.

Strategic planning, a long-term plan that forecasts more than 2 years into the future, is the process of determining what you want to accomplish, how to accomplish it, and how to implement it. Important components of strategic planning include thinking about diverse alternatives, weighing the strengths and weaknesses of each approach, and identifying the best approach in light of current as well as anticipated market conditions. According to Mintzberg and Waters (1983), strategy has four dimensions: (1) *strategy is a plan*, a set of guidelines intended to influence behavior in the future; (2) *strategy is a position*, the means to define or at least to identify an organization in an environment; (3) *strategy is a perception*, organizational strategy is how the members of an organization view their world, and (4) *strategy is a pattern*, synonymous with consistency, what actually happens in the organization. Although such retailers as J. C. Penney and Dayton-Hudson have been involved in strategic planning for decades, other companies have been unwilling to create these long-term blueprints. The article in Box 4.1 looks at what really happens in the strategic planning process.

BOX 4.1
Debunking the Myths of Strategic Planning

Strategic planning is attracting renewed interest among leading organizations. According to Bain & Company's fourth annual survey of management tools and techniques, 89 percent of the 870 international managers surveyed use strategic planning to drive success through their organizations. Much of the conventional wisdom about what strategic planning is, and does, is misplaced and inconsistent with what really happens. Here are some insights on recent trends in expectations, and myths.

Members of the board of the Toronto chapter of the Strategic Leadership Forum have seen strategic planning fluctuate and evolve for years now. Several volunteers, both past and present board members, recently joined in a discussion of strategic planning, reviewing recent trends in expectations and myths with respect to strategy. The purpose here is not to present the "how-to" manual of strategic planning, but rather to help generate an understanding as to why such a definitive "how-to" manual does not exist.

In recent years, there has been a wide spread shift from centralized planning departments to decentralized, shared responsibility for strategy across the senior management team. The gurus of contemporary wisdom promised that, by opening strategy development up to the entire management team, it would no longer be a black box, beyond the comprehension of 95 percent of the organization. The Strategic Leadership Forum, anticipating this trend, changed its name from The Planning Forum and advocated the learning and use of the best practices in strategic management throughout organizations. This trend was viewed as a positive acknowledgment that strategy had to be integrated with daily management decision making and cross-functional team problem solving in order to be successful.

But this positive change had some less than desirable results. In some organizations, the strategic planners, who had been schooled in the tools and techniques for facilitating strategy development, ended up being downsized. At the same time, senior managers, who had focused primarily on operational decisions, were asked to take full responsibility for strategy development. For many executives, the demands of today's decisions just did not allow for big picture, "what if?"-type discussions. As a result, strategic planning seemed to hit a lull for awhile. After sampling many management tools and techniques—some appropriately, others misplaced or poorly applied—organizations are once again turning to strategic planning as an additional robust approach to pull the organizational efforts together into a coordinated unit with a common focus and direction.

Understanding the Nature of Strategic Planning Better: The Eight Myths

Now that strategy is experiencing a rebirth, a few myths about strategic planning need to be examined. The emphasis on what strategic planning is, and does, is misplaced. The biggest contributions that planning makes to an organization are not the tangible ones that have been traditionally described. Many of the practices that are proposed by various practitioners are inconsistent with the way that planning really occurs. We have identified eight myths (among others) that we feel need to be examined under the light of day:

1. **You need a documented plan.** We started our discussion by asking, "What is the value of strategy?" In our collective experience, the strategic plan itself is not where the value lies, though it is often the most visible, tangible output. Rather, it is the development of the plan that provides the value-added. In other words, "it's not the breath but the breathing that's important." The value lies in developing a common language, articulating the assumptions held, and learning to make decisions together.

2. **A plan can describe all the things that must be done to succeed.** The ultimate objective of strategic planning is to close the gap between where the organization is now, and where it would like to be (the vision). The strategy describes what needs to be achieved; the oper-

ational plan, or tactical plan, describes how the gap will be closed. This distinction between strategy and tactics is important.

Strategy occurs at the strategic business unit level, crosses functional areas, and sets direction. Without a strategy, functional areas may make tactical resource decisions that inadvertently move the organization in a certain direction unilaterally, without reference to what will benefit the entire organization. Imagine a computer department designing an information technology data architecture that binds the organization to a specific set of technical capabilities and data views and, as a result, leaves others in the organization unable to respond to the needs of customers. Organizations without a strategic planning process can find themselves in just this sort of predicament.

The purpose of strategy is not to provide a comprehensive set of decisions on all actions that are required to be successful. A strategy sets direction and a context for decision making so that subsequent decisions at the subunit level can be made in harmony, with everyone "singing from the same song sheet" when making his or her respective tactical decisions. These operational or tactical decisions happen in real time. They are not encoded in the strategic plan.

3. **Strategy planning is a formal, analytical process**. In some organizations, the development of strategy, and the subsequent links to the operating plan and budget, have been reduced into a single annual effort. As a result, the linear, analytical characteristics of budgets have been incorrectly attributed to strategy. Strategy is inherently a creative process. Strategy deals with complexity and ambiguity. For many of us, this territory is uncomfortable and full of risk, particularly when combined with the myth that the plan is the important output from the strategic planning process. After all, one might argue, if the plan is cast in stone, one must have a high degree of certainty about its relevance and accuracy, otherwise it loses credibility.

However, if we accept that the value of planning is in the process, then we realize that the plan is never finished, and it need not be precisely accurate. We can accept the plan as being approximately correct, and of having "the right intent," at least for today's tactical decisions. This view places value on the creative nature of planning. In addition, it frees managers to make decisions that are appropriate to their circumstances. The complexity and ambiguity of the real world stimulates the creative process and the evolution of the plan.

4. **Plans are built solely on "facts" and "hard data."** No one would argue against the need of research and for measurement in assessing the organization's strengths and weaknesses, and the opportunities and threats facing an organization. This "SWOT" analysis is a common starting point for strategic planning. But it would be a mistake to think that a strategy can emerge solely from an examination of the tangible, proven acts and evidence. A strategy is a set of hypotheses about how the world behaves. Facts and hard data can be used to test the validity of a strategy, but it is the assumptions underlying the discussion that shape the strategy. Articulating and examining these assumptions helps turn facts into knowledge, and this is where emphasis needs to be placed.

A useful diagnosis of your organization's strategy is to look for gaps in the implicit assumptions underlying the strategy. For example, is there evidence that the organization thinks it has no competition? Is there an assumption that the company knows what the customer wants with no reference to the need for an ongoing scanning process to capture changing market demands? The fact finding can help you to find the gaps in these assumptions, and point to emerging trends.

The future is being created through the strategic process. The dialogue between people shapes our view and our assumptions and therefore our choices and behaviors. This process creates new realities which historical facts and evidence may not point to.

5. **The planning cycle runs on your financial calendar.** Mintzberg promoted the idea of emerging strategies, i.e., a dynamic process. This is indeed the case— strategic planning is not confined to the formally recognized planning cycle. New events and information cause us to reexamine and sometimes change our assumptions. The formalized cyclical process is useful for creating opportunities, time and space amidst the day-to-day operations for strategic thinking, but ad-hoc strategy is also important.

6. **The work is over when the plan is done.** Strategy must meet stakeholders needs. A strategy is working when shareholders, customers, employees, creditors, and other stakeholders see that their expectations of the organization are being met. A plan is not enough to satisfy these needs. A strategy must be put into action to meet today's needs and to adapt to changing needs.

Giving the strategy life is rarely achieved through distributing a plan. Management by objectives, performance measurement using balanced scorecards, and Hoshin planning are examples of techniques for engaging the organization in the discussion and application of strategy. They encourage conversations about the cause-effect linkage between actions and the satisfaction of stakeholders' needs within the business environment. Finally, the fact that stakeholders' needs change means that the strategic plan is never done.

7. **There is one right strategy.** The expectation of finding the "right" direction implies that there is one right strategy. We don't agree. Successful directions are created through interactions and conversations between stakeholders and understanding the implications of alternative strategic direction. Strategy is about identifying and creating more choice—increased degrees of freedom.

8. **There is one best process for building strategy.** Many schools of thought about approaches to strategy development exists—most are valid. No one "right" way to develop and implement strategy exists. The key to successful planning is to get the best fit between the chosen tools and techniques; the organization's current culture, capabilities, and business environment; and the desired outcome. Read; attend conferences; talk to other organizations about what they've tried. Test techniques in pilot areas for their fit with your organization.

Most practitioners would agree that strategic planning requires two equally important processes. The first stage is one of divergence, which harnesses creative thinking without undue regard for its realism, logic, or fit with current assumptions and beliefs. The second stage is convergent, using a set of filters and analytical tools to sort through the output from the divergent stage and create a set of assumptions consistent with the vision of the organization and today's realities.

Our experience suggests that benefits come from extended commitment to a chosen set of tools and techniques allowing for the development of a common language. But we also know that change is often a catalyst for creativity—an essential ingredient of planning. So keep what works, change what doesn't. The strategic planning process is robust, yet inexact. Introduce new ideas to keep the dialogue going. Document what you learn as a means of sharing and furthering the conversation rather than as an end in itself.

Adapted from: Gooderham, G. (1998, May 1). Debunking the myths of strategic planning. CMA, 72, 24-27 [On-line]. Available: http://www.elibrary.compuserve.com.

In the past, strategic plans seemed less important to retailers and manufacturers than planning day-to-day operations. As new and alternative methods of doing business emerge, however, more firms may see the need for strategic planning. The globalization of business necessitates a more strategic approach. This type of planning requires the involvement of all key personnel, since the nature and scope of the business will be affected.

Personnel Responsible for Promotion Planning

Promotion planning may take place at various departmental levels within the firm. The first step, therefore, is the selection of the proper organizational level at which planning will be focused. Promotion planning may be the responsibility of upper management. In a retail company this may include the chief executive officer (CEO), president, and vice president in charge of promotion. The corporate management team then translates the goals and objectives to the lower levels of management and operation. This represents top-down planning.

Promotion planning may alternatively be the responsibility of the individual managers who implement the promotional strategy. The advertising, public relations, merchandising, and marketing managers may be charged to submit plans to upper management. This flow of information represents bottom-up planning.

Should planning and communication occur in an upward or a downward course? In reality, information flows in both directions. Various interactions between top management and middle managers are necessary for the planning process to be successful.

A further discussion of top-down and bottom-up management approaches may be found in Chapter 5, on budgeting.

Assignment of personnel with the responsibility and authority for various promotion mix activities should take place during the planning stage. This involves designating particular obligations and accountability of specific individuals and departments. Many times a program is implemented without the proper delegation of responsibility, leading to unclear expectations. Assignment of personnel at the planning stage prevents confusion about the chain of command and frustration about failure to meet expectations.

A review of strategic plans from a variety of businesses shows the following areas are typically covered: strategic analysis, mission statement, goals and objectives, budget, strategies and tactics, personnel assignments, implementation time frame, and evaluation. Figure 4.2 shows the steps in the planning process. Promotion planning involves deciding what promotion actions to undertake, why they are necessary, when and where they will be accomplished, who will be responsible, and how they will be carried out. In this chapter, we focus on strategic analysis, development of the mission statement, defining the goals and objectives for promotion, determining who is responsible for promotion planning, and establishing a time frame using promotional calendars. Budget is covered in Chapter 5; strategies and tactics are discussed in Chapter 7; and promotion evaluation is the subject of Chapter 17.

Strategic Analysis

A **strategic analysis** is a statement of the historical events leading to the current condition of the organization. The checklist on page 97 identifies key elements for the business to consider in preparing a strategic analysis. This activity forces the firm to review relevant facts about the founding of the company; size and scope of its products and services; and, strengths, weaknesses, opportunities, and threats (SWOT) for the firm and the industry as a whole. Information necessary for the completion of the strategic analysis may come from internal and/or external sources.

Internal information is the type of data available from within the firm. This typically includes information that comes from employees or firm records. Senior managers and executives have knowledge about company origin, sales history, products or services offered, distribution methods, pricing policies, and promotional practices. Additional documentation should be readily available from internal sources such as annual reports, sales and stock statistical reports, or departmental records.

External information is material and facts from outside sources, often beyond the control of the firm. This type of information consists of knowledge about the economic, social, political, technological, and competitive environments in which the firm operates. This documentation is available from government materials, sociological reports, and economic statistical sources.

Figure 4.2

Steps in the Planning Process

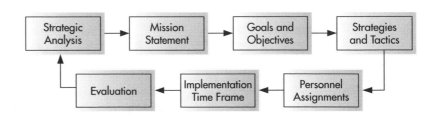

Strategic Analysis Checklist

The Company
- ❒ Historical development
- ❒ Size and scope of the firm
- ❒ Reputation of the firm
- ❒ Management strengths and weaknesses
- ❒ Profitability

Competitive Status
- ❒ History of the industry
- ❒ Characteristics of the industry: distribution patterns, promotional activities, geographical patterns, profit patterns
- ❒ Other firms in similar businesses: market share, growth potential, technological advances, and other contributions
- ❒ Strengths and weaknesses of competition

Sales History
- ❒ Sales records
- ❒ Cost and expense analysis: product costs and promotional expenses
- ❒ Market potential

Product or Service Records
- ❒ Product research and development
- ❒ Special sales features
- ❒ Technological developments: what improvements are planned?

Market
- ❒ Customer definition: who are the customers; what do they want; where do they wish to find it; when should it be available?
- ❒ Market share: history and potential

Distribution
- ❒ History and current position in the distribution channel
- ❒ Past policies: trade advertising, display resources, co-operative advertising or co-marketing activities

Pricing
- ❒ Price history: trends, relationship to competition, response to buyer's requests
- ❒ Past price objectives

Promotion Analysis
- ❒ Past advertising appeals
- ❒ Promotion expenditures
- ❒ Sales force: training and potential
- ❒ Successes and failures of prior promotional activities

Mission Statement

An organization's mission defines the purpose of the firm and what it wants to accomplish. Most large corporations formalize this explanation into a **mission statement**, which has been derived from the strategic analysis. The mission statement usually covers a discussion of the company's products, services, and target consumers. This guiding force for the company is frequently presented in corporate literature such as annual reports and newsletters. Often a significant aspect of the firm's plans and actions, the mission statement is frequently displayed in the retail store or manufacturer's offices. Heller Financial used the world's simplest corporate mission statement as the theme for its advertising, shown in Figure 4.3.

The Neiman Marcus Group is a retailing corporation consisting of four entities, Neiman-Marcus Stores, NM Direct, Bergdorf Goodman, and Bergdorf Goodman Man. This retailer, focused exclusively on the high-end segment of the specialty retailing marketplace, defines its purpose as follows:

> Our mission is to be the leading specialty retailer of fine merchandise to discerning, fashion-conscious customers from around the world. We will strive to exceed customer expectations for service, quality and value as we build upon our long-standing tradition of excellence. As we pursue this mission, we are guided by the following important values.
>
> • We will maintain an uncompromising commitment to quality and the highest levels of customer service in all of our businesses and endeavors.
> • We will adhere to the highest levels of integrity and ethical standards in dealing with all constituencies, including customers, suppliers and employees.
> • We will aspire to achieve a leadership position in every one of our operating businesses.
> • Our management decisions will emphasize long-term benefits to the value of our businesses, not short-term gains.
> • We will employ capable, motivated people; follow sound management practices; utilize new technology efficiently; and reinvest earnings and additional capital as required to grow our businesses and maintain the corporation's financial health.

Figure 4.3

An advertisement from Heller Financial promotes "The World's Simplest Corporate Mission Statement: Find a way to say yes."

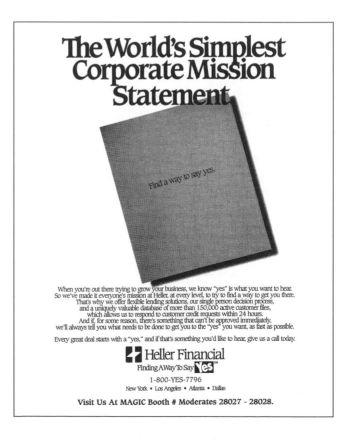

- We will strive to maximize the potential of all employees and maintain a professionally challenging work environment.
- We will be socially and environmentally responsible and support worthwhile causes, especially in those communities in which we operate ("Love Stories," 1996).

Professional organizations also define their purpose by writing a mission statement. The organization uses this information as a focus for its meetings, publications, and interactions with professionals. The mission statement for The Fashion Group International, a global nonprofit association established in 1931, with over 6,000 members in the fashion and related industries, is provided as an example.

The mission of the organization is:

- To advance the professionalism of fashion and its related lifestyle industries, with a particular emphasis on the role and development of women
- To provide a public forum for examination of important contemporary issues in fashion and the business of fashion
- To present timely information regarding national and global trends that have an effect on the fashion industries
- To attain greater recognition for women's achievements in business
- To encourage men and women to seek career opportunities in fashion and [its] related industries
- To provide activities and programs that enhance networking skills and encourage interpersonal contacts so as to further the professional, social and personal development of members
- To administer the activities of The Fashion Group International Foundation ("About FGI," 1998).

Since the mission statement drives the performance of a firm or organization, it also directs the planning for promotions that the firm undertakes. The mission statement determines the goals and objectives of the company or organization as well as the methods to achieve them.

Goals and Objectives

After the strategic analysis and mission statement are written, the firm's general goals and objectives are specified. **Goals** are the end results that a business wants to achieve. Goals are generally assumed to be in a long-term time frame. These strategic goals of a firm may be designated in periods from 2 years or longer. A retail store such as Eddie Bauer may establish the goal of becoming the industry leader in outdoor apparel, accessories and home furnishings. This is a fairly broad definition the firm would hope to achieve over a long term.

Objectives are outcomes desired by the firm within a short time period, typically 1 year or less. An objective established by Eddie Bauer might be, for instance, *to increase the number of retail branches by 25 units during the next 12 months.* This is a more specific, measurable business activity that is limited by time.

Many firms and people use the terms goals and objectives interchangeably. However, in this book we take the view that goals are long-term desired outcomes, whereas objectives are short-term desired outcomes, achievable in one year or less.

Marketing Objectives

Marketing objectives are statements that specify what is to be accomplished by the overall marketing program within a short time period. They are expressed as part of the planning process. Marketing objectives are measurable outcomes typically based upon such factors as sales volume, profits, returns on investments, and/or market share. An apparel manufacturer might establish a marketing objective of, for example, *increasing* *sales by 10 percent in Eddie Bauer men's sportswear division during the next 12 months.* This is an example of a broad, yet measurable, marketing objectives.

Integrated Marketing Communications Objectives

In addition to the marketing objectives, the business should be concerned with the integrated marketing communications (IMC) objectives. **IMC objectives** are statements about what various aspects of the IMC program will accomplish. An example of an IMC objective might be *to increase awareness about Eddie Bauer brands among 18- to 24-year-old males.* Guidance for the IMC objectives comes from the strategic analysis and mission statement. The article in Box 4.2 shows how defining clear IMC objectives will strengthen relationships between firms and their customers.

BOX 4.2

Clear Integrated Marketing Communications Goals Build Strong Relationships

As a business marketer, what do you really want to accomplish through an integrated marketing communications (IMC) strategy?

Using IMC to coordinate all the messages your company articulates through advertising, direct marketing, public relations (PR), and sales promotion will help you create a unified image and support relationship-building with customers and other stakeholders. The key, however, is to determine exactly what your IMC strategy should achieve.

The first step is to identify the specific members of the buying center you should target (initiators, users, decision makers, influencers, buyers, gatekeepers) and understand what each needs from your IMC campaign.

After you identify your audience, you are ready to set your goals. Broad IMC goals for business marketing fall into five categories, which are interrelated in their ability to create or enhance customer relationships. To sharpen your focus, concentrate on only one or two goals to avoid stretching your IMC strategy, and budget, to cover four or five objectives. Your choices include:

1. Build brand equity. By using IMC to reinforce your brand's unique value and identity, you increase awareness and encourage stronger preference among customers and prospects. Moreover, using IMC to build brand equity can give you a potent competitive weapon as well as a tool for strengthening relationships with distributors and other channel partners.

Consider the business-to-business ads for Scotchgard, the stain-protection product marketed by 3M to textile and garment industry customers. In the ads, 3M builds the Scotchgard brand by linking it prominently and positively to specific benefits that its customers value, such as keeping apparel in good shape by adding stain-shedding qualities.

2. Provide information. In the course of making a buying decision, business customers need a lot of information. Your IMC tactics can give the buying process a boost by offering details about product specifications and uses, availability, buying incentives, and other data.

Investigate what buying-center members need so you can provide what they want in a way that is most convenient for them. For example, Pall Corp.'s website attracts customers who are in the market for fluid filtration and purification products. Rather than organize information around its internal divisions, Pall organizes the site around industry theories. Research and development (R&D) staffers at client or prospect companies can then browse through the appropriate industry-related web pages or use the site's search function to find Pall products and technologies appropriate for solving their problems.

Just as important, clients and contacts can easily electronic-mail requests for sales contacts through the website.

3. Manage demand and sales. When you can't meet demand or have a temporary problem, you may need IMC to dampen sales or shift demand. Most of the time, however, companies use IMC to build sales by stimulating primary demand (for a relatively new or innovative product category) or selective demand (for your own brand in a more mature product category).

Look at American Express, which uses direct mail, advertising, and other IMC tactics to build selective demand for its corporate card. In a highly competitive market, Amex's IMC campaigns are designed to have a positive effect on cardholder acquisition and, by extension, on card use and market share.

4. Communicate differentiation and enhance positioning. What do your goods or services stand for and how are they better than your competitors' products? IMC helps you convey your most significant points of differentiation and contributes to your positioning in the marketplace. For instance, a current UPS ad stresses the range of guaranteed "urgent delivery" choices offered to business customers. Having same-day as well as next-day choices differentiates the company from its competitors while simultaneously positioning it as able to meet virtually any deadline—a powerful image for a delivery firm.

   5. Influence attitudes and behavior. You can use IMC to promote a favorable inclination toward your company and your products while encouraging buying-center members to take some action, such as recommending your services, contacting your representatives, or listing your products on a purchase order.

   For example, to support the introduction of a new two-color printing press, A. B. Dick created an IMC campaign targeting small printing firms, corporate printing departments, and large commercial printers. Using direct mail, PR, newsletters, and magazine advertising to lay a foundation for personal sales calls, Dick emphasized the new product's key benefit: making short-run color printing profitable. Although Dick traditionally has been known for its duplicating machines, this campaign helped establish the company as a maker of full-size printing presses and led to 350 orders totaling more than $20 million.

Marketing Lesson

- Once you chose from among five broad goals for your IMC strategy, you need to define specific, measurable, and time-defined objectives linked to your overall marketing and corporate objectives.
- Only by measuring your IMC results will you be able to evaluate your investment in IMC and check your progress toward starting relationships with new customers, strengthening relationships with existing customers, and jump-starting stalled relationships with former customers.

Adapted from: Wood, M. B. (1997, June 23). Clear IMC goals build strong relationships, Marketing News, 3. 11, 15.

   The IMC objectives are based upon four factors:

1. **Target audience:** the market segments the firm wants to attract, considering such factors as demographics and psychographics
2. **Product:** the main features, advantages, benefits, uses, and applications of one or more of the company's wares
3. **Brands:** the company's and competitors' brands
4. **Behavioral responses:** the responses sought from trial, repurchase, brand switching, or increased usage

   Communications-oriented professionals believe the objective of advertising and other promotional activities is to communicate information or knowledge about a product or service. This differs from the marketing-directed managers, who insist upon an evaluation of success based on some sales or sales-related measurement.

   Communications professionals base IMC objectives on one of the hierarchical models such as the one illustrated in Figure 4.4. According to such models, consumers generally pass through several different stages: (1) developing awareness, (2) becoming interested, (3) desiring to take action, (4) proceeding to take action, (5) making repeat purchases, and (6) becoming brand loyal. Making consumers loyal to a particular brand is the ultimate hope of most promotional sponsors.

   Figure 4.4 is an example of IMC objectives for marketing Sally Hansen ColorFast One Coat Fast-Dry Enamel to 18- to 24-year-old women. Notice how the objectives address the successive stages that consumers pass through in developing brand loyalty. The first level of an IMC objective would probably be expressed in terms of developing awareness in the desired target market. The next objective is to communicate benefits and features to arouse interest. Once advertising has brought the consumer from

Consumer Stage	Sample Objective
Developing awareness	*To create a 90 percent awareness of Sally Hansen ColorFast One Coat Fast-Dry Enamel among 18- to 24-year-old females during the first 6 weeks of the campaign.*
Becoming interested	*To communicate the distinctive benefits of Sally Hansen ColorFast One Coat Fast-Dry Enamel—that it provides a silicone protection and shine that dries in just 90 seconds, salon-style, in cutting edge colors, using 1 coat—to 75 percent of the target audience to interest them in the brand.*
Desiring to take action	*To create positive feelings toward Sally Hansen ColorFast One Coat Fast-Dry Enamel among 50 percent of the target audience and a preference for the brand among 25 percent.*
Proceeding to take action	*To use sampling to elicit experimentation with Sally Hansen ColorFast One Coat Fast-Dry Enamel among 15 percent of the 18- to 24-year-old females during the first 2 months of the product launch.*
Making repeat purchases	*To use cents-off coupons to elicit replenishment purchase of Sally Hansen Color-Fast One Coat Fast-Dry Enamel among 10 percent of the 18- to 24-year-old females during the first 3 months of the product launch.*
Becoming brand loyal	*To develop and maintain regular customers of Sally Hansen ColorFast One Coat Fast-Dry Enamel among 5 percent of the 18- to 24-year-old females.*

Figure 4.4

Sample IMC Objectives

awareness of the new product to knowledge of its benefits, the objective of the next level of the campaign is to create the desire to take action based upon a positive feeling toward the product. The point now is to turn a certain percentage of the target market toward purchase. This action stage is near the top of the hierarchy. Manufacturers may use sampling or coupons to stimulate action. Consumers will be influenced by the advertising as well as the potential savings with a trial sample or a cents-off coupon. After a certain percentage of the target market has purchased the product, the manufacturer will attempt to stimulate repeat purchases. Consumers might react to coupons or enticements to buy that are included inside the packaging of the product. The ultimate communications objective is to turn experimenters into loyal customers. It is hoped that once they use the product, consumers will continue to use it and will repurchase it. Nail enamel products are in a highly competitive market. The final objective during the product launch could be to retain a modest percentage of the target market as brand loyal consumers.

The top executives of a firm must determine how specific communication objectives will be carried out by which promotion mix activities. Promotion personnel in South Africa have studied this concern and have provided a tool for analyzing which promotion mix tools work best for various communication objectives. Table 4.1 features this objective-by-tool matrix.

The promotion planner must decide whether to use strictly marketing objectives, IMC objectives, or some combination of both. Not all marketing managers will accept communications objectives since they have been trained to think in terms of sales, profit, market share, or return on investment. Most likely promotion planners will use some combination of the marketing objectives and IMC objectives to evaluate the success or failure of a promotion program.

Table 4.1 **The Right Tools for the Job—an Objective-by-Tool Matrix**

Objective	Advertising	In-store Promotion	Branded Promotion	Price-off Promotion	Direct Response	Mailers	Events	Exhibitions	Public Relations
Create awareness	yes	yes	yes	yes	yes	yes	yes	yes	yes
Create trial endorsement	yes	yes	yes	yes	yes	yes	yes	yes	yes
Current users	yes	no	no	no	no	yes	no	no	yes
Expand users	yes	yes	yes	yes	yes	yes	yes	yes	yes
Expand usage/ users	yes	no	no	no	no	yes	no	no	no
Retain customer base	yes	no	no	no	no	yes	no	no	no
Create perceptions	yes	no	no	no	no	yes	yes	yes	yes
Change attitudes	yes	yes	no	no	no	no	yes	yes	yes

Adapted from: Interactive Financial Mall/Ad focus/Top Tables [On-line]. Available: http://www.fm.co.za/adfocus/tables/tools.htm.

Promotion Objectives

Common and universally accepted **promotion objectives** are consumer outcomes that can be represented by a hierarchy or pyramid (Fig. 4.5). Lowest level objectives make consumers aware of products or services, while the highest level objectives create loyal customers. Consumer responses are easier to accomplish in the initial stages than in later stages. It does not matter whether the organization is a profit-making corporation or a charity group; these objectives are the desire for any business or non-profit organization. The five *general* objectives of promotion are:

1. **To inform** or make target consumers aware of available products and services.
2. **To arouse interest** within the target consumer group.
3. **To persuade** the target groups to take some form of action.
4. **To encourage purchase** of the product or service offered by target consumers.
5. **To gain loyalty** of the consumer group due to the success of the first four steps.

These general objectives of promotion may be narrowed to *specific* objectives, focused on distinct activities that may require special projects or events to reach identifiable groups of customers. The nature and extent of each of the following specific objectives vary from company to company and product to product. The list is not meant to be comprehensive or required for all firms. These specific objectives are common in the merchandising environment:

- **To introduce new products.** All organizations, especially those in the fashion field, need to inform customers about new products and lines of merchandise. Information about seasonal style and color trends and new products should be conveyed to potential customers. Color Plate 2 shows the introduction of a new magazine.
- **To inform about merchandise assortment.** Some stores build a reputation by offering a complete line of merchandise under one roof. The range, depth, and variety of

Figure 4.5

Promotion Objectives Pyramid

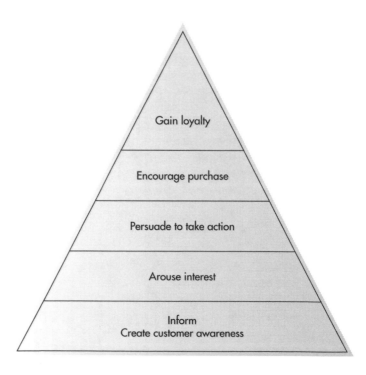

products offered at value prices are the hallmark of Target stores, for instance. The reputation of the firm for presenting quality merchandise at low prices draws customers to these stores. Other retail firms, such as Neiman Marcus, promote an elite selection of merchandise available at its branches, basing its reputation on exclusive lines of merchandise. A selectively stocked collection of exclusive merchandise is planned and promoted to meet the needs of the Neiman Marcus customer, while low prices and value-oriented products are advertised to the consumer at Target stores.

- **To establish fashion authority.** Building a reputation for fashion leadership is the specific objective of many celebrity designers and specialty retail stores. Well-known designers have the status to attract media attention. Popular-priced manufacturers and retailers follow or adapt the styles, colors, and fabrics featured by these famous innovators. Once a designer has established his or her philosophy of design and becomes successful, the position of authority and leadership is granted.

- **To present special merchandise, prices, or themes.** In a retail location there is a need to inform potential customers about unique products. A fiber producer may work in cooperation with a retail store to advertise products made from a unique fiber, such as Tencel. Attractive or temporary sale prices for an annual sale on hosiery or underwear may be promoted. Holiday or seasonal themes may also be featured to bring customers into the store.

- **To attract new customers.** All levels in the distribution system have the desire to sell merchandise and make a profit. Whether the company wishes to replace lost customers or find new customers, promotion will help to attract new clients.

- **To inform about public and community service.** In the contemporary social climate a commitment to the community in which a firm operates is essential. Retail stores, including Saks Fifth Avenue and Macy's, stage fashion shows for charitable organizations in communities where they have stores. These fashion shows raise money for such causes as AIDS or breast cancer research. The goodwill created by such sponsorship is translated into sales and support for the retail firm.

- **To provide education.** New products are created to meet the needs of a niche group. Women with sensitive skin represent a cohort group for the development of such products as the Estée Lauder skin care line called Verité. The research completed by the cosmetic giant indicated that most women needing this product were typically not department store shoppers. The firm had to create a communication package to inform customers about the benefits of the product and where to find it. Through promotion campaigns, product education takes many forms. A seminar for petite customers, informing them about new styles and how to wear them, is a popular promotional activity educating a specific customer. From *how to find a pair of jeans that fit* to *how to wear the latest accessory*, the list of educational promotional strategies is almost endless.

- **To reach persons who influence the purchaser.** Perhaps the most obvious example of this type of promotion is television commercials for toys and breakfast foods during Saturday morning cartoons. The child influences the parents to purchase the game or soft drink advertised, using persuasive techniques to sway parents to buy.

- **To identify and differentiate brands.** Manufacturers, designers, and retailers develop strategies and visual images to identify merchandise. Brand names such as Reebok, Liz Claiborne, or Hanes reflect and maintain an impression of that brand's quality or style. Firms protect and differentiate themselves through the use of corporate identity. Hanes Her Way advertising (Fig. 4.6) features the firm's logo to enhance the image.

Figure 4.6

Advertisement for Hanes
Her Way with corporate
logo prominently
featured

- **To build traffic.** This specific objective attempts to emphasize increased flow and movement of people into and through a retail store, bringing potential customers into the sales location. A store will monitor the number of sales transactions in a given period of time, frequently each hour. Comparative statistics are used to analyze the benefits of advertising, displays, or special events.

In addition to understanding the goals and objectives of promotion, it is important for us to understand each of the market levels where promotion takes place. Therefore, we will turn our attention to analyzing the various market levels in the distribution channel.

MARKET LEVELS APPLYING PROMOTION OBJECTIVES

Since promotion encourages the sale of all kinds of products and services, nearly every business is involved in the promotion process. The next section of this chapter identifies the most common channels of distribution where promotion objectives are applied. Promotion of fashion-oriented products and services takes place at four market levels: global, national, trade, and retail.

Global Markets

Global promotion takes place when manufacturers of internationally distributed merchandise and global retailers implement promotional programs aimed at consumers in several different countries. As we first learned in Chapter 1, global promotion may be accomplished with a standardized or an individualized approach.

A U.S.-based firm, such as Donna Karan, has worked with a variety of retailing firms in countries like England, France, or Japan to promote globally. The consumer might expect to see an ad for Karan's merchandise with Harrod's, the British department store or Printemps, the Paris-based retail company. French-based Chanel is internationally known due to its application of global promotion objectives. Clinique Moisture Control, a U.S.-manufactured cosmetic product, is available worldwide. Figure 4.7 is an ad for Clinique's *Bajo Control*, as featured in the Spanish edition of *Elle* magazine.

Domestic Markets

In the United States, market channels commonly used to advance promotional objectives are national, trade, and retail. **National promotion** involves planning and executing promotional activities by primary resources, secondary resources, and national retailers to the ultimate consumer. Primary resources (manufacturers) are the producers of raw materials. The primary resources in the merchandising environment include textile fiber firms, fabric manufacturers, and other producers of raw materials.

Figure 4.7

Global Product Ad: Clinique moisture control in *Elle,* Spanish Edition

Secondary resources include the manufacturers of finished goods, such as clothing, shoes, accessories, home furnishings, or cosmetics. National promotion is used to *pre-sell* the ultimate consumer. For example, a textile producer such as Monsanto promotes its fibers directly to consumers through consumer magazine or newspaper advertising.

Activities promoting products from one business to another business are known as **trade promotion**. This type of activity promotes a product from a primary resource or trade association to a secondary or tertiary resource. Retailers are considered tertiary resources. For example, a textile manufacturer such as Celanese (primary resource) advertises to an apparel manufacturer such as Vanity Fair (secondary resource) or a retailer such as Macy's (tertiary resource) in a trade publication such as *Women's Wear Daily*. Trade promotion may also involve a trade association, such as Cotton Incorporated, promoting to a retailer in a trade magazine such as *Home Furnishings Daily*.

Retail promotion involves stores promoting products and an institutional image to ultimate consumers. Retailers are the main distributors of fashion items and focus their promotion efforts toward consumers. An example of retail promotion is a Sunday newspaper advertisement featuring the newest Nautica sheets, towels, and comforter covers available at Dayton-Hudson.

These categories of market level promotion are not mutually exclusive. An advertisement may be both national and retail if the clothing manufacturer and retailer work cooperatively to develop and publish the ad. This type of collaboration is called **cooperative promotion**, activities jointly planned and paid for by members of the distribution channel, and is mutually beneficial from the expense and image enhancement points of view. In the previous example, the manufacturer creating Nautica home linens may cooperatively sponsor the advertisement with Dayton-Hudson. It is common in the merchandising environment for primary or secondary resources to work cooperatively with each other and with retailers to promote products.

PROMOTION CALENDARS

After decisions are made about which promotional activities will take place and which employees will be involved, promotion calendars are developed to keep everyone organized. Manufacturers, retailers, and advertising agencies rely on several **promotion calendars** to assist in achieving their promotional goals. Timing can make the difference between success and failure of any promotional activity. Scheduling annual promotional events, based upon previous timetables, assists professionals in planning the next year's events and activities. Consumers have relatively consistent buying patterns. Back-to-school shopping peaks in August and September, while home furnishings sales normally occur in July or August. Coat sales can be anticipated in October and clearance sales take place in January and July.

Calendars are prepared for various market levels and specific promotion mix activities. The most common planning calendars are the trade, retail, and individual promotion mix calendars.

Trade Calendar

The monthly guide to events occurring at the manufacturing level is the **trade calendar**. It is the listing of the major market weeks and generally precedes the retail calendar by 2 to 6 months. Merchandise presented and sold during a market week requires time to manufacture and import, and the paperwork must be processed far in advance of the shipment of the merchandise to the retail store. Merchandise arrival is timed so that it is available at the highest peak of consumer demand. It is the basis for the development of the promotional activities at the trade level.

The trade calendar is used by the buying staff, members of the fashion or marketing departments, and upper management of a retail store. Buyers plan trips to coincide with markets for the products they purchase. The divisional merchandise manager (DMM) or general merchandise manager (GMM) may accompany buyers from their divisions and work with several different buyers. Members of the fashion office may be assigned to specific divisions, or the fashion director may attend numerous markets, especially those that are most essential to the image of the firm.

The fashion director may visit the international designer shows in Milan, Paris, and London in addition to the New York shows. The fashion director may travel for several weeks each year. A fashion coordinator for a division such as children's or accessories may accompany buyers and the DMM to the children's or accessories market. These coordinators would not have as extensive travel schedules as the fashion director, who visits many markets.

Many professionals in the fashion industry are also familiar with *The Fashion Calendar*. This weekly calendar, published by Ruth Finley for more than 40 years, serves as a guide to market activities, focusing on the New York market center but also listing events in other cities across the United States and around the world. Retailers, manufacturers, and the press are apprised of dates and related information for key fashion events. This information helps to avoid potential scheduling conflicts.

The trade calendar is also used by manufacturers to schedule fashion shows and showroom activities. The New York fashion industry has pulled together under the auspices of the Council of Fashion Designers of America to produce 7th on Sixth, a week of fashion shows created to present new seasonal lines of merchandise two times each year. Many of the famous designers as well as up-and-coming designers come together to present fashion shows in tents at Bryant Park. Coordination allows members of the media and retail community to maximize the number of shows they can attend in a short period of time. A sample trade calendar produced by the *Apparel News Group* is provided in Figure 4.8.

Retail Calendar

The **retail calendar**, also known as the consumer calendar, indicates what merchandise is currently available in the retail store. It identifies what the consumer's fashion needs are throughout the calendar year and is the basis for the creation of all of the promotion mix calendars at the retail level (Fig. 4.9). Themes, activities, and events are all built from the basic elements of the retail calendar.

The retail calendar is planned to have broad classifications of merchandise in the store when consumers want them. For example, October traditionally marks the transition from fall into holiday, so a holiday dress may be purchased in October for the Thanksgiving and Christmas season. A new bathing suit may be purchased in February or March to anticipate the upcoming season or spring break. Although these broad classifications, such as dresses or bathing suits, are normally available during the retail calendar season, theme and promotion mix calendars are developed with the season's specific fashion trends in mind.

The retail and trade calendars have the most consistent schedules from year to year. These calendars represent the continuous flow of new merchandise from the designer and manufacturer to the retail store. Merchandise is presented as a broad classification,

Figure 4.8

Trade Calendar from the
Apparel News Group

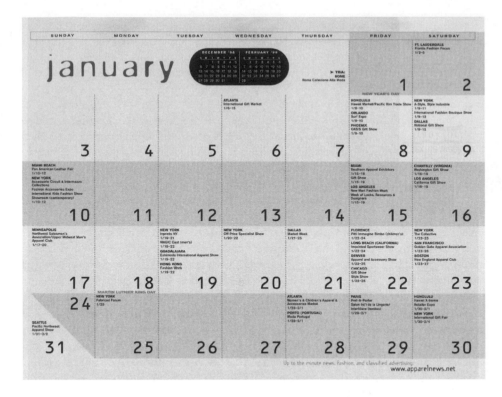

like active sportswear. After the lines are reviewed, creative fashion themes are interpreted about the seasonal styles, colors, fabrics, and accessories. Based on these trends
the fashion forecasters predict the themes, such as *Olympic Gold*, and the various promotional mix calendars are generated to serve as a guideline for the season's promotional activities.

Promotion Mix Calendars

Based upon the fashion trends of the season, in combination with activities at trade
and retail levels, various promotional projects or events are planned. For each of the
promotional areas in which the firm is involved, a separate calendar of events is proposed. These promotional mix elements may involve anything from advertising to special events. A retail firm may develop a fashion theme calendar as the basis for the advertising, special events, and visual merchandising calendars. A firm may utilize a single
promotion mix calendar or develop an individual calendar for each element.

Fashion Theme Calendar

The **fashion theme calendar** is a guide that indicates fashion trends and creative interpretations of basic categories. The retail and trade calendars are quite static, listing
the general categories of merchandise as they are presented at the trade and retail levels. These calendars simply list merchandise by classification such as "Men's Suits," "Junior Sportswear," or "Table Top," and do not take into consideration the more creative
elements of the season. Fashion trends reflect these creative interpretations of the ba-

January Spring Color Story Resort and Cruisewear Early Spring Bridal Fashions	**July** Early Fall Sportswear Registration Fall Bridal Fashions Fall Shoes Early Fall Sweaters and Knitwear
February Spring Color Impact Spring Dresses Spring Suits Spring Knitwear Spring Shoes	**August** Fall Color Story General Fall Sportswear Impact Fall Leathers and Suede Back-to-School Highlight Shop
March Spring Accessories Spring Coats Spring Intimate Apparel Spring Active Sportswear	**September** Fall Dresses Fall Suits Fall Accessories Evening Clothes Registration
April Prom and Graduation Dresses Swimwear Highlight Shop Opening	**October** Boots Evening Clothes Impact Holiday Fashions Skiwear Highlight Shop Opening
May Summer Color Story Summer Vacation Clothes Summer Vacation Highlight Shop	**November** Last Minute Gift Center Highlight Shop Opening
June Hot Weather Clothes Transitional Cotton Clothing Summer Shoes	**December** Holiday and Christmas Saturation

Figure 4.9

Sample Retail Calendar

sic categories. In a fashion theme calendar, the "Men's Suits" category becomes the *Moving to the Top*, while the "Junior Sportswear" classification reinforces the seasonal fashion trend called *Country Comfort Denims*.

Advertising Calendar

The **advertising calendar** for a retail firm identifies when, where, and what items will be advertised. This calendar is used by the promotion department to prepare ads or to send merchandise samples and product information to the advertising agency to create ads.

Store personnel also use advertising calendars. The dates and products on the advertising calendar are essential information for sales associates, who need to know what products will be featured so they can prepare displays of merchandise on the sales floor and gain product knowledge prior to customers arriving in the department. As customers arrive in the store the merchandise should be featured prominently in a high traffic area. If merchandise has been delayed, the advertisement should be pulled. But, if the ad could not be stopped, sales associates need to have information to properly handle customer inquiries.

Fashion Show Planning Calendar

Locations, themes, dates, and times for the planned fashion shows are included on the **fashion show planning calendar**. This tool is used primarily by the fashion and sales staffs to plan and perform the various steps in fashion show production. The fashion show calendar may be used as an organizational tool for delegating and following through on responsibilities.

Special Events Calendar

Guest appearances, product demonstrations, vendor promotions, and other special activities are coordinated by using the **special events calendar**. The promotion department or fashion office may maintain this calendar. Plans, as far as 1 year in advance, are not uncommon for retailers such as Macy's. For example, as soon as the Thanksgiving Day parade is presented, event planning for the following year is started. Coordination with the various departments is necessary in order to pull together seamless special events.

Visual Merchandising Calendar

The **visual merchandising calendar** (Fig. 4.10) is developed to organize visual presentations for the business. Visual presentations may be planned at the manufacturing or retail level. Manufacturers will put together displays in the showrooms prior to the start of a market week. Retail stores present merchandise as window displays, internal displays, or special theme shops.

Visual merchandising in the retail environment is frequently based upon the fashion theme calendar. Fashion window displays feature the fashion trends identified in the fashion theme calendar. The visual merchandising staff will take the major fashion themes and plan window treatments or interior displays to reflect these statements for approximately 2-week time periods.

VISUAL MERCHANDISING CALENDAR

MONTH: <u>March</u>

DATES:	March 1–14	March 15–29
PROMOTION THEMES:	<u>Wearin' the Green</u>	<u>Softly Pastel</u>

DISPLAY AREAS	MERCHANDISE TO BE FEATURED	
Main Street Windows	Donna Karan: Spring Designer Fashions	Gucci: Pastel Plaids
Junior Merchandise Windows	Quicksilver: Spring Green Dresses	Tommy Girl: Soft pink, blue, and yellow seperates
Men's Windows	Ralph Lauren: Green Blazers	Private Label: Pastel Polo Shirts
Internal/Aisle Presentations	Merchandise focus on: Spring Green	Merchandise focus on: Soft pink, blue, and yellow colors

Figure 4.10

Sample Visual Merchandising Calendar

If a storewide theme is developed, the internal displays will be set to match the overall theme. The theme *Summertime Blues* could be featured in every department from denims in the apparel departments, to blue plates, plastic beverage glasses, and picnic supplies in the home furnishings areas. With a storewide theme the trend can be shown in all areas. If a narrowly focused fashion trend is emphasized in the designer apparel section, perhaps color or fabric could be used to tie in other departments.

FUTURE TRENDS IN PROMOTION PLANNING

Strategic planning, first popularized in the 1960s, became overly bureaucratic, absurdly quantitative, and largely ignored within many firms. Countless 5-year plans, updated annually, were gathering dust due to unrealistic costs, prices, market share, and technology changes which were impossible to forecast. The old style planning has evolved into a new focus more accurately called strategic thinking. Executives use it to describe what a company does to become smart, targeted, and nimble enough to remain competitive in an era of constant change.

Managers who are able to expand their imaginations to see a wider range of possible futures will be in a much better position to take advantage of unexpected opportunities that will come along. There are a couple of emerging planning techniques that will enable managers to do just that. These techniques include scenario planning and strategic market modeling.

Scenario planning, a disciplined ten-step process for imagining possible futures, is a method companies have applied to a great range of issues. According to Schoemaker (1995), scenario planning is especially useful in industries, such as advertising, that are experiencing uncertainty in the marketplace. Scenario planning explores the joint impact of various uncertainties that are considered as equals. Scenario planning attempts to capture the richness and range of possibilities, stimulating decision makers to consider changes they would otherwise ignore.

Strategic market modeling (SMM) was developed in the late 1980s by Hewlett-Packard to generate and to test alternative business strategies for both itself and others (Schnedler, 1996). SMM uses several market research methodologies, including choice modeling, cluster analysis, and needs segmentation. Although these techniques are commonly used in consumer market analysis, Hewlett-Packard has applied these techniques to higher level strategic issues in more complex international markets.

With rapidly increasing technological advances and continued uncertainty in the marketplace, planners in the 21st century will most likely incorporate such activities as scenario planning and computer modeling. Strategic analysis and planning will continue to be a significant function of the promotion industry for a long time to come.

In this chapter we have reviewed the steps and tools for promotional planning. Each individual firm may decide how detailed its planning will be. Strategic plans serve as a map or guideline for an organization, outlining its mission, general goals, marketing, IMC, and promotion objectives. A number of different types of calendars were identified. These calendars should assist promotion personnel in accomplishing their goals and objectives.

SUMMARY

- Without advance planning, problems could occur and details could be overlooked. Events or promotional activities are not enjoyable for the clients (sponsors) or target audience (guests) without planning.
- The promotional planning process starts with a strategic analysis. This analysis leads to the creation of a mission statement, identification of goals and objectives to meet the needs of the organization, preparation of the budget, development of an implementation scheme, and establishment of a method to evaluate the effectiveness of the activities.
- Promotion personnel and their responsibilities are defined. The plan is implemented. Then, the process starts all over again.
- Promotional activities are planned at various market levels including global, national, trade, or retail.
- Manufacturers and retailers may keep the responsibilities for promotional planning and coordination of promotional activities inside the firm or hire an outside agency to plan promotion mix activities.
- Calendars are essential tools used by promotion executives to keep track of various activities at the retail and trade market levels.
- Trade and retail calendars are used to develop promotion mix calendars that are used for planning and implementing fashion themes, advertising, fashion shows, special events, and visual merchandising.
- Coordination of all promotional activities is necessary and made achievable by proper planning and attention to detail.
- Scenario planning and strategic marketing modeling (SMM) are two of the newer methods used to develop long-range plans.

KEY TERMS

advertising calendar	national promotion	special events calendar
cooperative promotion	objectives	strategic analysis
fashion show planning calendar	promotion calendars	strategic market modeling
fashion theme calendar	promotion objectives	strategic planning
global promotion	promotion planning	trade calendar
goals	retail calendar	trade promotion
IMC objectives	retail promotion	visual merchandising calendar
marketing objectives	scenario planning	
mission statement	short-term plan	

QUESTIONS FOR DISCUSSION

1. Why is it important to plan for promotion?
2. What are some of the methods of promotion planning, and who is responsible for carrying them out?
3. How is a strategic analysis developed and why is it important?
4. What is a mission statement and how is it used to direct an organization's promotional activities?
5. What are the differences between general goals and objectives, marketing objectives, IMC objectives, and promotion objectives?
6. Which market levels apply promotional objectives?
7. How are calendars used in promotional planning?

ADDITIONAL RESOURCES

Avery, J. (1997). *Advertising campaign planning: Developing an advertising-based marketing plan* (2nd ed.). Chicago: Copy Workshop.

Cooper, A. (Ed.). (1997). *How to plan advertising.* London: Cassell Academic.

Hameroff, E. J., and Gardner, H. S. (1997). *The advertising agency business: The complete manual for management and operation.* Lincolnwood, IL: NTC Business.

Steel, J. (1998). *Truth, lies, and advertising: New advertising and the art of the account planner.* New York: Wiley.

Steel, J., and Carr, N. (1996). *Account planning.* New York: American Association of Advertising Agencies.

Figure 5.1

Advertisement for Dazzling, the new Estée Lauder perfume, featuring Elizabeth Hurley

BUDGET

D azzling! Is that the name of the newest Estée Lauder perfume, or is it the reaction to the advertising budget for the product launch? The war chest, also known as the promotional budget, was estimated to be $20 million, with nearly $4 million allocated just to national print advertising (Born, 1998). The print ads (Fig. 5.1), which featured Elizabeth Hurley, were designed to portray a celebratory party image. In addition to print ads, TV advertising, and store catalogs, the firm experimented with innovative sampling techniques. How did the firm decide how much to spend and where to spend the money allocated for the launch?

After you have read this chapter, you should be able to:

Explain the significance of the budgeting process.

Implement various methods of budgetary planning.

Plan various methods of allocating budget to promotional activities.

Discuss how channel members share budget expenses.

Differentiate how agencies are compensated for their work.

Determining how much to spend on promotion is one of the most confusing and difficult tasks associated with merchandising management. Whether the firm is a small business with limited allocations for promotion, or a large company with global concerns and billion dollar budgets, personnel involved in planning must not ignore the importance of the budget.

As we discussed in Chapter 4, the budgeting process is based upon the plans that define the organization's mission, goals, and objectives. With the mission of the firm in mind, financial specialists establish overall budgets for its operations. Then, in consultation with promotion specialists, they allocate budgets for promotional activities.

Business professionals with an accounting background and the Internal Revenue Service view promotional costs as current business expenses, which are similar to travel or any other short-term expense. As a result of this, financial executives may handle promotional budget allocations as items that can be trimmed or eliminated as sales decline. Although this type of action is understandable, it does not take into consideration the long-term investment benefits of promotional activities.

The financial executive may understand that a new building or warehouse is a contribution to the future, but fail to recognize that promotion can also be an investment in that future. Advertising, one of the promotion mix elements, is used to encourage immediate action and sales, but it can also be more fully developed for a cumulative long-term effect. Building consumer confidence and brand preference, as well as promoting goodwill, are examples of how advertising can be used for long-term impact. Since advertising enhances the reputation and perceived value of a brand, consumers will trust the company and its product. Thus, they are likely to become repeat customers. Although advertising may be considered a current expense for accounting purposes, it is also a long-term investment.

This chapter focuses on how an organization develops the budget and allocation for each promotion mix activity. We start by looking at the theoretical background of sales response methods. Next, various approaches to budget allocation are discussed. Methods of allocating the budget to different promotion mix elements are also considered. Since payments to outside agencies are budget items for many manufacturers and retailers who use such services, compensation procedures for advertising agencies are also introduced. Techniques for extending the budget through cooperative ventures are explained. The chapter concludes with a discussion about the future trends in budgeting. Evaluation of the budget is discussed in Chapter 17 as part of the evaluation process.

THEORETICAL BACKGROUND: SALES RESPONSE MODELS

Before viewing the various pragmatic approaches to budgeting, it is helpful to understand something about how economists and advertising researchers view optimal expenditure. Researchers have developed two theoretical models to explain the relationship between sales response and advertising: the diminishing returns curve and the S-shaped curve. Although these models were developed with advertising in mind, they may also serve as a guide for most promotion mix budgets.

In the **diminishing returns model**, visually represented in Figure 5.2A by a concave-downward shape, sales are stimulated by the dollars spent on advertising. The more a firm spends on advertising, the more it will sell—up to a certain point. Then, the benefits of additional advertising expenses diminish. According to the early research conducted on the microeconomic law of diminishing returns (Simon and Arndt, 1980), as the amount of advertising increases, its incremental value decreases. This is because consumers with the greatest potential to purchase are more likely to act after initial exposure, while those who are less likely to purchase are not likely to change even with more exposure to advertising. The key is for promotion executives to determine at what stage this decrease occurs. This is not easy to do, because additional variables such as competitive products or price fluctuations can also influence sales. Budgeting under this model implies that fewer advertising dollars may be all that is necessary to achieve success.

The **S-shaped curve model** (Fig. 5.2B) also depends upon a relationship of sales to advertising expenditures. Advertising managers who subscribe to the S-shaped curve

Figure 5.2

Theoretical models:
A. Diminishing returns curve and B. S-shaped curve

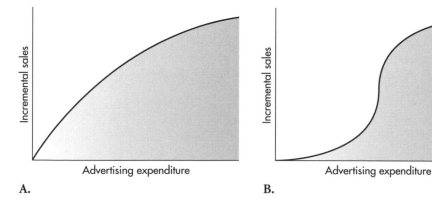

A.

B.

model believe that initial outlays of the advertising budget have little or no impact on consumers in the early stages of sales. This is indicated by the relatively flat sales curve at the beginning of the campaign. After a certain level of promotional expenditures, advertising efforts begin to have an impact on consumers. Thus, as additional money is spent on promotion and advertising, sales will increase. This incremental gain continues only to a point, then, the law of diminishing returns takes effect, suggesting that additional expenditures will have little or no impact on sales. In this case, there is no reason to spend any additional dollars on promotion or advertising.

To management these models might suggest spending on advertising until it stops working. However, practitioners recognize that these models have weaknesses and limited usefulness for practical measurement. For one thing, there are other factors that affect sales besides the amount of money spent on advertising, including better personal selling techniques, attractive stores, seasonal changes, or better-displayed merchandise. For another, it is unclear how advertising affects profit for a specific product, especially when a firm is likely to have several different products contributing to profits. How is one product measured against another?

Even though response models such as these might not be directly applicable to a professional manager's specific problem, study of the theoretical models could give managers insight into how the budgeting process works. Luchsinger, Mullen, and Jannuzzo (1977) studied the relationship of advertising to sales, which supported the S-shaped response curve. Their results, still relevant today, indicated that a minimum amount of advertising dollars must be spent before there is a noticeable effect on sales. Even though these models may not provide tools for directly implementing the promotion budget, we can use them as a theoretical guide for our appropriations.

METHODS OF BUDGET ALLOCATION

In actual practice, theoretical models are rarely used to determine the promotional budget. We now turn our attention to evaluating some of the methods currently being used. There are almost as many different approaches to budgeting as there are different firms. Large companies may use several distinct and scientific techniques, while some small businesses may use simple judgmental techniques or no budget planning at all. Regardless of the size or complexity of the organization, budgeting helps to indicate how, when, and where the firm intends to emphasize its promotional activities. Budgeting also provides a benchmark for evaluating effectiveness. Budget approaches may be considered top-down or bottom-up (Fig. 5.3). First, we look at the top-down approaches.

Top-Down Approaches

In approaches designated as **top-down**, the senior executives establish the budget amount for the entire retail corporation or manufacturing concern at the highest management level of the firm. The money is then allocated to the various departments or divisions. Top-down budget approaches are dependent upon the experience and knowledge of the top management. These techniques are also referred to as judgmental methods since they are contingent upon administrative opinion. The top-down methods include all one can afford, arbitrary allocation, competitive parity, percentage of sales, and return on investment.

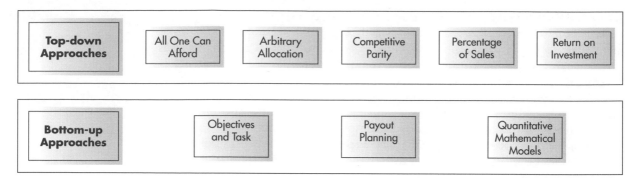

Figure 5.3

Methods of budgeting: Top-down and bottom-up approaches

All One Can Afford

The philosophy behind the **all one can afford** method, also known as the affordable procedure, is the belief that the portion of the operational budget allocated to promotional activities is the amount the firm can financially manage to spend. Actual tasks, specific projects, or methods of measuring promotional effectiveness are rarely taken into consideration with this simplistic type of planning. All one can afford budgets are often overestimated or underestimated. Overspending or underspending can easily take place in this type of planning, because guidelines for evaluating the impact of various promotional activities have not been established.

In the fashion business, new designers frequently fall into the trap of believing so strongly in the creative process that they assume their designs will sell themselves. They allocate most of their budget to product development. After creating the line there is little or no money left to promote and sell the line. Such start-up companies, with limited financial backing, often think, "we can't be hurt if we know what we can afford and do not exceed it." While this might be true from an accounting perspective, it does not reflect the significance of a communication and marketing viewpoint. Considering the S-shaped sales response model, this method might not allocate enough money to get the product off the ground. In other circumstances, sales might experience a slowdown in a tough market; this method would likely lead to promotional budget cuts at a time when budgets should be increased.

All one can afford techniques are frequently used in combination with other budgeting strategies. This strategy is often employed for new products where historical information and perspective are unknown.

Arbitrary Allocation

Although arbitrary allocation is one of the weakest methods of budgeting, it is commonly used in the merchandising environment. **Arbitrary allocation** simply means that the budget is determined by management solely on the basis of executive judgment. In this method, the budget is created by management's belief in spending what is necessary. The goals and objectives of promotion are not taken into consideration. These *feelings of intuition* provide an environment for controlling managers to maintain their power. Because this method is subject to judgment, it goes without saying that it is the least reliable or scientific of all budget approaches.

There is no good explanation why arbitrary allocation continues to be used except that it is cheap. It is not a highly recommended method. Our intent is to make people aware of its weaknesses and suggest more professional approaches.

Competitive Parity

Competitive parity is the first of the top-down methods to rely on objective data. **Competitive parity** takes into consideration the amount of money that a competitor spends on promotion and uses this information as a guide to promotional spending.

Although it might seem like corporate espionage, information about competitor's spending habits is readily available. Data can be found in advertising publications, trade association newsletters, government agency publications, and the Internet. Merchandising firms can fairly accurately estimate the amount that a competitor spends by tracking the advertising and promotional activities through a **clipping service**. This type of service cuts out competitors' advertisements from local or national print media. Since advertising rates are published information, the advertiser can determine the competitor's media budget and other expenses. Some retail stores assign this research task to executive trainees or assistant buyers.

Competitive parity offers several advantages. First of all, the competition is one of the major environmental factors influencing sales. In addition, competitors' use of promotional expenses is a guide to setting a merchandising firm's promotional expenses. Also, competitive relationships can be stabilized, minimizing aggressive market rivalry. Finally, unnecessary promotional expenditures are reduced.

Despite being a more scientific approach, competitive parity has its limitations. For one thing, this technique fails to recognize the specific goals and objectives of the promotional plan. As such, it would not be desirable in a firm committed to an integrated marketing communications (IMC) environment. It also does not fully appreciate the contributions of the creative process and allocation to alternative media choices. In addition, it does not consider failure of previous or competitors' promotional activities. It also assumes that firms with similar expenses will have equally effective programs.

The primary limitation of competitive parity, however, is the focus on the past. The ability to match competitors' expenditures is limited by the information available. Short of illegally placing a spy on a competitor's staff, it will be impossible for the merchandising firm to know what that competitor will do next. Competitors could take a more assertive stance or decrease their promotional expenses.

Executives and decision-makers must always be aware of what the competition is doing, but they should not just emulate them in setting goals and developing strategies. For this reason, it is unrealistic to use competitive parity as the only approach to promotional budgeting. Competitive parity is more frequently used in combination with another method, such as percentage of sales.

Percentage of Sales

One of the most common methods of promotional budgeting in the merchandising environment is **percentage of sales**. In this approach, the promotion budget is based upon a specific percentage of anticipated annual sales. Historical information about promotional spending is combined with sales forecasts to set the dollar amount for promotional expenses. This is a simple data-based application that requires the calculation of the amount of money spent on various promotional activities as a percentage of revenues. Even if an organization does not have its own historical data, the company can use industry standards, such as advertising-to-sales ratios developed annually by Schonfeld & Associates. Table 5.1 illustrates some of these ratios for 1997.

The percentage of sales method is widely used in the merchandising environment and is easily defended. First of all, it is simple to calculate. Managers use sales figures as the basis for establishing fundamental financial goals, such as gross margin and profit. It is second nature for management to think of promotional expenses as a ratio to sales

Table 5.1   1997 Advertising-to-Sales Ratios for Selected Industries

Industry	SIC Number[a]	Ad $ as Percent of Sales
Advertising	7310	0.5
Apparel and other finished products	2300	5.8
Apparel and accessory stores	5600	2.3
Catalog, mail order houses	5961	9.0
Department stores	5311	3.6
Dolls and stuffed toys	3942	15.3
Drug and proprietary stores	5912	1.2
Family clothing stores	5651	2.6
Footwear, except rubber	3140	3.5
Furniture stores	5712	7.6
Hobby, toy, and game shops	5945	4.5
Home furniture and equipment stores	5700	2.9
Jewelry stores	5944	4.3
Jewels and precious metals	3911	4.8
Knit outerwear mills	2253	3.1
Knitting mills	2250	2.3
Men, youth, boys furnishings; work clothing	2320	2.6
Miscellaneous business services	7380	1.6
Miscellaneous furniture and fixtures	2590	1.0
Miscellaneous nondurable goods—wholesale	5190	3.6
Miscellaneous retail	5940	2.6
Miscellaneous shopping goods—stores	5900	1.3
Newspaper publishing	2711	4.8
Pens, pencils, other office materials	3950	3.5
Perfume, cosmetics, toilet preparations	2844	8.5
Pottery and related products	3260	4.7
Radio broadcasting stations	4832	5.8
Radio, TV, consumer electronic stores	5731	3.4
Rubber and plastics footwear	3021	8.1
Shoe stores	5661	2.4
Soap, detergent, toilet preparations	2840	9.7
Sporting and athletic goods	3949	6.3
TV broadcasting stations	4833	1.7
Variety stores	5331	1.7
Watches, clocks, and parts	3873	15.9
Women's, misses', children's, infant's undergarments	2340	6.5
Women's clothing stores	5621	2.0
Women's, misses', junior's outerwear	2330	4.3
Wood household furniture, except upholstered	2551	3.2

[a]*SIC is the Standardized Industry Code.*
Adapted from: Schonfeld and Associates. (1997, June 30). 1997 Advertising-to-sales for the 200 largest ad spending industries. Advertising Age [On-line]. Available: http://www.naa.org/marketscope/databank/97ADV.htm. Reprinted with permission. Copyright, Crain Communications Inc., 1997.

in this manner. Many managers feel that this method is financially secure since promotional budgets are linked to sales revenues. The risks associated with promotional activities are minimized since that function is associated with revenues. Finally, budgets are relatively stable. Whether looking at past records or forecasting for the future, the budget will not vary drastically.

Despite the many advantages and consistency of the percentage of sales approach, it does have weaknesses. The very core of this concept is anticipated sales. This is somewhat like the tail wagging the dog. Letting sales levels determine the advertising appropriation reverses the cause-and-effect relationship between advertising and sales. It requires one to think of promotional expenditures as an expense of making sales instead of an investment, whereas sales are actually generated through the use of advertising and promotional activities. Firms that consider advertising and promotion as more of an investment are limited by this budget method.

Stability is another problem with the percentage of sales approach. Although stability is desired through a consistent percentage devoted to promotional activities, it is a limiting factor. It does not take into consideration changes in the market, nor does it allow for innovation by competitors or introduction of new products or novel retailing formats. Aggressive firms may wish to allocate more funds to introduce these new products or formats. Since new products do not have a past sales record, it may be difficult to forecast accurately the sales on which the advertising will be based. A start-up business cannot rely on historical records to develop its strategy using a percentage of sales budget analysis, whereas a firm with long-term accounting journals could more accurately utilize this method.

If promotional budgets are based solely on sales, promotional budgets are contingent upon sales. When an economic downturn takes place, promotion budgets will most likely be cut. In such times, it may actually be beneficial to maintain or increase advertising expenditures to assure visibility and protect a strong image. As the economy strengthens, the firm is still in the mind of consumers who now have the purchasing power. Box 5.1 looks at how specialty retailers establish their advertising budgets.

Although percentage of sales budgeting has both strengths and weaknesses, it remains one of the most popular techniques since it is so easy to use. For the greatest effectiveness it should be used in combination with other methods.

Return on Investment

In the **return on investment** (ROI) budget approach, advertising and promotion are considered investments. The key word here is *investment*. The assumption is that the investment—expenditures on promotion—will lead to some type of long-term return.

This method appeals to financial officers and accountants, who like to have a measurable objective. The expense of promotion is justified by the results of the actions. How to assess the impact of promotional activities is not considered. This method will be limited, as long as sales are the primary basis for evaluation. How to measure success and what the actual return is, will remain the primary limitations of this method.

Despite the limitations of top-down budget planning, the various top-down approaches continue to be widely used in the industry. Percentage of sales prevails as the most accepted top-down budgeting method. Alternative budget approaches begin at the lowest management levels, with managers who have the responsibility of putting the plan into action. Next, we look at the bottom-up budget techniques.

Bottom-Up Approaches

Bottom-up budgeting methods, also called build-up approaches, consider a firm's goals and objectives and assign a portion of the budget to meet those objectives. Rather than

BOX 5.1
Establishing an Advertising Budget

Advertising doesn't cost," the old saying goes. "It pays." The short-term dollar-for-dollar return on money spent for advertising may not be apparent, but in the long term, the money you invest in promoting your shop should be rewarded with increased sales.

Most specialty shops need to advertise in order to attract new customers and encourage existing customers to return. Good advertising increases awareness of your products and enhances your store's image. It should help differentiate your shop from the competition, especially the discount stores and category killers that advertise nothing but low prices. Use your advertising to let the public know about your style, service, selection, and knowledgeable staff.

There is no limit to the many different forms that advertising can take, from a Yellow Pages ad to a banner towed by an airplane. Signage, window displays, shopping bags, brochures, and public television underwriting can all be considered part of your advertising program. Think of advertising as a challenge to your creativity and imagination. How many different ways can you find to express the appeal of your store and your merchandise to the buying public? What is the image of your store that you want all your advertising to project?

Pace Your Spending

Most traditional forms of advertising are fairly expensive, so you must spend your advertising dollars wisely, especially at first. Experience, based on the types of advertising that produce the best results for your store, will help guide your future decisions.

An advertising budget normally ranges from 3 to 5 percent of total sales, but can be as high as 10 percent. Retailing marketing consultant Jeffrey L. Greene suggests that four factors be considered in setting the budget: (1) traffic, (2) marketplace awareness, (3) competition, and (4) price sensitivity. If you have high traffic, are well known in your market, have few competitors, and place little emphasis on price, you will not need to spend much on advertising.

A new store needs to advertise more aggressively than one that is well established. Some sources recommend doubling your advertising budget for the first year you are in business. Of course, unless you are opening a franchise or branch store, you will have little way of predicting what this first year's sales will be. Doubling an advertising budget based on a hypothetical sales figure can be dangerous. A leather goods store on our street spent $10,000 on tele-

vision advertising soon after opening, producing only $12,000 in sales. Had sales been $100,000, this might have been a wise investment. As it turned out, the store went out of business within a year. Check with other stores your size to get an idea of their advertising budget and the types of advertising that works best for them.

If your business is seasonal, budget more of your advertising money for the months when you are busiest. It is always tempting to run big ads to bring in business during slow times and try to increase sales of slow items by advertising them. But as a rule, you should use your advertising to sell what is selling when it is selling.

Allocating Your Advertising Money

There are countless ways to spend the dollars you have allocated to advertising. If you have never done any advertising before, you may be surprised at how little you get for your money. An ad you barely glance at as you read your morning paper may have cost hundreds of dollars. It pays to give careful consideration to getting the most mileage from your advertising money.

Advertising can help make new customers aware of your store, including where it is located, what it sells, and the services it offers. This is image advertising, and it is useful for building prestige and trust among existing customers as well as reaching new ones. A motto, or tag line, used in conjunction with your store name and logo can help create a memorable impression in this type of ad. Try to define your store in a few well-chosen words. If you use radio or television, your tag line can be part of a jingle to help listeners remember it.

A second type of advertising is product promotion, which highlights individual items. Many products, especially national brands, do their own product advertising. Suppliers with an advertising program sometimes allow a store name to appear in their product ads or underwrite store advertising featuring their products by providing an advertising allowance.

The third type is special event or sale advertising, encouraging customers to come in during a specific time. There has been such a proliferation of this kind of advertising from department stores and discounters that consumers have become a bit jaded. Specialty stores must offer an unusual twist to get today's shoppers excited.

Adapted from: Schroeder, C. L. (1997, October). Specialty shop retailing. In, Establishing an advertising budget. WWD Specialty Stores: A Special Report, 31.

viewing the process as a judgmental method, planners link appropriations to objectives and the strategies to accomplish them. This takes into consideration not only financial plans but communications objectives as well. The idea is to budget in such a way that the promotional mix strategies can be activated to accomplish the expressed objectives. These types of budget approaches work well in an IMC environment, because the budget allocations are associated with the firm's goals and objectives. The bottom-up approaches include objective and task method, payout planning, and quantitative models.

Objective and Task

The objective and task method requires that planning and budgeting go hand in hand. This is a bottom-up approach that takes the planning objectives as a significant reason for the budget. The **objective and task** method consists of three steps: (1) stating the promotional and communications objectives to be achieved, (2) developing the strategies and tasks necessary to accomplish them, and (3) estimating the costs associated with implementing these activities and reaching these objectives. The budget is an aggregate of the costs identified with the performance of the promotional activities.

On an intuitive level, the objective and task approach has the most validity of all of the methods described so far. It takes into consideration all of the specific objectives and develops strategies to achieve them; however, it assumes that the planners know how much it will cost to meet those goals. Herein lies the problem. Is the objective worth attaining? What is the best way to increase brand awareness by 30 percent? Should newspapers be used exclusively or should other media be utilized? Is it possible to determine the best promotion mix? Many alternatives and variable strategies to achieve objectives exist, and yet the objective and task budget method depends upon promotional executives to know which strategies and tactics will be able to meet the planned objectives.

Difficulties associated with the objective and task method can be overcome by recording the actual practices that take place. Realistic goals can be set after completing research, estimating costs, and aggregating the expenses to determine a suitable appropriation. This can be measured more accurately by an accumulation of data over time. Collecting and evaluating performance data will make this type of budget planning more realistic. Recorded historical data should provide invaluable information for future appropriations. Although objective and task is a superior method for budgeting, the difficulties associated with setting up this type of budget remain an obstacle to frequent application.

Payout Planning

Payout planning (Fig. 5.4) is a budgeting strategy used for the introduction of new products. The underlying assumption is that a new product requires up to 1.5 to 2 times as much promotional expenditure as an existing product. A budget is determined by looking at the planned revenues for a 3- to 5-year period. An expected rate of return is set and serves as a basis for creating the payout plan. Planners assume that the product will lose money during the first year, almost break even during the second year, and show profits by the third year. Advertising and promotion rates are the highest in the first year and decrease during the second and third years.

Payout planning is useful for new product budgeting. It may be used successfully in combination with another planning strategy, such as objective and task. The planners probably have some time frame in mind by which a new product must show a profit before the product is deemed unsuccessful and is abandoned.

Quantitative Mathematical Models

With the development of computer simulations and economic forecasting models, **quantitative mathematical models** have been introduced into the promotional bud-

Figure 5.4

Sample Payout Plan

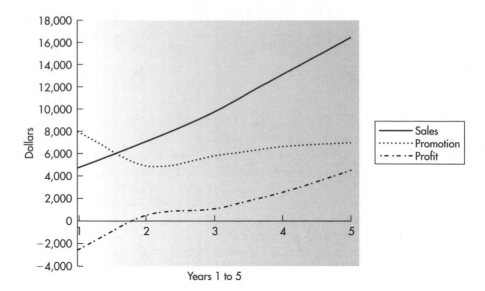

geting process. Techniques involving multiple regression analysis are used to analyze the relationship of variables to the relative contributions of promotional activities. More recently, computer simulations have been developed to relate awareness levels, purchase frequency, sales, and profitability to alternate television media schedules and other media placement.

Acceptance of computer simulations and economic forecasting models is limited in industry practice. For the most part, these techniques are time consuming and costly. Determining the relevant variables and validating their appropriateness have not provided enough evidence to confirm their effectiveness as predictors. Quantitative mathematical models have not reached their potential. As there is considerable interest in this approach, however, better models will probably be created in the future.

How Firms Choose Budget Approaches

How do firms decide which technique to use if each of the methods discussed has limitations? The top-down budgeting methods previously discussed are limited because they are judgmental and often lead to budget appropriations that are not linked to objectives and strategies. Tradition and top executives' desire for control are probably why top-down methods continue to be used.

Bottom-up budget methods take into consideration promotional objectives and expenses related to accomplishing them, but they too are limited. Problems associated with determining which tasks will be required and the costs associated with each are among the flaws associated with bottom-up methods.

By understanding the flaws of various methods, decision-makers can choose the best methods to use for their individual situation. Manufacturers, designers, and retailers select procedures to appropriate budgets for their promotional efforts based upon historical information and experimentation with newer techniques. Box 5.2 addresses the problems of choosing and using a budget approach.

No matter what method is used to establish the budget for promotion, the next step is to allocate it. The allocation decision distributes the promotion budget to the various elements of the promotional mix.

BOX 5.2
Does Budgeting Have to Be So Troublesome?

Many medium to large organizations are using budget plans that are incomplete and rarely accurate. Some diverse organizations have even gone so far as to discard budgeting as unworkable on all but an operational unit level, sacrificing a significant measure of managerial control. Why?

Budgeting Lies at the Heart of Business Management

"Budgetary planning and control is the most visible use of accounting information in the management control process. By setting standards of performance, and providing feedback by means of variance reports, the accountant supplies much of the fundamental information required for overall planning and control," say Emmanuel, Otley, and Merchant in their book *Accounting for Management Control.* Historically, a budget is simply a forecast of expenditures and revenues for a specific period of time. However, as the structure of businesses has become more complicated, the function, scope, and management of the budget have become accordingly more complex. Departing from its original function as a purely financial document, the business budget is now generally used as a tool to formulate intelligent decisions on the management and growth of a business venture, enabling businesses to set priorities and monitor progress toward both financial and nonfinancial goals.

Effective enterprise-wide budgeting is difficult. The problems encountered in what one industry analyst, the Gartner Group, has called this "painful annual ritual" are considerable: It is not uncommon for line managers and their staff to spend weeks preparing their budget submissions and for central budget managers or management accountants to spend at least as long consolidating, revising, and redistributing budget plans. In a 1995 benchmark exercise, Price Waterhouse reported that budgeting costs large multinational enterprises a median of $63,000 for every $100 million of base revenue within finance departments alone. Factoring in the considerable effort spent by multiple budgeting units would increase this cost many times over.

Most budget processes are inefficient as well as costly. The Price Waterhouse benchmark also found that budget preparation took an average of 110 days from start to finish, and reported that profit forecasts varied from actual results by a median of 10 percent.

Budgeting is troublesome because by its nature it is comprehensive and collaborative—according to the European economist Beatrice Loom-Din, "the budget is the sole corporate task that goes in depth and detail through the entire organization."

This article is intended to examine the problems encountered in preparing enterprise-wide budgets, and to show how software is key in improving the process and its results.

Budgeting Process

No single budgeting method prevails in large organizations. Techniques range from traditional methods focused on cost-center accounting, through project and fund budgeting, to activity-based budgeting (ABB), which is increasingly popular within service enterprises. The starting point for budget creation can be a strategic summary level (top-down budgeting) or come from a detailed operational level (bottom-up or zero-based budgeting). In practice most organizations use a combination of techniques, sometimes known as a "counter current" process. However, despite the range of techniques, most budgeting processes and planning requirements are the same for all companies. Budgeting, by its nature, tends to be:

- Hierarchical—with multitiered checkpoints and control levels
- Iterative—with multiple versions and layered consolidations
- Nomadic—with the sporadic involvement of many people some in remote locations
- Periodic—typically a once-a-year process with multiple re-forecasts
- Mutable—changing business conditions prolong the process

Budgeting Problems

In itself budgeting remains a conceptually simple exercise, whatever the size of the organization involved or the approach taken; it is the logistics of the process, the arrival at credible figures, that represents the source of difficulty. Again according to Emmanuel, Otley, and Merchant, "the two major problems in the accounting information itself relate to data collection and information disaggregation." This has serious implications because "it is possible that the lack of use of accounting information is as serious a problem as its misuse, particularly at the middle-management level. Line managers will ignore formally produced accounting information when they perceive it to be of little relevance to their tasks." The enterprise-wide budgeting process is difficult to manage, as it is:

- Detailed—requiring a large volume of data for accuracy
- Distant—often perceived as a finance "dictatorship" with little local relevance
- Dependent—relying on the information technology (IT) department and supporting technology
- Unpredictable—the number of cycles needed to agree a budget is unknown and erratic and may lead to significant deadline overruns

Budgeting Process Problems

In 1996 Hyperion Software undertook some research into large organizations' budgeting processes. Outlined below are five of the seven problem factors identified as the most commonly encountered in the process:

- **Lack of support from line managers**—"All I know is I've got to put numbers in this spreadsheet for Head Office. It doesn't reflect the way we do business here. . . ." *Implication:* Line managers feel disenfranchised, budget figures are produced grudgingly, and budget accuracy suffers as a result.
- **Lack of corporate control**—"I have no idea where my managers get the numbers from." *Implication:* The underlying detail used in the development of operational budgets is never collected or is lost during consolidation. As a result corporate finance has little understanding of how line managers have arrived at their budget submissions.
- **No communication of assumptions**—"Where do the figures come from? I think it's largely 'finger in the air' stuff." *Implication:* The top-level budget model does not tie back to the department managers' detail. Corporate finance spends countless hours trying to reconcile the two frameworks and "forcing" one to match the other. The resulting "plug" creates uncertainty in the plan or forecast and a lack of ownership of the goals by the organization.
- **Poor use of managers' expertise**—"I'm convinced our managers spend the entire budgeting period worrying about the budget, not the business." *Implication:* Managers manage the budget and not the business. As a result corporate finance, aware of this outcome, is reluctant to involve line managers in re-forecasts during the lifetime of the budget. Consequently these forecasts do not reflect managers' knowledge of changing business conditions and so may not improve ongoing budget accuracy as intended.
- **It takes too much time**—"How long is our budget cycle? Forever!" *Implication:* The law of diminishing returns sets in. The never-ending, attritional nature of budgeting can seriously undermine support for, and the subsequent effectiveness and accuracy of, the budgets produced.

Defining a Process Solution

Daniel Vasella, Novartis's chief executive, recently described management as a "top down, bottom up, top down process," supporting the view that business needs to take account of the views and expertise of operational staff to succeed in meeting its strategic goals. Likewise, line manager support is key to the success of enterprise-wide budgeting, and organizations should strive to establish a budget-friendly culture in which line-managers have:

- Ownership of their part of the budget
- Involvement throughout the process
- Belief that budgeting is meaningful and adds value to their operation
- Clear "downward" communication of strategy, targets, and changes
- Understanding of a sensible budget process that is logical and cohesive
- Comfort—the process should ideally be efficient, automated, and user-friendly

Organizations must also consider how they approach budgeting as an exercise in itself. According to the Hackett Group (Hudson, Ohio), a pioneer of innovative thinking in the financial function, improvements will occur by:

- Reducing the time allowed to build a budget. People will use up as much time as they are given, and they will continue to "finesse numbers."
- Reducing the number of iterations until the budget is finalized. The precision improvement in each cycle rarely justifies the extra effort.
- Reducing the "time boundaries" of the budget. Rolling forecasts, by quarter, will be much more accurate than a budget that "looks" 15 to 18 months into the future.

Budgeting System Problems

The procedural problems encountered in budgeting are often exacerbated by the technology used by organizations. The research carried out in 1996 by Hyperion Software found that two of the seven most common problems encountered in budgeting are directly related to the software used by organizations to manage the process:

- **Dependence on complex spreadsheets**—"My financial analysts are becoming spreadsheet macro programmers." *Implication:* Over time, budget spreadsheet formulas and macros become more and more complex and difficult to understand and maintain. It is a constant battle to force the spreadsheet system to conform to business and user needs. It is usually the case that only one person understands how the spreadsheet budgeting application works, leaving organizations' budget creation processes vulnerable.

  Spreadsheets are fully integrated into most organizational cultures—almost all managers use them. Erroneously, spreadsheets are perceived as having low maintenance and little or no development costs. As a result, most organizations rely on spreadsheet software to support their budgeting process. According to IDC, Visicalc, the Lotus 1-2-3 predecessor became the original "PC killer application" in large part because of its ability to participate in the budget process. This brings a number of problems—spreadsheets were not designed to support process driven functions like budgeting. Spreadsheets are personal productivity tools, not enterprise-wide "groupware" facilitators. Their use may, in fact, hinder rather than help in the management of enterprise-wide budgeting, as they become part of the problem rather than the solution.
- **Inaccuracies**—"It's a nightmare. We are constantly checking and rechecking the figures due to poor spreadsheet version control and multiple rekeying of data." *Implication:* Organizations are forced to undertake iterations of the budgeting round to correct data rather than to improve the long-term quality of the management information offered by the budget.

Problems Encountered Budgeting with Spreadsheets

- Little centralized control
- Poor data integrity
- Inflexible reporting
- Unmanageable consolidation mechanics
- Slow turnarounds
- IT department dependence
- Inability to react to and reflect change
- Lack of integration with other systems
- Lack of dynamic financial statements

- Rigid templates for each user involved
- Lack of security at the account level
- Lack of support for multiple line items in an account
- Little facility to view data across different dimensions

These problems are not limited to spreadsheets alone. Any software not specifically designed to support iterative, inclusive, enterprise-wide processes will struggle to meet the requirements of budgeting. In its 1996 report on Budget Management Software, IDC excluded all spreadsheets, proprietary general ledger-based systems, and other online analytical processing (OLAP) tools from evaluation altogether.

Inadequate and inflexible budgeting software has other implications. For example, it can limit an organization's ability to adopt other budgeting methods, such as ABB or fund budgeting.

Defining a Software Solution

The "ideal" budgeting software should offer:

- Flexible analysis, including line item detail, ongoing adjustments, what-if analysis, on-the-fly dimensional analysis, and the ability to satisfy unique budget requirements.
- Powerful automation, to support quick turnaround, consolidation, and distribution of budgetary information.
- Comprehensive reporting, both during the budget process and for ongoing updates.
- Secure control to give corporate finance centralized maintenance power and enable multitiered review points and budget version management.
- System integration, for data transfer from disparate supporting systems and to promote data integrity by removing the need for re-keying.
- User friendliness, so that all users, both finance and operational, no matter how infrequent their involvement, can produce good budget submissions easily.
- Enterprise-wide support that understands and supports the nature and process of budget preparation.

Conclusion

The majority of the problems encountered with budgeting arise from managing the process itself. Dedicated budget management software can alleviate many of these issues and help to establish a climate in which budgeting can move from being little more than "a big guesstimation" (R. J. Habig, chief financial officer, PepsiCo) to a much more useful and accurate management tool.

The bottom line, according to the Gartner Group, is that enterprises that do not rethink and retool their budgeting process will annually spend 75 percent more effort than enterprises that do. The choice for large organizations is either to lose many of the undoubted benefits in planning and control offered by budgeting or to apply a software solution to the process and make it less troublesome, less costly, and more effective.

Adapted from: Henderson, I. (1997, October 2). Does budgeting have to be so troublesome? Management Accounting (British) 75 (2), *26–27. Copyright 1997 the Chartered Institute of Management Accountants (UK).*

ALLOCATING THE RETAIL PROMOTION BUDGET

As we introduced in Chapter 4, retailers typically focus their planning on the short term by developing 6-month merchandising plans. The two 6-month periods, which last from February to July and from August to January, also serve as the scheduling timeline for allocating the promotion budget. Considering prior experience as a starting point, anticipating new trends, the staff allocates specific budgets to advertising, direct marketing, electronic media, fashion shows and special events, personal selling, visual merchandising, and any other designated promotion activities.

Advertising

Department store retailers have traditionally spent the highest percentage of their promotion budget on advertising. According to Competitive Media Reporting (1998), retailing organizations spent $9,375.5 million on advertising in 1996, up 6.8 percent from 1995. Table 5.2 shows a comparison of the amount of money spent by retailers and various manufacturers on advertising in a variety of media. Local newspaper advertising accounted for 50 percent of the retailers' advertising budget, supporting the premise

Table 5.2   **Total Measured U.S. Ad Spending by Category and Media in 1996**[a]

	Retail	Toiletries and cosmetics	Apparel, footwear, and accessories	Household furnishings, supplies, and materials
Measured Advertising	$9,375.5	$3,326.3	$1,357.2	$332.5
Consumer Magazine	320.9	992.5	664.1	167.5
Sunday Magazine	87.0	21.6	35.1	8.2
Local Newspaper	4,695.7	6.9	8.7	21.9
National Newspaper	50.9	1.3	7.6	4.2
Outdoor	112.8	6.6	13.7	.7
Network	776.2	1,350.7	386.7	61.0
Spot TV	2,523.2	269.0	70.2	38.3
Syndicated TV	75.0	290.5	27.0	5.4
Cable TV Networks	270.8	319.1	135.2	17.9
Network Radio	125.6	27.5	1.7	3.5
National Spot Radio	337.4	10.7	7.2	3.9

[a]*Figures are in millions.*

Adapted from: Competitive Media Reporting. (1998). Total measured US ad spending by category and media in 1996. Advertising Age [On-line]. Available: http://www.adage.com/dataplace/archives/dp208.html. Reprinted with permission. Copyright, Crain Communications Inc., 1998.

Table 5.3 **1996 Ad Spending and Revenues of the Top Ten U.S. Retail Companies**

Rank	Company	Company Revenue[a]		Measured Advertising[b]	
		1996	1995	1996	1995
1	Wal-Mart Corp.	$99,826	$89,882	$144.9	$143.1
2	Sears, Roebuck & Co.	34,848	31,628	588.1	556.3
3	Kmart Corp.	30,378	30,429	240.8	239.7
4	Dayton Hudson Corp.	25,371	23,516	270.8	259.3
5	J. C. Penney Co.	23,649	21,419	305.1	272.9
6	Federated Department Stores	15,229	15,049	405.0	407.4
7	May Department Stores	11,650	10,484	398.8	339.4
8	The Limited	8,645	7,881	20.6	21.8
9	Woolworth Corp.	8,090	8,150	47.1	33.9
10	TJX Cos.	6,689	3,975	54.5	54.9
Total		$264,375	$242,413	$2,475.7	$2,328.7

[a]*Revenue is U.S. and was obtained from annual reports and represents most recent full-year reporting period. Revenue is of all operations, not just retail, as are advertising totals. Revenue is in millions.*

[b]*Advertising is in millions of dollars.*

Adapted from: Competitive Media Reporting. (1998). Top 20 retail companies. Advertising Age *[On-line]. Available: http://www.adage.com/dataplace/archives/dp203.html. Reprinted with permission. Copyright, Crain Communications Inc., 1998.*

that retailers continue to use local newspapers as their primary advertising outlet. The next most popular media used by retailers was spot TV ads, accounting for nearly 27 percent of the advertising budget.

As illustrated in Table 5.3, the top ten retail advertisers in the United States spent nearly $2.5 billion on advertising in 1996. Wal-Mart Corporation had the highest company revenue at $99 billion, spending less than 1 percent of sales on measured advertising, whereas Federated Department Stores spent 2.6 percent of its revenues of $15 billion on advertising.

Retail advertising may also be called local advertising due to the emphasis on a local target market. Although some retailers, such as Sears and J. C. Penney, do advertise nationally, most retailers focus on the local or regional areas. Expenses for retail advertising fall into two categories: production and media placement. Production expenses consist of the costs associated with creating the ad, whereas media placement expenses are the costs of running the ad in a print medium or broadcasting a commercial on an electronic medium.

Retail advertising has been criticized for being less sophisticated and more utilitarian than national advertising (Wells, Burnett, and Moriarty, 1998). The short-term emphasis of retail advertising compared to national advertising is among the reasons identified to explain this. Most retail ads are designed to promote merchandise with price as a main feature. These retail ads are run for just a few days. In contrast, a national ad typically features a standardized message that may be used for several months or even years. National advertisers might spend $5,000 or more to produce a newspaper ad and spend an additional $200,000 to run it in 100 large markets. Local retailers simply cannot justify such high production costs for their advertising. A local retailer who places an ad in the local paper might have media costs of only $400, making it unreasonable to spend $5,000 on production. As we begin the 21st century, there are several other strategies vying for promotional dollars.

Direct Marketing

Direct marketing activities may be included in the advertising budget or considered as a separate promotion budget allocation, depending upon the firm. Direct marketing is one of the promotional mix methods that is attracting interest among retailers and manufacturers, who see the benefits of focusing their promotional attention on their target customers. Direct marketing is the topic of Chapter 10.

Electronic Media

Have you purchased a pair of khakis on line? Storefront retailers, such as the Gap, and direct response retailers like L.L. Bean think you will, if you have not done so already. E-commerce is a rapidly growing promotional strategy for fashion retailers. In it not unusual to see banner advertising on the Internet or website addresses in magazine ads for either of these established retailers. The Gap promotes its website at its retail stores, on Gap shopping bags, and through its print ads (Kaufman, 1999). Promotional budgets for these electronic sites were originally derived from the advertising budget. As Internet shopping and website advertising grow in popularity, the promoters of these technologies will demand and receive separate promotional budgets.

In 1995, Amazon.com went into the business of selling books with over 2.5 million titles (Topolnicki, 1998). Without a physical storefront or any actual inventory, Amazon.com built its virtual bookstore by offering on-line consumers a broad selection of books at a discount (Fig. 5.5). After a consumer ordered a book, Amazon.com ordered the book from a distributor or publisher. Once the book was at the warehouse, the firm shipped it to the consumer. The reputation for the firm was built through Web advertising. By 1998, Amazon.com was among the top 25 U.S. Web shopping sites, with more than 9 million visitors in December (Kaufman, 1999).

Spending for on-line advertising amounted to $1.5 billion in 1998, growing over 130 percent from $650 million in 1997. Industry analysts projected on-line spending for advertising to increase to $8.9 billion in 2002 (Cox, 1999). Whether used by traditional retailers, such as the Gap or L.L. Bean, or on-line retailers like Amazon.com, budgets for electronic media will grow with the demand for e-commerce.

Fashion Shows and Special Events

Depending upon the retailer's commitment to producing fashion shows or other consumer-oriented special events, a budget for these activities will be allocated to the fashion director, fashion coordinator, public relations director, or special events coordinator. There has been a trend in department store retailing to combine the activities of the fashion office with the special events and public relations office; as a result these budgets are likely to be merged.

The fashion director or special events coordinator is responsible for scheduling major and minor fashion shows, celebrity appearances, community service projects, or other activities to enhance the public image of the store. This coordinator works very closely with the advertising director and visual merchandising director to bring a coordinated image to the public.

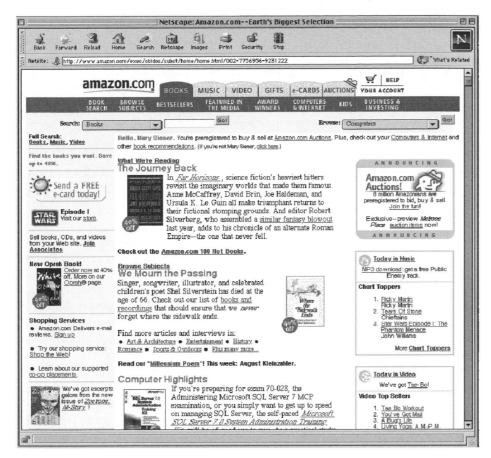

Figure 5.5

Amazon.com Homepage

Budget requirements for fashion shows include stage and seating requirements, lighting, music, model fees, props, and technical personnel. There may also be hospitality expenses such as food, refreshments, room rental, or decorations.

Special events may involve expenses related to physical presentation. This could be anything from a simple table to demonstrate a new cooking appliance to an elaborate stage setup, with a sound system, and security to launch a celebrity fragrance. Budgeting for fashion shows and special events needs to take into considerations the expenses required to accomplish the task. If the fashion show or special event is supposed to make money as a charity fundraiser, the person in charge of planning the budget must consider how revenues will be generated in addition to the anticipated expenses. The budget takes into consideration planned revenues and expenses as well as actual figures.

Personal Selling

Although personal selling is an essential element of the promotion mix, the allocation for it is not normally considered as part of the promotional budget. Personal selling expenses are usually considered as part of the personnel or human resources budget. This is because the human resources department has the responsibility for initial sales training. Regularly scheduled refresher seminars sponsored by the human resources division help sales associates keep up with the latest sales techniques and provide motivation.

Visual Merchandising

The visual merchandising department has expenses related to the physical presentation of merchandise on the sales floor. Props, signs, merchandise fixtures, and mannequins are part of the visual merchandising budget. Besides interpreting the tangible image of the store, this department works closely with advertising and fashion offices to coordinate a creative storewide image with visual tools in the stores. Additional expenses, incurred by the visual merchandising department, are required for the care and upkeep of existing materials.

ALLOCATING THE MANUFACTURING PROMOTION BUDGET

Primary promotion expenses for manufacturers and designers involve fashion shows, trade exhibits, and national advertising to introduce new designs and product innovations for the next season. Fashion show expenses are substantial at the designer level, providing an excellent opportunity to gain publicity for the new merchandise. Designers have put a high percentage of their promotional budgets into fashion shows that cost several hundred thousand dollars. Considering the high cost of hiring supermodels, trendy hairstylists, makeup artists, stage and set designers, and appropriate technical support staff, it is no wonder this promotional tool is so expensive. Figure 5.6 provides a sample breakdown of the expenses required to launch a big-scale fashion show at 7th on Sixth, the American ready-to-wear shows.

Manufacturers must also allocate a portion of the promotional budget to national advertising and cooperative advertising. Table 5.2, introduced earlier in this chapter, illustrates and compares media usage and spending patterns of four industries: retailing; toiletries and cosmetics manufacturing; apparel, footwear and accessories manufacturing; and household furnishings, supplies, and materials. Manufacturers and designers incur production and media expenses, in a similar manner to retail advertisers.

Manufacturers, designers, and retailers are able to extend their budgets by entering into cooperative arrangements. A discussion about entering into such cooperative arrangements follows later in the chapter.

We have identified methods of allocating budgets to promotional activities for both retailers and manufacturers. Budgets should also take into consideration the expenses related to hiring an outside advertising or promotion agency. The next section focuses on the traditional methods of paying for services and differentiates some of the other techniques used to compensate agencies.

ALLOCATING ADVERTISING AGENCY COMPENSATION

As we introduced in Chapter 3, the types of services provided by various advertising agencies differ according to the organization of the agency, actual services provided, and needs of the client. A variety of methods are used to compensate advertising agencies and other service providers. Payments may come in the form of commissions, fees, cost-plus agreements, percentage charges, or incentive-based compensation. These pay-

The following list is a sample breakdown of expenses for participating in 7th on Sixth, the big-scale fashion show in Bryant Park, which is run by the Council of Fashion Designers of America. In this example, the Tent, a venue with a capacity of 1,212, is used.

Invitations (for 2,000 guests)
- ❐ $5,000 for printing
- ❐ $5,000 for calligraphy at $2.50 per envelope
- ❐ $650 for postage
- ❐ Total: $10,650

RSVP Followup and Seating Arrangements (if done in-house)
- ❐ Hiring three people full-time to handle the volume of phone calls, for 6 weeks at $500 per week: $9,000

Venue
- ❐ $25,000 for the space which includes: official registered press list of about 1,500 names, venue seating plan, all 7th on Sixth Center services (credentials, radios, first-aid, lost and found, general information and assistance), private bonded 24-hour security, volunteer staff, sponsor services, production staff (producer, production manager, venue manager, site/security manager, volunteer coordinator), walkie-talkies on-site, food service program, travel and lodging assistance, press hospitality services, and inclusion in all official materials (print ads, T-shirts, signs, press materials, passport, etc.)

Music
- ❐ $5,000 for selection, timing, editing

Polaroid Film
- ❐ $700 for one case to style the show

Blown-Up Seating Chart and Stickers
- ❐ $400

Signage
- ❐ $1,000

Video
- ❐ $2,000

Still Photographer
- ❐ $2,000

Production Supervisor (if outside producers are hired—may also be done in-house.)
- ❐ $10,000 to $50,000 for Front-of-House (organizing mailing lists; sending invitations; coordinating RSVPs; handling press requests for interviews; previews; arranging seating charts; making sure the press folders, run-of-show lists, and goody bags are on seats; and working the day of the show) and Back-of-House (casting and booking models; hiring stylists, hair, and makeup; coordinating the sound, music, lighting; and styling the show)

Run-of-Show Credits
- ❐ $1,000

Press Folders
- ❐ $3,000

Models
- ❐ Total: $75,600 for 21 models. (For an average model, not a superstar, $1,200/hour; minimum 3 hours, $3,600)

Dressers
- ❐ $500 for the head dresser
- ❐ $8,400 for one dresser for each model @ $400 each
- ❐ Total: $8,900

Hair
- ❐ $5,000

Makeup
- ❐ $5,000

Food/Liquor/Champagne for Models at Venue
- ❐ $1,000

Transportation
- ❐ $1,000 for getting the collection to and from the venue

Total
- ❐ $166,250 to $206,250 (not including accessories, the party after the show is over, or a percentage of the rush work to get the sample collection ready)

Figure 5.6

Expenses for *7th on Sixth* Fashion Show

Adapted from: Pogoda, D. M. (1996, October 24). Costs of fashion shows keep piling up. Women's Wear Daily, 32 (Section II); and Pogoda, D. M. (1996, October 24). 7th on Sixth Package, Women's Wear Daily, 32 (Section II).

ments should be considered as part of the budget when a retailer, manufacturer or designer chooses to use an outside agency for promotion services.

Commissions

The once-standard practice for agencies involved in buying media was compensation through a commission. A **commission** is a percentage of money given to an agent who assists in a business transaction. The agency normally receives 15 percent from the media on any advertising time or space purchased for the client.

This type of compensation is easy to figure out. For example, an agency prepares a television advertisement for a client and purchases time for the ad to run. The television station bills the agency $85,000. The agency bills the client $100,000. The $15,000 difference is the payment for the agency, representing the 15 percent commission.

Compensation by commission has received a great deal of criticism in recent years. Concern is centered on how the commission relates to the services provided. If two different agencies require the same amount of effort to prepare an advertisement, the argument can be made that they should be compensated in a similar manner. The first agency is able to place the ad for $100,000, and the second agency places the ad for $1,000,000. The first agency receives $15,000 commission while the second agency is paid $150,000. Critics argue that agencies are forced to recommend high media expenditures to improve their commissions. Some clients feel that agencies are overly compensated due to high media costs. Additional debate results from the perception that noncommissionable media, such as direct marketing or sales promotion, are ignored by agencies unless the client specifies them.

There are proponents of the commission system, too. They argue that the commission system is easy and fairer to administer than other payment methods. Emphasis and higher costs are placed on accounts demanding more time and effort.

According to a study by the Association of National Advertisers, a New York-based trade organization, only 35 percent of advertisers paid their agencies based on media commissions. That was down from 61 percent 3 years earlier (Lauro, 1999).

In order to overcome the inequities of the commission system, many agencies and clients have developed alternative methods of compensation. These include fee or contract arrangements, cost-plus agreements, percentage charges, or incentive-based programs.

Fee Arrangements

A fee arrangement, or payment for services based upon a predetermined rate, may take several different forms. The first is a **fixed-fee rate**, also known as a straight fee. In this method, the agency charges a basic monthly rate for all of its services and credits any commissions earned to the client. The client and agency decide upon the exact work to be done and how much the client will pay for those services. This system assumes a long-term relationship between the agency and client.

In some situations, the agency may hire a specialized agency to provide limited services based upon a **contract**, a written agreement identifying the work to be accomplished, deadlines, and payments. This is a fee for specific activities such as management of a special event, production of a fashion show, or design of a direct-response mailer. A contract fee arrangement is established for a short-term project; it may be for one specific job or task.

Another system used by the agency and client is a **fee-commission combination**. In this instance, media commissions are credited against the fee. Payment is adjusted if the commission is less than the agreed upon fee. The client pays the difference. If the agency is involved in doing work in noncommissionable media, such as sales promotion, a fee is charged.

Fee arrangements require the agency to keep accurate records of the costs of providing services. By assessing these costs for a specified period of time or project, the agency will add the agency's desired profit to the expenses before billing the client. To avoid any problems or disputes, the fee arrangement should specify exactly what services would be performed by the agency.

Cost-plus Agreement

The **cost-plus agreement** requires the client to pay a rate based upon cost of the work plus an agreed-on profit margin, normally a percentage of total costs. This method requires the agency to keep track of the direct and indirect costs for accomplishing the task. Direct costs relate to the salaries of the personnel and the time it takes to produce the assignment. An allocation for indirect costs such as the agency overhead and administration need to be incorporated into the fees.

Many clients prefer a fee-based or cost-plus system because they receive a precise breakdown of where and how their promotion or advertising dollars are being spent. However, many agencies find these systems too complex because they must provide detailed cost accounting. The expenses of doing a project are often difficult to predict when the agency bids for a client's business. Also, agencies are reluctant to let clients view internal expense records.

Percentage Charges

Another method of compensating an agency is by adding a markup of **percentage charges** to costs for work done by outside suppliers. Services such as graphic design, photography, or market research are billed to the agency and the agency marks up that cost to the client in order to cover its administrative expenses.

This system is used when the agency has to employ freelancers to accomplish required tasks. These suppliers do not allow a commission, so the agency builds in a markup charge between 17.65 and 20 percent. A 17.65 percent markup yields a 15 percent commission. For example, a firm asks a graphic designer to produce an advertising billboard. The designer bills the agency $10,000. With a markup of 17.65 percent, the agency bills its client $11,765. The $1,765 markup is approximately 15 percent of $11,765. These markup charges allow the agency to cover its administrative costs and provide a reasonable profit for the agency's efforts.

Incentive-based Compensation

Since more clients are demanding accountability for their promotional activities, clients have tied payments to performance in some type of **incentive-based compensation**. The fundamental concept is that payment is based upon how well the activities meet a predetermined performance goal. For instance, an **event bonus** is a premium paid above the fixed fee, if the attendance goal for an event is exceeded. In the case of **media savings**, a new agency receives a share of the media savings it achieved over the previous agency. By using a **unit sales incentive**, a client pays the agency a base fee and a bonus for unit sales above the goal or target sales. In these alternative compensation plans, extra performance incentives provide additional motivation for an agency.

EXTENDING THE PROMOTIONAL BUDGET

Manufacturers, retailers and designers in the merchandising environment have been able to extend the value of the promotional budget by working in a cooperative manner. These activities not only extend the promotional budget, they also have the capability of enhancing the image of all cooperative partners in the marketplace. Popular cooperative strategies include co-marketing, co-branding, cooperative advertising, sponsorship and co-sponsorship, and strategic alliances. In the next sections, we provide a brief introduction to methods by which such cooperative activities may be used to extend the promotional budget.

Co-marketing

Co-marketing is the creation of cooperative efforts by which the manufacturer and retailer join forces to increase the revenue and profits for both parties. It involves a range of marketing activities, not just a prescribed activity. Co-marketing has gained popularity in the promotion of food products to the consumer market and in the promotion of electronic or personal care products to the business-to-business sector.

Traditional marketing was based upon the premise that manufacturers and retailers were not working together. Manufacturers emphasized increasing their sales to the retailer, a trade channel considered more important than the ultimate consumer. The retailer, on the other hand, concentrated on profit, which was realized from the ultimate consumer, and sought less expensive merchandise or discounts from manufacturers to improve the gross margin and obtain a greater bottom line. The product manager for Heinz ketchup, Mark Trumbull summed up the problem with the traditional marketing approach, "We focused on how much the retailer would buy rather than how much the consumer would buy. And the retailer was more focused on how cheaply he could buy, not on how much product he could move to consumers" (Marx, 1995). The concern was that neither the manufacturer nor the retailer was improving sales by working against each other.

Now mass retailers, such as Target, Kmart, and Wal-Mart, are working to find marketing programs that help differentiate their stores from each other. Co-marketing programs have been used to distinguish merchandise presentation. An example of a successful co-marketing program is that of Wal-Mart and L & F Products, makers of such brands as Lysol, Wet Ones, and Ogilvie Perms. L & F Products became the manager for the home permanents section located in the Wal-Mart stores, controlling the visual appearance as well as the distribution, pricing, promotion, and shelf management for its own as well as other products. The goal was to improve the top-line and bottom-line profits for the retailer in addition to expanding the return on investment for both the manufacturer and retailer. As a result of the co-marketing efforts, Wal-Mart was able to achieve double-digit increases in home permanent sales in the early 1990s, while

Ogilvie improved its market share volume. The market share grew from about 40 percent to from 62 to 67 percent share in 2 years (Marx, 1995).

Co-branding

Another example of cooperative efforts is the development of co-branded credit cards. **Co-branding** marries a card issuer, usually a bank that wants to increase its volume, with a consumer company in search of a market share boost. In cooperation with L.L. Bean, Visa developed a credit card that offers special shipping rates, discounts, and previews for sales events. This type of card is also used to provide frequent flier miles for a variety of airlines including Alaska Airlines, America West, and Delta. Figure 5.7 shows an example of an advertisement for a co-branded airline and bank credit card. According to Stephen J. Bartell, vice president of co-branding and affinity marketing for Master-Card International, "frequent flier cards, for example, can have 10 times the volume of standard cards" (Marx, 1994).

Co-branding has gained acceptance from manufacturers and retailers who act as two brands working together to gain equity and profits for both organizations. Although historically, relations between manufacturers and retailers have been based on mutual distrust rather than cooperation, practitioners of co-branding have benefited from teamwork. Both Sears and Wal-Mart launched co-branded MasterCards in 1996. Ac-

Figure 5.7

Co-branded credit cards offer consumers unique advantages.

cording to Dale Ingram of Wal-Mart, "we didn't test-market; we did consumer research asking our customers what they wanted in a credit card. Customers asked us for a way to save money while shopping with a Wal-Mart credit card" ("Sears, Wal-Mart unveil Co-branded MasterCards," 1996).

Cooperative Advertising

In **cooperative advertising** the manufacturer works with the retailer to develop an ad and shares in the cost of running that advertisement. The advertisement may be placed in local or national media. The brand name of the manufacturer is featured prominently in the ad along with the name of the retailer where the merchandise can be found. Primary or secondary producers may use this strategy to tie the image of the national brand to a particular retail store in a market area.

For example, a fragrance producer such as Chanel might agree to cooperatively sponsor an advertisement with retailer Neiman Marcus in *Vogue* magazine (Fig. 5.8). The share of the cost may be split 75/25 or any other ratio decided upon prior to running the advertisement. This means that Chanel pays for 75 percent of the cost, while Neiman Marcus pays the other 25 percent. Sharing the expenses has the effect of extending the budget for both the manufacturer and retailer.

Figure 5.8

Chanel and Neiman Marcus used cooperative advertising to extend each of their budgets for this ad, originally created by artist Andy Warhol.

Sponsorship and Co-sponsorship

Sponsorship may take one of two forms. The first form of sponsorship involves advertisers who lend their name to a sporting activity or another type of special event. The Fifth Annual Polo Sport Race to Deliver (Fig. 5.9) is such an event. As the main sponsor, Polo Sport was recognized in the name of the race. The cosponsors paid for ads, arranged for their placement, and generally supported the event. By participating in such activities, sponsors hope that participants will think favorably of them, and therefore become customers or, in the case of nonprofit organizations, contributors. Event sponsorship is discussed more fully in Chapter 14.

A second form of sponsorship, involves an advertiser who underwrites the cost of production for a television or radio program and its commercials. The commercials are fit into the program, when and where the advertiser wants them, as the program is broadcast. This is very costly; therefore, single sponsorships are rare and usually limited to special programs. AT&T, Xerox, and Hallmark are manufacturers that have been associated with this practice. To save costs and reduce risks, many advertisers decide to cosponsor programs. Why do they spend so much money on programs and advertising?

There are several important reasons why advertisers sponsor television and radio programs. First, advertisers believe the audience more readily respects the product(s) that are associated with an organization that sponsors high-quality entertainment. This

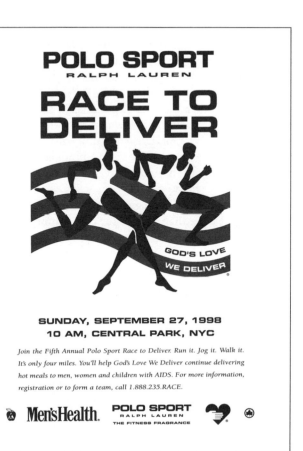

Figure 5.9

Ralph Lauren sponsors the Polo Sport Race to Deliver.

is true when there is prestige attached to programming. Second, the sponsor controls the timing and content of its commercials, so long as they remain within the network's or local station's regulations. If the sponsor wants to run a commercial longer than normal and offer fewer interruptions during the program, it may do so. Consumers, who respect this type of action, are likely to purchase products or services from the sponsor. Moreover, even though sponsorship is expensive, the advertiser is able to reach incredibly large audiences through sponsorship.

Strategic Alliances

Kurt Salmon Associates (KSA), a global management consulting firm specializing in consumer products and retailing, defined a **strategic alliance** as a partnership between a manufacturer and a retailer working in a particular supply chain that leverages the core competencies of each firm (1997). By combining their individual strengths and abilities, partners are able to create a supply-process synergy that results in increased profitability, efficiency, and market share for each firm, which results in greater value for the consumer. When implemented properly, the strategic alliance supply chain between the partners will look like a well-run vertical company. Sara Lee Intimates and Wal-Mart entered into a strategic alliance. Over their 8-year affiliation, the business has grown from an initial $134 million account to a $1 billion partnership (Kaplan, 1997). According to Jeff Stiely, a KSA manager, "the ultimate strategic alliance, which the industry has just begun to embrace, should completely redefine and reengineer the supply complex from concept to consumer" (Kurt Salmon Associates, 1997).

Partnerships between retailers and manufacturers began during retail consolidation in the 1980s, when retailers demanded that manufacturers perform *value-added* functions such as inventory management and in-store merchandising. By the 1990s, the power had shifted away from the retailer to the consumer, requiring manufacturers and retailers to work together to satisfy the same master. Strategic alliance partners benefit from manufacturers' knowledge about the product and how to display it, and they benefit from retailers' knowledge of how to develop and deliver a unique store personality and shopping experience. Together, they make an efficient and productive team with greater product sell-through, better assortments in stores, and an easier and more pleasant shopping experience.

Among the reasons for entering into strategic alliances listed in Figure 5.10, manufacturers and retailers identify several ways their businesses could improve through shared information and capital. By creating mutual sales and profitability goals, the partners can better meet the needs of consumers by working together. According to KSA (1997), the most practical areas for strategic alliances are: (1) assortment—category management, planning, and development; (2) introduction—product development, product testing, and marketing; (3) replenishment—in-stock and fast turns; and (4) promotion—advertising, direct marketing, sales promotion, and visual merchandising. Although a strategic alliance is not strictly a budget matter, each partner benefits financially from working cooperatively.

Advantages of Cooperative Arrangements

There are several advantages for both the manufacturer and retailer entering into cooperative arrangements.

- **Cooperative arrangements give the manufacturer and retailer extra exposure.** Sharing costs extends advertising expenses.

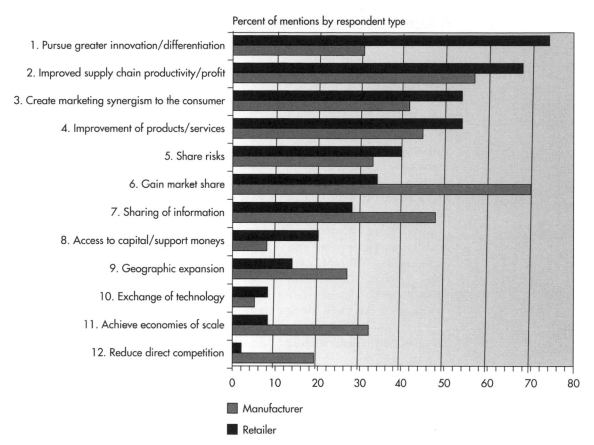

Percent of mentions by respondent type

1. Pursue greater innovation/differentiation
2. Improved supply chain productivity/profit
3. Create marketing synergism to the consumer
4. Improvement of products/services
5. Share risks
6. Gain market share
7. Sharing of information
8. Access to capital/support moneys
9. Geographic expansion
10. Exchange of technology
11. Achieve economies of scale
12. Reduce direct competition

0 10 20 30 40 50 60 70 80

■ Manufacturer
■ Retailer

Figure 5.10

Primary Reasons for Entering into Strategic Alliances

- **Images of a merchandise manufacturer and retail firm are mutually enhanced.** The label of a fashion designer, such as Calvin Klein, benefits when it is associated with an upscale retailer like Bergdorf Goodman. Both the designer and retail store profit from strongly linked images created for the product and the store.
- **Retailer and manufacturer benefit from lower advertising rates and better placement in publications.** Because the retailer and manufacturer work together, they are able to run ads more frequently. The more regularly ads run in certain publications, the more prominent their placement and the greater their discount.

Disadvantages of Cooperative Arrangements for Manufacturers

Substantial allocations for cooperative promotional activities are built into the budgets of fashion apparel, accessory, cosmetic, and related manufacturers. Although the advantages are clear, there are also several disadvantages to be considered.

- **Manufacturer identity may be lost in the layout.** Art, photography, copy, and store logo may be featured more prominently than the logo or name of the manufacturer. As a result, the manufacturer's identity may not play as dominant a role as the manufacturer would like it to.

- **Accounting records are a business expense.** Normally after an advertisement runs in a local newspaper, the retail store sends an invoice and "tear sheet" as proof of the co-operative advertisement. The manufacturer reimburses the store after receiving the invoice. Accounting procedures take time and expense to follow through.
- **Stores are late sending documentation.** Frustrations can easily erupt when the store sends proof of advertising after a lengthy period of time. Prompt attention to detail helps to overcome these frictions.
- **The manufacturer may have limited control over timing, style, identity, message, and content.** If the retailer maintains control over these factors, the manufacturer is at the mercy of the retailer who chooses when to run the advertisement. The retailer can also decide how much emphasis is placed on the merchandise or brand.
- **The manufacturer has no control over in-store merchandise placement.** The store may choose to run only an advertisement and fail to support the merchandise with in-store display and merchandise presentation.
- **Retailers may take advantage of the manufacturer by considering the advertising allowance as a discount.** Some retailers will ask for a percentage discount for advertising allowance. The manufacturer has very little control over what is advertised and when. A specific contract identifying the merchandise to be advertised and proof of run by a tear sheet will alleviate this problem. The manufacturer controls payment after receipt of documentation.
- **Competition may overstimulate promotional budgets.** The retailer may ask for more than the manufacturer has available for advertising expenses. Fear of losing out to the competition may make the manufacturer spend too much for cooperative advertising.

Disadvantages of Cooperative Arrangements for Retailers

On the surface, retailers may not perceive any problems associated with cooperative arrangements. The following list provides some caution regarding their use.

- **Cooperative advertising money becomes more important that the actual merchandise.** In an attempt to lower advertising costs, buyers are enticed to buy merchandise that does not meet the company's image. The buyer loses sight of the *nature of the merchandise,* choosing merchandise based on availability of cooperative advertising rather than the merchandise most preferred by the customer.
- **Manufacturer demands may not fit with retailer's style.** The manufacturer places requirements on advertising that may not fit with the type of advertising done by the retailer. The retailer may have a certain approach, such as using only photography as the art in newspaper advertising, whereas the manufacturer may insist upon line drawings. The continuity and identity of the retailer is lost in the transformation.
- **Manufacturer's message must be consistent with the retailer's communication.** The merchandise and sales communication between the two participating firms should be in harmony. The retailer could have a short-term product orientation, while the manufacturer is interested in building a long-term image, resulting in dissatisfaction by either party.
- **Approval for advertising should include the promotion director.** Internal friction could develop between merchandising and promotion personnel, if decisions regarding cooperative advertising ignore the input from the promotion director. Merchants, who desire the benefits of cooperative dollars, could encourage advertising that is inconsistent with promotional strategies established by the promotion division.

- **Cooperative advertising contracts are difficult to execute**. The complexities of the contracts discourage many retailers from participating.

Overcoming Disadvantages to Cooperative Arrangements

Generally the advantages of using cooperative advertising outweigh any of the disadvantages. The best way to overcome any of the limitations is to clearly state the terms of the responsibilities of the retailer and manufacturer in a contract prior to implementation. This contract should consist of terms, including scheduling, location of publication, size of the space, dates to be run, anticipated expenses, and the percentage of contribution by each party. The contract should further identify the type of advertisement. Is it a single-item ad, a part of a departmentalized promotion, or a storewide theme ad? The size and style of the logo or appropriate visual signature should also be stated. A written contract provides a description of the terms that were agreed upon. This should prevent any legal problems.

FUTURE TRENDS IN BUDGET PREPARATION

At the close of the 20th century, the advertising and communications industries are predicting a rosy future for increased promotion budgets. According to the eleventh annual *VS & A Communications Industry Forecast*, the communications field is projected to be the third-fastest growing major industry in the United States (Veronis, Suhler and Associates, 1997). With an expectation of 44 percent growth in communication spending by 2001, the communications industry will ride into the 21st century with a surge of support for interactive digital media, database information services, and advertising across a broad spectrum of media. Key findings from the *Forecast:*

- Rising corporate profits will induce U.S. companies to focus on sales growth, boosting spending on advertising, trade shows, and other tools used to generate sales.
- Audience fragmentation will stimulate advertiser spending for emerging media, such as interactive digital and subscription television, without adversely affecting traditional media.
- Substantial advertiser spending will sustain healthy growth for traditional media.
- Consumer on-line spending will triple by the year 2001.
- Total communications spending will grow at a compound annual rate of 7.6 percent to $419.6 billion by 2001, 44 percent above the 1996 total of $290.7 billion (1997).

In addition to strong budgetary support, improving computer models to help make the budgeting process easier is another future trend. Earlier in the chapter, we stated that the first attempts at quantitative budget models met with limited success, but it is believed that computer programmers and financial specialists will work to make these computer models more user friendly.

Because the budget is one of the most important planning documents an organization uses, the time and effort spent on developing a budget are definitely worth it. The budgetary process helps a firm to understand its past practices, current financial position, and opportunities for the future. A number of theoretical and practical methods of preparing a budget have been introduced in this chapter. A well-prepared budget will enable a firm to achieve its general as well as IMC objectives. Although some people think that budgeting is a confusing and boring task, a good budget will assist the organization in achieving its goals.

SUMMARY

- The budget is one of the most important planning documents a manufacturer or retailer can develop.
- Budgeting provides an opportunity for the firm to analyze its current position and past practices and set promotion objectives for the future.
- Budgeting forces executives to take into consideration changes in the economy and environment and assess their potential impact on the promotional plan for short- and long-range goals.
- Because budgeting is considered frustrating and confusing, many small businesses ignore the benefits of the budgeting process and simply follow their past practices.
- Researchers have proposed several theoretical models, such as the law of diminishing returns and the S-curve, that assist budget managers in preparing the plan.
- Whether the budget planners use one of the top-down or bottom-up methods, the firm will benefit from the analysis.
- After the appropriations are made to the promotion division, specific budgets for promotional mix elements are allocated. The firm sets priorities for advertising, direct marketing, fashion shows, special events, public relations, and visual merchandising.
- Manufacturers and designers also allocate the promotion budgets to their mix elements, from trade fashion shows to advertising and cooperative activities.
- The budget provides financial planning figures. These estimates can be compared to objectives and actual results as the season progresses. This planning tool is used to measure the success of promotional activities.
- During their budgeting process, retailers and manufacturers should consider agency compensation. Advertising agencies have traditionally been compensated through commissions, but controversy over commissions has lead to alternative compensation methods such as fee arrangements, cost-plus agreements, percentage charges, and incentive-based compensation.
- Manufacturers, retailers, and designers can extend the value of their promotional budgets by working in a cooperative manner. Co-marketing, co-branding, cooperative advertising, and sponsorship not only extend the promotional budget, they enhance the image of cooperative partners in the marketplace.

KEY TERMS

all one can afford
arbitrary allocation
bottom-up approaches
clipping service
co-branding
co-marketing
commission
competitive parity
contract
cooperative advertising

cost-plus agreement
diminishing returns model
event bonus
fee-commission combination
fixed-fee rate
incentive-based compensation
media savings
objective and task
payout planning
percentage charges

percentage of sales
quantitative mathematical
    models
return on investment
S-shaped curve model
strategic alliance
top-down approaches
unit sales incentive

QUESTIONS FOR DISCUSSION

1. Why is budgeting for promotion so important?
2. Who is responsible for competitive parity promotion budgeting?
3. What method of budgeting is the most common for retailers? How does each method compare with the other techniques? Which techniques might be better than others?
4. How do retailers, designers, and manufacturers extend budgets by sharing promotional expenses?

ADDITIONAL RESOURCES

Engel, P. H. (1996). *Budgeting and finance.* New York: McGraw-Hill.

Schonfeld Associates Incorporated. (Ed.). (1998). *Advertising ratios & budgets.* Lincolnshire, IL: NTC Business.

Tracy, J. A. (1996). *Understanding budgeting.* New York: Wiley.

Figure 6.1

A futuristic theme-based promotion campaign for Ferré.

PROMOTIONAL ASPECTS
OF FORECASTING

After you have read this chapter you should be able to:

Define forecasting and identify the personnel involved in this activity.

Correlate the business functions of forecasting and promotion.

Identify trend resources in the primary, secondary, and tertiary markets.

Discuss theme development in promotion planning.

Milan—Ferré photographed model Eva Witwoska clinging to the Eiffel Tower (Fig. 6.1) for a futuristic space and technology theme tempered with feminine clothing (Conti, 1998). The photos from the campaign were also placed onto Ferré's Internet site.

New York—Ellen Tracy decided to promote its two brands, the Ellen Tracy Collection and Company Ellen Tracy, in a series of ads with the tagline *One Vision, Two Views* (Lockwood, 1998c). Four-page inserts, created for fashion magazines highlighted both collections and featured model Christy Turlington. In addition, Ellen Tracy bolstered its outdoor presence with advertisements on buses, adding out-of-home media to the promotion mix.

Paris—A twist on five masterpieces provided the big story in fashion advertising for Yves Saint Laurent (Raper, 1998). The campaign featured model Kate Moss in well-known and immediately recognizable scenes from famous paintings. The art theme was an institutional campaign for YSL and appeared as double-page ads in traditional fashion magazines and as outdoor advertising.

These three vignettes describe promotion campaign themes and advertising strategies produced for the same fall fashion season. Milan designers featured futuristic themes, New York designers presented lifestyle themes, and Paris designers concentrated on beauty and art. The three themes are timeless and could have been created in the 1960s, 1990s, or in the year 2020. These campaigns, based on fashion forecasts, were created far in advance of the actual selling season. These programs are the communication tool sellers use to announce upcoming trends to the buying public.

This chapter begins by introducing forecasting and those involved in the business of forecasting. Next, we discuss the mutual dependence between forecasting and promotion. Although promotion specialists rely on media outlets to communicate trend messages, these same professionals depend on media outlets as sources for identifying and forecasting future trends. The next section of this chapter examines forecasting resources available to raw materials producers, designers and manufacturers, and retailers. In the final section of this chapter, we discuss theme development. Themes, based on forecasts, are important elements of promotion campaigns. The chapter concludes with a discussion of the future direction of forecasting and implications for promotion executives and consumers.

WHAT IS FORECASTING?

Forecasting is the activity of projecting trends. A **trend** is the general direction in which something is moving. Generating forecasts based on trend analysis has become a necessary management function in many industries. Using all available resources, a forecaster predicts the future. A stock analyst will forecast the direction of the stock market. A television meteorologist will predict the weather. Although predictions are made, forecasters must be ready to change course if the unexpected occurs.

A **fashion trend** is the visible direction in which fashion is moving. It may be a color, a fabric, or a style characteristic apparent for the coming season. A major trend is based on well-researched market information, has high sales volume potential, and test markets with positive results against direct competition. Analyzing fashion forecasts is similar to analyzing the weather or the stock market. A fashion director and buyer will decide on the general trends of a season to meet the expected needs of the store's target customer.

In Chapter 2, we discussed the well-defined product life cycle of a trend. A trend is given birth when a small group of leading-edge people get wind of the idea and try it. As the trend grows, it is discovered by more people. Articles are written about the trend and it is shown on broadcast spots. Fords emerge during this stage of the product life cycle. A **ford** is a best-selling trend with strong customer demand, available at several different price points, and produced by many different manufacturers.

As the trend reaches maturity, it is seen at chain stores in malls; it declines to the racks at deep-discount outlets; and it dies when it is available at flea markets (Hinds, 1994). A very short-lived trend is considered a **fad**. A fashion fad has quick acceptance and departure within the product life cycle. A trend that endures over a long period of time undergoing only minor changes as it progresses through the product life cycle is called a **classic**. But, where do trends come from?

Linda Allard, designer for the Ellen Tracy lines, was once asked in an interview if all designers got together and decided what the trends were going to be. It was true, as the questioner implied, that sometimes there appeared to be a conspiracy when every designer showed the same color, style, and silhouette for a season. In a response, still relevant today, Hinds (1994) reasoned that trends appear to be similar because the sources for inspiration are similar. Trends emerge from:

- **Society.** A trend can come from high up, the studios of top designers, or way down, what kids are wearing on the street.
- **Culture.** It can be global in its implications, or extremely individual, sparked by a rock star's wardrobe.
- **Designers.** Trends can come from the lifestyles of the designers themselves. The New York or Paris fashion scene is a tight-knit community that shares a wealth of common experiences. Designers go to the same museum exhibits, movies, and restaurants, and are going to be influenced by the same images.
- **Raw materials vendors.** Fabric fairs play a vital role, although they're not that well-known outside the industry. Held regularly in various countries, the fairs are where designers and manufacturers go to see the latest fabrics.
- **Publicity.** Headlines are almost as important as hemlines when it comes to style decisions.
- **Consumers.** The biggest motive in the creation of any trend is cash. New styles mean new reasons to make a purchase. Trends are the lifeblood of the fashion business. They

create consumer excitement and encourage customers to visit stores and buy new merchandise.

Consumer behavior is one of the most meaningful factors used to project trends. What better place to learn about consumers than from message sponsors and media who have an acute awareness of consumer behavior and can provide us with insight about society. Through research, promotion executives know what people are buying and what influences the purchase, where and how people are spending their time, what people are thinking and how society reacts, and what impact the government and the economy have on the consumer.

The current marketplace is driven by consumers. Trends appear when consumers take action in the marketplace as a reaction to work, home, or society. Streamline Incorporated, a computerized concierge service based in Westwood, Massachusetts, is an example of a business opportunity based on a consumer trend (Furchgott, 1998). The trend—consumers strapped for time—has resulted in home delivery services. Consumers order groceries, wine, pet supplies, and other items over the Internet and the items are delivered to their homes, freeing up time otherwise spent grocery shopping. Trend identification is based on professional analysis of consumers, the marketplace, the economy, and past experiences. Tracking trends to determine what will come next is the only way for many firms to stay ahead of the competition.

Since forecasts are predictions about the future based on research and best guesses, past statistics are helpful, but will not guarantee the future. Forecasters know a range of possibilities that may occur to confirm or oppose a projection. They select the best guess among many plausible alternatives. As a result, business leaders often plan for a future that never arrives, while a different future passes them by (Mahaffie, 1995). History is filled with forecasts that did not work out in the way the predictor intended. In 1876, Western Union predicted that the telephone would have too many shortcomings to be seriously considered a means of communication. Thomas Watson, chairman of IBM in 1943, predicted that there would be a world market for maybe five computers (Krantz, 1996).

The most common error in forecasting is overestimating the time it will take for forecasts to be implemented into society. Also, forecasters underestimate the wider implication and secondary effect that any forecast has on people and situations. John Mahaffie (1995), an associate with Coates & Jarratt, Inc., a Washington, D.C. research firm specializing in the study of the future gave eight reasons why forecasts fail:

- **Failure to examine assumptions.** On what does the forecast rest? Are there specific social or technological developments that will be required for the forecast to come true? Does the forecast assume things that seem unlikely, given your view of human nature or economic realities?
- **Limited expertise.** Some enthusiasts overshoot their expertise when making a forecast.
- **Lack of imagination.** Other forecasters have the opposite problem. They fail to explore more interesting possibilities for the future out of conservatism or timidness of thought. These tendencies misguide a forecast just as easily as over enthusiasm.
- **Neglect of constraints.** Forecasters are obliged to make predictions that are within the realm of possibility. This failure is summed up in the idea that "people just are not going to go for that."
- **Excessive optimism.** An excessively optimistic forecaster does not weigh the "downside risk." If a forecast does not consider the offsetting or limiting factors in a given potential future, it is likely to be flawed.

- **Reliance on mechanical extrapolation.** Extrapolation means to estimate by extending known information. This works for identifiable limiting factors such as population growth or market penetration. However, forecasters who use it for unknown factors miss the acceleration of the forecast.
- **Premature closure.** When developing forecasts, some researchers finish their work before all factors are considered. As a result, the more creative and far-reaching possibilities are never explored. Fear may be the reason for early closure and other narrowness of thinking.
- **Overspecification.** The danger in making a concrete forecast, such as an exact statistic or an exact fashion trend for a future year, is that it pushes the science of forecasting beyond its capabilities. It is not possible to have control over all variables that drive change, so no one can be utterly specific about most developments. The real value in forecasting is in showing the directions and characteristics of change.

For a forecast to be useful, Mahaffie (1995) suggested considering the following elements:

- **A clear statement of purpose.** Why was the forecast made? The purpose should give a clear sense of how the forecast is meant to be taken. Is the forecast a mind-stretching exercise or is it highly probable?
- **Clear assumptions.** The technological and social assumptions on which the forecast depends, should make it possible for users to evaluate the forecast and decide if they agree or disagree. Without clear assumptions, the users can only take the analyst's word that the forecast is plausible.
- **A time horizon.** Users cannot effectively interpret a forecast if they do not know when the developments it describes are supposed to happen. If no time frame exists, at least explain why.
- **Attention to discontinuities.** Discontinuities are breaks or gaps. Things that could speed up, slow down, or break the forecast should be discussed.
- **Adequate accounting for social and technological forces.** Social forces in technological forecasts, and technological forces in social forecasts, must be accounted for to ensure the full context in which developments will happen.

Any forecast that fails to cover these elements is suspicious, or at least flawed in its presentation. Users who demand forecasting to be a predictive science will be disappointed, but those who use forecasting as a tool to expand their thinking about change will be rewarded (Mahaffie, 1995). But, who are these individuals willing to take risks and predict the future?

Forecasting Personnel

There are professional forecasters, and there are professionals who forecast as a responsibility of their job. As it is used in this chapter, a **forecaster** is a nonspecific title given to any individual within an organization who is responsible for trend identification and image. In this section, we first discuss **futurists**, who make long-range forecasts for many industries. Then, we turn our attention to professionals in the fashion and promotion fields. These professionals, called **fashion forecasters**, work for fashion forecasting services or the forecasting division within retail, manufacturing, or advertising firms.

Many other fashion and promotion professionals forecast as a routine part of their job. We discuss these individuals at the conclusion of this section. Job titles include but are not limited to the following: designer, fashion director, buyer, assistant buyer, creative director, fashion coordinator, fashion merchandiser, stylist, store manager, and owner. Promotion specialists within promotion, advertising, and public relations departments who are involved with brand positioning and merchandise selection are also considered fashion forecasters.

Futurists

Futurists are self-proclaimed, forward-looking individuals who answer such questions as: Who will fight the next war in the Middle East? Where will the best jobs be next year? What will be the hot consumer-electronics products of the year 2008? (Krantz, 1996). Because the work futurists do is often categorized as economic forecasting or strategic analysis, profitability statistics are vague. However, it has become a very sophisticated business in high demand by such corporate giants as Coca-Cola, Pepsi, Monsanto, Avon, Rockport Shoes, General Mills, and Saatchi & Saatchi, among others.

Futurists have the ability to spot trends and translate them into real opportunities (Tillotson, 1998). They include successful people like Faith Popcorn of BrainReserve; Edie Weiner and Arnold Brown of Weiner, Edrich and Brown; and Vickie Abrahamson, Mary Meehan, and Larry Samuels of Iconoculture. These professionals, in addition to running successful consulting agencies, are popular media personalities and authors of best-selling books. Businesses hire futurists to help determine what new products and services consumers will buy.

Media outlets provide a major resource for the trend analysis conducted by futurists. Every month Weiner and her partner Arnold Brown read dozens of publications looking for new and offbeat ideas (Beck, 1996). The three partners of Iconoculture gather information from separate sources and compare notes for consensus. Abrahamson drives across the country reading local newspapers and shopping at local small-town stores; Samuels surfs the Net and keeps tabs on nightlife; and Meehan gathers information from newsstands, television, and conversations with a variety of people (Tillotson, 1998). Popcorn and her staff check hundreds of magazines, books, and newspapers for research to pinpoint trends (Koenenn, 1998). These professional forecasters do not start trends; they communicate the trends they see in consumer behavior back to clients. Each identified trend provides an opportunity for a forward-thinking promotion executive to get ahead in the marketplace by providing something new and interesting to the consumer.

Fashion Forecasters

Professional fashion forecasters work for independent fashion forecasting services or forecast divisions within retail or manufacturing firms or advertising agencies. Forecasting services contract with clients to provide trend analysis information. Clients either subscribe to, or hire consulting services from, the forecasting company. A forecasting division within a retail or manufacturing firm will provide the same services for its parent firm. Forecasting services operate at all levels of the fashion industry, assisting raw material producers, designers and manufacturers, and retailers. They include color and fiber associations, resident buying offices, and independent firms that specialize in apparel categories or home furnishings. Cotton Incorporated, the Tobé Report, D^3 Doneger Design Direction, and Promostyl are just a few examples of forecasting services. A listing of forecasting and reporting services is available at *http://www.fashiondex.com.*

The Tobé Report, published by Tobé Associates Incorporated, is one of the oldest forecast services, established in 1927. It publishes a weekly report containing illustrations, photographs, and editorials about merchandise trends for apparel and accessory markets. Fashion forecasters, including Tobé Associates, do not include advertising in their reports. This allows fashion forecasters to present a totally unbiased source of fashion information.

Many fashion forecasters work in international fashion centers to identify global trends. For example, Promostyl, a French-based forecasting service, has offices in Paris, London, New York, and Tokyo. Its forecasters attend trade shows, couture openings, and fabric fairs. They visit with new and established designers to learn where their inspiration comes from. Foreign publications are read and broadcasts are viewed for trend insights. Fashion forecasters watch consumers on the street to find out what merchandise and materials are selling fast, what merchandise boutiques cannot keep in stock, and what hot items from last season are out of fashion in the current season.

Fashion forecasters disseminate information about fashion trends through the use fashion trend portfolios. A **fashion trend portfolio** is a series of visual boards, slides, videos, or kits, projecting major trends in silhouettes, fabrics, colors, patterns, accessory treatments, catch phrases, and theme ideas. Additionally, fashion trend portfolios may include color cards or swatches, fabric swatches, yarn samples, and sketches or photographs of the fashion look. Texture, print, pattern combinations, and other aspects of the fashion image are also included in the fashion trend portfolio. Figure 6.2 is a photograph showing a fashion trend portfolio from D³ Donegar Design Direction.

Fashion forecasters are responsible for discovering new trends and interpreting specific characteristics of the trend that will be profitable for the firm or client. A clear understanding of the target customer and brand position of the firm or client are critical to trend interpretation. Although the same trend may be identified, it will be interpreted quite differently for a specialty boutique versus a mass merchandiser.

Forecasters

Fashion and promotion professionals forecast as a routine part of their job within many advertising, designer, and retail firms. These experts within the organization determine

Figure 6.2

A fashion trend portfolio from D³ Doneger Design Direction

the look of the firm. They include personnel from the fashion, promotion, advertising, or public relations departments, and department managers and buyers. Anyone involved in the brand positioning of a firm, including trend identification, merchandise selection, or image, is a forecaster.

Forecasters travel to domestic and international fashion centers to visit trade shows, manufacturers, and designers. They keep up to date by reading fashion publications and discussing potential trends with fashion editors. They subscribe to fashion forecasting services and watch their own customers to determine what is likely to be the next best-seller for their store. Forecasters also analyze store sales. Tracking the success of a specific style, color, or silhouette will give management an idea of what might potentially sell in the future. Electronic tracking is an easily accessible tool to statistically chart hot sellers. In addition to a store's own sales, the competition's sales may be a reference in forecasting future trends.

FORECASTING AND PROMOTION

Fashion forecasting and promotion are cyclical in nature. Fashion forecasters present upcoming trends to consumers through promotion channels. They review these same communication channels as resources to identify the next trend. Promotion is integral to this cycle.

Promotion as a Source

Promotion is the major communication tool used to inform consumers of the latest trends as shown in Table 6.1. If you doubt this statement, compare the September issue of any fashion magazine with any other monthly issue of the same publication. What do you see? A very large fashion handbook illustrating fall trends in clothing, accessories, makeup, entertainment, food, and home furnishings. Take a more in-depth look. The September issue will have more sponsors and more pages dedicated to advertising space than the other issue. Fashion forecasters, who have planned for this sell-

Table 6.1 **Source of Clothing Ideas for Women Ages 16 to 24**

Store display	60%
People seen regularly	43%
Fashion magazines	36%
Catalogs	31%
Commercials/ads	31%
Family members	24%
Salespeople	21%
Celebrities	19%

Adapted from: Lifestyle Monitor (1997, April 24).
A new source of fashion ideas? Women's Wear Daily, *p 2.*

ing season months and years in advance, are now dependent on promotion strategies to accurately communicate the season's trends to the consumer. All elements of the promotion mix are used to communicate trend messages to consumers.

Promotion as a Resource

Fashion forecasters are also dependent on promotion as a major resource to discover new and upcoming trends for future seasons. Editors look at the competition to see what they identified as the hottest trend of the moment. Publications outside of fashion are reviewed to identify cultural trends that cross product categories. Electronic media, covering the entire spectrum of attitudes and lifestyles, is constantly monitored for the discovery of the next new look in apparel, body adornment, body modification, and numerous other characteristics that define current culture.

Reading fashion publications is essential for anyone involved in forecasting. As one of the most readily accessible resources, they provide insight to the creative directions of fashion leaders. Creative fashion presentations, trade publications, newspapers, business magazines, foreign publications, consumer fashion publications, CD-ROMs, Internet sites, and other media provide valuable news about fabrics, styles, silhouettes, colors, and fads. Consumer publications interpret the fashion scene based on their readership. *Seventeen* will interpret a style to attract echo boomers. The same trend may presented on the cover of *Vogue* for a more sophisticated market. *Modern Maturity* may also highlight the trend, showing fashionable silver streakers wearing it.

There are numerous on-line sites that provide up-to-the-minute fashion news to assist forecasters in discovering trends. Figure 6.3 is an example of an on-line Internet site, *http://www.fgi.org,* that allows viewers to access The Fashion Group's trend reports and fashion forecasts. The Fashion Service offers fashion forecasters an interactive, computer-based CD-ROM called *Fashion Ink* that gives them immediate access to the runway shows of Paris haute couture, the New York and European ready-to-wear shows,

Figure 6.3

Forecasting information from The Fashion Group's website

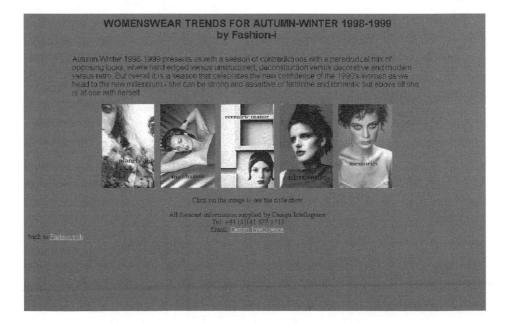

and latest street fashions. Because the CD-ROM is interactive, the viewer can jump to any point in the presentation at any time, to view colors, fabrics, and silhouettes.

But, how are trends introduced into the communication channel? In the next section we discuss the fashion industry market levels and explain the forecasting process from producer to consumer.

Research

Fashion forecasters must have a complete knowledge of the fashion industry and their consumers. They need to understand the distribution channel, structure, and timetable for each market. They must know the promotion strategies utilized by each market level to communicate to consumers. Each level of the distribution channel is responsible for communicating to the next level, and to consumers (Fig 6.4). Knowledge of the industry is gained through pure, applied, or action research. Previously we have discussed market research, used to gain insight about consumers in Chapter 2, and planning research to understand the strategic mission of a firm in Chapter 4.

Research is the investigation of a subject in order to understand it in a detailed, accurate manner. The purpose of research is to discover fresh information about the subject from history, science, literature, or other sources. Three types of research are used in the fashion industry: pure, applied, and action research. **Pure research**, also known as fundamental research, is scientific in nature and is conducted to find new knowledge about a subject. Textile companies use pure research to create new fibers and finishes. **Applied research** is the use of scientific methods to solve a problem that already exists. Apparel manufacturers use applied research to test sewn products to determine which is likely to fail first, the fabric or a stitched seam. **Action research** is a one-time study with a very narrow application. Forecasters use action research to learn about consumer wants and needs. A fashion count, used to determine the importance of a color or style, is an example of action research.

A **fashion count** is a research method used to survey what people are currently wearing. The fashion count is an organized plan of counting and classifying apparel

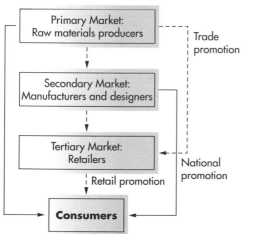

Figure 6.4

Fashion Distribution Channels

components. By counting components, a researcher can show the relative importance of different styles, colors, and fabrics worn by the specified group. Current fashion looks can be identified using a fashion count. Repeated at frequent intervals, a fashion count shows which styles, colors, or other trends are nearing the acceptance, maturity, or regression stages of the product life cycle. Fashion counts sum the components worn by consumers, or the number of times a component is featured in a fashion magazine.

The use of a fashion count is varied. For example, a Denver skiwear manufacturer was interested in forecasting style elements and color combinations for future skiwear. Forecasting teams were sent to three different Colorado ski resorts on the same weekend to take fashion counts of the skiwear being worn on the slopes. The three ski resorts were selected based on the different clientele each resort targeted. The first was a lower-price resort, frequented by the local skiing population and college students. The second resort was a mid-priced resort, visited by families for a ski holiday. The third resort was high priced, exclusive to celebrities and the wealthy. The manufacturer and research team determined the variables that were to be counted, and a tabulation sheet was formulated. The fashion count was taken, tabulated, and results returned to the manufacturer for evaluation. The three ski resorts provided quite different results based on their target customers. The manufacturer, who produced moderate-priced clothing, used the results from the high-priced resort to project what new apparel combinations and color combinations would trickle down to the mass market the following year. The manufacturer also determined what color combinations and apparel items were at the end of the product life cycle based on results from the lower price-pointed resort.

Gathering data on consumers' preferences is commonly called **market research**. Promotion executives depend on market research to determine market segments and properly position their brand to consumers. The demographic, behavioristic, and psychographic bases of segmentation, which we discussed in Chapter 2, are determined us-

Figure 6.5

Focus Group Flow Chart

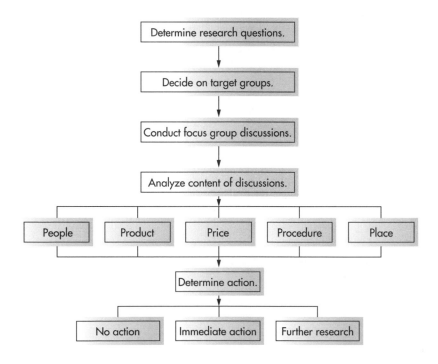

ing sophisticated market research. A market researcher does extensive analysis, documents facts, projects conclusions, and strives for a high degree of accuracy.

One method used to study customer likes and dislikes in the marketplace is through the **focus group**. This is a carefully planned discussion designed to obtain perceptions on a defined area of interest in a nonthreatening environment. Focus groups are commonly used to collect psychographic information from consumers, reflecting their true attitudes, opinions, and interests about the product or service in question.

Figure 6.5 is a flow chart illustrating the steps that a market researcher uses to conduct a focus group. Focus groups are generally composed of seven to ten participants who do not know one another. Participants are selected purposely, not randomly because of their common interest in the topic of the focus group. A moderator facilitates the focus group and creates an atmosphere that nurtures different perceptions and points of view without an intended bias (Krueger, 1988). Group members may influence each other by responding to ideas and comments in the discussion. Participants are not encouraged to reach consensus. The focus group is conducted several times with different participants to identify trends and patterns in perceptions. Careful and systematic analysis follow the focus group to determine how a product or service is perceived. For example, a retail store may ask local teens to participate in a focus group to identify trends for the junior market for the coming season.

FORECASTING FROM PRODUCER TO CONSUMER

As we have learned, fashion research takes place at all levels of the distribution channel. The **distribution channel** is the path through which goods are dispersed from raw material producers to retailers. Fiber companies, mills, converters, and yarn producers use research to develop new fibers, finishes, and construction methods. They research the use and care of products, along with color and design, in order to meet the needs of consumers. Designers research historical influences and important people, places, and events to determine future fashion direction. Apparel manufacturers use research to determine worldwide trends, fabrics and textures, colors, silhouettes and design details, and new products. Retailers use research to determine what products are selling and where buyers can source the goods; customer needs and wants; and elements of store operations, design, and security.

Each market in the distribution channel is responsible for forecasting trends to the next level. Adequate time must be allowed at each level to produce and promote goods. Figure 6.6 shows the forecast timeline and promotion schedule for the primary, secondary, and tertiary markets. Historically, retailers were the final link in the distribution channel directly responsible for selling to consumers. This is no longer true. Firms from all distribution channels have the opportunity to sell directly to the consumer on a national or global level.

Primary Market Forecasts

Primary market producers are the earliest market to project upcoming trends. The **primary market** is composed of raw material producers who sell to the secondary market, manufacturers and designers. They work 12 to 24 months in advance of the season to project color forecasts, fiber selection, and fabrication processes. Projections

		January	February	March	April	May	June
Primary Market Fibers, fabrics, and color	Color forecast	Color forecast presented 18 to 24 months in advance of the retail season.					
	Fiber and fabric forecast	Fiber and fabric forecasts researched 12 to 24 months in advance of the retail season.					
	Fabric presentation						Present Spring fabrics
Secondary Market Manufacturing	European market	Spring Haute Couture		Fall prêt-à-porter	Fall ready-to-wear		Resort
	Fashion shows	European		European	American		St. Tropez
	American market	Prepare Fall I		Show Fall I			Prepare resort and holiday
	Trade publication coverage	Show Summer	Prepare Fall II			Show Fall II	
Tertiary Market Retail Promotion	In-store merchandise		Spring				Fall I
		Resort			Summer		
	Special promotions	New Year's Clearance	Presidents' Day	Spring break Easter	Easter	Cinco de Mayo Mother's Day Memorial Day	Father's Day Weddings

Figure 6.6

Forecast timeline and promotion schedule for the primary, secondary, and tertiary markets.

Adapted from: Perna, R. (1987). Fashion forecasting. *New York: Fairchild.*

by primary market producers are unveiled to the secondary market manufacturers approximately 1 year in advance of the selling season. Projections made by primary market producers are not seen by the tertiary market, retailers, until buyers make selections at market, approximately 6 to 8 months in advance of the selling season. The general public is not made aware of the apparent trend until goods are available for sale in stores or catalogs.

Color

Fashion projections in the primary market begin with color, the first element that catches the eye of the consumer. Color forecasts are made the farthest in advance of the intended selling season, from 18 to 24 months. Color forecasts are projected using color stories. A **color story** is a collection of fashion, staple, warm, cool, neutral, and dark

		July	August	September	October	November	December
Primary Market Fibers, fabrics, and color	Color forecast	Color forecast presented 18 to 24 months in advance of the retail season.					
	Fiber and fabric forecast	Fiber and fabric forecasts researched 12 to 24 months in advance of the retail season.					
	Fabric presentation	Present Spring fabrics		Present Fall fabrics			
Secondary Market Manufacturing	European market	Fall haute couture		Spring prêt-à-porter	Spring ready-to-wear		
	Fashion shows	European		European	American		
	American market	Prepare resort and holiday	Show resort and holiday				
	Trade publication coverage	Show Summer	Prepare Spring		Show Spring		Prepare Summer
Tertiary Market Retail Promotion	In-store merchandise	Fall I			Holiday		
				Fall II	Resort		
	Special promotions	4th of July Clearance Sidewalk sale	Back to school	Labor Day	Columbus Day	Thanksgiving Hanukkah	Christmas Hanukkah

(Figure 6.6 continued)

colors, coordinated for the upcoming season, and different from the last season (Tate, 1989). A color story is used to introduce accurate values and intensities of color. For example, in one season, the neutral, off-white, may be darkened slightly and called natural, jute, sand, or stone. In another season, to make the color story different from the past season, off-white may have yellow added to it, and it becomes ivory, light sage, or cream. In one season, green may be a staple color like hunter, forest, or kelly, and in the next season it is a fashion color such as military, moss, sage, or pistachio. Fire engine red may imply a warm red for one season, followed by berry, a cool red, the following year.

Color forecasters develop descriptive names for the color story based on consumer trends. The descriptive names become tools to assist promotion staffs in creating the correct message to send to the consumer. In a season when environmental trends are influencing consumers, colors may be expressed as vegetable names, such as tomato, eggplant, and zucchini. In another season, green, purple, and red may be called emerald, amethyst, and garnet, reflecting a strong economy and the willingness of consumers to spend money on luxurious jewels. Descriptive words are used to highlight the warmth or coolness, brilliance, or dullness of a color. Even black, which has less variation than other hues, may be described as midnight in promotion materials and catalogs. The color story is also used to illustrate how the color might be used in fabrication. Hunter green may be represented in heavy flannel or wool fabrics, while moss green may be used to describe sheer, blouse-weight fabrics.

Color forecasting services distribute color forecasts to fiber, fabric, and apparel producer members. Internationally known color forecasting services include Intercolor, and the International Color Authority (ICA). Representatives from the fashion industry make up each of these organizations, meeting twice a year to determine specific color palettes for targeted retail seasons 2 years into the future. Intercolor representatives analyze the color cycle, looking at the natural evolution of color preferences. The International Color Authority establishes color predictions for fiber, fabric, and yarn producers and sends selected color palettes to members approximately 6 months after the meeting.

The Color Association of the United States (CAUS) is the chief domestic organization responsible for determining color forecasts for the apparel and home furnishings industry. The Color Association is a nonprofit organization made up of industry executive volunteers who evaluate everything from politics to societal issues to the economy to culture and the arts to determine the color climate of the country. Members pay dues to receive annual color forecasts represented by swatch cards that forecast colors for the coming 18 to 24 months. Over 700 companies are members of the organization, encompassing automobiles, home appliances, sporting goods, fashion products, and many other industries. CAUS archives contain individual forecasts and decade volumes dating back to 1915.

Pantone is a leading developer and marketer of products for the accurate communication of color in a variety of industries, including textiles. Pantone develops color communication tools, such as color swatch books, which can be used by professionals to standardize colors across vendors to insure accurate color matching of textiles, buttons, trim, zippers, and other component parts of fashion goods. Gretag Macbeth, the producer of the Munsell Color System, is also a color forecasting resource.

Fibers

Fashion projections in the primary market continue with fibers. Fiber forecasts are made 12 to 24 months in advance of the retail selling season. Primary market producers rely on fiber manufacturers, fiber trade associations, industry fairs, and trade shows for fiber forecasts. Fibers are categorized into natural and synthetic fibers. Synthetic fibers are generally produced by giant chemical companies, such as Du Pont. Synthetic fiber producers have always heavily promoted their products to the fashion industry and consumers. Promotion includes instruction of fabric manufacturers in how to process synthetic fibers into fabrics, creation of demand for synthetic textiles among garment and home furnishings manufacturers, and promotion of the benefits of synthetic fibers to the general public, creating consumer demand for synthetic fibers.

Both synthetic and natural fiber companies must be able to respond rapidly to consumer preferences for texture, color, weight, luster, care requirements, and other characteristics created at the raw material stage of production. The growth of the synthetic market has forced natural fiber producers to promote their products aggressively within the fashion industry.

Natural fiber trade associations are the promotion outlet used to forecast fiber trends to the fashion industry and consumers. Almost every natural fiber has a trade association made up of ranchers, fiber processors, and business and marketing professionals. Two strong trade associations include Cotton Incorporated and the American Wool Council. Each season, Cotton Incorporated forecasts colors, trends, fabrics, and silhouettes focusing on cotton as a fashion leader. It produces a fabric library called THE COTTONWORKS, tracking trends through 10,000 manufacturers, retailers, and designers who utilize the library. The American Wool Council produces a yarn library through its trend forecast service called the Wool Room. New fabrics are as important to apparel designers as the fibers they are made from.

Fabrics

Fabric manufacturers are a large segment of the primary market. As early as 2 years prior to a market season, textile producers create color stories and sketches of the important fashion trends. They suggest fabrics that will best interpret the projected season's fashion directions. For example, a seasonal trend may be chenille and other fabrics made from nubby, loopy yarns. Nubby, loopy yarns are most likely produced with staple length fibers. Fiber producers and knit fabric producers must forecast trends cooperatively to ensure the correct fiber length is produced for the projected fabric.

Textile collections are a source of inspiration for designers. They review past textiles to project future trends in fabrics. One such collection is at the museum of the Fashion Institute of Technology. The collection consists of 1,300 sample books and over 250,000 indexed swatches and larger textiles, dating back to the 19th century. To protect the swatches from wear and tear, the museum has put the collection on a series of CD-ROMs. The images have been arranged by themes and are cross-referenced so that one piece can be placed into as many categories as are appropriate. The images can also be downloaded into design software for use by textile designers in creating new patterns (Holch, 1996).

Fabric manufacturers show the latest trends in textiles at trade fairs such as the International Fashion Fabric Exhibition (IFFE). The IFFE, held in New York City, allows textile, trimming, and computer-aided design/computer-aided manufacturing (CAD/CAM) manufacturers, and fashion services to introduce the trends they have been creating over the previous 12 months. Apparel manufacturers, the secondary market, purchase the goods to create the next season's fashion line. Figure 6.7 shows designers reviewing fabric samples at a trade fair.

Secondary Market Forecasts

The **secondary market** refers to manufacturers, the distribution channel member between the primary market (raw material producers) and the tertiary market (retailers). Manufacturers are responsible for creating fashions using the forecasted colors and fabrics delivered by the primary market. Manufacturers produce items 6 to 12 months in advance of the selling season. They present the designed goods to retail buyers 4 to 6 months in advance of expected delivery. Manufacturers present a line that balances new fashion items with successful basic styles from the previous season. The collection must be worthy of promotion by the retailers who are going to invest in the look. There is a fine line for manufacturers between *playing it safe*, offering merchandise that is only slightly updated from the previous season and therefore less attractive in promotions,

Figure 6.7

Designers at a trade fair

and *going out on a limb,* offering merchandise that is so trendy it allows for exciting promotions but is likely to attract only a few consumers. Box 6.1 describes how hosiery manufacturer sales representatives introduce new trends to retailers using trend boards.

International Trade Shows

Forecast information sources at the secondary market level include international and domestic markets. Internationally, the fashion leader is France, introducing new haute couture fashions in Paris each spring and fall, usually before shows in any other fashion center. While Paris remains the most significant international city for haute couture fashion, Milan has superseded the Paris shows in recent years, with a more businesslike atmosphere and less panache and glitz surrounding the shows. Spring haute couture shows begin in January and include design houses such as Valentino, Saint Laurent, Lacroix, Versace, Dior, Balmain, and Ungaro. Fashion shows in London and Tokyo follow traditionally before the trends are presented on New York runways. As a result of the Paris shows, the same fabrication, silhouette, or color palette may be seen in New York, London, Paris, or Mexico City retail establishments. The cycle repeats itself in July, with showing of Fall haute couture merchandise.

Closely following the haute couture fashion shows, many designers, reveal their prêt-à-porter lines for international markets, or ready-to-wear lines for American markets (Fig. 6.8). These collections often reflect the same trends in more commercial price ranges. The prêt-à-porter shows attract the fashion press, who present the trends in industry and consumer publications such as *Women's Wear Daily, Bazaar, Vogue,* and newspapers, acknowledging their praise or disgust of the latest rage. *Allure* magazine publishes a special edition to cover the looks introduced at the runway shows. These major apparel markets attract international buyers, who identify the upcoming trends and distribute the styles in retail establishments throughout the world, testing potentially successful styles that were first noticed at the haute couture shows. It is not uncommon to

BOX 6.1
Trend Boards Make Everything Click

NEW YORK—Trend boards used to look like collages pasted together by teenage girls. But they have grown up. The seasonal image presentations have now become a key sales tool for many legwear vendors, especially those who specialize in casual looks.

Makers are trying to portray a more avant-garde image with edgy photos from hip magazines like *The Face, Arena, Loaded,* and *Paper.* The growing importance of the junior market—an area that is unfamiliar to many buyers—has prompted some vendors to explain it to them.

For its licensed Kenneth Cole Reaction line, DML Marketing spelled out its younger customers' interests—home, news, music, rituals, jobs, entertainment, food, spiritualism, and adventure—and used photos to illustrate them. Images of sushi, surfers, beer bottles, *South Park* characters, and rainbow color condoms were used to illustrate their varied interests.

"Trend boards are absolutely more important than they used to be," said Barbara Russillo, President of DML Marketing, which also makes Legale legwear. "It is really important to show buyers how the legwear works back into the ready-to-wear and sportswear that they carry in their stores. Stores need to be more focused on the major trends that are happening. When they see the boards, it all clicks."

While showing a store spring offerings, Russillo said the buyer balked at the henna-inspired looks. "When she said, 'Who is going to wear dragonfly prints?' and I reached back for my trend board and showed her photos of all the dragonfly stuff in the junior market," Russillo said, "then she understood."

Defining trends also helps retailers to be more concise with their merchandising, Russillo said. During market week, DML outlined everyday casual, career casual, and chino casual. By gaining a clearer understanding of the various casual options, retailers in turn can make shopping easier for their customers.

Hanes Hosiery has boards for colors, others for trends and, for the first time, ones for images of in-store displays. The company no longer pins socks to its boards—opting to show buyers bins of the actual products, said Deborah Boria, executive director of design and merchandising. "It makes buying the line easier. It helps them understand how their category relates to the realm of fashion," she said. "It gives them more confidence about why they buy what they did."

Having three different boards is particularly effective for its licensed Donna Karan legwear, since it helped to highlight the designer's focus for the season, Boria said. For its Hue legwear, Kayser-Roth Corporation is placing more fashion photos on its trend boards. Images pulled from British fashion magazines and, to a lesser degree, French publications are particularly popular.

"It is exciting for us because the whole market has not been that great," said Dana Feldman, design assistant. "It helps the stores to see the product in a different way, and that will help business." For example, showing stores shots of women wearing sportswear in spring colors encourages stores to buy legwear in similar hues. "The boards give vision to someone who might not have a lot of imagination," she said. "If a product is presented in its context, it is much more appealing than if it were on a hanger."

Unlike some of its competitors, Hue designers do not always piece together trend boards before they design a line. But, they always create color boards to show the season's direction. Using trend boards has been "a great selling tool" for Royce hosiery's licensed Nine West legwear, which was launched in 1997, said Pat McNellis, president. "It is a good way to introduce an account to the line," McNellis said. "It is a good way to see if our trends match their trends."

European trips, yarn fairs, and a dozen American, British, and French magazines are the primary sources of inspiration for the trend boards, according to Karina Dolgin, vice president of product development and design for Royce.

Royce's designers start working on trend boards 6 to 9 months before market. Before they get to work, Dolgin advises, "Imagine you are walking around with a big funnel on your head. Let everything fall in and then we will sort it out. This cannot go on all season, but it is a good start."

In the early stages, they post on corkboards photos from fashion magazines or snapshots of window displays of small European boutiques they visited. The finished product generally consists of four or five boards.

The responses from Royce's sales force and retail accounts are taken into account. After receiving a tepid response from a handful of retailers for its "Blue Lagoon" trend board, Nine West legwear decided to hold the group for fall, McNellis said.

Knowing some retailers want to know Hot Sox's direction weeks before market, the company provides certain sales reps with color photographs of its trend boards. "Not everyone is very visual. If we just lay the socks out and tell them, 'This is the theme,' they might not get it," said Susan Marchand, design director. "The visuals help buyers buy appropriately for each delivery, so it shows cohesiveness, and consumers will not get confused."

Each season The Hot Sox Company centers on four themes in its trend boards. A spring collection for example may have the key points of Cross Cultures, portrayed in intricate prints; Blooming—florals and other novelties; Metro, comprising sleeker styles; and Street Sports in athletic stripes. Each board has up to five photos and five to twelve socks. Until 2 years ago, Hot Sox designers used to sew quilts of fabric, photos, and embellishments to post on trend boards. To convey lingerie looks, for example, six or seven bras and corsets were sewn together. Unlike the current format, which takes a few hours, the quilts required a couple of days of sewing.

"It was so time consuming it is easier for our customers to get real information than a piece of art."

Marchand said. "We found references to actual fashion trends easier to digest."

Knowing some retailers reference their own trend reports and color palettes during legwear presentations, Jockey has redesigned its boards to convey a more unified presentation. The company has combined its trend and color boards and reduced the number of images on them because collages were too confusing for buyers, said Susan Williams, vice president and general merchandise manager for women's hosiery. Those presentations are now three-dimensional. Color patches, for example, might be mounted on a square of cardboard and then placed on the board to make it more interesting.

Adapted from: Feitelberg, R. (1998, August 17). Trend boards make everything click. Women's Wear Daily, 10, 22.

Figure 6.8

Advertisement for Paris
Prêt-à-porter trade show

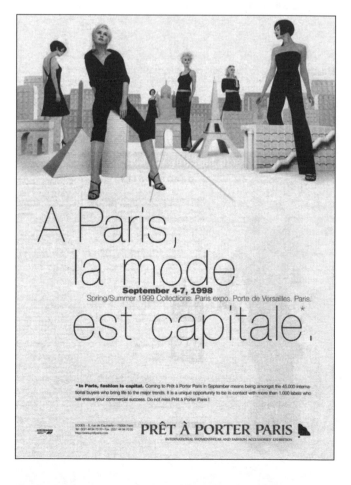

have nearly 1,000 exhibitors representing over 25 countries and hosting over 50,000 buyers at the Paris prêt-à-porter show held each September and March. Explaining the reason for attending the Paris prêt-à-porter show one vendor stated, "In the U.S., American companies can only go after a bigger slice of the same pie. But here in Europe it's a brand new market. American companies can compete on price and styling" (Weisman, 1996).

Domestic Trade Shows

Seventh Avenue in New York City is the center of the fashion industry for domestic manufacturers. Markets are generally categorized by the price points of goods sold: low-end, moderate, better, bridge, and designer. Forecasters cover the New York market along with regional and international markets. Major trade shows occur semiannually in New York—7th on Sixth, Fashion Coterie, In-Style Works, New York Premier Collections, and Showroom—presenting trends to specialty store buyers from around the country. Fashion Coterie features designer, contemporary, and bridge apparel; New York Premier Collections features classics; and Showroom features casual apparel.

Seventh on Sixth is a designer ready-to-wear show held at Bryant Park, usually timed to immediately follow the European shows. In an effort to gain more attention and revenues from retailers, who routinely view European shows first, some designers, including Helmut Lang and Calvin Klein, have begun showing their lines in New York 2 weeks prior to the 7th on Sixth market week. These shows are creating two fashion weeks in New York and pre-empting the European shows. American designers are in favor of this move because it strengthens their image as trend setters. They have been considered followers of European trends since the 1950s (White, 1998a).

In-Style Works is a New York-based trade show held in September and February featuring the collections of young designers and new designers in the bridge and contemporary sportswear and accessories market. To accompany the trade show, In-Style Works also offers a collection of services to benefit exhibitors and buyers, including a website at *http://www.StyleWorks.com;* vendor catalogs and line sheets featuring digital photographs that retailers can take with them; fashion trend presentations; and a customized beauty program that vendors can offer to accounts. At its website, In-Style Works promotes each exhibitor by presenting four looks from each vendor, information about the resource, and a salesperson the viewer can contact.

Regional markets offer market weeks and information sources for upcoming trends. New York is still the center of attention for designer and bridge merchandise but regional marts, including Dallas (Fig. 6.9), have become the focus for swimwear, dresses, and accessories bought outside of New York. Each regional market has its own specific influences, which are represented through its merchandise lines. Regional marts include San Francisco, Los Angeles, Atlanta, Dallas, Las Vegas, and Chicago, among others, which feature smaller, more specific shows in a location more convenient and economical for smaller retailers.

Tertiary Market Forecasts

The **tertiary market** refers to retailers, who are responsible for communicating trends, developed previously by primary and secondary producers, to consumers. Based on information about their customers, retailers forecast what the best-selling items will be for their stores in the upcoming season. Each retailer will interpret trends in a slightly different way to match the brand position of its organization. Buyers for retail stores

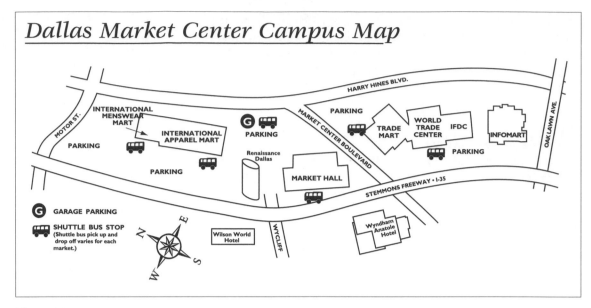

Figure 6.9

The Dallas Market Center

view fashions 4 to 6 months in advance of the expected delivery and make their forecasts. Buyers whose primary customers are fashion innovators will expect very early delivery of goods prior to the start of the selling season. They will make their forecasts based on expected sales. Buyers purchasing goods for the fashion majority will purchase items closer to the selling season and make forecasts based on tested trends from the fashion innovators.

Retailers make their forecasts based on merchandise previewed at market weeks, and buying trips to designer showrooms. They also base forecasts on advice from resident buying offices.

Resident Buying Offices

Resident buying offices, once primarily used to bring buyers and manufacturers together, have expanded their services into forecasting (Diamond and Diamond, 1997). The increase in private label merchandise by retailers has caused the growth in resident buying office services. Resident buying offices are located in major manufacturing locations such as New York, Dallas, and Los Angeles, and their personnel have knowledge about supply conditions. Resident buying offices provide varied information, including availability of products; reliability of suppliers; present and future supply trends; and special deals, prices, promotions, and services offered by suppliers (Lewison, 1997).

Retailers depend on resident buying offices to assist in determining trends. At the end of the 20th century, Doneger Design Group, based in New York, is the world's largest privately owned resident buying office ("Style," 1997). It is one example of a resident buying office that provides forecasting services. Its forecasting division is called D^3 Doneger Design Direction and its approach, similar to that of other forecasting services, is highlighted in Box 6.2. A fashion trend portfolio from this company was shown in Figure 6.4. The company provides the following promotion-based materials in the trend portfolio, as part of its services to clients:

- **Color forecasts** presented in palette format to show color stories, illustrated with photographs, color swatches, and yarn samples.
- **Fashion trend forecasts** published as books illustrated with photographs, yarn color samples, and fabric swatches.
- **Newsletters** covering designer shows, trade fairs, hot trends seen in global fashion centers, and merchandising and display concepts.
- **Slide libraries** of international designer collections available for research and duplication as slides or prints.
- **Workbooks** filled with photographs, and sketches depicting key colors, fabrics silhouettes, and design details.

Each forecasting service provides information in a slightly different presentation format to distinguish its image from that of the competition. Color forecasters, fiber producers, designers and manufacturers, resident buying offices, and retailers creatively package their forecasts around themes to communicate trends to their customers.

BOX 6.2

Style Gazing: How a Fashion Forecasting Service Looks into the Future

President Abbey Doneger created D³ Doneger Design Direction in the early 1990s to provide a more commercial, versus fantasy, approach to fashion forecasting. As a resident buying office, her company is rooted in the reality of retailing, and therefore is highly sensitive to shifts in buying and selling patterns. It is able to factor in business reality with the creativity of fashion.

How does D³ forecast fashion's future? It starts with color. Color is the starting point of any season. Separate ranges are developed for women's wear, menswear, and children's wear. The colors are targeted to the season, meticulously dyed and re-dyed to meet exact specifications. Colorists travel to the world's fashion capitals, attending fashion shows and trade fairs. They also research carefully the colors that are currently selling. Once colors are selected, then the fabrics and designs quickly follow. An amazing amount of information is accumulated by the creative team in order to project fashion forward. David Wolfe, Creative Director of D³ is oft-quoted as saying, "Fashion is the result of many forces, a fascinating mix of style, economics, history, politics, weather, science, sex, and a sense of humor." Firsthand observations are important, so staffers travel to Paris, London, and Milan; to South Beach, Los Angeles, the French Rivera, and less "chic" destinations like suburban malls. They are constantly on the alert, trend-spotting on the streets, in stores, restaurants, and theaters, and attending concerts and films as well as scouting nightclubs.

On their regular reading list is everything from general news magazines to specialized publications like *Women's Wear Daily* and even the *National Inquirer*. The Internet is fast becoming a hot source of information. Even watching TV is considered a vital activity, another way to check how the public pulse is coursing.

Wolfe assimilates all the different aspects, and with his team analyzes the information and creates trends that become the basis of a series of booklets, slide presentations, and newsletters. Gae Marine, vice president of fashion marketing states, "The published products are 50 percent of what our clients buy . . . the other 50 percent is a relationship." That client relationship is nurtured through frequent slide shows and special one-on-one meetings where information is tailored specifically to various clients' own business needs. Answering clients' needs has put the company into another arena, that of special projects that range from conducting consumer surveys to creating websites.

According to Wolfe and Marino of D³, fashion trends today are not what they were in the 1970s when everyone wanted to dress like a gypsy one season and an Indian princess the next. Their approach to trends is all about the big changes that really will affect everybody, whether it's a color or a societal change.

Adapted from: Style gazing: How a fashion forecasting service looks into the future. (1997, February). The Magic Guide *[Show guide.] MAGIC International, 6200 Canoga Ave., Suite 303, Woodland Hills, CA 91367.*

Buying Trips

Buyers return from buying trips filled to the brim with potential new trends, so they must sift through to determine what is right for their organization. After reviewing notes, slides, videos, and other materials, buyers identify trends—fashions and fads—that they will invest in for the coming season. Buyers have the opportunity to support or weaken a fashion look through their power to place orders. They may place small or large orders, or no orders at all, if they determine the look will not work for their store's retail position. After reviewing all possible sources, the anticipated forecast is presented to top management and marketing and promotion departments of the organization so they may begin to design themes and other creative elements that must accompany the merchandise within the store.

THEME DEVELOPMENT

To test their projected forecasts, retailers bring merchandise into their stores 2 or 3 months ahead of the anticipated season. Fall merchandise will appear in stores in June and July, spring merchandise will appear in stores in January. Retailers use themes to communicate messages about the new merchandise to consumers. A **theme** is the re-occurring idea that is seen in color, silhouette, fabric, and other design components. The theme may be based on style, economics, history, politics, weather, science, humor, or some other aspect of society. Box 11.1, later in this book, shows how sales promotion products are selected around a theme. As we discussed in Chapter 4, the themes are planned on a fashion theme calendar. Manufacturers also use themes to create a feeling about merchandise presented to buyers. When organizing a line, designers coordinate groups of styles so that the styles reflect a theme (Tate, 1989). The three vignettes at the beginning of this chapter describe promotional themes designers hoped would be attractive to consumers for that selling season.

Each season, themes are prevalent in all merchandise categories: women's, men's and children's apparel, soft goods, and home furnishings. These themes are promotional tools used to create moods and prepare consumers for what they will see in the marketplace.

Retailers and manufacturers have the opportunity to position their brand as different from their competitors by developing promotional themes. Themes help the firm create a look and image that can be carried through advertising, signage, visual merchandising, fashion shows, and other special events, helping to build brand reputation. In developing a theme, many retailers piggyback themes created by manufacturers or designers. Designer fabric and color stories present themes that are easy for a retailer to adapt in presenting their own merchandise. Shared themes may be part of a co-marketing effort by producers and retailers to increase the brand awareness of a product. As discussed in Chapter 4, both sponsors may use the same theme in advertisements, displays, or at special events.

Themes should be creative and imaginative to strengthen advertising messages and promotions. Themes should influence consumers to buy. Ideas for themes should be current and timely. *The Colors of Summer* leads into such themes as *In the Pink, Country Road Red, Summertime Blues,* or *Naturally Neutral.*

In a retail environment, themes may be created for a single department or as a storewide event. In a manufactured line, themes may be specific to merchandise categories such as women's or men's, or designed around a fabric and carried across all cat-

Table 6.2 **12-Month Color Themes**

Timing	Theme Name	Colors Presented
January	*Dawn*	Next-to-nothing nudes
February	*Day Break*	Pale tints
March/April	*Day Light*	Whitening tones
May/June	*Sun Up*	Clear brights
July	*High Noon*	Neon brights
August/September	*Dusk*	Spice tones
October/November	*Deep Darks*	Deep darks
December	*Twilight*	Rich hues

egories, such as the use of gray flannel. A theme may be short, lasting several weeks, or longer, lasting through an entire season or a year, depending on the promotion strategy of the retailer. Table 6.2 is an example of a color theme moving from neutral winter colors to bright summer colors to darker fall colors. The theme is presented over 12 months, but updated every 2 months to look new to the customer. Retail and/or manufacturing themes may be categorized in any of the following ways:

- **Storewide theme.** A storewide fashion theme involves a broad focus to be used throughout the entire store, including all apparel and home furnishing departments. For example, a *Sophisticated Safari* theme may be featured in apparel departments for men, women, and children, incorporating khaki safari jackets with trousers, skirts, or shorts. The accessory department may add safari hats, knapsacks, totebags, and sunglasses. The home store would contribute wicker picnic baskets, travel coolers, and linens. The furniture department would be decorated with wicker, earth tone sheets, mosquito netting, and plants. Virtually every department may contribute some article to the extensive theme.

- **Color theme.** Trends relating to color offer endless suggestions for themes. March brings to mind green for Saint Patrick's Day and the start of spring. Pastel colors frequently replace the darker colors of winter so retailers present a pastel color story around the Easter holiday. Fashion statements such as astro-brights or vegetable colors may be trend features. The theme may apply to ready-to-wear, cosmetics, accessories only, or may be extended over all product categories. For example *Holiday Jewels* may show bright ruby red, emerald green, and sapphire blue in the ready-to-wear, intimate apparel, and costume jewelry departments.

- **Fabric theme.** A fabric theme is based upon the popular fabric of a given season. A fabric theme may be created in one specific department or by a specific designer. Juniors might feature *Work Out*, with stretch fabrics that cling to the body. Men's apparel might stress *The Naturals*, with natural fibers of cotton or linen in neutral shades. Cashmere sweaters may be the item of choice in *Sweater Weather*.

- **Lifestyle theme.** Meeting the needs of a particular focus group of consumers involves a lifestyle theme. The trend for physical fitness has led to seminars with sports figures and trend shops with leotards, tights, and workout equipment located in one spot. Another popular lifestyle theme shows working women what to wear for business activities. *Women Incorporated* may feature seminars on money matters or balancing home and work needs, as well as on appropriate fashions for work.

- **Special occasions.** The special occasion theme emphasizes clothing and other items related to unusual or traditional events. One of the most popular special event occasion themes combines all of the elements required for a wedding. From selection of the bridal gown to the caterer, this event requires more planning than the average consumer is used to arranging. The photographer, music, attendant and parent apparel, household items, and more are all under consideration. *An Affair to Remember* bridal event brings together all of the components necessary to plan a wedding and start a new life as a couple. Other popular special occasions include baby showers, back-to-school, and holidays.

The fashion story presentation, including a theme, should be reflected throughout the entire promotion mix. The forecast checklist below includes trend resources, trend

Forecast Checklist

Resources to Investigate for Trend Ideas
- ❐ Primary market (color, fibers, fabrics)
- ❐ Secondary market (global and domestic markets)
- ❐ Tertiary market (buying trips and resident buying offices)
- ❐ Previous sales figures
- ❐ Competition
- ❐ Market research about consumers (demographic, psychographic, behavioristic)
- ❐ Fashion publications
- ❐ Forecast services
- ❐ Influences from society, media, arts, music, the Internet
- ❐ Other industries
- ❐ Observations of others
- ❐ Your intuition

Elements of a Trend
- ❐ Influence
- ❐ Silhouette
- ❐ Fabrication
- ❐ Pattern or texture
- ❐ Color story
- ❐ Descriptive color names
- ❐ Details or trim
- ❐ Promotional theme

Trend Presentation through the Promotional Mix
- ❐ Advertising
- ❐ Direct marketing
- ❐ Sales promotion
- ❐ Publicity and public relations
- ❐ Personal sales
- ❐ Special events
- ❐ Fashion shows
- ❐ Visual merchandising

elements, and how the trend is presented through the various promotion mix components. As a primary element of the promotion mix, advertising should document the latest trend in print media, including newspaper, magazine, and direct-response campaigns. A store with in-store video-wall capabilities should highlight the trend through broadcast video clips aimed at a specific market segment. Themes for seasonal events and fashion shows should indicate the trend using lighting, music, and props that accent the trend on the runway. Sales personnel should be thoroughly knowledgeable about the trend and illustrate appropriate trend influences to prospective customers. Packaging and gift-with-purchase displays should feature the trend. Publicity for the vendor should always have the trend depicted formally or informally to the media and consumers. Visual merchandising displays throughout a store should have the trend featured prominently to every customer who walks into the department.

FUTURE TRENDS FOR FORECASTING AND PROMOTION

At the turn of the 21st century, three distinct societal trends are merging that will have a long term impact on marketing and promotions, according to Peter Judy (1996), vice president at MHW Advertising and Public Relations, in Cleveland, Ohio:

1. **Society is in a perpetual state of change.** Consumers are no longer merely modifying tastes but rather are transforming their value systems, resulting in changes in behavior and purchasing habits.
2. **Technology has made society more interactive and informed.** The availability of multimedia has conditioned consumers to desire more data and expect direct interaction with companies before purchasing products.
3. **Media are becoming increasingly integrated.** Advertising messages and editorial messages are becoming less distinct to the consumer. Media giants are emerging as vehicles that deliver news and entertainment; they are buying alternative sources such as Internet companies that create news and entertainment. Media messages are present everywhere in the form of logos.

How will the merging of societal changes, technology, and media affect marketing? Judy (1996) suggested the following insights, which remain applicable today for marketing and promotion specialists. Manufacturers and retailers will need to:

- Continue to differentiate through brand positioning.
- Recognize the competition, no matter where it comes from.
- Identify changing channels of distribution.
- Know the changing values of consumers and be ready to react to these changes.
- Include interactive communication as a continuing part of a marketing strategy.
- Be cognizant of the consumer's desire for information.
- Be prepared to respond electronically to any news that can affect their company's reputation.

Trends do not appear out of thin air. As we have seen in this chapter, they are changes brought on by consumer preferences and behavior. The development of a trend forecast is based on knowledge of consumers, brand positioning, and industry resources. A fashion forecast for the primary, secondary, or tertiary levels reflects up-to-the-minute fashion trends grounded in research. Using forecast research techniques, the fashion forecaster identifies information about fashion trends directed at the firm's selected target market. Data is collected on the important fabrics, colors, textures, and patterns and combined with information on the latest silhouettes and accessories. Societal and cultural concerns of the season are blended into the forecast, and together with the promotion team, forecasters determine the company's fashion story, which leads to the promotion strategy for the coming season.

SUMMARY

- Forecasting is the activity of projecting trends.
- A fashion trend may be a color, a fabric, or a style characteristic apparent for the coming season.
- A major trend is based on well-researched market information, has high sales volume potential, and test markets with positive results against direct competition.
- Trends emerge from society, culture, designers, raw material vendors, publicity, and consumers.
- There are professional futurists and fashion forecasters, and professionals who forecast as a responsibility of their job.
- Fashion forecasters work for fashion forecasting services or forecasting divisions within retail, manufacturing, or advertising firms.
- Forecasters present upcoming trends to consumers through promotion channels and review these same communication channels as resources to identify the next trend.
- The forecaster must have a complete knowledge of the primary, secondary, and tertiary markets.
- Each market in the distribution channel is responsible for forecasting trends to the next level.
- Central to the promotional strategy is the theme.
- Forecasters use every source available to research and predict trends.
- Forecasting services are available to clients wishing to buy commercially produced information on trend projections.
- Trends should be reflected throughout the entire promotional mix.

KEY TERMS

action research	fashion trend	primary market
applied research	fashion trend portfolio	pure research
classic	focus group	research
color story	ford	secondary market
distribution channel	forecaster	tertiary market
fad	forecasting	theme
fashion count	futurists	trend
fashion forecaster	market research	

QUESTIONS FOR DISCUSSION

1. What are the similarities and differences between futurists, fashion forecasters, and forecasters?
2. How is forecasting influenced by promotion?
3. How is promotion influenced by forecasting?

4. What distribution channel do consumers rely on for fashion forecast information?
5. What is the importance of a theme to the promotion strategy of a manufacturer? A retailer?

ADDITIONAL RESOURCES

Hanke, J. and Reitsch, A. (1998). *Business forecasting.* Upper Saddle River, NJ: Prentice-Hall.

Meehan, M., Samuel, L., and Abrahamson, V. (1998). *The future ain't what it used to be.* New York: Riverhead Books.

Perna, R. (1987). *Fashion forecasting.* New York: Fairchild.

Popcorn, F. (1992). *The Popcorn report.* New York: Harperbusiness.

Popcorn, F., and Marigold, L. (1998). *Clicking: 17 trends that drive your business and your life.* New York: Harperbusiness.

Tain, L. (1998). *Portfolio presentation for fashion designers.* New York: Fairchild.

Underhill, P. (1999). *Why we buy.* New York: Simon & Schuster.

Wheelright, S., Hyndman, R., and Makridakis, S. (1997*). Forecasting: Methods and applications.* New York: Wiley.

Promotion Mix

Figure 7.1

Tommy Hilfiger launched his line of fragrances and better women's apparel with these ads in 1996.

chapter 7

ADVERTISING AND
THE CREATIVE PROCESS

Advertising is very expensive. Besides all of the creative production costs, there are media placement expenses. Tommy Hilfiger (Fig. 7.1) had a budget of $25 million to launch his line of women's better apparel and fragrances in 1996, while Ralph Lauren and its licensees spent more than $130 million in fiscal 1997 to promote and advertise the company's brands worldwide (Lockwood, 1997b). The *Super Bowl*, the American football championship game, has perhaps the most expensive advertising placement costs. In 1998, 33 companies paid a record $1.3 million for each 30-second commercial (Elliott, 1998b).

Is it really worth all of the time and money it takes to plan and implement an advertising campaign? "Advertising can be effective when it's done right, when it's done creatively, and when it's presented in the right media. But it depends on what you want to get out of it," according to David Bender, president and chief operating officer for Mediamark Research Incorporated (Waldrop, 1994).

This chapter on advertising begins Part III of the text, which focuses on each promotion mix technique in detail. Advertising, one of the most widely used promotion techniques is so broad that we devote three chapters to it. After introducing advertising and the creative process in this chapter, Chapter 8 considers advertising media in general as well as specific print media. Then, Chapter 9 expands our knowledge of advertising by examining broadcast media. Other promotion mix techniques that will be discussed in Part III of this text are direct marketing, sales promotion, publicity and public relations, personal selling, special events, fashion shows, and visual merchandising.

The goal of this chapter is to introduce advertising, any nonpersonal information paid for and controlled by the sponsoring organization, and the creative process, a standardized plan of action for developing a creative strategy. We look first at creative strategy, the foundation for all advertising and promotion campaigns. Creative strategy depends upon appeals—the reasons for customers to buy—and approaches—the ways appeals are presented. They are examined as part of the creative process that will assist creative personnel in selecting the best advertising approach for their products or services. After establishing this foundation, we define the functions and classifications of advertising, examine characteristics of successful advertising, and forecast future trends in advertising creativity.

After you have read this chapter, you should be able to:

Explain what advertisers mean by creativity, the creative process, and creative strategy.

List and describe the primary functions of advertising.

Distinguish among the various methods of classifying advertisements.

Name the different types of retail and manufacturer advertisements.

Identify the characteristics common to successful advertising.

CREATIVE STRATEGY

Creativity is difficult to define, and many individuals look at it from very different perspectives. Some traditional retailing and marketing executives think of the creative members of the staff as the quirky and unconventional people, who wear unusual clothing. In other settings, however, the creative staff may dress and act more conservatively, even though they are responsible for innovations and novel approaches to problem solving. In this text, **creativity** is viewed as a quality manifested in individuals that enables them to generate clever or imaginative approaches or new solutions to problems.

After reading a newspaper, watching television, or surfing the Web, the average consumer easily recognizes that there are unlimited ways to send and convey advertising messages. Behind each of these communications is a **creative strategy**, a plan for determining what the message will say, and a set of **creative tactics**, steps for implementing the message strategy.

Finding a way to create advertising messages that will break through all of the communication clutter in our modern society is becoming more and more difficult. Although the marketing profession has not been known to nurture creativity, Laurie Tema-Lyn (1997), founder and president of Practical Imagination Enterprises, offers tips for encouraging creativity.

- **Use paradigm-breaking language.** *Why?* It is the word of childhood. *Why is the sky blue?* Similarly, we need to question underlying assumptions about a product, its value, target markets, and so forth. *What if?* It is the phrase of permission, speculation, and imagination. What if we could eat snacks that protect us against colds? *Who?* In an age of narrowly defined target customers, it is remarkable to see who best represents a sea of millions of consumers who are willing to spend money on your product or service.
- **Graze for information.** Scanning information from an array of media beyond your normal professional sources is a way to open a new window to ideas. Website visits, as well as reading issues of nontraditional media, may uncover interesting language and insights about consumer perceptions.
- **Walk on the wild side.** Getting out of the office and exploring new environs recharges your creative batteries.
- **Cross-fertilize.** What can we learn about distribution from the world of ants? How can we connect promotional strategies from the auto industry to advertising jeans? Creative professionals transfer knowledge from fields and industries that are seemingly different.
- **Diversify the team.** It is acceptable to bring together a range of disciplines in the organization. Personnel from research, finance, sales, and customer service to outsiders, who are not afraid to tell the emperor he is not wearing any clothes, bring original ideas to the process.
- **Explore.** Creative firms have developed physical spaces for teams to come together to jam ideas. The Creativity and Innovation Lab began as a division of Polaroid and is now an independent operation. Set up like a grown-up's kindergarten, it is a large room filled with crayons, magazines, toys, and music, free from the distraction of ringing phones. The space symbolically sets the tone that it is safe to explore ideas.

These kinds of activities and ideas promote the flow of creativity, which is necessary to develop and implement advertising and promotion strategy. Next, we look at the creative process.

Creative Process

Following a standardized plan of action can be helpful for advertising executives developing a creative strategy, although many feel that creativity should not be approached in such a structured manner. James Webb Young, former creative vice president of J. Walter Thompson advertising agency, developed a classic model for approaching the creative process in advertising. Young (1975) felt that the process of creativity should be viewed in a manner similar to assembly line production. Rather than putting together Ford automobiles, creative personnel are assembling ideas. Young's paradigm of the creative process has five steps.

1. **Immersion.** Collect current and historical information through background research, and then embed yourself in the problem.
2. **Digestion.** Look over and review the information, then attempt to comprehend it.
3. **Incubation.** Put the problem out of your conscious mind and let your subconscious mind do the work.
4. **Illumination.** The *Ah-hah* moment or birth of a creative idea.
5. **Reality** or **verification.** Study the idea to see if it will solve the problem. Does it still look good? Then, shape the idea to make it useful and practical.

   This model is useful for organizing the unorganizable. Developing a creative answer to a marketing question can be an overwhelming task without a starting point. Young's model gives advertising personnel that starting point. The following information guides us through the steps in the creative process. We start by identifying and locating background information and appropriate research.

Background Research

It is impossible to develop a creative strategy without background information about the client and the industry, including general trends, conditions, and developments in the client's industry. This research can be conducted in numerous ways. First, read anything and everything related to the product or market through books, trade publications, business publications, general interest magazine articles, research reports, scholarly journals, government documents, and so forth. Publications, such as *Advertising Age* and the *Wall Street Journal,* as well as industry groups, such as the American Association of Advertising Agencies or the Magazine Publishers Association of America, provide general articles about advertising strategies.

After this overview is completed, the creative specialist can interview personnel related to the product. From the designers and manufacturing personnel, to the sales associates and consumers, these people have intimate knowledge about the product and its benefits. They can also point out weaknesses in design, packaging, distribution, or use.

Heightened awareness of the product and industry should enter into the consciousness of the creative specialists. Visiting stores or malls where the product is sold and listening to what people are saying about the product can also be helpful. Listening to what the client has to say can be especially informative, since the client knows the market better than other resources.

The creative specialist can also become more familiar with the product or service by actually using it, thus acquiring firsthand knowledge. Going one step further, the specialist may be able to work in the client's business to better understand the product and target consumer.

This preliminary background research combined with product or service specific research will help the creative specialist with the preplanning stages. It is during the preplanning stages that creative processes of immersion, digestion, incubation, and illumination take place.

Product or Service Specific Research

Individual studies conducted on the product or service, the target audience, or a combination of both is known as product or service specific research. The commonly used research methods for this stage include qualitative and quantitative consumer attitude studies, market structure and positioning studies, focus group interviews, and demographic and psychographic profiles of users of a particular product service or brand. These research projects may be completed by large advertising agencies, educational institutions, or government agencies as secondary research. Research undertaken by an advertising agency specifically for the client is considered to be primary research.

Product or service specific research can yield information that is beneficial to the creative team. The advertising agency BBDO developed **problem detection**, a system for finding ideas that could stimulate the formation of creative strategies (Norris, 1975). In this still relevant process, BBDO asked consumers to identify things that caused them frustrations while using a product or service. An exhaustive list of consumers' annoyances gave researchers input into how to improve products, reformulate products, and design new products to better serve the target customers. This research also provided information regarding attributes or selling features to emphasize in advertising. It also furnished ideas and guidelines for repositioning existing brands or positioning new brands.

During the product or service specific research step of the creative process, the creative team reviews the potential appeals and approaches as they relate to the product or service to be advertised. Different appeals and approaches are discussed later in this chapter.

Verification and Revision

During the verification and revision stages, ideas generated through the illumination stage of the creative process are evaluated and modified, as necessary. Inappropriate ideas are rejected, while the remaining ideas are refined and polished into final products. A variety of methods are used in the evaluation. Focus groups are used to evaluate creative concepts, ideas, or themes. Message communication studies, portfolio tests, and other tools are used to measure viewer reaction.

At this stage of developing the advertising program, the creative team is attempting to find the best creative approach prior to producing the actual advertisements. Understanding the roles of appeals and approaches assists with this effort to select the best approach based upon product dimensions. The verification and revision stage may include formal or informal pretesting before a final decision is made. Further discussion of the techniques used to pretest advertising concepts is found in Chapter 17. For a global comparison, the article in Box 7.1 discusses how French advertising executives view the creative process.

Appeals: The Reasons for Customers to Buy

Motivations are the reasons why consumers buy. They are described as the drives within people that stimulate wants and needs. Consumers have individual motivations, but patterns of motivations may develop within groups. Based upon the motivations of target consumer groups, the advertiser develops appeals to meet those motivations. In simple terms, **appeals** are the reasons to buy given by the advertiser.

BOX 7.1
How the French Develop Creative Strategies

An automotive brochure is a house. Plastic wrapping surrounding packaged salad is a windbreak. An industrial machine can be your mistress. Such metaphorical thinking—in which one thing stands for another—sound strange to U.S. advertisers, but these examples represent the way French advertising professionals think about products and how they should be presented to French consumers. Each example was revealed by its creator in a study of French advertising professionals conducted in the cities of Paris and Montpellier in May 1994.

Hall and Hall (1990) noted in their study of French businessmen that the "most common complaint we have heard about American advertising is that the heads of French subsidiaries . . . have great difficulty persuading American headquarters to accept their advice about appropriate advertising in France." To succeed in France, U.S. businesspeople must understand French consumers' expectations of advertising, as well as the ways French advertising professionals plan and execute advertising.

French advertising, in comparison to U.S. advertising, is said to be more emotional, to be subtle, to use symbolic references and linkages to historical events and literature, to use sex appeals, to tell a story, to appeal to individuality, and to make exaggerated promises. Like U.S. advertising, French advertising uses humor, often in the form of jokes or manipulations of shapes and names.

The Study

The research was a qualitative exploration of how French advertising professionals define the creative process and French advertising. The authors sought to understand the cultural categories and principles that define advertising creativity as viewed by the creators of advertising. Participants were a strategic planner, a research director, a creative director, five general managers or owners of advertising agencies, and managers of a public relations agency, a directory publishing firm, and a media-buying service. Interviews were conducted in French or in English, depending upon the preferences of the participants.

In addition to conducting the interviews, the authors examined the strategy planning documents produced by the organizations; documented photographically more than 50 posters appearing on mass transit vehicles and in stations and waiting areas in Paris, Lille, and Montpellier; and observed advertising in *les grands media* (newspapers, magazines, television, radio, cinema, outdoor) during the 3-week research period. Discussion centers on the material gathered through interviewing, with analysis drawn from the interviews and from advertisements documented photographically.

The Findings

Using analytic induction, the authors discovered four broad categories central to the French professionals' construction of creative strategy and advertising. These included French and U.S. models of strategy development, characteristics of French advertising, perceptions of French consumers, and perceptions of U.S. advertising.

Strategy Development

French advertising professionals work under two distinct and separate models of strategic development. One model was labeled the "American approach" or the "Anglo approach" because its strategic path so closely resembles advertising practiced in the United States. The second model was labeled the "French approach" because its strategic path is based in semiotics and linguistics of the French culture. Regardless of the strategic model followed, the advertising executions produced by the two approaches are very similar. The basic distinction between the two models involves the nature and type of research conducted to form the knowledge base for creative decision.

In the American model, adherents practice social science survey and focus group research that has come to dominate and inform U.S. strategic thinking. This type of research is client driven. In the French model, intimate knowledge of French culture and reliance on intuition and experience are hallmarks. Intuitive decision making is captured in the phrase, *"Je me sens,"* which translates at "I sense (it)," "I feel (it)," or "It needs no explanation".

Characteristics of French Advertising: *La Fleur et le Fruit*

After asking participants to describe the unique characteristics of French advertising, participants were able to describe good advertising. "Good advertising works to achieve its immediate objective as well as build image over time. . . . It's both flower and fruit." Consistency of answers among participants revealed four closely related characteristics: *la seduction, le spectacle, l'amour,* and *l'humour.*

La seduction

The French verb *seduire* does not always carry the same connotations as the English word "seduce." It commonly means to tempt, to fascinate, to attract, to charm, or to entice. A good French advertisement is one that tempts the consumer with its offering; a fashionable product may be referred to as a seduction. For example, EuroDisneyland advertised a combination price for park admittance, hotel, and breakfast as *nouveau et seduisant* (new and enticing).

Le spectacle

Spectacle incorporates the meanings of sight, an attraction, a show, a play, a story, and a lavish production, with high production values. A good French advertisement is one that has the drama, entertainment value, production values, and excitement of the theater. In Paris, *affiches* (posters) announcing performances of the opera, ballet, theatre, museum exhibits, movies, and other cultural events are commonly placed on *colonnes Morris* (cylindrical outdoor posting sites) near the street.

L'amour

Outsiders sometimes characterize the French as being obsessed with sex, romance, and innuendo. But these characteristics are integral parts of French culture and as such form an integral part of French advertising. *Un café nomme desir* (the coffee of desire) may express irrelevancy between product and claim to an American, but to French consumers it brings together two cultural expectations: (1) romantic notions should be expressed whenever possible, and (2) advertising should not focus on product functions.

L'humour

Participants described humor as central to French advertising. French advertising may be considered shocking to Americans, but to the French humor with language is necessary, expressed in playful use of words or amusing associations. To illustrate the compatibility of one brand of computers with software applications and to communicate the idea of "productive relations," one agency visually presented the computer as human sperm with computer plugs as sperm tails and the applications as human eggs.

Perceptions of French Consumers

French practitioners often discussed their view of French consumers when defining and explaining creative strategy and advertising. They perceived French consumers to be more "savvy" about advertising, than their American coun-terparts. The French television channel M6 airs a weekly 25-minute program on advertising strategies, *Culture Pub*. Because French consumers are somewhat knowledgeable about the advertising process, French advertisers rarely engage in direct persuasive attempts. More common is the attempt to entice or charm the consumer into buying.

Perceptions of U.S. Advertising

Because the French practitioners perceived consumers to be somewhat knowledgeable about advertising, they viewed U.S. advertising as largely inappropriate for the French market. Compared with French advertising, U.S. advertising executions were considered, "boring, unoriginal, stupid, silly, predictable, laughable, untruthful, horrible, and lacking big ideas." In addition U.S. executions were perceived as lasting too long and being too direct.

Management Implications

The findings have implications for manufacturers who want to enter the French market. For advertisers who want to build demand through advertising in the French market, the following suggestions and observations are offered:

- Advertisers should rarely, if ever, use an informational approach and should not focus on the product. A creative strategy that blends the ideas of *la seduction, le spectacle, l'amour,* and *l'humour* has a much greater chance of succeeding in the French market.
- The tone should not be direct. "Soft sell" outsells "hard sell" in France.
- The French sense of aesthetics leads to artistic expectations about the design of advertising. Advertisers should pay careful attention to the ad's image.
- If television is part of the media mix, advertisers should think in terms of messages that can be conveyed in very short time periods. The modal French television commercial has dropped from 30 to 20 seconds and many advertisers are experimenting with 5-second and 3-second commercials.
- Given a choice, French advertising professionals rely more heavily on intuition and experience for developing strategy than on American-style research.

Adapted from: Taylor, R. E., Hoy, M. G., and Haley, E. (1996, March 1). How French advertising professionals develop creative strategy, Journal of Advertising, *1–15.*

Also cited: Hall, E. T., and Hall, M. R. (1990). Understanding cultural differences. *Yarmouth, ME: Intercultural Press.*

If the advertiser understands motivations, which are established by the consumer, the advertiser can develop reasons to buy the product to meet these needs. The advertiser establishes the appeal. The appeal is used to stimulate a consumer's attention, interest, desire, and action.

Selling Points

Appeals may take the form of **selling points**, the features and characteristics of the merchandise that make it desirable. Why would anyone want to buy this product? The design, reputation of the manufacturer, color, fabric, comfort, versatility, size, or price may be the outstanding feature. These are the factors the advertiser must consider relative to the target audience. Determining which characteristics are most important to the target audience is essential so that the main appeal is derived from the most important selling point.

Unique Selling Proposition

When the advertiser concentrates on a single main appeal, that appeal is frequently referred to as the **unique selling proposition** or **(USP)**. A USP stresses the most important reason for a consumer to prefer this product to all others. Rosser Reeves, former chair of the Ted Bates agency, developed the concept of the USP. In his book *Reality in Advertising*, Reeves (1961) noted three characteristics of USPs:

1. Each advertisement must make a proposition to the consumer. For example, the advertisement must say to each reader, *Buy this product and you will get this benefit*.
2. The proposition must be one that the competition does not or cannot offer. It must have unique characteristics in the brand or claim.
3. The proposition must be strong enough to move mass consumers; that is, pull new consumers to the advertiser's brand.

For this appeal to work there must be a truly unique product or service attribute, benefit, or inherent advantage that can be used in the message. The ad featured in Figure 7.2 offers a unique service for people with unusual shoe sizes. With over 64 different shoe sizes, the USP of the Rockport Concept Store is to provide comfortable, attractive shoe styles for each individual. Considerable research about the product and consumer may be necessary, not only to determine the USP, but to document the claim. Some companies have sued competitors for making unsubstantiated uniqueness claims.

The producer must also consider whether or not a USP can be maintained in a highly competitive market. Will competitors be able to match the distinctive brand features, making the USP obsolete? Procter & Gamble invented a combination shampoo and conditioner product as a way of revitalizing its Pert brand. The new product, named Pert Plus, was introduced and its market share grew from 2 to 12 percent. But, despite its initial popularity, it could not sustain its growth when competitors Revlon and Suave quickly launched similar shampoo-conditioner products (Swasy, 1990).

Brand Image

With so many similar products within a merchandise category, it is often difficult to differentiate between brands. Any name, trademark, logo, or visual symbol that identifies a product or group of products by a specific manufacturer or identifies a specific retailer and helps to differentiate the product(s) or retailer(s) from competitors is a **brand**. Brands may be classified as global, mega niche, national, regional, or private

Figure 7.2

Rockport Concept Shoes has the unique selling proposition of providing comfortable shoes that will fit virtually everyone.

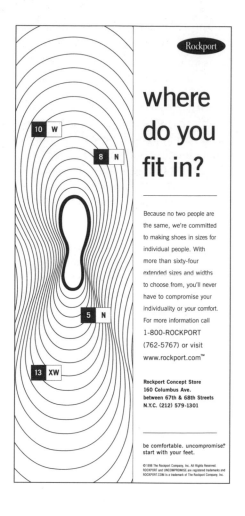

label. Unbranded or generic products may also be sold in retail stores as a value or budget-priced product. Box 7.2 offers suggestions about how to build a brand.

Global Brands   Manufacturers or retailers with merchandise in international distribution struggle to develop recognizable identities. It is the ultimate goal of these organizations to establish an identity for the product or service so consumers immediately think of and prefer it to all others. **Global brands** are broadly distributed throughout many parts of the world. Such products and retail stores as Lancôme, Levi's, Hermès, and Benetton have gained international or global brand status. Levi's, a name known throughout the world, has become almost synonymous with jeans. Levi's has protected its brand name to avoid falling into a state of commoditization, a situation where brand names no longer matter and competition deteriorates into price rivalry rather than brand rivalry. Examples of products whose brand name has become identified with the *product* rather than the manufacturer include Kleenex and Scotch tape.

Mega Niche Brands   The **mega niche brand**, also called the 3-D brand or universal brand, involves taking a successful brand name and launching it into a broad number

BOX 7.2
How to Build a Brand

Private label. Price wars. Rising cotton prices. Shrinking margins. What is a brand to do?

With all the competition for a piece of the action in the denim industry today, it is not enough just to churn out reliable product. To thrive, existing brands are finding they must put time and money into building their names. Without at least a few new strategies in play at all times, say top denim companies, brands will fade faster than an indigo stonewash.

"It used to be, if you made a good quality jean, you stood out in the pack," said Robert Luehrs, president of Chic HIS. "Now, a lot of people make a good quality jean. That's a given."

One of the must-have strategies today is advertising. Others include focus groups to pinpoint new trends, international expansion to tap new consumers, and electronic data interchange (EDI) and Quick Response, to keep retailers in stock at all times.

In fact, EDI has become so important that Levi Strauss chief executive officer Robert D. Haas admitted that his company had fallen behind in that area, while rival VF Corp.'s state-of-the-art systems are a jewel in the manufacturer's crown.

"It is much more important to invest in a brand," says Mackey McDonald, president and chief operating officer of VF Corp. "Just putting a label on a product is not going to be successful. Consumers are much more value-conscious, and they are formulating their methods of determining the value of their products."

What do some of denim's big guys think are the main strategies to keep their brands ahead of the game today? Following are a few ideas.

1. Advertise, Advertise, Advertise.

"You must develop the brand name through advertising," said Luehrs. "You have no lasting life in this business unless you advertise. There are only two products in all of apparel where the consumer buys by name—sneakers and jeans. Unless you have very, very good quality and low, low prices, you don't have to advertise. But if you don't have those, you better have a name."

And an attention-getting campaign can go a long way toward reviving a name.

"Our first step was to change our image," said Jack Gross, president of Gloria Vanderbilt. "After we redid the packaging and the logo, our next step was to advertise."

In 1995, Gross launched a new Gloria Vanderbilt campaign featuring top model Helena Christensen.

Being adventurous helps, according to Eric Rothfeld, president of Sun Apparel, which manufactures the Code Bleu and X-Am lines and holds the license for Todd Oldham and Sasson jeans.

"We were the first apparel brand to go into comic books, which is a great way to get to the young male audience," he said. "We also try to do cross-marketing with other brands, such as sporting goods. It's important to have consistency of theme. If you choose purple, for example, it has to pervade your marketing."

2. Develop a Unique Relationship with the Stores.

VF Corp., which owns such brands as Lee and Wrangler, has executives who work with accounts to merchandise the entire denim department, not just their own brand. That helps lift sales for the entire category, not just one label, according to McDonald.

"Retailers, in order to be successful, have to invest in brands," said McDonald. "In the long run, they've got to make some investment to continue to grow and be viable."

Private label, said McDonald, is "growing, but replacing brands that aren't doing these [marketing strategies]. It's with those brands that you'll see a decline. Our solution to a consumer looking for value is to form a stronger partnership with retailers. We have a system that allows the store to have the right product at the right time. When we go through one of these cycles, like the most recent back-to-school cycle, it becomes evident how important that is."

Sasson president Linda Elton said one of her brand's strongest areas is marketing, but not just to the consumer. Elton will work with stores to create unique advertising campaigns, product mixes, and promotions.

"We treat each store as a separate corporation, from the standpoint of product, in-store events, advertising, everything," said Elton. "We'll do that for the local stores as well as the national chains. For instance, each product is merchandised separately so that when it hits a store, it's not competing with another store."

Sasson also supports the retailers through linked advertising. One example, she said, is sports marketing. Sasson has an ongoing campaign that mentions the brand and the local retailer in major-league arenas around the country.

"That has been incredibly effective for us," said Elton. "We also have fashion presentations to our stores twice a year, which helps them see the whole concept."

Beyond sophisticated sales response systems, there are also in-store techniques that brands employ. Vanderbilt's Gross uses techniques made popular in the beauty industry such as sweepstakes and gift-with-purchase. However, those are sometimes stunted by reluctant retailers, he said.

"People are too used to doing things the way they've always done them," said Gross. "You really have to be innovative. Wal-Mart does things that people said couldn't be done, and that's why they're successful."

Gross said that when he proposed a promotion that would allow customers to enter a sweepstakes for a car just by trying on a pair of Vanderbilt jeans, top level retailers were excited.

"But the first response I got from the middle management was, 'How are we going to do that?'" he said.

3. Have Up-to-Date Systems Response.

"Just a few years ago, Quick Response was a luxury," said Chic's Luehrs. "Now, it's a necessity, or you're dead in the water. Now we're moving toward a new development, VMI—vendor management inventory—where the manufacturer plans the needs of the store by style, size and color. For example, if Kmart moves 2,400 pairs of jeans a week, we'll plan their inventory on a weekly basis."

"It's pretty difficult, but we'll be studying sales of our accounts on a weekly basis, and we'll be able to determine what their needs are, what their base inventory per store should be and how we maintain that. We also have to be able to ship a complete order within 5 to 7 working days of receiving it."

4. Bring Value to the Market.

"The ability to be competitive and really give the consumers excellent value is very important," said Rothfeld. "Whether you're high or low, you have to make the best possible product for your price point. You have to be consistent in fit, which is critical in the denim market, as well as finishing and fabric. When a consumer picks up a size 10 and tries it on, that same size has to fit the same way when she comes back the next time."

"By owning our own manufacturing facilities, we get the highest degree of consistency we can."

5. License.

From department store lines such as Guess to the mass market brands such as Sasson and Chic, licensing is a way to keep the name in front of the consumer as well as bypassing the ebb and flow of the denim market.

"It's not mandatory, but we do a lot of it," said Chic's Luehrs. "More and more mass merchants want coordinating products to go with denim jeans. We'll do $100 million in wholesale volume in licensing this year, and it helps the brand grow. We'll do $130 million or $140 million next year."

"Getting the name on different types of product validates the name," said Rothfeld, adding that if one product category is weak, other product areas are likely to still be going strong.

But haphazard licensing will backfire, said McDonald, if the basic business is not there.

"A dependence on licensing without building the product value will not be successful," he stated. "Consumers are conscientious, and there has to be a high value equation."

6. Go International.

Europe, Asia, South America—they all have a taste for American denim. "It's becoming more and more important to be in other parts of the world," said VF's McDonald. "The trends that we see in the U.S. are happening worldwide. We feel there are tremendous opportunities globally for our brands."

"In Western Europe, we already have a strong presence, and we continue to invest there. In Eastern Europe, we have new opportunities in Poland and Hungary, and we continue to evaluate there. In Asia, there are a number of growth opportunities. We are working on a joint venture in China, and we have new partners in India. South American is an important area that we are now pursuing."

7. Once It's Built, Protect It.

Levi Strauss registered its Arcuate back pocket stitching pattern as a trademark in 1873 and has been monitoring its use ever since, said Ruth Meyler, chief intellectual property council for Levi's and co-leader of the Brand Protection Team, which tracks counterfeiting worldwide.

"There's no company in the world that doesn't have Levi's counterfeit," she said, noting that on any given business day, Levi's is pursuing 200 civil cases and at least twice as many criminal cases worldwide.

"It's exploding now. The more successful we become, the more counterfeit we see."

Counterfeit—an attempt to recreate the product identically—is a criminal offense, noted Meyler. Infringement, or an attempt to create a link in the consumer's mind with the copyrighted product, is less serious and is prosecuted as a civil offense.

"If we didn't do this, ultimately the consumer would not be able to tell the difference between our product and someone else's," said Meyler. "Part of being a strong brand is being able to distinguish yourself in the market. To me, this is as much a part of business as the marketing and advertising and retail sales."

So no matter how intense the pressure gets on the selling floor, brands that work to maintain their businesses will always be a draw.

"The stores have to realize they need us," said Gloria Vanderbilt's Gross. "Brands are what bring in the feet."

Adapted from: Ozzard, J. (1995, October). How to build a brand. Denim Network (Special Report). Women's Wear Daily, *10, 22.*

of different merchandise categories. Ralph Lauren, Donna Karan, Calvin Klein, Tommy Hilfiger, Liz Claiborne, Nautica, and The Gap are companies with at least half a billion dollars in sales, that have expanded their lines of merchandise beyond initial product offerings. For example, brand extension at Ralph Lauren has enabled growth from the core business of Polo ties and men's wear in the early 1970s to include women's apparel, children's apparel, boys' wear, footwear, home collection, fragrances, jeans, and infant and toddler apparel (Fig. 7.3). They also have retail stores throughout the United States and in such international cities as London, Paris, Milan, and Shanghai. Additional licensing agreements have been made for men's and women's intimate apparel and casual footwear. Brand names include but are not limited to Polo, Chaps, Ralph Lauren Home Collection, Safari, Double RL, RALPH by Ralph Lauren, and Ralph Lauren Polo Sport.

Ralph Lauren's incredible expansion is just one example of the mega niche brands. While it is not new to the fashion industry, brand extension reached new heights in the 1990s. Categories such as furniture, paint, candles, and floral arrangements have

Figure 7.3

Mega niche brands, such as Ralph Lauren, have spread powerful, generic images of a variety of products into consumer consciousness.

enlarged Lauren's brand recognition beyond traditional licensing agreements for cosmetics, fragrances, and accessories. Table 7.1 summarizes the categories of merchandise promoted and sold by the leading mega niche firms.

National Brands   **National brands** are available anywhere in the United States. Often these products with a national image are also sought in the international marketplace. As a result, it has become difficult to sort out some national brands from global brands. National brands may be a product or a retail store. Examples of U.S. national brands include Martex, Bobbi Brown, Fitigues, Healthtex, and Nine West.

Regional Brands   **Regional brands** are products and distributors located in one region or district in the United States. These products may gain widespread recognition, and consumers in that region may think of these products in as strong a position as many national brands. Retail stores may concentrate in a part of the country where they have established a favorable identity. Paul Harris is a women's apparel chain located in the Midwest. Dallas-based brand Isabel is a best seller at Jacobson's, a 25-unit chain with stores in Michigan, Indiana, Ohio, Kentucky, Kansas, and Florida. Gottschalks, a 35-unit regional department store based in Fresno, California, developed a regional brand relationship with Graff of California, a misses sportswear line in prints and wovens targeted to women in their fifties and older.

Table 7.1   Categories of Merchandise Promoted and Sold by Mega Niche Producers

Product	Ralph Lauren	Donna Karan	Calvin Klein	Tommy Hilfiger	Liz Claiborne	The Gap	Nautica
Designer men's	✓	✓	✓	✓			
Designer women's	✓	✓	✓				
Bridge men's	✓	✓	✓	✓			✓
Bridge women's	✓	✓	✓		✓		✓
Better	✓		✓	✓	✓	✓	✓
Moderate					✓	✓	
Accessories, men's	✓	✓	✓	✓		✓	✓
Accessories, women's	✓	✓	✓		✓	✓	✓
Footwear—athletic, casual	✓	✓		✓	✓	✓	✓
Footwear collection	✓	✓	✓				
Footwear, bridge		✓	✓	✓		✓	
Jeans wear	✓	✓	✓	✓	✓	✓	✓
Fragrance	✓	✓	✓	✓	✓	✓	✓
Beauty		✓					
Hosiery, socks	✓	✓	✓	✓	✓	✓	✓
Eyewear	✓	✓	✓	✓	✓	✓	✓
Activewear	✓	✓		✓	✓	✓	✓
Home	✓		✓		✓		✓
Bed and/or bath	✓		✓		✓	✓	✓
Children's	✓	✓	✓	✓		✓	✓
Intimate apparel, underwear, loungewear	✓	✓	✓	✓		✓	✓
Handbags, leather goods	✓	✓	✓	✓	✓	✓	

Adapted from: Ozzard, J., and Seckler, V. (1996, September 19). Fashion revolution: The 3-D mega niche. Women's Wear Daily, *9.*

Table 7.2　**Brands That Register Higher Regional Consumer Awareness
(vs. overall national awareness for the brand)**

Northeast	North Central	South	West
Champion	Cabin Creek	Love Pats	Pendleton
Totes	Riders	Lady Manhattan	Cheetahs
Woolrich	Cricket Lane	Bonjour	Cherokee
Ann Taylor	Impressions	Vanity Fair	Brittania
L.L. Bean	Playmate	Jerzees	Ocean Pacific

Adapted from: Regional brands can be local champs. (1996, September 11). Women's Wear Daily,
32–33.

Some national brands may actually find better acceptance in certain geographical areas of the country. Table 7.2 reports brands with higher regional consumer awareness. Brands such as Pendleton and Cherokee register higher consumer awareness in western states, while Woolrich and L.L. Bean are more highly recognized in the Northeast.

Private Label Brands　　Many stores create an image of exclusivity through **private label brands**, merchandise manufactured for a specific retailer. Corporations such as The Limited—which owns Express, Victoria Secret, and Lane Bryant among others—may carry products manufactured by their own production division called Mast Industries. Other retailers, such as Kmart (Fig. 7.4), commission manufacturers to produce exclusive merchandise just for them. Nordstrom features collections known by the brand names Nordstrom, Brass Plum, Classiques, and Preview Basics. The store may use its

Figure 7.4

Private label brands, such as Kmart's Jaclyn Smith women's wear line, offer consumers products associated with a name they recognize.

name or create a separate brand identity. This method insures store and brand loyalty since no other store carries the exact same merchandise. Some customers may not realize that the product is a private label and may try to purchase it at another location. For example, a customer who seeks Brass Plum from a Macy's store will not be able to purchase it there.

Generic Brands **Generic brands**, also known as unbranded merchandise, are especially popular in the retailing of food and some beauty products. The primary benefit of generic products is the normally low or budget price. Although the quality of unbranded products has been questioned, pharmaceutical and beauty industries promote generic products as a more economical alternative to brand names.

Positioning

Trout and Ries introduced the concept of positioning as the basis for advertising strategy (1972). The foundation of positioning is that advertising is used to establish, or *position,* the specific product or service in a particular place in the mind of the consumer. Thus, positioning involves the image consumers have of the brand in relation to competing brands within the product or service category. As we learned in Chapter 2, products can be positioned by attributes, such as price and quality, use or application by product user, product class, or the competitor. Any of these positioning characteristics can ignite a major selling idea that can be developed into a creative strategy, resulting in a brand occupying a particular place in the mind of the consumer.

What makes a consumer choose among Levi's, Calvin Klein, and Arizona brand jeans? The creative strategy used to sell these products is based on the development of a powerful, unforgettable identity for the brand through **image advertising**, advertising that creates an identity for a product or service by emphasizing a symbolic association with certain values, lifestyles, or an ideal. Image advertising has been used as the main selling idea for a wide variety of products and services. From soft drinks, automobiles, airlines, and financial services to perfumes, cosmetics, and clothing, image advertising has helped to differentiate brands. Many consumers choose certain brands of clothing or drink specific brands of beer based upon the image of these brands.

Approaches: The Way Appeals Are Presented

The **approach** is the way an advertiser chooses to present the appeal. Experienced sales personnel and advertisers know that the way they present their sales message is an important factor, influencing a consumer's response. In personal selling, the salesperson is able to modify his or her appeals and approaches in response to the customer's feedback. In advertising, the appeal and approach must be carefully developed with the customer profile in mind since changing the advertising approach cannot be as immediately or directly responsive to consumer feedback.

The seven approaches or manners of presentation discussed here were originally identified in *The Management of Advertising* (Simon, 1971). These approaches, with minor modifications for the 21st century, include information, argument, emotional attraction, repeat assertion, command, symbolic association, and imitation.

Information

Information ads are presented as straight facts. The relevance of the facts is not necessarily explained, since the reasons for advertising are generally quite obvious. Classified and Yellow Pages are top examples of this approach. Many other straightforward ads are also informational. For example, *Threadz announces the arrival of Nine West Shoes,* or *Ralph Lauren Paints are now 20% off.*

Argument

The argument approach is presented as a logical statement or reason why a consumer should purchase the product or service. The justifications used may be facts or expected benefits to the consumer. Benefits could be in terms of social standing, improved health or beauty, or any other improvements. Argument ads will frequently feature some type of question that a consumer can answer. Figure 7.5 illustrates an argument ad.

Emotional Attraction

Emotional pleas are the basis of motivation in emotional attraction advertising. The product image is enhanced by the attachment of a pleasant emotional connotation. Emotional attraction ads depend upon a mood created by the advertisers, making the product desirable. Cosmetic, cigarette, and alcohol advertisers depend heavily on mood advertising. Advertising for health-related issues also use emotional appeals. A corporate sponsor may draw on the target audience member's interest in particular social or health issues to attract attention. Figure 7.6 uses an emotional attraction to ask con-

Figure 7.5

An argument approach provides a rationale for buying the advertised product or service.

Figure 7.6

The emotional attraction approach uses psychological pleas to gain consumer attention.

sumers to use a Spiegel MasterCard that will benefit the National Alliance of Breast Cancer Organizations for their purchases.

Repeat Assertion

The hard sell approach to advertising is known as repeat assertion. The statements in these ads, as well as the reasons why the statements are held to be true, are usually unsupported by facts. Nonprescription drug producers and cosmetic companies are frequent users of this type of advertising. The assumptions here are that people will believe a statement if they hear it frequently enough and have no intrinsic interest in the product message. The advertiser is interested in getting the most memorable line to the audience through repetition.

Command

A command advertisement orders or reminds us to do something. The assumption with this approach is that the audience is suggestible. Examples of the command approach include: *Give to the United Way,* or *Drink Pepsi, get stuff.* Command ads work best with products the audience knows and already respects. Clairol uses a command approach, telling the consumer to *Work yourself into a lather,* and *Feel what it does for your hair* (Fig. 7.7).

Symbolic Association

Using a more subtle variation of the repeat assertion ad, symbolic association intends to get across one piece of information about the product by linking it to something the consumer knows and likes. By linking the product to a person, musical piece, or situation with a positive circumstance, the product and the situation become highly interrelated. Popular comedian Jerry Seinfeld has been linked to the VISA credit cards through humorous situations. By bringing together the actor and financial service, the two have been linked in symbolic association.

This approach has strong ties to emotional appeals, since many of the situations are associated with good times. For example, long-distance telephone services link positive interactions between friends and family to the telephone, a very emotional approach.

Imitation

Imitation ads attempt to present people and situations for the audience to imitate. The assumption with this approach is that audience members will wish to be like people that they admire. Celebrities are typically used for testimonials or status appeals. If "James Bond" wears a certain type of watch, as in Figure 7.8, or drives a certain type of car, the audience will wish to imitate him, buying that watch or that car.

Selecting the Best Approach Based upon Product Dimensions

Simon (1971) also noted a number of dimensions that could be used to assist the creative team in selecting the best approach for the specific product or service being advertised. These dimensions, suggested by such product or market conditions as industrial versus consumer goods, product characteristics, stage in life cycle, stage of brand acceptance, price, or other market categories, give advertisers methods to activate interest in these products or services. Thus, the classification of a product, service, or market situation can provide a logical way to plan the advertising message.

Figure 7.7

Command approaches often demand that the consumer try the product.

Figure 7.8

Imitation builds on the consumer's desire to look or act like another person.

Industrial or Consumer Goods

Products promoted to the industrial market typically are best served by the information or argument approaches. Due to the complexity of the products, high dollar value of the products, and risks associated with selecting the wrong products, industrial product ads, by necessity, need to provide facts and rational arguments.

Approaches to promoting consumer goods are not as clear-cut; almost any of the activation approaches can reasonably be used for consumer advertising. We must examine other dimensions, such as product characteristics, stage in life cycle or brand acceptance, price, or other characteristics in order to decide which approach to take.

Fashionable or Functional Merchandise

Is there a word that best characterizes the product? If that word is fashion, advertisers tend to select imitation, emotional attraction, or symbolic association as the approach. Fashion-oriented products are often promoted with an image that conveys a sense of the product rather than specific information. On the other hand, if that word is functional, implying products such as computers or cars, advertisers frequently use information or argument approaches. Statistical data is frequently used to justify the reasons to select the advertiser's functional product. Advertisers of products with sensory characteristics, such as perfume or soap, tend to use symbolic association, emotional attraction, or imitation. These types of products demand advertising that goes beyond words. If service is the primary characteristic, advertisers generally depend upon information or argument, because the audience needs to know what the service is and how it will benefit them. Hidden benefit advertisers often choose information, argument, or emotional attraction. Nonprescription drugs, cosmetics, financial services, and foods are among the vast number of products with hidden benefits. Target audiences must be informed of these benefits and persuaded that they are important through argument or by appealing to emotion.

Luxury or Necessary Products

Typically, luxury products use symbolic association or imitation approaches. Luxury products are designed to provide a prestigious element, making it necessary for the advertiser to create an atmosphere of status. Also, since the product is so far removed from being a necessity, the advertiser will most likely need to create a demand for the product. The advertiser can use emotional attraction to entice the luxury buyer to action.

Products deemed necessary or convenient are less likely to require such stimulation. The advertiser is more inclined to use information or argument approaches because emotional attraction is not likely to be used for necessity or convenience goods.

Stage in Life Cycle

The product life cycle was introduced in Chapter 2. As the product is introduced to the marketplace, consumers need reasons for buying it. Products in the introduction and rise stages generally use information, argument, or emotional attraction to stimulate interest and action. As the product matures into an acceptance stage of the life cycle, consumers need less information and other types of encouragement. Assertion, imitation, symbolic association, or command approaches are more commonly used with mature products.

Stage of Brand Acceptance

When a brand reaches a mature stage in the product life cycle, there is enough consumer demand to introduce a new brand. Thus, in a similar manner to products in the introductory stages of the product life cycle, new brands would benefit from information, argument, or emotional attraction approaches. Older brands are treated like products in the mature stages of the life cycle.

Price Range

Advertisers of high-priced products tend to use information, argument, and emotional attraction, since people need reasons to pay higher prices. Products with lower prices tend to be impulse purchases, so symbolic association, command, and repeat assertion are more likely approaches.

Similarity to Competition

If the product has unique characteristics, differentiating the brand will be easier. These specific product characteristics can be reported through information, argument, or emotional attraction techniques. Products with similar characteristics to the competition must rely on other methods to create desire.

Repeatability of Purchase

Shampoo, toothpaste, and coffee are examples of products with short repurchase cycles. Consumers need to replace these basics often. Advertisers use symbolic association, command, repeat assertion, or imitation approaches to attract consumers to these products needing regular replacement. Items with long repurchase cycles, such as coats, diamonds, and cars are more likely to depend upon information or argument.

Method of Completing the Sale

Products sold through direct marketing strategies, such as mail-order or item-of-the-month clubs (e.g., books or coffee), require the consumer to take action. These action-oriented ads are more likely to use argument or psychological approaches. These ads must complete the selling process on their own and therefore can use many of the other activation techniques too.

Market Share Held by Brands

Advertisers with brands that dominate their markets may wish to gain the whole market. In such instances, the advertiser would use information, argument, or emotional attraction—methods typically associated with products in the early stages of the product life cycle.

The foundation, established by a product-market interrelationship analysis, can assist the advertiser in selecting the appropriate message activation method. Within each of these categories there are unlimited methods to create ads. Words, colors, and graphics can be used in millions of different ways. Other dimensions such as humor, using a spokesperson, or placing the audience into a real-life situation are also options. This plan does not limit the advertiser's need for creativity; it simply provides a framework to aid our understanding of the process.

Creative Strategy Development

After all of the background research material is evaluated, and the appeals and approaches have been considered, the creative strategy is developed. This strategy focuses on what must be communicated to the consumer and will guide the generation of all messages used in the campaign. Creative strategy is based upon several factors that originated with identification of the target audience, the basic problems and/or opportunities, major selling ideas or key benefits, and any supportive information. Once these factors have been determined, the advertising agency should develop a creative strategy statement, outlining the message and suggesting a style that will be used. Many advertising agencies outline these factors in a written format known as the copy platform.

Copy Platform

The **copy platform** is a document, typically prepared by an account representative or creative manager, which specifies the basic foundation of the creative strategy. Some agencies may refer to this manuscript as a creative platform, work plan, creative blueprint, or creative contract. Individuals from the advertising agency's strategic planning or research departments and members of the account team, which includes creative personnel such as copywriters and media planners, may also have input into the copy platform.

Although there are many different ways to present the copy platform, it generally consists of six parts:

1. **Executive summary**—a statement which defines the basic problems or opportunities the advertising must address
2. **Advertising and communication objectives**—statements about the intended outcome of the advertising program, defined in Chapter 4

3. **Target audience**—the consumer the advertising is designed to attract
4. **Appeals**—the major selling points or key benefits to be communicated
5. **Creative strategy**—the statement, which includes campaign theme, approaches, and execution techniques to be used
6. **Supportive information**—additional documentation that includes such information as brand identification, disclaimers, and so forth

The sections on problems or opportunities, general and communication objectives, and the target audience are written as part of the planning process discussed in Chapter 4, Planning. In addition to developing the creative strategy, writing the sections on the appeals (the selling points or key benefits) and creative strategy (the central themes, approaches, and execution techniques) are typically the responsibility of the creative team or specialists. These strategies form the basis of the advertising campaign.

Once the agency has prepared the document and samples of creative production, the advertising staff presents the copy platform to the client. The advertising, marketing, or product manager who represents the client is typically given the responsibility of approving the copy platform.

Advertising Campaigns

Most advertisements are part of a series of messages coordinated into an **advertising campaign**, which consists of multiple messages presented in a variety of media. These messages focus on a central theme or concept. Critical components identified by the copy platform, such as the central theme, idea, position, or image, drive the development of the creative aspects of the advertising campaign. Some campaigns are long lasting, while others survive for short periods of time. *Just another Avon Lady,* is a successful theme that has survived several seasons, whereas the Timex watch theme, *Takes a licking and keeps on ticking,* has endured for decades. Next, we look at the reasons why advertisers are willing to spend large amounts of money on advertising campaigns.

FUNCTIONS OF ADVERTISING

Firms such as Tommy Hilfiger and Ralph Lauren have made huge financial investments in producing advertisements and buying time or space for placement, confirming a confidence in the importance of advertising. Product acquisition, part of the consumer behavior process of consumption that we discussed in Chapter 2, is searching, evaluating, and choosing among alternative items after need is established. The consumer can benefit from the information made available through advertisements and other promotional materials, if the ultimate goal of the advertiser is to have the consumer purchase its goods and/or services.

Advertising is valued for its contributions to communication by providing new information, persuading customers to buy merchandise, reminding customers of product attributes and availability, introducing product innovations, and assisting with other company efforts as part of a total integrated marketing communications (IMC) package.

Providing New Information

Advertising creates awareness about new products, informs consumers about attributes of specific brands, and educates the public about product features and benefits. When a manufacturer or designer launches a new spring or fall fashion line or seasonal cosmetic colors, advertising can help consumers learn about the new features. As the firm Nautica diversified into the home furnishings market, the advertising campaign featured the tag line, *Introducing The Home Collection.* Consumers were notified about the availability of sheets and towels with this brand that was more closely associated with apparel.

Persuading Consumers

Persuasion involves causing someone to do or believe something by using strategies of reasoning, urging, or convincing. Customers may be persuaded to try products through effective advertising. Persuasion may take the form of primary or secondary demand. Primary demand creates demand for an entire product category. In this case, the advertiser promotes desire for a broad category such as coats.

Secondary demand creates demand for a certain firm's brand and for the product category only secondarily. Here, the firm is asking the consumer to buy the brand name when selecting a piece of outerwear. Secondary demand is used more frequently than primary demand, because the advertiser is more interested in persuading the consumer to buy its brand.

Reminding Consumers

Advertising helps to keep the product fresh in the mind of the consumer. When an individual needs a new or replacement product, advertising helps to keep the merchandise in the consumer's memory. This may be used effectively for mature brands, making them recognizable and encouraging the consumer to switch brands. The institutional ad in Figure 7.9 reminds current customers about the store's extensive service and range of products.

Introducing Innovation

Innovating, improving quality, or altering consumer perception are ways a firm may add value to its products. These concepts work interdependently and are frequently used for personal care products.

Innovations in some skin care products are geared to the adult and silver streaker markets. One skin care firm developed a cream-gel to firm and smooth aging skin. The advertisement in Figure 7.10 was created to introduce this innovative product with the offer of a complimentary sample.

In another example of product innovation, consumers liked the long-lasting lipsticks, but they did not like how dry their lips felt. Through its advertising, Revlon let consumers know about the improved quality of its Colorstay Lipcolor with added moisturizers.

The advertiser tries to change consumer perception through innovations and quality improvements. Neutrogena introduced a deep-cleansing wash called Deep Clean, demonstrating its benefits through advertising. Without such promotion of a product's improvements, the consumers' perception may actually diminish rather than increase.

Assisting Other Company Efforts

Advertising is only one type of promotional activity in the mix contributing to a firm's overall IMC plan. Although advertising may be the primary promotional mix element used by the firm, in certain instances advertising may be used to support other mix

Figure 7.9
This retailer's ad reminds current and potential customers that the store stocks a variety of products to meet their needs.

We have a most unique clientele. People with superb taste. A flair for individual style. And a high regard for quality.

And to satisfy each and every one of them, we offer thousands of hand-crafted silk, paper and string shades. Plus, specialized services such as custom-made shades, lamp restorations, repairs and mountings.

Some come to New York's premier resource for custom shades and services.

But, please, no dancing in the store.

Whatever your style, we have your shade

ORIENTAL
LAMP SHADE CO.
Over 85 years of handcrafting quality lamps and shades.
CUSTOM SILK, PAPER AND STRING SHADES. MOUNTINGS. REPAIRS. RESTORATIONS.
816 LEXINGTON AVE. (BETWEEN 62ND & 63RD) 212.832.8190
223 WEST 79TH ST. (BETWEEN B'WAY & AMST) 212.873.0812
OPEN 10–5:30 MON THRU SAT

elements. Advertising may be the technique used to distribute coupons for sales promotion activities or it may be used to assist other promotional goals by preselling products, making the job of the sales representative easier. Prospects are informed about the features, benefits, and costs prior to the sales representative's visit, giving the rep additional credibility during the personal sales presentation. Advertising enhances the overall IMC effort. Advertising can be classified into several different categories, which we examine next.

ADVERTISING CLASSIFICATIONS

The desired outcome of advertising differs according to the promotional objectives of the firm presenting the advertisements. These objectives may vary from one firm to another or within a company with various advertising needs. One firm may seek to in-

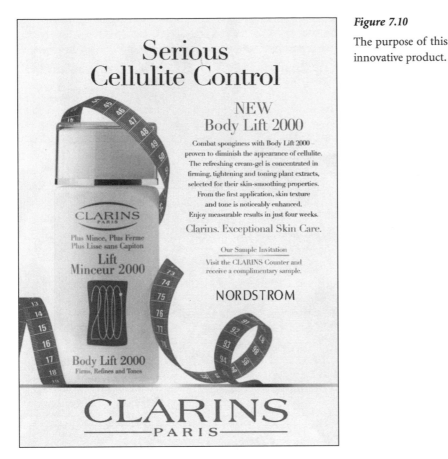

Figure 7.10

The purpose of this advertisement is to introduce an innovative product.

crease awareness about a new product with an aggressive product launch targeted to a specific customer group. Another firm may want to develop enhanced community perception over a period of time by creating a strong institutional image.

Since the nature and purpose of advertising may vary, advertising may be classified by several alternative models, including target customer, geographical location, and purpose. These classifications are not mutually exclusive; an advertisement may be defined by its target customers in addition to the geographical location, type of media where it is placed, and its purpose. A particular advertisement such as the one for Louis Vuitton briefcases in Figure 7.11 is targeted at men, as shown by the headline and visual image. It may be classified geographically as international; stores in Canada, Mexico, Bermuda, and Bogota, as well as many U.S. cities are listed. The advertisement is placed in a magazine for the purpose of encouraging the purchase of briefcases made of a particular leather.

Target Customer

The study of consumer behavior taught us that successful advertising programs are frequently aimed at segmented population groups. An advertisement may not appeal to each member of the general population but rather to the target customer, a particular segment of the population. Take baby lotion for instance. The product may be advertised to two different target markets. When that product ad features the traditional

Figure 7.11

This Louis Vuitton briefcase advertisement may be classified as an international consumer advertisement placed in a magazine to encourage the purchase of merchandise.

primary benefits for babies, it attracts the audience of new mothers. A television commercial, featuring baby lotion as an after-sun skin soother, appeals to the junior market. There are two ways of defining target customers for advertising purposes: consumer and trade.

Consumer Advertising

Advertising directed toward the consumer, the ultimate user of the product, service, or idea is known as consumer advertising. Advertising that is directed to the consumer audience may be sponsored by the manufacturer or the retailer, or as a cooperative venture between the manufacturer and retailer. Much of consumer advertising is placed in the mass media, such as newspapers, magazines, television, or radio. Direct-response, a promotional technique using catalogs, flyers, or other direct-mail media, is intended to solicit a response from the consumer by phone, mail, Internet, or personal visit. Direct-response advertising is also used by consumer directed advertisers. An advertisement for Oneida flatware placed in a consumer magazine such as *Elle Decor, House & Garden,* or *Martha Stewart Living* is representative of a consumer-oriented advertisement.

Trade Advertising

Business-to-business directed advertising is known as trade advertising. A textile producer that creates primary level fibers or fabric promotes its products to sheet and towel manufacturers or retailers in *Home Furnishings Daily.* This is an example of trade advertising. Trade advertising is focused toward professional journals, trade magazines, business publications, and through direct-response materials in contrast to much of consumer advertising, which is concentrated in consumer-oriented mass communication channels. Since trade advertising is targeted toward professional or trade publications, the ultimate consumer is not usually aware of this type of advertising.

The difference between consumer and trade advertising is demonstrated in Figure 7.12. The Swiss Army brand can be compared through its consumer and trade advertisements. The consumer-directed ad, Figure 7.12A, could be found in many different consumer publications from *Self* to *Time.* It informs the consumer about the quality and uses for the original Swiss Army knife. The trade ad, Figure 7.12B, was published in the trade paper *Women's Wear Daily.* This ad let merchants know about concerns related to counterfeit watches and actions taken to protect the brand.

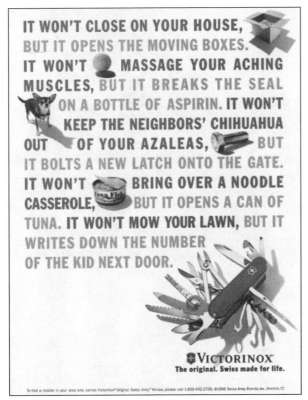

A.

B.

Figure 7.12

Consumer and trade advertisements by Swiss Army can be compared. The consumer-directed ad is illustrated in A. while the trade ad is illustrated in B.

Geographical Location

Another method of classifying advertising is by its geographical orientation. Four classifications of advertising are associated with the geographical location: global, national, regional, and local.

Global Advertising

In recent years products and retailers have expanded beyond traditional national borders. L.L. Bean has stores in Japan, and Bally the shoe manufacturer is available throughout the world, not just in Switzerland. The need for international or **global advertising** is an increasing market. The advertiser must make the choice whether to follow a global or local approach in presenting international products. For instance, Johnson and Johnson, internationally known producer of baby shampoo, chose to take the same theme used in its American commercial showing a new mother singing to her newborn and translated it into a localized advertisement by re-shooting the same commercial using Japanese language and actors.

With increased globalization of media and merchandise, it is often difficult to determine where an ad or a product originated. Figure 7.13 features U.S. apparel in a French publication. Could a French student think Gap products are created in France?

Figure 7.13

With so many firms operating in today's global marketplace, it is not unusual to see ads for American brands in French publications or vice versa.

GapKids est maintenant ouvert au quatrième étage des Galeries Lafayette Haussmann.

Les collections Gap pour femme sont aux Galeries Lafayette Haussmann et Montparnasse.

Gap est aux Galeries Lafayette

National Advertising

National advertising generally promotes consumer products or retail stores that are widely available throughout the United States. Although some authors say that national advertising is only done by manufacturers or designers, national advertising can also be done by retailers or as a cooperative activity among a manufacturer, designer, and retailer.

Regional Advertising

Through **regional advertising**, manufacturers, retailers, and advertisers can take advantage of more widely distributed media within a limited geographical region. A newspaper with statewide or regional distribution may be chosen as the medium for advertising for a regional department store chain or mall. A Mother's Day promotion may highlight gift suggestions from many different stores within a regional shopping center.

Several national magazines offer regional advertising opportunities for advertisers through regionally distributed editions. A store with outlets located only in the northeastern United States may purchase advertising space in a magazine that would only be distributed to readers in that part of the country.

Local Advertising

Local advertising is developed for an immediate trading area. The owner of a junior specialty store with one outlet in the historic district of a small university town targets her advertising to students through the college newspaper. A manager of a locally owned furniture store places television ads during programs popular with his target customers, new homeowners and newlyweds.

Product Orientation

As we discussed in Chapter 4, the advertiser defines the goals and objectives for advertising. Some ads are created to promote goods (products), whereas others are developed to promote the company (institution) through its services and image.

Promotion of specific goods or services is the objective of **product advertising**. Advertisements for sunglasses manufactured by Donna Karan, a fragrance sold by Revlon, and a scarf by Hermès are examples of product ads. The focus with this type of advertising is to urge consumers to take quick action toward purchasing a product. The primary objective of product advertising arouses instant interest in the merchandise and, therefore, it has a short-term emphasis. In the world of fashion advertising, this sense of urgency is emphasized due to the sometimes short-lived nature of fashion products.

Retail Product Advertising

Retail product advertising is a form of consumer merchandise advertising sponsored by a retailer. Retail stores typically spend most of their advertising budget on the merchandise currently available for sale. Retail advertising may be categorized by the conditions of sale or by merchandise category.

Conditions of Sale   Conditions of sale advertising consists of four types: regular price, special price, clearance, or mail order. **Regular price advertising** features merchandise that is in the introductory or rise stages of the fashion cycle, and seasonal or holiday merchandise. Fashionable trends are introduced to increase awareness of the new colors, prints, or silhouettes for a season. These ads attract the fashion leaders and innovators, shoppers who select merchandise during the introduction and rise stages of the

Figure 7.14

This ad is used to introduce a
new season's merchandise at
full price.

fashion cycle. Seasonal selections of swimwear or outerwear announce the change in
time. *Father's Day* merchandise is advertised in various publications for several weeks
prior to the holiday. The example in Figure 7.14 illustrates regular price merchandise
offered at the beginning of the fall season.

Advertisements featuring regular price merchandise are generally presented in large
formats, such as full-page ads in a magazine or newspaper. Elegant illustrations or photography may also be presented in full color to improve the impact of such advertisements.

Regular price ads generally include information about the sizes, colors, price, and
manufacturers of the merchandise. Additionally, regular price ads may include benefits
or fashion trend information. How much information is placed in the copy is dependent upon the target customer and the store's image.

Special-price advertising promotes merchandise that is offered as a special purchase to build store traffic and sales. Special-price merchandise results from the retailer negotiating a less than normal price from the manufacturer and passing that savings onto the consumer. For instance, the retailer may receive a shipment of winter coats or boots in July. Although the selection may not be very deep, the manufacturer may want to test the popularity of a few styles prior to the start of the regular selling season. A 20 percent discount may encourage early shoppers and provide information regarding color and style trends to the retailer and manufacturer. The retailer may be able to adjust its orders to fit the anticipated demand based upon preseason sales, while the manufacturer may alter their production.

In another scenario a retailer may receive a discount before the end of the season. This can be especially important during the Christmas gift-giving period. Time limits are frequently used to motivate customers to action. Copy such as *TWO WEEKS ONLY* is employed to encourage movement of the merchandise. The clearance ad in Figure 7.15 is intended to reduce the inventory of women's Halloween costumes before the holiday. After Halloween, this merchandise will be virtually unsaleable.

Figure 7.15

Price reductions are offered by retail stores in clearance ads.

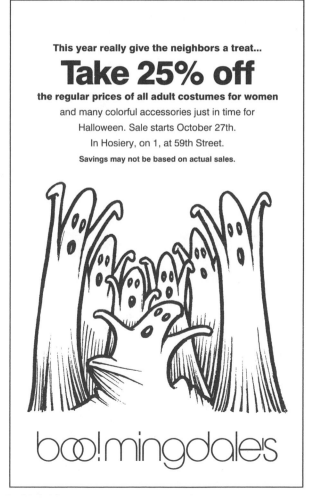

Special-price advertisements are also developed for annual or semiannual sales of basic stock such as socks, men's furnishings, household linens, or intimate apparel.

Clearance advertising is used to promote end-of-the-month or end-of-the-season stock. The retailer needs to clear merchandise from the shelves to make room for the next season's inventory. Clearance ads are also used during slow sales periods.

Art used for clearance ads may *represent* the category rather than feature any specific product. Many clearance ads use copy without any artwork to emphasize the sale prices. The point for the retailer is to get rid of the merchandise. A customer may be disappointed if a particular style is depicted and it is not available when he or she arrives at the store. An empty clothes rack or stacked shoeboxes represent the typical merchandise, not specific styles, colors, or sizes available.

A retail firm offering merchandise through nonstore sales sponsors **direct-response advertising**. This is an alternative to bringing the customer physically onto the sales floor. Mail-order advertisements offer convenience for customers with limited free time or mobility for shopping. Products may be similar to ones offered in the store or they may be items only available through mail order. These advertisements may be presented in newspapers, magazines, and television or through direct-response catalogs or billing inserts.

Firms may use mail order as a method of stimulating business from customers who do not live within a commuting distance of the store. Rural customers or those outside the traditional trading area may become new clients. Some retailers conduct their business primarily or exclusively through catalog orders. Mail-order ads, such as the one shown in Figure 7.16, often include a form to mail back to the sponsoring firm or a toll-free telephone number.

Merchandise Orientation   Merchandise orientation of retail advertising involves more definitive classifications of merchandise. These classifications give a clearer picture of the intention or purpose of the ad. Merchandise orientation for advertisements includes single-item, assortment, related-items, vendor, theme, departmental, or volume.

Figure 7.16

This postage-paid card, inserted in magazines, is part of a direct marketing strategy, encouraging the consumer to make a purchase directly by phone or mail.

A **single-item advertisement** focuses on one piece of merchandise. This type of advertising is reserved for seasonal trends, products from well-known designers and manufacturers, or bestsellers. These product ads often feature color, price, size, and trend information in the advertising copy. Artwork may be as sophisticated as full-color photography or as simple as line sketches.

Assortment advertisements are generally larger in size than single-item ads, featuring a range of merchandise from within a retail department, product division, or unrelated departments. These types of ads emphasize the breadth of merchandise available in the firm. In a shoe advertisement, several styles of women's shoes may be shown or a single category such as a sandal may be shown from the men's, women's, and children's departments. Unrelated merchandise may be coordinated as a vendor ad.

Copy for assortment ads may consist of descriptions of individual styles or general text indicating a range of products. Artwork may show specific styles of merchandise or general categories of merchandise such as wedding or prom dresses, representing the assortment of wedding or prom dresses carried by the store.

Related-items advertisements feature merchandise from a store's retailing division, which is not always purchased by the same buyer. For instance the store may have separate buyers for infants', toddlers', girls' apparel, boys' apparel, and children's sleepwear and accessories. The related-item ad could feature merchandise from the children's division, including knit apparel or back-to-school merchandise from each of the different buyers.

Advertisements featuring merchandise from one single manufacturer or designer are considered to be **vendor advertisements**. Merchandise from the vendor Perry Ellis may be available in the cosmetic/fragrance, men's tailored apparel, women's accessories, active sportswear, and luggage departments. An advertisement coordinating these different products through the use of the vendor name would fit this variation of an assortment advertisement.

Groups of products from individual departments, divisions, or the entire store could be coordinated as **theme advertisements**. Themes may be based upon fashion trends, such as *Café Au Lait* or *Stripe it Rich;* seasons, as in *Back-to-School, Christmas,* or *Easter;* special and annual events, as a *White Sale* or *Anniversary Sale;* or an international promotion, as in *Bon Jour France* or *British Designer Week.*

Departmental advertisements present merchandise from a specific department. Artwork may either coordinate the merchandise into one image or be presented as various products in graphically separated segments of a larger layout. A variation of a departmental ad places several single-item products from one department as ads on one page.

Volume advertisements are created for best-selling products. These items such as polo shirts in the summer or wool pullover sweaters in the winter are classically styled items that remain popular for many years. These volume ads feature the latest as well as traditional colors, emphasizing price and/or quality and immediate availability. Another clue for identifying volume ads is the fact that products are offered in a wide range of sizes from extra small to extra large in a broad range of fashion and basic colors. A volume ad, offering the consumer selections of swimsuits in a broad range of brands, styles, colors, and sizes is shown in Figure 7.17.

Manufacturer and Designer Product Advertisements

Manufacturers and designers use consumer ads to presell their brands to the target customer at the national and international market levels. Designers can make consumers aware of their lines of merchandise by placing ads in national magazines such as *Vogue, Harper's Bazaar, Mademoiselle,* or *Jane.* The manufacturer of home linens, such as

Figure 7.17
Volume ads are designed to remind consumers about the availability of bestsellers.

Martex, may present the latest line of sheets, pillowcases, and bed coverings in *Elle Decor,* or *House and Garden* magazines.

Institutional Orientation

If the ad promotes an image or the company's commitment to social causes, it is no longer a product ad. Advertising that is geared toward building the reputation of the firm, enhancing civic sponsorship and community involvement, and developing long-term relationships between customers and the firm is classified as **institutional advertising**. This form of advertising is more closely associated with long-term objectives for the advertiser; therefore, institutional advertising focuses on company policies, physical facilities, the image of the merchandise assortments, departmental features, customer, and selling services. The firm seeks to convince the clientele of the firm's fashion leadership and authority as well as of its services.

Retail Institutional Advertising

At the retail level the store wants to create an image for the firm, showing the customer what the firm stands for in terms of fashion merchandise leadership, community social responsibility, and store services.

Fashion leadership can be advertised in the form of **prestige advertising**, introducing new lines of merchandise or designer special appearances. Although prestige ads may also draw customers to products, they are created as part of a long-term effort to build and maintain a fashionable reputation.

Institutional advertisements may also promote community service projects. Community service projects may take the form of a high school art contest for safety posters or a fund-raising fashion show for the area symphony guild. Or, a store may simply invite the local high school choir to sing Christmas carols during the weekend before the holiday.

Institutional advertising increases customers awareness of the availability of store services, which are conveniences that make shopping easier and more pleasant. These services are gift-wrapping, credit services, charge accounts, hair salon, post office, home delivery, and other such aids. Consulting and planning advice in terms of interior design, cosmetic colors, skin treatments, bridal registry, career dressing, or wedding apparel are all store services that might enhance consumer patronage.

Manufacturer and Designer Institutional Advertising

Institutional ads produced by the manufacturer and designer markets stress the manufacturer or designer's reputation for design innovation, product quality, or social commitment. Design innovation may be emphasized in trend report advertising for a top designer such as Karl Lagerfeld, while product quality and fit may be highlighted by Timberline, the shoe manufacturer. Estée Lauder emphasizes social commitment with the *Pink Ribbon* campaign for Breast Cancer Awareness month. All of these promotions are designed to differentiate products and brands.

Commercial or Nonprofit Advertising

Commercial advertising is directed toward the profit-making sector, whereas **nonprofit advertising** is used by nonprofit organizations. Nonprofit groups such as Goodwill Industries International, through their regional agencies, use advertising to increase donations of used products or cash, promote sales of used goods in their retail stores, or gain volunteer support for their efforts to help disabled and disadvantaged populations.

CHARACTERISTICS OF SUCCESSFUL ADVERTISING

John Wanamaker, the founder of Wanamaker's Department Store, once said, "I know half of my advertising is wasted. The trouble is I don't know which half." Are we really able to measure the effectiveness of advertising?

A simplistic way to view an advertisement's success is to measure whether the ad met the advertiser's sales objectives. This approach defines success simply as sales revenue generated by the act of publishing or broadcasting an ad. Actually, advertising success should be the function of a fully integrated marketing communications package and measured in that context.

While it is more difficult to establish criteria for assessing advertising in terms of the composition of the advertisement, there are several identifiable qualities that can improve an advertiser's chances for accomplishing its goals. Many of these attributes may be common throughout most effective advertisements. Those considerations customarily associated with successful advertisements are:

- **Consistency with marketing strategy.** A well-coordinated marketing communications strategy should be developed and serve as a plan, integrating advertising into

Checklist for Planning Effective Advertising

☐ **Determine the function of the advertisement.** Is the function to inform, persuade, remind, add value, or assist other company efforts?

☐ **Determine the advertising classification.** Is the advertising directed toward a particular target consumer or trade customer? Is it directed to a particular geographical location? Which advertising medium was used and was it the most effective outlet? For what purpose was the advertising created (product vs. institutional, commercial vs. nonprofit)?

☐ **Identify and evaluate the appeal, approach, and selling points.** Do these conditions meet the wants and needs of the target customer?

☐ **Identify the relationship between the visual and verbal.** Is the ad attractive, using an appropriate combination of art and copy or video and sound? What attention-getting devices are used? Are they appropriate in relationship to each other, the product, and the target customer?

☐ **Determine if there is a unique selling proposition (USP).** What is the primary benefit? How does the product stand out from all of the others?

☐ **Identify how image and continuity are achieved.** How does the advertiser create a consistent identity through the use of a logo, layout, artistic style, or other mechanism? Does the ad build on previous ads and build for the future?

☐ **Determine the nature of the requested response.** What is the consumer being asked to do? Request? Buy? Remember?

☐ **Evaluate whether the selling message is obvious or lost in creativity.** Did the advertiser use a whimsical theme or humor in an appropriate manner to encourage the desired action from the consumer? Or did the advertiser use ingenuity for the sake of ingenuity?

the package. Thus, the advertising is compatible with all of the other elements of a correlated communications program.

- **Obvious intention.** The reader or viewer of an ad should be left with a lasting impression of the product or service being promoted. The main message or idea should be apparent to the audience. The first television advertisements for Infiniti automobiles were so obscure that audiences were not sure what product was being promoted.

- **Evident objective.** Is the advertisement consumer or trade oriented? Is the purpose of the advertisement to produce merchandise sales or to develop an institutional image? What is the advertiser trying to communicate? If the objective of the advertisement is difficult to identify, the ad cannot be very productive.

- **Consistent identity.** By using a consistent visual or audio style throughout various advertisements, the sponsor's ads can immediately be recognized. The layout, graphics, artistic style, copy, typography, sound effects, or video effects contribute to an identifiable image. Consistency gives a positive, easily recognized image to the advertising.

- **Continuity.** The advertisements build upon each other. With a theme or consistent graphics program each advertisement benefits from prior ads and builds for the next ads. Taster's Choice coffee developed a soap opera scenario for its two main characters. The audience anticipated the newest installment of the television commercial.

- **Good relationships between the visual and verbal elements.** In a print ad the visual elements include the artistic elements, and the verbal element is the copy. Advertising copy can be enhanced by appropriate visual stimulus. In a television commercial the spoken words or music reinforces the video. Music from the 1960s and 1970s is used to promote products aimed at baby boomers.

- **Targeting the consumer's point of view.** The needs, wants, and values of the consumer take precedence over those characteristics of the advertiser. The consumer purchases products based upon his or her perceptions.
- **Simplicity.** Although repetition and superfluous language have entered the advertising world, today's sophisticated consumers appreciate simple, concise, and direct language and advertising production styles.
- **Creativity secondary to advertising strategy.** Creativity enables the advertiser to bring humor and/or charming themes into the advertisement. But, an ad should not be cute for cuteness's sake or humorous for humor's sake. When consumers remember the ad for its creativity and cannot remember the product, it is ineffective.
- **Delivery of what it says it can.** Good advertising never promises more than it can deliver. Consumers learn very quickly when they have been deceived or mislead, causing resentment toward the advertiser. These customers will not trust or continue to purchase from such an unethical advertiser. The snake oil salesman in the Old West was likely to be run out of town when consumers found out about the deception.

A checklist for planning effective advertising is shown on page 212. Using this examination technique can be helpful in creating ads as well as evaluating and critiquing ads. Students and advertisers may wish to develop their own criteria or add to these.

FUTURE TRENDS IN ADVERTISING AND THE CREATIVE PROCESS

Globalization is one of the significant trends in advertising. Firms such as Hermès based in Paris have boutiques all over the world, from New York and Washington, D.C., in the United States to Japan, England, Italy, and Australia. Attempting to coordinate an image that is consistent with the high quality associated with the product mix is truly an international problem. Although each boutique has the ability to develop its own local advertising, it must be in line with the global image originated in Paris. The challenge for the future is to create and implement international advertising programs while maintaining local integrity.

According to Wall Street analysts, mega niche brands will continue to have a significant influence on consumer demand, attracting support from all ages and economic groups (Brady, 1996). Most of the mega niche brands have a quality product and the capital to effectively reach consumers with a desired, highly controlled image. According to Elizabeth Eveillard, managing director at Paine Webber, "Clearly these brands represent not only a certain quality and taste level, they represent a certain image, and people are buying that image" (Brady, 1996). The big brands are anticipated to continue to grow because consumers at the end of the 20th century were trading up; they were buying fewer items, but they were buying more expensive nationally known products.

In addition to growth of mega niche brands, private label programs are also anticipated to grow for the more price sensitive and less image conscious consumer. Chains, such as Sears, Roebuck and J. C. Penney, have effectively created powerful private brands. Sears' Canyon River Blues and Arizona from J. C. Penney have become popular with middle market shoppers. These private label products are expected to be popular well into the 21st century.

In order to maintain leadership, mega niche brands will continue to use creative strategies to set their names apart from the competition. Peter Arnell, chairman and creative director of the Arnell Group said, "The difference between creating an image and establishing an image is the difference between presenting a singular idea that can be utilized once or presenting an idea that has many executions" (Parr, 1996). Thus, according to his theory, the brand should have repeated applications, but the original concept remains unchanged. Mega nichers following this formula include Tommy Hilfiger (the spirited, slightly mischievous American), Donna Karan (the belief in female potential), Calvin Klein (the power of sensuality), and Ralph Lauren (the fruits of the good life). Regardless of what the image is or how the agency spins it, it must strike a cord with the public, whether they are buying candles, dresses, or shoes.

In this chapter, we have shown how creativity helps creative strategists come up with their plans. We have also looked at the functions of advertising. Defining the classifications of advertising helped us to distinguish the various roles of advertising. The future looks strong for creative personnel working on a variety of projects, especially for mega niche and private label brands.

SUMMARY

- Creativity, a quality manifested in individuals that enables them to generate clever or imaginative approaches as solutions to problems, can be nurtured and developed in any individual. Creative strategy determines what the message will say, while creative tactics deal with how the message strategy will be implemented.
- Appeals are the reasons people chose to buy based upon the selling points, unique selling proposition, brand image, or position in the market.
- Approaches are the way the appeal is presented to the customer. The basic approaches may be categorized as information, argument, emotional attraction, repeat assertion, command, symbolic association, or imitation. Approaches may be selected based upon product dimensions.
- The copy platform is the document that specifies the basic foundation of the creative strategy that has been determined by background research, product/service specific research, verification, and revision.
- Manufacturers, designers, and retailers have identified several functions that advertising helps them accomplish, which includes providing information, persuading consumers to try their products or services, reminding consumers about the brands, adding value by improving the image or quality of the product/service, and assisting the company's overall marketing efforts.
- The targets for advertising energies are private end-users known as consumers or business users identified as trade consumers.
- Advertising may be directed toward any number of different geographical regions from global to national, regional, and local.
- Advertising may take the form of product, which primarily involves selling merchandise, or institutional, which primarily involves selling long-term goodwill and company image.
- Advertising is considered valuable for both commercial, profit-oriented businesses and nonprofit organizations.
- The growth potential for creative advertising looks very strong for the 21st century.

KEY TERMS

advertising campaign
appeals
approach
assortment advertisements
brand
clearance advertising
commercial advertising
copy platform
creative strategy
creative tactics
creativity
departmental advertisements
direct-response advertising
generic brand

global advertising
global brand
image advertising
institutional advertising
local advertising
mail-order advertising
mega niche brand
motivations
national advertising
national brand
nonprofit advertising
persuasion
prestige advertising
private label brand

problem detection
product advertising
regional advertising
regional brand
regular price advertising
related-items advertisements
retail product advertising
selling points
single-item advertisement
special price advertising
theme advertisements
unique selling proposition
vendor advertisements
volume advertisements

QUESTIONS FOR DISCUSSION

1. Why do manufacturers and retailers advertise?
2. How does product advertising differ from institutional advertising in the retailing environment? In the manufacturing environment?
3. Why would an international firm advertise differently in one country than in another?
4. What is creativity? Why is it so difficult to define?
5. What are the steps in the creative process?
6. What are the differences between motivation, appeal, and approach? Who has the responsibility for each?
7. How does creative strategy development in France compare with that in the United States?

ADDITIONAL RESOURCES

Arens, W. F., and Bovée C. L. (1994) *Contemporary advertising.* Burr Ridge, IL: Irwin.

Jewler, A. J., and Drewniany, B. L. (1997). *Creative strategy in advertising* (6th ed.). Belmont, CA: Wadsworth.

Shimp, T. A. (1997). *Advertising, promotion and supplemental aspects of integrated marketing communications* (4th ed.). Orlando, FL: Dryden Press.

Sutherland, M. (1994) *Advertising and the mind of the consumer: What works, what doesn't and why.* Boston: Allen & Unwin.

Tellis, G. J. (1997). *Advertising and promotion strategy.* Reading, Mass: Addison-Wesley.

Trout, J. (1997). *The new positioning: The latest on the world's #1 business strategy.* New York: McGraw-Hill.

Von Oech, R. (1992). *A whack on the side of the head: How you can be more creative.* New York: Warner.

Williams, R. H. (1998). *The wizard of ads.* Austin, TX: Bard Press.

Winters, A. A., and Winters, P. F. (1996). *What works in fashion advertising.* New York: Retail Reporting Corporation.

Ziccardi, D., and Moin, D. (1997) *Masterminding the store: Advertising, sales, promotion and the new marketing reality.* New York: John Wiley.

Figure 8.1

Coach changed its logo and advertising strategy with the *Living Legends* campaign.

chapter 8

PRINT MEDIA

Coach, the American manufacturer of high quality leather goods, introduced a new contemporary logo with its advertising campaign *Living Legends*. It was the company's hope that changes in logo design and the print advertising campaign would boost its transition to a younger, more of-the-moment firm (Hessen, 1997). It was their first new logo in 70 years, and the advertising campaign (Fig. 8.1) was designed to attract a youthful international audience. The campaign, which targeted Japan as well as the United States, consisted of print ads in *Elle, Vanity Fair, Vogue, W*, and *In Style* in addition to the *New York Times Magazine* and other regional publications. Outdoor media was incorporated into the promotion mix, highlighted by a billboard at 59th Street and Lexington Avenue in New York City. How did Reed Krakoff, senior vice president and executive creative director for Coach, decide on which media, actors, models, and advertising themes to use?

After you have read this chapter, you should be able to:

Use the basic terminology related to media and media planning.

Evaluate and select various media to be used for advertising.

Differentiate among the categories of print media used by advertisers.

Evaluate the advantages and disadvantages of each print medium.

Explain the print media creative process.

The purpose of this chapter is to answer the questions about media in general and about print media specifically. The creation of an effective media plan, deciding which media to use, is vital to any marketing or merchandising program. Thus, it is fitting to move toward analyzing basic media terminology. Next, we assess the formats of traditional print media, which includes newspapers and magazines. The advantages and disadvantages of these media outlets are discussed, because these factors contribute to media selection decisions. Finally, we look at the future trends in print media.

MEDIA

The broad term **media** refers to the mass communication organizations whose function is to provide information or entertainment to an audience of subscribers, viewers, or readers while furnishing advertisers an environment to reach the audience with print and/or broadcast messages. The singular form of the word, **medium**, is used to describe a particular communication category such as newspapers, magazines, television, or radio. A media outlet is the specific newspaper, magazine, television show, or radio program used to communicate an advertising message.

Executives in the promotional field have many choices as to where to place their advertising message, from traditional media to alternative media. Examples of traditional print media include newspapers, newspaper supplements, and magazines.

Broadcast media formats, such as broadcast television, cable television and radio, are covered in Chapter 9.

Print Media Costs

The expense associated with the placement of an advertisement in a print or broadcast outlet is known as the media cost or simply cost. The cost of doing any promotional activity is closely tied to the promotional budget, established early in the planning process. Key executives need to have a basic knowledge of media costs, since the costs will most certainly affect the selection of which media the sponsoring organization will be able to utilize.

Print media cost relates to the price paid for space, a full or partial page, in a newspaper or magazine. The costs associated with print media placement vary from the type of medium to the complexity of the visual message to be reproduced.

The **media buyer** is the executive in charge of media placement who must deliberate the pros and cons of each medium in relationship to the advertising budget. Each specific medium, whether it is television, newspapers, or any other, provides potential advertisers with information about the circulation or size of the medium's audience via its distribution. The top 20 U.S. daily newspapers by average daily circulation are identified in Table 8.1. From the circulation information the media buyer assesses the potential customers that can be expected to respond to the advertisement, also known as the maximum **rate of response**.

One method used to make comparisons between media and competitors within a medium is to calculate variations in cost and circulation. One common measurement used in the print media, particularly in magazines, is to evaluate the **cost-per-thousand** or CPM. This measurement, determined by dividing the medium's audience into the cost for space or time, is the cost of attracting 1,000 readers, viewers, or listeners.

A comparison between two publications will show how a print media buyer would use a CPM analysis to select an appropriate publication for the advertisement. The media buyer for a children's apparel manufacturer wishes to consider two different magazines for placement of a full-page, four-color launch for a line of back-to-school fashions.

Magazine A has a general circulation of 2 million readers with an advertising rate of $25,000 for a full page, four-color ad. The CPM calculation follows:

$$\frac{\$25,000}{2,000 \text{ (circulation in thousands)}} = \$12.50 \text{ CPM}$$

The media buyer needs to have additional information from an alternative choice in order to make a decision. Magazine B provides the following circulation and rate data. This publication has a circulation of 2.5 million readers. Nearly 50 percent of the audience are mothers with school-age children between 6 and 18 years of age. An advertisement meeting the buyer's specifications costs $29,000. The media buyer considers the CPM for the general readership and mother audience. The two formulas are as follows:

Magazine B General audience	**Magazine B** Mothers with school age children
$\dfrac{\$29,000}{2,500} = \$11.60 \text{ CPM}$	$\dfrac{\$29,000}{1,250} = \$23.20 \text{ CPM}$

Table 8.1   **Top 20 U.S. Newspapers by Circulation**

Rank	Newspaper	Average Daily Circulation[a]
1	*Wall Street Journal*	1,774,880
2	*USA Today*[b]	1,713,674
3	*New York Times*	1,074,741
4	*Los Angeles Times*	1,050,176
5	*Washington Post*	775,894
6	*Daily News,* New York	721,256
7	*Chicago Tribune*	653,554
8	*Newsday*	568,914
9	*Houston Chronicle*	549,101
10	*Chicago Sun-Times*	484,379
11	*San Francisco Chronicle*	484,218
12	*Dallas Morning News*	484,032
13	*Boston Globe*	476,966
14	*Phoenix Republic*	437,118
15	*New York Post*	436,226
16	*Philadelphia Inquirer*	428,223
17	*Star-Ledger,* Newark, NJ	406,010
18	*Star-Tribune,* Minneapolis	387,412
19	*Detroit Free Press*	384,624
20	*Plain Dealer,* Cleveland	383,586

[a]*Average for 6 months ended September 30, 1997.*

[b]*Adjusted circulation.*

Adapted from: Newspaper Association of America and Audit Bureau of Circulations, ABC FAS-FAX. (1998). Top 20 US daily newspapers by circulation [On-line]. Available: http://www.naa.org/info/facts/14.html.

In order to have a more complete comparison, the media buyer asks Magazine A for the number of readers who are mothers with children in the target ages. This magazine provides data that out of the 2 million readers, 75 percent meet the additional criteria. The new calculation shows a CPM of $16.67 ($25,000/1,500). Armed with the comparative information, the media buyer has better data to make a decision.

	Magazine A	Magazine B
CPM for general circulation	$12.50	$11.60
CPM for mothers with school age children	$16.67	$23.20

These statistical facts help the advertiser to make an informed decision. Based upon the data for general circulation, the media buyer might select Magazine B as the better choice because the CPM for the general circulation is less. After further analysis, however, the executive selected Magazine A, because the targeted customer, mothers with school-age children, reading Magazine A make the cost-per-thousand contact lower.

Like magazines, newspapers use the cost-per-thousand as a measurement of cost effectiveness. The following example shows a comparison between newspapers. If all other factors were equal, the advertiser would find Newspaper B to be more cost effective than Newspaper A.

	Newspaper A	Newspaper B
Cost-per-page	$23,000	$10,800
Circulation	425,000	380,000
Calculation	23,000/425	10,800/380
CPM	$54.12	$28.42

Comparison between media outlets can be very helpful as a decision making tool. It does make sense to compare one magazine to another, but it is misleading to draw conclusions between media. Television is able to provide sight and sound, while newspapers provide advantages of immediacy and relatively low costs. Other characteristics besides cost-effectiveness must be considered when making media selections. Magazines have a longevity not experienced by TV or newspapers. Additionally, magazines have a pass along rate, an estimate of how many people read the magazine without buying it. Individuals may see it and read it in a medical office waiting room or share the copy with roommates and family. But, there are many other factors besides cost and cost-effectiveness that impact an advertiser's decision to select a particular medium.

Reach, Coverage, and Penetration

Reach, coverage, and penetration are all related to the audience or potential audience that an advertiser is trying to attract. Although many people use these terms interchangeably, it is important to understand the distinctions.

Reach describes the percentage of target audience, homes, or individuals exposed to an advertiser's message at least once in a period of time, usually 4 weeks. Thus, reach represents the number of target customers who see or hear the advertiser's message during the designated time period. Advertisers want to know how many people a media outlet can reach without counting individuals more than once. Reach is normally expressed as a percentage of the total audience of different homes or unduplicated individuals who are exposed to a message.

A variation of reach is a cume, or **cumulative audience**. This refers to the total number of different people who are exposed to a schedule of commercials. The term cumulative audience implies that additional unduplicated individuals will be added to the reach as the time period progresses. Consideration of unduplicated and duplicated research figures into reach analysis. Unduplicated reach symbolizes potential new exposures, while duplicated reach provides a gauge of frequency.

Coverage refers to the potential audience that might receive the message through a media outlet. Most advertisers are interested in choosing media that will communicate or "cover" all of the advertiser's active and potential target audience. Coverage is frequently expressed as a percentage of a population group. For instance, the estimated population for a target group is 1.2 million. A magazine declares a readership of 72,000 fitting within that target population—or 6 percent coverage. Coverage relates to potential audience, whereas reach reports the actual audience delivered. Therefore, reach is always smaller than coverage.

Penetration refers to the total number of persons or households that are physically able to be exposed to a medium by the nature of that medium's geographical circulation or broadcast signal. Television penetration is the percentage of total households that own at least one television set reached within a specific geographical region. Billboard penetration is the percentage of drivers and passengers that are exposed to a billboard within a specific geographical area.

Frequency and Scheduling

Advertisers typically want to have their message in front of consumers at all times, reminding them about the features and benefits of their product. But, it is unrealistic and unaffordable to maintain such a constant pace for promotional communication. Frequency and scheduling are ways advertisers plan the pace of media exposure.

Frequency is defined as the number of times the receiver is exposed to the media outlet within a specified period of time. Frequency increases the chance that target audience members will be reached. An advertiser running an advertisement in the local newspaper on a weekly basis will reach additional target customers by adding ads to the Sunday magazine supplement. Frequency is closely related to scheduling.

Scheduling involves setting the time for advertisements or commercials to run. The primary objective of scheduling is to time promotional efforts to coincide with the period when the target audience can be attracted. For some products the scheduling is obvious, for others it is not so clear. Currently, three scheduling strategies are used by media planners: continuity, flighting, and pulsing.

Continuity

Continuity refers to a steady placement of advertisements over a designated period of time. This pattern could mean every day, every week, or every month. The fundamental factor is regularity in the pattern so that no gaps or lapses occur. Merchandise ideally suited for this pattern of scheduling are products consumed on a regular basis without regard for seasonality. Skin care items, shampoo, and basic stock items such as white shirts, hosiery, undergarments, towels, and sheets benefit from continuity scheduling.

Flighting

Flighting uses a much less regular schedule, involving periods with moderate to heavy exposure followed by a hiatus or lapse prior to restarting the advertising schedule. Sometimes there are substantial advertising expenditures followed by periods with limited expenses. Seasonal items such as skis, ski apparel, and accessories benefit from a flighting scheduling pattern for promotion. Between October and April, ski-related manufacturers advertise heavily, but they rarely spend any promotional money during the spring and summer.

Pulsing

Pulsing, the third method of scheduling, is a combination of the first two methods. An advertiser using a pulsing strategy maintains a continuity of advertising with a step-up effort at certain times of the year. Fragrance and cosmetic lines use a pulsing strategy. Although fragrance and color cosmetics are advertised regularly, manufacturers increase advertising during holidays such as Christmas and Mother's Day, gift-with-purchase promotions, or at the start of a fall or spring fashion season.

The scheduling strategy used by an advertiser depends upon several factors, such as the media objectives, consumer buying cycles, and budget among other concerns. Since advertisers have differing objectives and always have budget limitations, they find themselves deciding between reach and frequency. The advertiser faces trade-offs between having the message seen or heard by more people and having a smaller number of people exposed to the message more often.

Measuring the Media

In addition to the cost analysis previously discussed, supplementary methods are used to evaluate media choices. Ratings, gross rating points, and share are some of the various tools used by media measurement services to provide this additional information. Most of these terms originated in the broadcast industry but are used by almost all media today.

The audience size, an estimate of the total number of homes reached expressed as a percentage of the total population, is known as ratings or **program ratings**. Ratings are established by an independent research service, such as Nielsen Media Research. A rating of 20 equals 20 percent of all people in the market. The program rating is calculated by dividing the number of households (HH) tuned to a particular show by the total number of households in the area. If 10 million households watched a particular television show, the national rating would be 10.6. The calculation follows:

$$\text{Rating} = \frac{\text{HH tuned to show}}{\text{Total U.S. HH}} = \frac{10,000,000}{94,000,000} = 10.6$$

The next example shows how this information can be used by an advertiser to predict reach. Assume there are 94 million homes with television sets in the United States and a TV program has a rating of 25. The advertiser can estimate the potential audience. The calculation is 25 percent of 94 million (0.25 × 94 million), or 23.5 million homes.

Another method of measuring media involves **gross ratings points** (GRPs), the sum of all ratings delivered by a commercial schedule. This information helps the advertiser and media buyer know how many potential audience members might be exposed to a series of commercials. This measurement combines the program's rating with the average number of times the home is reached during the defined time period (frequency of exposure). The calculation for GRPS is as follows:

$$\text{GRPS} = \text{Reach} \times \text{Frequency}$$

GRPs show the number of listeners or viewers that radio or television schedule might be reached by a media schedule, using a duplicated reach estimate. In order to determine unduplicated reach, media specialists look at target ratings point. **Target ratings points** (TRPs) refer to the number of people in the primary target audience the media buy will reach. Unlike GRPs, TRPs does not contain waste coverage.

Just what do these ratings points mean? A purchase of 100 GRPS could reflect several conditions. In one instance, it may mean that 100 percent of the market is exposed to the message once. In other cases, it may mean 50 percent of the market is exposed twice, 25 percent is exposed four times, and so on.

A sample media buy can be described as follows. Revlon purchased 1,800 GRPs during a 4-week period to introduce *Stone Edge: Nature's Muted Tones Bring Color Down to Earth*, the latest line of lip, nail, and eye color cosmetics (Fig. 8.2). This purchase consisted of 50 separate magazine advertisements, estimated to reach 96 percent of the target audience on average of 12 times. Prior to the buy, the media planner needed to determine whether or not this would be an effective purchase. Certainly a reach of 96 percent is desirable, but is the frequency level too high or not high enough? Does this level of GRPs impact consumer awareness and make them more likely to purchase the product?

Researchers at Foote, Cone & Belding advertising agency and others have explored these questions. David Berger, vice president and director of research, determined that 2,500 GRPs were likely to lead to an approximate 70 percent probability of high aware-

Figure 8.2
Advertisement for
Revlon's Stone Edge
colors.

ness, but 1,000 to 2,500 would yield about a 33 percent awareness, and less than 1,000 would impact virtually no awareness (Berger, 1987). In this still relevant type of analysis, if an increased awareness level leads to trial, then it would be desirable for Revlon to increase its GRPs.

In terms of media planning, **share** refers to the size of an audience for any given time period. This figure, also originated in the broadcast industry, considers variation in the number of sets in use and the total size of the potential audience, since it only considers the households that have their televisions turned on. It is also expressed in terms of a percentage, as follows:

$$\text{Share} = \frac{\text{Number of TV household tuned into a program}}{\text{Number of households using TV at that time}} \times 100$$

Next, we turn our attention to media planning and strategy development. Media planning evolves from overall strategic planning for all promotional and marketing activities. Once the marketing strategy has been developed, the advertising strategy is planned with the appropriate selection of media as a coordinated effort. Thus, advertising objectives, budget decisions, message, and media strategies evolve from the firm's overall promotional and marketing strategy.

Responsibility for Media Analysis

The executive designated with the responsibility for developing the media plan is known as a media planner. This executive has the difficult responsibility of analyzing the appropriate media location for the message, which requires careful quantitative and qualitative research. The ultimate desire is to attract the target customer with a minimum of waste and a maximum of efficiency. The media planner not only has to select between the various media, but also between alternatives within the same medium. Should the planner choose to place the advertisement in *House and Garden* or *Metropolitan Home?* Media planning is the task of deciding when, where, and how the advertising message will be delivered. New computer models have been developed to enhance the researchers' capabilities in assessing which media to use. These computer models are discussed later in the chapter.

Media Objectives and Strategy

Developing media strategy and objectives is a complex and involved process, made more difficult with inconsistent terminology, the introduction of alternative media technologies, and evolution of existing media. As the media planning process takes place, ideas are generated, evaluated, altered, used, or abandoned. This process leads to a media plan.

Media objectives are the goals to be attained by the media program that should be accomplished by media strategies. Media objectives are determined by a media situational analysis, a process similar to the marketing situational analysis discussed in Chapter 4. Planning media objectives is a part of the *big picture*, assisting the firm to attain its communication and marketing objectives. The purpose of media objectives is to translate marketing objectives and strategies into goals that media can accomplish. An example of a media objective follows: *Create awareness of Swatch Irony Metal Collection Watches* (Fig. 8.3) *in the target market of men and women between the ages of 18 and 32 years through the following strategies:*

- *Utilize magazine print medium to provide coverage of 80 percent of the target market over a 6-month period.*
- *Reach 60 percent of the target audience at least three times over the same 6-month period.*
- *Concentrate heaviest advertising during fall and winter with lighter emphasis in spring and summer.*

The article in Box 8.1 provides information about matching the media with the ad copy objectives.

Media strategies are definite plans of action designed to achieve these media objectives. Media strategies translate media goals into general guidelines that will control the planner's selection and use of media. The best alternatives should be selected. Media strategy specifies target audience, defines the media objectives, selects the media categories to be used with specific outlets, and directs media buying. Broad media classes and specific media are recommended. If magazines are to be used, then which ones should be used? If radio or television was recommended, which markets will be used? Additional decisions involve determining media schedules, allocating the media budget, and choosing the appropriate geographical locations for the advertising message.

The media plan formalizes the planning process into a plan for selecting the best method for getting an advertiser's message to the market. Thus, the basic goal of the

Figure 8.3

Advertisement for
Swatch's Irony Metal
Collection

BOX 8.1

Match Your Media Choice and Ad Copy Objective

Working recently on a Yellow Pages advertising project, it struck me how many display advertisers —from the local retailers and industrial suppliers to national brands—emphasize messages inappropriate to the medium.

Running awareness-oriented advertising in a directory provides a marketing benefit, but it appeals weakly to the audience's foremost need: finding a supplier for a specific purchase already in mind. Directory ads should promise specific solutions and unambiguously ask for a response.

Hardly limited to Yellow Pages, running ads not tailored to the medium is a common mistake in business-to-business communications. Often the culprit is a limited budget that stretches one ad across different types of media.

Available cash notwithstanding, advertisers should know better. One often hears of business-to-business marketing managers hoping to create awareness in inquiry-oriented media, or generate leads from publications better suited to image building. Their advertising is not working as hard as it could.

A rule of thumb about the advertising media most appropriate to ad copy objectives can be useful at the start of communications planning. To simplify a business-to-business example, assume the copy objective is either building awareness or generating qualified sales leads:

- Awareness advertising strives to put a company or brand identity and position—what it stands for in the marketplace—in the forefront of sales prospects' minds so they will recall the name if and when they consider a purchase.
- Lead-generating ads inspire target prospects to ask the company for more information and identify themselves for sales follow-up. They emphasize action that will solve a reader's immediate, top-of-mind need.

Although an ad's primary objective should be either awareness or leads, well-crafted messages can contribute to both.

Further simplifying this business-to-business example, let's consider only vertical business publications that focus on specific industries or product categories. They are the workhorse media of business marketing. Vertical business publication editorial fare appears in two main flavors that determine how audiences use them.

- Article-oriented periodicals stress industry news or service journalism designed to be read. The article topics draw readers to those publications.
- Product tabloids and directories list new products and sources of supply. Immediate buying intentions motivate people to scan the pages, seeking suppliers with solutions to specific problems.

There is plenty of gray area between those extremes. New product sections of article-oriented publications invite scanning. Also, how-to articles aimed at solving specific problems create a natural environment for advertising proposing branded solutions to the same problems. And business-buying influencers whose jobs require staying abreast of technology frequently flip through product tabloids without having a specific problem in mind.

Two extremes of media performance and two extremes of copy objective create a classic two-way space, or matrix.

- An awareness campaign in an article-oriented publication is a natural fit, reaching readers thinking about their jobs, industries, careers, and other strategic issues in a generalized way. An appropriate ad headline might read: "How to master the new widget technologies before they master you."

- A lead-generation campaign in a product tabloid or directory is another slam-dunk match of copy and medium. Readers want a specific fix to a specific problem now. An appropriate headline would get right to the point: "Same day service for X-class Widgets—at the old low prices."
- A lead-generation campaign in an article-oriented publication tends to reach readers less likely to pounce on a specific product or service offering. The copy should build awareness about a class of solutions offered by the vendor. An exemplary headline could offer a booklet of genuine reader value: "How to determine whether X-class widgets are right for you."
- An awareness campaign in a directory or product tabloid publication is not likely to be a strong fit of copy objective to the medium. Readers are more likely to have purchase specifications, not brand imagery, in mind. Copy faces an uphill task trying to wedge a positioning statement and a specific performance promise into the reader's head simultaneously. The headline will have to be provocative: "Before you jump for any X-class widget, benefit from Harry Smith's nightmare," for instance.

Like all rules of thumb, these are rough guides, and you may have plenty of legitimate reasons for not following them. But, when you break the rule, be able to explain the reasons why.

Adapted from: Donath, B. (1998, June 8). Match your media choice and ad copy objective, Marketing News, 6.
Bob Donath of Bob Donath & Company Inc. in White Plains, New York, is a consultant and writer specializing in business marketing and communications.

media plan is to identify and articulate the most worthwhile combination of media, or media mix, that enables the advertiser to communicate the message in the most effective manner to the largest number of potential customers at the lowest cost. The media plan serves as the guide for media selection and placement.

Difficulties in Media Planning and Strategy Development

A number of problems make development of media objectives and implementation of a media strategy arduous.

- **Inconsistent terminology.** Many of the terms associated with the media are confusing and may be used incorrectly. Terms such as reach and coverage may be used synonymously, adding to the confusion.

- **Inconsistent measurement tools.** The methods for evaluating cost of using a particular medium may be inharmonious with evaluation in other media. Magazines commonly use CPM, as previously noted in this chapter, while broadcast media refer to cost per ratings point (CPRP), and outdoor media use the number of showings. The cost-effectiveness measure for newspapers is based upon the daily inch rate. How can a media planner compare number of showings to CPM, CPRP, or a daily inch rate?

- **Lack of information.** Even though there is a tremendous amount of information about markets and the media, media planners often require more than is available. Timing of the measurements for television audiences are during sweeps periods: February, May, July, and November. During these times the television networks offer many highly attractive special programs, exciting sporting events, and new episodes of popular shows instead of reruns, trying to obtain the highest audience numbers possible. These measurements are generalized for the following months, but might not take into consideration popularity of certain programs without competition from special programming that ran during sweeps. Planning decisions are based upon historical data, created during especially strong program periods. Lack of information is also a problem advertisers face during the introduction of the new fall programs. Although the advertiser has an opportunity to preview the new program, it is untested with the consumer market. The advertiser does not have actual audience measurements.

- **Time urgency.** Advertisers are always in a hurry, working under tight deadlines. Print schedules, competition actions, and the general nature of the advertising business place a huge time pressure on promotional executives. Whether the pressure is real (as when a competitor offers a price break) or imagined, media selection without proper planning and analysis cannot lead to the most effective placement of creative strategy or budget.

- **Difficulty measuring effectiveness.** Because there are many problems associated with evaluating the effectiveness of promotional and advertising activities in general, we can assume that this difficulty is also associated with measuring the effectiveness of the various media or media outlets. How can the media planner assess the effectiveness of running an advertisement in *Vogue* versus *Elle*? Because of an inability to quantify the differences, the media planner must usually guess at the impact of one outlet versus another. To complicate the evaluation process, how does the media planner compare the print ad placed in a magazine to a television commercial?

- **Lack of information about untested or emerging technologies.** Statistics regarding increased use of the Internet and projection of its growth are staggering as this book is being written. How can an advertiser anticipate just what kind of impact this emerging technology will have on his or her promotional planning? The great anticipation for home shopping via interactive television has not lived up to the expectations. Will advertisers flock to the alternative media such as CD-ROM when even the best forecasters cannot anticipate its future?

Media Measurement Services

Independent research companies provide unbiased evaluation of consumers and their use of media. Mediamark Research, Inc. (MRI) and competitor Simmons Market Research Bureau (SMRB) provide lifestyle information in addition to media usage characteristics. MRI annually surveys 30,000 consumers throughout the continental United States and provides comprehensive information on demographic, lifestyle, product usage, and media data to subscribers. Some data from MRI are available free via publications and Internet access. Such information relates to magazine audiences, cable television audiences, and demographic statistics of Internet and Online Service Usage.

Newspapers use circulation statistics, certified by the Audit Bureau of Circulation, as the consumer use information. Scarborough Research Corporation and Media Audit attempt to find out detailed information about consumers who read newspapers. Scarborough Research surveys consumers in 58 markets. Randomly selected consumers are asked about their socioeconomic profiles, shopping habits, what newspapers they read, what radio and TV stations they tune to, and the kinds of TV programs they watch. Media Audit conducts similar research in 55 markets.

Traffic Audit Bureau conducts research for the outdoor media industry, while magazine statistics are gathered by Simmons Market Research Bureau, Mediamark Research, and Standard Rate and Data Service. Local advertisers can obtain market profiles from Media Audit.

Media Selection

As we can recognize, the task of the media buyer is a complicated one. Planning and placement of the media budget is critical to the success of an advertising program. The checklist below can serve as a guide to the selection of media. The questions posed must be considered prior to making final media decisions.

Media Selection Checklist

- ❑ **Who is the target customer?** The target customer should be defined in terms of demographics and lifestyle. The customer could be a prospect, regular user, or an inactive customer. The media buyer should take into consideration any primary or secondary research accumulated about the customer or potential customer. Additionally, the geographical location of the consumer must be considered in light of the media options.
- ❑ **What are the advertising and media objectives?** Is the advertiser interested in selling merchandise or the institution? Is the advertiser interested in creating advance awareness for a new product? Does the advertiser want to emphasize the image of the designer, manufacturer, or retailer?
- ❑ **What type of message is the advertiser sending?** Is the advertisement for a product or service? Is the emphasis on value, quality, prestige, service, or some other characteristic?
- ❑ **What are the product's properties?** At what stage of the product life cycle is the merchandise? Is it a new product or an established brand? Is the merchandise in a highly competitive or exclusive environment?
- ❑ **Is the particular medium suited to the merchandise or producer?** The audience for a particular publication should be interested in the category of merchandise. It seems obvious that Coach leather handbags would receive a more positive response in *Vogue* rather than *Details.*
- ❑ **Who is the competition and where do they advertise?** Understanding the role of the competition and estimating the expenditures of the competition helps the media buyer justify maintaining a competitive stance.
- ❑ **How much does it cost to advertise in a particular medium?** How does that relate to the advertising budget? Can the advertiser afford the expenses for creative development and placement?
- ❑ **Where is the business located?** If the business is in a high traffic area, perhaps advertising is not as essential as it would be if the advertiser is in an out of the way location.
- ❑ **What has the advertiser done in the past?** What media placement has been successful versus ineffective in past advertising programs?

Table 8.2 **Rank Order of Information Sources for Women's Fashions**

Information Source	1979	1987	1996
Going shopping in the store	1	1	1
Looking through catalogs	8	3	2 (T)
Observing what other women wear	2	2	2 (T)
Sales promotions/flyers	NM	NM	4
Newspaper fashion advertising	3	4	5
Discussions with other women	7	5	6
Television fashion advertising	9	6	7
Reading magazines other than those which are fashion-oriented	6	8	8
Reading fashion articles in newspapers	5	7	9
Reading fashion magazines	4	9	10
Speaking with clothing salespersons	10	10	11
Fashion advertising on radio	11	12	12
Discussing women's fashion with men	12	11	13

NM, not measured; T, tie.
Adapted from: Chain Store Age Chicago Apparel Study. (1996, October) Chain Store Age, 22B-23B.

The media planner can also use outside research results as a source of information when planning which media to use. For example, the Chicago Apparel Study conducted for *Chain Store Age* asked women consumers about their lifestyles, interest in shopping, and interest in fashion trends. When asked to assess their level of interest in women's fashions compared to other women, 59 percent of the apparel shoppers described themselves as being about as interested as most other women, while 30 percent said they were less interested than other women (Chain Store Age Chicago Apparel Study, 1996). With this in mind, the shoppers were asked to rank order their sources of information to ascertain clothing trends; the results are shown in Table 8.2. Although top sources of information, "going shopping in the store" and "observing what other women wear" were non-media sources, more than half (54 percent) of all respondents reported having visited a store as a result of seeing a newspaper insert. Figure 8.4 shows media that were most effective in bringing consumers into the store, and media that were most effective in turning the shoppers into purchasers. This type of research helps the media planner to select the most effective media outlets.

Computers in Media Planning

Significant quantities of information about media, target audience, reach, frequency, ratings, and other relevant factors can be overwhelming to the media planner. Advanced planning models such as linear programming, simulation, and iteration have been around since the early 1960s with limited success. Computer models have been able sort through data, significantly improving the quantitative information available to managers for decision-making purposes. Attempts to improve the media buying process through computer simulation models have received a great deal of attention.

As indicated earlier in the chapter, MRI provides consumer demographic information, product statistics, and media usage characteristics. Access to the MRI database is available through several computer applications, including MEMRI, MEMRI 2, and

Figure 8.4

Effective Advertising
Media.

Source: Based on
Chain Store Age. *(1996,*
October), 22B–22B.

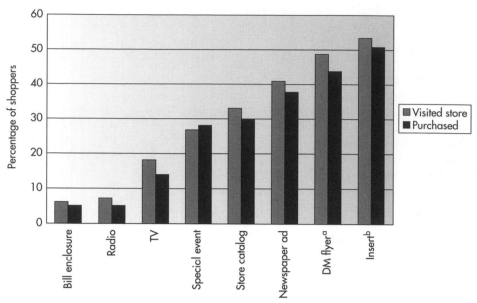

[a]Direct mail store flyer
[b]Special store newspaper insert

Mediamark Reporter. MEMRI allows subscribers such as marketing specialists and media planners access to MRI's consumer database. MEMRI 2 provides an updated Windows environment, making the data easier and more flexible to use. This information is delivered via CD-ROM, installed on the subscriber's computer or local area network (LAN), eliminating third-party vendors, telephone and on-line charges, and computer queues. Mediamark Reporter information is distributed on diskette or CD, allowing the user to manipulate report data in methods not possible through printed books. Data may be retrieved by keyword, rows and columns can display only the specific data needed, report headings can be customized, and data can be exported to spreadsheet and presentation packages. All of these benefits were made possible through the introduction of computer technology into consumer and media analysis.

Other market analysis programs are also available. ClusterPlus and Market America include demographic, geographical, psychographic, and product and media use statistics that can be used in media investigation. Computer programs can be used to cross-tabulate media and demographic data, estimate reach and frequency and rank costs, in addition to numerous other applications. This type of information can help planners determine which markets should be targeted in addition to selection of the appropriate media objectives and placement. Now that we have a basic understanding of the media, we will turn our attention to newspapers, one of the most important print media outlets.

NEWSPAPERS

Newspapers are the primary advertising medium used by retailers and the medium with the highest share of advertising expenditures in the United States. According to the Newspaper Association of America, in 1996 daily newspapers reached $38,075 million, or a 21.8 percent share of the $174,904 million spent on advertising in all media

(Newspaper Association of America and McCann-Erickson, 1998). These statistics reflect the advertising expenditures from all types of businesses, not just fashion retailers and are shown in Table 8.3.

Although newspapers are the primary print medium selected by retailers, manufacturers and designers rarely use local or regional newspapers. Unless they are participating in cooperative advertising with a retailer in the local trading area, most manufacturers and designers have national advertising goals, placing advertisements in widely distributed newspapers with broad circulation.

Newspapers are low in purchase cost, and many U.S. citizens read the local newspaper as a chief source of news and information about their local communities. According to the Newspaper Associaton of America (1998), nearly 59 percent of all adults in the United States read weekday newspapers, while 68.5 percent read Sunday or weekend newspapers (Table 8.4). Demographic studies, reflected in Table 8.5, indicate that the population reading newspapers tends to be better educated, with higher household income, higher home values, and higher job responsibility. Newspaper readership extends beyond the person purchasing the paper, because the paper is passed on to others. With more than 36 million newspapers sold daily, the average daily readership extends to an average of 2.16 readers per copy. This means that more than 78 million adults read the newspaper on a daily basis. These statistics rise to 91 million adults on Sundays ("Newspaper Readership," 1996).

Table 8.3 **U.S. Advertising Expenditures—All Media**

	1996[a] (millions)	% of Total	1997[b] (millions)	% of Total	% Change
Daily newspapers total	$ 38,075	21.8	$ 41,341	22.1	8.6
National	4,667	2.7	5,322	2.8	14.0
Retail	18,344	10.5	19,257	10.3	5.0
Classified	15,065	8.6	16,762	9.0	11.3
Magazines	9,010	5.2	9,975	5.3	10.7
Broadcast television	36,046	20.6	37,145	19.9	3.0
Cable television	4,472	2.6	5,275	2.8	18.0
Radio total	12,269	7.0	13,180	7.1	7.4
Direct mail	34,509	19.7	36,925	19.8	7.0
Yellow Pages	10,849	6.2	11,470	6.1	5.7
Miscellaneous total[c]	22,263	12.7	31,575	16.9	41.8
Total—national	103,307	59.1	110,432	59.1	6.9
Total—local	71,597	40.9	76,454	40.9	6.8
Total—All media	$174,904	100.0	$186,886	100.0	6.9

[a]*Revised data.*

[b]*Preliminary data.*

[c]*Includes weeklies, shoppers, pennysavers, and bus and cinema advertising. Estimates include all costs: time and talent, space, and production.*

Sources: NAA (newspapers) and McCann-Erickson Inc. (all other media).

Adapted from: Newspaper Association of America and McCann-Erickson. (1998). U.S. advertising expenditures—all media {On-line}. Available: Http://www.naa.org/info/facts/09.html.

Table 8.4 **U.S. Daily and Sunday/Weekend Newspaper Reading Audience**[a]

Year	Weekday Readers % of Total Adult Population	Sunday/Weekend Readers % of Total Adult Population	Year	Weekday Readers % of Total Adult Population	Sunday/Weekend Readers % of Total Adult Population
1970	77.6	72.3	1989	63.6	67.0
1977	68.5	67.9	1990	62.4	67.1
1980	66.9	67.4	1991	62.1	66.9
1982	67.0	66.6	1992	62.6	68.4
1984	65.1	65.4	1993	61.7	69.0
1985	64.2	65.1	1994	61.5	70.4
1986	62.9	64.1	1995	64.2	72.6
1987	64.8	65.7	1996	58.8	68.5
1988	64.2	64.0	1997	58.7	68.5

[a]*Aged 18 years and over.*

Sources: W.R. Simmons & Associates Research Inc. 1970-1977, Simmons Market Research Bureau Inc. 1980–1994, Scarborough Reports–Top 50 DMA Markets 1995–1997.

Adapted from: Newspaper Association of America. (1998). U.S. Daily and Sunday/Weekend newspaper reading audience [On-line]. Available: http://www.naa.org/info/facts/02.html.

Table 8.5 **U.S. Daily and Sunday Newspaper Readership Demographics**

Education Level	% Daily	% Sunday	Household Income	% Daily	% Sunday
College graduate or beyond	67	77	$75,000 or more	69	78
Attended college (1–3 years)	61	71	$50,000 or more	66	76
High school graduate	59	67	$40,000 or more	65	73
Less than high school graduate	43	47	Less than $40,000	53	60
Age			**Job Responsibility**		
18–24	48	59	Professional/managerial	68	78
25–34	48	62	Technical/clerical/sales	58	69
35–44	60	68	Precision/craft	56	63
45–54	64	70	All other	53	58
55–64	66	71	**Home Value**		
65+	68	68			
			$200,000+	68	75
			$100,000–$199,999	66	74
			$50,000–$99,999	63	70
			Less than $50,000	53	59

Source: Simmons Market Research Bureau, Spring 1997.

Adapted from: Newspaper Association of America. (1998). U.S. daily and sunday newspaper readership demographics [On-line]. Available: http://www.naa.org/info/facts/03.html.

Newspaper Formats

Newspapers in the United States fall into one of two different formats. A paper is either a **broadsheet**, the large standard size six columns wide, or a **tabloid**, approximately half the size of a broadsheet with five columns. The *New York Times, Wall Street Journal,* and *Los Angeles Times* fit the broadsheet category. Tabloids have been popular in the trade press. *Women's Wear Daily* and *Daily News Record* are published as tabloids. The *Rocky Mountain News* is an example of a daily newspaper that publishes in the tabloid format. Some local papers with a high number of commuters sell tabloid size newspapers, making it easier for train or bus riders to read during their commute.

The image associated with tabloid formats has been negative, because many people view tabloids as a sensationalistic type of journalism. This was especially so in 1997 after the death of Diana, Princess of Wales, when unregulated paparazzi photographers were blamed for provoking the automobile accident that killed Diana, her male companion, and her driver. In this text, however, tabloid refers to a newspaper format, not necessarily to the style of journalism presented in the sensational press.

Newspaper supplements are targeted special issues covering any topic from shopping themes such as wedding planning, home improvements, back-to-school, traditional fashion season change, to photographic displays, entertainment sections, or Sunday news and feature magazines. Newspapers, including the *San Francisco Chronicle* and the *New York Times,* publish a magazine supplement each Sunday. The Sunday magazine published by the *Denver Post* is called the *Empire Magazine.* Other papers insert national newspaper magazines, such as *USA Today* or *Parade,* into their Sunday papers.

The *New York Times* publishes several special fashion supplements to its Sunday magazine annually. *Fashions of the Times* are presented at the beginning of the fall and spring seasons; publication dates are in August and March. The women's fashion supplement has editorial features on trends for the upcoming season and advertising from major retail stores, designers, and manufacturers of apparel. Additional supplements cover the men's, home interior, and children's markets. Special issues such as one on *The American Store* have also been distributed (Fig. 8.5).

Since supplements are directed to a special interest group, they may be used to target a specific audience for advertising. The wedding planning supplement is an ideal place for photographers, musicians, rental halls, or bridal stores to advertise. Stores such as Target, Sears, and Wal-mart provide color inserts to local papers on higher quality stock than typical newsprint. These inserts enable the advertiser to use color more effectively with high impact for the consumer. These supplements take on some of the advantages of magazines with longer lives and higher quality printing.

Newspaper Advertising Costs

Each newspaper has a rate schedule that specifies the cost of space in that publication. These costs are directly related to the size, the amount of space the advertisement fills, the circulation, or number of the newspaper's distribution and readership, and the position of the ad in the newspaper, or the place or location it occupies.

The **standard advertising unit** (SAU) is used to measure the space by which advertising is sold. Ads are measured by column width and depth in inches. The greater the number of widths and inches the ad spans, the greater the cost. Prior to 1984 news-

Figure 8.5

Trade advertisement for *New York Times Magazine* supplement, *The American Store.*

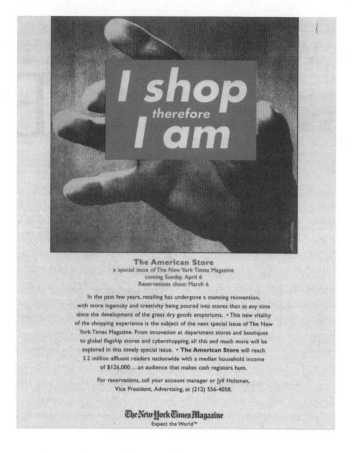

paper space was sold by agate line, causing problems with inconsistency since newspapers used columns of varying width. In order to make newspaper advertising rates more comparable, the Newspaper Advertising Bureau led the newspaper industry toward the SAU as the universal measurement system. Under this system all newspapers use column widths of 2 1/16 inches wide, making broadsheet papers six columns wide and tabloid formats five columns wide. The column inch is the unit of measurement, standardized into 57 units or format sizes (Fig. 8.6). The column inch is 1 inch deep and one column wide.

This system of measurement allows a national advertiser to prepare an ad in a particular SAU, and it can be used in any newspaper that accepts SAUs. Since nearly 90 percent of the daily papers in the United States use SAUs, rates quoted on that system permit national advertisers to produce consistent advertisements. The production and purchase processes have been simplified tremendously.

In addition to the considerations of column inch and SAU, newspapers offer other options and considerations to the media planner. Many newspapers offer flat rates, which means they do not offer any special discounts for quantity or regularly scheduled space purchases. Other publications offer open-rate structures, allowing discounts under specific conditions. These conditions usually are granted to advertisers buying frequent or bulk amounts of space, determined by the number of column inches purchased in a year.

Newspaper advertising rates may vary due to special requests from the advertisers. These requests include such factors as the position where the ad is placed or the use of

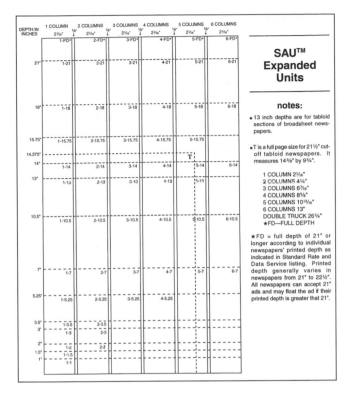

Figure 8.6

Standard advertising units are used to measure advertising space in newspapers.

Source: 1999 Editor & Publisher International Year Book. *Reprinted with permission.*

color. Basic advertising rates established by the newspaper are for the run of paper (ROP), which means that the ad can be placed on any page or section, determined by the newspaper. The advertiser desiring a specific page or news section is required to pay a higher price for this preferred position, which may be the back page of the front section or some other highly demanded position. Color advertising may be available for higher impact. These pages may be limited to certain positions, through preprinted inserts or in the Sunday supplements.

Advertisers may be able to buy newspaper space based upon combination rates whereby a discount is offered when the advertiser agrees to purchase space in several newspapers. Thus, combination rates may apply when the newspaper publisher owns several newspapers.

Types of Newspaper Advertising

The major classifications of newspaper advertising are display, classified, public notices, and preprinted inserts. Different types of ads are used by advertisers to achieve their various goals.

Display Advertising

A display advertisement includes copy and artistic elements, such as illustrations, photography, headlines, and/or other visual components. Display ads vary in size and appear in all sections of a newspaper except on the front page, the editorial page, and the first page of major sections. Display ads may be black-and-white, or color may be introduced. Although a display ad does not require *pictures,* they normally will contain some type of art through a logo, photograph, or drawing.

Display ads are purchased by amounts specified on **rate cards**. These documents list the costs for space, production (mechanical and copy) requirements, deadlines, and other publication information such as preferred position and circulation, discussed earlier in the chapter.

Classified Advertising

Classified advertisements differ from display ads because they normally contain only copy. They provide a community marketplace for goods, services, and every type of opportunity, from real estate and used cars to garage sales. Classified ads are organized under subheads that describe the class of goods or services to be offered. For example, people who are looking for a job will look for the subhead labeled *Help Wanted.*

Classified ads are purchased by the number of lines the ad occupies and the number of times it runs. Rates may also depend upon the category where it is placed. Since classified ads provide a significant source of advertising revenue for a newspaper, the classified section is generally a significant portion of the paper. Some papers also accept classified display advertisements, which run in the classified section of the newspaper. These ads feature slightly larger type sizes and may include photos, artistic borders, white space, and possibly color.

Public Notices

Newspapers carry legal notices for a fee. These public notices inform the citizens about changes in business or personal relationships, public government reports, notices by private citizens, and financial reports.

Preprinted Inserts

Sometimes advertisers prepare an advertising document, which is delivered to the newspaper. The document is then inserted into the newspaper as a preprinted insert before the newspaper is delivered to readers. Inserts vary in size, ranging from a postcard to a flyer, catalog, brochure, or sheet of coupons. Some newspapers allow advertisers to limit the circulation of these inserts to specific circulation zones or to home subscribers only. Some firms find that it is less costly to distribute flyers this way than by mail or door-to-door delivery.

Advantages of Newspapers for Advertising

Newspaper advertising provides many benefits to the advertiser. Besides the widespread acceptance and readership of the medium, newspapers offer the following advantages:

- **Immediacy**. Daily newspapers have relatively short lead times for the insertion of an advertisement. This short time period allows for quick response to product or service announcements, fast testing of consumer interest, or rapid switching of advertising needs to meet the current conditions in the community. Marketing tie-ins can be immediately covered with extensive, next-day editorial coverage of such activities as sporting events, political ceremonies, or special events such as presentation of the Oscars or other award ceremonies. Appropriate sports apparel may be advertised during the regional Special Olympic Games. Accessories or designs associated with a political figure may show up in newspaper advertisements after a local personal appearance. Weather tie-ins are triggered by weather-related conditions. After the first snowfall, advertisements for winter weather apparel or snow blowers may be featured.

- **Local emphasis.** Many newspapers are still focused on a city or town rather than a state or large geographical region. City newspapers offer benefits to small retailers wishing to place the core of their advertising close to their local target market. The exceptions to the local press are such publications as the *New York Times, Washington Post, USA Today,* and *Wall Street Journal.* These papers have national distribution.
- **Flexible production.** Production of the ad can be adjusted to the budget of the advertiser. Newspapers offer a wide range of sizes from as large as two full pages to something as small as a business card. The advertisement may be developed with a lot of copy or limited copy. It may be created with drawings or photography. Preferred position has the highest visibility, either in the first few pages of the general news section or in the Lifestyle, Fashion, or Art sections where fashion-related news appears. Customers may learn to associate advertising from a particular retailer with a specific position. A top department store may always place a full-page ad on the back page of the first section of the paper. Thus, the budget of the advertiser may be met with position, size, and style variables taken into consideration.
- **Short closing times.** Deadlines for submitting advertising material for publication are known as closing times. Daily newspapers rarely have closing times that exceed 24 hours. This allows the advertiser to make changes in copy or art right up to the last minute, an advantage when the product has not arrived from the manufacturer in time for the advertisement. Closing times for Sunday papers are frequently longer, ranging from 4 to 6 weeks for Sunday supplements.
- **Geographical target market flexibility.** Newspapers published in large metropolitan areas have recognized the need for targeted coverage. As a result many newspapers offer **zone editions**, providing news and advertising focused to an area within the city. For example, the *Chicago Tribune* has offered several zone editions and supplements to specific neighborhoods and suburban areas. The city zone is the area defined by the corporate limits of a community, while a retail trading zone includes a geographical area around a central city.
- **Credibility.** Newspapers are believed to be a source of credible information. Although research may not be able to prove the veracity of the printed word, it is recognized as a believable resource. This attribute has been known to carry over to the products and services advertised within the newspaper's content.
- **Reseller support.** Dealer and local distributors work together with newspapers as the most frequently used medium for reseller support. Cooperative advertisements with shared costs, identification and promotion of a local dealer for a national product, promotion of quick action through coupons, and other means to join dealer support are all methods used for reseller support.
- **Color reproduction.** Ninety-three percent of newspaper readers prefer color advertisements, while 92 percent perceive color ads to be more effective than black and white ads ("Strength of Color," 1997). Since standard color printing in the run of paper has become more common, advertising has benefited. Approximately 90 percent of all newspapers offer black-and-white plus one ROP color: nearly 70 percent offer black-and-white plus three ROP colors. This allows for more realistic color reproductions, despite the porosity of newspaper stock, called newsprint. Newsprint is an off-white pulpy stock made from inexpensive paper. Newsprint comes in various qualities, light to heavy and smooth to rough. Truly accurate reproduction is not technologically possible using newsprint, and the cost of running a full-page ad in full color (black plus three colors) runs roughly 30 percent higher than for a black-and-white ad. Many advertisers desiring color sophistication revert to supplemental inserts.

Disadvantages of Newspapers for Advertising

Every advertising medium has limitations. The following list provides some of the disadvantages of advertising in newspapers.

- **Short shelf life.** Newspapers are typically read and tossed into the recycle bin; they are not retained for very long. Since the exposure is limited to a short period of time, advertisers have little opportunity for repeated exposure for their ads. Magazines are the print medium to use to overcome this obstacle.
- **Reproduction problems.** Printing techniques prevent high quality reproduction and printing errors do occur. Due to the quick turnaround, detailed preparation and care in production are not as strong as in other media.
- **Clutter.** Each ad competes with editorial content in addition to competing with other ads on the same page.
- **Small shared audience.** Sharing issues of a publication are referred to as the pass along audience. The pass along audience of newspapers is much smaller than through other media such as magazines.
- **High costs of reaching a national audience.** Reaching a national audience by newspapers is more costly in comparison with national media such as network television or magazines. National newspaper coverage costs more than other nationally produced media does.
- **Inability to show products true-to-life.** All print advertising is limited by the ability to show the product in three dimensions, and the product cannot be seen in action with the advantages of sound and motion.

MAGAZINES

Although newspapers remain the primary resource used by retailers for print advertising, manufacturers and designers prefer to use magazines. There are many characteristics that make magazines the natural choice for firms desiring a national or international audience. Customers familiar with national or global brands are likely to translate that increased awareness into sales for prestige-oriented products. Despite increased postage rates, magazines show continued strength and vitality in the international marketplace, with many new magazines introduced each year. The article in Box 8.2 features opinions about magazines from serveral creative directors of advertising agencies.

Magazines may be published on a weekly, monthly, bimonthly, or quarterly basis. Purchase price and perceived strength of the advertising are related to the frequency of publication. The amount of time an advertiser has to prepare and submit layouts to the publication will also vary with the amount of time between publication.

Fashion magazines consist of editorial content and advertising. Editorial content involves the feature stories and fashion spreads controlled by the magazine editors, staff writers, and photographers. Editorial credit is given to manufacturers and retailers within the fashion articles. Advertising includes the pages and partial pages paid for by the companies wanting to promote their products and services.

Fashion magazines are distributed by two different methods: through subscription or over the counter at a variety of retail outlets, such as a newsstand, grocery, discount store, or drugstore. The magazine will be able to provide the potential advertiser statistics about the primary method of sales. Magazines with a higher percentage of subscriptions can provide a more consistent target audience with well-defined demographic information.

BOX 8.2

The Ad Maker's Passion

What do you like best about creating ads for magazines? What, in your view, makes a magazine ad powerful? These are some of the questions the Magazine Publishers of America has asked dozens of ad agency creative directors over the past 8 years for it's popular trade advertising services, "I Wish I'd Done That Ad." The series featured magazine ads so good they were picked by top creatives who had not done them, but wished they had.

"I gobble magazines, tons of magazines," says Donny Deutsch, chief executive officer of Deutsch Inc. "I roam and graze for news value—editorial value—ad value—page-page-page-page-stop! With magazines you can stop where you like—at any spot that feels relevant to you."

Deutsch also uses magazines as a talent barometer. "When I'm hiring, I don't look at reel—I look at print books," he says. "With a TV commercial you've got 74 other creative players who are involved. But in a magazine ad it's person-tool-paper—period. End of story."

He's not alone in his magazine appreciation. "Print is where you find out if somebody has ideas and can really craft a message," says Nina DiSesa, executive creative director at McCann-Erickson New York. "Making a magazine ad come alive is the most exciting thing creative people do."

"Secretly, creative people prefer doing a great magazine ad to any other medium. It's gratifying and it's yours. You can carry it around with you and mail it to your mother," says DiSesa, who has had a tattered ad for Body-slimmers hanging on her office door for years. The ad copy reads: "While you don't necessarily dress for men, it doesn't hurt on occasion to see one drool like the pathetic dog that he is." Above the ad sits a caricature of Nina's head attached to an idealized body, creating the impression that she's posing. "That ad refuses to be ignored; it's intelligent, sexy, not bimbo sexy, and it's going to stay up there forever," she says.

In some ways, magazine ads may be harder to do than TV commercials, says Judy Lotas, creative partner at Lotas Minard Patton McIver. "A magazine ad absolutely comes down to the idea. You have no music, no big production, no place to hide."

Lee Clow, TBWA Chiat/Day chief creative officer, North America, calls magazine ads, "an acid test of a creative person's talent and judgement. You craft the ad and move the picture an eighth of an inch and decide how big the logo should be and whether you've got the right photograph and the right typeface. TV is more collaborative."

"Print is personal—one-on-one—you're trying to connect with somebody. Nowadays, when we're surrounded by screens, interactive media, TV, and CD-ROMs, I think people will discover it's a real luxury to spend time with the printed page. You know, go sit outside in the sun and not turn on anything that has a tube attached to it. You'll find me on a Sunday with a wonderful magazine in my lap. It's very time-relaxed. A good environment to meet a brand."

Kirshenbaum Bond & Partners co-chairman Richard Kirshenbaum revels in this luxury. "If I could get a telephone, fax, stereo, computer all hooked up in one and was able to buy everything from this technical piece of wizardry, I still wouldn't stop reading magazines. I take home ten at a time and digest them all—every kind. There's something great about settling in a bath or on your couch and just kicking back and seeing what's up."

The reader's unhurried approach is the magazine medium's trump card. "The reader's 'hand speed' is leisurely, so an advertiser has time to stop you—and then leave a lasting impression," noted Jerry Della Femina.

From an advertiser's standpoint, a "real benefit of a magazine ad is that you can stop people for a moment to reflect on a universe you've constructed," said Sean Fitzpatrick, executive vice president/vice chairman at McCann-Erickson North America. "It can make you stop and think and begin to change your perceptions. When the ad feels like it was created for you and your way of life—you have a sale."

And readers "can rip out the ad, keep it as a reminder," says John Ferrell, president and chief creative officer, Ferrellcalvio Communications. He was won over by an ad for Royal Viking Star and wound up taking his family on a cruise.

Ferrell's personal experience has been appreciated collectively by readers of the Absolut Vodka campaign. "It's convinced me that there's no other vehicle of communication that people take as personally as their magazine," says Arnie Arlow, who while at TBWA worked on Absolut. "People have an especially intimate relationship with their magazine. You come home, pick up your magazine, settle into your favorite chair, spread those pages open before you and lose yourself in the experience."

Ken Mandelbaum notes that his voracious magazine reading—probably 50 titles a month—is "creating a veritable windfall for my recycling company." The chief executive of Mandelbaum Mooney Ashley when he did his MPA "I wish" ad, Mandelbaum professes to "love going to the newsstands and buying esoteric hobbyist magazines aimed at specialized audiences—magazines that let me eavesdrop on some weird subculture of society."

Mandelbaum says that although people may be talking about television's 500-channel future, "I can't help thinking that magazines surpassed that mark a long time ago."

Adapted from: The ad maker's passion: It's not just marketers who like magazines (and the way ads work in them). (1997, October 20). New York Times (Advertising Supplement), 14.

Consumer or Trade Orientation

Magazines may be classified as either consumer or trade oriented. Trade publications direct the flow of information from business to business situations. Whether the publication is a trade association magazine or one business entity directing information to a particular market, the primary audience includes businesses wanting information about products and services related to that industry. Examples of trade magazines are *Stores,* the publication of the National Retail Federation, *Visual Merchandising and Store Design (VM + SD),* published by ST Publications, Inc., representing the display and store planning industries, and *Daily News Record,* the Fairchild publication directed toward the men's wear industry.

In contrast, consumer publications are directed to ultimate consumers. These publications are classified as general interest, news, fashion, sports, or any other special interest. General interest magazines, such as *Life,* have been declining in popularity as special interest magazines gain acceptance. Examples of news publications include *Newsweek, Time* and *U.S. News and World Report.* Besides general news topics, these publications regularly contain articles relating to the fashion industry, making them resources for apparel, home furnishings, or cosmetic advertisements.

Promoters wanting to attract a fashion or home decor-oriented audience may select a fashion or home furnishings magazine in which to target advertisements. Fashion magazines may be further targeted to a specific target audience. *Glamour* and *Mademoiselle* are focused toward college students and women entering careers. *Vogue, Harper's Bazaar,* and *Elle* strive to attract a slightly older and sophisticated target market, while *Seventeen* and *Teen People* appeal to the teenage market. The audience for *Latina Vanidades,* and the Spanish edition of *Cosmopolitan* (Fig. 8.7) is Hispanic women. *Elle Decor, Metropolitan Home,* and *House and Garden* are known as shelter magazines because they target consumers interested in residential interior design and gardening.

Figure 8.7

Fashion publications for Hispanic women include *Latina,* a bilingual magazine; the Spanish language edition of *Cosmopolitan;* and *Vanidades,* a Spanish language magazine.

Specialized Features

Magazines offer advertisers a variety of creative possibilities through some technical or mechanical features. These features include bleed pages, cover positions, inserts, gatefolds, and special sizes. Next, we will briefly introduce these features.

Bleed pages are a technical feature that allows the dark or colored background to extend to the edge of the page. It is said to *bleed* off the page. Although many magazines offer this option, it costs the advertiser 10 to 15 percent more to print these types of pages. Bleeds offer greater flexibility for advertising expression, with a slightly larger printing area, and a more dramatic effect.

Cover position offers a more desirable position for an advertising message. Publishers are willing to sell the first page inside the magazine (second cover), the inside back cover (third cover), and the back cover (fourth cover) for a premium. The highest price is for the back cover, considered to be a prime location for advertising.

Rather than buying a standard advertising page, an advertiser may purchase an **insert**, which is an ad printed on high-quality paper stock. This type of ad adds weight and drama to the message. The advertiser has an insert printed separately and sent to the magazine for insertion at a special price. Another option is a multiple-page insert, devoted to one brand or manufacturer. Despite high costs, these multiple-page inserts offer a particularly strong focus for the advertiser.

A **gatefold** is a special kind of insert, created by extra-long paper. The sides are folded into the center to match the size of the other pages. When the reader opens the magazine, the folded page swings out like a gate to present an oversized ad. Gatefolds are dramatic methods of magazine advertising that are sold at a substantial premium. Not all magazines provide gatefolds.

International Magazines

At one time consumer magazines were directed only toward a domestic audience, but now magazine distribution has been influenced by the trend toward globalization. The Greek fashion magazines shown in Figure 8.8 incorporate English and French words and phrases into the editorial and advertising copy. In 1998, *Fortune* magazine, the biweekly business magazine, announced it had opened six new international bureaus, expanded its Asian and European editions, launched a Chinese-language edition, and started *FORTUNE Americas,* Spanish and Portuguese biweekly supplements distributed by newspapers throughout Latin America (Sykes and Pepe, 1998).

Vogue, one of the leading fashion magazines, originated in the United States during the 19th century. The popularity of the publication led to the establishment of ten international editions. British and French editions can be found throughout newsstands in the United States. There are also editions of *Vogue* in such Asian markets as Taiwan, Korea, and Japan.

Elle started in France after World War II and has also expanded into many other countries. Editorial staff and content are determined by the publication within a particular country and are not likely to be exactly the same throughout the world.

The three leading Spanish language fashion magazines are *Cosmopolitan, Vanidades,* and *Harper's Bazaar* (Lockwood, 1997a). The editors of the Spanish editions of *Cosmo,* Sara Maria Castany, and *Harper's Bazaar,* Laura Lavida, indicated that they are striving to bring their publications editorially and photographically to the level of their parent publications. International designers and top international fashion models are featured in these publications, emphasizing the topics Latin American women are interested

Figure 8.8

Greek fashion magazines

in—particularly fashion, beauty, the arts, men, careers, family, and celebrities. Even the ads from international companies, including Lancôme, Chanel, and Estée Lauder, are similar to U.S. versions. All three of these publications are divisions of *Editorial Televisa,* the largest publisher of Spanish language magazines in the world and leader in Latin America. Growth potential for the Hispanic market has spurred the growth of these publications.

Italian Vogue, Marie Claire, and Elle are considered to be the big three fashion magazines in Italy. In addition to these monthly fashion glossies, there are countless other weekly and monthly publications in Italy (Conti, 1997). The launch of *Io Donna* and *D Donna della Repubblica,* fashion magazines distributed once a week with daily newspapers, sparked major changes in the weekly fashion publications in Italy. A fresh and more dynamic approach to fashion presentation led to updates in the more traditional *Grazia, Anna,* and *Amica.* Updated versions of the weeklies are easy to read and provide editorial content on how to wear the latest trendy as well as practical fashions.

In the 1990s French fashion publications struggled, and many of the top magazines, including French *Glamour, Maison & Jardin,* and *Vogue Hommes,* closed (Aktar and Raper, 1997). Attracting advertisers who had shifted their dollars into other media such as outdoor advertising was difficult for French magazines. To combat the problem, *Jalouse, DS,* and *Femina* were launched at a price of 10 to 15 francs, much less than the 30 francs charged by French *Vogue,* the most expensive fashion magazine in France. Editorial content mixed social issues with fashion, travel, and beauty articles.

Fashion magazines are available almost anywhere in the world. Most of the top international publications have jumped into markets such as Russia, never thought to be strong fashion markets. Russian trendsetters have been seen carrying glossy fashion magazines after they were launched. *Cosmopolitan* published an 850-page issue to coincide with Moscow's 850th anniversary in 1997 (Singer, 1997). In addition to the usual fashion, beauty, and advice pages, the issue covered Moscow nightlife and contained large advertising spreads from such advertisers as Revlon, Nivea, Avon, Sonia Rykiel, Clinique, Estée Lauder, Lancôme, Maybelline, and Yves Saint Laurent. Other international publications that have launched Russian versions in Moscow include, *Harper's Bazaar, L'Officiel, Elle, Good Housekeeping, Men's Health,* and *Vogue.* The debut of the French shelter magazine *Maison Française* had 224 pages of editorial content with 7 pages of ads. Half of the content was taken from the French edition, whereas the remainder was produced by the Russian staff. With an initial circulation of 50,000, a full-page ad ran $14,000 (Singer, 1997).

Magazine Promotional Tie-ins

Magazine publishers strive to improve the circulation and advertising revenues by participating in a variety of tie-ins with other media and with retailers. *Vogue* magazine featured images of fashion personalities Isaac Mizrahi, Dolce & Gabbana, Gianfranco Ferré, Shalom Harlow, and Christy Turlington on 95 New York City buses. *Vogue* also featured a 14-by-48-foot billboard of Amber Valetta, the magazine cover model for a *See You in September* advertising campaign. In addition to these aggressive advertising strategies, publisher Ronald Galotti noted that *Vogue,* in cooperation with the Chambre Syndicale, brought six French fashion designers to Bergdorf Goodman to do fashion and trunk shows.

In Style teamed with *Entertainment Weekly* to sponsor an AIDS fund-raiser at the Boathouse in Central Park, while *Seventeen* brought its editorial pages to life for its teen readers with fashion shows in 20 retail stores. *Rolling Stone,* in cooperation with *Men's Health* and *Esquire,* produced a point-of-purchase gift video for Haggar. This *how-to* lifestyle piece showed hip and fun fashions for nineties men.

The types of advertising and promotional activities used by magazines are varied to meet the needs of the target audience. Whether the promotion is a long-standing annual promotion, such as *Glamour's* "Top Ten College Women of the Year" or *YM's* unconventional decision to put promotional dollars into researching the youth market, magazines make significant contributions to the promotion industry. They are not only a place to buy advertising space, they also stimulate the promotion industry by promoting themselves.

Magazine Media Costs

Magazines provide potential advertisers with advertising rate cards, providing information about the cost of black-and-white or color ads. Discounts may be given if an advertiser purchases ads in continuous issues. Certain positions in the magazine command higher price. The preferred position for advertising includes the back cover, inside the back cover, and inside the front cover.

In 1997, a single full-color, full-page advertisement in *Harper's Bazaar* cost $52,805 compared to $66,140 for the same type of ad in *Vogue.* Ad costs increase for placement on an inside cover, while the back cover demands the highest price. In order to show how advertising costs compare, Table 8.6 illustrates the costs for a full-page, four-color ad in selected magazines. The table also provides cost per 1,000, an important tool for the media planner, and audience size ("Simmons Study," 1998).

Advantages of Magazines for Advertising

Magazines offer advertisers a number of strengths and benefits. These advantages include:

- **Selective audience.** Magazines provide detailed analysis of the readership of its audience to potential advertisers. Demographic as well as lifestyle information is available in addition to statistics on the size of the magazine's circulation. The advertiser can know the percentage sold to subscribers versus over the counter sales, which will indicate the regularity of the audience.
- **Geographical editions.** Magazines have traditionally reached a broad market with general interest publications. As magazines have focused toward more specific topics and target audiences, they have started to narrow even more to meet the regional demands for readers and advertisers. *Better Homes and Gardens* has 145 regional editions. **Split-run advertising** allows an advertiser to elect to advertise in one or more geographical editions depending upon the advertiser's needs. Small premiums may be charged for regional advertising, but advertisers feel that it is worthwhile to increase the efficiency of reaching the target audience. Figure 8.9 shows the geographical split-run regions for *Glamour*.
- **High-quality reproduction.** In comparison to newspapers, magazines use higher quality stock and reproduction techniques. Magazine printing technology can provide more true-to-life illustrative reproduction.
- **Long life and pass along audience.** Magazine reproduction quality is so good, that many readers may wish to keep magazines for a long period of time. The life of a magazine may last several months to several years. In addition to the individual that purchased the copy, research indicates that three to four other adults will read the

Figure 8.9

Split-run regions for *Glamour* magazine.

Table 8.6   Simmons Study of Media and Markets:
Audience, Advertising Rates, Age, and Income for Selected Media

Magazine	Audience (in thousands)	Cost of Page (4-color, $)	Cost/1,000 (4-color, $)	Median Age	Median Household Income ($)
Total Adults	192,463	n/a	n/a	41.8	38,418
Allure	2,192	44,910	20.49	27.8	44,796
Architectural Digest	5,430	53,410	9.84	43.0	66,636
Bon Appetit	5,780	49,180	8.51	43.0	60,984
Bridal Guide	3,563	21,375	6.00	30.3	41,352
Business Week	5,702	77,100	13.52	41.3	67,088
Cosmopolitan	16,967	94,100	5.55	31.5	41,883
Country Home	8,830	72,200	8.18	43.9	42,518
Country Living	12,307	80,175	6.51	44.6	46,386
Ebony	12,928	48,519	3.75	38.3	26,529
Elle	4,682	55,540	11.86	29.6	44,034
First for Women	4,178	28,060	6.72	36.3	43,385
Flower & Garden	6,101	21,000	3.44	46.8	40,095
Forbes	5,567	59,340	10.66	42.5	68,837
Fortune	4,256	60,800	14.28	38.8	68,241
Glamour	11,709	85,080	7.27	31.0	40,524
Gentlemen's Quarterly	7,057	49,540	7.02	30.7	50,001
Harper's Bazaar	3,201	52,805	16.50	40.0	46,312
House Beautiful	6,946	68,795	9.90	45.7	47,323
Kiplinger's Personal Finance	4,082	46,580	11.41	47.0	67,064
Ladies Home Journal	16,559	127,000	7.67	46.4	40,014
Mademoiselle	5,636	55,910	9.92	27.5	44,276
Martha Steward Living	7,461	93,328	12.51	42.6	57,727
McCall's	17,815	113,120	6.35	46.0	36,035
Men's Health	5,570	72,135	12.95	35.7	49,334
Metropolitan Home	2,221	48,300	21.74	42.3	66,247
Mirabella	2,484	39,550	15.92	29.5	54,532
Newsweek	21,424	148,800	6.95	42.8	52,654
People	39,913	125,000	3.13	39.0	45,785
Self	4,318	59,380	13.75	29.9	57,171
Seventeen	7,630	71,115	9.32	27.3	42,039
Teen	3,646	53,250	14.61	28.9	41,021
Time	26,885	162,000	6.03	42.9	47,293
Town & Country	3,494	43,805	12.54	44.0	50,721
Traditional Home	2,681	49,600	18.50	41.8	52,331
Vanity Fair	5,329	67,890	12.74	37.1	49,846
Victoria	3,159	49,980	15.82	42.7	53,889
Vogue	10,155	66,140	6.51	32.5	45,717
Working Woman	3,250	43,800	13.48	39.6	44,041
YM	4,293	73,270	17.07	22.0	44,968

Source: Simmons Study of Media & Markets for Spring 1997 [On-line].
Available: http://www.amic.com/amic_mem/scoreboard/sm97sa.html.

publication. Each reader takes more than 3 days to read a magazine, spending 60 to 90 minutes. This long life and multiple readership provides more opportunities for the reader to view advertisements.

- **Controlled circulation and receptivity in some business magazines.** The audience for trade and business publications purchase these magazines because they want to keep up to date with current trends within the industry. Editorial content has a high degree of credibility. Advertisers benefit from this attitude, making their advertisements have more perceived believability.

Disadvantages of Magazines for Advertising

Despite their many strengths, magazines also have several limitations. These disadvantages are as follows:

- **Inability to show products true-to-life.** As with all print advertising, magazine advertising is limited to a two-dimensional image. Motion and sound cannot help the audience interpret the product or service. Improved product sampling techniques have helped cosmetic advertisers with this problem by providing fragrance tester strips and eye shadow samples. Other products have not been able to overcome this limitation.
- **Expensive.** Full-color advertising in national magazines is expensive. *Mademoiselle* charges $55,910 for a 1-page, four-color advertisement. *Cosmopolitan* charges $94,100 for the same type of ad ("Simmons Study," 1998).
- **Long lead time.** In comparison to newspapers, magazines have a substantial lead time. The lead time varies with the publication schedule. Weekly magazines have shorter lead times than monthly publications.
- **Editorial and advertising conflicts.** Magazine editors have been criticized for writing articles featuring producers, designers, or retailers who are heavy advertisers in the magazine. Thus, the selection for editorial credit and articles can be perceived as biased toward firms that buy advertising on a regular basis.

CREATIVE DEVELOPMENT FOR PRINT MEDIA

Print advertisements are prepared for publication in newspapers, magazines, outdoor media, and direct marketing materials as catalogs, billing inserts, and the like. Whether a print ad is placed in a trade or consumer-oriented publication, it consists of three elements: copy, art, and space. Every print ad starts with space, the blank canvas on which the verbal component is created by copy, and the visual component is built through artwork. The shape of the space is determined by the size of the pages of newspapers and magazines.

One of the first questions to be answered in the development of a print ad is, What are the dimensions of the ad? The amount of space an advertiser purchases from a publisher is an important consideration. How big is the space? Where will in be located on the page or within the publication? How will it be noticed?

The space of an advertisement that is not occupied with artwork or copy is referred to as white space. These *unused* areas of the ad are created by the placement of the copy and artistic components. Such variations can be used to stimulate eye movement, attract attention to the copy, and provide distinctiveness in the style of the ad. Next, we look at the various components of copy and art that contribute to the finished print ad.

Copy

The verbal component of a print advertisement is called the **copy**. Copy consists of all of the words used to articulate the advertiser's message. In print advertising this is all of the reading material in the ad, consisting of the headline, subheadlines, body copy, and advertiser's slogan. Each of these segments contributes to clarifying what the advertiser wants the customer to know. Figure 8.10 shows the various components of a print advertisement.

Headline

In print ads, the **headline** is the boldest statement. The headline is written taking into consideration what would have to be said if only one or two lines of space were available for the message. The copywriter puts forth the main theme in a few words.

Headlines should be written to attract attention and work with the visual elements to generate consumer interest. Many copywriters feel the most effective headlines emphasize the primary selling point or main appeal of the merchandise, giving the consumer a reason to respond to the ad. It is also common to include the name of the brand, manufacturer, or retailer in the headline.

Headline information can be used for several purposes. Here are seven of the most common types of headlines.

- **Advice.** This headline offers advice to the consumer, for example, *You owe it to yourself to try Nail Strength*. It is normally followed by a subheadline that offers some type of claim or promise, such as, *You will have stronger, prettier nails in just 2 weeks*. A properly developed advice headline appeals to self-interest or self-improvement, helping the consumer to solve a problem or improve health.

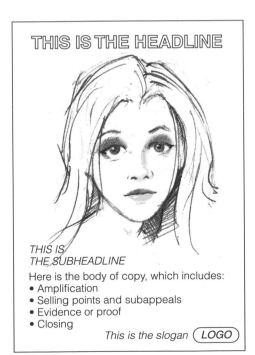

Figure 8.10

Components of a print advertisement

- **Command.** The command headline uses the hard-sell approach. The consumer is told to act before the offer is over, as in, *Use this coupon on November 25th or 26th to save 15% off the regular price.*
- **Curiosity.** The curiosity headline is considered to be the most provocative approach, attempting to arouse interest in the unusual. Frequently it is presented in the form of a question. *Where do you want to go today?* has been the stimulant for Microsoft Internet Explorer. The audience members can decide for themselves just what Internet categories interest them. The risk in a curiosity headline is that it is often used strictly for novelty. Novelty without meaning is useless as an advertising tool.
- **News.** The news headline is the most straightforward technique, playing a role similar to a headline for a news story. The news headline should be direct and timely, frequently featuring a brand name. For example, *97% of Prizm Owners Would Recommend Prizm to a Friend.*
- **Product claim.** The product claim headline is similar to the advice headline, as in, *It works with your skin, not just on it.* Although many product claim headlines are successful, this approach has been weakened by advertisements that make unrealistic or irresponsible statements. Unrealistic statements for weight-loss products have made many consumers wary. If this approach is taken, the advertiser should take care to supply supporting documentation in the body copy.
- **Product or company name.** The name of the brand may be so significant that it is used as the headline for the advertisement. This approach may be effective when the product is so timely that merely mentioning it will be sufficient to arouse interest. *Lord & Taylor: The Signature of American Style* is an example.
- **Prospect selection.** Products that have a specific target audience may use the prospect selection headline, in which the target customer is mentioned. Because very few products are of interest to everyone, this headline helps to direct the ad to consumers who are interested in or need the product. A headline that starts, *For women with sensitive skin . . .* or *Parents with toddlers . . .* attracts those audience members fitting into specific categories.

Subheadlines

Subheadlines are secondary statements that are used when the primary headline needs further clarification or there is a secondary appeal or selling point. Although subheadlines are not always used, they can be helpful in providing backup to the main headline. Product claim, advice, or curiosity headlines might need a follow-up. For example, the curiosity headline *How do you top a luscious cheesecake yogurt?* is followed by the subheadline, *Discover all the ways Dannon tops yogurt.* The subheadline is the connection between the headline and artwork in this ad.

Body Copy

Body copy is additional copy created to support and reinforce the headline. By attempting to stimulate desire in a product or response to ideas, body copy adds selling points, offers evidence or proof of claims, provides subappeals to the main appeal, or asks the consumer to take action.

Copywriters are increasingly faced with knowledgeable consumers who demand more factual information. Information that will assist the copywriter in preparing the written portion of the ad is found in the Copywriter Background Information Checklist on page 249. Statistical documentation and research that supports the claims featured in the headlines are ways copywriters can include hard information on the product and its benefits throughout the message.

Copywriter Background Information Checklist

❏ **Target audience:** Who is the target customer? An accurate demographic and psychographic profile of the customer should be available.

❏ **Positioning of the product or service**: What are the key appeals or selling points of the product or service in terms of quality, value, price, and so forth? What is the target customer's point of view of these factors?

❏ **Position of the competition:** What are the selling points of the competition and how can the copywriter point out differences?

❏ **Objectives:** What are the advertising objectives and creative strategy? Is this a single ad or will it be a part of a series? Is the emphasis on product or image? Is it part of a campaign? Are the goals long or short term?

❏ **Copy platform:** What is the basic foundation of the creative strategy? The copy platform should include a discussion of the appeals and approaches in order to develop catch phrases or ideas to be included in the advertising.

❏ **Media style:** Which medium will be used? What is the editorial style of the publication or programming? This enables the copywriter to tailor the message to the medium being used. The medium's editorial content or programming style sets the tone for the copy.

❏ **Response desired:** What is the reader or viewer expected to do? The feelings and preferences of the consumers should be taken into consideration as the copy is developed.

It may be helpful to classify the different approaches that can be used in developing body copy.

- **Direct-selling news copy.** This method presents the message in a straightforward, factual manner. Using the newspaper story as a guideline, news copy is written as an article with informative content. Details about new products are frequently presented in this manner.

- **Implied suggestion.** In contrast to the direct-selling news copy approach, implied suggestion provides an opportunity for the reader to draw his or her own conclusions from the points presented. The copywriter tries to make the details so obvious the reader will draw a favorable conclusion about the product or service.

- **Narrative description.** A human experience with some type of problem and a solution involving the product or service is created by the copywriter of a narrative description. Hopefully, the reader will see a connection between his or her problem and the favorable use of the advertiser's product. A variation of narrative description is the storyform, in which human experience using the product is also told in a straightforward description. This may involve an analogy between the story and the product benefits.

- **Monologue and dialogue.** The presentation by an individual about the benefits of merchandise or services from a personal point of view is a monologue. If the story is told by two or more people it is a dialogue. This format is often presented as a testimonial message. A testimonial suggests the reader can emulate or imitate the person giving the statement. By following the exemplary behavior of the authority, the reader can achieve the same benefits or results.

- **Humor.** Product value can be enhanced by utilizing a humorous situation. Although some critics, including advertising executive David Ogilvy, believe that humor does not sell, humor has been used to successfully entertain and provide information about products and services (Ogilvy, 1983). A television commercial, such as the one in which men shopping with their wives are sucked into the display window of a Radio Shack store, may cause consumers to remember the product as a result of the humorous scenario.

- **Comic strip or continuity.** Fictional or cartoon characters have gained popularity as product or service spokespersons. Snoopy has become a spokesperson for financial services, while Bugs Bunny and Daffy Duck have been used in VISA commercials.

Slogans

Slogans are repeated selling points or appeals that are primarily associated with the product, brand, or company. Slogans are words creatively combined to embody the company or product image. Generally slogans are short and to the point and feature the name of the company or brand. Through repetition, a slogan becomes familiar, provoking prompt consumer recall of the advertiser's message.

Slogans may be developed for specific products or institutions. Successful slogans may remain popular for many years. The slogan for DietCoke, *Just for the taste of it*, is an example of a product slogan that has been popular for a long time. Sears revitalized interest in its apparel and merchandise softlines with the slogan, *Come see the softer side of Sears*. Slogans may be so powerful that they become part of popular culture. *Just Do It*, has become a slogan for more than just the Nike corporation.

Legal protection for slogans was awarded under the Lanham Act of 1947. If a business registers its slogan and certain additional conditions are met, legal protection is guaranteed.

Art and Design

Advertising depends heavily upon the use of visual arts to produce aesthetically pleasing and creative advertisements. Design elements consist of the core components of design—color, shape, texture, and line—and design principles are standards for visually organizing all design elements into a unified composition. The design principles are balance, contrast, emphasis, proportion, rhythm, and harmony.

Organization of the different design elements and principles is used to achieve an integrated, tasteful end product. Effective visual messages combine creative strategy with design and copy to complete the process. Several ideas are worked up into preliminary ideas and tested in the first steps of advertisement development. As ideas become solidified into a prospective ad, final presentations are shown to the client for approval. Next, we look at the visual components of the print ad.

Layout

Layout is the arrangement of the physical elements of art, copy, and white space within the boundaries of the print advertisement. The layout becomes the blueprint where the elements of art and copy are placed. Layout assists art and copy to complete the selling job more effectively. Planning steps in developing the layout include the design of thumbnail sketches, roughs, and the comprehensive.

Thumbnails are preliminary unpolished designs produced in a small size so several versions can be tried. A variety of alternatives are evaluated and a few of the designs are chosen to be worked up. **Roughs** are workups of the chosen thumbnails, rendered in actual size to represent where the art, headlines, copy, and logo will be placed. Figure 8.11 shows a series of thumbnails and a rough.

After the rough is approved, the layout artist does a comprehensive layout. The **comprehensive** will give a realistic impression of the final ad. Testing, evaluation, and revision may be done throughout this entire process.

Figure 8.11

Thumbnails and a rough

Typography

Typography involves the selection and setting of a **typeface**, the style of type, to be used in headlines, subheadlines, body copy, or logos. One of the most important considerations in selecting a typeface is its readability. The type style, boldness, size, length of line, and spacing between letters, words, and paragraphs are all factors that need to be taken into consideration as the typeface is selected.

There are five common groups of type styles used today. These include Roman, Gothic, square serif, cursive or script, or ornamental. Roman is a popular type style with good readability, distinguished by serifs, extra small lines or tails. Serifs finish the ends of the bold strokes of letters in various designs or sizes. Gothic, a sans serif style, is also referred to as block or contemporary. The style is characterized by bold and clean strokes without serifs. Although it is not as readable as roman, Gothic is the second most popular style due to its modern appearance. Square serif styles are a combination of sans serif and roman styles, resulting in even letter strokes. Cursive or script type most closely resembles handwriting. Letters connect and offer a more feminine feeling, but these styles are not as readable as other typefaces. Cursive type can be successfully used in headlines, announcements, or invitations. Ornamental type covers a wide variety of novel styles. It can offer special effects, but generally is not very easy to read.

In addition to considering the typeface style, the designer also needs to consider which elements within a type family will best assist in the overall design. Each typeface has variations in proportion, weight, or slant of the letters. The type may be light, medium, bold, extra bold, condensed, extended, or italic. These variations enable the typographer to provide contrast or emphasis without changing the type family. A **font** refers to a complete range of capitals, small capitals, lowercase letters, numerals, and punctuation marks for a particular typeface and size.

Type size is measured in points. There are 72 points to an inch, so one point is equal to 1/72 of an inch. Typically text material is printed as a measurement of 8 or 10 points. Larger sizes are necessary for headlines, subheadings, and logos. Figure 8.12 shows different typefaces and styles.

Figure 8.12

Typefaces and styles in several sizes.

E	8 Point	**San Serif:**
E	10 Point	This line is set in Helvetica.
E	12 Point	*This line is set in Helvetica Italic.*
E	16 Point	**This line is set in Helvetica Bold.**
E	20 Point	This line is set in Futura.
E	24 Point	***This line is set in Futura Italic.***
		This line is set in Futura Bold.
E	36 Point	**Serif:**
		This line is set in Times New Roman.
E	48 Point	*This line is set in Times New Roman Italic.*
		This line is set in Times New Roman Bold.
E	60 Point	**Square Serif:**
		This line is set in Serifa.
		This line is set in Serifa Italic.
		This line is set in Serifa Bold.
E	72 Point	*script:*
		This line is set in Caflisch.

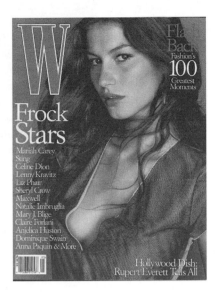

Figure 8.13

W's logo remained the same even though the format changed from newspaper to bound magazine.

Logos

Logos are graphic symbols or distinctive typefaces that represent a company's name, mark, or emblem. Graphic symbols may be incorporated with the typographic signature to complete the logo. Bloomingdales, Macy's, and Dillard's are department stores that use specialized lettering as their signature in ads. Lord and Taylor includes a single red rose with its distinctive script signature. A graphic symbol such as the NBC peacock or the CBS eye is shown often enough for the viewer to associate the visual image with a particular company. The swoosh created by Nike is so memorable that an ad with the symbol does not even require a headline. Figure 8.13 shows how the logo for *W* maintained the identity of the publication even though it switched from a newspaper format to a bound magazine.

Logos are first associated with print media. But, logos can also be developed or adapted for electronic media. In the broadcast field, a logo can be created by a musical song or jingle, and visual images can be animated.

Photography

Photography is a process for visual reproduction of a pictorial image. The process was originally created by reproducing images on a light sensitive material. Modern technology has taken that process from one requiring film to one that goes directly to a digital image. Photographs present the most realistic image of products but have limitations in the reproduction process.

Photographs cannot be reproduced in newspapers without using a halftone process. The halftone process converts photographic images using screens, which break up continuous tones into dots. Solid areas are dots in close proximity, while lighter shades are made up of dots that are farther apart. Blacks are not truly black, nor are whites absolutely white. The human eye sees the dots as black, white, and shades of gray. That is why a photograph reproduced in a newspaper is not as sharp and clear as the original.

There are several advantages of using photography in print ads. First, photography shows the actual product, not an artistic interpretation. This results in the most realistic representation of the merchandise. Photography can also be used to create dramatic moods and provide true-to-life impact. Photography is a mainstay in advertising apparel and fashion-related goods, especially popular in magazines and other publications where the reproduction justifies the expense associated with photography.

The disadvantages of photography prevent some advertisers from selecting this illustration form. The cost of a photo shoot includes many people above and beyond the photographer and his or her photo assistants. Models must be hired, and photo stylists provide behind the scenes production assistance. Stylists generally work as freelancers, helping with everything from making location arrangements and furnishing props to hiring models and hair and makeup personnel. In addition to the costs, photographs do not reproduce in newspapers as well as line drawings. The halftone process limits the details that can be seen in newspaper reproductions.

Illustration

Artistic illustrations for print ads can be created by line drawings or halftone illustrations. **Illustrations** are visual matter used to clairfy or decorate the text in an ad. **Line drawings** are made using lines to represent the pictorial image, whereas **halftone illustrations** use shades or tones created by watercolor, chalk, pencil, markers, or other art medium to illustrate the image with tonal qualities.

Line drawings reproduce better than halftone illustrations or photography in newspapers. Greater detail is possible with line drawings since the halftone screens are not used. Because halftone illustrations and photography can be used to create dramatic moods and image development, they are more likely to be used in magazine ads. Although each of the methods of presenting images is used in various media, the strengths and weaknesses of each illustration style direct their use.

Illustrations can also be categorized as either pictorial or symbolic. Pictorial illustrations are descriptive, portraying merchandise in a true-to-life manner (Fig. 8.14). Customers can see how a product looks and may be used. A pictorial illustration is generally accompanied by direct and clear copy, persuading customers to make up their minds to purchase merchandise by seeing and reading the advertisement. Pictorial advertisements are best used for merchandise with immediate sales impact.

In contrast, symbolic illustration (Fig. 8.15) is more decorative and fundamentally impressionistic. It seeks to create an atmosphere, mood, or image. As such, symbolic illustration suggests the nature of the merchandise but leaves the details to the viewer's imagination.

Paste-up

After all the decisions regarding layout, copy, use of logos, and style of artwork are made and the roughs have been tested, the ad is put into final format. This format is called a **paste-up** or **mechanical**. The paste-up shows the format of the art, copy, and logo in its presentation layout. In addition, the copy has been converted into the desired typeface. The final paste-up should be **camera ready**, meaning that it is ready to go to the printer. No additional changes are made to camera-ready paste-ups.

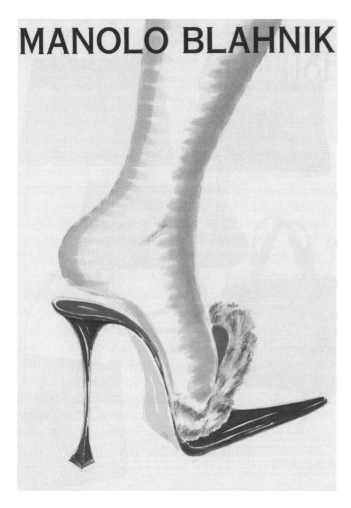

MANOLO BLAHNIK

Figure 8.14
Pictorial illustration.

How the artwork will be used, determines what happens next. If the ad is a black-and-white ad in a newspaper, the camera-ready art may be taken to the newspaper office as a paste-up or sent as an electronic file from a computer. A variety of methods are used depending upon the technology used by the designer and publication site. Color printing can be delivered as a mechanical or electronic image.

Visual Formats for Print Advertisements

Art directors and graphic designers may be able to use visual formats that can be classified according to features or other techniques of presentation. The following list illustrates common visual formats that are used for print ads.

- **Single product.** This powerful presentation of the product is shown without background or setting. This simple visual form emphasizes the intrinsic characteristics that command attention. Distinctive items such as fine jewelry or designer apparel and similar products can attract attention without the use of a background that may detract from the product.
- **Product in a setting.** In order to give the target customer an idea of how the product can be used, the advertiser places the product in a background. This setting may imply using the product in a pleasant or satisfying environment. Sporting equipment

Figure 8.15

Symbolic illustration.

or apparel, such as skis with outdoor clothing, is placed on models using the merchandise in a realistic winter scene.

- **Product in use.** This widely used visualization places the product in service by individuals representing the desired consumer. The reader is stimulated by identifying with the product user and identifies him- or herself as the recipient of its benefits.
- **Product benefits.** Positive results derived from product use are depicted. Hopefully, consumers will see themselves as the ones who will benefit from product use.
- **Need dramatization.** The potential customer may realize that he or she has a need for a product illustrated in a dramatic manner. Customers may not even be aware that they could benefit from the use of the product. Typically baking soda is used as an ingredient for food. Need dramatization gave potential consumers the idea of using baking soda as a refrigerator deodorizer.
- **Product use explanation.** By explaining how the product is used, consumers without knowledge of its use may be more likely to try it. If the consumer has used the product incorrectly in the past, getting poor results, proper explanation of use can help to overcome objections to trying it again. Furthermore, consumers may have a limited view of how the product should be used and the advertiser shows alternative methods of using it.
- **Product details.** A frequently used advertising theme centers on an improvement of some product detail. The detail may be enlarged or a cross section profiled to call attention to that detail.
- **Dramatization of evidence.** In order to support claims made by the advertiser, effective illustrations can be created to support claims with supplementary evidence.

- **Comparison.** This technique shows a comparison between a competitor's brand and the advertiser's brand, or before and after pictures are compared to make clear *how* the product can improve appearance or performance.
- **Headline dramatization.** An illustration can effectively strengthen a headline by communicating what the headline states in words through a visual presentation.
- **Symbolism.** Advertisers can use a symbol to associate the product or service with some basic concept. Using a visual symbol such as an eagle represents strength and patriotism.

FUTURE TRENDS IN PRINT MEDIA

We are able to observe many trends within the broad category of print media. Changes are taking place in how media buying and planning are done. Alternative media are challenging traditional print media outlets, causing newspapers and magazines to look for ways to meet these challenges. First, we look at changes in media buying and planning.

Media buying, once a job performed primarily by the advertising agency, is now, generally, a separate function. Duties of handling media strategy (planning) cross over to the duties of media execution (buying). When Procter and Gamble restructured, it decided to place tactical planning functions for print with its print buying agency, Starcom, and its TV planning function with its TV buying agency, TeleVest (Mandese, 1998). It used the rationale that media buyers had a better grasp on real-time media marketplace conditions, information P & G considered essential for optimizing plans. Many other advertisers are watching to see if this works and if strategic planning should reside with the media planners.

Other companies are also integrating media buying and planning. In an attempt to gain greater control over media strategy, as well as have more flexibility in managing its creative assignments at agencies, Coca-Cola maintains a media planning role with its corporate media staff. "Three years ago, we were faced with an environment of an increasing number of agencies handling our media and creative. We had as many as nine agencies handling media," according to Chris Gagen, director of U.S. media at Coca-Cola. "We felt the core competencies of these agencies varied dramatically and with the complexity of the media environment, we needed to take a bold step into the future." Coca-Cola pulled its media planning responsibilities from its brand agencies and consolidated it at D'Arcy Masius Benton & Bowles in 1996 (Mandese, 1998). Coca-Cola has already seen some positive results from the shift. Although buying and planning disciplines have unique and distinctive roles, Coca-Cola executives felt they were blurring the lines between planning and buying. One of the key goals that this accomplished was to get media planners to think more about local media strategies.

Newspaper circulation, battered by a decade of decline, as seen in Table 8.4, started to show improvements at the end of the 20th century. Eleven of the United States' five largest newspapers showed increases in 1998: *USA Today* (3.2 percent increase for the Monday-through-Thursday issues), the *Los Angeles Times* (2.45 percent increase for daily papers), the *New York Times* (2,975 gain for a weekday circulation of 1,110,143), the *Daily News* of New York (increased weekday circulation by 2,600 to 730,761) and the *New York Post* (up 4,300 to 432,707 weekday circulation) (Barringer, 1998).

While newspapers looked forward to greater circulation, they face threats from new and emerging alternative media. Internet-based classified advertising is evolving so rapidly that newspaper executives began to worry about the competition. Since classified ads, on average, represent 37 percent of newspaper's total advertising income, newspaper publishers needed to decide whether to expand in cyberspace or focus on protecting traditional print classifieds ("Online Classifieds," 1996).

The future of magazines was the topic of discussion debated by several industry leaders toward the close of the 20th century. The fact that magazines are visually stimulating and portable were among the reasons cited for magazine survival into the 21st century. According to David Altschiller, chairman and chief creative officer of Hill, Holliday/Altschiller, "By the year 2006, magazines that are very heavy in text information will have been replaced by the Internet and cable TV" (Lockwood, 1996b). Steve Klein, partner and media director of Kirshenbaum, Bond & Partners, predicts niche publications including epicurean, home decorating, gardening, and personal finance magazines will be thriving into the next century. Faith Popcorn, futurist and author, forecasts that magazines will be available through a virtual reality room, a 3-D space where viewers will be able to see the magazine articles acted out and where they will be able to ask different types of questions of holograms. Her futuristic view will make the on-line content at the end of the 20th century look like ancient history.

Every print advertisement starts as a blank space and is shaped into a creative message through artwork and copy. The artwork and copy in one print advertisement may be minimal, using few words and images, while a contrasting advertisement may be very busy with multiple images and detailed copy. Both creative messages are effective in attracting the attention of the consumer because the creators have balanced the visual and verbal components of the advertisement into meaningful communications.

These meaningful communications are placed in a variety of media. It is difficult to predict exactly what types of media will be available in the future. However, the basic understanding of current media terminology and practices presented in this chapter can help us look into the future trends. What magazines and newspaper formats will you be reading in the next few years?

SUMMARY

- Advertising media are the places where advertising messages are placed. These range from the print to broadcast or electronic sources. Traditional advertising media includes newspapers, magazines, radio, and television. Innovative technologies are providing alternative places to advertise.
- Newspapers have been one of the most significant print media used by retailers for advertising. With high readership and low cost, newspapers are ideal for product advertising.
- Magazines are another popular print medium, primarily used by manufacturers and designers. Magazines offer a variety of formats suited to targeting specific markets.
- Print media uses the copy platform as a guideline to design art and copy into an advertising layout.
- Copy, the verbal component of a print advertisement, consists of all of the words used to articulate the advertiser's message. In print advertising this is all of the reading material in the ad, consisting of the headline, subheadlines, body copy, and advertiser's slogan.

- The visual arts, including design elements, color, shape, texture, and line—and design principles—balance, contrast, emphasis, proportion, rhythm, and harmony—are used to produce aesthetically pleasing and creative advertisements.
- Advertising media is being modified due to influences from the changing roles of media planners and buyers and to the challenges posed by emerging technologies. There will be changes in the role of advertising media in the future.

KEY TERMS

bleed pages	illustration	rough
broadsheet	insert	scheduling
camera ready	layout	share
comprehensive	line drawing	slogan
copy	logos	split-run advertising
cost-per-thousand	mechanical	standard advertising unit
coverage	media/medium	subheadline
cover position	newspaper supplement	tabloid
cumulative audience	paste-up	target ratings points
font	penetration	thumbnail
frequency	photography	typeface
gatefold	program ratings	typography
gross ratings points	rate cards	zone editions
halftone illustration	rate of response	
headline	reach	

QUESTIONS FOR DISCUSSION

1. Who is responsible for evaluating and selecting media outlets? Why is that job so important?
2. How should advertisers select appropriate media for their advertising message?
3. Newspaper advertising has been a significant media outlet for retail advertisers in the past. Is retail newspaper advertising still justified?
4. What are some of the future trends in advertising media anticipated at this time?

ADDITIONAL RESOURCES

Herzbrun, D. (1997). *Copywriting by design: Bringing ideas to life with words and images.* Lincolnwood, IL: NTC Business Books.

Kaye, J. R. (1998). *Layout (graphic idea resource).* Glouster, MA: Rockport Publishers.

McDonald, C. (1995). *Advertising reach and frequency: Maximizing advertising results through effective frequency.* Lincolnwood, IL: NTC Business Books.

Sissors, J. Z., and Bumba, L. (1996). *Advertising media planning.* Lincolnwood, IL: NTC Business Books.

Surmanek, J. (1995). *Media planning: A practical guide.* Lincolnwood, IL: NTC Business Books.

Swann, A. (1991). *How to understand and use design and layout.* Cincinnati, OH: North Light Books.

Turk, P. B., Jugenheimer, D. W., and Barban A. M. (1996). *Advertising media sourcebook* (4th ed.) Lincolnwood, IL: NTC Business Books.

Figure 9.1

Elsa Klensch cooperated with CNN to pioneer a weekly 30-minute television program about fashion and related topics.

Source: Courtesy of CNN's Style with Elsa Klensch.

chapter 9

BROADCAST MEDIA

E lsa Klensch and CNN (Fig. 9.1) pioneered fashion television coverage in 1980 with the 30-minute program *Style.* Toronto-based *Fashion Television* began in Canada and Europe in 1985 and was picked up by American VH-1 in the early 1990s. *FTV,* which has grown in international popularity, is now watched in over 100 countries worldwide (D'Innocenzio, 1998). *Fashion File, Joan & Melissa Fashion Review,* and *Video Fashion* all debuted in the mid-1990s, but the intensity of interest in fashion coverage increased dramatically in the last 2 years of the 20th century. E! Entertainment Television, a cable network, expanded its fashion coverage in 1998 to include 28 half-hour programs, 33 percent more than the previous year. E! also added *Style,* a 24-hour cable network that focused exclusively on style, fashion, and home design. The cable network Lifetime added *New Attitudes* to its lineup. Inspired by the original *Attitudes,* a program that went off the air in 1987, *New Attitudes* hired three reporters to cover the fields of fashion, health, and finance with more of a hard-news edge. And VH-1, which produced the popular *Fashion Awards,* launched *Fashion Kingdom,* a documentary series that offered an inside look at the fashion world (D'Innocenzio, 1998).

After you have read this chapter, you should be able to:

Discuss the different television and radio formats.

Evaluate the strengths and weakness of each broadcast medium for advertising.

Explain how broadcast media are measured.

List the broadcast media measurement services.

Explain how broadcast commercials are produced.

Why was there such an increase in the interest of fashion topics on television as the 20th century drew to a close? TV executives cited celebrity designers and entertainers, who attended or modeled in fashion shows and intrigued their viewers. With enhanced fashion awareness, producers of apparel and related products, who had not normally advertised on TV, increased their television advertising budgets. The Gap introduced its easy fit jeans through a TV campaign, featuring such diverse entertainers as Lena Horne, L. L. Cool J., and Luscious Jackson. "All of a sudden people in small towns everywhere know us," said Bob Fisher, head of the Gap division (Munk, 1998). The success of Gap's television commercials supported growth of its advertising budget to more than $300 million in 1998, 4 percent of annual sales, an increase over the $175 million, or 2.7 percent of sales, the firm spent during the previous year.

The purpose of this chapter is to analyze broadcast media used by retailing and manufacturing firms that merchandise fashion-oriented products. First, we discuss television, from the different television formats and advertising categories to how television influences fashion trends and brand globalization. Advantages and disadvantages of using this medium are explored. In addition to television, radio offers opportunities for fashion advertisers. Radio formats, programs, sponsorship, and scheduling are introduced prior to analyzing the advantages and disadvantages of using radio for advertising. General issues of broadcast media, including costs and media measurement, are then presented. Creative production of television and radio commercials is presented before the chapter concludes with a discussion about future trends in broadcasting.

TELEVISION

Could you live without television? One-quarter of Americans said they would not give television up, even for a million dollars. An additional one-fifth of all Americans would not give it up for a penny less, according to a survey conducted for *TV Guide* (Montague, 1993). Television has a significant role in our everyday lives; it is the primary source of news, information, and entertainment for many people. Television is the broadcast medium in which sight is combined with sound and motion to provide the most realistic reproduction of life. It is this combination of visual images with sound that attracts and holds the attention of the viewer. Table 9.1 illustrates how television usage in U.S. homes grew from 32.5 hours per week in 1950 to 50 hours per week in 1996.

Television has several different formats that must be considered when analyzing the medium as a potential resource for advertising. Television programming consists of four formats, including networks, local stations, syndication, and cable and satellite. Table 9.2 provides an estimated share of U.S. TV home set usage by program source.

Network Television

A network is formed whenever two or more television stations broadcast the same program, which originates from one source. Network television is an alliance between regional television stations, called **affiliates**, and one of the national television companies. A national television company normally provides entertainment, news, and sports programs of national interest. Although it is assumed that affiliates will broadcast all of the programs offered nationally, it is up to the affiliate to decide which network programs to show and what local programming should be offered.

Table 9.1 **Weekly Channel Tune-in**[a]

Year	Weekly Set Usage per Home	Channels Available per Home	Channels Viewed Weekly	Time Spent per Channel Viewed Weekly
1950	32.5	2.9	2.8	11.6
1960	36.5	5.9	4.2	8.7
1970	42.0	7.4	4.5	9.3
1980	46.5	10.2	5.6	8.3
1990	48.5	27.2	8.8	5.5
1996	50.0	43.0	10.3	4.9

[a]*In hours per U.S. TV homes.*

Source: http://www.telmar.com/amic_mem/rates/md1.html.

Table 9.2 **Estimated Share of U.S. TV Home Set Usage by Program Source**[a]

Media	Early 1950s	Mid 1990s
ABC/CBS/NBC	60%	27%
DuMont	4%	—
FOX	—	4%
Other on-air networks	—	4%
Network affiliates[b]	30%	17%
Independent stations[c]	6%	14%
PBS	—	3%
Pay cable	—	4%
Basic cable[d]	—	23%
VCR play	—	6%
Video games	—	1%
Pay-per-view	—	<1%
Average Hours of Set Usage Weekly[e]	35 hours	56 hours

[a]*Annual averages.*

[b]*Includes syndicated shows.*

[c]*Excludes WTBS and FOX or other on-air networks; includes syndicated shows.*

[d]*Includes WTBS.*

[e]*Counts multiple-set usage to different sources at the same time as separate exposures.*

Source: http://www.telmar.com/amic_mem/rates/md3.html.

For decades network television consisted of three major networks. These national networks, known by their initials, include NBC (National Broadcasting Company), ABC (American Broadcasting Company), and CBS (CBS officially changed to this designation from Columbia Broadcasting System in 1974). NBC, ABC, and CBS each own 15 regional stations and have approximately 150 affiliates.

National advertisers may purchase time from any of the networks, enabling their message to be broadcast across the nation through local affiliates. Network advertising represents a mass medium since the commercial is shown simultaneously throughout the country. The affiliates, who pay a fee to the networks for their programs, receive a percentage, usually 12 to 25 percent, of the revenues paid to the network by national advertisers.

Television sponsorship is an arrangement whereby the advertiser takes full responsibility for the production of the program and provides the accompanying commercials. As a sponsor, the advertiser generally has input into the program content as well as the advertising that appears during the broadcast. In the early years of television, most programs were created for advertising sponsors. Examples of early sponsored television programs include *Bonanza,* sponsored by Chevrolet, and *Hallmark Hall of Fame.* Sponsorship has a powerful impact, but it is very expensive—too expensive for most advertisers today. Although sponsorship was widespread during TV's infancy, most shows are now produced by the network or by an independent production company.

At the end of the 20th century, sponsorships represented less than 10 percent of network advertising (Wells, Burnett & Moriarty, 1998). The rest of network television advertising is sold as **participations**, in which advertisers pay for commercial time during one or more programs. This time is sold as 15-, 30-, or 60-second commercials.

Public Broadcasting Service (PBS) is the television network with the specific mission to present programs that educate and entertain, inform, and inspire—free and accessible to everyone. Programs consist of documentary, art, news, public affairs, and children's presentations. Although many people consider public television to be "commercial free," a ruling by the Federal Communications Commission (FCC) in 1984 liberalized the guidelines (Wells, et al, 1998). PBS stations were allowed to reinterpret the distinction between underwriting and outright sponsorship. Current FCC guidelines allow ads to appear on public television only during the local 2.5-minute program breaks. Each station develops and maintains its own specifications for acceptability. While some PBS stations may choose to run commercials that have been broadcast on network or local programs, other stations will not run any ad that has been shown on commercial television. These stations run "value neutral" ads, featuring messages that include nonpromotional corporate and product logos and slogans. In other words, there is no attempt to "sell" through these "ads." Because public broadcasting reaches affluent, educated households, as well as minority and low-end consumers, PBS is an attractive medium for advertisers.

The very nature of traditional network television underwent dramatic change at the close of the 20th century. The "big three" networks were challenged by newer national broadcasting companies, including FOX and UPN; by other forms of television, including cable, syndication, and cable networks; and by other electronic media.

Local Television

Local television stations serve a regional geographical area and may be affiliated with a national network or broadcast independently. If the station is affiliated with a national network, it will most likely run locally produced shows in addition to network shows. For example, WICU-TV is the local affiliate for NBC in Erie, Pennsylvania. Independent channels, such as KTVK-TV—Channel 3 in Phoenix—offer locally produced programs and syndicated shows; these are discussed in the next section of the chapter.

Advertising on local channels is sold as spot announcements. These local spots are sold for a specific amount of time, usually 10, 20, 30, or 60 seconds. Spots may be sold to national, regional, or local advertisers, although local buyers dominate local spot slots. Time for spot advertising is negotiated and purchased directly from local television stations. A station rep is an individual who acts as the sales representative for local stations, enabling national advertisers to buy local spot time.

Syndication

Syndicated programs are shows that are sold and distributed to local television stations to fill open hours. Syndicated programs have boomed because of growth in the number of independent television stations and the prime-time access rule, which forbids network affiliates in the 50 major U.S. television markets from broadcasting more than three hours of prime time programming in any one 4-hour slot. There are several categories of syndicated programs, including off-network, first-run, and barter syndication.

Table 9.3   Trends in TV Network, Cable, and Barter Syndication Ad Revenues[a]

Year	ABC, CBS, NBC	FOX	WB, UPN	AD-Supported Cable Networks	Barter Syndication	Unwired Networks	Total	ABC, CBS, NBC, Share (%)
1980	4,827	—	—	50	25	—	4,902	98.5
1985	7,592	—	—	625	550	5	8,772	86.5
1990	8,750	360	—	1,375	1,250	95	11,830	74.0
1995	10,040	1,130	95	2,655	1,800	265	15,985	62.8

[a]*In millions.*

Source: http://www.telmar.com/amic_mem/rates/md2.html.

Off-network programs consist of reruns of network programs, old or current, that are bought by individual stations. FCC regulations require that at least 88 episodes of a network show must exist before it can be syndicated. Reruns of shows such as *M*A*S*H*, *NYPD Blue*, and *Home Improvement* continue to be attractive to local audiences.

First-run syndication refers to shows that are produced specifically for the syndication market. Some shows that are dropped by the networks continue to create new episodes in syndication. These shows, such as *Rescue 911* and *Too Close for Comfort*, continued production in syndication because they had not met the 88-episode rule imposed by the FCC. Popular syndicated shows include talk shows, news, game shows, entertainment news, comedies, or dramas. These shows are *sold* to local channels and may or may not be viewed on a national network affiliate.

Under the barter syndication system, both off-network and first-run syndicated programs are offered to local stations for free or at a reduced rate if the station gives the syndicator a portion of its commercial time instead of cash. The syndicator negotiates a price with the station by dealing with cash, barter, or a combination of the two. The cash deal is obvious; the syndicator grants the stations the rights to run the show for a specified period of time for a cash license fee. Syndicators are able to do this because some of the advertising is already presold to national advertisers. Typically half of the advertising is presold, allowing the local station to sell the other half. Benefits are gained by national advertisers who are able to break into the local markets and by local stations that receive free programming and time to sell local spots. Trends in TV network, cable, and barter syndication ad revenues are illustrated in Table 9.3.

Cable and Satellite Television

Early cable television channels were developed to broadcast signals through wires rather than airwaves to geographically isolated regions. Programming for these pioneer channels frequently consisted of reruns of network programs. However, alternative programming, with an emphasis on information and entertainment and targeting of specific markets, has led to rapid growth of cable television. Cable television has evolved into a mass broadcast medium, offering programs for both niche and general markets. Cable television is extremely popular with over two-thirds of the 95 percent of U.S. television homes with cable access subscribing to the service (Piirto, 1995).

Table 9.4   **Common Television Dayparts**

Morning	7:00 A.M. to 9:00 A.M.	Monday through Friday
Daytime	9:00 A.M. to 4:30 P.M.	Monday through Friday
Early fringe	4:30 P.M. to 7:30 P.M.	Monday through Friday
Prime-time access	7:30 P.M. to 8:00 P.M.	Sunday through Saturday
Prime-time	8:00 P.M. to 1:00 P.M.	Monday through Saturday
	7:00 P.M. to 11:00 P.M.	and Sunday
Late news	11:00 P.M. to 11:30 P.M.	Monday through Friday
Late fringe	11:30 P.M. to 1:00 A.M.	Monday through Friday

Source: Belch, G. E., and Belch, M. A. (1995). Introduction to advertising and promotion: An integrated marketing communications perspective *(3rd ed.) Chicago: Irwin. Reproduced with permission of the McGraw-Hill Companies.*

Cable subscribers pay a monthly fee for which they receive an average of 30 or more channels. The local cable system broadcasts local network affiliates; independent channels; various cable networks, such as CNN, ESPN, CNBC, or MTV; and local cable channels. Subscribers may also select premium channels for additional fees. These channels include HBO, Showtime, and the Movie Channel.

Cable channels such as CNN and CNBC also broadcast internationally. The impact of global brands is enhanced with television commercials that are simultaneously broadcast to several countries. This is particularly significant in the European markets, since television commercials for brands ranging from Nike to Johnson's Baby Shampoo are simultaneously broadcast to several countries at one time.

At first cable channels were dependent upon wires. As technology evolved, network and cable television began to use satellites to broadcast signals and the era of satellite television began. Consumers were able to purchase personal satellite dishes to receive these signals. To protect the cable industry, scramblers were added to the sites, requiring consumers to purchase contracts similar to monthly cable charges in order to unscramble the signals.

TV Commercial Scheduling

The cost of buying advertising time on television varies with the time of day, the type of program, and length of the commercial. Since the demographics and size of the audience changes throughout the day, TV time is divided into **dayparts** or time periods. Dayparts may vary from station to station, but the common classifications for a weekday are shown in Table 9.4. **Prime time**, programming that is broadcast between 8 P.M. and 11 P.M., delivers the largest audience and has the highest commercial placement costs.

Advertisers are also interested in who specifically watches the different programs offered. Individual television stations can provide target audience information for potential advertisers.

Most television commercials are sold in 15-, 30-, or 60-second time periods. For many people, the start of a television commercial provides a signal to grab the remote or bolt to the kitchen for a snack. But a few advertisers are experimenting with snack-proof and zap-proof ads: the 1-second commercial. **Blink ads**, as they are called for obvious reasons, depict an advertiser's image in a flash. Master Lock, the Milwaukee, Wisconsin–based manufacturer of locks, used the quick pitch—showing the company's signature image, a bullet shredding, but not opening a lock, with its logo—in a 1-second commercial. The ads are part of a campaign that also uses 30-second spots for Master Lock padlocks. According to Richard Kirshenbaum, co-chairman of Kirshenbaum, Bond & Partners, blink ads cannot introduce products, but they can certainly reinforce such icons as McDonald's Golden Arches (Christopher, 1998).

Television Influences on Fashion and Brand Globalization

Television and fashion have been inevitably linked from the start of the medium. Fashion has influenced television audiences and helped establish trends, creating bestsellers ranging from the *Y necklace* and Jennifer Aniston's haircut from *Friends* to *shoulder pads* as worn by Crystal Carrington, a character on *Dynasty*. Fashion influences have helped create story lines and television characters on such programs as England's *Absolutely Fabulous,* Canada's *OohLaLa,* and America's *Just Shoot Me* and *Suddenly Susan.* Fashion has become the primary topic on such reality-based programs as Canada's *Fashion Television* and CNN's *Style* with host Elsa Klensch. Whether it is involved in creating fashion trends, bestsellers, and entertaining characters, or providing information, television has an impact on fashion and vice versa.

Television, perhaps more than any other medium, has had an impact on worldwide trends, creating a global village. Worldwide access to commercial television has influenced the growth of global brands. It is not surprising that teenagers in Bangkok are just as aware of such brands as Levi's and Calvin Klein jeans, Timberland boots, and Adidas and Nike footwear as their counterparts in America. One of the most important sources of brand information comes from television commercials broadcast internationally.

Historically, major jeans manufacturers such as Levi Strauss and Lee have been among the few apparel manufacturers willing to spend large sums of money for television ads. But bridge labels, such as Ellen Tracy, experimented with 30-second spots for a 2-week period. The Ellen Tracy television commercials, used in combination with print ads and transit media, were concentrated in five metropolitan markets—New York, San Francisco, Dallas, Atlanta, and Los Angeles. According to Donald Ziccardi, president of Ziccardi & Partners, Ellen Tracy's advertising agency, this integrated marketing communications approach used television commercials as an image-building tool (Socha, 1997).

MTV has significantly contributed to the globalization of the teenage consumer market. The music network has established separate networks in international regions such as MTV Latino, MTV Brazil, MTV Europe, MTV Mandarin, MTV Asia, MTV Japan, and MTV India. Although music tastes are locally programmed and produced, there are common themes in clothing and style shared around the world. The network has the ability to reach a large proportion of the world's youth markets in a matter of minutes (Walker, 1996).

Advantages of Television Advertising

Television offers a number of benefits to advertisers. These advantages include:

- **Audience size.** Television reaches a large audience. Networks have a vast amount of research on the size and demographics of the audience and make this information available to potential advertisers. Both national and local advertisers are able to target specific viewers.

- **Versatility and flexibility.** Messages, creative innovation, and technical capabilities are unlimited. Television commercials may use still photography, video, action, or any combination of techniques.
- **Ability to show products true-to-life.** Television brings the combination of sight and sound to the message. Viewers can see a fairly realistic representation of merchandise, increasing the impact of the message and improving the chances for response.

Disadvantages of Television Advertising

Even though television offers advertisers many benefits, it also has some weaknesses, which are illustrated next.

- **Television advertising avoidance.** With the introduction of television remote controls and with so many choices on television, the audience can easily switch channels, mute the sound, or leave the room during commercials. Consumers zip or zap commercials. VCRs have also created an atmosphere where the audience can avoid the advertising message. Nearly 80 percent of VCR users admit they always or sometimes fast-forward through commercials (Kneale, 1988). Zipping occurs when consumers fast-forward through commercials during the playback of a previously recorded program. Zapping takes place when the consumer uses the remote control to change channels during a commercial. Either way, the consumer avoids watching the commercial.
- **Costly.** Television air time and the production of TV commercials is very expensive. Hiring competent personnel, from on air talent to technicians, is costly. Skilled experts are required to complete professional quality television advertising.
- **Long response time.** Writers, actors, musicians, photographers, and editors require time to produce television commercials. It may take as much as 3 to 4 weeks to produce a commercial before it is ready for broadcast. This long response time prevents quick response to meet current market conditions.
- **Limited amount of broadcast time.** Most advertisers want the impact of running commercials during prime time. There are a limited number of time slots during prime time. These spots are frequently purchased by large network advertisers, making cost higher due to high demand.

RADIO

Radio is the broadcast medium that allows sound to travel via electrical impulses called signals. Electromagnetic waves with height (amplitude) and width (frequency) transmit these signals. The **radio frequency** is the number of radio waves a transmitter produces in a second. Thus, a radio station assigned a frequency of 107,000 cycles per second (megahertz) can be found at 107 on your radio dial. The FCC assigns these frequencies so radio signals will not interfere with each other.

Radio stations are designated as AM or FM. An AM, or amplitude modulation station, uses ground waves during the day and sky waves during the evening. That is why nighttime listeners of AM radio are able to pick up signals from transmitters beyond the daytime range of the station's ground waves. An FM, or frequency modulation station, differs from AM in that the frequency is adjusted rather than amplitude. An FM station signal remains constant from day to night. Because the signal put out by an FM station follows the line of sight, the distance of a signal depends upon the height of the antenna; typically 50 miles is the maximum signal distance.

In addition to AM and FM delivery systems, cable radio was launched in the 1990s. This technology uses cable television receivers to deliver static-free radio programs via wires plugged into the cable subscribers' stereo.

Upon first consideration, it does not make too much sense to advertise such visually oriented products as apparel and home furnishings on the radio. How can advertisers translate such strong visual images into a medium such as radio? According to research conducted by Jack Trout, however, "there is much evidence that the mind works by the ear, that thinking is a process of manipulating sounds rather than images (even when pictures or photographs are involved). As a result, you see what you hear, not what the eye tells you it has seen" (Trout, 1995). Repeated studies show that the ear works much faster than the eye, making radio an ideal medium for advertisers. According to the Radio Advertising Bureau, representing 4,600 stations, radio is an ideal medium to use to attract highly selective target audiences. Radio reaches 77 percent of all consumers every day and 96 percent every week ("1997 Radio Marketing Guide," 1997). With numerous radio formats and so many places to listen—from the home, car, or office to just walking around with personal earphones—radio is available anywhere. Radio has the ability to affect all ages and interests through its specific listenership, as the article in Box 9.1 demonstrates.

BOX 9.1
Why Radio Thrives

As media wars rage around them, traditional radio formats survive by adapting quickly to changing listener needs. Radio audiences have eerily consistent audience demographics. New technology may change radio, but the medium's personal, adaptable nature is the secret to its survival.

Eerily Consistent

In some ways, radio listeners act more like magazine subscribers than television viewers. They tend to listen habitually, at predictable times, to stations with narrowly targeted formats. They are loyal, identifiable, and cheaper to reach than are TV audiences. The average person listens to two or three different stations, according to the media measurement service Arbitron, but one station is usually the favorite. "People develop a special relationship with one station," says Gary Fries, president of the Radio Advertising Bureau (RAB). "They talk about a favorite station as if they own it."

"Women who listen to country music have very different attitudes from our listeners," says Danny Clayton, program director of WKTI in Milwaukee. The core audience for WKTI's Top-40 format is women, aged 18 to 34. Country listeners are also likely to be women, but they are concentrated in the 25-to-54 age group and have lower incomes than do Top-40 listeners. More important, says Clay-

ton, is an attitudinal difference: country listeners may be more prone to a melancholic outlook than Top-40 fans. "We're the up, bright, fun spot on the dial," he says.

One advertiser recently capitalized on WKTI listeners' demographics—and their frisky nature—with a highly successful promotion. Warner-Lambert's goal was a 3 percentage point increase in the Milwaukee market share for e.p.t., an over-the-counter pregnancy test. Thomas McMillian, zone manager for e.p.t., used WKTI exclusively because it the highest rated station in the area among women in the peak childbearing ages, 18 to 34.

The ad featured five women and one man asking, "Am I pregnant?" It was coupled with a promotion called "The Baby Derby," during which three couples competed to conceive for big cash prizes. During the 2 months it took for a couple to get pregnant, listenership and media interest climbed. As the couples became Milwaukee celebrities, e.p.t. got free publicity on local television shows and newspapers. When it was all over, the product's local market share had jumped 20 percentage points. "It sometimes helps to be a little offbeat," says Todd Gatzow, WKTI account executive. "Some people called it risqué, but it really got people listening."

The story illustrates a good rule of thumb about buying time on the radio. Advertisers get more bang for their buck when their product plays a role in the station's programming, instead of just filling time on a commercial break.

Personal Connection

Radio is a personal medium because music is personal; it can be an important part of a person's self-image or membership in a social group. Music "is like a common language," says Fries. "People with common musical threads seem to have common social threads." Radio audience profiles show that 25 years after Woodstock, Americans still use popular music to choose their tribes.

The Progressive or Alternative radio format is packaged and sold to young rebels. Its format, featuring the loud, raw sounds of bands like Pearl Jam and Nirvana, draws baby busters (now aged 18 to 29). Other popular formats with young listeners, according to Simmons Market Research Bureau, are Classic Rock, Top-40, New Age, Spanish/Latino, and Urban Contemporary.

If you want to attract young people with music, you have a lot of choices. But if you want to chase them out of your store and replace them with seniors, put on some Benny Goodman. And, what about the Woodstock Generation? The two most popular formats with the middle market, aged 25 to 64, emphasize Classic Rock, Golden Oldies, and Jazz.

Talk Radio

Popularity of AM radio stations declined 48 percent between 1981 and 1992. One reason for AM's decline was due to the technical sound superiority of FM. "People tune into FM because it sounds better," says Larry Rosin, vice president of Bolton Research in Philadelphia. But there's a silver lining to that dark cloud, and it's called talk. All-News and News/Talk formats are taking over more AM stations, and high fidelity isn't as important to talk as it is to all-music formats.

News/Talk is one of the best all-around radio formats, according to Simmons. It is popular with older audiences, but a decent proportion (22 percent of listeners) is aged 18 to 34. Its listeners tend to be relatively well educated; 36 percent have completed 4 or more years of college, compared with 21 percent of all Americans aged 25 and older. News/Talk radio is also a good choice for multimedia advertising campaigns, as listeners are 51 percent more likely than average to be heavy newspaper readers.

Secret to Survival

In the 1980s, talk radio helped AM survive the challenge of FM. Today, both bandwidths face new challenges from technology. A few years ago, for example, industry pundits boldly predicted that Digital Audio Broadcasting (DAB) would make over-the-air radio obsolete. The technology digitizes an audio signal, changing it into a series of ones and zeros much like the stream of data that pours from a computer modem. When a DAB transmitter meets a DAB-equipped receiver, the sound quality of an AM and FM signal is equal. But DAB is now embroiled in a regulatory battle, and "it'll be years before anything comes of it," Rosin says.

Satellite and cable are two ways to send and receive digitized radio signals. But each DAB delivery option has a fatal flaw; it will cost more than broadcast radio. Several companies now send digitized CD-quality music over cable to subscribers for $10 a month. But so much radio listening occurs in cars or at work that cable radio at home is not much of a threat. "The people who will pay to get music piped into their homes are audiophiles," says RAB's Laura Morandin. "They are probably listening to CDs anyway."

Rosin predicts that in 5 years, broadcast radio will exist just as it does today—with formats continually adapting to meet new audience needs. "Radio is like an alley cat with nine lives," he says. It's a survivor. You can't ever kill it."

Source: Piirto, R. (1994, May 1). Why radio thrives. American Demographics, 16, 40 [On-line]. Available: http://www.elibrary .com. Reprinted by permission of Rebecca Piirto Heath.

Although retailers rarely use radio as their exclusive advertising medium, radio is a media outlet that is used in combination with other media to present a communication package. There is an immediacy about radio—the audience feels that it is current and timely—making it a good vehicle for a coordinated advertising program.

Radio Formats

Radio advertising is available on national networks and through local markets. Network radio, similar to television networks, consists of a group of local affiliates connected to one or more of the national radio networks through telephone wires and satellites. The four major radio networks include Westwood One, CBS, ABC, and Unistar. Radio networks also use syndication, a distribution method introduced under the discussion about television.

More than 20 different radio formats have been identified on a national level, from Alternative to Contemporary Hits, Country, and Jazz. Radio formats have been developed to fit every possible interest. Locally operated radio stations may follow these more common models or vary from these national formats. Table 9.5 shows the radio formats and audience age as profiled by the Radio Advertising Bureau. This information helps an advertiser select the most appropriate format to reach the target audience.

In a manner similar to television, radio broadcasters use dayparts as time blocks or periods that break up the broadcast day. These radio daypart classifications are divided into five different segments. The most common dayparts for radio are illustrated in Table 9.6.

Table 9.5 **There's a Radio Format for Everybody**

Age	Adult Contemporary %	All News %	Album Rock (AOR) %	Alternative/ Adult Alternative %	Classical %	Classic Rock %
18–24	17.0	2.6	26.8	34.9	10.9	21.2
25–34	30.8	18.7	41.8	41.2	17.9	36.4
35–44	25.4	24.2	20.3	16.9	23.6	32.3
45–54	14.4	20.6	8.3	5.0	20.5	7.7
55–64	6.5	12.7	1.8	1.0	10.9	1.3
65+	5.9	21.2	1.0	1.0	16.2	1.1

Age	Contemporary Hits (CHR) %	Country %	Easy Listening %	Full Service %	Jazz %	Modern Rock/ New Age %	News/Talk %
18–24	35.5	14.8	12.4	8.6	13.1	27.0	5.7
25–34	34.4	25.8	17.0	9.4	22.6	33.8	17.8
35–44	19.0	22.5	16.6	17.8	39.6	21.1	24.6
45–54	6.7	17.3	17.7	6.9	14.7	11.7	18.5
55–64	1.4	10.0	16.0	32.1	5.0	3.5	12.3
65+	3.0	9.6	20.3	25.1	5.0	2.9	21.1

Age	Nostalgia %	Oldies %	Religious %	Rhythm & Blues %	Soft Contemporary %	Spanish %	Urban Contemporary %
18–24	6.2	12.5	10.2	13.4	10.4	26.3	30.7
25–34	6.1	24.6	24.1	25.8	26.6	26.9	30.1
35–44	10.0	30.1	27.7	30.3	30.8	23.8	22.7
45–54	14.7	21.9	14.8	14.6	15.6	10.9	10.3
55–64	21.2	5.8	11.0	7.1	7.1	6.2	2.5
65+	41.8	5.1	12.2	8.8	9.5	5.9	3.7

Source: Simmons. (1996). Radio marketing guide and fact book [On-line]. Available: http://www.rab.com/station/radfact/fact36.html.

Table 9.6   **Common Radio Dayparts**

5:00 A.M. to 10:00 A.M.	Monday through Saturday
10:00 A.M. to 3:00 P.M.	Monday through Saturday
3:00 P.M. to 6:00 P.M.	Monday through Saturday
6:00 P.M. to 1:00 A.M.	Monday through Saturday
5:00 A.M. to 1:00 A.M.	Sunday

Source: Belch, G. E., and Belch, M. A. (1995). Introduction to advertising and promotion: An integrated marketing communications perspective *(3rd ed.) Chicago: Irwin. Reproduced with permission of The McGraw-Hill Companies.*

Drive or **traffic time** is the period when radio listenership is the highest. This prime time for radio often features news and weather reports and corresponds to the transition from home to work and work to home. Although these hours may shift in one region versus another, drive time usually falls between 6:00 A.M. and 9:00 A.M. in the morning, while the evening drive time is normally between 4:00 P.M. and 7:00 P.M.

Radio stations sell advertising time to national firms as well as regional and local advertisers. Typically radio commercials are sold as 60-second or 30-second announcements, but shorter commercial lengths, such as 10, 15, or 20 seconds, may be available from some stations. Although costs do vary by length, they are not proportionally priced. A 30-second announcement usually costs between 75 and 80 percent of a 60-second announcement.

Radio Programs and Sponsorship

Radio stations present regularly scheduled feature programs such as news, weather, traffic reports, sporting events, or other special-interest programming such as gardening or syndicated music programs. Advertising time may be sold as spots or through **program sponsorship**, which may include an opening mention, a commercial during the program, and a closing credit. Sponsorship is a long-term commitment (13 to 52 weeks) at premium rates. Commercial times and length are subject to variation in different markets and from station to station.

Another way a radio advertiser can tap into regularly scheduled programs, without investing in sponsorship, is to buy **adjacencies**, commercials sold at a premium rate, to run just before or after a program. This is another way to secure some of the advantages of advertising during a program without the expense and commitment of sponsorship.

A local retail firm or regional shopping center can tap into a local promotion by using a **remote**, a live broadcast on location. The radio station sends the station's announcers to the store, mall, or other designated location for a promotional event. While broadcasting regular news and music, the announcers promote the retailer or mall and may have merchandise specials or giveaways.

Radio Advertising Scheduling

Radio scheduling techniques are similar to the methods used by other media, with some alternative strategies. In addition to continuity, flighting, and pulsing techniques, discussed in Chapter 8, the radio industry uses blinking/bunching, bursting, and sliding. A blinking/bunching approach schedules advertising activity over a short period, involving 1 week on, 1 week off, and so forth. Bursting is a pattern in which heavy advertising is concentrated over a short period, placing one week's advertising within a 4-day period. Sliding occurs when the frequency of advertising is changed over the course of the advertising campaign. Normally an advertiser using a sliding strategy launches the campaign with heavy advertising and decreases the quantity of advertisements as the campaign progresses, with a possible hiatus between schedules.

Advantages of Radio Advertising

Some of the advantages radio offers advertisers follow.

- **Specific audience.** Since each station programs to a very specific audience through one of the focused radio formats, the audience demographics for a radio station are readily available to an advertiser. With the turn of a radio dial, audiences for country, news/talk, hard rock, or adult contemporary can be easily selected.
- **Nearly universal medium.** The Canadian Radio Marketing Bureau estimates that radio reaches 90 percent of all adults and teens weekly. Canadians over the age of 12 listen to an average of 23 hours of radio each week ("1997 Radio Marketing," 1997). The average American listens to the radio more than 3 hours on weekdays and nearly 6 hours each weekend. Listeners tune in at home, at work, and during leisure activities in addition to listening in their cars, while commuting, or shopping.
- **High degree of frequency.** Radio builds top-of-mind awareness with repetition. Repetition builds awareness through affordable frequency.
- **Timing is more immediate.** Although most retail advertising is planned long in advance, there may be occasions when an advertiser needs to bring an advertising message to the audience immediately. An unplanned celebrity personal appearance or weather changes can lead to an unanticipated opportunity. A radio spot can be produced, scheduled, and aired more quickly than through print media or television.
- **Cost-effective.** The relationship between low costs and highly selected audience are documented through research studies. Radio delivers more advertising impressions than other media for the same budget. In addition to the cost advantages associated with reach and frequency, radio commercials have a much lower production expense than other media. This allows the advertiser to change the message, or develop creative messages to match the format and demographics for each radio station used.
- **Least ignored advertising medium.** Research studies show that while almost 60 percent of television audiences switch channels during advertising, only 28 percent of radio listeners avoid advertising messages.
- **Audience consistency.** People listen to the radio to find out about community events. From traffic reports to school closures, the audience tunes in to find out what is happening daily in their communities. This interest is consistent from day to day and throughout the year. Unlike other media, such as television, with a summer decline in audiences, radio listeners tune in all year long.

Disadvantages of Radio Advertising

The following list identifies some of the weaknesses associated with radio advertising.

- **Inability to deliver a visual image.** Research shows that a visual image is suggested through sound, but it does not provide the subtleties that can be furnished with a visual image. Colors, silhouettes, and other product characteristics cannot be visually represented by sound alone.

- **Lack of listener attention.** Radio is a companion medium; in other words the listener is involved in more than one activity at one time. Because the radio is *on* during times that the listener is at work or driving, it may serve as background noise to the primary activity. Under those conditions, the listener may be distracted by other actions as the advertising message is run and may tune out the commercial.
- **Nonretrievable format.** While clipping services help print advertisers save copies of advertising messages, radio commercials are typically aired and the tape is lost or forgotten. Archival copies are not generally available.

BROADCAST MEDIA ISSUES

Because television and radio are the dominant broadcast media, they share some similarities. Evaluating media costs and analyzing techniques to measure media effectiveness are among the media issues common to television and radio.

Television Media Costs

Television media use **cost per ratings point** (CPRP) for cost comparison figure. This measurement, also known as **cost per point** (CPP), is based upon the following formula:

$$\text{CPRP} = \frac{\text{Cost of commercial time}}{\text{Program rating}}$$

Advertising in a local television market can be used as an example. A men's wear specialty retailer wants to run a 30-second ad prior to Father's Day. The retailer has information about the cost of commercial time and the program rating provided by the television station. The results of the analysis indicate that the spot advertisement would be less expensive to reach an individual audience member on Program B, but Program A would provide the larger audience reach.

	Program A	Program B
Cost per 30-second spot ad	$8,000	$2,000
Rating	18th	6th
Reach (total persons)	325,000	138,000
Calculation	8,000/18	2,000/6
CPRP	$444.44	$333.33

While the costs for network and local television are considered to be very high, cable operators offer retailers and manufacturers more reasonably priced television commercials. Next, we will consider cable television costs.

Cable Television Costs

Cable television has proven successful for a variety of retailers. For example, Betsy Robbins, owner of Shoemaker's Warehouse, a shoe store tucked away in an industrial part of Atlanta, has been singing the praises of cable advertising. Robbins had always relied upon radio and newspaper advertising to draw customers to her store. Then she tried cable TV and was pleased with the results. Prime-time spots cost her $50 to $150, and she indicated she got better and more measurable results from her cable ads. Local television stations have been able to rent cameras and a crew for as little as $65 per hour, making the production costs affordable for small retailers (Updike and Schatz, 1997).

Radio Advertising Costs

Similar to the other media, radio stations generally publish their advertising rates on a rate card. The radio industry offers several different rate and package plans. First, the **single price cards** reflect a single price for each of the dayparts, time periods, and days of the week. This is the simplest and most direct method of pricing advertising.

Some stations offer a second method, **grid cards**, a multi-level rate card, in which the rates for each time period vary, week to week, depending upon available air time. In this system, an advertiser wishing to book time on very short notice may pay a higher rate than an advertiser willing to wait a while.

A package plan known as a **total audience plan**, **guaranteed audience plan**, or **reach plan** is a rate given for a combination of time periods. The distribution of announcements to be run in each daypart is determined by the station. This strategy uses a broad combination of dayparts intended to give the advertiser an increased opportunity to reach more potential customers than it might by a schedule limited to breakfast time.

Other scheduling formats, such as **run-of-schedule** (ROS) or **best time available** (BTA), are forms of package plans that typically offer lower rates than the total audience package plan. ROS or BTA plans may run at any time between 5:00 A.M. and 1:00 A.M. with no guaranteed distribution by daypart. The positive aspect of lower cost may not be worth it to the advertisers if they cannot be promised ideal timing for their commercials. Each advertiser will have to measure the tradeoffs with this system.

Broadcast Media Measurement Services

In addition to firms that take a broad consumer and mass media view, individual media use measurement services specific to their medium. Television and cable industries determine the size of their audience by subscribing to Nielsen Media Research. A. C. Nielsen is the research firm known for evaluating television ratings. These ratings have become the currency used by buyers and sellers of advertising time and program sponsorship to evaluate potential as well as achieved audiences through Television Audience Measurement. This famous television research firm affixes black boxes to television sets randomly selected in the 30 largest geographical markets. In these markets, the local stations and their advertisers have data on the size of the audience every day of the year. In smaller markets, Nielsen sends diaries (Fig. 9.2) to homes selected at random four times each year. The results are quarterly reports on the size of TV audiences, defined primarily by age and sex. There is little in the way of socioeconomic information and no comparisons to other media. Local advertisers would need to find other qualitative resources to provide a broad picture of local consumers and their media use.

As the demand for information grows globally, Nielsen has expanded its services to provide data from 93 different countries. Television Audience Measurement is now conducted in 25 different countries.

Television advertisers may also use SQAD, the acronym for Spot Quotations and Data. Each month SQAD publishes a report of spot TV cost-per-point projections. The data provides average costs for 30-second television commercials, without information about specific products, brands, or individual stations. The data is provided confidentially from advertising agency buy data for spot TV purchases and is meant to be viewed as a benchmark, not a listing of the lowest prices in a market. Subscribers receive printed

Figure 9.2

A sample Nielson TV diary

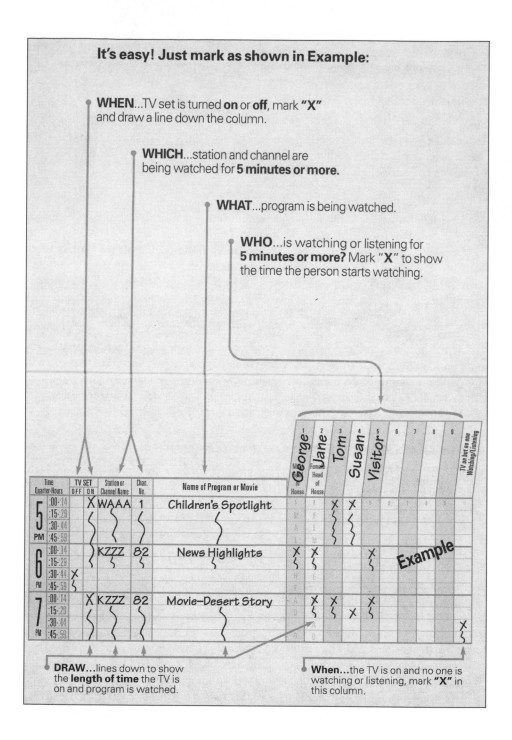

reports or Windows- or MAC-compatible diskettes. Automated or hard copy delivery systems reflect technological developments in the media measurement industry.

In Canada the industry association for commercial television broadcasters is the Television Bureau of Canada (TVB). TVB, also known as Bureau de la Télévision du Canada, was incorporated in 1962 to provide (1) leading edge research and information about television advertising, and (2) video services to its member stations, network and sales rep organizations, and agencies and advertisers. TVB supplies the most up-to-date research to its constituencies, houses Canada's TV commercial archive, with over 26,500 commercials, and manages two high profile commercial awards shows, the Bessies and Retail Comp ("Television Bureau of Canada," 1998).

Radio stations must also subscribe to a ratings service to find out about their audiences. The leading radio research service is The Arbitron Company, which measures radio audiences in more than 260 markets. In a manner similar to Nielsen, diaries are sent to randomly selected households. Each person over the age of 12 is sent a diary to record for 1 week, noting when he or she listens to radio, the station listened to, and where the listener is located—at home, in the car, or at work. The top 94 markets receive reports each quarter with monthly updates. Smaller markets receive reports once or twice each year.

In Canada, the Bureau of Broadcast Measurement (BBM) provides ratings analysis. This nonprofit research company surveys and reports radio listening habits across Canada.

CREATING BROADCAST COMMERCIALS

As we learned in Chapter 3, in a large full-service advertising agency with a complex corporate structure, the head of creative services focuses on creation and execution of the advertisements, while gaining marketing, management, and account services from other divisions. In a smaller firm, the owner may have complete responsibility for every aspect of creative development in addition to running other functional operations.

Coordination between the creative strategists, copywriters, artists, freelance workers, talent, production workers, and copywriters is the responsibility of the creative services director. This director, who sets the tone for the creative strategy of the organization, is responsible for the overall creative and aesthetic quality of advertising production under his or her leadership, and typically supervises verbal and visual personnel in the organization. From idea individuals to visual and verbal experts, a variety of people with unique skills must be pulled together to execute creative advertisements.

Creating Television Commercials

With the advantages of site, sound, color, and movement, television offers an exceptional method of presenting an advertising message. Television incorporates all of the elements of copy, art, and layout previously discussed in relationship to print and radio advertising along with live-action, and special effects or animation. In print advertising, the relationship between copy and art may be considered the visual interpreting the verbal. However, in television the relationship between art and copy could be viewed as the verbal interpreting the visual.

Creation and production of television commercials demand a complex combination of skills. Acting, art directing, casting actors, directing, designing graphics, filming, film editing, musical directing, producing, set designing, and writing are just some of the creative expertise needed to produce television commercials. Both radio and television commercials depend upon hiring the right talent, which includes actors, announcers, disk jockeys, celebrities, singers, dancers, and models, to bring the concept alive.

An outside director may be hired to turn the creative idea into a commercial. In the 1990s, television commercials were beginning to look a lot like movies. This trend was due to movie directors moonlighting in advertising. The article in Box 9.2 reveals more about this practice.

Retailers or manufacturers rarely produce television commercials with an in-house staff, relying on advertising agencies and television production specialists to produce ads. With the high costs of maintaining electronic equipment, studios and specialized personnel, retailers, and manufacturers have found hiring outside personnel to be more cost effective in meeting their needs.

BOX 9.2
Hot Spots

"It used to be that 'commercial' movies meant movies that made lots of money," says Ted Sann, chief creative officer and co-chief executive officer (CEO) of BBDO/New York. "Now we mean they *look* like commercials."

Sann was talking about a growing trend on Madison Avenue. More and more top-flight directors are shooting commercials in between movie projects. Depending on whom you talk to, such moonlighters either create advertisements so great they should be on the big screen, or movies that do not linger in the mind for longer than 30 seconds. Or both.

Since the 1970s, at least, Hollywood has looked to advertising as a potential training ground for directorial talent. The brothers Ridley (*Alien*) and Tony (*Top Gun*) Scott as well as Adrian (*Fatal Attraction*) Lyne and Alan (*Evita*) Parker all cut their teeth doing commercials. What is new about the current crop of directors, however, is how nimbly they jump between Sunset Boulevard and Madison Avenue.

Leading the pack is Spike Lee, who has recently been anointed creative director at his own spin-off agency, Spike/DDB. Then there is Joe Pytka, who says he is "in shock" over the enormous success of *Space Jam* but is continuing to churn out TV spots anyway, for clients such as HBO and Pepsi. David Fincher (*Seven*), Michael Bay (*Bad Boys*), and Barry Sonnenfeld (the Addams Family pictures and *Get Shorty*) are all currently shooting commercials, or will be in the near future.

"Feature-film directors know how to find a magic moment, something that isn't even in the script," says Keith Reinhard, DDB/Needham's chairman and CEO. "Bill Bernbach, who founded this company, always said you can't storyboard a smile." And Hollywood-trained maestros have something else: an expertise in getting the best performance out of actors. "People who do only commercials tend to be more design-driven," says Stephanie Apt, director of broadcast production at J. Walter Thompson/New York, who was so impressed by the ensemble acting in Stanley Tucci's *Big Night* that she hired him to direct a series of upcoming TV spots for New York Cares.

The availability of such high-powered directors leaves some ad execs feeling a bit starstruck. "It's as if Bill Clinton showed up and told a mayor he's willing to run his city for a while," says Barry Hoffman, a creative director at Young & Rubicam. "Suddenly, everyone is for sale." For the right price, that is. With fees reaching as high as $20,000 a day, a hot director can earn substantially more for his time doing a commercial than directing a movie.

Michael Bay, however, says it is not about money. "I already make plenty from doing features," he states so matter-of-factly, it hardly seems like bragging. Then why after his huge hit *The Rock* does Bay seek out 30-second jobs? "Because I love to shoot, and commercials present a new challenge," he explains. "Billy Wilder said he was always amazed at how ad guys could communicate so much information so quickly. Every second must convey something."

Bay's experience is typical of this new breed of double-threat director. He recently shot the sexy "elevator ride" spot for Levi-Strauss—a young couple's first glance, first kiss, first child, all in half a minute. But this month, it is on to a new movie, about which he remarks, "Let's just say it's heroic—and will cost about $100 million."

Blue jeans one day, blockbusters the next. Less-established directors dream of such mobility. Stavros Merjos, whose production house, HIS, has recently formed a new division to groom advertising directors who want to enter film, thinks the trend is a positive one for a simple reason. "Directing is a technical skill," he says. "Practice makes perfect. The guys who shoot all the time are the best directors."

Merjos's clients include Roman Coppola, Matthew Rolston, and Samuel Bayer—who did Nike's emotional "If You Let Me Play Sports" ads, which aired during the [1996] summer Olympics—and he believes all of them are poised for a leap into feature-film work.

Space Jam's Joe Pytka also approves of the trend, and sounds an even more pragmatic note. "Directors used to shoot two or three movies a year," he says. "Now it can take two or three years to develop a single project." So Pytka uses advertising assignments to keep his favorite crew of designers and cinematographers together, and also as a way to keep abreast of new technologies, especially in CGI, or computer-generated imagery.

Commercials, these directors agree, actually have a more demanding audience than movies because viewers will see a TV spot dozens, even hundreds, of times. (Who, other than someone in thrall to *Paris Is Burning* or *Valley of the Dolls,* would sit through a film that many times?) "It's the repeat viewership that kills us," says Johnny Semerad of Quiet Man, a New York special-effects company. Semerad shudders when recounting his travails in syncing dialogue to the lips of "talking" chimps in Pytka's recent HBO commercial.

On an afternoon in December, Semerad sat before the Flame, a computer that manipulates digitized film or video, putting the final polish on a commercial that debuted during the [1997] Super Bowl. Observers were sworn to secrecy, so suffice it to say that the spot (also directed by Pytka) includes an homage to a popular sci-fi movie of a few years back. It turns on a kind of in-joke—that the commercial's enormously sophisticated visuals weren't technically possible when the movie being spoofed was first released. Blow-you-away clever, the ad will leave viewers wondering, "How'd they do *that?*"—just as they were after seeing the postproduction wizardry Semerad had done for Tostitos, Lincoln Mercury, and Pizza Hut.

"Which came first?" Semerad asks pointedly, "the Diet Pepsi spot with James Cagney, or Tom Hanks and JFK in *Forrest Gump?*" The answer of course: Diet Pepsi.

Clayton Hemmert, Semerad's partner at Quiet Man, is similarly brash in claiming a pioneering role for advertising as he demonstrates the ability of an AVID editing machine to "composite," or mix live-action footage with cartoons, mattes, and blue- or green-screen photography. Hemmert refers to such cinematic trickery as "the cheat of it," and says, "Adding flash to save a weak idea is much easier than it was five years ago."

Exactly the problem, says Barry Sonnenfeld, whose movie *Men in Black,* a comedy with Tommy Lee Jones and Will Smith, came out in the summer of 1997. "The reason films are getting more and more horrible is because of commercials," he argues—even though his own impressive client list includes Reebok and Dr. Pepper. Sonnenfeld claims to like postproduction more than any other part of filmmaking but is leery of relying on special effects, as they can shift a director's focus away from the set.

"Rather than getting the best performances while actors are there," he explains, "some directors will shoot lots of coverage (the same scene shot from multiple angles), with plans to whip up excitement during editing."

He contends that many of today's films, as a result, have a visual style similar to TV commercials: a too-frequent use of close-ups and hyperactive editing. "All those explosions and stunt men flying through candy glass!" Sonnenfeld exclaims, "I wouldn't know how to make such a movie."

Michael Bay, who clearly does know, is quick to defend what he has learned from his advertising jobs. How to shoot efficiently, for instance. A complicated car chase like the one featured in *The Rock* might have taken a director with less experience 4 weeks, he points out, but he shot it in 10 days.

While Bay admits to being irked by some of the harsh reviews his films have received, he says his gloom has not lasted for long. "Reporters love to trash commercial directors," he says, "but I added up the other day, and the combined gross of my first two movies is somewhere near half a billion dollars."

An impressive track record, but Bay still probably could not get work from Nina DiSesa, executive creative director at McCann-Erickson. (McCann, you'll recall, just happens to be the agency that lost the Coca-Cola account a couple of years back to Mike Ovitz's CAA—an ignominy that in many ways presaged L.A.'s muscling into advertising.) Unlike her peers who are anxious to hire a director fresh from a movie job, DiSesa prefers to use people who have a "commitment to the work, and aren't just filling in their schedule." Furthermore, she is skeptical of whether Hollywood talent can really deliver the goods.

"I've seen it succeed, and I've seen it fail miserably," she says, reeling off a few choice examples of recent campaigns. "Spike Lee and Nike, or the Coen Brothers and Dime Savings Bank? If you've got a good match-up like these, there can be magic," says DiSesa. "But when you have David Lynch doing an Alka-Seltzer commercial, that's a waste of his talent, and the client's money."

Creative Development for Television

The creative staff pulls together the concept for the television commercial and presents it to the client through the storyboard. **Storyboards** are graphic presentations, part advertising layout and part script, the written copy to be read by performers, that describes television commercials of any length. The storyboard is exhibited as a strip of video visuals, either rough sketches or photographs, similar to a cartoon strip. The storyboard for a television commercial is a layout that is comparable to a print layout or radio script, functioning as a part of the planning procedure.

An audio script includes other visual and verbal components that accompany the storyboard. Visual components include camera direction and descriptions for actors and sets. Verbal elements include the characterization of the voice-overs, sound effects, and music. As the planned commercial is presented to the client, the agency will probably produce an audio tape to simulate the sound that will be incorporated into the final production.

Television Production Techniques

The three major categories of production techniques used today are live action, animation and special effects. **Live action** portrays people, animals, and objects as life-like in everyday situations. It is the most realistic format, but it lacks the distinctiveness created by animation or special effects. **Animation** uses illustrated figures, such as cartoon characters or puppets, inanimate objects come to life. Popular with children's advertising, animations are created as cartoons, photo animation, stop-motion photography, or computer-generated video animation. **Special effects**, such as moving titles, whirling logos, and dissolve images have been developed as a result of computer technologies. **Digital video effects units** are able to manipulate graphics in a number of ways, from fades to wipes, zooms, rotations, and other effects. Music and sound can also be digitally manipulated. Color Plate 4 shows how Target stores used the medium to imprint its logo on the minds of consumers.

Historically, advertisers had to choose between live action and animation. With newer technologies, both strategies may be employed. Bugs Bunny and Daffy Duck can be merged into a television commercial with a human. The possibilities are unlimited.

Television Commercial Production Stages

Television commercial production goes through three states: preproduction, production, and postproduction. Once the client has approved the storyboard and script, the preproduction stage begins. This stage includes all the work done prior to the actual day of filming, such as casting, arranging for locations, estimating costs, finding props and costumes, and other related preparations. A team including a writer, director, producer, art director, and musical director is assembled. A studio is selected through a bid process followed by casting talent. Every aspect of production is planned during the preproduction phase.

Production of a television commercial may take a day or more, depending on the complexity of the commercial and where it is being shot. The production of television commercials has become similar to production of a television show or a movie, incorporating the activities of cinematographers, sound specialists, stage set designers, and talent.

Once all of the scenes are recorded, the commercial enters the postproduction phase, in which the film editor, sound mixer, and director actually put the commercial together. Film or videotape is edited into a **rough cut** for review or testing prior to making the final commercial. The rough cut may have scenes substituted, music or sound effects added, or last-minute changes incorporated. After the client approves the final commercial, copies are made for delivery to television stations and networks.

Most national commercials are still shot on film, because film is extremely flexible and versatile. It can be used for a variety of optical effects. Film prints are less expensive than videotape dubs. In recent years, videotape has gained in popularity, especially for local productions. Video offers a more brilliant picture and better fidelity than film. It looks more realistic and tape quality is more consistent than film stock. The chief advantage of video is its immediate playback function, greatly speeding the editing process.

Creating Radio Commercials

Radio commercials are dependent upon voices, sound effects, and music to communicate the advertiser's message. The advertiser must get the message across in 30 or 60 seconds, which requires as few as 125 words. Intriguing sound effects, ranging from animal sounds to footsteps walking across a wooden floor, must be skillfully blended with music and voices into a successful radio commercial.

Radio advertising is directed to a targeted customer as defined by the demographic information about the audience compiled by the radio station. Thus, the radio commercial needs to be developed with a specific listener in mind.

The radio commercial normally consists of announcements read from scripts with or without the use of special sound effects, singing, or music. Radio personalities, station announcers, disk jockeys, news commentators, the advertiser, or actors read announcements. These people are considered the talent for a radio production. Professional actors can imitate the voices of famous celebrities or create multiple voice dialogues. On-air personnel may read some radio commercial announcements live, while others are taped in advance at a studio and replayed during the scheduled time. Commercials involving sound effects and/or music should be done in advance rather than *live*. Editing can help make these commercials sound more professional.

The copywriter for a radio commercial works with the copy platform to prepare a script. The radio script will include information about any special sound effects or music in addition to the announcement to be read. Figure 9.3 is an example of a radio script.

Narrative Dramatization
The **narrative dramatization** is a form of radio commercial with actors portraying individuals in real-life situations. These sequences may use music or sound effects to give listeners a slice-of-life experience. Although challenging, it is possible for a dramatization to demonstrate the use of products through visualization in sound.

Musical Commercials
Singing or music are vivid attention-getters. A **jingle** is a catchy verse or song with an easy rhythm that is used to create a verbal link to a product. When a jingle is amateurish it can be irritating, but a well-produced musical interpretation has the capability of preparing the audience with a recognition factor. Many popular musical artists have lent their expertise to the creation of jingles, elevating the professionalism of the approach.

Figure 9.3

A sample of a radio script

Sample Radio Script	
Client:	Favorites to Wear
Product:	Spring Floral Dresses
Agency:	Indelible Ink
Title:	Spring Is Here
Length:	30 seconds
Music:	"Favorites to Wear" theme song
1st Female Voice:	It finally feels like spring. Have you seen the tulips blooming in front of the bookstore downtown?
2nd Female Voice:	Yes, and these warm and sunny days are too hot for my winter clothes. I'm dreaming about soft . . . flowing . . . cool dresses.
1st Female Voice:	I know what we need. "Favorites to Wear" has put floral dresses in their window. Let's head over there on our lunch break. I'm ready for a change too!
Announcer:	The newest floral print dresses have arrived at "Favorites to Wear." Come to historical downtown Cambridge and see all of the new Spring merchandise.
Music:	"Favorites to Wear" theme song

Radio Production Stages

In a manner similar to television, radio goes through three stages of production, which include preproduction, production, and postproduction. During the preproduction stage, a radio producer is hired to estimate costs, prepare a budget, select a studio, and find a casting director. Music and talent are coordinated during a rehearsal. Production involves cutting the spot, or actually recording the commercial. Sound recording takes place at a recording studio. The postproduction stage is the finishing phase where sound engineers mix voices, music, and sound effects into the finished commercial. A radio spot is much easier to produce than a television commercial.

Creative development for electronic media differs from print media through the addition of sound and movement as imaginative variables. Radio creates images with sound, but without a visual element. Television is able to use the benefits associated with sound and movement to enhance the selling opportunity. Electronic technologies identified with the computer, including CD ROMs or the Internet, now are able to incorporate video and sound into advertising and promotion, opening up a wide range of creative opportunities.

FUTURE TRENDS IN BROADCAST MEDIA

Dramatic changes are taking place in both radio and television. Competition for audience attention has taken many forms. Alternative electronic media, including the Internet, CD ROMs, and other media innovations, are taking the audience in new directions.

In attempts to compete for viewership with the other electronic media, the major networks have diversified into other electronic media. ABC, NBC, CBS, and FOX have each launched Internet websites, offering up-to-the minute news, weather, sports, and entertainment in addition to **chat lines**, which feature on-line discussions with celebrities from the network's programs. In 1989, NBC started a cable channel (CNBC), offering in-depth news targeted to an upscale audience interested in financial and business information. In cooperation with Microsoft, NBC launched MSNBC in 1996. MSNBC, a 24-hour, all-news cable television network, also debuted as an Internet news service on the World Wide Web.

Cross-media and cross-marketing ventures are not limited to television networks combining with Internet sites. Magazines have also crossed traditional lines. In 1998, a partnership between *Condé Nast Traveler,* a travel magazine, and the Travel Channel, the travel and tourism TV network and a part of Discovery Communications, was formed to offer a prime-time travelogue series. The first collaboration was an hour program called "Condé Nast Traveler Presents Amazing Destinations," hosted by Thomas Wallace, editor of *Condé Nast Traveler* (Elliot, 1998d). Cross-marketing packages encouraged marketers to advertise on the series as well as in the magazine. Sponsors agreed to participate in print, television, and on-line advertising.

Global concerns, discussed throughout the text, are also a future trend in broadcast advertising. The New York–based Multichannel Advertising Bureau International is a trade group that announced it will increasingly focus its efforts on working with U.S.-based agencies and advertisers that control and influence 70 percent of all international media budgets. This strategic focus was approved by the board of directors to maximize the trade group's impact on the growth of multichannel TV advertising globally, pan-regionally, and nationally. The group created an annual survey, conducted by Price Waterhouse, to track multichannel TV revenue growth in Asia, Latin America, and Europe ("Multichannel TV Trade Group," 1998).

At the end of the 1990s we observed the breaking down of traditional media lines. Television networks are involved in website development and cable news channels. Here are just some of the media predictions:

- **High definition television (HDTV)** will come to the broadcast industry. Although it is not yet available to the consumer, predictions are that HDTV will provide crystal clear visuals through higher resolution.
- **Videocompression** or **multiplexing,** which technically combines radio and TV signals to allow more than one channel to beam on a frequency width, will enable TV sets to play several channels at once.
- **Fiber optics,** the technology of light transmission through very fine, flexible glass or plastic fibers, will enable telephone and cable television companies to offer as many as 500 different channels in some U.S. markets. These companies should be expanding to other regions.
- Satellite technology will be miniaturized. Uplink transmitters and downlink receivers will continue to see reductions in prices, making them more affordable.
- Palm-size video projectors, approximately the size of a shampoo bottle, will be able to throw an image 3 feet wide onto a wall.

This chapter has focused on the two main broadcast media, television and radio. Whether we want to admit it or not, both play a significant role in our lives every day, as communication sources that provide news, information, and entertainment. Accompanying the news, information, and entertainment are sponsored messages designed to grab the attention of the listener or viewer. We wake up to these media, listen and or watch these broadcast vehicles throughout the day, at work and at home, and use these formats as entertainment during leisure hours. The creation and production of radio and television commercials are highly complex and require expertise in broadcast strategy and creativity. Even with all of the interest in the newest emerging technologies, existing media cannot be ruled out. Several studies indicate that the traditional media will continue to receive the bulk of media placements.

SUMMARY

- Broadcast media, similar to print media, uses the copy platform as a guideline to create television and radio commercials.
- Television plays a significant role in the everyday lives of people throughout the world and has contributed to the globalization of everything from fashion to music.
- Television advertising makes product information available to people of many cultures throughout the world.
- Although radio may not seem like an ideal medium for visually oriented products, its ability to target specific groups keeps it a thriving advertising medium.
- Television and radio advertising media costs are determined by the time of day, called dayparts, when the commercial is broadcast.
- A. C. Nielsen and SQAD are firms that measure television audiences.
- Radio audiences are measured by The Arbitron Company in the United States and by the Bureau of Broadcast Measurement in Canada.
- Television and radio commercials are written as scripts and through performance are brought to life.
- Television and radio commercials go through three stages, which are preproduction, production, and postproduction.
- Alternative media are increasingly competing with television and radio to attract audiences.

KEY TERMS

adjacencies	fiber optics	radio frequency
affiliates	grid cards	reach plan
animation	guaranteed audience plan	remote
best time available	high-definition television	rough cut
blink ads	jingle	run-of-schedule
chat lines	live action	single price cards
cost per point	multiplexing	special effects
cost per ratings point	narrative dramatization	storyboard
dayparts	participations	total audience plan
digital video effects units	prime time	traffic time
drive time	program sponsorship	videocompression

QUESTIONS FOR DISCUSSION

1. What are the steps in creating a television commercial?
2. What are the steps in creating a radio ad?
3. In what ways is technology challenging and changing broadcast commercials?
4. What are the similar and different characteristics of print media and broadcast media?
5. What does television syndication mean? What is the difference between off-network and first-run syndication?
6. Think of a television commercial that you have seen recently. Was it effective? What made it effective? How long do you think it took to produce? How much do you think it cost to produce and broadcast it?

ADDITIONAL RESOURCES

Anderson, R. K., and Schiller, H. I. (1995). *Consumer culture and TV programming*. Boulder, CO: Westview Press.

Baldwin. H. (1989). *How to create effective TV commercials*. Lincolnwood, IL: NTC Trade.

Book, A. C., Cary, N. D., Tannebaum, S. I., and Brady, F. (1996). *The radio and television commercial*. (3rd ed.). Lincolnwood, IL: NTC Business Books.

Maitland, I. (1997). *How to plan radio advertising*. London: Cassell Academic.

Rutherford, P. (1994). *The new icons? The art of television advertising*. Toronto, Canada: University of Toronto Press.

Schulberg, B., and Schulberg, P. (1996). *Radio advertising: The authoritative handbook*. Lincolnwood, IL: NTC Business Books.

Figure 10.1

Harrods' Christmas merchandise was presented to consumers by catalog and by a CD-ROM with promotional copy on the package liner.

DIRECT MARKETING

Harrods Christmas Collection 1998, was an example of an integrated marketing communications promotion, produced by the legendary London retailer Harrods Knightsbridge and developed to allow domestic and international consumers an opportunity to do their holiday shopping from home. Harrods presented thousands of gift ideas from fragrance to food, women's apparel to children's toys. Consumers in London, Japan, and the United States could simultaneously browse among the many items to fill their shopping lists. When consumers were ready to order, they simply dialed a toll-free telephone number, a sales representative took their order, and the merchandise was delivered to their home. So, what was unique about this promotion? This was the first time in history that Harrod's presented its holiday merchandise on a CD-ROM (Fig. 10.1). The copy for the CD-ROM read, "This is shopping from home for a new generation." The CD-ROM was part of a direct marketing campaign that also included catalog distribution. Catalogs and CD-ROMs are two examples of direct-response media that can be used to deliver promotional messages to consumers.

After you read this chapter, you should be able to:

Incorporate direct marketing into a promotion plan.

Contrast the different direct marketing strategies available to promotion specialists.

Examine the components of successful database management.

Every day, consumers are asked to sort through an incredible number of direct appeals in search of those that interest them. Over 11 million pounds of mail, with a direct advertising message, are delivered to homes in the United States daily. Included within this advertising mail are catalogs, coupon packages, free samples, image identifying brochures, service commitments, solicitation appeals from institutions and nonprofit organizations, questionnaires, and hundreds of other requests for recipient response. Beyond mail, solicitations are sought over the phone and through television, radio, computer, and outdoor media. These forms of appeal are components of the process known as direct marketing.

This chapter explores the role of direct marketing in promotion. We consider the major direct marketing strategies as they relate to promotion. Then we look at database management as the key function by which direct marketers successfully do their job. The chapter concludes with a look at trends and future directions in this area. Many of the strategies discussed in this chapter are emerging technologies that only came about in the mid- to late 1990s.

ROLE OF DIRECT MARKETING AS A PROMOTION TOOL

Direct marketing is the marketing process by which organizations communicate directly with target customers to generate a response or transaction. The direct marketing request may be a sponsored advertisement or an unsponsored publicity promotion. Traditional promotional plans included activities that require an intermediary, such as a retail store or a manufacturing firm, to take the message to the consumer. Direct marketing goes directly from the sponsoring company or organization to the consumer to generate a behavior response to the promotion. **Direct sellers**, companies that sell directly to the consumer, such as Mary Kay and Avon, rely heavily on direct-response methods to reach their clients. **Direct-response** describes the method of distribution whereby a sale or solicitation is initiated and completed through advertisements or promotions that require a direct reply. Consumers will use return mail, a toll-free number, or an interactive link to make the direct response. Direct marketers use a set of direct-response media as tools to implement the promotion strategy. Direct-response media include direct mail, print media, telemarketing, broadcast media, on-line computer services, and out-of-home media, among other media. They are intended to solicit a response from the consumer by phone, mail, computer, or personal visit. Color Plate 5 shows some of the direct response media used by ABC to promote its soap operas, *General Hospital* and *Port Charles* and to publicize a charitable campaign to raise money for AIDS research.

Direct marketing may also use support advertising. Support advertising does not solicit a response from the consumer, but rather asks the consumer to watch the mail for an upcoming direct mail appeal. Publishers Clearing House has long used supportive advertising in print and broadcast to supplement its direct-mail appeals.

Direct marketing appeals generally follow a one- or two-step approach. An appeal that directly obtains an order uses a **one-step approach**. Catalog shopping is an example of a one-step approach. The consumer browses the catalog of promoted merchandise and responds by making a purchase using a credit card or other payment agreement. The objective of a one-step approach is to gain an immediate sale.

An appeal that first identifies and/or qualifies potential buyers and then follows up with a second request to generate a response uses a **two-step approach**. Two-step approaches are often targeted to a specific market and must be well prepared and well researched to be successful. Book, music, and movie clubs use this marketing strategy often, enticing potential buyers with free trial offers. In step one, the promoter makes the promotional offer to readers through magazines or newspapers. The consumer responds to the offer by sending in an attached coupon, or calling a toll-free number to join a club at a free or minimal charge. In step two, the promoter sends the consumer additional movies, CDs, or books that must be returned during a specified time period or bought at the regular price, generating repeat sales. Two-step approaches offer the opportunity for repeat sales because the customer, who responds to step one of the promotion, is predisposed to respond positively to the step two communication.

GROWTH OF DIRECT-RESPONSE ADVERTISING

A rapid growth in the use of direct-response advertising and promotion occurred in the 1990s as a result of emerging technologies that allowed more efficient ways to target specific audiences. Direct-mail operations, cable television, community-based shop-per newspapers, radio, Yellow Pages, and on-line computer services began competing for advertising dollars that had previously been allocated to newspapers, television, and periodicals ("Services," 1997). Advertising spending forecasts through year 2002 predict an increase between 5 and 7 percent each year, with most of that growth coming from direct marketing and promotions, rather than the traditional forms of advertising. Direct mail, television infomercials, and on-line retailing will account for most of the increase in advertising spending. The top 10 U.S. direct-marketing agencies are highlighted in Table 10.1.

Countries outside the United States are also potential markets for direct marketing. For example, direct marketing offers good opportunities for U.S. firms that want to do business in Mexico, because the Mexican Foreign Investment Law allows for 100 percent foreign ownership of direct marketing and advertising services ("Services," 1997). U.S. firms that can obtain effective Mexican partnerships to handle cultural differences and regulations will continue to develop direct marketing strategies. Products that are not readily available in stores, such as electronic equipment, answering machines, and fitness equipment represent good opportunities for direct mail and telemarketing in Mexico and other foreign countries in close proximity to the United States.

Direct marketing strategies are becoming increasingly important in the promotion mix. Advertising sponsors are turning to this promotion strategy to reach consumers where they live. Changing attitudes of consumers, sophisticated marketing techniques, and an improved image of direct marketing techniques have contributed to the increase in direct marketing strategies used by retailers and wholesalers to directly influence the consumer to respond to promotional appeals. Although many direct marketing programs are implemented to generate sales or charitable contributions, some programs

Table 10.1 **Top 10 Direct-marketing Agencies, 1998**

Rank	Agency	Direct Marketing Revenue[a]	U.S. Agency Revenue[a]
1	Brann Worldwide	$287,580	$287,580
2	Draft Worldwide	142,641	180,558
3	Rapp Collins Worldwide	126,148	167,148
4	Bronnercom	124,200	124,200
5	Wunderman Cato Johnson	120,495	140,110
6	Harte-Hanks/DiMark	90,538	90,538
7	Grey Direct Marketing	82,740	82,740
8	OgilvyOne Worldwide	77,200	77,200
9	Carlson Marketing Group	75,757	254,096
10	MRM/Gillespie	48,600	48,600

[a] *Dollars are in thousands.*

Adapted from: Direct marketing agencies. (1999, May 17). Advertising Age *[On-line]. Available: http://www.adage.com/dataplace/archives/dp337.html.*

seek to build a company's image, maintain customer satisfaction, or educate the consumer. In the next section we discuss specific direct marketing strategies.

DIRECT MARKETING STRATEGIES

Various direct-response media are used to accomplish direct marketing promotional objectives. Each direct-response outlet offers the consumer an opportunity to purchase directly from a manufacturer or retailer, and each allows the sponsoring firm to be creative in its appeal. Direct-response media services are designed to sell a product or service immediately, identify a lead, or generate store traffic. These include direct-response print media, telemarketing, direct-response broadcast media, direct-response on-line marketing, direct-response out-of-home media, and other direct response media.

Direct-response Print Media

What came in your mail today? Hopefully a personal letter, maybe a bill, and probably several promotions and catalogs. The promotional pieces are considered direct-response print media, which are devices, delivered to the consumer, encouraging the recipient to respond directly to the manufacturer or retailer by telephone, return mail, or by visiting a store location. These print media include any form of printed material that requests a direct response. Examples include direct mail, "take one" brochures at stores, package inserts, sales promotion premiums such as matchbooks, Yellow Pages, newspaper advertising inserts, and direct-response advertising space in newspapers and magazines. The mail is not the only delivery mechanism. Consumers may encounter direct-response print media at stores from sales associates or as freestanding displays, as package inserts in purchased goods, or through marketplace advertisements distributed in newspapers or magazines.

Direct-response print media in newspapers and magazines is highly competitive because of the large number of advertisements in any particular issue. The cost of newspaper and magazine space is often more expensive than other media and return rates and profits may often be lower (Belch, 1995). Direct-response print campaigns are often more successful in magazines tied to a specific interest than in general or news and business weeklies, because they can target a specific audience with their product or service. Newspaper and magazine advertising space has been previously discussed in Chapter 8. "Take one" displays, package inserts, and sales promotion premiums are all subjects of sales promotion, which is discussed in Chapter 11. Here, we focus on direct mail and Yellow Pages.

Direct Mail

Direct mail is all direct response communications delivered through the mail. It includes catalogs, cards, card decks, letters, brochures, pamphlets and flyers, video tapes, CDs, diskettes, and other sales promotion items.

There are several advantages to using direct mail. It can cover a wide audience and offer the audience an opportunity to read and reread the message, allowing a more permanent sales appeal. It is ideal for merchandise that is easy to visualize and has well-known characteristics. Direct mail also can be used to enhance the image of an organization and showcase products, service commitments, quality guarantees, or other promotional goals. Consumers use printed materials as one way to judge the credibility of an establishment. Although they may dislike the volume of direct-mail appeals they receive, it does add to the trustworthiness of the firms sponsoring the pieces.

Direct mail has a relatively low cost per piece produced. Printed pieces can be mass produced in high volumes for relatively little expense. Videos, computer discs, and CD-ROMs have higher production costs, but potentially offer a greater return for the sponsoring company.

There are disadvantages associated with direct mail. For one thing, direct mail is a relatively impersonal sales approach, even if the piece is personalized. For another, as opposed to personal selling, there is no opportunity for immediate feedback to the sponsoring company. Additionally, direct-mail pieces do not always spark a sense of urgency and excitement in the reader, and the rate of return is often low. Last of all, there is always the possibility that the direct-mail piece will be discarded before being read.

In international regions, such as Europe, that have reliable and inexpensive postal services, widespread rural populations, and efficient delivery mechanisms, direct mail is proving to be an up-and-coming industry ("Services," 1997). Direct mail offers the same advantages to foreign countries that it does in the United States, including target marketing and accurate assessment at low cost. Catalogs are one of the most popular direct-mail outlets in the United States and are growing in popularity in European countries.

Catalogs   The growth of catalog marketing has paralleled the development and expansion of the U. S. Postal Service, which has made catalogs widely available to rural and metropolitan residents. A catalog is a published list of items for sale, usually including descriptive information or illustrations (Fig. 10.2). In 1997, catalog sales hit an all-time high of $78.6 billion (Furchgott, 1998). The Direct Marketing Association projected catalog sales of $95 billion in sales by year 2000. There are over 8,000 titles devoted to every imaginable product line offered by small and large retail and manufacturing firms. Small businesses, in particular, use catalogs as a way to gain national exposure and distribute new products. Catalogs feature men's, women's, and children's apparel, home furnishings, electronics, auto accessories, power tools, and recreation equipment, among many other product lines and categories. Consumers like catalogs because they can find unique and specific items that may not be available in their local market area. Additionally, catalogs provide descriptive details to help the consumer visualize the product. Catalogs are one of the most popular direct-mail outlets to solicit customer response.

Catalog shopping saves time, is stress free, and is convenient for families and individuals who have less time to shop or cannot shop. The average catalog shopper is a career woman, nearly 40, with a family, and a household income of over $40,000 ("Lifestyle Monitor," 1997). Catalog shopping is particularly popular with special size customers who cannot find their size in a store. Another target market continually tapped for mail-order purchases includes people who have no choice but to purchase from catalogs because they cannot shop elsewhere. These markets include rural residents, elderly people, people with disabilities, or others who have difficulties leaving their home.

Catalogs have multiple advantages, including convenience, availability of hard-to-find merchandise, ability to comparison shop with other catalogs, and easy payment opportunities through the use of credit cards. Return policies are generally easy to implement. New customers have an opportunity to become acquainted with a retailer by reviewing a catalog and current customers can be introduced to the new trends of the season. Increasingly, companies are using catalogs to offer special incentives and sales promotions to their customers. The catalog featured in Figure 10.3 invites customers to *buy now, pay later*.

Figure 10.2

Pottery Barn, a retailer of
home furnishings,
supplements its
promotion mix strategy
with a catalog.

Catalogs can be an image-building tool as well. Through creative use of design, photography, and copy that provide a strong fashion statement and illustrate a fashion direction, a company can build one-on-one communications with the customer. For example, Esprit launched a new catalog in October 1997, after a 10-year break. The company's reason for reviving the catalog was as an image-building tool to re-establish a relationship with a consumer by putting a certain look, style, and lifestyle in front of them (Parr, 1997c). The image of the catalog was intended to show consumers the new energy of this long established firm. As an integrated strategy, the catalog was also available in retail stores and advertised on Esprit's website.

Junior catalogs have entered the market, targeting the Generation Y population, 10 to 24 year olds (Parr, 1997b). Junior catalogs include *Delia's, Girlfriends L.A., Zoë, Airshop and Alloy,* and *Wet Seal.* These catalogs are advertised in popular teen magazines. They ask teens to use 800- or 888-numbers to order catalogs; in this way, the firm creates a database list of potential customers. The demographic information sought from the junior market differs from that for the adult market. Companies are interested in the schools that their consumers attend, and whether junior consumers use their parents' or their own credit cards. Junior catalog marketers also track the purchasing record of young consumers, since these consumers generally will not have a purchasing record anywhere else. Junior catalogs are intended to transfer purchase decisions from the parent to the teen.

Figure 10.3
Incentives offered by catalog vendors encourage consumers to respond directly to the advertisement.

There are also disadvantages to catalog shopping. These include inability to touch or feel the products, or to try products on for size before placing an order. Also, although companies allow for exchanges or refunds, this may be a time-consuming and a costly experience for the purchaser of an unsatisfactory product.

Europeans consumers have been more hesitant than American consumers to grasp the idea of catalog shopping. According to Stewart-Allen (1997), there are several reasons for this. First, Europeans, more than Americans, have the need to socialize as part of the shopping experience. Catalog shopping does not accommodate this. Second, Europeans as compared with Americans are more skeptical of new and different things. In their minds, they associate new and different with cheaper, lesser quality goods, which will probably perform more poorly than merchandise sold through traditional distribution channels. However, based on U.S. models of mail-order operations and distribution centers, European-based retailers are becoming more successful with catalog sales. Stewart-Allen (1997) has identified four competencies that are keys to successful European mail order:

- **Database management.** Keep the customer databases clean and current.
- **Customer service.** Staff the catalog with knowledgeable sales people who are given the freedom to solve customer problems immediately without manager intervention.
- **Local market customization.** Adapt to the local operating environment of the target country, including cultural and sizing differences; speak the local language; and reflect prices and sizes in local terms.

Figure 10.4

Brochures sent through the mail can inform consumers of special sales.

• **Product ranges matched to the market.** Ensure the product range is well matched to the local market tastes.

A vendor who follows these competencies should succeed in global catalog marketing. Catalogs will assume ever greater importance in the United States and abroad as consumers gain confidence in shopping by mail. Merchandise offerings are not limited to catalogs. A vendor may consider a multitude of other print options.

Other Direct-response Print Media   In addition to catalogs, many other forms of print media arrive through the mail to promote local businesses, tell residents about upcoming special events, and advertise merchandise. Figure 10.4 is a example of a co-marketed brochure advertising back-to-school sales from retailers at a regional mall. The format for printed media is varied and includes cards, card decks, letters, brochures, pamphlets, and flyers. All of the print media contain promotional information and product details. Cards are flat, rectangular pieces of stiff paper, cardboard, or plastic. A product or service is highlighted on one side, with postal markings on the other. Card decks are a set of cards, usually bound or cellophane wrapped, offering product advertisements on both sides of the card. Letters are written communications, generally with a personalized message, addressed to a specific individual or organization. An unbound printed work, usually with a paper cover is considered a pamphlet. Brochures are folded pages that create messages on panels. A flyer is a lesser quality, nonpersonalized, printed notice intended for mass distribution that is usually single sided, with mailing information on the reverse side if needed. Each print medium is created following a similar format and using creative elements of print media as explained in Chapter 8. A checklist for creating direct-response print media is shown on page 295.

Printed pieces are created to offer a benefit for the person who reads the piece. For vendors who offer limited products, or higher priced items, singular printed pieces may be more cost-effective than a catalog. For example, Figure 10.5 is a three-panel, direct-mail brochure promoting a software program used in multimedia productions. In this ad, the software sells for $199.95. The vendor, Buz, hopes that the creative photo will capture the attention of the consumer, who will read the message and determine the benefits of owning the software, and then consider the price that is printed in smaller

Checklist for Creating Direct-Response Print Media

Printed Piece
- ☐ Determine quantity.
- ☐ Determine components (cover letter, brochures, flyers).
- ☐ Determine direct-response device (800 number, return mail, store visit).

Format
- ☐ Design rough draft.
- ☐ Write text.
- ☐ Determine creative work (photography, illustrations).

Materials
- ☐ Select colors.
- ☐ Select paper.
- ☐ Determine label printing (personalized printing, sensitized labels).
- ☐ Confirm size of the total package for postal conformity and cost per piece.

Before Going to Press
- ☐ Is the stock correct?
- ☐ Is the press layout correct?
- ☐ Does each two-sided piece back-up correctly?
- ☐ Does the color register properly?
- ☐ Proofread the document.
- ☐ Cut and fold the sample.
- ☐ Weigh the sample for postage.

Figure 10.5

An eye-catching graphic encourages the consumer to read direct-response offers.

type on an inside panel. Individual printed pieces are also used by sponsors who are promoting services or events that are singular opportunities.

Video tapes, compact disks (CDs), and diskettes are also produced for products or services and may be delivered through the mail. They are considered direct-response electronic media and are discussed in that section of this chapter. There is an alternative direct-response print medium that a vendor may choose; that is the Yellow Pages.

Yellow Pages

Yellow Pages are considered a direct-response print media. Yellow Pages are a volume or section of a telephone directory that lists businesses, services, or products alphabetically according to field. Consumers frequently use Yellow Pages to locate businesses or the services they desire. According to British Telecommunications, Yellow Pages are used 1.4 billion times every year in the United Kingdom. On average, 88 percent of business information seekers refer to the Yellow Pages regularly (Sorkin, 1998). The top 10 Yellow Pages advertisers in the United States are featured in Table 10.2. Advertisers may choose to simply include the name of their business with a phone number or to purchase a display advertisement in color.

In addition to the traditional telephone directories, Yellow Pages are showing up on the Internet (Fig. 10.6). Most regional Bell companies, as well as new media competitors such as BigBook and WorldPages, have their own on-line Yellow Pages ("Bell," 1997). Internet guides are also bound into the regional Bell print Yellow Pages. They contain information on hardware and software requirements for getting on-line, a glossary of terms, tips on shopping for an Internet provider, and a list of recommended websites. With this emerging technology, finding businesses and individuals may no longer be limited to printed directories. Internet Yellow Pages can be updated and linked, providing instant information to users.

There are several advantages to using the Yellow Pages as a direct marketing strategy. They include the generation of inquiries that bring in new customers. A British kitchen planner and installation firm believes that 75 percent of its inquiries were gen-

Table 10.2 **Top 10 Yellow Pages Advertisers**

Rank 1996	Advertiser	Yellow Pages **Spending 1997**[a]
1	General Motors Corporation	28.0
2	U-Haul	27.3
3	Sears, Roebuck & Company	25.6
4	Midas International	17.8
5	Ford Motor Company	16.6
6	Servicemaster Company	16.0
7	Ryder Truck	15.0
8	Chrysler Corporation	14.0
9	Allstate Insurance Group	13.5
10	Volunteer Hospitals of America	13.5

[a]*Millions of dollars*

Adapted from: Top 25 Yellow Pages advertisers. (1998, September 28). Advertising Age *[On-line]. Available: http://www.adage.com/dataplace/archives/dp252.html.*

Source: Yellow Pages Publishers Association.

Figure 10.6

An advertisement in the print Yellow Pages for Internet Yellow Pages

erated by Yellow Pages, and it converts a high percentage of those inquiries into customers. Additionally, Yellow Pages are a strong medium for local and small firms. Many small firms do not have big budgets for promotion and may use the Yellow Pages as their sole promotion tool. Small business owners believe that many customers are brought into their local retail firm though Yellow Page ads more often than from other methods.

As with all direct-response advertising, there are disadvantages with this strategy. Yellow Page ads have to conform to strict requirements in size and printing capabilities and therefore creativity is limited. Also, not all consumers have access to telephones and directories, and directories are not always available at pay phones. Finally, regulation of Yellow Pages is increasing. For example, since Yellow Pages are alphabetical, some businesses have added A's to their name so that consumers will view their ads first. However, Yellow Page publishers are limiting the number of A's that can be used in an advertisement so advertisers will be held in check. Aaron's or AAA Travel will still be accepted, but AAAAAAA Publishers will not. Direct-response print media, including Yellow Pages, is the most popular form of direct marketing used by sponsors. However, telemarketing is nearly as popular as a direct-response media.

Telemarketing

Telemarketing is the selling of products or services, or fundraising for an organization or institution, using the telephone to contact prospective customers. Telemarketing includes all out-bound direct-response advertising communications conducted over the telephone using telecommunications services. **Out-bound calls** are initiated by the vendor, but telemarketing operations may also be responsible for in-bound calls. **In-bound calls** are initiated by consumers who voluntarily phone into the company with a merchandise order or a consumer question. Figure 10.7 illustrates the direct-response device (800 number) that consumers can use for an in-bound call. Nearly all companies have set up an 800- or 888- toll-free phone number to stimulate calling.

Figure 10.7

800- and 888- phone numbers are direct-response devices used for in-bound calls.

As with other direct-response advertising methods, telemarketing has seen a boom in the 1990s as a result of new technologies. Software that skips busy signals and brings up a customer's transaction history with just a few key strokes is now available. The resulting increase in productivity has made telemarketing a very reasonable option for an increasing number of large and small companies (Seiler and Martinez, 1997).

Telemarketing is a very widely used method of direct marketing. It is considered to be as profitable as any of the direct marketing strategies. Cotton Incorporated uses telemarketing extensively to survey consumers about their attitudes and preferences toward clothing and fashion. After surveying consumers, Cotton Incorporated reports the results in the *Lifestyle Monitor* featured in *Women's Wear Daily*. This direct marketing promotion tool is used to build consumer demand for U.S. cotton.

The advantages of telemarketing include a personal approach by the caller, instantaneous feedback, and the chance for multiple sales. As with direct mail, a wide audience can be marketed through this approach. Disadvantages of telemarketing include a higher cost than direct mail, difficulty in reaching potential customers due to telephone answering machines, and customers who do not accept telephone solicitation.

The following components should be considered when developing an effective telemarketing program:

- Companies must be willing to devote time and money to secure all available phone numbers.

- Callers should be trained thoroughly and continually updated.
- Callers should have as much information as possible about the potential customer, including demographic information and lifestyle characteristics.
- New products and product characteristics should be part of every training session.
- Problem-solvers should always be available to answer product specification questions or verify services.
- Follow-up should be immediate through product delivery or action to the customer concern.

In the United States, telemarketing has proven to be an effective and cost-efficient means of advertising, and therefore, the market has grown accustomed and even tired of this direct marketing strategy. However, it has not yet caught on in many countries, and there are good growth opportunities throughout the world ("Services," 1997). Potential telemarketers need to study possible markets to ensure a country has adequate or reliable telephone service and does not charge exorbitant rates for telephone service. Additionally, the region needs to have adequate mail or delivery services.

In recent years, telemarketing has come under fire because of the unethical practices of certain companies, who telemarket unethically to the senior citizen market. These companies may promise travel packages, specialty products, and/or investment opportunities to senior citizens in return for a large amount of money but then pocket the money without producing the promised product or service. Anyone, senior citizen or not, can ask for his or her name and telephone number be removed from a solicitation list, and the vendor must comply. If a vendor does not comply, it can be reported to the Better Business Bureau which, in return, can have the business investigated. In some situations, the firm can be brought up on charges of fraud by the federal government.

Telemarketing and catalogs are traditional forms of direct marketing. Catalogs have been around for over a century, and telemarketing began with the invention of the telephone. Next, we look at direct-response broadcast media, introduced into marketing strategies in the recent past.

Direct-response Broadcast Media

Direct-response broadcast media includes all direct-response advertising communications conducted through local, national, or cable radio and television channels. Television is the major medium for direct marketers who use broadcast media because radio listeners are often too preoccupied with other things to record an address or telephone number (Wells et al., 1998). However, some local marketers have had success with at-home listeners who will take the time to note the message. When radio is used, it can be highly targeted to a very selective market based on radio station formats.

Technological developments have led to alternative methods of direct-response advertising to business and consumer markets. These advances are so new that *Advertising Age* did not begin keeping statistics on many segments of the interactive industry until 1994. Table 10.3 is a summary of the estimated dollar size of selected segments of the interactive industry from 1994 to 1998. Projections into the next century can be charted from this historical data. The table applies to this discussion and to later discussions about direct-response on-line and electronic media.

There are two major direct-response television outlets: home shopping networks and infomercials. In 1994, the size of the infomercial and home shopping industry together was $2.8 billion. By 1998, these industries had risen to $5.4 billion, an increase of 92 percent.

Table 10.3   **Estimates of the Dollar Size of Selected Segments of the Interactive Industry**

	1994	1995	1996	1997	1998
Commercial On-line Services[a]	$795 million	$1.1 billion	$1.6 billion	$1.8 billion	$1.7 billion
Internet[b,c]	$366 million	$771 million	$1.5 billion	$2.4 billion	$3.7 billion
CD-ROMs[d,e]	$2.5 billion	$2.8 billion	$3.1 billion	$3.3 billion	$3.5 billion
Infomercials and Home Shopping[d]	$2.8 billion	$3.3 billion	$3.9 billion	$4.6 billion	$5.4 billion

[a]*Source: Forrester Research, Cambridge, MA.*

[b] *Includes revenues for expertise, access, software, content, and commerce.*

[c] *Source: Goldman, Sachs & Co., New York.*

[d] *Wholesale revenues for CD-ROM software, semiconductors.*

[e] *Source: Dataquest, San Jose, CA.*

[f]*Source: Paul Kagan & Associates, Carmel, CA.*

Adapted from: Estimates of the dollar size of each segment of the interactive industry. (1995, May 1). Advertising Age *[On-line]. Available: http://www.adage.com/dataplace/archives/dp002.html.*

Home Shopping Networks

Television shopping networks originated in the 1980s. QVC and the Home Shopping Network dominate the industry. QVC, the largest home shopping cable network, broadcasts live 24 hours a day, 364 days a year (excluding Christmas Day). In addition to the cable shopping service, QVC, the West Chester, Pennsylvania–based firm operates divisions in the United Kingdom and Germany and on the Internet.

Home shopping networks broadcast programs with hosts in a manner similar to a talk show. Hosts converse with designers, such as Bob Mackie or Diane Von Furstenburg, while promoting various items of merchandise. The celebrities and hosts interview shoppers who call into the show to make purchases. Sales of $1.8 billion were achieved in 1996 by QVC ("QVC," 1998).

The success of QVC has spurred other companies to enter this market. Although forecasters thought this would be a very lucrative market, many firms have found it difficult to compete with such a dominant force.

Infomercials

An infomercial is a program-length product demonstration that often looks like a TV show. These demonstrations were introduced to the television medium in the 1980s, as long commercials that typically last 30 minutes. The top 10 grossing infomercials for 1997 included fitness programs, a speed reading course, weight loss programs, hair removal systems for women, cooking products, and a course on money making opportunities ("The Ten," 1998). Innovators of this medium were primarily unknown companies selling skin care, treatments for baldness, exercise equipment, teeth whitening, and other health-related merchandise. With the success of these firms and a growing respectability, better known brands have started to promote their products via this outlet. Avon, Clairol, Braun, Sears, and Procter & Gamble have experimented with this medium.

In contrast to the traditional 15-, 30- or 60-second television advertisement, the infomercial can be more detailed, informative, and imaginative. The format generally consists of a news or talk segment combined with some form of entertainment. These "programs" may run on network, local, or cable stations. The sponsors of this form of direct marketing hope audience members will turn on and find the show so persuasive that they will watch the entire program. With the excitement generated, they hope viewers will pick up the telephone and order the product. During an infomercial, consumers are asked to respond by calling a toll-free 800- or 900- number to place an order. Some consumers dislike infomercials because of their similarity to regular programming. They look like a reliable (objective) TV report when, in fact, they are a paid advertisement. These ethical concerns are discussed in Chapter 18.

According to the National Infomercial Marketing Association, the average production costs for a half-hour infomercial are $450,000, though on a per-minute basis, infomercials are approximately one-fifth the cost of a 30-second commercial ("Infomercials," 1997). Although audiences for infomercials are not as large as during national network prime-time programming, the program-length commercials are a popular alternative advertising medium, here to stay.

Infomercials are certainly not limited to the United States. China entered this market in 1995 with *China Shop-A-Vision*. The Shanghai firm started broadcasting 10-minute infomercials with products ranging from exercise equipment to spray-on hair. The lack of telephones and credit cards in China have been obstacles to this developing medium.

Direct-response On-line Marketing

Direct-response on-line marketing is an even more recent development than direct-response broadcast media. Direct-response on-line media includes all direct-response advertising communications conducted over the computer. **On-line** means that data and graphics are transmitted from an interactive electronic computer network over telephone or cable lines and displayed on a user's computer terminal screen. For consumers in their homes, this communication medium joins individuals and companies with a computer and a modem. Businesses often have an Ethernet connection to facilitate on-line communication. Companies and consumers can access on-line services in one of two ways: either by commercial on-line companies or through the Internet.

Commercial Companies

Commercial on-line companies are private companies that provide on-line information for a fee, such as America On-line, among others. They charge subscribers a monthly fee and provide subscribers with e-mail, shopping services, dialogue opportunities (such as bulletin boards and chat rooms), entertainment, and other Internet connections. Companies can advertise on commercial on-line services by placing ads in the classified section of the on-line service, in newsgroups that are set up for commercial purposes, and on on-line billboards. Table 10.3 (see p. 300) shows the growth in dollar size of commercial on-line services, which grew from $795 million in 1994 to $1.7 billion in 1998.

Internet

The **Internet** is a global data communications system of over 45,000 computer networks (Wells et al., 1998). The Internet is publicly held by several communications giants, including AT&T and Sprint among others. The growth in dollar size of the Internet is also shown in Table 10.3. In 1994 the size of the industry was $366 million, but by 1998 the industry was $3.7 billion.

Besides needing a computer and modem, users need an Internet Service Provider (ISP). The ISP may simply provide connections to the Internet or may additionally provide original content. ISPs may be local or national companies that charge subscribers monthly or hourly rates. Many communities will have their own ISPs that can be found in the Yellow Pages. On-line commercial services, universities, or libraries may also provide Internet services, making Internet access available to nearly everyone.

Both commercial on-line services and the Internet allow participants to communicate via e-mail and the World Wide Web. E-mail is the term commonly used for electronic mail, a method of communicating with other users on a worldwide basis. Many people use the terms Internet and World Wide Web synonymously, but they are not interchangeable. The Internet is a vast system, while the World Wide Web (www) is a part of that system in which commercial operations occur. Within the Web, participants have an address which is called a site, homepage, or page. An example of a Web address is *http://www.gap.com/*. We have used many sites as examples in this text.

A wide variety of data that could previously be found in books and libraries, product information, and retail merchandise offerings can be found at various websites. Web users find the system to be mesmerizing, yielding answers to questions they did not even know they had, or frustrating when they cannot find things they want. However, unlimited resources for information on any topic or merchandise—from endless numbers of manufacturers and retailers—is available on the Web.

Consumers can visit their favorite international retailers, find fashion trend information from the international trade shows immediately, do research on an educational topic, join a chat line, or find a biography of almost any designer or celebrity. Instant global communication is a significant attribute of the Internet. The Italian Fashion Industry sponsors a homepage for the Camera Nazionale della Mode Italiana at the following address: *http://www.intalycollections.it* (Fig. 10.8). This homepage offers a cal-

Figure 10.8

The Camera Nazionale della Mode Italiana is one of many international sites available to visitors on the Web.

endar of fashion show schedules and fashion stylist pages. Stores from throughout the world, including England's The Conran Shop, offer on-line catalogs with price lists and ordering information. An individual can order merchandise from almost anywhere in the world on the Web, from Denmark's Royal Copenhagen porcelain to America's Land's End sweaters.

The introduction of World Wide Web addresses has affected direct marketing in a positive way by giving advertisers a new and efficient way to market their products (Turley and Kelley, 1997). Placing an Internet address in an ad enables the reader to acquire additional information about the product or sponsor at a time convenient for the consumer. These addresses are now appearing in print media, broadcast media, sales promotion premiums, and various other sources. Direct marketers have reported promotion cost savings associated with the use of World Wide Web and Internet addresses in advertisements. Color Plate 5 shows the role that the ABC network's website played in an IMC promotion.

There are several ways direct marketers can advertise on the Internet. They can communicate via e-mail, place a direct-response ad on-line, or set up an electronic storefront on a website. E-mail can be used by a firm to inform subscribers about merchandise, news topics, chat sessions, or service special offers. For example, the company Express maintains lists of interested individuals and notifies these people about new styles, colors, or special offers aimed directly at e-mail consumers.

On-line Advertising

On-line advertising is becoming a popular way for sponsors to communicate their message to consumers. **On-line advertisements**, also called **banner advertisements**, are sponsored messages that appear on websites by third-party vendors. Sponsors hope website visitors will click on on-line advertisements to learn more about products and purchase them.

In 1997, consumer Internet advertising revenue totaled $544.8 million, up 147.1 percent over revenues in 1996. During the late 1990s, Internet advertising was dominated by technology and services vendors. Computer and software vendors contributed $275 million, or 50 percent, of all Internet advertising in 1997. Financial services were the second leading category, contributing $42 million, or 7.7 percent, of Internet advertising and telecommunications was third, spending $33 million, or 6 percent, of Internet advertising. However, product categories such as skin care and education (including universities) are emerging categories. In 1996, skin care marketers spent nothing on Internet advertising. In 1997 they spent $500,000 advertising creams, lotions, and oils over the Internet. In addition to on-line advertising, sponsors have the opportunity to set up website storefronts on the Internet to generate direct-response sales (Maddox, 1998).

Table 10.4 shows the top 25 Internet advertisers of 1997. The significance of this data is illustrated by the extremely large percentage changes in Internet advertising by some companies. The top Internet advertiser, Microsoft, increased advertising by 136.8 percent and the second largest Internet advertiser, IBM, increased advertising by 178 percent. General Motors Corporation, Sony Corporation, and ivillage increased Internet advertising expenditures by more than 400 percent and US Robotics Mobile Communications Corporation increased Internet advertising over 1000 percent. This data shows the emergence of Internet advertising as a powerful promotional tool at the end of the 20th century.

In addition to banner advertising, companies on the World Wide Web have entered into agreements with affiliate networks to get other companies to do their marketing. **Affiliate networks** entice on-line shoppers to click over to another website to make a

Table 10.4   **Top 25 Internet Advertisers**

Rank 1997	Advertiser	Internet Advertising		% change
		1997	1996	
1	Microsoft Corp.	$30.9	$13.0	136.8
2	IBM Corp.	20.1	7.2	178.0
3	Excite Inc.	11.7	6.9	69.2
4	Yahoo Corp.	8.6	3.9	117.1
5	Netscape Communications Corp.	8.4	5.7	46.9
6	Infoseek Corp.	7.6	5.1	49.8
7	Lycos Inc.	6.7	3.9	72.3
8	General Motors Corp.	6.9	1.2	460.8
9	AT&T Corp.	6.8	7.3	−7.2
10	Compaq Computer Corp.	6.1	2.6	130.1
11	CBS Corp.	5.7	2.4	134.6
12	Ziff-Davis	5.5	2.0	171.0
13	Ford Motor Co.	4.9	1.2	314.6
14	Intel Corp.	4.5	1.6	179.0
15	Bell Atlantic Corp.	4.3	4.1	5.1
16	Toyota Motor Corp.	4.0	2.2	83.2
17	Hewlett-Packard Co.	4.0	0.8	369.2
18	Song Corp.	4.0	0.8	412.8
19	Walt Disney Co.	3.5	0.8	313.5
20	iVillage	3.5	0.6	455.2
21	Visa International	3.4	0.4	671.8
22	Amazon.Com Books	3.2	1.6	91.6
23	US Robotics Mobile Comm. Corp.	2.9	0.2	1070.1
24	Honda Motor Co.	2.9	1.0	182.4
25	Donaldson Lufkin & Jenrette	2.7	0.6	356.5

Dollars are in millions.

Source: InterMedia Advertising Solutions, a sister company of CMR [On-line] Available: http://www.adage.com/ dataplace/archives/dp251.html.

purchase. Each affiliate earns commissions on the sale up to 15 percent (Schwartz, 1998). A newspaper and a bookseller provide good examples to illustrate affiliate networks. Book reviews are common features of on-line newspapers. If the on-line newspaper is part of an affiliate network, a banner advertisement will appear in the book review that allows the viewer to immediately go to a website that has that particular book for sale. Amazon.com, a leading on-line book seller had signed up 100,000 affiliates by 1998. The main goal of affiliate programs is to lure first-time on-line consumers to check out retail websites that they might not go to otherwise.

On-line Retailing

Does this sound familiar? Your friend has just told you about a great new book she is reading that is full of history, romance, and adventure. You cannot wait to get your hands on a copy! But, it is 10:00 at night and the local bookstore closed an hour ago.

Just log onto the Internet. There you can find a virtual bookstore, place an order, pay with your credit card, and have the book delivered to your home in just a few days. If this doesn't sound familiar yet, just wait. This is an example of on-line retailing, also know as Internet Shopping, Internet Retailing, and Internet Commerce or e-commerce to the consumer.

On-line retailing is the selling of goods to the consumer via an interactive computer network. On-line retailing is an example of a one-step approach. Users of L.L. Bean's on-line catalog, Quickstop, for example, can electronically order any item featured in the catalog by entering an item number. A photograph of the item is shown and on-line shoppers are asked to choose the appropriate size and color and then order the item by credit card. Product availability is confirmed on-line while customers wait; purchases are shipped within 24 hours of ordering ("L.L. Bean's On-line," 1997).

On-line retailing has emerged as a major shopping channel with the power to assist and increase sales of a growing range of products. As we have mentioned throughout this chapter, the industry is very new, having only emerged as a direct-response marketing strategy in 1995. In 1998, *Stores* magazine issued its first special report on Internet Shopping ("Internet Shopping," 1998) and *Time* magazine featured on-line shopping as a cover story (Krantz, 1998). Both these publications illustrated the importance of this emerging technology.

While the outlook for on-line retailing is positive, Krantz (1998) reported several reasons consumers gave for not buying on-line. The reasons include:

- Fear of hackers
- Lack of products
- Inability to see the products
- Need to reveal personal information
- Poorly designed sites
- Companies' reputation
- Fear of money or merchandise getting lost

In another move to show the importance of this emerging technology, the National Retail Federation formed a Virtual Retailing Council to address the issues of visual merchandising, sales promotion, and physical distribution associated with Internet retailing ("Internet Shopping," 1998). The council was established for retailers, to help promote understanding and reduce the risks associated with Internet retailing.

The ability to reach a global consumer is one of the most positive aspects of on-line retailing. Almost half of Web sellers' sites are accessible outside the United States ("Internet Shopping," 1998). One-fourth of retailers and 46 percent of manufacturers target international on-line sales. Forty percent of U.S retailers and manufacturers with internationally accessible sites say some of their Internet orders are from global consumers. Firms use this direct-response strategy as a service to global consumers who would otherwise have to pay for a phone call to order merchandise. Additionally, firms use the Internet to offer consumers closeout merchandise. It is too expensive to mail international customers direct-mail informing them of sales, but the Internet allows firms access to global consumers. U.S. companies are not the only sellers participating in on-line retailing. European-based and China-based sellers, among others, are participating in Internet commerce.

Other Direct-response Electronic Media

Besides the computer, there are other direct-response electronic media available for vendors to use as direct-response media. Videotapes, CDs, and diskettes can be used to deliver advertising messages to consumers, delivered through the post office as direct mail or through other delivery means. Videotapes are a recording medium that electronically records sounds and images simultaneously, produced for playback with a video cassette recorder (VCR) on a television set. CDs (compact disks) are small optical disks that can have music or data encoded on them, produced for playback on a CD player or computer. CD-ROMs are compact disks that function with read-only memory. Harrod's use of a CD-ROM as a direct-response medium was the topic of the opening vignette. A diskette is a flexible plastic disk coated with magnetic material and covered by a protective jacket, used in computers to store data magnetically. Videotapes, CDs, and diskettes are potentially more entertaining to the audience than print media, because they offer sound and even lifelike visuals.

With advances in television technology and computers, advertisers have used these newer resources to attract potential customers. The invention of the VCR has created opportunities for videotaped commercials. The videotape market started with simple home videos showing still photographs of merchandise in a manner similar to mail-order catalogs. These videos have evolved into professionally produced programs that appear similar to television programs. Celebrities offer endorsements on every product imaginable from exercise equipment and skin care to home furnishings and sunglasses.

Videotapes have advantages similar to television's, showing products in a realistic setting. This form of advertising features key audio and visual information about brands. Since more than 90 percent of American households own at least one VCR, the video advertising medium is capable of reaching an enormous audience. Consumers are less likely to throw away videos delivered to their home or office than other unsolicited media.

CD-ROM is a form of computer software that runs on multimedia computers, systems that are capable of providing both video and sound. In 1998, wholesale revenues for CD-ROM software, drives, sound boards, and semiconductors were $3.5 billion, up from $2.5 billion in 1994, a 28 percent increase (see Table 10.3). Some mail-order firms including L.L. Bean and Tiffany have participated in CD-ROM catalogs. Users can select the products they wish to review in this medium. As larger numbers of households and businesses elevate their computer capabilities, CD-ROM has the potential to grow as an alternative to traditional media.

Diskettes are also sent through the mail as direct-response advertising. America On-line, a commercial Internet service provider, uses direct mail to provide potential customers with 10 free hours of on-line use via computer discs sent through the mail and included in magazine subscription packaging (Fig. 10.9).

Direct-response communication is not limited to media that reach consumers in their homes. It can be advertised on sidewalks and highways through direct-response out-of-home media.

Direct-response Out-of-home Media

Outdoor media may be among the oldest forms of advertising. During the 17th and 18th centuries, shopkeepers used signs to attract consumers to their stores. Because so many individuals could not read during that era, signs and symbols were used to identify businesses. Perhaps one of the most famous shopkeeper symbols was the red and white striped barber pole. Customers could find the place for haircuts and shaves by looking for this symbol. Now, outdoor media is used in fashion promotion. In the opening synopsis of Chapter 6, both Ellen Tracy and Yves Saint Laurent were including outdoor advertising in their promotion strategies. The top 25 outdoor advertisers are highlighted in Table 10.5. Phillip Morris Companies is identified as the top outdoor

Figure 10.9

Direct-response diskette
sent through the mail to
encourage consumers to
enroll in on-line services

advertiser on this table. On April 21, 1999, tobacco advertisers were required by the settlement of a lawsuit by state governments to remove all tobacco ads from billboards. In some instances the tobacco ads were replaced with anti-smoking messages, and in other instances, the billboards were removed completely. The tobacco advertising dollars that were spent on out-of-home media were redistributed into magazine and newspaper advertisements ("New York Times pulls tobacco ads," 1999).

Consumers encounter printed advertising messages at bus stops and train stations, in addition to signs placed above the seats in subways, buses, or trains. These constitute **transit media**. These messages represent and out-of-home direct-response advertising. **Out-of-home media** are advertising displays that reach consumers on the move through placement on bus shelters, bus exteriors, taxi tops, kiosks, street furniture (newsstands and benches), indoor out-of-home (airport or mall), spectaculars, painted walls, and even toilet stalls. Blimps (Fig. 10.10) are a modern out-of-home medium. These media have been gaining in popularity in the United States and international cities that have a large population base. Color Plates 2 and 6 show effective use of out-of-home media.

The Outdoor Advertising Association of America distinguishes on-premises signs from outdoor advertising. Signage used to promote goods or services offered by businesses on the property where the sign is located is considered to be **on-premises signage**. For example, the store sign with a business logo such as Niketown is on-premises signage. Out-of-home advertising promote products and services that are not available for sale at the location and are considered to be remote or off-premises signage.

One of the most famous places for out-of-town media is Times Square in New York City. Billboards for Tommy Hilfiger, Calvin Klein, Liz Claiborne, Perry Ellis, Banana

Table 10.5   **Top 25 Outdoor Advertisers**

Rank[a]	Advertiser	Spending on Outdoor Adverstising[b]
1	Phillip Morris Cos.	$76.4
2	RJR Nabisco	42.1
3	B.A.T. Nabisco	32.6
4	McDonald's Corp.	18.8
5	U.S. dairy producers, processors	17.1
6	Seagram Co.	16.7
7	General Motors Corp.	14.7
8	Cendant Corp.	14.6
9	Anheuser-Busch Cos.	13.0
10	Diageo	12.7
11	Loews Corp.	12.1
12	Walt Disney Co.	11.6
13	Bass plc	8.8
14	Choice Hotels International	8.2
15	SBC Communications	8.1
16	U.S. Government	7.9
17	Nike	6.2
18	Allied Domecq	6.1
19	Wendy's International	5.7
20	Shoney's	5.7
21	AT&T Corp.	5.6
22	Red Roof Inns	5.6
23	Blue Cross & Blue Shield Association	5.1
24	Cracker Barrel Old Country	5.0
25	Sony Corp.	4.8

[a]*In 1997.*

[b]*Dollars are in millions. Source:* Competitive Media Reporting.

Adapted from: Top 25 outdoor advertisers. (1998, September 28). Advertising Age [On-line]. Available: http://www.adage.com/dataplace/archives/dp259.html.

Republic, Levi's jeans, and the Wonderbra have appeared there (Fig. 10.11). Because 20 million tourists visit Times Square each year, advertisers will pay as much as $1.2 million a year to have their corporate images or their products on display in this area (Holusha, 1996). In addition to signs, Times Square is home to a 35-by-27-foot animated screen operated by Panasonic and NBC. The NBC-TV network, through its local affiliate in New York City and other NBC ventures, broadcasts news and public service announcements over this screen as out-of-home media.

London's Piccadilly circus and central areas of Paris and Los Angeles have also become centers for apparel advertising billboards. Even Berlin has endorsed fashion-oriented billboards. Famous male models and actors have been used to advertise men's underwear lines for such designers as Calvin Klein. Attractive female models wearing the latest creations from Victoria Secret have been featured in London. Both the scantily clad

Figure 10.10

The Tommy Hilfiger blimp—one of many forms of out-of-home media

Figure 10.11

Billboards on Times Square

Sources: Sherwood Outdoor (left) and © New York Convention & Visitors Bureau (right)

men and women caused controversy and were said to be the cause of several traffic accidents. The Gap used billboards to introduce the opening of a new store in Tokyo. Color Plate 6 is a dramatic example of an outdoor sign used by Pretty Polly in the U. K.

Outdoor advertising revenues have grown at an annual rate of 7 percent since 1993 (Edmondson, 1998). This includes 400,000 billboards and 37,000 buses plastered with billboard-sized ads. To maintain growth in the direct marketing out-of-home media, billboard companies have started target marketing. The market they are targeting is drivers, particularly drivers with cell phones. These consumers have been labeled **direct-response driver-consumers** (Edmondson, 1998). Nine out of ten American adults drive, and they typically spend more than an hour a day behind the wheel, according to the Department of Transportation. Two-thirds of all car trips are made alone. If drivers see a billboard or hear a radio commercial that promises to fill an immediate need, he or she might be persuaded to pick up the phone and directly respond to the advertising. This phenomenon is described in Box 10.1.

There are several advantages to using out-of-home direct-response media. For one thing, outdoor advertising can provide broad coverage of local markets. The advertisements selected for these media can be targeted to the selected market within local geographical areas. By specifying a billboard location on a specific bus route, the advertiser has the ability to direct who sees the ad.

The large size of the ads make outdoor advertising media big, bold, and hard to miss. High quality images are possible using the industry's latest printing technology. Transit media have a high frequency of exposure and repeat exposure. Research has indicated that more than 60 percent of all adults in the selected market will have seen the message within the first week. By the end of the month, close to 90 percent of the adults will have seen the message. Close to 40 percent of the adults will be able to recall the message content. According to the Outdoor Advertising Association, outdoor advertising costs 80 percent less than television, 60 percent less than newspaper, and 50 percent less than radio advertising ("Industry," 1997).

Disadvantages of other direct-response media are common with out-of-home media as well. First, there is the attitude of the consumer. The consumer in transit is faced with many distractions, from heavy traffic to scenery, to unpleasant weather. These distractions and stress can put the consumer in a bad mood, making him or her unresponsive to outdoor media. Second, there are creative limitations with out-of-home media. A strong first impression to the consumer must be created in a very brief period. The type of copy and artwork are limited to a few words and/or a strong graphic image to capture the interest of the passerby. Third, as with other media, out-of-home may have a negative image. The federal government enacted the Highway Beautification Act, requiring state governments to provide control of outdoor advertising and junkyards on interstate and primary highway systems. Provisions of the act restrict outdoor advertising in commercial areas and attempt to stop the proliferation of signs. Many people want to limit or eliminate billboards from the nation's highways and some states have enacted stronger limitations than the federal laws.

Other Direct-response Media

There are other types of direct-response media that you may never have considered. One example is at the movie theater. **On-screen entertainment** is the slide show that previews before the movie. These presentations are created by the National Cinema Network (NCN) and show ads along with trivia and tidbits about Hollywood to

BOX 10.1

In the Driver's Seat

When I'm driving, I think about what I have to do next. After that, I daydream and listen to the blues," says Jack Jensen. He drives about 400 miles a week for his job as a federal housing official. That is an hour or two every workday spent planning projects, dreaming, and singing the blues, often at speeds exceeding 55 miles an hour. Jack is a typical American guy.

Nine out of ten American adults drive. Men who drive spend an average of 81 minutes a day behind the wheel, and women drivers spend 64 minutes a day. This is more than the average American spends cooking or eating. It is more than twice as much time as the average parent spends with his or her children. And two-thirds of all car trips are made alone, with only the radio and billboards for company.

Thanks to the construction of interstate highways, the entry of women into the workforce, and several other social revolutions, driving has become America's most important source of quiet time. Between 1969 and 1995, the number of drivers in the United States increased more than three times as fast as the population, and the number of household vehicles increased six times as fast. The three-decade surge in driving has slowed slightly in recent years, although forecasts call for continued growth. We are approaching one car for each licensed driver in the United States. Home may be where the heart is, but a driver's car is her castle.

The boom in daily travel has been good for several industries, and none has benefited more than companies that sell out-of-home advertising. The revenues of outdoor advertising firms have been growing at an annual rate of 7 percent since 1993. Outdoor advertising is projected to reach $4 billion in 1998, which would account for 3 percent of all advertising expenditures. But, the industry's growth is not concentrated among the 400,000-odd billboards scattered around the country, some of which have been carrying advertising for more than a century. The growth is with advertising that shows up in nontraditional, less regulated places like taxi tops and toilet stalls. Of the 60,000 buses in the United States, for example, 37,000 are now plastered with billboard-sized ads.

The billboard trade has grown with the driving boom, and outdoor advertisers have aggressively created advertising spaces in new places. But when it comes to understanding their audience, billboard marketers have fallen behind the times. Most out-of-home ads are still marketed as a mass medium, with the price of space usually set according to traffic counts and the estimated number of daily "impressions" a billboard makes. While other media have developed sophisticated models to put specific advertising messages where potential customers are likely to see them, most outdoor advertisers still play a simple numbers game. In print and broadcast media, toll-free numbers have become a standard marketing tool. But even through three in ten drivers now carry working telephones, relatively few billboards invite viewers to make an immediate response. To maintain their growth, billboard companies must turn to target marketing. They must understand the hearts and minds of drivers.

Most Americans hold fairly positive attitudes toward driving, and most are tolerant of outdoor advertising. About one in ten adults does not drive. Another four in ten are light drivers, putting in fewer than 100 miles a week behind the wheel. People in these groups are likely to be elderly and have low incomes and they are unlikely to hold full-time jobs.

Heavy drivers (those who drive more than 100 miles a week) tend to be the most desirable consumer targets—middle-aged, middle-class, and employed full-time. But they are also the group most likely to be annoyed by billboards, and their negative attitudes become stronger with each advance in income and age.

About three in ten drivers fall into a fourth segment that uses technology to stay in touch on the road. The number of drivers with a working cellular telephone in the car is growing rapidly. Most of them are also heavy drivers. But this is a younger group, and they are more likely to hold positive attitudes toward billboards.

The growth of "wired" drivers is another lucky break for outdoor advertisers. Telecommunications tools are transforming the driving experience, and the cellular phone is the first wave of the transformations. Once they are wired, solitary drivers are no longer isolated. If they see advertising that promises to fill an immediate need, they might be persuaded to pick up the phone. They could become a whole new market: direct-response driver-consumers.

The Phone

Jack Jensen's first cellular phone was purchased for him by his employer. He was careful to use it only for important business calls, because each call costs at least a dollar. But now he makes about five calls a day, with only three business calls, and he pays for them himself. "I need to keep in touch with my friends and my kids, not just my clients," he says.

In 1988, about 2 million cellular phones were in use in the United States. That number has doubled every year since, and it shows no sign of slowing down. As the number of cellular-phone subscribers continues to grow, cellular-phone users will turn more billboards into direct-response advertising. Also, a billboard that is linked to a telephone number is more accountable to advertisers. Instead of relying on an estimated number of "impressions" based on traffic counts, the client will know exactly how many calls, and how much revenue, each billboard produces.

As the number of cellular phones increases and their cost declines, their use will trickle down from more affluent to less affluent drivers. It will also trickle up the age ladder, as young adults get hooked on cellular phones and grow older. This means that out-of-home advertisements linked to phone numbers will get an immediate response from two desirable consumer segments—the rich and the young. And as the cellular-phone boom continues, ads linked to a phone number will begin to appeal to more mainstream groups.

Jensen, 41, says that he makes a point of never buying anything over the phone. But, if you press him, a different story emerges. In about a year of cellular-phone use, he remembers reporting a drunken driver, confirming hotel reservations, and ordering take-out food. "If I'm not careful, I don't even think about how expensive it is to use," he says. "A phone is a phone."

One of the chief tasks facing outdoor advertisers in the next decade is how to design advertising that will persuade people like Jensen to stop daydreaming, pick up the phone, and buy a product. To answer this question, it is necessary to learn what is on people's minds as they drive. What images and messages are most likely to make them respond?

Successful messages from out-of-home ads should consider the purpose of the intended customer's trip, and whether or not the driver is likely to be alone. Commuters might respond best to ads that celebrate feelings of solitude, reflections, and quiet enjoyment. When potential customers are on their way to the mountains or the beach, most are not alone—so billboards will make a positive impression if they stimulate game-playing and pleasant conversation in the car. Whether they are alone or not, people

like to be taken away from their cares. They may not drink while they drive, but they do daydream.

How They View Ads

Many outdoor advertising companies believe success depends on putting up more billboards, making them bigger, and loading them with ever-more elaborate gimmicks. You can see the results just south of the Seattle-Tacoma airport on Interstate 5. It is a full-color electronic billboard—in effect, a color television screen—that is about 7 percent larger than a full-sized traditional billboard. It plays more than 6,000 advertising spots a day, with each spot lasting about 7 seconds.

Every year, ads like these are honored with "Obie Awards" at a huge industry banquet. But to ordinary Americans, more billboards and louder billboards will just add to clutter, no matter how good-looking or creative they are.

Most Americans do not appreciate the artistic or entertaining qualities of outdoor ads. Yet they do not hate billboards, either. They see outdoor advertising as marginally useful to their lives, and they accept it as a consequence of the free enterprise system. Four out of five consumers are open to the messages they see in outdoor advertising. But only a minority appreciate beautiful or entertaining images, and a majority are interested in information they can use.

Every Driver Is Different

The trend toward more travel may even continue after boomers retire, because boomers will be a different breed of retiree. Educated Americans are more likely to participate in leisure travel, and they are more likely to refrain from smoking and otherwise preserve their health. So outdoor ads should continue to have larger and larger audiences, with more older eyes behind the wheel.

Outdoor ads may also have increasingly appreciative audiences. Drivers now under age 34 are most likely to be cellular-phone users who could make an immediate connection to a business after seeing a billboard. Second and more important is that young drivers have a more positive opinion of the medium than older drivers do. Young adults grew up in an advertising-saturated culture. Most of them accept billboards as part of the driving experience, some even enjoy them as art, and they are the group most likely to begin using outdoor ads as interactive purchasing tools.

The cellular-telephone boom is only the first in a series of high-tech opportunities for drivers and outdoor advertisers. In a few years, it may be common for bill-boards to establish electronic links with navigation systems and on-board video screens in cars. And if the era of "smart cars" comes true, drivers will be free to relax and daydream on the freeway while their cars drive themselves. Then outdoor messages could become more detailed, and the audience may become as attentive as they are now captive.

Although technology may bring the loneliness of the long-distance commuter to an end, the challenge to bill-boards will remain the same. Jack Jensen says that if his car could drive itself, "I would pay even less attention to bill-boards. I'd read or work on my laptop computer."

Adapted from: Edmondson, B. (1998, March 1). In the drivers seat. . . . American Demographics, *46–53.*

movie-goers ("Field of View," 1998). According to the NCN, the potential audience for prefilm ads is close to 90 million a month. Those who benefit most from this advertising are small businesses that occupy space near theaters.

The dry cleaner provides another source of direct-response media. Look World-wide, a Miami-based advertising agency, has coordinated more than 10,000 dry cleaners in the largest metropolitan markets into the International Cleaners Advertising Network ("Ads Are Coming," 1998). Marketers can place ads on cleaners' plastic bags, paper-covered hangers, and protective paper garment covers, as well as offer samples that come in bags attached to the hangers. Benefits of the network include reaching professional, higher-income consumers, as well as "repeat impressions" as dry cleaning goes from store to home or office.

WHY USE DIRECT MARKETING?

In this chapter we have introduced direct-response media. So why should vendors use direct-response promotion strategies in their business? Because direct marketing allows businesses to create relationships between the company and its customers. This is a strong advantage of a direct marketing program.

Advantages of Direct Marketing

Other advantages of direct response promotions include:

- **Shopping convenience.** Foremost for customers, direct marketing offers increased shopping convenience and service by allowing individuals to shop at home using a catalog, telephone, computer, or other delivery vehicle during leisure time, rather than shopping at a retail establishment. This method is particularly popular with working women, who may not want to invest time searching for parking spaces, standing in line at over-crowded stores or malls, or shopping after work hours when the risk of theft or harm may be higher.
- **Instant payment by credit card.** Most direct-response promotions offer the consumer the opportunity to pay by credit card. Credit cards are the dominant payment form for low-and high-end merchandise by a majority of the population. Sellers encourage the use of credit cards as a guarantee that they will be paid. As we will discuss in Chapter 11, credit cards are offered as part of customer incentive programs and are becoming increasingly popular among retailers to encourage brand loyalty.

- **Selective reach and segmentation.** Direct marketing appeals can be addressed to a specific individual or family, zip code area, or other segmented population, rather than a general audience, allowing for selective reach. The advertisement is sent only to those consumers the promoter wishes to contact, eliminating waste. The coverage may be broad through a television broadcast, or selective to individuals identified as members of a specific organization. The segmentation capabilities are limitless based on consumer demographics and lifestyle characteristics.
- **Frequency.** Direct marketing offers the opportunity for the sponsor to develop frequency levels. Frequency levels are the number of times a consumer is exposed to an appeal in a specified time. Recent purchasers will have a higher frequency level than consumers who have not made a purchase within the last 12 months. Higher frequency may result in more sales. However, receiving too many exposures, such as duplicate catalogs or repeated broadcasts of infomercials, may turn consumers off.
- **Effectiveness.** Results of each direct marketing transaction can be evaluated for success because each transaction requires action on the part of the customer by return mail, sending in a coupon, making a telephone call, responding over the computer, or some other direct response. In addition, this direct interaction between company and customer allows the company to create a customer database for use in promoting future products or services.

Disadvantages of Direct Marketing

Although direct marketing is gaining popularity and market share in the advertising arena, there are disadvantages associated with this promotion mix element. They include:

- **Image.** The image of direct marketing has not always been positive. Many consumers consider direct marketing appeals as uninvited solicitations. Direct-response advertisements received in the mail are referred to as "junk mail," and oftentimes get filed in the trash. Telephone call solicitations are met with even less enthusiasm by consumers. Early infomercials and cable shopping networks were produced as low-budget productions adding to consumer's negative opinions of direct-response broadcasts.
- **Accuracy.** Although direct marketing allows the sponsor to target specific audiences, if the list used to target the audience is not kept up-to-date, accuracy becomes a problem.

In order for any direct marketing campaign to be successful, the following five components should be carefully considered and executed. They include:

- **The list** must be properly managed, and contain well-researched, potential and repeat customers.
- **The offer** must match the intended outcome of the promotion, generating immediate sales or building long-term customer relationships with the consumer.
- **The format** must create an urgency in the consumer's mind to respond.
- **The follow-up** must ensure that requested products or information are sent within 48 hours of the request.
- **The analysis** must keep the database current.

A sponsor who follows these recommendations should have a successful campaign.

We hope you have noticed a theme running through this chapter as we have discussed the different direct marketing strategies. That theme is accurate database management, and it is the subject of the next section.

DATABASE MANAGEMENT

The key to successful direct marketing strategies is target marketing through segmentation. Target marketing is achieved by using a consumer database to identify the specific population of customers to receive the promotional appeal. A **database** is a collection of data arranged for ease and speed of search and retrieval. Within a database, a computerized record of each previous buyer and/or potential prospect is maintained. This record includes the customer's background, purchase patterns, and interests, which serves as a source for future targeted marketing efforts. The database allows a company to identify the individual characteristics of each consumer and serve his or her needs. Instead of sending a large general merchandise catalog to someone who may want to buy only one particular item, a company can use a computerized database to identify consumers who should receive product-specific catalogs.

Beyond market segmentation, effective database management can stimulate repeat purchases. It has been proven that once consumers have made an initial purchase, they are more likely to make repeat purchases using the same direct-response media, if the experience has proven easy and reliable. Effective database management can also stimulate cross-selling. **Cross-selling** is the sale of additional products and services to the same customer. Cross-selling merchandise may be additional merchandise from the same company or merchandise from a different company with products that appeal to the same demographic or psychographic characteristics of the individual. When customers respond by telephone, sales representatives may offer special sales on merchandise available only during the phone call. It is a common practice for companies to sell or rent lists that are then used to cross-sell. For example, after ordering from a catalog, consumers are often sent unsolicited issues of other catalogs to influence similar purchases.

Manufacturers and retailers who use direct marketing strategies must research their current and potential customer base to identify spending habits and customer loyalty. Research should encompass demographic data, lifestyle information, and information about the trading area of the business. Demographic and lifestyle factors were discussed in Chapter 2. A checklist on page 316 suggests categories of demographic information that should be retained in database records. The information should include name and address, as well as other demographic and socioeconomic indicators about the individual. The individual's name should be spelled correctly, with the preferred salutation of that individual. Businesses should track the recency of purchase, frequency of purchase, dollar amount, type of payment, type of products purchased, and motivation for purchase. Demographic information may be obtained from direct contact by personal observation of the client, through government data resources, such as the U.S. Census *(http://www.census.gov)*, or from companies that specialize in supplying data, such as Market Statistics.

Businesses may segment customers based on values, attitudes, fashion awareness, or other lifestyle characteristics. Patterns of behavior can be determined by knowing what foods people like, what movies and other forms of entertainment people participate in, and how they decorate their homes. By understanding the lifestyle characteristics of an individual, a business can focus on specific products and promotions that are most likely to increase purchases by the consumer.

A company's database should include characteristics of the business' trading area. A **trading area** is the city, county, state, or region a company services. A trading area for a convenience store may be only a few blocks in the surrounding neighborhood. A

Checklist for Database Record Management

Name
- ❐ First
- ❐ Middle initial
- ❐ Last

Address
- ❐ Street address
- ❐ City
- ❐ State
- ❐ Zip code

Phone
- ❐ Area code
- ❐ Phone number
- ❐ Work or home identification

Demographics
- ❐ Age
- ❐ Gender
- ❐ Marital status
- ❐ Ethnicity
- ❐ Education level
- ❐ Income level
- ❐ Home ownership

Payment information
- ❐ Payment amount
- ❐ Payment method
- ❐ Date of payment

---

trading area for a company, such as Levi Strauss or Nike, may be worldwide. Businesses should be able to plot the boundaries of a trading area on a map and identify by zip code or other geographical factors the location of heavy spenders. Promotion and advertising decisions can then be based on patterns within the trading area.

The information collected in a company database has far-reaching implications for an integrated marketing communications plan. Beyond a direct marketing campaign, data about specific target markets can assist businesses in determining store locations, merchandise selection, store layout and visual merchandising, personal selling and service opportunities, and potential special events and other sales promotion activities.

In-house List Development

Companies that engage in direct marketing have the option of creating their own in-house database list or purchasing database lists from list brokers. **In-house lists** are developed, owned, and maintained by the company. For example, the retailer Carson Pirie Scott replaced its vendor-maintained list with an in-house database for several reasons, including more easily targeting specific customers based on purchasing habits and monitoring effectiveness of promotional events (Zimmerman, 1998b). In-house lists are generated using customer information retained through previous contacts with the customer or through voluntary participation by the customer. Previous contacts with the customer may include past sales for which purchase history is recorded, personal contact lists managed by sales consultants in retail stores, or referrals through in-bound toll-free numbers or other direct-response media.

A consumer may voluntarily participate in list generation by filling out surveys or response cards, ordering merchandise through direct response, or filling out a credit card application for a specific company. Land's End creates its own in-house lists for specialty catalogs by using direct-response customer information from its general merchandise catalog.

When creating an in-house list, the merchant should record the last contact made with the specific customer and the direct-response media used. Customer names should be purged or marked inactive if they have not made a purchase within a specified time period, usually 12 to 18 months, or if the consumer has asked to be removed from the list. Individuals can remove their names from the mailing list of companies that subscribe to the Direct Marketing Association's Mail Preference Service by sending their name, address, and zip code to: Mail Preference Service, Direct Marketing Association, PO Box 9008, Farmingdale, N.Y. 11735–9008. Consumers may also request that companies not rent or sell their name. Many direct-response printed materials offer this option by allowing the consumer to check a box. Merchants are obligated by law to comply with the request of a consumer to be removed from direct marketing lists. Ethical considerations concerning list management are discussed in Chapter 18.

Brokered Lists

Direct marketing companies that choose not to maintain an in-house list may purchase brokered lists. **Brokered lists** are database lists offered for sale or rent through negotiation of a contract in return for a fee or commission to a list broker. List brokers act as purchasing agents for the database. A list broker is commissioned by a company or list owner to offer the list for rent or sale. A company that wants to purchase a list contacts the broker who, in turn, contacts the list owner. The list owner will decide if the list can be shared. Upon sale or rental of the list, the broker receives a commission.

List owners are companies that compile, promote, and maintain the integrity of a database for sale or rental to others. List owners frequently ask to review proposed marketing materials before selling or renting a list to ensure the offer is not offensive or too competitive with other products being offered to individuals on the list. National Demographics and Lifestyles (NDL) is a segmentation and lifestyle marketing company and list owner. One example of a list offered for sale by NDL is the Lifestyle Selector. Lifestyle Selector is a national database composed of consumers who have voluntarily returned questionnaires answering demographic and lifestyle-oriented questions about interests and hobbies. The questionnaires, which have been inserted into packages of consumer retail products, allow NDL to segment the data and offer it for sale to publishers, fund-raiser companies, catalog distributors, travel companies, retailers, and insurance and financial industries, among others.

The U.S. Census Bureau, the U.S. Postal Service, and various professional organizations are also common sources for direct marketing lists. Universities may occasionally provide lists of graduates or enrolled students to companies for solicitation purposes, if a return is brokered with the institution to benefit scholarships or other institutional needs.

Lists are generally sold per 1,000 names. It is essential to test a list by sampling before purchasing it. Using a sample set, a prescribed group of elements is selected and analyzed to estimate the characteristics of a population. A sample set of names is purchased and those people are contacted using the proposed direct marketing strategy. Results are analyzed, and if a positive direct-response return is made from the sample, the entire list or a larger proportion of the list may be purchased.

Electronic information processing capabilities are essential for the success of any direct marketing program. Today, companies rely heavily on database management systems to drive programming. Information management needs must allow for efficiency, accountability, and selectivity. With companies entering and leaving the industry on a daily basis, it is important for businesses to work at the highest efficiency possible. Often, evaluation within a business is at least in part based on the quality of the database management system. Box 10.2 highlights how Sears saved its Canadian-based catalog through efficient database management.

For companies to remain successful, their ultimate responsibility is to be accountable to their customers. Particularly in direct marketing, where customer decisions are based on reliability and competence, the sponsoring company should pay attention to detail through information management. Selectivity is necessary when using a database. Retrieval capabilities are very important to a database management system. A good system has built into it fast turnaround and response times.

BOX 10.2
Back from the Brink

Arthur Hughes was lucky to get the details on a very fortunate example of database marketing at its best: the Sears Canada catalog story.

Sears Roebuck terminated its big catalog in the United States several years ago, but the book is still going strong in Canada—it is currently the largest mail-order catalog in the country. At the same time, Sears is also a big retailing presence in Canada, with 110 retail stores and 1,800 catalog agents.

In the mid-1990s, the retail stores were in trouble. Profits had dropped 73 percent and Sears had eliminated 1,200 jobs. Things did not look good. With retailing in trouble, Sears looked to the catalog business to pull the company out of its hole.

A Somewhat Dated Operation

Sears hired a list manager for catalog marketing with a mandate to implement a new marketing database for the catalog business. When the list manager took a look at the Sears database, he knew that some changes had to be made.

The database was stored on a mainframe computer, using 30-year-old software. It took 120 people to do the manual file maintenance. The file itself was loaded with duplicates. It was not on-line, and could be accessed only through hard-copy reports that took a week to produce.

The list manager decided to make a business case for a new database system with modern software, and on-line access to do counts, reports, and selects. He showed that he could pay for the system just by finding and eliminating the estimated 10 percent of duplicate names on the system.

He set up a system whereby the data from the mainframe could be viewed by a client server through a simple spreadsheet. The new system permitted the company employees to look at circulation, media, performance analysis, growth and response rates, and track of promotions.

With the new system, the 7-million-name database could be updated weekly in about 2 hours, and produced all sorts of reports.

The mainframe was not replaced. Sears still uses it to hold all of its data. The list manager set up a separate marketing database on a file server that met the needs for modern database marketing without interrupting the ongoing operational mainframe system. Sear's three calling centers take more than 18 million calls a year. Data from these calls and all retail and catalog transactions is kept in the database. The mainframe sorts the transaction data and summarizes it for the client server.

The client server software system, called Archer, was developed by Retail Target Marketing Systems. It is a marketing selection tool that is used to study the RFM (recency, frequency, monetary value) segments into which Sears customers are now divided. The system is plugged into a local area network (LAN) so that a large number of Sears marketers can access and play with the data. The marketers can use macros and sorting on their spreadsheets to manipulate the customer data in a wide variety of ways.

Tracking Customers through the Segments

Before the list manager arrived, active customers were defined by the company as people who had shopped with Sears in the last 12 months. During the previous decade, the active file had been going down 3 percent per year. The decline had to stop.

First, duplicates were removed. Next, the practice of dropping people who had not bought in 12 months was stopped. It is very difficult to maintain or build any kind of relationship with customers, or to develop any kind of long-term learning process about them, when you dump their data after a year.

Sears needed to understand customer segment behavior so that it could begin retention activities, reactivation, and catalog cross-shopping promotion. This required knowing how many customers Sears had, and what they were doing. The old system classified customers as active, inactive, one-order customers, and two orders-plus. A new model that included 189 RFM segments was developed on the new system based on customer's lifetime value and the amounts they spent on catalog items.

The segments tracked response rate, average order, and dollar per book across all 189 segments for every one of Sears's 13 catalogs. All the variable costs of each promotion, whether it was a catalog or a direct-mail promotion, could be applied to each of the 189 segments to forecast segment profitability. This told Sears whether it would be profitable or not to mail to each segment. The company could understand the ramifications of what it was doing for each major promotion, and accurately forecast sales at the end of the year.

The RFM segments themselves were not cast in stone. If a Sears customer had a lifetime spending of $2,500 and had made a purchase in the past 3 months, the customer would be in a specific RFM segment. If there was no purchase in the next 3 months, the customer would move to a lower RFM segment. Sears marketers could track customer migrations through all the segments on a weekly basis. They were able to learn where the customers were coming in, how they were moving around in the file, and what their performance was.

Using the new system, it was possible to do stimulation activities. Analysts could identify Sears customers who left and start reactivation programs. In addition to RFM, they also developed a predictive model. They were able to forecast an annual file growth projection on a weekly basis. They were able to know whether they were growing or shrinking, and where they needed to worry and replan.

Early Warning System

With the new system in place, if a business was starting off below the marketing plan, Sears could readjust and reallocate marketing expenses to deal with it. Customers could be compared not just by RFM segment, but also by media. Do people perform better with a wish book, a sale book, or a spring and summer book? What kind of merchandise do they buy? Do they buy just men's clothing or women's or children's? Do they buy appliances through the catalog?

Analysts could also look at segment payment methods: Sears credit card, third-party card, cash, and how performance differs among them. They could also look at performance by catalog distribution method.

By tracking sales, Sears learned that the half-life of a catalog was 20 days after it was mailed. That means that after 20 days, the company had received half of the orders that it was going to get from that particular catalog. Tracking meant it could determine the entire success of the book by sales made during the first 20 days.

Sear's investment in database marketing paid off:

- Customer activity is now going up, not down as it did for the last decade.
- Sears sales were found to parallel customer activity. Sales are also up.
- Sales from every single catalog but one went up after the database kicked in.
- The Fall and Winter catalog had a 10 percent increase in sales.
- The Christmas Wish Book sales increased 26 percent.
- The first reactivation book went out to people who did not receive the regular catalog. The break-even response rate was 3.5 percent. The actual response rate was 4.5 percent. Sears reactivated 12,000 customers, and made a profit while doing it.

101 Uses for a Database Marketing System

Having tasted success, Sears has set a series of ambitious goals for the future:

Integration of Data. The goal now is to put data about customer behavior on the screens at the telemarketing call centers, so Sears can start target marketing program scripts at the beginning of the calls. Sears also wants to put this information onto the screens of the 1,800 catalog agents who talk to the people when they pick up their packages. Sears wants to take competitive advantage of its data to build relationships that will surprise and please customers.

Migration to Retail Stores. Sears hopes to adapt the database program to its retail operation in the very near future, linking customer data to the point-of-sale system. When you walk into a Sears store and pay for something at the cash register, you will be treated in ways that are distinctive to you, based on your preferences and purchasing behavior.

A Corporate Picture of Customer Behavior. Sears is really three companies: a credit organization, a catalog organization, and a retail organization. The customer, however, sees Sears as one company. Some customers only shop by catalog, some only shop in retail stores. Some shop both.

Suppose that a catalog-only customer spends an average of $100. A retail store-only customer may spend $165 in the store. But a cross-shopper who uses both channels spends $235 in retail and $140 in catalog, for a total of $375 for both channels. These cross-shoppers are Sears core customers. They represent 30 percent of the entire database.

Sears's goal is to market to these valuable people. But the current Sears organization, with its three separate entities, was not built to take advantage of this situation. Sears is going to have to change the corporate culture. Examples of what is being planned include:

- **Specialty programs.** Sears now has a solid business case for a reactivation and prospecting endeavor. It is working on a retention model.
- **Distribution management.** Sears has eight different distribution methods and 13 catalogs. It is building a distribution table to support and manage distribution to reduce the cost.
- **What-if strategies.** Sears now has an improved testing capability. At any given catalog mailing, it can do up to 99 different tests. Sears also has the capability to start developing new catalog media based on the data available on the 7 million names in the database.

The Brighter Side of Sears

Sears Canada is certainly a terrific example of what can be done in database marketing. The list manager had to apply a set of skills that all successful practitioners must master:

- Creating a *marketing* database, instead of relying on an operational system that could not support marketing requirements;

- Cleaning up the data and eliminating duplicates on an old neglected database;
- Developing a new RFM segmentation system;
- Provide marketers with easy access to data that had previously been locked inside a mainframe;
- Using the data to develop essential tools for analysis: lifetime value, RFM predictive modeling, test and control groups, promotion half-life calculation, break-even response rates;
- Using these tools to create innovative programs, including reactive mailings, new distribution and payment methods, and studies of customer behavior by catalog, region, age, family composition, and lifestyle.

Finally, the list manager had to introduce new ways of thinking and cultural change in a large organization with years of history behind it.

Looking at what was able to be done in Canada, one has to wonder what would have happened if the method had been applied to Sears USA when the decision to scrap the U.S. Sears big book was made.

Adapted from: Hughes, A. (1998, March). Back from the brink. Marketing Tools, 5(2), 14,16,18–19.

Arthur Middleton Hughs is executive vice president of ACS, Inc., a database marketing company in Reston, Virginia.

FUTURE TRENDS IN DIRECT MARKETING

Direct-to-consumer marketing is a trend in direct marketing. Many product categories have traditionally had an intermediary that made purchase decisions for the consumer based on advertising that was directed to the intermediary. One example is prescription drugs. The sponsor advertised to the doctor, who then wrote a prescription for the advertised drug to the consumer. The consumer did not participate in the brand decision. **Direct-to-consumer** advertising aims sales to the consumers (Fig. 10.12) who make the purchase. Sponsors of direct-to-consumer advertising believe it is beneficial to the consumer because it encourages dialogue between intermediary and consumer. This trend has developed as a result of the Food and Drug Administration's relaxation of rules governing prescription drug ads on television. In order to advertise prescription drugs to the consumer, however, the FDA has declared that TV commercials must also include information about the potential risks associated with the drugs (Elliott, 1998e). This marks the first time that an advertisement has had to include reasons why not to buy the product.

Figure 10.12

Direct-to-consumer print ad for Claritin.

Implications for direct-to-consumer advertising go beyond prescription drugs. Direct marketing will continue to expand into more direct-to-consumer markets, and advertisements will continue to be monitored to ensure that consumers are receiving accurate information about these products.

Another trend in direct-response media is interactive television. **Interactive television (ITV)** is a form of television entertainment in which the signal activates an electronic apparatus in the viewer's home or the viewer uses the apparatus to affect events on the screen, or both, allowing for viewer control. The user is no longer simply the receiver of the message in the traditional communications model. The user helps to define the amount or type of information he or she wants to receive. The user can choose a brief encounter or seek information over a significant period of time. The request for additional information may take the form of a computer, the touch of a screen, or the push of a button. The user and the source are involved in give and take of data.

Interactive television involves two-way communication between the sponsor and the user of the message. An early use of ITV has been in the academic world. Professors have been able to communicate class lectures through television to remote sites, enabling students in distant locations the opportunity to participate in the educational process. Interactivity allows students at remote locations to fully participate in the class, asking questions of the professors. In turn, the instructor can actively involve students from many different locations.

Viewer control can be achieved in one of three ways (Wells et al., 1998):

- **Video-on-demand (VOD).** Viewers control what and when they watch a specifically televised show such as **pay-per-view (PPV)** movies or sporting events. Pay-for-view allows consumers to watch shows at times predetermined by the entertainment or sports producer.
- **Electronic box.** This system stores information at the television set and allows viewers to choose programs from the box in their home much in the same way that VCRs work.
- **Simulcast.** This system transmits digital information in conjunction with an actual broadcast. Simulcast viewers control the programming by punching in choices on a keypad. Examples include finding out more information during a documentary.

Interactive television has been off to a slow start, but one company has started to deliver. CableSoft Corporation of Burlington, Massachusetts, provides a free interactive service to its cable subscribers along with local weather, traffic reports, classified ads, business listings, and results of local sports at a click of the remote control (Malik, 1998). CableSoft makes money from two advertising sources: local business listings and classified ads, which are very similar to the Yellow Pages. In the future the company hopes to sell banner ads.

On-line retailing will continue to be the trend of the future for direct-response marketing. Table 10.6 is a snapshot of the on-line retailing industry as it was in reported in 1998. The median age of on-line shoppers was 33 with an average household income of $59,000. Over half (57 percent) were college educated and a larger proportion (59 percent) were single. Travel was the leading industry for on-line shopping with $2,091 million in revenues. Consumers ordered $270 million worth on groceries over the Internet and $71 million in clothing.

Table 10.6   **Summary of the On-line Retailing Industry**

Profile of On-line Shoppers in the U.S.		Estimated On-line Revenues by Industry (1998)	
		Industry	Amount[a]
Median age	33	Travel	$2,091
Average household income	$59,000	PC hardware	1,816
Single	59%	Groceries	270
Married	41%	Gifts/flowers	219
Children under 18 at home	34%	Books	216
College degree	57%	PC software	173
Professional	30%	Tickets	127
		Music	81
		Clothing	71

[a]*In millions of dollars.*
Adapted from: Krantz, M. (1998, July 20). Click till you drop. Time, *34–37.*

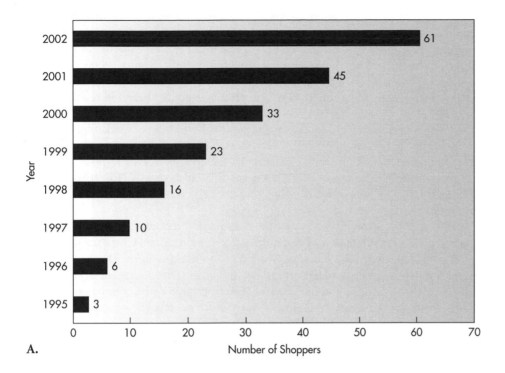

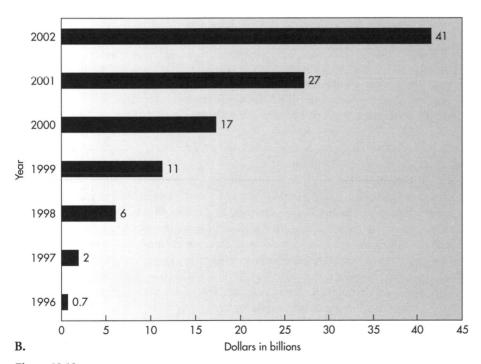

Figure 10.13

A., estimated number of on-line shoppers and B., estimated total on-line shopping revenues (1996–2000).

Adapted from: Krantz, M. (1998, July 20). Click till you drop. Time, *34–37.*

Figure 10.13 projects the number of on-line shoppers and the amount of on-line shopping revenues for each year from 1996 through 2002. It was estimated that in 1998, 16 million consumers were on-line shoppers. The number was projected to rise to 33 million in year 2000, and 61 million shoppers in year 2002 (Krantz, 1998). Total on-line shopping revenues were $.7 billion in 1996, the first year they were reported. Shopping revenues rose to $6 billion in 1998, and estimates predict they will reach $41 billion in 2002.

As with all marketing programs, companies involved in direct marketing must determine which markets to target with which strategies, and then evaluate the effectiveness of the direct marketing program. Computer technologies have improved the quality of print and broadcast messages and led to creative and alternative advertising media. The Internet, CD-ROM, and on-line shopping have all been made possible due to improvements in computer technologies.

Because of the strong emphasis on the consumer, direct marketing works well as a tactic in an integrated marketing communications environment where the same message must be repeatedly and continually delivered to the consumer. Direct marketing strategies rely heavily on understanding the consumer. Direct marketers use a consumer database to identify the specific audience to receive a promotional appeal and to select the direct marketing techniques—such as direct mail, telemarketing and electronic advertising—most likely to bring the promotional message to the consumer's attention.

SUMMARY

- Direct marketing is a promotional strategy created by the sponsoring company or organization to inform consumers in a direct manner.
- Direct-response media include direct mail, print media, telemarketing, broadcast media, on-line services, and out-of-home, among other media.
- Direct mail is all direct-response advertising communications delivered through the mail, including catalogs, cards, card decks, letters, brochures, pamphlets, flyers, video tapes, diskettes, and promotional items.
- Direct-response print media includes any form of printed material that requests a direct response including direct mail, "take one" brochures at stores, package inserts, sales promotion premiums such as matchbooks, Yellow Pages, newspaper advertising inserts, and direct-response advertising space in newspapers and magazines.
- Telemarketing is the selling of products or services, or fundraising for an organization or institution, using the telephone to contact prospective customers.
- Direct-response broadcasting includes all direct-response advertising communications conducted through local, national, or cable radio and television channels including home shopping and infomercials.
- On-line marketing is the newest direct-response marketing strategy. Companies can advertise on commercial on-line services or on World Wide Web sites using banner advertisements or through affiliate networks.
- Direct-response out-of-home include displays that reach consumers on the move through placement on bus shelters, bus exteriors, taxi tops, kiosks, street furniture (newsstands and benches), indoor out-of-home (airport or mall), spectaculars, painted walls, toilet stalls, and blimps.

- Sponsors are continually developing other direct-response media to promote their message to consumers.
- The key to successful direct marketing is efficient and effective database management.
- Target marketing is achieved by using a consumer database to identify the specific population of customers to receive the promotional appeal.
- A database is a collection of data arranged for ease and speed of search and retrieval.
- Direct-to-consumer advertisements and interactive television are future trends in direct marketing.

KEY TERMS

affiliate networks	direct-to-consumer	on-line retailing
banner advertisements	in-bound call	on-premises signage
brokered list	in-house list	on-screen entertainment
cross-selling	Interactive television	out-bound call
database	(ITV)	out-of-home media
direct response	Internet	page
direct-response driver-	one-step approach	pay-per-view
consumers	on-line	trading area
direct sellers	on-line advertisements	two-step approach

QUESTIONS FOR DISCUSSION

1. Why is direct marketing effective as a promotion strategy?
2. What challenges are inherent in direct marketing strategies?
3. What are the strengths and weaknesses of various direct-response promotion strategies?
4. What makes a database list effective?
5. What are the pros and cons of maintaining a database list in-house?
6. How can vendors acquire names for a database?
7. Identify other product categories (besides prescription drugs) that have a traditional intermediary (e.g., doctor) between the advertiser and the consumer. What is the probability of the advertisers' going directly to the consumer with their messages?

ADDITIONAL REFERENCES

Cohen, W. A. (1996). *Building a mail order business: A complete manual for success* (4th ed.). New York: Wiley.

Eicoff, A., and Eicoff, A. (1995). *Direct marketing though broadcast media: TV, radio, cable, infomercials, home shopping and more.* Lincolnwood, IL: NTC.

Evans, R. C. (1993). *Marketing channels: Infomercials and the future of televised marketing.* Upper Saddle River, NJ: Prentice-Hall.

Hallberg, G. (1995). *All consumers are not created equal: The differential marketing strategy for brand loyalty and profits.* New York: Wiley.

Hawthorne, T. B. (1997). *The complete guide to infomercial marketing.* Lincolnwood, IL: NTC.

Hughes, A. (1996). *The complete database marketer* (2nd ed.). New York: McGraw Hill.

McDonald, W. (1997). *Direct marketing: An integrated approach.* New York: McGraw Hill.

Reitman, J. (1996). *Beyond 2000: The future of direct marketing.* Lincolnwood, IL: NTC.

Figure 11.1

A vending machine that dispenses merchandise from Polo Jeans Company is an attention-grabbing sales promotion vehicle.

chapter 11

SALES PROMOTION

Everyone is familiar with vending machines, those devices stationed in high traffic areas that spit out drinks, chips, or candy. Now, adding a new twist to an old standby, the Polo Jeans Company has introduced vending machines that, with the swipe of a card, dispense clothes, accessories, or prize certificates (Coin-op, 1999). The PJC vending machine (Fig. 11.1) is the size of a standard beverage vending machine and is illustrated with images of the current advertising campaign as part of an integrated marketing communications promotion. When the machine was featured at a trade show, VIP customers received a collectible PJC single-use swipe card through the mail. These limited edition collectible VIP cards gave added value to recipients for future retail promotions. According to Michael Nash, Public Relations Director for Polo Jeans Company, the purpose of the promotion is "to provide for exciting and interactive POP, in-store, and specialty distribution programs, while reaching out to VIP customers and rewarding the growing clientele base" (personal communication, April 20, 1999). The vending machines were mass distributed at surprise locations in the fall of 1999 and included product giveaways and contest redemptions. Polo Jeans Company planned to use the vending machines for promotions 5 months per year and for sales of limited edition apparel the other 7 months. The PJC vending machine is one example of a sales promotion technique used to encourage brand loyalty.

After you have read this chapter, you should be able to:

Discuss the role of sales promotion activities in integrated marketing communications.

Examine the growth of sales promotion.

Describe objectives of consumer-oriented sales promotions.

Explain consumer-oriented sales promotion techniques.

Describe objectives of trade-oriented sales promotions.

Explain trade-oriented sales promotion techniques.

This chapter begins by defining sales promotion and discussing the significance and growth of sales promotion as a marketing activity. Next, we evaluate consumer-oriented sales promotion and describe the techniques of consumer-oriented sales promotion. Consumers are not the only target market for sales promotion. Trade-oriented sales promotions are another part of the promotion mix that is discussed, including techniques for trade-oriented sales promotion. The final segment of this chapter concentrates on sales promotion management. The chapter concludes with a discussion of the future direction of sales promotion.

ROLE OF SALES PROMOTION

Sales promotion refers to those activities that provide extra value or incentives to the sales force, distributors, or ultimate consumer. It is a set of paid marketing endeavors, other than advertising and personal sales, sponsored by the vendor, to encourage buyer action through a direct incentive intended to add extra desirability to a purchase. Table 11.1 features the top 20 sales promotion agencies.

As we learned in Chapter 7, appeals are used to provide consumers with a reason to buy a service or product. Once the consumer has a reason to buy the product or service, sales promotion is used to prompt its actual purchase. The **incentive**, something put in place to induce action or motivate effort, is the chief element of the promotion and is used to attract the consumer with a promise of reward. Incentives are used to stimulate an immediate sale. Incentives take on various forms, including coupons, price reductions, gift-with-purchase, purchase-with-purchase, refunds, rebates, opportunities to enter a contest or sweepstakes, or an extra amount of the product. Cosmetic companies give away free samples of fragrances and other products to encourage

Table 11.1   **Top 20 U.S. Sales Promotion Agencies**

Rank 1997	Agency	U.S. Sales Promotion Gross Income, 1997[a]
1	Carlson Marketing Group	$160.2
2	Alcone Marketing Group	115.5
3	Gage Marketing Group	85.0
4	Frankel & Company	77.7
5	TLP Inc.	51.0
6	HMG Worldwide	45.8
7	Cyrk Worldwide	42.8
8	Integer Group	33.0
9	GMR Marketing	31.9
10	Ryan Partnership	28.3
11	QLM Marketing	27.4
12	Draft Worldwide	27.2
13	Ross Roy Communications	27.1
14	Aspen Marketing Group	24.0
15	Dugan Valva Contess	23.1
16	Flair Communications	21.1
17	Clarion Marketing & Communications	19.9
18	J. Brown/LMC Group	19.0
19	Market Growth Resources	18.6
20	Eison Freeman	17.1

[a]*Dollars in thousands*

Adapted from: Top 25 sales promotion agencies 1997. (1998, April 27). Advertising Age *[On-line]. Available: http://www.adage.com/dataplace/archives/dp282.html.*

purchases of the sampled product. Producers may couple sunscreen and after-sun moisturizing lotions in specially priced promotional packages of other products to stimulate sales of both products.

Calvin Klein used a very sophisticated incentive program to create publicity at the spring 1998 presentation for Calvin Klein accessories. Fashion editors whom Klein considered opinion formers and influencers were given free shoes. Each editor was invited to order from a choice of seven styles that ranged in retail value from $145 to $210. The event was used to promote Calvin Klein shoes by putting them into the wardrobes of these influential fashion editors (White, 1997b).

Incentives have become so important to trade consumers in corporate America that a trade group, the Incentive Marketing Association, was formed in 1998 to represent incentive merchandise and service providers and expand the incentive market customer base.

Sales promotion activities may also be used to encourage the consumer to purchase an image. Image is a strategy used to position a company as completely different from the competition. Many companies include image development in their corporate mission statement. Sales promotions designed to promote an image may include opportunities for the consumer to purchase a specific image-oriented gift. Selling promotional CDs that were music collections, compiled to represent the image of the retailer, was a trend in the late 1990s. Pottery Barn, a home furnishings company, used this sales promotion technique to establish a new, more *chic* image. To get its new image across to customers, it sent them home with *Martini Lounge,* a jazz CD. According to one store manager, the retailer was transforming its style from rustic to city, changing the dress code from khaki to black and white, and jazz went with the new lounge image (Levy, 1997). Other retailers that have been successful using this sales promotion technique include Williams-Sonoma, Banana Republic, and Starbucks.

Retailers may also promote a corporate image through contributions to nonprofit causes, such as the Children's Miracle Network or Save the Rainforest. Retailers may use their willingness to contribute to the cause as an incentive for consumers to purchase certain items or make an additional contribution at the point-of-sale. These retailers may use point-of-purchase displays to sell merchandise specially manufactured for the promotion, or ask consumers to add an additional amount to their payment. In both cases, the contributed amount would go to the nonprofit cause. In a third scenario, retailers promote their image as a good community partner by contributing a percentage of sales during a 1-day or several-hour sale to the nonprofit cause. This is used as an incentive to encourage consumers to buy during these times.

Sales promotion activities are designed to encourage buyers to make purchases. For example, extra incentives are used to encourage consumers to purchase larger quantities of the product. By encouraging the consumer to buy immediately, the vendor is shortening the purchase cycle. The **purchase cycle** is the interval of time between acquisition and replacement of the same or a similar product in a routine manner. The purchase cycle of health and beauty products may be several months, whereas the purchase cycle of a winter coat may be 2 or 3 years. Certain sales promotion techniques boost the consumer to replace a product before he or she has completely finished the current supply. Coupons with an expiration date or limited time offer are examples of sales promotions used to accelerate the purchase process.

Sales promotion is also used in simplified selling situations. **Simplified selling** allows the customer direct contact with the merchandise through "self-service" (Fig. 11.2) In these situations, sales promotion displays and incentives can provide consumers with

Figure 11.2

Self-service display units encourage consumers to buy by simplifying the selection of merchandise.

information and encourage them to make purchases. Retail firms that concentrate on the sale of convenience goods, items purchased at the most convenient acceptable outlet, will use the simplified method of selling. A sales incentive such as a coupon or a bonus pack can influence the purchase, causing the customer to change brands or purchase a larger quantity of the item. Most items purchased at a grocery store are considered convenience goods. Convenience goods are often lower priced merchandise and the simplified method of selling allows retailers to reduce their selling costs associated with these items.

Both retailers and customers find simplified selling to be more efficient for merchandise categories that are already packaged and presold through extensive sales promotion generally at the national level. Hosiery is always prepackaged and displayed in units that allow for easy access to the product. Lingerie manufacturers, including Playtex and Maidenform, box their products. Brand-loyal customers trust the product to be consistent from purchase to purchase.

SIGNIFICANCE AND GROWTH OF SALES PROMOTION

In the 1990s, the importance of sales promotion activities increased significantly (Belch and Belch, 1995). While consumer promotion stayed relatively constant, trade promotion has increased greatly, displacing advertising expenditures. According to Donnelley Marketing, in the mid 1980s marketers allocated 26 percent of their marketing budget to consumer promotion and 37 percent each to advertising and trade promotion. By

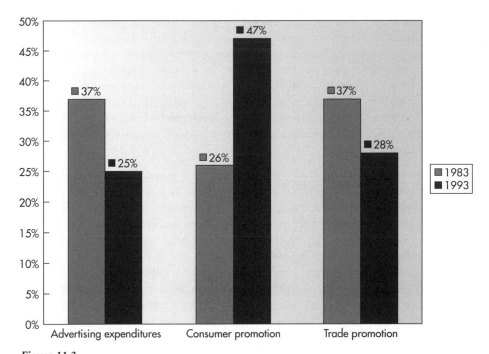

Figure 11.3

The change in trade and consumer promotion and advertising expenditures over a 10-year period.

Source: Belch, G.E. and Belch, M.A. (1995) Introduction to advertising and promotion: An integrated marketing communications perspective *(3rd ed.). Chicago: Irwin.*

the mid 1990s companies had shifted allocations. They slightly increased their consumer promotion to 28 percent, and greatly increased trade promotion to 47 percent. Increased sales promotion forced advertising expenditures to decrease to 25 percent of the total marketing budget. This change is reflected is Figure 11.3.

There are two reasons for the shift from advertising to sales promotion. First, there has been a transfer of power from manufacturers to retailers. Consumer product manufacturers for many years had power over retailers in the form of information. Manufacturers knew which brands sold well because they created demand for these brands by using advertising and consumer-oriented promotions, such as coupons. Retailers relied on the manufacturers to provide sales analysis and did very little research on their own to determine which brands were good performers and which were poor performers in the marketplace. With the development of optical checkout scanners and computers, however, sales analysis information became available to retailers. Retailers have the tools within their stores to track good and poor performance of products. Roles have reversed and retailers are now in a position to tell manufacturers which products they will carry instead of accepting the manufacturer-determined product assortment. A manufacturer who is able to provide discounts and promotional support will be given shelf space; a manufacturer who does not comply will have less space or may even be dropped. The advertising budget that a manufacturer once used to promote a specific brand to the consumer has now been replaced with a trade discount to the retailer.

Second, branding, discussed in Chapter 7, is another big influence on the shift from advertising expenditures to sales promotion expenditures. Individuals within an organization responsible for managing the marketing program for a specific brand use sales promotion techniques in an attempt to keep loyal customers and to gain new customers. Using the focus group method, Langer Associates conducted research on consumer preferences for branded merchandise (Shermach, 1997). Results clustered consumers into several categories based on their loyalty to branded merchandise. The clusters include steadfast consumers, loyalty minimizers, category contingent consumers, and image rejectors.

- **Steadfast consumers** declare their loyalty to a brand as a sign of character. It is highly unlikely that sales promotion will change the attitude of a steadfast consumer.
- **Loyalty minimizer consumers** consider themselves free agents willing to shop for the best price. However, they will return to their favorite brand if price is not substantially different. Sales promotion techniques aimed at price reduction have an opportunity to influence loyalty minimizers.
- **Category contingent consumers** are semiloyal based on the product category. If a product is important to them and they perceive a difference among brands, the category contingent consumer will be loyal to his or her preferred brand. Sales promotions may be used to reinforce to the consumer the perceived difference between brands.
- **Image rejecter consumers** have no loyalty to brands and base every buying decision on product characteristics and price.

Two concurrent phenomena in the 1990s concerning branded products have influenced the growth of sales promotion. First, the number of new brands introduced by manufacturers has saturated the marketplace. Often these brands have no distinguishable attributes in the minds of the consumer. This causes advertising to be less effective. Second, the saturation of branded merchandise within the marketplace has caused consumers to become less brand loyal. Modern consumers are more interested in price, value, and convenience. As a result, advertising dollars that in the past were used to persuade a customer to purchase a specific brand name product are now being transferred to sales promotion to persuade consumers to try new brands. This is because the added value of a sales incentive has more influence in creating sales than do advertising messages.

The growth of sales promotion in the 1990s effected both consumer-oriented and trade-oriented sales promotion. Next we discuss these two types of sales promotion.

CONSUMER-ORIENTED SALES PROMOTION

Sales promotion activities exist at both the consumer and trade market levels. The ultimate consumer or product user is the target of consumer-oriented sales promotion. These activities include contests, coupons, gift-with-purchase, purchase-with-purchase, point-of-sale displays, refunds, rebates, sweepstakes, and sampling. These activities encourage prompt purchase of the product and improve short-term sales.

Victoria's Secret Fashion Show. The Internet is an emerging global medium. It is also emerging as an essential tool in integrated marketing communications campaigns. Victoria's Secret used the Internet to broadcast a live fashion show. The fashion show was considered the most watched Internet fashion event to date in 1999. Much of the show's success can be attributed to the IMC campaign that was staged prior to the event. The *Wall Street Journal* was lined up as a corporate sponsor. Print ads such as this one from *BusinessWeek* and on-line banner ads were used to publicize the event. Additionally, in one well-placed broadcast ad, the fashion show was promoted during the 1999 Superbowl, one week prior to the fashion show. The IMC campaign combined traditional and non-conventional promotion mix tools to sell Victoria's Secret's image and merchandise to the world.

High Tech
High Fashion

Hi Wall Street

See the Victoria's Secret Fashion Show LIVE online.

This Wednesday, tickers will be racing after the markets close. The Victoria's Secret Fashion Show will be broadcast LIVE, online, for the first time ever. Stephanie, Tyra, Laetitia, Karen, Daniela, Heidi, and twenty more of the most beautiful women in the world hit the runway on February 3, at 7 pm, EST. So get to **www.VictoriasSecret.com**. It's proof positive that you can turn more than profits on the internet.

VICTORIA'S SECRET
A division of Intimate Brands, Inc. / NYSE: IBI

Jane, a consumer lifestyle magazine targeting women 18-34, features articles on fashion, beauty, and celebrities. The premier issue was published in 1997. Fairchild Publications developed a campaign using the image of a nametag with the slogan *HELLO my name is JANE* to promote the publication. In addition to print ads, media placement included out-of-home media using signage on storefronts, New York City buses, and highway billboards. The campaign was successful because it had a simple idea and a high frequency rate to presell the magazine.

Color Plate 3

Givenchy Haute Couture Collection 1999. Haute couture, considered the highest quality fashion design and construction, pushes the limit of fashion twice a year with shows in Paris and Milan. Colors, fibers, and fabrications are combined to make beautiful, if not extravagant designs, which will be the inspiration for trends that trickle down to ready-to-wear, bridge, and moderate lines. In 1999, Alexander McQueen showed his collection for Givenchy on mannequins that rose up at intervals through the floor, creating an exciting new presentation approach for haute couture fashions.

Source: Photos by Giannoni Giovanni and Stephane Feugere for Women's Wear Daily.

Target, pronounced "Tar-zhay" with a French accent by its many fans, leads discount retailers with its *Cheap is Chic* products. In order to promote its trendy clothing and household designs, Target has held fashion shows in Manhattan, introduced housewares designed by architect Michael Graves to compete with Kmart's Martha Stewart products, and produced television commercials that feature the red and white Target logo.

Source: © 1999 Dayton Hudson Brands, Inc. Agency: Peterson, Milla, Hooks.

The Sixth Annual Nurses Ball on *General Hospital* and *Port Charles,* the ABC soap operas, was a merging of real-life and fictional promotion campaigns. Characters on the shows wore a T-shirt to promote the event, a fundraiser for the fight against AIDS. In the real-world campaign, which lasted from mid-June through August 1999, the T-shirt was sold via print ads and promotional spots on TV featuring a toll-free phone number, as well as on the abc.com website. A portion of the proceeds was donated to organizations combating the disease. This charitable promotion also provided publicity for the shows and the network.

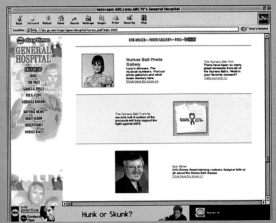

Source: © American Broadcasting Company, Inc. Not to be reprinted without permission.

Color Plate 6

Pretty Polly, well-known U.K. hosiery brand, was successfully reintroduced to the British market after years of declining sales. Helen Atkins, Pretty Polly's marketing director, devised a relaunch that included product and package redesign, point-of-purchase presentations, advertising, public relations, and sales promotion. With a limited budget, the new image was presented on 60-foot billboards placed in high traffic areas and attached to a helicopter flown over parts of London. The traffic stopping signs created newsworthy stories that were featured in the British press and on television.

Source: Courtesy of Sara Lee Corporation

Color Plate 7

Intel **Bunny People.** As a promotion tool, fashion shows create one of the most spectacular atmospheres to excite consumers. Fashion shows combine lights, music, and models to entertain and electrify audiences about merchandise. Realizing the effect fashion shows can have on an audience, Intel created an advertising campaign for the Pentium II processor that featured models in flashy colored cleanroom suits carrying processor chips as props down the runway. It is a compliment to this promotion mix tool that a supplier of nonfashion goods would use it in a successful campaign.

It's the new look.

The Pentium® II processor for a whole new style of computing.

Intel's engineers have done it again. Their latest design, the Pentium® II processor, is unlike anything you've ever seen—from its unique package to the amazing effect it has on your multimedia applications. That's because it's been designed with new architectural features, plus Intel MMX™ media enhancement technology. Now, enhancing your favorite photos or making a video phone call on your PC is better than ever. The Pentium II processor. You'll love what it does for your image. ▶ www.intel.com/home

The Computer Inside.™

Explore II, the 800-square-foot museum store at the Pacific Science Center in Seattle, was selected by the Institute of Store Planners and editors of *VM + SD* as the 1998 Store of the Year in the category of specialty stores under 2000 square feet . Because the store would not be advertised and exterior store signage was restricted, Smash Design, the project architects and designers, were challenged to make the space memorable. Fixtures, which included the green "Blades" and orange "Whale," were inspired by modernist sculptor Alexander Calder. Three columns, made from glass mosaic tiles, were created to draw attention to the store and provide lockable display space for small merchandise.

Source: Courtesy of Smash Design, Seattle, WA. Photo by Rex Rystedt/seattlephoto.com.

Objectives

There are many different sales promotion techniques to encourage consumer purchase of products and services. Each technique or incentive is established with a specific objective in mind. Objectives of consumer-oriented sales promotion include trial and re-purchase of a new or existing product, increasing consumption of an existing brand, defending current consumers from the competition, and strengthening advertising and marketing efforts.

Trial

Influencing a consumer to make a **trial purchase** of a new or improved product is the objective of many sales promotion techniques. When a new brand does not have distinguishable attributes in the mind of the consumer, the manufacturer must use techniques other than advertising to encourage purchase of the new products. The consumer is encouraged to test a trial-size portion of the new product. The trial size is often free or discounted significantly to avoid risk on the part of the consumer.

Repurchase

Increasing consumption of an established brand through repurchase is a major objective of sales promotion. Competition between established brand names is strong. Consumers have tried different products and are content with their choice. With established brands, advertising as part of the integrated marketing communications approach is used to maintain brand awareness. Sales promotion can also be used to increase sales of the established brand and defend the brand against competitors.

Increasing Consumption of an Existing Brand

Increased sales of an established product may be generated through showing the consumer a new way to use the product. Recipes or other materials identifying the new use may be accompanied by a sales promotion coupon. Increased sales of an established brand may also be generated by attracting nonusers of the product. Sales promotions used to attract nonusers must be designed to change the mind of a nonuser who sees no need for the product. It is often easier for a brand manager to attract customers who use the competition than it is to attract nonusers.

Defending Current Consumers from Competition

The best way for a brand manager to dissuade current customers from purchasing competing brands is to keep the consumer stocked with the manager's brand at all times. Special incentives may load consumers up with the product before they have a chance to buy the competing brand. Additionally, brand managers may offer to redeem a competitor's coupon to defend against the competition. Sales promotion techniques encourage consumers to buy the product early and often to ensure that a brand will keep its current customer base.

Strengthening Advertising and Marketing Efforts

A successful IMC promotion package will use sales promotion techniques to strengthen the advertising and marketing efforts that are already in place. These sales promotions may include sweepstakes or contests in which the consumer is asked to read an advertisement in order to learn the rules or fill out an entry blank. Forcing the consumer to read the advertisement will reinforce the message. Sweepstakes and contests are only two of many techniques used in consumer-oriented sales promotion that are discussed next.

Techniques

Various sales promotion techniques are used to accomplish the consumer-oriented sales promotion objectives discussed in the previous section. These appeals include sampling, coupons, premiums, gift-with-purchase or purchase-with-purchase programs, contests and sweepstakes, refunds and rebates, bonus packs, price-off deals, reward programs and frequent-buying clubs, deferred billing, and event sponsorship.

Sampling

Sampling is a sales promotion technique in which a small quantity of a product is given to a consumer at no charge to coax a trial use. Companies evaluate the possibility for sampling of a product based on three factors:

1. The product has a relatively low unit cost so that samples will not be too expensive for the producer to manufacture.

Figure 11.4

A magazine insert with a fragrance sample. Fragrance testers are not limited to women's scents.

2. The product is easily divided into small sample sizes that are adequate to demonstrate the brand's features and benefits.
3. The purchase cycle of the product is short so that the consumer will consider an immediate purchase of the sampled product.

Samples are distributed through direct-response marketing efforts, at in-store demonstrations, or on the packaging of other products. Mailed samples are generally small, lightweight, and nonperishable. Sampling through the mail is controlled through the use of segmentation tools described in Chapter 2. Zip code and income level are common segmentation factors for mailed samples. Increasing postal rates and expanded postal restrictions are detriments to mailed samples.

Fragrance strips are a common product sample inserted in magazines (Fig. 11.4). In 1965, 3M developed the first scratch-and-sniff test strip, called Microfragrance. Arcade, an international scent sampling manufacturer, introduced Scent Strips into magazine advertisements in 1979. The Scent Strip allowed mass distribution of fragrances away from the retail fragrance counter for the first time by developing an accurate rendition of the fragrance between two sheets of paper. Arcade has produced more than 20 billion scented samples in various forms since the first Scent Strip. The samples can be inserted in magazines, store handouts, catalogs, envelopes, direct mail, hang tags, postcards, and other formats. Air France has put fragrance samples in its ticket jackets. The American fragrance industry has tripled retail sales volume to an estimated $6 billion since the introduction of the Scent Strip (Larson, 1997), showing a correlation between sampling and industry growth.

In-store sampling is a technique in which samples are distributed in the retail environment. In-store sampling has become increasingly popular to test food products. Consumers are becoming aware of this sales promotion technique and depend on certain retailers to always have samples available. Benefits of in-store sampling include immediate availability of the product if the consumer decides to purchase the sampled item. In-store sampling requires planning to ensure tables, trash receptacles, and electricity are available if needed. Selling space must be used to accommodate the demonstration. If consumers do not choose to buy the product, in-store sampling may be viewed as a sales promotion technique that is too expensive.

On-packaging sampling refers to a trial size sample that is placed on the product or within another product. On-package sampling is very effective for a specific target market that already uses the accompanying product. On-packaging sampling does not work for the nonuser audience.

More than other sales promotion techniques, sampling works cross-culturally, because the product, such as a fragrance or a lipstick color, does not have to rely on language to represent it. The scent or the color and the vendor logo provide enough information and do not have to be translated into other languages. Because of this, sampling is on the rise internationally, particularly in France and Poland (Fine, Dang, and Todé, 1997).

Sampling is the most successful sales promotion technique used to encourage the use of a new product, because it offers a risk-free opportunity for a nonuser to try the product. However, the cost to produce trial samples, including product and packaging, and the fact that trial samples given away provide no revenue, cause sampling to be a very expensive sales promotion technique. This may prevent some retailers and manufacturers from using this technique.

Figure 11.5

Coupons encourage consumers to shop during special hours or on special days.

Coupons

Coupons are printed forms or vouchers that entitle the bearer to certain benefits, such as a cash refund or a gift when redeemed. A coupon may also be attached to a product and be redeemed for a cash discount. C. W. Post Company began using this price-reduction technique in 1895, by offering a penny-off coupon for breakfast cereal.

Manufacturer coupons are a very popular sales promotion technique for both new and established products. Coupons controlled by the manufacturer do not rely on the retailer for cooperation. Coupons allow the price-sensitive consumer to purchase a product at a reduced cost, while not decreasing the cost to all consumers. Those consumers who are not as price-sensitive will overlook the coupon but will still buy the product at the producer's regular marked price. As with sampling, a coupon can reduce the perceived risk to the consumer, encouraging the consumer to try a new product. Coupons are also incentives for the repurchase of a product once a sample has been tried.

Retailer-sponsored coupons are becoming popular to entice consumers to shop at their store during busy selling seasons. During the high-volume selling period between Thanksgiving Day and Christmas Day, department stores use coupons to encourage customers to shop during 2-hour, 1-day, or weekend-only sales (Fig. 11.5). Advertisements complete with coupons may invite customers to shop at the *biggest sale of the year when you bring in this coupon,* or may tell customers, *You will receive the lowest prices of the year with this coupon.* Catalog retailers use coupons as direct-response media to stimulate buyers who have not made recent purchases. Promotional messages may state, *We haven't heard from you in a while . . . use the attached coupon to receive 15% off your next purchase.* This is a recent trend, and such coupons are expanding rapidly as a new approach to generate repeat sales from proven customers.

Coupons are distributed through newspapers, magazines, and direct-response, or are enclosed in product packaging. The most popular distribution channel is through freestanding inserts within newspapers. Newspaper distribution causes brand awareness in consumers who purposely look for coupons in Sunday editions or on "food day," the day in which all grocery store ads appear in the paper, usually Tuesday or Wednesday. Manufacturers also place coupons in or on the packaging of the same or similar products. This method is popular because there are no additional distribution costs. A coupon that is good for redemption of the same product is called a **bounce-back coupon**. It encourages the consumer to repurchase the same brand. A **cross-ruff coupon** encourages the consumer to buy a different product manufactured by the same producer. An **instant coupon** is a form placed on the outside of a package to encourage the consumer to immediately redeem the coupon.

The advantage of coupons is the ability to offer price reductions to those targeted customers who need this incentive to purchase the product. By searching for and using a coupon, consumers self-identify their need for the incentive. Consumers who would purchase the product anyway do not need the incentive and are less likely to use the coupon, and the cost associated with the promotion is not wasted on these consumers.

A disadvantage to coupons is tracking. It is impossible to know when a consumer is going to use a coupon. Although expiration dates are printed on some coupons to accelerate the purchase of the product, response is rarely immediate. Additionally, coupons that are intended to attract new buyers are often redeemed by current users of the product. Instead of increasing market share with new users, coupons decrease profit margins when redeemed by current users. In recent years coupons have become less important to consumers, and therefore, some food and household supplies manufacturers have considered eliminating coupon programs, using the dollars saved from this trade promotion to reduce the retail price of the product.

Premiums

Have you ever been offered a free travel clock when you renewed a subscription? Or, been offered a free T-shirt if you present a card at a new store opening? The travel clock and the T-shirt are premiums. **Premiums**, also known as **ad specialties**, are gifts or merchandise offered free or at a reduced price as an inducement to buy something else. We are all familiar with the prizes that appear in Cracker Jacks. These were the first premiums, developed in 1912. Premiums can be almost anything from logo coffee mugs, mousepads, pens, book bags, caps, and T-shirts to other novelty items. They may be given away or included in a package or sent to consumers, who mail in a request and a proof of purchase. Use of premiums as incentives is on the rise. Premium incentives accounted for 29 percent of all expenditures on promotions, or $20.5 billion dollars, in 1996, a 90-percent increase from 1990 (Heath, 1997). Customers who receive premiums will reorder sooner than those who received a coupon. Breakfast cereals use premiums as a popular incentive to purchase brands.

Premiums can be expensive for a vendor to produce and to package within a product. Children are more enticed by premiums than adults. A particularly poor premium, because of selection or quality, targeted to adults may do more harm for a product than good. Sales promotion premiums play an important role in encouraging consumers to buy a product. But a business must be careful that the premium does not backfire, either by being too costly or turning off the consumer. Daly (1998) has provided seven ways that a business can get positive results from using consumer-oriented sales promotion products. These techniques are highlighted in Box 11.1.

BOX 11.1

How to Turn Yesterday's Giveaways into Today's Promotional Power

Industry spends an estimated $2 billion a year on promotional products or "ad specialties." Produced by the millions, they range in price from pennies a piece to literally thousands of dollars each.

Almost without exception, these products are "imprinted with a company name or message." Most of these items are viewed as "goodwill builders," "gimmicks," or "giveaways" for attracting attention.

To describe them as essential to promoting a business would be a substantial exaggeration in the minds of most ad specialty or promotional product buyers. In good times, when there is plenty of money in the company coffers, buying giveaways can be justified, but when things get tight, forget about the pens, T-shirts, coffee mugs, and colorful sunglasses.

Yet there are significant examples of how promotional products can play an integral role in setting the stage for companies to increase sales. In effect, the power is not in the promotional product, but in the way a particular product or item is used. Many firms are getting positive results from carefully crafted promotional programs built around the right promotional product.

Here are seven ways to put the persuasive power of promotional products to work:

1. Choose a Product with the Correct Fit for What You Want to Accomplish

A business owner took delivery of a new Lincoln Continental several years ago. He had dreamed about the moment he would be handed the keys to his first luxury automobile. The day arrived and the car was delivered to his office by the salesman. But, he will never forget when the keys were dropped in his hand, attached to a cheap, plastic key holder. He had spent more than $30,000 for the car and the dealer had diminished the importance of the sale by giving him a 19-cent key ring!

On the other hand, an aggressive insurance broker offered custom T-shirts at a landscape contractor trade show for completing a brief information form. The shirts went like hotcakes because the company invested time, effort, and money in creating a shirt with attractive, colorful artwork and an appropriate, creative message: "We dig landscaping." Every contractor wanted a shirt. It could be worn anytime, anywhere, because it told the contractor's story and, by implication, it sent the landscapers a message about the insurance agency.

At a very small show, this insurance agency wrote five new accounts and received an additional 26 qualified leads. Each shirt cost about $10. Was it worth the money? Yes! The insurance agency has already signed up for the next landscapers' trade show.

By making the promotional product fit what you want to accomplish, you actually build business. By the way, the auto dealer could have accomplished his goal of impressing the customer by using a leather key holder imprinted with the customer's name and placing it in a presentation case.

2. Build Your Promotion around a Theme

More often than not, it is not the promotional product itself that turns out to be the problem. It is the way it is used that renders the item ineffective.

A bank in Miami, Florida, did it the right way. When the bank moved one of its branches, the marketing director realized most of the customers were senior adults who might be wary of going to the new location, even though it was less than a mile away from the old office. The bank's marketing agency came up with a comedy theme, "Laugh All the Way to the Bank," for a promotional program designed to appeal to the senior market and acquaint the older customers with the new locations. Customers were given a fun (but inexpensive) gift—hand buzzers, whoopie cushions, windup "chattering" teeth, bent pencils—each time they came in and used a banking service at the new branch. The promotion resulted in retaining the current customers and actually introducing many to banking services they had never used. When the promotion came to an end, the results were positive for both the bank and its customers.

3. Make Sure to Do a Good Job Connecting the Promotional Product with Your Business

Just handing out pens or mailing calendars is not enough. There is nothing to connect the gift with your company, yet it is the connection that makes the difference.

A marketing services firm wrote an article asking the question, "What does every customer want?" the answer was "ESS," which stands for enthusiasm, solutions, and service, the three qualities customers expect from people they do business with. When clients asked what ESS stood for, the firm offered them a gold "ESS" lapel pin, attached to an attractive, colorful card explaining ESS.

As a result of the article being published, the marketing firm has, over the past few years, distributed several thousand ESS pins, which have come to symbolize its creativity and understanding of what customers expect. In other words, a simple three-letter pin has come to express a company's philosophy—and the company name does not appear on it!

4. Use the Promotional Product to Get Attention

Cutting through all the clutter and getting the customer's attention is the key to marketing today. If used correctly, promotional products can make the difference between dull and innovative.

A financial services company had spent millions of dollars in print advertising in an unsuccessful attempt to get the attention of companies relocating to areas where the firm has offices. The company's ad agency came up with another approach, which was highly focused and aimed at just six people—the key executives of an international firm. Each one received a $400 leather briefcase filled with an exciting array of executive gifts and pertinent information about the company and the area. The briefcases provided the recipients with a thorough "briefing" for both relocating and for doing business with the company.

So impressive was this rather unorthodox presentation that one company officer receiving a briefcase called the financial services firm and made arrangements to deposit $18 million! A $10-million advertising campaign could not get the attention of the right people—a briefcase with the right message did.

5. Take Advantage of the Power of Personalization

What should be the most obvious benefits of a promotional product is often missed. It is the use of the recipient's name, whether it is an individual, a company or an organization. Everything from pencils to plaques can be personalized.

Tens of thousands of coffee mugs are given away every day. Some are used in offices, others are taken to someone's vacation cabin, while a majority wind up on a shelf somewhere. But not the 400 mugs presented to the employees of a manufacturing company in Massachusetts.

As part of a major safety program, the employees received coffee mugs, individually personalized with their names. Instantly, the mugs became personal property, as if a "this is mine; do not touch" sign went on each one. More than anything else, personalized gifts are perceived to be of more value. They go beyond just giving something. Those receiving the gifts know someone took the time to think specifically of them. That is what gives the personalized gift its unusual power.

6. Enhance the Impact of a Promotional Product by Giving It Special Value

Magnets are particularly popular today. Refrigerators and filing cabinets are covered with them. But does anyone really read what they say? Or is their value inherent in what they do—hold pages, notes, orders, and whatever? In other words, magnets may be seen and used, but that is where it ends.

This need not be the end, however, as a regional accounting firm has discovered. Instead of choosing some cute little magnet, the firm decided on one that measures 3 3/4 [inches] by 8 [inches]. Designed specifically for the front of filing cabinets, the magnet lists which financial records should be kept for what periods of time in order to meet tax requirements.

Are these magnets useful? Absolutely. Will the accounting firm's name be on display in dozens and dozens of offices? Of course. But it is not only the firm's current clients who are requesting the magnets. Others want them, too. As a result, the magnets are actually creating leads.

What is important to note is that lists of records to keep have been around for decades. No one could remember where they were filed. Now, they are right where they belong—on the front of the file drawer—along with the accounting firm's name and telephone number.

7. Finally, Remember that "Memorable" Is of Far More Value than "Useful"

"We want something that will be used on a person's desk," is the common request. If it meets the "useful test," it is considered a valuable promotional product. In many situations, passing the "memorable test" is far more important to achieving the goal. The briefcases were memorable first and useful second.

Soon after the Gulf War ended, a marketing services firm ordered 100 "Desert Storm" camouflage pens, with the company name imprinted in gold. The pens were sent to prospects with an accompanying letter indicating that a marketing firm's role is to increase the visibility of its clients, while it stays in the background unseen. More than a year later, people were still talking about the camouflage pens. The mailing was memorable.

The president of the company that mailed the pens opened an envelope one day from someone who had received a pen. But the sheet of letterhead inside was blank, so he called the prospect. Instantly, the prospect's secretary started to laugh over the phone stating, "He wrote the letter with invisible ink from the camouflage pen." Memorable makes the difference. When that particular prospect became a client, the agreement was signed in real ink. The purpose of a promotional product is to actually promote the company and its products and services. In the final analysis, it is not the product that has the power, it is the impact of the gift on the recipient.

Whether it is persuading customers to come to your business, to your party, to your store opening, or to think of you when they need what you do, promotional products can help give power to your message.

Adapted from: Daly, E. (1998, March 1). How to turn yesterday's giveaway into today's promotional power. American Salesman *43 (7), 24.[On-line], Available: http://www.elibrary.com.*

Ellen Daly is manager of The Bankette Co., located in Quincy, MA. The firm is a leading resource for promotional products.

Direct premiums are attached to or placed inside the promoted item and available immediately to the consumer upon purchase. **Mail-in premiums** require the consumer to send in a proof-of-purchase to receive the gift. Generally they require more than one proof-of-purchase. These premiums encourage repeat purchases and brand loyalty.

Figure 11.6

Barbie and Hot Wheels are offered as mail-in premiums as an incentive to purchase Cheerios.

However, the consumer must take the initiative to send away for the premium and the immediate reward for the consumer is lost. Figure 11.6 offers the consumer a free Barbie doll or Hot Wheels car by sending in two proofs-of-purchase from a Cheerios box.

Self-liquidating premiums require the consumer to pay for the cost of the premium. Payment may be money, or points earned from purchasing the product. Points are commonly printed inside packages, bottle caps, beverage cups, or game cards. Generally, self-liquidating premiums are higher-priced goods, such as sports figure posters, jackets or hats, or sporting equipment. Vendors usually do not attempt to make a profit but do want to cover costs. Pepsi Stuff is a self-liquidating premium intended to enforce brand positioning of Pepsi products.

Gift-with-Purchase or Purchase-with-Purchase Programs

Gift-with-purchase or **purchase-with-purchase programs** are incentives used by retailers to create immediate or limited-time sales. Customers are offered a special gift or bonus package if they buy merchandise over a certain dollar amount. They may receive the gift free or be given the opportunity to purchase an item from the product line at a discounted price. Cosmetic companies use this sales technique extensively. Estée Lauder originated this promotional device. Many cosmetic lines offer gift-with-purchase opportunities biannually in selected department stores. The cosmetic companies promote the gift-with-purchase through co-op ads in the print media, and the retailers send preferred clients direct-response mail to inform them of the incentive.

Gift-with-purchase incentives have long been used as a sales promotion technique in the moderate priced market. However, in 1997 Karl Lagerfeld introduced the gift-with-purchase concept to haute couture ("Scoop," 1997). Haute couture shoppers on the Rue Cambon were given a little quilted handbag adorned with a nameplate in solid gold. The quilted handbag has become a signature piece for the House of Chanel.

Contests and Sweepstakes

Contests are promotions in which consumers compete for a prize based on skill and ability; winners are determined by judging entries and determining the best match based on predetermined criteria. Contests generally require a proof-of-purchase or entry form that a consumer acquires from a vendor or advertisement to enter. **Sweepstakes** are promotions in which winners are determined solely by chance and a proof-of-purchase is not required as a condition of entry. Because no skill or proof-of-purchase is required, sweepstakes are more popular than contests with many consumers. Contests and sweepstakes are beneficial in getting the consumer involved with a specific brand. Consumers like sweepstakes and contests because they have the opportunity to win something. Vendors like contests and sweepstakes because they increase brand awareness and relationship with the consumer. More importantly, they allow the vendor an opportunity to collect data about the consumer using the registration card.

In a highly unique contest opportunity, Peugeot and L'Oréal cooperated in launching the car manufacturer's Speedfight scooter, priced at $2,400. As part of a Father's Day promotion, a month-long contest was held in France, Portugal, Belgium, and Italy, with winners to receive a black scooter with L'Oréal's Drakkar Noir fragrance name emblazoned on it. The contest was held at Drakkar Noir outlets, where contestants completed an entry form to participate in a drawing without purchase requirements. A French radio station conducted the drawing and awarded one scooter per day to listeners, distributing 200 Peugeot scooters ("Drakkar's," 1997).

A growing number of companies are using sweepstakes in their on-line ads as an entree into the Internet advertising arena (Tedeschi, 1998). The strategy is to attract consumers with big prizes such as trips, laptop computers, or large sums of money, hooking them with promotional offers, and then use any information gleaned from the registration process to bring them back again. The sweepstakes work for two reasons. First, the firm establishes relationships with consumers by encouraging them to invest their time. Second, the firm is more likely to receive accurate data for its database because consumers will provide accurate information if they might win something. Contests and sweepstakes are a good way for companies to start a relationship with consumers. However, consumers want value and convenience more than anything else, so contests and sweepstakes should be replaced with incentives such as samples, rebates, or free shipping if the firm wants to build customer loyalty.

The downside of contests and sweepstakes is the fact that in some cases a consumer is more interested in the contest or the prize than the product being promoted. In these circumstances, the game has not generated any after-promotion effectiveness. Additionally, there are numerous legal considerations that must be followed when designing and administrating contests and sweepstakes. Specific laws within each state and several federal agencies regulate contest and sweepstakes. The Federal Trade Commission (FTC) has rendered various decisions concerning contests and games of chance, relating to the disclosure of the number of prizes to be awarded plus the odds of winning each prize, in addition to other regulations. Advertisers should make certain any contest or sweepstakes conforms to FTC requirements as well as to local and state laws.

Refunds and Rebates

Refunds and rebates are offers by the manufacturer to return a portion of the product purchase price. A **refund** is money given directly to the consumer at the point-of-purchase. Vendors use refunds to entice consumers to try a new product or encourage a consumer to switch brands.

A **rebate** is a price deduction given upon proof-of-purchase. Rebate requests are generally mailed in by the consumer. Rebates are often perceived by the consumer to be an immediate price savings, although the consumer has to mail in proof-of-purchase in order to receive the incentive. As with premiums, the rebate must be worth the time and effort of the consumer because immediate reward for the consumer is lost. The time between the mailing in of the offer and the return of the incentive is a detriment to many consumers.

Bonus Packs

Bonus packs are extra amounts of a product, given in addition to what is expected. Manufacturers offer consumers a larger quantity of a product at the regular price. Products may claim *25 percent more free* or *get one free, when you buy two* in specially wrapped packages. Bonus packs may include a larger volume of a consumer good such as hosiery, socks, or other staple items, or an extra item in specially packaged goods. By receiving a larger portion of the product at the point-of-purchase, a consumer sees an immediate value to the incentive.

Manufacturers use bonus packs as leverage against a competitor's promotions, using value to reinforce loyalty of a known brand to the consumer. This is an advantage of the technique. A disadvantage of the technique is that bonus packs are more attractive to current users than to nonusers.

Price-off Deals

Price-off deals reduce the price of the offered item, offering an immediate incentive to the consumer. Price-off deals differ from rebates because the consumer does not have to mail in a proof-of-purchase to receive the price-off deal. It is the marked down price of the item. The price-off reductions are offered on the package of specially marketed items. Reductions generally come from the manufacturer's profit margin to keep the retailer's margin at the appropriate level, which encourages cooperation from the retailer for current and future promotions. The advantage to using price-off deals is their immediacy. Price-off deals are immediately evident to the consumer, who can view the price reduction along with the regular-priced merchandise from the competition. Price-off deals may also encourage the consumer to buy a larger volume of the merchandise, diminishing possible sales from the competition. A disadvantage of price-off deals is the reduced profit margin for the manufacturer.

Reward Programs and Frequent-Buying Clubs

Reward programs and **frequent-buying clubs** reward frequent buyers for their purchases with incentives of money-off coupons, gifts, invitations to special members-only events, or other benefits. The concept of reward programs was first used in the airline industry, rewarding frequent flyers with free flights or upgrades. In the past few years retailers have adopted this incentive strategy to increase customer loyalty. Neiman Marcus, Saks Fifth Avenue, Sears Roebuck, and numerous other retailers have programs that reward loyal customers with gifts or discounts good for future purchases, based upon customer spending.

Customers may present a frequent-buyer card at the point-of-sale and earn points. For each dollar they spend, they earn an increment of one or more points. When consumers have earned a certain number of points, they receive the incentive. Retailers include discount coupons for their establishment and for other noncompeting industries to encourage repurchase from their store. Examples of incentives are airline or restaurant discounts, discounts on floral bouquets, or free phone cards. Eddie Bauer Rewards offers members gift certificates valued at $10 after the accumulation of 5,000 points. Additional benefits include member-only offers (Fig. 11.7), advance notice of new products and sales events, and points toward reduced-priced merchandise. Points may be earned by making in-store or catalog purchases.

The increased interest in loyalty programs is based on widely held beliefs about customer loyalty. Dowling (1997) documented these beliefs:

- Many customers want a relationship with the brands they buy.
- A proportion of these buyers are loyal to the core and buy only one brand.
- The hard-core, loyal buyers are a profitable group because there are many of them and they are heavy or frequent buyers.
- It should be possible to reinforce these buyers' loyalty and encourage them to be even more loyal.
- With database technology, marketers can establish personalized dialogues with customers, resulting in more loyalty.

Figure 11.7

Direct-response advertisement sent to members of the Eddie Bauer frequent-buyer program

Neiman Marcus has developed a loyalty program that rewards repeat shoppers with gifts, discounts, and other prizes tied to an American Express customer database (Zimmermann, 1997b). This loyalty program differs from others because it is triggered automatically when customers use their American Express charge cards. Unlike many competing loyalty programs, shoppers are not required to present an additional card at the point-of-sale. The rewards program is linked to the shopper's American Express account, and AmEx maintains the database. Loyal customers are identified by purchasing guidelines set by the retailer. At the test sites equipped with the technology, clerks are alerted by the point-of-sale system each time a Neiman Marcus customer uses his or her AmEx card to make a purchase. Then, the clerks offer these repeat customers a choice of gifts, which might include tote bags, cosmetics, and restaurant discounts.

Consumers, choosing to participate in a rewards program, may increase their opportunities for incentives by using a credit card issued by the retailer. For example, L.L.

Bean offers an Outdoor Advantage Program. Members who choose to participate in the program use an L.L. Bean Visa card to earn points towards L.L. Bean products and services. Points are issued on coupons which are redeemable at stores, through the mail, or by phone.

The advantages of reward programs include sustained customer loyalty and less consideration by the consumer to shop at the competition. If, as mentioned earlier in this chapter, brands are becoming less differentiated, reward programs are replacing brand differentiation in the mind of the consumer. The products may be similar but the retailer with the reward program will get the business because of the reward.

Reward programs can be quite costly to a company if participating consumers do not increase their purchasing behavior with program membership. If consumers do not consider the reward certificate to be of great enough value, then the company is out the cost of the program and the opportunity lost with expected sales. These are all disadvantages of the program.

Deferred Billing

Deferred billing is the opportunity for the consumer to postpone or delay payment of a purchase. This incentive is used to accelerate purchases when money is limited. Deferred billing may be promoted on the cover of a catalog or in a print advertising message or a broadcast promotion. Catalogs distributed in August may state, *Buy now, don't pay until next year.* Other slogans may state, *Buy now, no interest charged for the first 6 months.* An example was shown earlier in Figure 10.3 (see p. 293). This incentive is advantageous to a retailer or manufacturer because it gains additional revenue in the form of interest on the sale. However, if a consumer is a credit risk, the retailer may loose interest revenue and the cost of the good if the consumer defaults on the bill.

Event Sponsorship

Event sponsorship, which involves company support of an event through monetary and/or in-kind contributions is becoming an important sales promotion technique used in IMC promotions to entice consumers to buy certain products and promote the corporate objectives of the institution. For a complete discussion of event sponsorship, refer to Chapter 14.

The industry uses many consumer-oriented sales promotion techniques to entice consumers to purchase goods. However, just as important as the consumers are resellers who stock the shelves in the first place. In the next section, we discuss reseller support, known as trade-oriented sales promotion.

TRADE-ORIENTED SALES PROMOTION

Trade-oriented sales promotion, also referred to as **reseller support**, is directed to distribution intermediaries, including manufacturers, wholesalers, distributors, and retailers, to support the efforts of their resellers. Resellers, motivated by trade sales promotions to carry a product, make an extra effort to promote the product to their customers. Activities aimed at the trade include promotional and merchandising allowances, price deals, sales contests, special counter displays or fixtures, and trade show discounts.

Objectives

There are many different sales promotion techniques used to encourage retailers to carry manufacturer's products. Each incentive is established with a specific objective in mind. Objectives of trade-oriented sales promotion include supporting new products, supporting established brands, encouraging retailers to promote brands, and building inventories.

Supporting New Products

Just as retailers use incentives to encourage consumers to buy certain products, manufacturers use incentives to encourage retailers to buy items for resale. Retailers have limited shelf space where each product category and accompanying brands may be allocated. New products are often considered a risk by retailers who have no sales history on which to base decisions. In order for manufacturers to encourage retailers to stock untested products, trade incentives can be offered to participating retailers to compensate for the financial risk the retailer takes for stocking a new product.

Supporting Established Brands

The support of established brands is as important as the support of new brands. Brands that have established themselves as mature products within the product life cycle are susceptible to losing market share from new products. Mature products are also likely to have fewer advertising dollars. Trade promotions can compensate a retailer for the smaller percentage of sales they are likely to generate with a mature product. They also compensate for decreased sales due to diminished advertising.

Encouraging Retailers to Promote Brands

Sometimes it is not enough to get a retailer to stock a product. Additional trade-oriented sales promotions can be used to encourage the retailer to display the product prominently and actively encourage consumers to buy the product. Incentives may be in the form of money, display fixtures, or other sales promotion tools. Displays that have the greatest chance of generating additional sales are placed away from the regular shelf position in a high traffic area. At holiday time, department stores set up one-stop shopping displays at the entrance of the store, promoting moderately priced gifts, such as gloves and slippers, cosmetic packages, or plush toys for children and adult consumers. Retailers are encouraged by the manufacturer, through trade incentives, to display the selected items.

Building Inventories

It is the nature of manufacturers to want retailers to have large inventories of stock. Large inventories will guarantee a retailer the necessary stock during high-volume selling periods and contribute to a more balanced production cycle for the manufacturer. Additionally, a retailer with a large inventory is more likely to push the merchandise to reduce warehousing costs. Manufacturers can encourage retailers to build their inventories through the use of trade-oriented sales promotions.

Techniques

Various sales promotion techniques are used to accomplish the trade-oriented sales promotion objectives discussed previously. These appeals include trade allowances; incentive programs; display and point-of-purchase materials, training programs, contests and incentives; and cooperative advertising.

Trade Allowances

Trade allowances offer the retailer a discount as an incentive to stock and display merchandise from a specific vendor. Trade allowances include buying allowances, promotional allowances, and slotting allowances. A **buying allowance** is a price reduction on merchandise purchased during a limited time period. The discount may be a certain dollar amount or percentage off the invoice price stated as an off-invoice allowance. Buying allowances may also be extra amounts of merchandise included with the purchase of a certain volume, stated as, *With every purchase of 12 dozen shirts, receive an additional half dozen free.* Buying allowances are well received by retailers and easy to implement by distributors. Retailers are predisposed to expect buying allowances and use them as a factor in selecting merchandise. Trade allowances are frequently negotiated at trade shows or during market weeks to encourage buyers to write orders at the market rather than waiting until they return home.

Promotional allowances are incentives from manufacturers for performing certain promotional activities to support their brand or product. Manufacturers design promotional guidelines that retailers must follow to receive the promotional allowance. The guidelines may specify the location of a sales floor display, directions for an in-store promotional program that may or may not include consumer-oriented sales promotions, or the use of a product in paid advertisements. The allowance must be offered equally to all resellers that carry the merchandise. In return for performing the promotional activities, the retailer receives a fixed amount per case or percentage deduction from the list price for merchandise ordered during the promotional period.

To encourage retailers to stock untested products, manufacturers can offer distributors trade incentives called **slotting allowances**, also called stocking allowances, introductory allowances, or street money. These allowances are fees paid to retailers to provide a position or "slot" to accommodate the new product. Slotting allowances are controversial because some marketers believe them to be a form of bribery. Retailers believe they need the money, which can range from a few hundred to several million dollars, to compensate for costs associated with introducing a new product to customers and company employees. Retailers who believe they can get slotting allowances will continue using shelf space as their base of power. Manufacturers with popular brands feel less threatened by slotting allowances and refuse to negotiate using the power of their brands to assure shelf space.

Incentive Programs

Incentive programs, which will be discussed in more detail in Chapter 13, are motivational tools generally designed to increase the sales productivity of sales associates at the retail level. Manufacturers sponsor sales training programs as a trade-oriented sales incentive for the retailer. Sales training assistance may take the form of classes or training sessions to increase the sales associate's product knowledge and usage. Incentive programs may also include sales contests, in which sales associates compete against one another, against other stores within the chain, or against established goals to increase sales. The manufacturer may create the contests and sponsor prizes associated with the contest as a sales incentive for the retailer.

Point-of-Purchase Materials

An often used promotional technique at the trade level is point-of-purchase display materials. **Point-of-purchase** (POP) materials are merchandise presentations of products at the point where the sale is made, such as a checkout line or a cosmetic or jewelry counter. Point-of-purchase displays are designed to promote or sell a specific product or brand. These are discussed in Chapter 16.

Cooperative Advertising

Cooperative advertising is a sponsored promotion in which the manufacturer works with the retailer to develop an ad and shares in the cost of running that advertisement. The most common form of cooperative advertising is the trade-oriented form, in which a manufacturer shares the cost of advertising with a retailer as an incentive to carry the product. Cooperative advertising was discussed in detail in Chapter 5 as part of the budgeting process.

FUTURE TRENDS IN SALES PROMOTION

Sophisticated sampling techniques are one of the major trends in future sales promotion. For instance, cosmetic companies are experimenting with foundation and lip color samples. Arcade, Inc., has developed a device called BeautiSeal, which adheres a single-use foundation sample to a magazine advertisement at a cost of 12 cents per unit. Prior to this new technology, very small packettes of product were available only through direct-response or in-store distribution and cost approximately 25 cents each. If used

Figure 11.8

Consumer advertisement using lip color sampling technology

in magazines, they caused the publications to be mailed "third class" rather than the standard "second class," adding a fee of $100,000 per magazine issue. BeautiSeal has the same opportunity as the Scent Strip to reach a mass audience through magazine promotions. The manufacturer Revlon has developed a similar technology for sampling lip color (Fig. 11.8).

Another major trend in the future of sales promotion is incentive programs. Retailers have realized that customers are becoming less loyal to a store or a brand and will switch brands based on a special promotion by the competition. Wendy D. Farina, a director at Coopers & Lybrand Consulting in New York, considers loyalty programs a megatrend. Loyalty programs are a way for retailers to establish dialog with customers and determine the best ways to promote to them (Zimmermann, 1997b).

The sophistication of loyalty program technology will also increase in the future. Currently, many programs consist of a plastic card much like a credit card that is presented at the point-of-sale. The cash register tracks the purchase, locates the information in the company database, and sends the customer a written statement and/or coupon periodically. GraphiCard has introduced a preferred customer card that is a readable and rewritable magnetic card (GraphiCard, 1997). Using specialized software, messages can be changed on the card each time the card is inserted in a scanner/reader at the point-of-sale. The card is immediately updated with purchase information and a message, such as *John Smith, save 50% on your next visit,* is imprinted on the card.

Sophistication in the delivery of coupons is also a sales promotion trend of the future. Retailers and manufacturers are experimenting with the Internet as a vehicle for distribution. Benefits include cost reduction and improved ability to target likely customers. Detriments include a security system that has not been fully developed to protect manufacturers against the fraudulent use of coupons. Box 11.2 highlights the considerations for Internet couponing.

BOX 11.2
Internet Seen Offering Opportunity, Risks for Coupon Distribution

Although the Internet has the potential to become an important way of getting coupons into the hands of consumers, its use also presents retailers and manufacturers alike with myriad challenges. The benefits of using the worldwide matrix of computer networks to distribute coupons include greatly reduced costs and an improved ability to target likely customers. But the risks of fraud are also substantial and could impede progress of the medium until new security measures are devised.

The cost-effectiveness of Internet couponing is a major reason the idea is gaining ground. Once necessary systems are put into place, the incremental expense of distributing coupons on-line falls to almost zero. Additionally, large volumes of coupons can be disseminated at a nominal cost.

Collecting e-mail addresses at site registrations yields marketers lists of current users who can be targeted with site-specific mailings. By tracking consumers' Internet activity, companies can send shoppers the coupons and promotions they are likely to use.

Retailers and coupon processors currently are reluctant to accept black-and-white coupons, for fear that they are counterfeit. Since creating bogus black-and-white coupons is not difficult on a computer, a way to distinguish legitimate Internet coupons from counterfeit black-and-white ones must still be developed.

Simple "cut and paste" desktop publishing techniques, moreover, can make it easy to alter the graphics and value of black-and-white coupons. Unless retailers and manufacturers find a means of quickly identifying these changes, they may incur unbudgeted coupon liability.

Another fraud-related complication is the location where coupons are redeemed. To minimize fraud, some Internet couponing programs are designed so that coupons are redeemable only at a particular retailer or individual store. Not all merchants have adopted the common practice of accepting competitors' coupons, however, and for those that do not, Internet coupons compound that problem.

Black-and-white coupons also can lead to significant handling problems. Cashiers will need to be retrained to recognize the coupons at the checkout counter, and may have to take extra time to scrutinize every black-and-white coupon for legitimacy. Such "hard to handle" coupons run counter to the industry goal of clearing coupons electronically at the point-of-sale.

Bar code readability is an equally important concern. The quality of Internet coupons generally depends on home printer quality, and poorly printed bar codes could necessitate additional handling during transactions and in the clearing process.

The practice also raises significant legal issues. While no lawsuits have been brought against firms engaged in on-line couponing, both the Federal Trade Commission (FTC) and the states are likely to scrutinize Internet coupon programs closely for deceptive or misleading content. They are likely to be especially vigilant with regard to deceptive or misleading offers of free or discounted merchandise. Accordingly, companies offering coupons on-line should closely study the FTC's guidelines for using the word "free."

On-line couponing also raises a number of other security concerns. Notably, the interactive nature of the Internet may provide considerable leeway to defraud coupon-issuing manufacturers. Some individuals and companies might also attempt to obtain confidential information about their competitors' promotions.

Anyone who uses the Internet to commit fraud would be subject to prosecution under the federal wire fraud statute and unauthorized interceptions of Internet communications are prohibited by the Electronic Communications Privacy Act. However, after-the-fact criminal prosecutions may be inadequate to remedy the commercial harm suffered by companies that fail to take adequate measures to protect the integrity of their on-line couponing programs.

Privacy matters are also part of the equation. Because the Internet enables companies to collect useful data about consumers who view their websites, some groups have called for guidelines to protect children against surreptitious gathering of personal data.

Intellectual property and antitrust issues come into play as well. Copyright and trademark infringement laws apply to communications on the Internet, and on-line couponing is subject to the same antitrust rules as conventional couponing practices.

A task force plans to continue studying regulatory and legal issues in order to fully understand the legal risks relating to Internet couponing. It also urges government officials to share information on emerging legal standards and model statutes on Internet misuse.

The task force's plans also call for:

- Developing a communications strategy to inform the industry about Internet couponing.
- Communicating with trade groups and the media.
- Collecting information about Internet coupons, including polling industry participants.
- Working with current and emerging Internet coupon providers.
- Exploring the legal issues in cases of fraud.
- Developing standards and guidelines for the data elements, design, and coding in Internet coupons and the clearing and payment processes.

Ross, J. (1997, February). *Internet seen offering opportunities, risks for coupon distribution.* Stores, 36–37.

Sales promotion activities are very important to retailers and manufacturers to encourage consumers to buy specific products or brands by adding extra value to the product. Branding has become a big influence on the shift from advertising expenditures to sales promotion expenditures. Since brand managers have the responsibility to manage the marketing program for a specific brand, they alone cannot market merchandise effectively. Sales promotion techniques directed at the trade and consumer are most effective when combined with an advertising campaign as part of the IMC promotional package. Figure 11.9 is a trade advertisement illustrating a fully integrated promotion campaign that was orchestrated in 1998, the year the movie *Titanic* won the academy award for best movie. The promotion offers in-store merchandising and sampling as

Figure 11.9
Print advertisement explaining the integrated marketing communications promotion campaign set for Max Factor cosmetics and the movie *Titanic*.

sales promotion techniques, TV and print advertising, and publicity for a new Max Factor makeup collection.

Trade-oriented sales promotion is used as an incentive to increase purchasing activity at the retail level. Incentives used at this level in the distribution channel motivate retailers to buy more products. However, as manufacturers and retailers realize that consumers have the final word, the trend is shifting from trade-oriented sales promotion to consumer-oriented programs. Through incentives, consumers are encouraged to try a new product, increase their consumption of an existing brand, or keep from switching to the competition's brand. Traditionally, manufacturers have used sales promotion techniques such as coupons and samples as short-term incentives to encourage consumers. However, in contemporary society, firms are realizing the importance of retaining customers as a long-term investment and are using incentives such as reward programs and frequent buyer clubs to establish long-term relationships with consumers.

SUMMARY

- Sales promotion is a set of paid marketing endeavors, other than advertising and personal sales, taken on to encourage buyer action.
- Sales promotions are designed to encourage consumers to buy a specific product or service through a direct incentive, intended to add extra value to a purchase, or to purchase an image.
- Over the past decade, sales promotion activities have grown and advertising expenditures have decreased.
- Objectives of consumer-oriented sales promotion include trial, repurchase, increasing consumption of an existing brand, defending current consumers from competition, and strengthening advertising and marketing efforts.
- Sales promotion techniques used for consumer-oriented appeals include sampling, coupons, premiums, gift-with-purchase or purchase-with-purchase programs, contests and sweepstakes, refunds and rebates, bonus packs, price-off deals, reward programs and frequent-buying clubs, deferred billing, and event sponsorship.
- Trade-oriented sales promotion is directed to distribution intermediaries, such as manufacturers, wholesalers, distributors, and retailers to support the efforts of these resellers.
- Objectives of trade-oriented sales promotion include supporting new products, supporting established brands, encouraging retailers to promote brands, and building inventories.
- Sales promotion techniques used for trade-oriented appeals include trade allowances; incentive programs; display and point-of-purchase materials, training programs, contests, and incentives; and cooperative advertising.
- Future trends in sales promotion include increased sophistication and/or improved technology in sampling techniques, expansion of loyalty programs, and delivery of coupons via the Internet.

KEY TERMS

ad specialties	incentive program	rebate
bonus pack	instant coupon	refund
bounce-back coupon	in-store sampling	reseller support
buying allowance	mail-in premium	reward program
contests	on-package sampling	sampling
coupons	point-of-purchase	self-liquidating premium
cross-ruff coupon	premium	simplified selling
deferred billing	price-off deal	slotting allowance
direct premium	promotional allowance	sweepstakes
frequent-buying program	purchase cycle	trade allowance
gift-with-purchase program	purchase-with-purchase	trial purchase
incentive	program	

QUESTIONS FOR DISCUSSION

1. Why has sales promotion replaced advertising expenditures?
2. What are the advantages and disadvantages of using each type of consumer-oriented sales promotion?
3. What are the advantages and disadvantages of using each type of trade-oriented sales promotion?
4. What role does technology play in sales promotion techniques?

ADDITIONAL RESOURCES

Block, T. (Ed.). (1997). *The only sales promotion techniques you'll ever need.* Chicago: Dartnell Corporation.

Edwards, P., Edwards, S., and Douglas, L. (1998). *Getting business to come to you.* New York: Putnam Publishing.

Kockan, N. (Ed.). (1997). *The world's greatest brands.* New York: New York University Press.

Robinson, W., and Hauri, C. (1995). *Promotional marketing: Ideas and techniques for successful sales promotion.* Lincolnwood, IL: NTC Publishing.

Tellis, G. (1997). *Advertising and sales promotion strategy.* New York: Addison-Wesley.

Totten, J., and Block, M. (1994). *Analyzing sales promotion text & cases.* Chicago: Dartnell Corporation.

Figure 12.1

Gianni Versace was featured on the cover of *Women's Wear Daily* the day after his murder.

chapter 12

PUBLICITY AND PUBLIC RELATIONS

Publicity takes many forms. While most publicity is coordinated to coincide with a planned happening, no person or firm prepares for unexpected tragedy and the publicity that occurs as a result. On July 15, 1997, Gianni Versace, one of the most important and successful fashion designers in the world, was murdered outside his home in Miami Beach, Florida. The story made the cover of numerous national and international newspapers and magazines, including *Women's Wear Daily* (Fig. 12.1), *Time, Business Week,* and others. Nearly 40 national and international camera crews set up at the steps of Versace's home; CNN, MSNBC, and other networks devoted large blocks of time to coverage of the story. Broadcast organizations, ranging from *World News Tonight* and *NBC News* to *Inside Edition, Entertainment Tonight,* and *WCBS News Radio,* and numerous websites raced to update the story by interviewing fashion designers, writers, and editors. This served as background material to tell of Versace's colorful career.

While the newsmakers were covering the story, public relations (PR) professionals in both the United States and Europe, who specialize in crisis management, were planning the right moves for the Versace company. The image the PR team had to emphasize to the buying public was of a stable company that would survive the tragedy and become even more powerful.

> **After you read this chapter you will be able to:**
>
> Describe the purpose of publicity and public relations.
>
> Differentiate among publicity, advertising, and public relations.
>
> Describe personnel involved with publicity and public relations.
>
> Identify media outlets available to receive publicity.
>
> Create press releases, press photographs, and press kits.

This chapter explores publicity and public relations and their roles in promotion. We consider the purpose of publicity and discuss the differences among publicity, public relations, and advertising. The chapter then focuses on media outlets for publicity. Then we look at the vehicles for transmitting publicity material from publicists to editors. The chapter concludes with a discussion on the future trends in publicity and public relations.

PURPOSE OF PUBLICITY

Publicity is nonpaid, unsponsored information initiated by the party seeking to tell others about a product, service, idea, or event and delivered to the public at the discretion of the media. The information is disseminated through media to attract public attention, and as a result of public interest, awareness about the event or organization is

Figure 12.2

A press release is the source for news reported in the media.

achieved. Although it is the intent of every publicity director to promote a positive image of the firm through publicity, media outlets may turn publicity around and use it to further a negative image of the intended subject.

A well-executed publicity campaign will persuade the public to take action as a result of what they have heard or seen from the publicity. Publicity may focus on merchandise, information, or events, or be used to build traffic for a specific retailer or department within a store. Common uses of publicity include introducing new products or indicating the depth, range, and variety of product assortments. Fashion information or instruction on product use may be distributed through publicity. Publicity may also take the form of event sponsorship or media events to get the attention of media outlets within a community. Figure 12.2 is a press release announcing a store event sponsored by Perry Ellis and Bloomingdale's to kick off the holiday season. Print or broadcast spots that run free of charge to charitable organizations are considered **public service announcements (PSAs)**.

Newsworthiness

A publicity campaign will always use the media as the resource to inform the public about the happening. A publicity campaign may include press releases, press kits, press conferences, or sponsored events to attract the attention of the target market. Written materials or photographs are submitted to the media outlet for publication, but it is at the discretion of the media outlet that the materials are run.

Is the happening of sufficient interest or importance to the public to warrant reporting in the media? This is the question that every editor or producer will ask when reviewing publicity materials, and it is the question every publicist should answer before submitting the publicity materials. A happening of sufficient interest or importance to the public is considered **newsworthy**. The illustration of billboards for Pretty

Polly hosiery (Color Plate 6) is an example of an event that the British media deemed worthy of news coverage. It is a subjective evaluation based on what the editor believes to be of value to his or her readers. Fashion stories of genuine interest and value to readers generally fall into the following categories:

- **A fashion trend.** *Red, fashion's favorite color of the moment.*
- **An improvement to a product, product lines, or service.** *Jockey. Let 'em know we're hosiery, too.*
- **A blending of related matters into one story.** *Vests are becoming a mainstay for all consumer groups.*
- **A response to current lifestyles.** *DKNY appeals to echo boomers.*
- **A major business move.** *Talbot's plans to open a second store in London.*
- **A *first* or an *exclusive*.** *Elizabeth Arden has entered into talks with the Spice Girls about future initiatives.*
- **Promotion or election of the firm's personnel.** *William Dillard elected president of the National Retail Federation.*

Another factor that editors and producers consider when deciding whether or not to feature publicity is the presence or absence of other news for the day. Publicity pieces have a greater chance of running when no other events of greater importance have occurred on the same day. Publicists cannot plan for unexpected national events, such as terrorist bombing or fluctuations in the stock market, that take dominant space in newspapers and on broadcasts. However, they can plan around scheduled events and place their publicity in the hands of an editor or new director on a day when other events are not likely to happen.

Media Contacts

Each media outlet has its own style and ideas on what to report. The people responsible for maintaining the editorial focus for the news organization are called **editors**, and they control the content and subject matter of all stories. Small organizations may have one person responsible for this task while large organizations will have a team. Team members of a print news organization might include the publisher, editor-in-chief, senior, associate, and assistant editors. The **publisher** coordinates all organizational and functional components of the medium. Although he or she generally does not have newsroom responsibilities, the publisher is a good publicity contact because of his or her stature in a community. The person in charge of all aspects of reporting the news is titled an **editor-in-chief**. Individuals who manage a news section, such as business, fashion, or travel, will have the title of **senior editors**. These people are also excellent contacts for fashion- or business-related publicity. **Associate editors**, often reporters, are assigned to cover certain topics and events. In communities where many events happen on a regular basis, associate editors are good publicity resources because they are likely to consistently cover the same type of events. Never underestimate the employee at the bottom rung of the ladder. At print media organizations, this is the **assistant editor**, who is responsible for reading all press release submitted to the organization and reporting the newsworthy pieces to the more senior editors. Often publications will have criteria that press releases must meet to be considered newsworthy. The assistant editor is most likely the person who will know these criteria and be able to assist **publicity writers,** who are seeking recognition for their event or products, in meeting the criteria for publication.

There are similar personnel in broadcast organizations. A **producer** is like an editor-in-chief, a top manager. Depending on the size of the news organization, this person may also have responsibilities similar to the publisher of a print medium. The **assignment editor** has control over the flow of information and assignments and, as such, is probably the best connection at a broadcast news outlet. Similar to the senior editors, **associate producers** are specialists in particular subjects and may also be good resources for publicity, if they regularly report on fashion or business.

The media can be a friend or a foe. A press release or publicity photo may be run as submitted, cut, rewritten, or ignored completely by the editor or producer of a media outlet. If a publicity piece is used, the producer or editor may use it just as it was presented for publication or develop the item into a news article. The press release may take the form of a news story, a feature story, or a news/feature story. A **news story** is information about recent events or happenings. A **feature story** is a prominent or lead article. A **news/feature story** combines information from a news story with the special emphasis of a feature article. The editor will base his or her decision about the form on the newsworthiness of the publicity.

We have all heard the saying, *she was at the right place at the right time!* The same can be said about publicity. It is critically important that press materials land on the desk of the "right person." The job of a publicist is to determine who the right person is and make the proper contact with that person. Publicity personnel should know each editor or producer for the media outlets they are interested in using. Editors or producers may review all publicity presented for publication or airing, or they may delegate subject areas to specific reporters. Publicists should know which reporter is most likely to want the subject matter they are presenting as well as the most convenient time to contact the reporter. A publicist should make every effort to develop friendly but professional relationships with important reporters and editors within the community. For publicity to have the greatest chance to be aired or published, it should be written in a professional manner, on a consistent basis, and delivered to the right person at the right time. Donna Carlson, president of DRC Communications and previously a technology editor, summed up how she was able to select the 20 press releases that would be published from the hundreds she received each month (1996). Her rules of thumb were:

- **Is the mail addressed to me?** If the release is addressed to a previous editor, the author probably does not read the magazine. The release is ignored.
- **Does the release give me the most important information in the first paragraph?** If I do not know why I should be concerned about this product by the second sentence, chances are my readers will not care either.
- **Does the writer present this news in context?** In other words, how does this new product or service affect the industry? If the release reflects little or no urgency, I am likely to let it pass.

Created and Covered Publicity

Within any firm, situations of interest to the general public routinely occur. The construction of a new parking lot, the implementation of a new service, or personnel changes within a business may be important to customers of the firm. Publicity writers determine the news value of each situation and write about it in a publicity release. This type of publicity is considered **covered publicity**. Publications may compile several covered publicity releases into a single column.

Other situations that, by themselves, may have little news value, may be made newsworthy by creating a special event around the situation. For example, a local specialty store may expand its selections of petite and plus-size merchandise. A publicity release stating the new size offerings may not have enough interest to warrant coverage in the local paper. However, a publicist may use this opportunity to plan a fashion show featuring the petite and plus-size merchandise, inviting the public to attend. A publicity release alerting the press about the fashion show will have news value and be passed on to the public. This type of publicity is considered **created publicity**. Created events are of interest to the public and warrant coverage using publicity.

Created publicity may also be corporate sponsorship of special events. By creating publicity for an event, the corporate sponsor has the opportunity to enhance the company image, improve customer relations, increase employee morale, and fulfill its civic responsibilities. Figure 12.3 shows a ceremony at the Smithsonian Institution, where President and Mrs. Clinton thanked designer Ralph Lauren for his corporate donation to the Star-Spangled Banner restoration project. Event sponsorship is discussed in more detail in Chapter 14.

Publicity can enhance the advertising budget and marketing efforts of any company that chooses to use this promotion technique. Published articles that incorporate information about brands, products, services, or the firm can raise awareness and interest in the product or firm and give an implied third party endorsement from the media outlet. Advertising and public relations are often used in coordination with publicity. Mass media are outlets of the public relations effort. According to the Bureau of Labor Statistics, public relations will be among the fastest-growing professions in the United States through the year 2005 (Mieszkowski, 1998). Supporting this trend, Fortune 500 companies increased their public relations spending by 65 percent between 1993 and 1998 ("Majority," 1998).

Companies are realizing the important role public relations has in achieving corporate objectives. The key to a successful public relations campaign is the integrated marketing communications approach set forth by management. The company's key product and corporate message, position within the marketplace, image, and identity should be coordinated throughout each publicity vehicle and media outlet to present the same

Figure 12.3

Ralph Lauren created publicity through Polo Ralph Lauren's corporate sponsorship of the Star-spangled Banner restoration project.
Source: AP/Wide World Photos

message to the public. Public relations materials must present the same message as the direct-mail campaign; advertising materials should look and feel like the website. The coordinated message should be reflected in sales promotion efforts, visual merchandise presentations, and special events. Effectiveness of the public relations campaign can be measured using public opinion polls and interviews with the targeted market.

PUBLICITY VERSUS ADVERTISING

Every organization segment within the fashion industry uses publicity as a short-term promotion strategy. Although two other promotional tools, advertising and public relations, are often used with publicity, the three terms are not synonymous. Advertising and publicity are vehicles of the public relations effort. Distinct differences exist among the three promotional concepts.

Advertising, as discussed in Chapter 7, is information paid for and controlled by the sponsoring organization. Like publicity, advertising is used to attract public attention to a product or business; unlike publicity, the sponsor pays for the announcements. A public relations department will use the tools of publicity and advertising to create or maintain a positive image for an organization, product, or brand.

There are basic differences between advertising and publicity. Advertising is a message from the interested party; publicity is a message from a public information medium about the interested party. Figure 12.4 illustrates this concept. In the selected story, *Glamour* (the public information medium) informs the reader about color selection in women's athletic shoes. Within the story, Foot Locker is complimented for a wide assortment of choices, and Avia and Adidas shoes are pictured. Foot Locker, Avia, and Adidas are represented in the story as the interested parties and benefit from the publicity given to them by *Glamour* in the form of an endorsement. This is an example of a publicity endorsement that was not initiated by a press release, but rather by news interest of the reporter.

In contrast, advertising is precise and controlled by the paid sponsor. Whatever leaves the advertising department, as approved by the sponsor, is exactly what will be seen on a prearranged date in the periodical, or heard on television or the radio or viewed on the Internet. As long as the advertiser can pay for the ad, and the ad complies with the acceptable standards of the medium, the advertisement or commercial will be printed or broadcast as submitted.

Publicity, if run, may take a form that is very different from the way it was submitted to the media. Although specific times for publication may be printed on the press release, an editor or program director may run the publicity when it is most convenient. A publicist may send the same press kit promoting a fashion show to several different print and broadcast outlets. At one outlet, the publicity may be used as a feature article, while at another, it may become a small news story in the fashion section. One broadcast outlet may consider the fashion show to be worthy of a live remote broadcast, while another station may only read the press release as a public service announcement, and yet another station may not mention the fashion show at all.

Although it may be more difficult to get publicity into media outlets, there is a benefit to the hard work. Publicity is perceived by the public to be a more credible source than advertising. Publicity, although generally written and submitted to the media outlet by a sponsoring firm, is not perceived by the public to be from the firm but rather

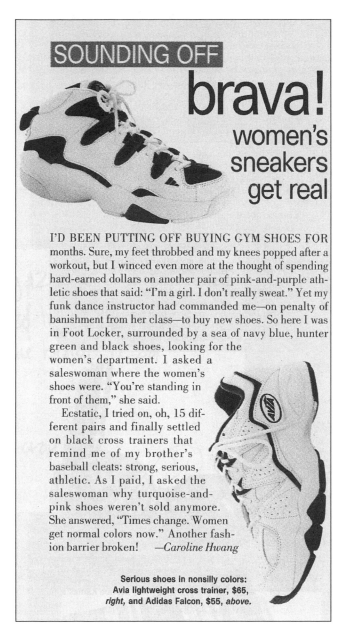

from the media outlet. The public has higher regard for the opinion of the media (an outside source) than for the firm.

Publicity is not free advertising. While the air time or column space do not have to be purchased, the effort and materials used to create the publicity must be accounted for in the budgeting process. For example, staff time, volunteer or paid, must be used to write press releases and create press kits; and sponsoring organizations may have to pay for presentation materials, giveaways, or coupons included in the publicity materials.

PUBLIC RELATIONS

Establishing and promoting a favorable public image about the event, product, brand, or company and generating good relations between the business and its customers are the role of the public relations department. Public relations involves the interrelationship between service providers and the public, to project a positive image of an organization through all levels of communication. For example, Timberland, a footwear and apparel manufacturer uses Cone Communications, a public relations agency, to promote its products, brand, and the company's commitment to community service ("Timberland," 1998). Public Relations is a function of management and is concerned with the long-range image of the firm. As a unit, the public relations office is responsible for the planned and continual effort to maintain and/or improve the institution's understanding of its public and, conversely, the public's understanding of the institution. The public of a company includes customers, potential customers, employees, vendors, educators, the community where the business is located, governments (local, regional, or national), stockholders, and possibly the competition. Table 12.1 highlights the top 20 PR agencies in the United States.

Several methods and activities are employed to establish and promote this agreeable relationship with the public. Public relations may analyze public opinion. By eval-

Table 12.1   **Top 20 PR Agencies, 1998**

Rank	Agency Name	Employees	1998 Fees
1	Burson-Marsteller	796	$141,996,000
2	Fleishman-Hillard	945	$136,272,000
3	Hill & Knowlton	555	$113,000,000
4	BSMG Worldwide	708	$109,537,000
5	Edelman PR Worldwide	1025	$105,377,523
6	Ketchum	799	$101,485,000
7	Shandwick	820	$91,485,000
8	Porter Novelli	737	$85,235,570
9	Weber PR Worldwide	430	$57,866,544
10	Ogilvy PR	441	$54,457,700
11	Golin Harris International	430	$52,973,267
12	Manning Selvage & Lee	366	$50,173,300
13	Ruder Finn	386	$45,601,000
14	GCI Group	382	$44,539,245
15	Waggener Edstrom	431	$40,900,000
16	Cohn & Wolfe	192	$25,981,360
17	Copithorne & Bellows	202	$23,563,683
18	Morgen Walke Associates	156	$23,143,604
19	Cunningham Communications	134	$20,437,000
20	The MWW Group	127	$17,220,267

Source: Inside PR 100 1998. [On-line]. Available: http://www.prcentral.com/ipr100_98.htm.

uating public opinion, the company defines programs and specific activities to generate and maintain improved relationships with its public. Allowing customers the opportunity to *tell us what you think* on a comment card is a common PR program used to improve relationships.

Public relations may measure success by obtaining public opinion through the media and the public. For example, a company may survey consumers to determine how much attention the media is giving to the company's publicity efforts. One U.S. company held simultaneous press conferences in New York City and Paris to introduce six new products. The company then evaluated press coverage in 12 countries in an effort to compare how different media in different sections of the world handled the story ("PR Evaluation," 1996). The company was also able to identify the public perception of the product launch in the 12 countries.

Public relations is an ongoing effort to explain the image of the business through communications designed to create public understanding and acceptance. Public relations is not promotion; however, public relations uses promotion to get the message of image or understanding across to its constituents. A public relations program will use the elements of publicity and advertising to promote the image of the firm and meet objectives established by management. Public relations is a long-range program designed to provide the public with the widest possible overview of the company's policies and activities.

It is also the role of the PR team to maintain a steady flow of positive information about a firm during times of economic downturn or disaster. Every company should have in place a public relations risk management plan for dealing with a disaster. Disasters may not always be as shattering as the death of Gianni Versace, but they can occur as the result of misjudging a fashion trend, a strike by the primary shipping firm, a safety issue at a manufacturing plant, or public comments by a distraught employee. Box 12.1 lists guidelines for a public relations risk management plan.

BOX 12.1

Don't Wait for Disaster; Have Your Crisis Plan Ready

All your marketing achievements—all the effort, the financial expenditure, and the energy spent in cultivating a high profile—can be dashed by one ill-handed communication disaster. All it takes is a single episode of product tampering apparently "covered up." One safety foul-up pushed under the rug. One employee talking cavalierly instead of thinking clearly.

Enlightened companies, from neighborhood restaurants and retailers to multinational merchants and manufacturers, have a risk management plan for dealing with a disaster. They buy insurance in event of fire, make contingency plans for failed equipment, train management personnel to carry on during labor strikes, code products to track sales and expedite a recall if necessary.

But as much thought as they have given to *overcoming operations disasters,* many of those companies have

given little thought to *how to communicate* during the emergency; how to let their consumers know "the food you ate here last night was not tainted," assure their employees that "everything's under control at the XYZ plant," tell their neighbors that "secure safety measures are in place."

Simple, clear-headed, advance preparation of a crisis communication plan is required in today's disaster-prone business climate. Although the specifics of each crisis communication plan depend on many factors (the size of the company, its distinct corporate culture, the product or service it delivers), there are some essential rules that all contain.

The following seven steps should guide you in preparing a basic plan so that you can communicate efficiently, effectively, and forthrightly at the moment an emergency hits your organization. You will get your company through the incident with its image intact or even enhanced.

1. **Name the crisis.** Identify all the disasters that conceivably could confront your company. Include the routine crisis your particular business might face (a trucking company might anticipate a highway accident or hazardous waste explosion) and the unexpected (such as the untimely death of the CEO). You will not be able to predict them all, but from discussion with all your firm's executives you can assemble a fairly comprehensive list. Practice formulating responses to these potential crises. That exercise alone will demonstrate where you are most vulnerable. Rehearsing what you would say also will give you some valuable testing ground for how competently you would express yourself in a real crisis.

2. **Who's up to the microphone?** Identify the person who should be your company's spokesperson. This should be someone high enough in the corporate structure to be believable, and someone who is comfortable in the public role. Be prepared to relieve this individual of all other duties for the duration of a major crisis in order to concentrate on communicating accurately and sincerely. Only one person should have the role of spokesperson in a disaster in order to present a consistent, cohesive message and prevent the spread of rumors. However, identify one or two alternates to cover if the principal spokesperson is ill, on vacation, or unavailable for some other reason. Look at the time lost in getting TWA's message out early in the flight 800 disaster because the CEO was in London and the other principal spokesperson was away from the home office at a retirement party. Arrange professional media training for everyone who may be considered for spokesperson. This training will give each person the confidence to stand up to challenging questions from reporters and others. It will prepare him or her to communicate your company's urgent messages in a clear and quotable way.

3. **Who's our real audience?** In highly public crises, such as Johnson & Johnson's harrowing experience with poisoned Tylenol capsules, the media would appear to be the most important audience. But it is necessary to calculate all the different "real" audiences you might need to reach and to figure out, in advance, how you would reach them. For example, in recalling its product, J & J had to communicate with retailers who had Tylenol on their shelves. It had to advise telephone receptionists where and how to route calls from consumers, sales reps,

and shareholders as well as reporters. It had to convey accurate information to every employee so each would feel the company was doing all in its power to manage the situation and could, in turn, handle the inevitable questions from families and neighbors. A key component of your crisis plan is to analyze each relevant constituency you serve and to organize in advance efficient vehicles (memo, fax, phone, in-person meeting, 800-phone line, teleconference, and videoconference) to reach these audiences.

4. **Put it in writing.** Build your crisis communication plan on computer or on paper and assemble it on a disk or in a looseleaf notebook for ease of organizing and editing. If it is to be user-friendly during a crisis, the plan must be well indexed, with clear instructions that are easy to access. Determine companywide guidelines for communicating with the media. Decide who should talk with the press on routine matters as well as crisis situations. Distribute written instructions regarding how media calls should be channeled to the appropriate spokesperson. Identify a crisis communication team and delineate specific communications roles. In addition to the spokesperson, perhaps you will assign one individual the role of assembling relevant information as the crisis heats up, another the task of setting up a pressroom, and a third the responsibility of internal communication. Develop contact lists of relevant media outlets, government authorities and regulators, key vendors and customers, industry groups, shareholders, and any other audience you need to reach.

5. **Collect in advance.** Assemble material you may find to be relevant in a crisis, either as background for reporters or as quick reference for yourself. This may include company literature, media kits, photographs of products or key personnel, industry/government rules and regulations, leases and other vital documents.

6. **Do it again.** Make duplicates of everything and store them in a safe place off-site. In the event of a fire, explosion, or other disaster that keeps you from your office, you will be able to move your vital communication operation to another location.

7. **Not in the storage vault, please.** No matter how comprehensive, a crisis communication plan is a living document and needs to be revisited regularly. Review your plan annually. People move around, so update contact lists. Bring newcomers to the organization up to speed on the rationale and procedures of the plan. Arrange a refresher media training to keep your spokesperson and alternates finely tuned.

Finally, on an ongoing basis, cultivate relationships that will aid you in a crisis. Get to know members of the media one-on-one. Meet in person or by phone with key community officials, vendors, and customers to develop a rapport and let them know yours is a caring company. This personal interaction can buy you a lot of support in the eye of the storm.

Adapted from: McGrath, J., and Pederson, M. (1996, December 2). Don't wait for disaster; have crisis plan ready. Marketing News, 30 (25), 6.

Joan McGrath and Myrna Pedersen are the principals of Pedersen/McGrath Associates Ltd., Chicago.

PUBLICITY AND PUBLIC RELATIONS PERSONNEL

Public relations for a company may take two forms: an in-house public relations department, which concentrates on the public opinion for the company, or an outside public relations firm hired for a period of time. The decision to engage in an outside firm is usually based on need and circumstances. A top-notch outside agency can be a very powerful tool, bringing specialized expertise, a wealth of new contacts, and a dispassionate assessment of the organization and its marketing strategy (Koprowski, 1997). Below is a checklist outlining components of an ideal client-agency relationship. A public relations firm (or advertising agency) should regard its clients as if they were part of the firm and evaluate its success directly in proportion to the success of the clients' public image. Public opinion research should evaluate a company's total image with the public, reviewing each separate component and the whole. Public relations is affected by anything that adds or detracts from the company's relationships with its public.

Publicity and public relations may be the responsibility of an in-house department. In-house departments are well versed in the organizational vision, corporate culture, and standard operating procedures. The structure of in-house departments is as varied as there are firms within the fashion industry. Figure 12.5 depicts a typical promotion structure for a large company. Such a company will have a **promotion vice president** who is responsible for the publicity staff, consisting of the advertising department, the

Checklist for Ideal Client-Agency Relationship

❏ Great communication
❏ Mutual respect
❏ Ability to listen
❏ Ability to hear
❏ Ability to agree and disagree
❏ Understanding of each work environment
❏ Measurable objectives, agreed upon before the work begins
❏ Defined chain of command and decision makers on each side
❏ Proper use of people. The agency must assign enough people to do the job, and the client must use them in the way their expertise was meant to be used.

Adaped from Nixon, G. (1997, February 3). Is your agency a keeper? Marketing News, 31 (3), 4.

Figure 12.5

How public relations and publicity fit into organizational structure of a promotion division in a large company

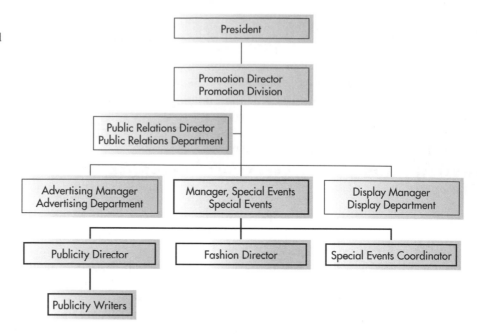

visual merchandising department, and the office of special events. Under the office of special events the firm may have a **fashion director**, responsible for fashion direction and leadership, a **special events coordinator**, responsible for directing all special events, and a **publicity** or **public relations director**, responsible for the firm's public relations. Publicity writers will be on staff in very large departments.

Large corporations will also have a public relations director who reports to the promotion director. However, the public relations director will also work very closely with the market research department to understand the perceptions of the public toward the institution. In smaller companies, a public relations and/or advertising individual may be responsible for all publicity, public relations, and advertising. A corporate office may create national publicity pieces, while local branch departments may be responsible for locally publicized events. **Publicists** may work for a public relations agency or work as freelance consultants. They work to sell the client or the client's product through good publicity.

All personnel involved with publicity must be completely familiar with the fashion press and incoming trends. They should work with fashion editors, subscribe to color and trend services, and use all research tools available to understand fashion influences for the season. Based on knowledge of the fashion industry, these individuals create professional press releases, photographs, and press kits that are most likely to create needed publicity for the client or the firm.

PUBLICITY OUTLETS

A **publicity outlet** is any mass communication medium used by a firm or agency to communicate with the public about a product, service, idea, or event. The same outlets that are used for advertising are also used for publicity. Publicity outlets include print, broadcast, and on-line media. A publicist for an agency or a publicity director for a firm must know where to send publicity to assure the greatest opportunity for publication or broadcast.

Publicity materials must be planned and written with the specific medium and type of story in mind. The type of story may be determined by the content, such as fashion product news, fashion collections, institutional information, fashion trends, and lifestyle news or personal interviews. Print materials should be prepared specifically for a column, department, editorial, or magazine photo layout. Broadcast materials should be designed for radio or television, as commentary or a news show.

Newspapers

Newspapers are a standard outlet for publicity and fall into three categories:

- Daily regional newspapers
- Daily or weekly local newspapers
- Industry or trade newspapers

Most large metropolitan areas have one or two competing leading daily newspapers with expanded Sunday editions. These papers have a regional readership beyond the metropolitan area. For example, in Colorado two large newspapers, the *Denver Post,* and the *Rocky Mountain News,* both published in Denver, have distribution throughout the entire state. Publicity sent to large newspapers must be of interest to a larger geographical population in order to get published. Table 8.1 lists the top 20 national newspapers by circulation.

Smaller communities typically have a daily or weekly local newspaper. The hometown human-interest story is more likely to catch the eye of an editor for community papers. Weekly newspapers may be published for special interest groups such as a "singles" population or an ethnic group in a non-English format. Weekly newspapers may also highlight segmented activities, such as arts and entertainment, within a community. Many communities throughout the country publish weekly or quarterly newspapers with information about cultural events happening in the area.

Industry newspapers are also published as trade journals. The fashion industry depends on *Women's Wear Daily (WWD)* to keep designers, manufacturers, suppliers, and retailers informed about the business of fashion on a daily basis. *WWD* targets a selected merchandise classification each day of the week.

- **Monday**—accessories, innerwear, and legwear
- **Tuesday**—ready-to-wear and textiles
- **Wednesday, Thursday**—sportswear
- **Friday**—beauty

In addition to coverage of specific merchandise classifications, *WWD* devotes issues to specific regional markets such as Dallas, Chicago, and California. Monthly supplements cover issues of interest such as merchandise associations and consumer market segments to the readership. Industry-based newspapers by their nature will create a higher level of interest in publicity for their industry. *WWD* features a high level of fashion-related publicity.

Other trade publications include *Daily News Record,* covering news and features on men's wear, retailing, apparel, fibers, and fabrics. The sporting goods industry is covered in a trade publication called *Sportstyle. Footwear News* is the leading publication in the international shoe industry. A weekly news publication featuring news in furniture, housewares, textiles, consumer electronics, and computers for the home products industry is called *Home Furnishings Network*. Nearly every industry has a trade newspaper that senior managers, buyers, merchandisers, designers, and key executives will use as a resource to know their industry.

Newspapers publish two types of stories: general and departmental. **General stories** are prepared for the main news section of a paper and include changes in policy, administration or personnel, business-related news, and announcements of special events of interest to the general public. **Departmental stories** are written from the viewpoint of a specific section or column of the newspaper, such as fashion, lifestyle, travel, state and local, finance, sports, or entertainment among others. The manner in which the story is written will determine its placement as a general or departmental story. Although a story on Gianni Versace might be considered departmental news, his death was such a newsworthy event that it appeared as a general story within the main news section of most papers.

The advantages of newspaper publicity include providing a good medium for conveying information to a community. Many papers are considered the best source for information within their communities. Newspapers provide intense coverage of events important to their readership. The detail in a newspaper story is usually more in-depth when compared to magazines or broadcast media. Newspapers have a professional staff to provide polish to submitted publicity. The newspaper audience is very selective and demographically definable.

Although text is very easily reproducible in newspaper publicity, visual reproduction is often of poor quality. Other disadvantages of newspaper publicity include the short life span of a newspaper piece and the haste with which readers often view the paper, missing important information.

Magazines

Magazines predisposed to run fashion news fall into six categories:

- Trade magazines, such as *Stores* and *Visual Merchandising and Store Display*
- Consumer fashion magazines, such as *W, Elle, Gentleman's Quarterly,* and *Marie Claire*
- Women's interest, including *Self, Heart & Soul,* and *New Woman*
- Home and living, such as *Bon Appetit, Architectural Digest* and *Country Living*
- General national consumer weeklies, including the *New Yorker*
- News and business weeklies, such as *Newsweek, Time,* and *BusinessWeek*

Although only a few magazines are listed, many more within each category exist and are outlets for publicity. Table 12.2 lists the top 30 national magazines by circulation.

As with newspapers, it is important to write publicity materials specific to the selective audience of each magazine. As compared with newspapers, magazines are more likely to define an editorial style for the publication. For example, *Glamour,* a Condé Nast Publication, and *Cosmopolitan,* part of Hearst Magazines, are both fashion consumer magazines considered to be the biggest and most profitable magazines of their parent companies (Lockwood, 1998a.) However, the editorial style for each publication is quite different. *Cosmo* is known for its strength in covering relationship and sexual issues, whereas *Glamour's* strengths are its coverage of careers and women's issues.

Magazines, particularly those published in a monthly format, have a longer preparation time for publication. The lead time for most magazines is 3 to 4 months before the publication date. Therefore, publicity submitted to a magazine will more likely run as editorial matter. Feature stories promoting yearly special events have a better chance at publication than time-specific news articles.

Table 12.2 **Top Magazines by Circulation**[a]

Rank	Publication	Circulation	Rank	Publication	Circulation
1	Modern Maturity	20,402,096	16	Playboy	3,151,495
2	TV Guide	13,085,971	17	Redbook	2,854,448
3	National Geographic Magazine	8,783,752	18	The American Legion Magazine	2,691,252
4	Better Homes & Gardens	7,616,114	19	Cosmopolitan	2,581,985
5	Family Circle	5,005,084	20	Via Magazine	2,489,605
6	Ladies' Home Journal	4,521,970	21	Southern Living	2,470,202
7	Good Housekeeping	4,517,713	22	Seventeen	2,437,194
8	McCall's	4,239,622	23	Martha Stewart Living	2,235,723
9	The Cable Guide	4,169,103	24	Glamour	2,208,926
10	Time	4,124,451	25	National Enquirer	2,206,747
11	Woman's Day	4,079,707	26	U.S. News & World Report	2,201,351
12	People	3,719,925	27	YM	2,170,687
13	Sports Illustrated	3,269,917	28	Smithsonian	2,088,299
14	Newsweek	3,227,729	29	Money	1,935,014
15	Prevention	3,152,814	30	Star	1,900,615

[a]*6-month averages ended June 30, 1998. Top paid-circulation magazines for the first half of 1998 based on Audit Bureau of Circulations and BPA International figures. ABC and BPA also audit non-paid circulation.*

Adapted from: Top magazines by circulation: six-month averages ended June 30, 1998 (1998, September 24, 1998). Advertising Age. [On-line]. Available: http://www.adage.com/dataplace/archives/dp271.html

The advantage of magazine publicity is the extreme audience selectivity that can be targeted through magazines. Magazines have a longer shelf life than newspapers, causing the publicity to have a longer period of effectiveness. In the minds of readers, magazines are seen as having greater credibility than newspapers. Reproduction of publicity pieces for magazines is very high in quality.

Although magazines can be very focused on specific audiences, a disadvantage of magazine publicity is the duplication of audiences, because readers generally refer to more than one magazine within a category to gain information about the subject. The same publicity piece is likely to be seen in *Vogue, Elle,* and *Glamour,* depending on the subject matter. Because magazines have a long lead time, another disadvantage is less flexibility in publicity materials and lack of immediacy of the event.

Radio

Radio broadcasts are another outlet for publicity materials. Radio show formats consist of:

- Conversation and debate shows
- Talk, interview, and phone-in shows
- Music shows hosted by a disc jockey
- News and radio "magazine" shows
- Public interest programming

Radio publicity is similar to newspaper publicity in that hometown interest stories are more likely to capture the attention of a news editor. A press release for a radio broadcast may be written in the form of a script and/or delivered as an audiotape. The publicist may have a particular commentator or "personality" in mind when writing the release who may add credibility or validity to the event. The publicist may go as far as to suggest the "personality" to deliver the message.

The advantage of radio publicity is that mobile audiences can be reached when television or print media is not an option. Drive time can be used to the advantage of a publicist. Radio listenership is very specific to a station based on the music/news format of the station. Publicity can be focused to a very select audience.

Disadvantages of radio publicity include the fleeting nature of the messages to an audience that may be only partially paying attention to the publicity spot. Additionally, the entire message may not be heard due to other distractions.

Television

The most specialized publicity coverage occurs on television, network or cable. Publicity delivered to television stations may take the form of audio/video-scripted storyboards, slides, clips, videotape, or film. **Video news releases** are publicity pieces created by publicists and delivered to television stations as news stories. For example, Edgewater Television Productions, a Florida-based company, shoots, edits, and delivers video news releases in professional formats for broadcast affiliates. Neither the television station nor the video news release mention that the firm seeking the publicity created the program. Television show formats consist of:

- News shows
- Morning interview and talk shows
- Public interest shows
- Television "magazine" shows
- Game shows
- Public access programming
- Special interest programs

The advantage of television publicity is its strong personal impact on the viewer. Information seen on television is perceived as highly believable by the public and has the ability to reach the mass population. Also, audiences are more likely to remember information seen on television than that received through other media outlets. A disadvantage of television publicity is the fleeting nature of the message to an audience that may not be paying complete attention. Additionally, television is influenced heavily by entertainment. It may be difficult for a publicist to have a message appear on television if the appeal does not have strong entertainment value.

In this discussion, we have identified media outlets that may be suitable for publicity. However, news organizations will not accept publicity submitted in an incorrect format. In the next section, we discuss the proper format for publicity submissions.

PUBLICITY ELEMENTS

Publicity is presented to media outlets using common delivery vehicles, including press releases, press photographs, and press kits. The format and contents may vary, but the essential style remains similar with certain elements common to all publicity vehicles.

Press Release

A **press release** or **publicity release** is the form used to pass information from the sponsoring party to the media outlet.

While the style (how a topic is expressed) and content of each press release may differ, the format (layout) remains the same with certain common elements. The elements have been established to make reading press releases as easy as possible for editors and producers. The following guidelines provide assistance in writing press releases (Fig. 12.6).

- Type copy on 8 1/2- by 11-inch white paper, using only one side of the page.
- Double-space copy with generous margins to allow for editing and revisions. Top and bottom margins should be 2 inches; left and right margins should be 1 inch each.
- Begin actual copy approximately one-third of the way down the page.
- Indent the first line of each paragraph five spaces.
- Add an extra single line space to the double space at the end of a paragraph.
- Repeat a two- or three-word heading at the left-hand top corner of the second and successive pages if more than one page is needed.
- Number all pages after the first page at the upper right corner.
- Use the word "MORE" centered at the bottom of any page when copy is continued on the next page.
- At the conclusion of the last page, use "###" centered to signify the end.
- Avoid dividing paragraphs from one page to another.
- Type the company name and address, single-spaced, within the margins at the top left-hand corner, when not using letterhead.
- If a publicity agency is involved, place the phrase "From: X Publicity Agency" on one line, followed on a second line, by "For: X-Corporation" stating the firm the agency is publicizing.
- Below the name and address, separated by a single space, list the contact person and telephone number.
- At the upper right-hand corner within the margins, place the release date as "For release: date/month/year." While some firms use the phrase "for immediate release," most editors do not like this because it places the decision about when to run the article on the editor rather than the publicist.
- Center a headline, typed all in capital letters, underlined, and placed approximately one-third down the page. The headline should present a comprehensive message of the prime news interest of the story. It is not the headline the editor will use in the publication.
- Begin the actual copy with the lead. The **lead** is one or two sentences that summarize the news, including who, what, where, when, and how. Should an editor or new director need to edit or cut a story, the essence of the message would still remain within the lead. **Amplification** fills out the rest of the story following the lead. All information and facts presented in the amplification section should be written in diminishing order of importance.
- Mail first class or hand deliver the press release. Do not use bulk mail rates because it takes too long for bulk rate to be delivered. While bulk rate delivery time has improved in the last several years, a bulk rate piece may still be held up to 3 weeks or more during a heavy mail season.

2 inches

Name of Organization
Address of Organization
[This is not necessary if letterhead is used]

Contact: *Name of publicist*
Phone No: (000) 555-0000

For release: date/month/year

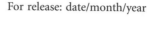

2 inches

<u>TYPE THE HEADLINE IN CAPS (UNDERLINED)</u>
[The headline should be placed approximately 1/3 of the way down the page or two inches below the contact information]

The first paragraph should contain the who, what, where, when, why, and how of the newsworthy event. The press release should be double-spaced with left and right margins of at least one inch, top and bottom margins of two inches.

at least
1 inch

The paragraphs should never be split between two pages. An extra space between paragraphs help to set them apart and allow for editing. The word MORE indicates that there are more pages to follow.

at least
1 inch

On the second page, a brief two- or three-word heading, repeating important words from the headline, should be placed in the upper left corner of the page.

The news release should be written in the third person. The press release should end with ### or -30- centered under the last line of copy.

###

at least
2 inches

Figure 12.6

Press release format

Organization and clarity of content are essential if the press release is to be read. Press releases are written with the editor or producer in mind. The publicity writer should write the press release in an objective manner, in the third person, as if it were a matter-of-fact news story. Subjective opinion based on emotional ties to the product or events should not be evident in the press release. "I," "we," or "you" should never be used. Opinionated words such as "spectacular" or "wonderful" will be rejected by an editor as self-serving to the firm seeking publicity. The publicity writer must determine what the media outlet wants and write in a style as near to those needs as possible. Editors want facts, not opinions, and will trust publicists who present professional press releases that do not promote insignificant happenings. A press release that allows the editor or producer to immediately grasp the story is a sign of professionalism and is appreciated by the editor.

The timing of a press release should be as close as possible to the actual event. The document may be written in the form of an advance announcement, informing the public of a future event or in the past tense, sharing the news of a past event. A magazine press release should be sent 3 to 4 months in advance of the event, based on the lead time for the magazine. A newspaper or broadcast press release should be sent 1 to 2 weeks in advance of the publication date on the press release. Regular contacts at publications or broadcast outlets can provide publicists with exact timelines for press release delivery. It is the responsibility of the publicity writer to determine the timeliness of the story and give a release date that allows the editor to run the story as close to the happening as possible, creating a more newsworthy happening.

Media outlets may publish style guides. A style guide is a set of rules mandated by the outlet so all copy reads the same. Media outlets or firms with established logos or other trademarked symbols may create style guides. The guides help to develop clarity and consistency in a message by providing accurate use of abbreviations and addresses for the firm, accurate reproduction of logos, and other information that may be necessary when writing to a particular media outlet or about a particular firm.

Publicity Photographs

Publicity photographs accompany press releases and are prepared with the format or visual style of the publication in mind. A drawing may be presented in place of a photograph if it is appropriate to the publication. Figure 12.7 is an example of a publicity photograph from Gap jeans. *Boot Cut Jeans $48.00 rinsed* is the caption on the back of the photograph featured next to the Gap logo. Many fashion publications have staff photographers who have developed individualistic styles for the publication. If the subject matter is of strong interest, a staff photographer from a publication or broadcast station will be sent to shoot the media outlet's own photographs.

As with press releases, publicity photos have specific requirements that should be followed for ease of printing. General requirements that assist the publication of publicity photographs are:

- Black-and-white photography is preferred but color may be submitted.
- Portraits should be 8-by-10-inch or 5-by-7-inch glossy stock; news photographs should be 4-by-5-inch glossy stock.
- Photographs should emphasize people and fashions, deemphasizing backgrounds.
- Fingerprints should not be left on photographs.
- Photographs should be identified on the back with a preprinted label or a felt tip pen to avoid making an impression on the photograph.

Figure 12.7

Press photograph for Gap
jeans

- Each photograph or drawing should be accompanied by a simple caption, with or without the association of a press release.
- Captions should consist of five or six lines and be written following the same stylistic guidelines used for a press release.
- Captions should be typed using the same identification lines as a press release, if accompanying a press release.
- Captions should be attached securely to the back of the bottom of the photograph or drawing with rubber cement.
- People should be identified from left to right with full names, titles, and affiliations.
- Model release forms should be obtained for each individual within a photograph.
- All syndicated or stock news service photos should be credited.
- Press photographs are exclusive to each publication. A press release may be common to several publications.

Press Kits

A collection of publicity materials delivered to the press as a single unit is called a **press kit**. Press kits are prepared for the most important news. A press kit may contain some or all of the following features about the product, service, or event being publicized:

- News stories and/or feature stories written in the style of a press release
- News photographs with captions

- Biographies and photographs of important people
- Company profiles or historical information
- Brochures, CDs or videos, samples, or giveaways, such as pencils, buttons, cups, T-shirts, or other promotional items.

A comprehensive press kit will also include a table of contents and a fact sheet to increase the editor's or producer's understanding of the product or event. A **fact sheet** is a detailed glossary of significant facts contained in the press kit. Publicity kits are presented in graphically attractive folders, representing the theme of the product or event, and include the business card of the publicity liaison for the firm or the publicity agency representing the firm. Figure 12.8 is a press release distributed from the Boston headquarters of the U.K.-based retailer NEXT.

Figure 12.8

Press kit from NEXT USA. The complete press kit included two press releases, history of the company, fact sheet, press photographs, photographs featuring celebrity endorsements, and a published article from print media.

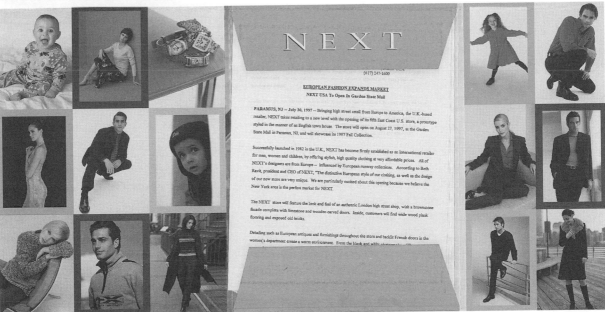

The goal of a press kit is to impress the editor to a greater degree than a single press release or press photograph could. The overall theme and graphic design developed for the press kit are used to reinforce the importance of the news. The key to a successful press kit is creativity. Anyone can come up with an idea, but how that idea is promoted and shared with the media and the public will determine how well the idea catches on with the buying public.

Press Conference

A **press conference** is a gathering held by a firm seeking publicity about an event or happening for news reporters. Press conferences are intended to create publicity about an event in the media to increase consumer awareness and interest. A press conference is held only when the firm seeking the publicity is confident that the happening or event is of such newsworthiness that the news reporters will attend the conference. For example, Bob Mackie used press conferences in major markets to launch a new fragrance. The press events were held at department stores carrying the Bob Mackie line. Models, adorned in his gowns, provided excitement by passing through the audience offering samples. Because the press conference was held in a retail department, customers who happened to be shopping that day were also treated to special samples and giveaways. Press kits were distributed to guests of the press, and they were allowed a private meeting with Bob Mackie to answer questions that later could be used in news or feature stories.

Editorial Credit

When publicity generated by fashion manufacturers appears in newspapers or magazines, it is the obligation of the editor to inform the readers where they can purchase the merchandise. The naming of retailers in such publicity is an editorial credit. The publicity may be featured within the fashion pages of a magazine, in an accompanying shopping guide at the back of the magazine, listing where the merchandise is available, or both.

In addition to stores, **editorial credit** may include the name of designers and suppliers of other accessories featured in the publicity. Retailers should be made aware of editorial credit and make necessary arrangements to have the cited merchandise in stock and available to customers who shop as a result of the publicity.

Product Placement

We have all seen it on television shows. The actor drinks a Pepsi or eats a Baby Ruth, or works at a Gateway laptop computer. The placement of a branded product versus an unbranded generic product as a prop in a movie or a television show is an example of **product placement**. Product placement has become a popular avenue to increase product or brand publicity.

Product placement may be planned or unexpected. For example, Laundry, a dress manufacturer, had success with unexpected publicity through product placement when the *New York Times* published a photograph of five bridesmaids wearing the same Laundry dress, in its weddings and engagements column. Loyal Laundry customers immediately recognized the dresses.

Product placement can also be planned. Public relations personnel representing clothing lines contact set designers and wardrobers to put their clothes on movie and television stars. Loyal customers will be validated in their purchase behavior by seeing their favorite lines on TV and movie stars. Product placement further promotes brand names to consumers. Box 12.2 discusses how fashion product placement has become a strong marketing strategy.

BOX 12.2

For Fashion Designers, the Big Screen Becomes a Celluloid Runway

New York—"Action!" Chris Columbus bellowed, shifting forward in his director's chair and keeping a watchful eye on Julia Roberts, who plays a fashion photographer in *Stepmom*, which was shooting the other day in a Manhattan studio. Just behind the director, in a chair of honor all his own, sat the designer Valentino, his famously hooded eyes just as intently fixed on the star.

For good reason. The scene showed Ms. Roberts making tiny modifications at a computer to a fashion advertisement, which, should the scene make the movie's final cut, will play to an audience of millions with Valentino's name written large over the heads of six long-stemmed models decked out in his trademark firehouse red.

In the high-stakes world of fashion product placement, as it is called, Valentino has scored a big coup, inserting not just his clothes but his high-status corporate emblem into a film from the director of *Home Alone.*

Famous designers have been providing the wardrobes for the occasional movie for years. The practice dates at least to the 1960s, when Audrey Hepburn and Hubert de Givenchy collaborated on a signature style for the star. It gained more attention in the late 1970s, when Giorgio Armani created the scene-stealing wardrobe for Richard Gere in *American Gigolo,* the movie that made the reclusive designer an American household name.

But not until recently has fashion product placement become a full-fledged marketing strategy, with designers and apparel giants that include the likes of Ralph Lauren, Levi's, and Nike jostling for position on the giant screen. As most of them well know, the payoff can be staggering, something Ray-Ban demonstrated when a tie-in with *Men in Black,* featuring Tommy Lee Jones and Will Smith in Ray-Ban sunglasses, brought a sales increase that the company put at threefold.

Such windfalls have hardly been typical in the rarefied world of luxury designer goods, where placement in a film has traditionally been a low-key affair, with correspondingly low-key rewards: a designer's credit flashing briefly on the screen, or a glimpse of a garment so fleeting as to be almost subliminal.

But there's nothing subliminal about the exposure that fashion designers are now chasing. Valentino is one of dozens of designers who are engaged in or considering aggressive strategies, from cultivating relationships with costumers and studio executives to employing outside specialists to insure that their glad rags land on the screen and are recognized by the masses.

To a degree, these gambits seem to work. Thanks to publicity about Gwyneth Paltrow in the modern-day version of *Great Expectations,* many filmgoers are likely to know that its star's chic wardrobe is by Donna Karan. Many also know Kristin Scott Thomas wore Calvin Klein in *The Horse Whisperer.* And with the release of *Tomorrow Never Dies,* it will be the rare film viewer who does not recognize James Bond's Omega Seamaster watch, thanks to a splashy Omega ad campaign featuring Pierce Brosnan, the latest Agent 007.

Few designers share Omega's agenda—to actually sell the product seen on screen—and few have such hefty advertising budgets. Providing wardrobes to film stars is only the latest wrinkle in a decade-long strategy by fashion to take in Hollywood glamour. Earlier efforts have included giving stars front-row seats and first-class airfare to runway shows, and dressing them for gala dinners and televised award shows.

Now, by placing their wares directly in films, designers are following the well-trod path of such champion marketers as Coca-Cola, Anheuser-Busch, IBM, and Ford Motor. The clothiers face a challenge: unlike most consumer products, their goods are not emblazoned with a product name or emblem. (One obvious exception is Tommy Hilfiger, who signed a deal with the William Morris Agency that included pursuing movie tie-ins.)

"Most people who go to the movies are not fashion conscious," said Dean Ayers, president of the Entertainment Resources and Marketing Association, a 104-member product placement trade group. "They won't know a Hugo Boss suit from a Brooks Brothers, and frankly they may not care."

Aye, there's the rub. Few filmgoers sit through the final credits to see who designed the clothes. To get their products recognized, many designers have piggybacked screening, premiers, and elaborate retail promotions onto a film's release.

"Product placement is all about marketing extension," said Michael Nyman of Bragman Nyman Cafarelli, a public relations and marketing company in Los Angeles. "That no longer means just PR and advertising; once the film comes out, it's getting the star to wear your clothes to the premier or on the publicity junket, and on posters in the stores. The more promotional vehicles you can use, the better off you are."

Adapted from: La Ferla, R. (1997, December 14). For fashion designers, the big screen becomes a celluloid runway. New York Times [On-line]. Available: http://www.nytimes.com/yr/mo/day/news/style/actors-fashion.html. Copyright © 1997 by the New York Times Co. Reprinted by permission.

FUTURE TRENDS IN PUBLICITY AND PUBLIC RELATIONS

Sharing the occurrence of an event with the public through the media will always be the mission of publicity departments and publicity writers. However, trends are changing in the way publicity is delivered to the media. The Internet is the newest publicity outlet available to publicists to promote their client or business. The Internet offers two distinct opportunities for publicity. Companies with websites may look to public relations firms to promote their websites or public relations firms may look to websites as a publicity outlet. Websites allow anyone to get information about anything at anytime. Just as a publicist compiles a list of potential broadcast and print outlets, he or she may also compile a list of potential submission sites that consumers may readily visit for information on products or services.

Magazine and newspaper editors have started broadcasting their publications over the Internet, opening the opportunity for on-line publicity through these media channels. Figure 12.9 promotes *Women's Wear Daily* on-line. Subscribers can pay to read the newspaper or magazine on a computer screen instead of in a print format. On-line publications are gaining popularity because of the immediate availability to view new fashions. According to Scott Omelianuk, style editor for *GQ* magazine, "there's no rush to print with the first look now, because the first look is already out there" (Tyre, 1997). On-line technologies are emerging as a compliment to print media. According to Omelianuk, on-line technologies are allowing the audience to view fashions instantly; in turn, the audiences are relying on print media to explain how to wear the fashions and give them a reason to buy.

Companies are also choosing to put media kits on-line or on CD ROMs. On-line media kits may include the same components as a printed media kit, including press releases, photographs, and news and feature articles along with graphics and logos. Figure 12.10 shows the *New York Times's* on-line media kit. A potential client wanting to promote its product or firm on the *New York Times's* website can gather needed information about demographics, statistics, and reporting needs through the on-line media kit.

Some CD-ROMs allow the user to download information while others are read-only. National distribution of a CD-ROM is less expensive than elaborate traditional media kits, but can create the same sense of excitement in the viewer to learn more

Figure 12.9

WWD on-line
subscription information

about the subject. With an on-line media kit, the company or individual seeking the publicity information can download only the pieces of information it wishes to use. The company offering the media kit does not have to pay reproduction costs for the materials. As compared with printed materials, a CD-ROM allows the viewer to be interactively involved with the subject presented. For example, a CD-ROM presenting ready-to-wear collections unlike a two-dimensional press photograph, allows the viewer to see the movement and flow of the fabrics.

Publicity and public relations can enhance the communications message of any company that chooses to use these techniques in its promotion strategy. Published articles raise awareness and interest in the firm's products or objectives and give an implied third party endorsement from the media outlet. The integrated marketing communications strategy set forth by management is key to successful promotion and should merge into a whole publicity and public relations campaign. The company's corporate message, position within the marketplace, and image should be coordinated throughout each publicity vehicle and media outlet to present the same message to the public. Publicity materials and the public relations campaign must present the same message as direct marketing, advertising, sales promotions, special events, and visual merchandising presentations.

Figure 12.10

The *New York Times* on-line media kit.

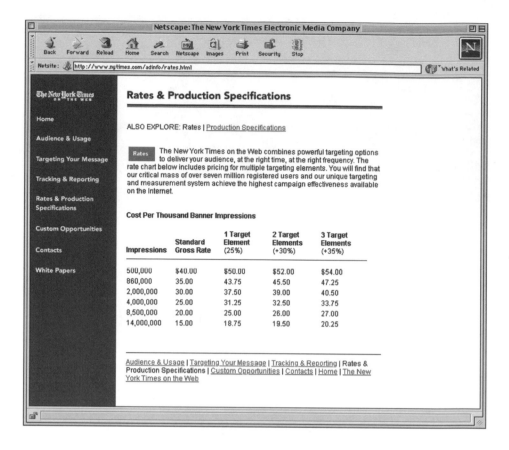

SUMMARY

- Publicity is nonpaid, unsponsored information initiated by the party seeking to tell others about a product, service, idea, or event and delivered at the discretion of the media.
- Publicity is disseminated through the media.
- The editor or producer will make a decision about whether to run the publicity based on his or her perception of the newsworthiness of the publicity.
- Publicity may be written after the fact to cover an event, or used before an event to create interest about the subject.
- Publicity, advertising, and public relations are distinctly different. Advertising and publicity are vehicles of the public relations effort.
- Public relations is the interaction between service providers and the public, as it relates to the image of the organization through all levels of communication.
- Publicists perform public relations functions at an outside agency.
- Specific guidelines are used to create press releases, press kits, and press photographs.
- New technologies for distributing press materials include the Internet and CD-ROMs.

KEY TERMS

amplification	feature story	public relations director
assignment editor	general stories	public service announcement
assistant editor	lead	publicists
associate editor	news story	publicity director
associate producer	news/feature story	publicity outlet
covered publicity	newsworthy	publicity photographs
created publicity	press conference	publicity release
departmental stories	press kit	publicity writers
editor	press release	publisher
editorial credit	producer	senior editor
editor-in-chief	product placement	special events coordinator
fact sheet	promotion director	video news release
fashion director		

QUESTIONS FOR DISCUSSION

1. Why might a firm use publicity and public relations?
2. What are the similarities and differences in the roles of publicity, public relations, and advertising?
3. How do created and covered publicity differ?
4. How can an item be made newsworthy?
5. What is the relative importance of the various types of media outlets where publicity can be submitted?
6. What role does technology play in distributing publicity and public techniques?

ADDITIONAL RESOURCES

Bivins, T. H. (1996). *Handbook for public relations writing.* Lincolnwood, IL: NTC.

Ellsworth, J. H., and Ellsworth, M. V. (1995). *Marketing on the Internet.* New York: Wiley.

Evans, F. J. (1987). *Managing the media.* New York: Quorum Books.

Henry, Rene A., Jr. (1995). *Marketing public relations.* Ames, IA: Iowa State University Press.

Janal, D. S. (1997). *Online marketing handbook.* New York: Van Nostrand Reinhold.

Lewis, H. G., and Lewis, R. D. (1997). *Selling on the net: The complete guide.* Lincolnwood, IL: NTC.

Loeffler, R. H. (1993). *A guide to preparing cost-effective press releases.* New York: Haworth Press.

Smith, R. (1996). *Becoming a public relations writer.* New York: HarperCollins.

Figure 13.1

Star sales associate in Neiman Marcus's shoe department

Source: Photograph by Steve Erle for Vogue *Magazine.*

chapter 13

PERSONAL SELLING

I t's 3 P.M. on Wednesday and the grandly remodeled shoe salon at the Beverly Hills Neiman Marcus seems strangely quiet. Two women wander about and one picks up a style she likes. "Do you need assistance?" asks a salesperson politely. She cuts him off, "No thank you." As the salesperson retreats, the customer turns to her friend and asks, "What day is it?" Her friend replies, "Wednesday." A gloom settles as both women realize their favorite shoe salesman has the day off (Rust, 1998). What makes this salesperson so popular? He offers such impeccable customer service that clients know they can count on him (Fig. 13.1)! This is an example of excellent customer service, a promotion technique that is gaining significance as marketers move away from a focus on the product, toward a targeted and personalized communication with the consumer.

After you read this chapter you will be able to:

Discuss the importance of personal selling.

Explain the buying and selling process.

Demonstrate elements of a sale.

Provide closure after a sale.

Differentiate between personal selling opportunities in the marketing channel.

List attributes of successful selling.

Handle various customer types.

In Chapter 1, promotion was defined as all activities initiated by the seller to inform, persuade, and remind the consumer about the products and services offered by the seller, including personal and nonpersonal selling approaches. Personal selling can be used to promote sales by informing, persuading, and reminding the consumer about products or services. Thus, using this definition, personal selling is a form of promotion.

This chapter begins by discussing the importance of personal selling and its place in the retail and wholesale marketing channels. It then examines the buying and selling process, discusses elements of the sale, and explains how to handle customer problems. The chapter concludes with a discussion of the future trends in personal selling.

SIGNIFICANCE OF PERSONAL SELLING

Communication experts believe the first contact is the most important contact two people can make. First impressions make or break lines of communication almost immediately. If a first impression is less than polished, a second encounter may never happen. This is especially true in buying and selling environments.

Personal selling is the direct interaction between the customer and the seller for the purpose of making a sale. This person-to-person communication encourages the seller to assist, and even persuade, a prospective buyer to make a purchase or act upon an idea. Through personal selling the seller can see or hear the potential buyer's reaction and assess the success or failure of the sales message. This feedback allows the seller to adapt the message to the client's needs. Personal selling allows more direct and accurate feedback about the sales message than any other promotion mix technique.

Many promotion mix techniques discussed in this text concentrate on the activities and procedures of nonpersonal selling, including advertising, sales promotion, publicity and public relations, visual merchandising, special events, and fashion shows. The purpose of nonpersonal selling is to bring customers to the point-of-sale. Nonpersonal selling (or simplified selling, as we discussed in Chapter 11) is very effective in certain selling environments, such as grocery stores. While we do need assistance occasionally in these environments, we would not want a sales associate to assist us through person-to-person communication with every item on our shopping list.

However, in other shopping environments, personal selling is often necessary to close the sale. Clothing and electronics departments are just two of many retail environments where sales associates assist customers in purchase decisions. Telemarketing firms rely solely on the customer service representative to provide adequate information and service to complete customer sales. In both environments, sales associates should have complete knowledge of their product, have a high level of self-confidence, and be personable, polite, and outgoing.

To a customer, the salesperson represents the entire organization and is responsible for building customer loyalty and creating customer satisfaction. If a salesperson projects a positive impression to the customer, the customer will likely return to do business with that firm and tell friends and colleagues to buy from that firm, as well.

Personal selling is often a function of the marketing process and at times falls short in its effectiveness. Salespeople often cannot answer questions about merchandise or may not be available at the right moment to assist an impatient customer. A retail salesperson or a manufacturing rep who is poorly trained or has a bad attitude will likely cause customers to find alternative shopping environments and share their bad experiences with their friends and associates.

Developing and maintaining a successful sales staff is one of the most difficult challenges facing retailers, but this does not mean all salespeople are inadequately trained. Retailers such as Nordstrom and Neiman Marcus have built retailing empires based in part on excellent customer service. In his book, *Minding the Store*, Stanley Marcus stated "we have one inviolable rule in our organization—that the customer comes first—and any staff meeting can be interrupted to meet the call of a customer" (Marcus, 1974, p. 107).

Sales associates provide customer service, stimulate sales, generate add-on sales, encourage repeat business, and control inventory shrinkage (Schmidt, 1996). The key to a successful personal selling team is the integrated marketing communications approach set forth by management. Sales associates should have access to all advertising and publicity materials and tell the same story to create a uniform image of the firm in the customer's mind. The company's key product and corporate messages, positioning, image, and identity should be articulated by each sales associate to present the same message to the public.

PERSONAL SELLING IN THE MARKETING CHANNEL

Within the fashion industry, personal selling exists at all levels of the marketing channel. Retailers rely heavily on the selling skills of their sales staffs to close sales within each department. At the manufacturing level, personal selling exists through wholesale representatives, who use their selling skills to sell clothing and accessory lines to potential retail buyers.

Retail Selling

Retail firms that focus on specialty goods will incorporate personal selling into the promotional mix. **Specialty goods** are products aimed at a narrowly defined target market. The target market is generally very knowledgeable about the product in question, has strong brand preferences, and is unlikely to accept merchandise substitutes. Specialty store customers most often prefer personalized selling and use the criteria of personal service in store selection. Department stores use personal selling for staple goods to help customers find what they want in a quick and efficient manner. Through personalized selling, salespeople can close sales and more readily suggest additional purchases, such as accessories or coordinating items.

There are many reasons a customer may need the assistance of a sales associate. Schmidt (1996) has developed several general categories of customer contact situations. They include the following:

- **Customers seek items with little specificity.** These customers do not know what they want so they ask a sales associate for assistance or an opinion.
- **Customers are especially particular about what they want.** They ask a sales associate for assistance in finding the item or for an opinion about the specific item.
- **Customers ask for items that are not available.** These items may not be made or carried by the particular firm or may be available only through catalog sales.
- **Customers have unusual needs or make requests for unusual items.** These requests may be for special sizes or styles of clothing.
- **Customers request services beyond the scope of services ordinarily provided by the sales associate.** These may include special assistance outside of the department, special deliveries, or just to spend time talking with the sales associate.
- **Customers need assistance overcoming personal problems that make it difficult to shop.** Examples include physical, mental, or language barriers or unruly children.
- **Customers want to negotiate a transaction with the sales associate that is not normally considered legitimate under store policy.** Returning merchandise under questionable circumstances or buying flawed items at a discount represent this type of contact situation.
- **Customers are upset, angry, irritated, or complaining.**
- **Customers are caught in illegal acts.**

Personal selling is a very successful form of sales promotion as it enables the salesperson to promote the characteristics of a product and overcome any objections the customer may have about the product or service. Customers in some instances see the personal attention they receive as validating their selection and decision to purchase the product. Sales initiated through other sales promotion activities, such as displays, advertising, special events, or fashion shows, are more likely to be completed through personal selling by a sales associate.

In addition to creating a positive first impression with the customer, sales staffs that participate in personal selling have the opportunity to gain feedback about customer needs and wants. Sales associates are in a unique position because they have knowledge of the product, the retail environment and the consumer. They know why decisions were made to carry certain merchandise and why certain store policies are established. The sales associate is able to ask questions about specific brands, styles, and color preferences that appeal to or are rejected by the customer. The sales associate can ask customers if they were drawn into the store by advertising or other special promotions. Sales associates also know the clientele of the store because they interact with customers on an ongoing basis. By having knowledge of all three components, sales associates are able to view how different customers react to different products or management policies and, in turn, report this information back to the buying office or the management staff. This firsthand knowledge passed to retail management can help determine future directions in merchandise selection and the promotion mix.

Historically, sales associates have not had as much direct contact with customers in discount and drugstores where items such as cosmetics or personal care products were prepackaged. However, drugstore chains have started adding sales staff to the previously "self-service" format in beauty and photo departments as a tool to differentiate themselves from their competitors. The addition of sales associates in these departments allows retailers to enhance service and in some cases increase the opportunity to stock upscale product lines.

Personal Shoppers

In an effort to provide increased customer service and retain store loyalty, larger retailers have introduced personal shoppers into the store service program. **Personal shoppers** are sales associates who assemble items for specific customers prior to or in place of a visit to the retail store. Some retailers even provide for personal shoppers to visit the customer's home or office with the selected merchandise.

Personal shoppers are also available to accompany customers through the store, offering assistance and identifying suitable merchandise. A personal shopper generally has good knowledge of the specific customer's preferences for brands, styles, and color and will coordinate merchandise groupings that are likely to appeal to the consumer. Personal shoppers may also call customers when new merchandise arrives in the store that may appeal to a specific client.

Printemps department store has taken the role of personal shopper to a new dimension in its Paris flagship. The store has given Internet shoppers their own personal in-store shoppers (Printemps, 1999). Cyberclerks, as they are called, wear bright red and yellow padded uniforms and rollerblades and carry laptop computers and miniature TV cameras (Fig. 13.2). Customers call up the website to communicate with these personal shoppers. The cyberclerks skate throughout the store, suggesting items by using the camera to show them to the client. The first test of the system, which took place over 2 1/2 days, resulted in 430 connections, servicing of 92 clients, and seven sales. Printemps anticipates late night shopping by overseas clients, who will be able to work with a cyberclerk even when the store is closed.

Direct Sellers

In addition to providing personal service to customers within a retail store, personal selling can take place individually through direct selling channels. Direct sellers are companies that sell directly to the consumer, bypassing a retail distributor. Individuals involved in direct selling often refer to themselves as **image consultants**. Avon, Mary Kay cosmetics, and Beauty Counselor are long-established companies training sales associates to be image consultants. Image consultants are experts who help individuals create a positive self-image. Areas of consultation include skin care, health, fitness, beauty, cosmetics, apparel, color, wardrobe, and personal and professional etiquette. Image con-

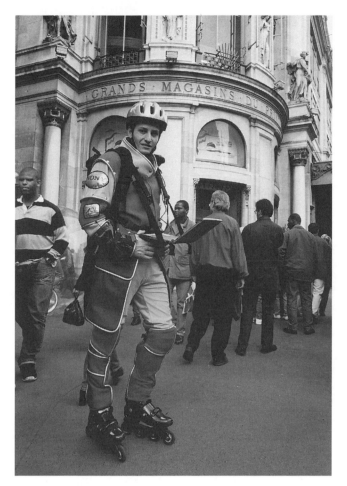

Figure 13.2
Cyberclerks are the personal shoppers of the future.

sultants may assist customers with basic information through color draping or extensive assistance, including complete wardrobe analysis and makeovers for hair and beauty. In addition to retail selling, sales personnel also work for manufacturers and designers.

Wholesale Selling

Personal selling at the wholesale level commonly is done by a **manufacturer's sales representative (rep)**. Representatives may work in manufacturers' showrooms or cover specific geographical territories, traveling to resident buying offices, trade shows, or retail establishments (Fig 13.3). All product categories require representatives to show the manufacturer's products to potential retail buyers. Responsibilities of a manufacturer's sales representative are varied but include many one-on-one communications with clients. Reps meet with buyers in person to show the latest lines. Complete familiarity with the line is essential for sales representatives. Reps and buyers work in close contact, touching the product line, discussing details of the product, which include findings and fabrics, and coordinating color and style features to create the assortment a buyer wishes to have available in his or her retail store. Reps write orders, complete follow-up work, and occasionally model garments for buyers. Reps may also commu-

Figure 13.3

A manufacturer's sales rep and a client

nicate with buyers on the phone to place reorders or discuss a product detail brought to their attention by retail customers. Manufacturing representatives must provide quality service to buyers if they want their lines represented in retail stores.

As the marketplace becomes global in nature, vendors from other countries are looking at the way U.S. sales representatives are trained. Miller (1996) contrasts several characteristics of U.S. and Chinese sales representatives and offers solutions to the Chinese way of doing things. Characteristics include:

- **Relationships.** Chinese business relationships are more personal than American business relationships and are not developed with regard to the business potential of either person. Solutions include teaching Chinese sales representatives to ask relevant, business-related, probing questions rather than social questions.
- **Price.** Chinese sales representatives have historically sold products solely on the basis of price, not qualifying potential customers. To qualify a buyer, it is necessary to determine the decision-maker within the firm. This is even more difficult in China than in the United States because for Chinese people to admit they do not make the decisions would involve a loss of face. Chinese vendors must constantly emphasize the necessity of identifying the decision-maker to achieve efficiency.

- **Training.** U.S. sales representatives are often trained through role-playing and problem solving, with heavy emphasis on in-depth product knowledge and its use in helping the customer understand product benefits to ensure sales. This is in contrast to the Chinese tendency to resort to price cutting in the face of any objection to making a purchase. The solution to this problem requires constant drills on product benefits and close supervision to ensure these features are emphasized. This solution complements the Chinese education method of rote memorization.

Miller suggests that Chinese vendors adapt training to fit cultural constraints, while working to modify Western techniques to obtain better results from sales representatives. These are just a few of the problems facing cultures as they become members of the global society. While the American way of doing business is not always the right way, it can be used as a model for other countries because we have been at it longer and have had successes.

Retail sales associates and wholesale sales representatives perform important duties for their employers. Before we discuss the attributes that make these sales personnel successful, it is necessary to look at the buying and selling process that involves both the customer and the sales associate.

BUYING AND SELLING PROCESS

When a salesperson becomes involved with a potential customer who is faced with a buying decision, two separate and distinct processes take place:

1. The customer becomes occupied with product acquisition (described in Chapter 2 as the process of searching, evaluating, and choosing among alternative products).
2. The salesperson becomes concerned with the buying/selling process.

The **buying and selling process**, illustrated in Figure 13.4, is the method used by a salesperson to encourage a customer to reach a buying decision about a product or service. Researchers in sales literature refer to this as the AIDA model, which stands for *a*ttention, *i*nterest, *d*esire, and *a*ction. Some researchers have added a fifth element, satisfaction, because it is necessary for evaluation.

The buying/selling process involves five steps, as follows:

1. Get the **attention** of the consumer.
2. Create customer **interest** in a product or service.
3. Form **desire** on the part of the customer for the product or service.
4. Stimulate customer **action** to purchase the item or service.
5. Create customer **satisfaction** to ensure continued loyalty in the firm.

Figure 13.4

The AIDA model of the buying and selling process.

All forms of selling include a buying and selling process. The process may be implemented entirely through personal selling or through a combination of personal selling and other elements of the promotion mix, such as advertising or visual merchandising.

Attention

The goal of a salesperson is to match the elements of the acquisition process (see Chapter 2) with the elements of the buying and selling process in order to satisfy customer needs and generate sales. Figure 13.5 shows the interaction between the buying and selling process and the product acquisition process. At the beginning of the process, the customer recognizes the need for a product. The consumer will peruse catalogs or go shopping at the mall for the item. He or she may be influenced by a window display or direct-response mailed message. A sales associate makes first contact with the customer as he or she enters a store or by answering an inbound call. In a retail environment, the salesperson should get the customer's attention by introducing, demonstrating, or offering samples of a product. A customer calling in response to direct marketing efforts has already taken notice of the firm's merchandise, but a sales associate can draw the customer's attention to additional products or services. Through curiosity, or appreciation of specific features, the customer may consider the product or service for possible examination.

Interest

Following the recognition of a need, the consumer usually wants to know what products might fill his or her need and begins gathering information. During this phase, it is the role of the sales associate to provide enough information about the product to arouse the consumer's interest. A sales associate may explain the expected benefits from the item and describe what the customer will gain by owning the product.

Desire

As the momentum of the acquisition process continues, a consumer will turn interest for a product into conscious desire for the product and begin choosing among alternatives. The sales associate may use the opportunity to explain the enjoyment and satisfaction the product promises in its attainment. The sales associate may also offer extra information about incentives associated with the product or service that were not evident to the customer.

Figure 13.5

Interaction of the acquisition process and the buying and selling process

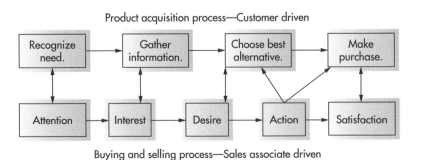

Action

At a certain point, the sales associate must shift the customer from choosing among alternatives to making a purchase. The sales associate should make every effort to stimulate action in the customer to buy the product through further explanation of specific features or details of the product. The salesperson may speak about or demonstrate the ease of assembly, explain specific care requirements, or explain a convenient feature not previously mentioned. If the client is a regular customer, the sales associate may suggest how the item will complement other items already owned by the customer. Action may also be accomplished by formalizing details of packaging, shipping, or other elements of the transaction. Through personal interaction with a sales associate or service representative, the customer chooses the best item for purchase to satisfy his or her need.

Satisfaction

The last and most important element of the buying and selling process is customer satisfaction. To assure customer satisfaction, the sales associate may offer to exchange the item or take it back in return if the customer is not completely satisfied with the product. Additionally, the sales associate may offer a coupon or free sample to the customer. This is also a good time to distribute customer surveys as a gesture of goodwill by the firm to ensure customer satisfaction and continued patronage. The handshake is a universal symbol of thanks and appreciation for loyalty. A salesperson may not complete each sale with a handshake. However, customers appreciate a friendly smile, and a sincere thank-you. The satisfied customer leaves the store and through use or wear of the item begins postpurchase product evaluation.

ELEMENTS OF THE SALE

The buying and selling process is used to persuade customers to reach a buying decision about a product or service. This sounds easy, but just how do sales associates go about making a sale? In this section, we discuss the elements of a sale.

There are four steps involved in making a sale. They include, (1) sales approach, (2) merchandise presentation, (3) handling objections, and (4) closing the sale. The interaction between the buying and selling process and these elements is illustrated in Figure 13.6.

Elements of a sale—Sales associate action

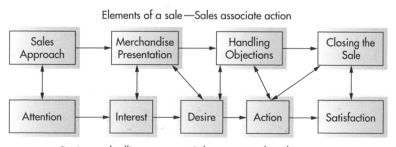

Buying and selling process—Sales associate thought process

Figure 13.6

Interaction between the buying and selling process and elements of a sale.

Sales Approach

The **sales approach** is the opening recognition and greeting of a customer. At this step, the sales associate is responsible for gaining the attention of the customer. Each customer who makes contact with a firm should be treated as a guest. Whether in person or through phone communications, sales associates should greet customers as friends with respect and courtesy. Mervyn's has trained its sales associates to refer to every customer as a guest. The sales approach may involve personal communication between the salesperson and customer through a greeting such as, *How are you this evening?* or a comment about merchandise such as, *These sweaters have just arrived in new fall colors.* The Gateway computer company has trained its sales representatives to greet each phone customer by asking if he or she is a member of the Gateway family.

An incorrect approach can easily bring forth a negative response from the customer. The question, *May I help you?* will almost always be answered with an abrupt no, (as shown in the opening vignette). A sales associate should express simple greetings such as *Good afternoon,* or ask questions that must be answered in a positive manner such as, *Are you trying to match a particular color?* These are examples of a **greeting approach**, a pleasant salutation expressing good wishes to the individual.

The alternative to a greeting approach is a **merchandise approach** that directly makes reference to the merchandise at hand. Phone representatives are experts at this method when they ask customers what page they are referring to when ordering merchandise. In most cases, the merchandise approach is more effective than using the greeting approach in getting the attention of the customer since it gives each party something positive to discuss.

During the sales approach, the salesperson should become aware of the customer's reaction to the merchandise. The salesperson should listen to the customer, asking minimal questions to determine specific preferences of the customer, such as color or price, and migrate with the customer toward the described merchandise.

A well-phrased, appropriately timed question is a very effective sales tool. Kahle (1997), president of DaCo Corporation, a firm specializing in systematic approaches to sales, offers the following tips about good questions.

- **Good questions direct customer thinking.** When you use a good question, you penetrate your prospect's mind and direct his or her thinking. For example, instead of asking a customer, *Do you need a new pair of athletic shoes?* ask, *What is more important to you, ankle support or a cushioned sole?* The salesperson's question helps customers to direct their thinking about the product they are interested in and conversation naturally proceeds based on the first answer.
- **Good questions will help collect information necessary to construct a sale.** How do you know what a customer thinks, or what his or her situation is, unless you ask a question? For example, if you are selling small kitchen appliances, you need to ask questions to determine whether the customer has counter space for the appliance or needs a space saver appliance. You must discover the concerns of the client so you can point out special features of the item to meet those needs.
- **Good questions build relationships.** The act of asking a good question shows you care about the person and his or her problems. The more questions you ask about your customer, the more he or she feels your interest, and therefore, becomes interested in you.

• **Good questions convey the perception of confidence.** Your customer sees you as competent and trustworthy—not necessarily by what you say—but rather by what you ask. For example, suppose a potential customer needs calendar refills from an office supply store. The customer asks the salesperson where refills are located in the store. One possible reply would be Aisle 3. A better reply would be, *What is your preferred brand? Day Runner or Daytimer, or something else?* This question conveys the perception to customers that you understand their needs and shows that you are competent at fulfilling their needs. Mastering good questions will increase the likelihood of completing a sale.

Merchandise Presentation

Once a salesperson has recognized the needs of the customer, he or she should begin presenting suitable merchandise to attract interest within the client. The sales associate should lead the customer to the merchandise rather than point to a rack across the room and expect the client to find it. Many successful retail salespeople use the **soft sell** approach, presenting merchandise in a discriminating, not forceful way. Advantages of the product are pointed out to the customer with slight encouragement to purchase the item now rather than postponing the purchase. Most customers are turned off by the **hard sell** approach, which pushes customers to buy a product they may not want.

The salesperson should lead the consumer to the appropriate merchandise, being selective in offerings, careful not to overstimulate or confuse the consumer by presenting too many items. Touching and feeling the merchandise will encourage customers to try on items for fit and color selection. The customer should be told what he or she most wants to hear about the product. If the customer has asked about price, do not continue to speak about product features. A salesperson should always be alert to tell clients what the product or service will do for them, fulfilling unmet needs.

The presentation should begin with medium-priced merchandise and, upon reaction from the customer, move up or down to fit the budget. Merchandise presentation is the perfect time for a sales associate to learn the tastes of the client and offer appropriate merchandise for the customer's consideration. **Trading up** is the process of substituting higher-priced merchandise for lower-priced merchandise during presentation. Upon assurance from the customer, verbal or nonverbal, that the price is not too high, the salesperson should begin to trade up, showing the customer similar but higher-priced merchandise with more fashion forward appeal.

Handling Objections

As customers move from interest to desire, they may develop questions or objections that the sales associate must be ready to handle. Consumers often attempt to object to a sales associate's offer for assistance by replying they are "just looking." Other common objections by consumers include requests for out-of-stock merchandise, or for merchandise not carried, or resistance to the price of selected merchandise. It is important for the salesperson to answer objections before they are raised, by watching the customer and preparing an answer to the possible question. If a customer is looking for a certain size, the sales associate should come to his or her assistance by showing the correct location for the size or by offering to find the correct size in reserve inventories. If it is necessary, agree with the customer about the objection and point out a superior feature or alternative product. A sales associate should never argue with the customer. By arguing, sales associates leave a negative impression about themselves and the retail establishment, influencing the customer's decision not to return to the establishment in the future.

Closing the Sale

Either a sales associate or a customer can determine when it is time to take action and close a sale. A customer will often signal he or she is ready to close the sale by a statement or action called a **buying signal**. A buying signal may be a question such as, *Can I charge this?* or a statement, *This will look great in my apartment.* Customers may also show they are ready to close the sale through nonverbal actions such as appearing restless when additional merchandise is shown, setting one item aside from a group of items, or nodding approval to the sales associate. If several customers are shopping together, a companion may suggest the close of a sale by reaffirming the buyer's decision or moving to a different department within the store.

A sales associate may close the sale by stopping the presentation of additional merchandise, narrowing the selection of items, and concentrating on those in which the customer has shown the greatest interest. This may be done by asking the customer which item he or she prefers. Promptly remove merchandise that has proven to be unsatisfactory to the customer. Ask the customer how he or she intends to pay for the merchandise and reassure customer about the decision through a statement such as, *Those earrings are a perfect match with your dress.* The sales associate should be conscious of the customer and avoid hurrying the decision of the customer or pressuring the customer into a sale.

Once the decision to buy has been reached, getting the customer through the checkout quickly is critical to closing the sale. In a study conducted by *Women's Wear Daily,* 62 percent of specialty and department store customers indicated that they sought a salesperson for fast checkout. The study concluded that 19 percent of the consumers surveyed said they would leave the store empty-handed if the checkout lines were too long. Positive interaction was also rewarded; 39 percent of the shoppers said if a salesperson was helpful and friendly they often ended up spending more (Schneiderman, 1997).

At the close of a sale it is appropriate for sales associates to suggest additional items or accessories for the customer to consider, but they should avoid suggesting alternative merchandise. **Suggestion selling** includes offering related merchandise, such as accessories, larger quantities of the same merchandise in other colors or styles, promotional merchandise, or advertised merchandise. The customer always receives suggestions better if the salesperson shows the merchandise rather than asking if he or she wants to see additional items or directing the customer to another area of the store to search for it without assistance from the salesperson. More than any other selling technique, successful suggestion selling can increase the profitability of the store and the productivity of the sales associate. These benefits cannot be overstated.

AFTER THE SALE

A common practice used by sales associates in specialty and department stores is to keep **customer directories** for future sales opportunities. Each salesperson develops his or her own customer directory with names, addresses, telephone numbers, and important details about the customer's purchases and preferences. Details may include sizes, color preferences, and style details that are of particular interest to the client, and any other information that might be helpful in creating potential future sales. The directory may also include anniversary and birthday dates as reminders to the sales associates and other appropriate people including spouses, other relatives, and friends. An accurate directory can be a valuable resource to a sales associate when new merchandise arrives, assisting the associate in identifying a potential customer. Jeffery Kalinsky, owner of three stores in Atlanta (Box 13.1), mails follow-up notes, answers phone calls, and sends gifts to clients to show his appreciation for their business. Kalinsky illustrates how a firm can achieve success if it concentrates on customer service.

ATTRIBUTES OF SUCCESSFUL SELLING

When making a purchase by phone, have you ever been asked by the customer service representative, *Can this phone conversation be recorded for quality assurance?* If you have, you should be pleased that the firm thought enough of customer service to want to improve its methodology and training. Retailers and manufacturers put a great deal of time and money into establishing store image through the promotion mix. This image is wasted if a customer is met by an uninformed or disinterested sales associate. Here are just a few of the many reasons retail sales are lost by sale associates:

- No salesperson in sight
- Salesperson chatting with co-workers
- Salesperson not available at the checkout
- Salesperson's bad attitude or physical appearance
- Customer has to ask for assistance
- Salesperson jumps too quickly to close the sale
- Salesperson unable to locate advertised merchandise
- Salesperson ignores a complaint or concern
- Salesperson has insufficient product knowledge
- Customers do not feel comfortable in the store
- Salesperson attempts to serve more than one customer at a time
- Salesperson is busy with something else
- Salesperson services a customer on the phone before the customer on the sales floor

Sales are also lost during phone transactions for various reasons, including:

- Customer put on hold for too long
- Sales associate has insufficient product knowledge
- Sales representative unable to make immediate decisions regarding a consumer's question about the merchandise
- Sales representative lacking good listening skills

Identifying quality individuals and training them properly is extremely important to retailers and others in the distribution channel. A successful business must incorporate a planned program of sales training into its marketing plan. A training program should educate the employee on store policies and procedures, interpersonal communications, and the goals and objectives of management. Quality training programs include role playing, active listening, feedback, videos, quizzes, and team exercises.

BOX 13.1
A High Fashion Destination Worth a Detour

On a sweltering Saturday in midsummer, when the department stores in many big cities were dead, Jeffrey Kalinsky's Atlanta mall boutique, which sells some of fashion's most desirable designs, was jammed with customers.

They were not bargain hunters at an end-of-summer sale, but style mavens in search of full-price fall clothing from Helmet Lang, Jil Sander, and Comme des Garçons. The customers were so numerous that the stockroom, bathroom, and manager's office served as dressing rooms. The floor was littered with Manola Blahnik shoes, the counters and benches piled high with castoff Lucien Pellat-Finet cashmere sweaters and sumptuous Dries van Noten skirts. It felt like the backstage commotion of a runway show, with women in mismatched outfits, scrambling to pull jackets and pants off the racks.

"Come on, work yourself, girl," Kalinsky chided a customer, turning the collar of a Prada coat she was trying on.

Kalinsky, a former shoe buyer for Barneys New York, arrived in Atlanta in 1990, a Pied Piper of high fashion, convinced that a desire for sophisticated apparel was not limited to Manhattan. His insight, coupled with extraordinary personal attention to customers—he sometimes flies them to Europe to view runway shows with him—has built a mini-empire of fashionable clothing below the Mason-Dixon line.

Kalinsky, who grew up in Charleston, South Carolina, said he worked from a young age in the first Bob Ellis shoe store, which his father opened nearly 50 years ago. It sold designer shoes and hard-to-find sizes. After graduating from George Washington University in 1984, he continued, he worked as a shoe manager at a Bonwit Teller branch near Philadelphia. Within months, he moved to Bergdorf's in New York, followed by 5 years at Barneys.

He owns three stores: Jeffrey, a multidesigner boutique; Bob Ellis shoes, a branch of his family's shoe-store chain, and a Jil Sander boutique. All are connected in Phipps Plaza, a mall on Peachtree Street in the Buckhead section of Atlanta.

"It is the opinion of most people in the fashion industry that if it's not in New York or L.A., then it doesn't exist," Kalinsky said. "We have a ton of people in Atlanta and everywhere who have good taste and want nice things. You'd be shocked where my customers come from— Dothan, AL, and Rome, GA. A woman in Mobile, AL, who has money buys from me. She goes to Barneys in New York, she calls Jil Sanders in San Francisco, and then she ulti-mately comes back to me because she realizes she doesn't have to go anywhere else."

With a reputation spread by word-of-mouth, even among fashion insiders in Manhattan, Kalinsky's stores make more than 50 percent of their multimillion-dollar yearly sales to out-of-town customers. He handpicks items with a customer's shape and tastes in mind, then sends off a package of clothes for her to try on. Other customers fly to Atlanta expressly to visit his shops.

"I came to Atlanta today to shop," Ellen Carey said, standing before a mirror in an ivory Jil Sander skirt and sweater. Ms. Carey owns Seed, a wholesale and public relations company in New York for young clothing designers.

"It's been a well-kept secret," she said of Kalinsky's stores. "Jeffrey runs around and encourages you to try things you'd never try. He has a total vision: the bag, the shoes and what else he's bought, and puts it together in an amazing way. The joy of Jeffrey is he does know what you want in New York." She added, "Also, you feel really glamorous flying to Atlanta for the day to shop."

Jackie Reses, an investment banker at Goldman, Sachs in New York, accidentally discovered Kalinsky's stores on a business trip. Now, she makes it a point to route her travel through Atlanta whenever possible. "I literally will go out of my way to go to the store if I'm in Atlanta," said Ms. Reses, who considers Kalinsky's shoe selection the best in the country. "If I were on a Delta flight going toward the south, I would stop in Atlanta for the store."

After the 1994 Super Bowl and 1996 Olympics were held in Atlanta, Kalinsky's mailing list expanded to include celebrities, musicians, and athletes' wives.

"I probably buy half my wardrobe through him," said Ann Tenebaum, of Manhattan. "In New York, you can buy whatever you want, but it can be a hassle here. Jeffrey makes it easy. He sends me these huge boxes. In the beginning of the season, he could send me a box with 30 things in it, sometimes with an additional 10 pairs of shoes. It's like the store comes to you. I pick a few pieces and send the rest back."

Both immensely accommodating and shrewd at business, Kalinsky mails follow-up notes advising a customer how to wear her new purchases, answers late-night emergency phone calls about shoes, and lavishes flowers and other gifts on preferred customers. He also trains his 28 employees in the art of personal service and requires them to attend Saturday-morning style clinics at the store, complete with a makeshift runway and models. "If I don't explain the clothes to my sales associates, how could they understand Comme des Garçons?" he said.

Bergdorf Goodman president Dawn Mello said Kalinsky "really knows what people want to wear," adding: "He's up to the minute in the sense of style, but he's not extreme. It's right on target."

Taking customers with him to Europe for the fashion collections or paying for airline tickets for a shopping spree at his stores might seem extravagant, but it pays off. "To spend $300 on a plane ticket for someone who spends $16,000—who cares?" Kalinsky exclaimed. "Free gift with purchase!"

Adapted from: Hayt, E. (1998, August 23). A high fashion destination worth a detour. New York Times [On-line]. Available: http://www.nyt.com/yr/mo/day/news/style/kalinsky-fashion.html. Copyright © 1998 by the New York Times Co. Reprinted by permission.

The National Retail Federation (NRF) has determined that sales training is of such importance that the organization has developed a certification program for training sales associates through the King of Prussia Retail Skills Center in Pennsylvania. The training program is a partnership among the NRF, Kravco Company, American Express, and the State of Pennsylvania to raise standards for the retail industry. The center has been established to help retailers find, select, and motivate professional retail employees. Workers are trained to increase their employability, raise their retail skills, and improve their knowledge of the industry. Additionally, educators have teamed up with the retail industry to develop programs to help students gain real-life job training. More information about this training program can be found at the National Retail Federation website at *http://www.nrf.com* (Fig. 13.7).

Providing high-quality service is a mind-set that has long been used by U.S. companies to differentiate products. In Europe, however, recognition of customer service to differentiate products is just emerging as a strategic option. Stewart-Allen (1996) highlighted several characteristics fundamental to customer service in the United States that can have positive results in Europe, as follows:

- Realize the importance of customers.
- Survey customers' attitudes and behaviors.
- Take ownership at the front line for customer problems.
- Take a proactive approach to suggesting solutions to customer problems.
- Make a statement to customers that they are valued and essential to the firms.
- Give customers the option to provide feedback about the firm.

Stewart-Allen suggests that knowing what good customer service looks like and surveying customers and clients' opinions regularly will help European vendors raise the standards of customer service. Effective sales associates broadcast the following positive attributes to each customer they meet: They are well groomed and attractive; have a good working knowledge of the merchandise and retailing environment; have a good rapport with customers; and are motivated and persistent in creating opportunities for sales and excitement in selling.

Personal Appearance

Personal qualities required of individuals in a personal selling situation include excellent appearance and grooming, strong fashion sense, outgoing personality, poise, artic-

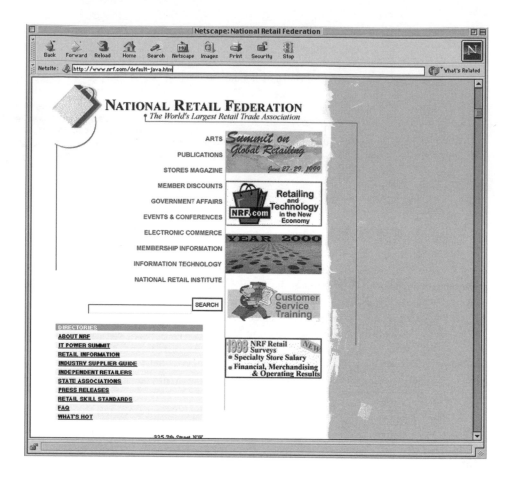

ulateness, quick-thinking, social ease, and self-confidence. Research has shown that personal attractiveness enhances personal communication and contributes to persuasiveness. Sales associates at all levels must have immaculate grooming and appearance. This does not mean sales associates must be beautiful or take on the image of a fashion model. They must, however, dress in a professional manner appropriate to their environment and have the restraint not to wear unattractive or inappropriate clothing.

Individuals must have a standard of cleanliness. Hair for both men and women should be clean and styled, and men with beards or mustaches should keep them trim and neat. Fingernails should be groomed. Polish, if worn, should be in good taste and not chipped or otherwise unattractive. Colognes and fragrances, if used, should be subtle, not overwhelming. Clothes should be clean, pressed, and in good shape, not tattered or worn. Sales personnel must be in good health and have the stamina necessary to stand for long hours and lift and move merchandise.

Knowledge

Knowledge of the merchandise, the retail policies, and the customer is critical in a good salesperson. Based on the assumption that customers want help in choosing the right merchandise, merchants and vendors have striven to improve the product knowledge of sales associates in recent years (Schneiderman, 1997).

With the volume of advertisements and promotions transmitted through print media, broadcast media, and the Internet, it is rare when a customer knows nothing about the product he or she is purchasing. Knowing more about the product and understanding the qualities of the merchandise that are particularly critical to the consumer are essential if a salesperson is to make a positive impression on the consumer. Salespeople should be familiar with every detail of the product, what the product does and does not do, the merits of particular items, and the benefits each item has to the purchaser.

Sales associates should be able to answer frequently asked questions concerning brands and manufacturers, sizes and colors available, fabric and fiber contents, and care requirements of merchandise, and should be able to use these features as selling points. In addition, a sales associate should be aware of the competition's product and the overall market so he or she can respond to concerns of the consumer who may be comparing products. The sales staff should be fully aware of fashion information concerning current trends and know where coordinating accessories, jewelry, shoes, and other items are available in the store. A salesperson who is perceived by the customer as an expert about the merchandise or service being offered has a much greater chance of making a sale. Figure 13.8 shows the Cyber Beauty Advisor, a point-of-purchase interactive video prepared by the cosmetics firm English Ideas. While waiting to be served by a live sales associate, a customer can access a mini-lesson about common makeup problems by touching the screen. The image of Rebecca Pflueger, the company presi-

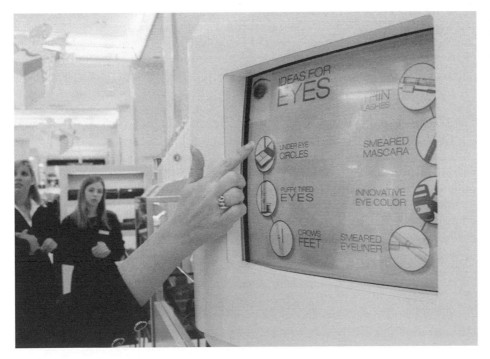

Figure 13.8

This point-of-purchase interactive device supplements the service of a knowledgeable sales associate.

Source: S. Farley/NYT Pictures

dent, presents information about products for lips, face, brows, or eyes. Both customer and sales associate can save time when the Cyber Beauty Advisor imparts this product knowledge. Then the sales associate can supplement this information with answers to specific questions and advice tailored to the customer's needs.

A good sales associate will be aware of store promotions, point-of-purchase displays, advertised merchandise in print media, billing inserts, and catalogs, and be ready to assist customers who have questions. He or she should be aware of merchandise displayed in windows or remote locations and where the customer may find the merchandise in-house or at branch locations. Buyers and merchandisers should meet regularly with sales associates to share their enthusiasm for the merchandise. Accessories and coordinating pieces should be shown to sales associates with information on where the pieces are located within the store. Reliable communication from the buying office should inform sales associates of ordered stock and estimated time of arrival in the store so they will be able to answer potential questions from customers.

Customer Savvy

Have you ever heard someone exclaim, *She has a lot of savvy!* This complement means the person is well informed and perceptive, a shrewd businesswoman. Sales associates who can obtain this trait are invaluable to selling firms. A credible salesperson is believable, trustworthy, and honest in dealing with customers and has a good sense of **salesmanship**, the ability to sell goods in a fair, sincere, and distinctive manner. The purpose of salesmanship is to provide assistance to customers during the buying and selling process so they will be satisfied with their purchase decisions. The viewpoint of the customer, not the salesperson, should be the driving force behind good salesmanship. Customers should be given reasons why, and encouraged to purchase because of what the product or service can do for them. Customers are not dumb and should not be treated as such by the use of a mechanical "canned" sales pitch. Salespeople should approach customers with genuine interest in the customer and not persuade a customer to purchase merchandise he or she really does not want. Figure 13.9 alludes to the importance placed on the customer in Japan: *Never, ever is the buyer put in a position of disrespect.* It has been wise for U.S. companies such as Saturn to adopt this philosophy, because they have reaped the rewards of satisfied customers in a product category that was known for less than positive customer experiences in the past.

Savvy sales associates are also taking advantage of the power of personalization. The easiest way to do this is by using a customer's name. A specialty store sales associate who keeps a reference list of loyal customers will have easy access to this information. Stores that participate in loyalty programs or frequent-buyer programs also have immediate access to the names of customers who participate in these programs. Addressing customers by name is also becoming more common by mass merchandisers. Sales personnel in these environments have access to the customer's name when the customer's credit card is swiped through the point-of-purchase system. This allows the clerk to conclude the transaction by saying, *Thank you, Ms. Smith.*

Today's customers are increasingly sophisticated in their needs and rushed in the time they can devote to satisfying their needs. They know what they want and have less store loyalty than previous generations. A professional salesperson will understand the demographic and lifestyle nature of his or her customers and offer merchandise to the customers' liking. Customers should not be stereotyped in terms of price, probable intentions to buy, or other characteristics that may be false assumptions. A salesperson should know the customer and the service expectations of the customer. A successful salesperson will help spend the customer's time profitability for both parties by offering merchandise that fits his or her consumer profile.

Motivation

Motivation of sales personnel is vital to the well being of the individual and the retailer. Motivated sales associates will show their enthusiasm for the retailer and for their role within the institution to each customer who enters the store. Unmotivated sales clerks will also convey their boredom and disrespect for their employer to customers who, in turn, are less likely to make a purchase.

George Gillen, executive vice president of Management Horizons, a consulting division of Price Waterhouse, has suggested the following strategies for transforming associates into "charming, efficient, and persuasive salespeople" (Emerson, 1995). According to Gillen, "great customer service is more than a list of do's and don'ts. It's an attitude—a state of mind—carried by the sales associate and fostered by the store environment itself." Here are just a few of the recommendations made by Gillen for a successful sales staff:

Figure 13.9

Saturn's commitment to personal service is illustrated in this advertisement.

- The easiest way to mobilize your store to provide great customer service is to hire people who are truly customer-oriented, which will show through during an interview and discussions about the business.
- The best way to encourage sales associates to provide excellent customer service is to treat them with respect.
- Have sales associates think in terms of the potential value a single customer can bring to the store. Staff will find that customers can bring in more profit if they are treated as they expect to be treated. These customers will return to the store.
- Provide response cards to the customer. If associates know customers are encouraged to give feedback, they will be motivated to provide the best possible service.
- Encourage sales associates to build relationships with customers and reward the associate who is responsible for bringing customers back.

Sales personnel motivation is the responsibility of management. It may take the form of training sessions and incentive programs designed to generate sales. Sales meetings should be regularly scheduled with sales associates to inform them about new merchandise, specific promotions, and store services.

Incentive Programs

Incentive programs are motivational tools generally designed to increase the sales productivity of each sales associate. Incentive programs can take the form of training sessions, sales contests, or salary enhancements.

Training Sessions

Well-executed training sessions are one of the best motivational tools a company can participate in. As we discussed in Chapter 11, sales training may be a trade-oriented incentive offered by manufacturers. Regardless of who sponsors the training program, it is an excellent resource for sales associates. Training sessions may take the form of a breakfast or luncheon meeting that focuses on product knowledge or usage. All sales associates are encouraged to attend to view the latest trends, hear comments from senior management, or learn about the firm's most recent promotion campaign. In Box 13.1 Jeffrey Kalinsky held style clinics for his personal service team.

A typical training session to introduce new trends may include a fashion show or display of new merchandise. The buyer will be the spokesperson, discussing each item of merchandise and answering questions from sales associates about the item. Discussion points may include new fabrications and colors, coordinating pieces, determining the correct size, and proper accessories for the item. Certain merchandise categories, such as shoes or bras, require hands-on fitting demonstrations to train associates. These can also be incorporated into a training session.

Training sessions are important for sales representatives, too. Rebecca Pierson, National Retail Merchandise Manager for regional JNCO, flew 26 coordinators to Los Angeles for a training session with a focus on negotiation skills, time management, presentation skills, and the customer experience. There is always a lot of excitement at training sessions. Senior management wants to energize the team and create enthusiasm about the merchandise.

Spiffs

PMs, which stands for push money or prize money, are salary supplements used to reward sales associates for pushing the sales of certain merchandise and often are used to encourage multiple sales. **Spiffs**, as they are also called, may be given to employees in the form of extra money, additional discounts, or merchandise whenever sales of specific items are made. Incentive rewards may be designed to increase the number of sales, the dollar volume of each sale, or multiple sales. PMs can have a negative effect on the retailer if sales associates use the incentive to push unwanted merchandise onto customers. When this occurs, the customer loses confidence in the retailer and the retailer loses a return customer.

Sales Contests

Incentives may also take the form of **sales contests** in which sales associates compete against one another, against other stores within the chain, or against established goals to increase sales. The winning employee or store may receive monetary or merchandise rewards. Sometimes these rewards are generous vacations or other large ticket items. Sales contests are generally designed to increase total sales for a salesperson during a given time or the sale of a particular item during a given time. Sales contests designed to promote competition between branch stores have the advantage of team building among associates within the same branch.

Salary Enhancements

Employers may use salary enhancements to motivate sales associates. **Salary enhancements** are special bonuses, merit pay, or salary incentives used to motivate employees.

Bonus   A sum of money or the equivalent given to an employee in addition to the employee's usual compensation is considered a **bonus**. Bonuses are commonly distributed at the end of the calendar year or the end of a fiscal year to employees and are based on length of service with the organization, not sales. Bonuses are often given as a reward to a team, a department, or the entire staff.

Merit Pay   **Merit pay** is extra pay awarded to an employee for outstanding past performance. Merit pay may take the form of a one-time payment, an increase in base salary, or a percentage of commissions earned. Merit pay is usually distributed on a individual basis as a way for the company to recognize superior performance by the employee.

Profit Sharing   Some companies use profit sharing as a motivation for the sales staff. **Profit sharing** is a plan that offers employees a chance to purchase stock in the company and an opportunity to receive shares of any profits earned by the company. With profit sharing, employees receive payment in addition to their regular salary when the company shows a profit increase. Profit sharing encourages employees to build long-term loyalty and work hard for the company, since they share directly in the profits.

Salary Plus Commission   **Salary plus commission** is an incentive used by some retailers or departments in which employees are given a base salary plus an additional percent based on sales generated. Salary plus commission guarantees a minimum level of income and also allows the salesperson to increase his or her earnings on the basis of sales performance. Macy's department store uses this sales incentive to stabilize earning for its sales associates and cultivate a better-informed team of sales personnel ("Department Stores," 1996). Nordstrom has long used this incentive as a way to encourage salespeople to work as a team as compared with straight commission, which encourages competition and can result in poor customer service.

Human resources expert Wilfred Roy has found that a good reward system should be based on the following characteristics ("Department Stores," 1996):

- It should be a reflection of the corporate culture of the firm. In the case of Nordstrom, the company culture stands behind the salesperson and will support satisfying the customer, sometimes even at a substantial cost.
- It should take a linear direction from the sales floor up so that everyone has the same focus.
- It should be at least 20 percent of the base pay to change behavior.
- It should have safeguards to prevent windfalls from events extraneous to effort.

But even the best trained and most motivated sales associate will occasionally come into contact with a difficult customer. We discuss some of the typical customer types in the next section.

HANDLING VARIOUS CUSTOMER TYPES

The selling environment is dynamic and ever changing. No two customers are the same, and a salesperson must be ready for any situation, routine or unusual, that may occur. Customers may be anxious to buy and pleasant to the sales associate or unfriendly toward the sales associate and not satisfied with any solution offered. A sales associate must be persistent and attempt to fulfill the needs and wants of each customer, using the positive energy while brushing off the negative stigma of the previous customer.

Every customer is different and should be treated as such. However, certain types of behavior among customers become recognizable to salespeople once they have familiarized themselves with the buying population.

Eccentric Shopper

The eccentric shopper compulsively shops, but never buys. Eccentric shoppers visit retail stores regularly and become known to the sales associates, who learn quickly that the eccentric shopper is not likely to make a purchase. They will find some excuse to put off the purchase, sometimes waiting until the sales associate has written up the sale. Sales associates should acknowledge the eccentric shopper and show him or her a few pieces and then politely move to the next customer where a sale is more likely to occur.

Browser

The browser is a shopper who will peruse merchandise in a leisurely and casual way. Browsers may be considered bothersome or beneficial, contingent upon their inclination to buy. A nonbuying browser may just be killing time with no intention of making a purchase. However, a browser may enjoy shopping and spending money, and thus is capable of making a purchase if the merchandise is appealing. The disinterested browser will have a detached attitude recognizable by the sales associate. A sales associate should be watchful to identify the potentially interested browser and provide enticing merchandise.

Bargain Hunter

The bargain hunter can be identified as wanting the best quality for the least amount of money. They show up for sales, but they also shop during nonsale periods looking for value investments. Bargain hunters enjoy saving money as a matter of principle and will not be influenced to purchase items they do not believe are worth the price. Some bargain hunters complain about pricing even after discounts or expect the discounted good to be of the same quality standards as the full-priced merchandise. Because bargain hunters are potential purchasers, sales associates should show them merchandise, pointing out details but refusing to argue or negotiate about price, quality, or other selection factors.

Serious Shopper

The serious shopper wants or needs a specific item and will not be influenced by alternatives. A sales associate should listen carefully to the serious shopper to determine what available items might satisfy his or her needs. A serious shopper who leaves a store without making a purchase is more likely to return to the store if the sales associate has been honest in explaining that the store does not have what the customer wants at the moment and has suggested an acceptable alternative.

Pressured Shopper

The pressured shopper is always in a hurry and pressured to make an immediate purchase. Because time is limited, pressured shoppers are often irritable, distracted, and indecisive in their purchasing decisions. The pressured shopper often expects the sales associate to solve his or her purchasing dilemma with little information or time spent evaluating comparative products. Pressured shoppers may need a gift for a birthday or anniversary; others may need items for a vacation or special occasion. A mindful sales associate can lead pressured shoppers to the correct department, then show merchandise in a rapid manner to help them make a decision.

FUTURE TRENDS IN PERSONAL SELLING

Personal selling is a fundamental element of retail promotion. Although emerging technologies, including Internet shopping and cable home shopping networks, have entered into the marketplace, they have not replaced the sales associate. Trends in personal selling involve the way sales associates are acquiring knowledge about products, trends, floor presentations, and selling techniques. Bloomingdale's has experimented with sales training through coast-to-coast video conferencing. The retailer has been conducting electronic meetings with staff at all its stores on a regular basis. The 21 branch stores are equipped with voice-activated microphones and large-screen TV monitors, which are brought together in an "interactive boardroom" (Zimmerman, 1997a). Bloomingdale's has saved a significant amount of travel expense by using this means of communication.

Future applications for video conferencing include sharing data and applications on personal computers. For example, a store manager in Minneapolis will be able to transmit weekly sales reports to all stores and illustrate a point during a live discussion about sales trends. Additionally, Bloomingdale's is considering using wireless cameras to convey visual images and audio from remote sites to the video conference audience. With the wireless camera, for example, footage of runway shows can be captured and shared with the entire sales staff.

In an effort to improve efficiency and effectiveness in sales associates, Federated Department Stores has tested **computer-based training programs** (CBTs) using interactive CD-ROM technology. The new programs for sales associates cover employee orientation and professional selling methods (Tosh, 1997.) According to Federated, the programs help new associates feel more comfortable on the selling floor faster. They give sales associates a boost in their confidence. The training includes a "virtual store tour" with full-motion video that introduces new employees to department managers and describes specific job responsibilities. Trainees also take a 1-hour professional selling course using video simulations that focus on greeting, selling, closing, and satisfying the customer. Forty core customer transactions and typical sales procedures are also taught via the CD-ROM training program.

The Internet also offers advancements in personal selling, introducing the "virtual makeover," which replaces the need for a personal image consultant. Cover Girl, Clinique, and Revlon are all offering customers the ability to identify the correct lipstick, eye shadow, powder, and rouge based on responses to questions on skin, eye, and hair type via the Internet. Websites walk customers through a network of makeup choices, skin-care tips, and entertainment tidbits. In 6 months the Cover Girl site doubled its number of visitors from 40,000 to 80,000. Researchers predict that the traditional department store cosmetics customer will slowly die out and be replaced by the Web customer (Hendren, 1997).

Merchants that have developed on-line retailing services are also realizing the importance of salesmanship by their customer service representatives. Figuring out how to better serve on-line shoppers is a trend in personal selling and is highlighted in Box 13.2.

Personal selling is one-on-one communication between a manufacturer or retailer, and a customer. Although often overlooked as a promotion technique, personal selling is an important tool in communicating a sponsor's message to a customer. Using the elements of the buying and selling process—attention, interest, desire, action and satisfaction—a sales associate has the opportunity to share a firm's message with the customer and complete a sale through personal communication.

Good salesmanship does not just happen. It takes dedication from both the company and the salesperson to do a good job. Marketers must combine personal selling with all other elements of the promotion mix to encourage positive, direct interaction between the customer and the seller and to create a homogenous image of the firm. Sales personnel can have the greatest influence on consumers by interacting in a polished and professional manner. A firm has no greater asset than an effective sales associate.

BOX 13.2

Internet Merchants Seek New Ways to Improve On-line Customer Service

As they move further into on-line retailing, companies such as Eddie Bauer that have built their specialty store business on an unyielding commitment to customer service are seeking new ways to ensure that conviction will resonate with their Internet customers as well.

"Customer service on-line goes beyond selection, easy navigation and order confirmation," says Judy Neuman, divisional vice president–interactive media for the Redmond, Washington-based retailer. "We're trying to look at our site through the value-added lens of the customer and figure out exactly what she wants."

Figuring out how to better service on-line shoppers, who are quickly becoming as diverse as store-based shoppers, is a top priority for all virtual retailers. E-mail increasingly is being used for customer support, but rarely includes immediate interaction between customers and retailers. Overloaded call centers, moreover, can be a source of long "hold" intervals and growing frustration—hardly the hallmarks of good customer service.

Aware that Net-based customer service can be a strategic differentiator, on-line merchants are exploring means of upgrading customer service. Many are looking closely at the growing list of new software programs from companies including Silknet, Acuity (formerly Ichat), Sitebridge, and Aspect Technologies, which promise to help them integrate on-line customer support into their existing customer service operations.

Silknet Software calls its solution eService. This enterprise solution, created exclusively for the Web, is billed as a comprehensive multimedia customer service solution designed to complement or even replace traditional telephone-based call centers. The software enables retailers to take advantage of all of the Internet's capabilities, including text, graphics, audio, and video, to provide customers with more robust answers to their questions than they had typically received through a call center.

"The essence of eService is that it puts the customer in control," explains Michael Bettua, marketing and communications director at Silknet. "If they have a question they can manage the interaction required to get them the desired answer. Chances are that if they search the eService knowledge base for answers they'll come up with one. If not, they can also choose how they would like a service rep to respond: e-mail, Internet conference, conventional telephone or via the Web."

The Silknet program is in sync with the self-service shopper who thrives on the thrill of the hunt for information on-line. The extensive knowledge base, far exceeding the typical Frequently Asked Questions, enables customers to dig deep into a subject until they find their answer. If they choose, they can opt for personal interaction, but Silknet's real strength is its ability to engage customers and draw them further into a website.

SiteBridge's CustomerNow program and Acuity's WebCenter software, by contrast, put the accent on real-time, interactive customer service, typically delivered via a call-back button or other customer link. The SiteBridge system is designed to allow home users with a single phone line to receive one-to-one service without disconnecting from the Net. WebCenter has three elements: a self-help system, a Web automated call distributor that routes inquiries to specific agents, and several chat options.

Some experts feel that allowing consumers to communicate directly with on-line retailers through chat functionality will be a boon for service and sales as a whole. Much of their theory springs from a study called "Revenue Prospects for On-line Chat," released by Juniper Communications.

The study argues that business-related chat has the potential to advance the competitive positioning of commerce sites, and that service-related chat would foster better client relationships and would aid in marketing products, closing sales, and promoting cross-sell opportunities.

While Neuman at Eddie Bauer admits that type of technology has value, her view of the new software tends to be more cautious. "Decisions about integrating new software are always complex, and this one has huge financial implications," she says. "For example, a tremendous amount of back-end infrastructure would have to be in place to support the idea of real-time chat. For starters, the idea of service-related chat on-line requires 24-hour round-the-clock help. We're not a 24-hour facility right now. Just the staffing would be a huge cost."

Eddie Bauer currently is evaluating its shopper support and trying to figure out the right formula for customer service on-line. Neuman points out that while some customers feel that on-line shopping can be impersonal and prefer to talk to a real voice, there is another group that is content with deeper levels of product information. "Customers are unique in their needs and habits and we have to be sensitive to that as we look at the service quotient," she says.

While SiteBridge allows shoppers to interact with an on-line customer service representative without leaving the Web environment, it is an exception. For home users with only one phone line, using the callback button requires them to disconnect from the Net in their quest for an answer, then get back on line to place an order.

On-line retail consultant Lauren Freedman urges retailers entering the "next phase" of Internet-based retailing to concentrate on the fundamentals.

"Shoppers need confirmation of their order and the ship time, and they want the ability to track a package. These should be readily available—not something the consumer has to chase down."

Adapted from: Internet merchants seek new ways to improve on-line customer service. (1998, August). Stores, *62–63.*

SUMMARY

- The salesperson represents the entire organization to a customer and is responsible for building customer loyalty and creating customer satisfaction.
- Personal selling involves direct interaction between salesperson and customer, initiated by either party, and finished at the completion of the sale.
- Personal shoppers are available at some retail establishments to shop with or for customers.
- Direct sellers, such as image consultants, offer personal service about beauty and fashion on an individual basis.
- All forms of selling include a buying and selling process: (1) getting the attention of the consumer, (2) creating interest, (3) forming desire, (4) stimulating action, and (5) creating customer satisfaction.
- Elements of a sale include: (1) sales approach, (2) merchandise presentation, (3) handling objections, and (4) closing the sale.
- Personal selling is used at both retail and wholesale levels.
- Qualities of a successful salesperson include excellent personal appearance and grooming, along with knowledge of the merchandise, the retail policies, and the customer.
- Employees are motivated to do a good job through incentive programs such as spiffs, sales contests, or salary enhancements, which include special bonuses, merit pay, profit sharing, and salary plus commission.
- Understanding customer types, such as eccentric shoppers, browsers, bargain hunters, serious shoppers, and pressured shoppers, can aid the salesperson in generating sales.
- Future trends in personal selling include video conferencing, CD-ROM training programs to assist in sales training, and "virtual makeovers."

KEY TERMS

bonus	image consultants	salary plus commission
buying and selling process	manufacturer's sales	sales approach
buying signal	representative	sales contests
computer-based training	merchandise approach	salesmanship
program	merit pay	soft sell
customer directories	personal shoppers	spiffs
greeting approach	profit sharing	suggestion selling
hard sell	salary enhancements	trading up

QUESTIONS FOR DISCUSSION

1. What is the importance of personal selling as a promotion strategy?
2. Explain the AIDA model. What fifth element have researchers added to the model, and why is this element important?
3. What are the elements of a sale?
4. What should a sales associate do after a sale is complete?
5. Discuss positive and negative attributes of sales associates. What solutions can you suggest for the negative attributes that were discussed?
6. What kinds of information should sales associates give and receive from management? Give examples.
7. What are some examples of good incentive programs you have participated in?

ADDITIONAL RESOURCES

Alessandra, T., and Barrera, R. (1993). *Collaborative selling: How to gain the competitive advantage in sales.* New York: Wiley.

Beckwith, H. (1997). *Selling the invisible: A field guide to modern marketing.* New York: Warner.

Bixler, S., and Nix-Rice, N. (1997). *The new professional image.* Holbrook, MA: Adams Publications.

Coscia, S. (1998). *Customer service over the phone.* San Francisco: Miller Freeman.

Gitomer, J. (1998). *Customer satisfaction is worthless, customer loyalty is priceless.* Austin, TX: Bard.

Hyatt, C. (1979). *The woman's selling game.* New York: Warner.

Jacoby, J., and Craig, C. S. (1984). *Personal selling: Theory, research, and practice.* Lexington, MA: D. C. Heath.

Johnson, S. (1984). *The one minute sales person.* New York: Avon.

Nix-Rice, N. (1996). *Looking good.* Portland, OR: Palmer Pletsch.

Wilson, L. (1997). *Stop selling, start partnering.* New York: Wiley.

Figure 14.1

The Fairmont Hotel's annual Christmas event

Source: Courtesy of the Fairmount Hotel, San Francisco.

chapter 14

SPECIAL EVENTS

After you have read this chapter you will be able to:

Explain the purpose of special events.

Examine goals of special events.

Describe the various types of special events.

Incorporate a feasibility study into event planning.

Discuss the personnel involved in special events.

Explain financial considerations for special events.

Evaluate the need for event sponsorship.

Review the evaluation process for special events.

Every year on the first Sunday of December, the Fairmont Hotel in San Francisco kicks off the holiday season. It treats guests to eggnog, apple cider, and sweets. Carolers, dressed in red velvet, serenade the visitors who stroll through the lobby admiring an elaborately decorated Christmas tree and registration area decorated as Santa's workshop (Fig. 14.1). This special event is intended to put travelers in a festive mood and motivate them to begin their Christmas shopping at the nearby shopping areas.

Retailers and manufacturers put considerable time and money into creating special events that will entice consumers to participate and ultimately buy products from the sponsor. From small events, such as product sampling stations at grocery stores, to large month-long retail celebrations featuring merchandise from other countries, special events play a significant role in promotion strategy.

The creation of special events is an integral part of the promotion mix. This chapter discusses special events in general, and Chapter 15 will discuss the fashion show, a long-established special event specific to the fashion industry. We begin this chapter with a discussion of the role of special events. Special events are produced to fulfill corporate goals, and these goals are the subject of the next section. Then we discuss some of the many types of special events. Next, we assess the need for a feasibility study for special events and, after that, focus on the personnel involved in special event planning. It takes many people to put on a special event. The chapter concludes with a discussion of event sponsorship and future trends in special events.

ROLE OF SPECIAL EVENTS IN PROMOTION

If you have never participated in the coordination of a special event, you should—it is one of the most rewarding (and one of the most nerve-racking) promotion strategies you can participate in! Special events are planned activities intended to encourage individuals or groups to gather at a specific time and place because of a shared interest. Some special events are intended to generate sales, while others are intended to communicate a positive image. They can create a dynamic impression of a sales promotion, team, atmosphere, or shopping season; a product or service; or a business, charity, or community event or be used for numerous other reasons. Corporate funding or support for a special project may also constitute a special event. All industries use special events as marketing tools to increase awareness of product or services, enhance brand or company image, or raise funds. One proponent of special events, Abbey Doneger, of The Doneger Group (highlighted in Box 6.2) advises store managers to stage clever special events because community involvement is essential for specialty store business (Moin, 1998).

The variety of special events a firm may choose to produce is limitless. Creativity abounds in special event planning and almost any circumstance a firm finds itself in can be turned into a successful event. Just a few of the numerous types of special events are listed here, including:

Anniversary Sale	Cook-off	Informal Modeling
Athletic Event	Employee Training	Luncheon
Banquet	Exhibit	Men's Night
Beauty Week	Extended Hour Sale	Musical Performance
Blood Drive	Fair	Parade
Brand Awareness	Fashion Show	Product Demonstration
Promotion	Festival	Product Launch
Breakfast	Fund-raiser	Retreat
Cause Awareness Day	Gala	Ribbon Cutting Ceremony
Celebrity Appearance	Gift-with-Purchase Event	Sidewalk Sale
Civic Responsibility	Girls' Night Out	Stockholder Meeting
Conference	Grand Opening	Tour
Contest	Holiday Celebration	Trade Show
Convention	Improvement Project	Workshop

As discussed in Chapter 12, special events lend themselves to *created* publicity. Situations that, alone, may not be considered newsworthy can be made newsworthy by the attention the special event created. For instance, local newspapers may not find product launches to be newsworthy, but if a celebrity is in town to promote a product launch, the appearance of the guest would be considered newsworthy and be given coverage. Store openings, anniversary celebrations, product launches, community action kick-offs, long-established charity events, and special-interest group recognition events can become special events with a planned promotion as part of the integrated marketing communications mix. Color plate 5 shows how a fictional special event, the Nurses Ball on *General Hospital*, promoted the ABC soap opera as well as a real life fund raising campaign for AIDS research.

Special events are an effective mechanism to persuade and inform target markets because they can come in any size or shape, frequency or format (Radman, 1997). An event can be modest, such as the Fairmont Hotel example, or splashy and exclusive, such as sponsorship of nationally televised happenings. Events are designed to promote products by linking them to highly visible activities, issues, or ideas of interest to target audiences. Some events are used as tools to persuade, educate, and provide added value to a particular organization's product or service offering. But behind the glamour, crowds, and product displays, all special events strive to perform the same function: to effectively communicate a message (Radman, 1997).

Special events are gaining importance as part of an IMC mix. According to IMC expert, Don Schultz, the strategically planned use of short-term or long-term events can build links that connect a product or brand to an event of public interest. In turn,

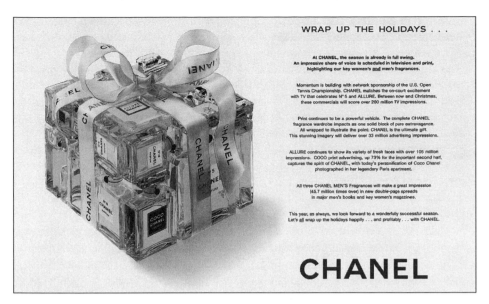

Figure 14.2

Chanel's integrated strategy for a fragrance promotion including event sponsorship.

these links can help a firm to establish rapport between customers and its product or service (Radman, 1997). Combining advertising, sales promotion, personal selling, and visual merchandising along with publicity can help create interest, awareness, and acceptance by the target market. An event hosted by Saks Fifth Avenue will serve as an example. In order to bring awareness of its assortment of British designer merchandise to its customers, the Saks Fifth Avenue flagship store held a 10-day event celebrating British fashion, art, and photography called *Cool Britannia* ("September Event," 1998). The special event combined window displays, personal appearances by celebrities, trunk shows, a photographic exhibit sponsored by the Wool Bureau, and a benefit party for the Ovarian Cancer Research Fund. The event was covered in trade and consumer publications as created publicity in advance of the event. In another example, Chanel developed an integrated promotion strategy for its men's and women's fragrances. The strategy for Chanel's vendors, outlined in Figure 14.2, included print and television advertising and corporate sponsorship of the U.S. Open Tennis Championship.

GOALS OF SPECIAL EVENTS

Special events are planned to fulfill one or more specified business goals. Such goals include the following:

- **Enhance the image of the company to customers or the general public.** Beginning in the 1980s and continuing today, there are many more sellers than buyers in the marketplace; therefore, producers, manufacturers, designers, and retailers have had to look beyond their products and focus on their consumers in order to distinguish themselves from the competition (Schultz & Barnes, 1995). Special events are a promotional strategy that can allow a company to distinguish itself from the competition. The event may enhance the image of a company or a brand the company offers to customers, employees, and the general public. These types of events are planned to communicate a positive image or impression of a company. Because retailers, manufacturers, and designers are so heavily dependent on public acceptance, they have become one of the most aggressive and constant users of special events.

- **Sell large quantities of products or services in a short time period while promoting future sales.** The goal of any promotion strategy is to have consumers respond to products, services, and ideas that are for sale. Special events have become a routine technique used to sell products. As part of doing business, retailers purchase large quantities of products based on a good price, a trade promotion incentive, or a hot seller in the marketplace. As a result of the larger than normal inventory, a special event will be used to sell it in a short period of time. This is a particularly popular technique used at holidays. During these high traffic periods, prewrapped items will be displayed on tables throughout the store as gift reminders for consumers.

- **Reach specifically targeted market segments.** Differentiation is the name of the game. Special events can be used to differentiate a firm from its competition, or differentiate specific target consumers who have potential to benefit the organization. Some special events are planned for the whole population, while other events are targeted to certain customers. Men's nights for example, are popular events hosted by retailers before Christmas and Valentine's day. A yearly ski swap, hosted cooperatively by a local retailer and its vendors, is another example of an event reaching a specifically targeted market segment.

- **Exhibit good corporate citizenship, giving back to the community from which one's customers come.** Malls, retailers, and supermarkets especially dependent on consumers must be particularly watchful of their impact on a community and exhibit good corporate citizenship. They may do so by coordinating special events that will promote an increased quality of life for their customers and employees. An example of a special promotion organized to provide enhanced quality of life for community customers and employees is illustrated in the following example. A regional supermarket chain has a box display naming each of the local elementary and secondary schools by a specific box. For a specified period of time customers are encouraged to deposit their cash register receipts into one of the boxes as they leave the store. At the conclusion of the time period, the supermarket totals the receipts for each school and makes a monetary donation to each of them. Following the promotion, special events are held at each local school to present the contributions.

- **Enhance customer and VIP relations to preferential and potential customers.** Every firm has special customers, or VIPs, that it wishes to impress. Events may be held for these people to show them how important they are to the firm. Invitation-only events, such as galas or premier showings by designers, illustrate their preferential status. For example, Lee Jeans and The Catalyst Group, a Los Angeles-based product placement company, hosted 110 Hollywood costumers and product resource executives for lunch at the House of Blues. The event goal was to introduce Lee Jean image and styles to the movers and shakers in television who wardrobe actors. By strengthening the relationship with the industry, Lee Jeans hoped to get more placement on leading television shows ("Lee Does," 1996).

- **Contribute to community's economic development.** Contributing to the community's economic development is also a goal of special events. Firms cannot exist in a community without contributing back to the economic enrichment of that community. One way for a firm to contribute is to increase sales revenue coming into the community. This can be accomplished by hosting special events that attract certain groups, such as tourists. The tourists will spend money at the event and at other businesses such as hotels and restaurants within the community, thus contributing to economic development. For example, a regional retailer in a resort community may sponsor a juried arts festival over a 3-day weekend to attract out-of-town guests. The tourists spend a day at the festival and another day shopping at local shops and boutiques including the retail sponsor. The community benefits from the economic boost from the tourists, and the retailer benefits from increased name recognition and sales.

- **Promote a charitable cause.** Increasingly, special events are being used to promote charitable causes. Firms ask their customers, employees, and senior management to get involved and take action in response to a concern or a crisis. Many of the examples that are used in this chapter have a cause associated with them. Causes that have particular support from the fashion industry include AIDS and breast and ovarian cancers, because these diseases have disproportionately affected the industry. AIDS has become very important to the fashion world because so many creative, successful, and influential men in the industry have lost their lives to the disease. Because a majority of the people who consume fashion are women, and the fashion industry employs more women than many other sectors of commerce, the industry has become very involved in public awareness for breast and ovarian cancers. Figure 14.3 illustrates Lee's National Denim Day and the international pink ribbon campaign that supports research for breast cancer. Box 14.1 describes some of the ways in which retailers are helping to support breast cancer awareness through programs and special events. Also note how the retailers integrated the special events with other promotion strategies, including print and broadcast advertising, public relations, sales personnel involvement, and direct mail. Although Box 14.1 highlights retailers' contributions, producers, wholesalers, manufacturers and designers are as involved in event planning to support causes that are important the industry.

Figure 14.3

Print advertisement for Lee National Denim Day, displaying the international symbol for breast cancer awareness, the pink ribbon

BOX 14.1

Retailers: In the Front Lines

Retailers are front and center in the fight against breast cancer, a disease that is expected to strike over 180,000 women each year. Perhaps it should be no surprise that breast cancer prevention, early detection, and research have been embraced by department and specialty stores. After all, they cater primarily to women, who have made the cause a priority among health issues.

The Susan G. Komen Breast Cancer Foundation gets the lion's share of support from many chains. Education takes precedence, with stores sponsoring lectures from cancer survivors and medical experts and distributing preventative literature.

From local events to corporatewide sponsorships, retailers across the country are throwing considerable muscle behind the cause. Here's how several of them have gotten involved.

Nordstrom partnered with Lifetime Television to promote the Gift, a self-detection guide and kit developed by In Your Corner, the company formed by Nancy Brinker, founder of Susan G. Komen. Nordstrom sold the kit, for $19.95 in its lingerie department. The chain was the exclusive retailer of the Gift for the month of October (nationwide breast cancer awareness month). Nordstrom also scheduled wellness symposiums with Brinker as a keynote speaker in several stores across the country, and Evelyn Lauder spoke about her survivor experiences at Nordstrom stores. Nordstrom also asked local health experts to speak on subjects such as nutrition and hormone replacement therapy.

The service-oriented store also had prosthesis coordinators available at all its stores to help with customer fittings. "They act not only as a fitter, but coordinate with insurance companies and file the paperwork," the spokeswoman said of the sales associates. "We are a provider for some health care plans, so that way, the customer doesn't even have to deal with the reimbursement. In all our stores, we can handle Medicare claims."

Nordstrom has also taken the unusual step of operating mammography centers in partnership with local hospitals in four of its stores; Skokie, Ilinois; Glendale and Riverside, California; and Littleton, Colorado. The mammography centers are usually located off the cosmetics area. Nordstrom provides customers with beepers so they can shop until the center is ready for them. "The essence of the idea came from a hospital, which approached us with the idea of creating a more accessible, more comfortable environment for women to have mammograms," the spokeswomen said. "We create the space for the facility and the partner hospital operates it day to day."

Henri Bendel hosted its annual *Shop for the Cure* shopping party to benefit the New York *Race for the Cure's* breast health program. It also hosted a *Shop for the Cure* party in Boston after realizing that many of the people involved in the Susan G. Komen Foundation were its customers. Bendel's donated 10 percent of sales on the evening of the event to the cause. The retailer also supported the event by sending direct-mail pieces to customers. As a specialty store focusing exclusively on women, Bendel's believes it is important to remain involved with women's issues. Bendel's had several exclusives for the event including a special scarf designed by Susan Lazar for the *Race for the Cure*. Sales associates wore the pink ribbon that signifies breast cancer month and told customers about the party. The night of the party, the front of the store was gelled pink [lit with pink filters in spotlights to created a colored ambiance] for the cause. "This is part of our ongoing effort to reach out to our customers and appeal to their sense of intelligence," the spokesperson said. "As we all know, its not just about clothes."

On the main floor of Macy's Herald Square, jewelry designer Carolee Friedlander hosted a wardrobe seminar where customers purchased a limited-edition champagne bottle pin designed exclusively for Macy's. Carolee signed certificates of authenticity for each pin purchased and a portion of the sales were donated to SHARE, Self Help for Women with Breast and Ovarian Cancer.

Ann Taylor was a platinum sponsor for the *Race for the Cure*. The chain's involvement went beyond donating money, however. Ann Taylor motivated its troops to participate in the race and was the recipient of the largest corporate team award 2 years in a row. In 1997, 641 associates took part in the race. In addition, Ann Taylor hosted a survivor's reception at its Madison Avenue store. Throughout the month of October, Ann Taylor gave out pink ribbons and shower cards in its stores that explained how to do self-examinations.

J.C. Penney Company's top-level sponsorship of the Susan G. Komen Breast Cancer Foundation *Race for the Cure* is only one of the ways in which the company got behind breast cancer awareness month. Penney's is the sole presenting national sponsor of the 15-year old race. By sponsoring what is actually a series of fund-raising races across the country, the company could summon a tremendous amount of support for breast cancer awareness. Penney's has stores in all 77 cities where there are races, except for Aspen, Colorado.

About 80 percent of J.C. Penney's customers are women, and the company believes that breast cancer should be openly discussed. It wanted to highlight breast cancer as a women's issue and a family issue, and to highlight the race as a wellness issue.

To further support the *Race for the Cure*, Penney's promoted upcoming races in the areas where they were held, via in-store videos, and ran newspaper ads in some of those markets. The company also produced public service announcements to hawk the races on local TV in the cities where the event is held.

In the 3 years since Penney's signed on as the national presenting sponsor, it has seen the number of Komen races run climb to 77 from the 46 held in 1994. They expected 422,500 participants in 1997. Past years' races raised $9.5 million that was allocated in grants to 315 local groups and 42 national organizations that are dedicated to breast cancer research and education. Typically, 75 percent of the funds raised in the contests are given to local groups.

Penney's promoted the races through credit card statements that were mailed to people in the locales where the events were held. In addition to the race sponsorship, Penney's also supported breast cancer awareness month with the purchase of an ad in *Newsweek* that featured a special section on breast cancer. Penney's also backed a series of cable TV programs, shown in October, under the banner "Lifetime Applauds the Fight Against Breast Cancer."

Uptons, a 75 unit chain based in Norcross, Georgia, outside of Atlanta, participated in Lee National Denim Day to support breast cancer research and education initiatives. The chain, a division of the American Retail Group, raised $2 million in a single day. All donations went to the Susan G. Komen Foundation. For the entire week prior to Lee National Denim Day, a purchase of a pair of men's or women's Lee jeans from any Upton store resulted in a $2 donation to the foundation. Also, customers purchasing Lee denim received pink ribbon lapel stickers, the universal symbol for breast cancer awareness. Uptons associates were encouraged to support Lee National Denim Day. In exchange for a $5 contribution to the foundation, employees were permitted to wear denim to work. Upton matched the employee contributions. David Dworkin, president and CEO of Uptons, said in a statement that "our participation in this important event is one more way we can demonstrate our commitment to our customers and their concerns."

Breast cancer is the leading cancer among American women and second only to lung cancer in all cancer deaths, the Komen group has found. By the end of the decade, approximately 1.8 million women and 12,000 men will be diagnosed with this serious disease.

Sears, Roebuck & Company aided in the breast cancer cause through ongoing support of Gilda's Club, a support group for cancer patients and their family and friends. According to Sears' research, about 75 percent of all families eventually will be touched by cancer, and the company felt it was in a position to provide family support. The clubhouses run by Gilda's Group provide a venue for relaxation and social interaction among people touched by cancer. The club is named for Gilda Radner, the comedienne and original cast member of *Saturday Night Live* , who died of ovarian cancer. Sears raised $80,000 in 6 months through the sale of Gilda's Club Neckwear ties and scarves, available exclusively in the chain's stores. A donation of $2 was made from the sale of each $20 tie and $10 or $12 scarf. Celebrities, including Jason Alexander, Katie Couric, and Gene Wilder, who was married to Radner and is co-founder of Gilda's Club, designed some ties. During the fourth quarter, Sears has intensified its fund-raising effort and kicked off a Sears Card promotional tie-in, and added Gilda's Club concept shops to 12 of its stores. The concept shops merchandised articles such as T-shirts, hats, and other logoed apparel. Half of the shops were in stores that were located in markets with a Gilda's Group clubhouse. The first clubhouse was launched in New York in 1995. Sear's also benefited Gilda's Club by marketing a 7-inch, plush snowman figure between Thanksgiving and Christmas. Sears estimated it could raise $250,000 with the sale of the snowman.

Adapted from: Seckler, V., Edelson, S., and Moin, D. (1997, October 6). *Retailers: In the front lines.* An Industry Aware, Women Wear Daily *[Special Report]*, 2.

All of these goals are important and a company must consider each goal when planning a special event. A firm may plan an event to accomplish one or more goals. Once a firm has established the goals for a special event, the next step is to determine what type of event to host. We discuss categories of special events in the next section.

TYPES OF SPECIAL EVENTS

Special events occur at the primary, secondary, and tertiary levels of the fashion industry. Raw material producers may use events to promote new discoveries in fibers or fabrics to manufacturers and consumers. Manufacturers use events to create interest in buyers to select their line for distribution in retail stores. Retailers use events to encourage consumers to shop at their locations. Figure 14.4 shows an event that promotes both a designer and a retailer.

Special events may be classified into two types—institutional events or merchandise-driven events—based on the intent of the event to influence the sale of merchandise or bring attention to the company. Attention to the company may be promoted through institutional features or attractions, specific customer services, special shows, or celebrity appearances. The sale of merchandise may be promoted through product displays, merchandise clinics or demonstrations, fashion shows, sales inducements, or free samples. These classifications are not mutually exclusive. Many special events may be developed as a combination to sell merchandise and bring recognition to the designer or retailer. In one instance, a store opening may be used to strengthen the image of firm, in another instance, to sell merchandise.

Institutional Events

Institutional events are planned to bring attention to the company. They may be produced to enhance the company image, exhibit good corporate citizenship, embellish customer relations, contribute to the community economic development, or promote a charitable cause.

Figure 14.4

A special event, the appearance of designer Karen Neuberger at Lord & Taylor for a pajama party, where sales associates join her in modeling her new lines of sleepwear

One longstanding special event used to promote an institution is the Macy's Thanksgiving Day Parade. Over 2 million people line the parade route and over 35 million people view the parade on television, extending the Macy's name beyond local New York residents. Macy's employees work on the parade year round, auditioning bands, designing floats, and creating the famous cartoon character balloons that fly high above the parade route. Over 3,000 employees are trained as volunteer clowns, dancers, and balloon handlers in the parade. Additionally, Macy's transformed a former candy factory into float central where each float in the parade is designed and assembled by Macy's employees. Other examples of institutional events include museum exhibits, gallery exhibits, in-store exhibits, musical performances, and anniversary celebrations. These are discussed as a sample of the many kinds of events that can be produced to highlight an institution or brand.

Museum Exhibits

A museum is an institution devoted to the acquisition, conservation, study, exhibition, and educational interpretation of objects having scientific, historical, or artistic value. Fashion items have always had great historical and artistic, as well as scientific, value. Museums may provide a unique exhibit space for clothing or unusual products. A **museum exhibit** is a presentation of fashion items in an interpretive setting at a museum. The opening of a fashion exhibit as a special event at a museum may create excitement and institutional recognition for a designer, retailer, or publisher beyond the walls of the institution. According to Melissa Leventon (1995), of the Costume Society of America, costume exhibits are among the most popular "art museum" events, drawing people who otherwise would not be exposed to such media. Clothing is displayed on mannequins arranged in attractive vignettes with narrative provided on signage and programs available from the museum. Retrospective books have been sold as part of the event to generate sales and create an ambiance for the showing. The opening night of museum exhibits is usually a gala party that serves as a fundraiser for the museum or other charity.

Fashion designer exhibits have been a longstanding tradition at the fashion wing of the Metropolitan Museum of Art in New York (see Fig. 1.7). An annual exhibit and gala are presented each year. These exhibits have honored such designers as Yves Saint Laurent, Chanel, and Christian Dior. Such an exhibit was staged in 1997, to memorialize Gianne Versace following his death. In this instance, the annual gala benefited from the added news value of his death. The opening, a $2,000-a-plate dinner, raised $2.3 million for the Costume Institute at the museum (White, 1997a).

Gallery Exhibits

Museums are not the only locations for fashion-related events; galleries also provide a unique location for special events. Galleries are rooms or buildings designed for the exhibition of artistic work. A **gallery exhibit** is a presentation of fashion items in an artistic setting at a gallery. The Art Directors Club in Manhattan featured a special exhibit devoted to products by, for, and from Levi Strauss & Company. The exhibit included posters, advertising, retail displays, commercials, memorabilia, and two pairs of the world's oldest Levi's jeans, circa 1886. The exhibit was designed to commemorate the club's presentation of its 1997 Management Award for Achievement in Brand Advertising and Design Communications to Levi Strauss.

In-store Exhibits

In-store exhibits, defined as special presentations of fashion items in a retail setting, are used to entice regular and new customers into a shop. The customers attend the event and view merchandise offered by the firm. Saks Fifth Avenue in Phoenix, Arizona, held an in-store event titled the *Faces of Fashion* to honor Adel Rootstein, the creator of Rootstein mannequins. Twenty-four Rootstein mannequins were displayed in and around the women's better designer sportswear departments on the third floor. Customers had to walk through the store to reach the display, and had the opportunity to shop on their way.

Musical Performances

Musical performances are entertainment presentations hosted by a retailer or manufacturer. A retailer may invite a local musical group to perform in the retail store for the benefit of shoppers to enhance a season or promote a cultural event. Manufacturers may sponsor a musical performance by a well-known popular singer or host a special viewing of a Broadway play to bring name recognition to its firm at a trade show.

With proper publicity and advertising, the retailer may increase traffic and promote goodwill by sponsoring the local musical organization. The simple addition of background music may enhance sales activities. Nordstrom's entertains customers with live piano performances. The success of the pianists in the flagship store was so great that Nordstrom now has piano players in several of its branch locations.

Anniversary Celebrations

Anniversary celebrations are special events used by companies to bring attention to their longevity in the community. Hudson's Bay Company celebrated its 328th anniversary in Toronto, Canada, by sponsoring institutional events to benefit Canadian charities ("Investor Relations," 1998). One event was an Annual Fashion Cares Gala benefiting the AIDS Committee of Toronto. The event has raised over $2 million dollars since its inception in the mid-1980s. A second event involved Hudson's Bay retail division, Zellers Incorporated. Zellers' associates participated in an employee fund-raising initiative called Moonwalk, which is a national walk-a-thon for the Canadian Cystic Fibrosis Foundation. The support by employees of the organization added to the credibility of the corporation in the eyes of the community. Both events fulfilled the special event goal of being good corporate citizens.

Beginnings and endings are often celebrated with anniversaries; these are usually good times to look back and forward at the same time. The turn of the 21st century was a prime opportunity to do this. The millennium added a unique twist to event planning. It provided a once-in-a-lifetime occurrence that gave companies the opportunity to look at their "corporate memory" and to use an anniversary celebration as a marketing tool. According to Phyllis Barr (1996), a New York-based consultant, using a company's past as a promotion tool in the present can bring attention and business to the company by illustrating the one thing that sets the company apart from every other company—its history. History can be used to respond to people's desire for reliability by telling how long a company has been in business and what it has done. History can also be used to bring renewed attention to long-established brand names by capitalizing on their record of reliability. Consumers are also likely to be drawn to history and nostalgia. By using a nostalgic theme for an anniversary event, the audience can look both backward and forward.

In 1998, the Ferragamo Company, an Italian shoe, accessories, and clothing manufacturer, celebrated the 100th birthday of Salvatore Ferragamo, the founder of the company. In an integrated promotional strategy, special events were planned to honor the founder and the company's values, culture, and products. To kick off the centennial celebration, the firm sponsored the first Salvatore Ferragamo International Competition for Young Shoe Designers. Students from 30 worldwide fashion and design colleges were invited to design sandals for the competition. Another event highlighted the firm's history. This event, a retrospective exhibit "1898–1998—Salvatore Ferragamo—The Art of the Shoe" opened in Tokyo and traveled to several other countries (Fig. 14.5). As a climax to the year of celebration, the company designed the shoe for the 1998 movie *Ever After*. The shoe was the main character of the movie. It was worn by Drew Barrymore and took over 50 hours of labor, 200 silver pearls, 1,000 tiny glass beads, and meters and meters of silver thread to make ("Ever After Ferragamo," 1998). Ferragamo hosted the International preview of the film and sponsored a ball at the Salvatore Ferragamo Museum in Florence, Italy. The company produced a 24-page special promotional section that was featured in consumer fashion magazines to announce its celebrations. The promotional supplement explained the year's events, interspersed with pictures of Ferragamo products and copy stating the firm's commitment to quality.

Merchandise Events

Merchandise events are planned to influence the sale of goods. The goals they fulfill include selling large quantities of products in a short time period, reaching specifically targeted market segments, enhancing customer relations, or promoting a charitable cause.

Figure 14.5

A print advertisement for "Art of the Shoe" exhibit celebrating 100 years of Salvatore Ferragamo

Retailers sponsor activities to attract customers into their stores in order to generate store sales. The activities range from large storewide promotions to small endeavors such as product demonstrations. Special events are an especially important device during off-peak selling seasons. For example, home shows and boat shows at malls are scheduled to bring people in during slower selling seasons. Store anniversary sales are not necessarily celebrated on the actual day of incorporation, but rather during a period in which sales need a boost. As one example, Siefert's, a midwest retailer, always promotes a Columbus Day coat sale to increase sales during a minor holiday, not typically associated with retail sales. Cosmetic companies use events such as facials or beauty seminars to coincide with gift-with-purchase and purchase-with-purchase sales events to increase traffic and move merchandise. Special events can also increase traffic to dispense merchandise rapidly during peak periods. For example, university bookstores always set up extra checkout lines during the first week of classes to accommodate higher numbers of customers during a rush period. Examples of merchandise events include store openings, celebrity appearances, product launches, vendor or category weeks, and product demonstrations. As with institutional events, this is only a sampling of the different types of events that exist to sell merchandise.

Store Openings

Special events are always planned for a store or boutique opening. **Store openings** are celebrations that introduce customers to a new merchant. The merchant may have the store stocked and ready for sales, or show the space where a future store will be located. Special sales, refreshments, and product demonstrations encourage consumers to shop in the new environment. Some events are planned to show consumers the space, rather than sell merchandise. For example, to open her Berlin store, Donna Karan turned the 5,000-square-foot empty space, located in a high-end mall, into a night club complete with a sushi bar and a disco dance floor. Over 1,000 guests attended, including the mayor of Berlin, bankers, politicians, artists, filmmakers, and entertainers (Drier and Ozzard, 1997).

Large chains, such as Target, plan several store openings at once across the country and have special store savings at every location. Special events include refreshments, activities for children, and a fireworks display. When REI, a Seattle-based outdoor gear and clothing chain, opened its new flagship store, it celebrated with a entire week of activities (Fig. 14.6), including a grand opening sweepstakes, a photo exhibit by Art Wolfe, and daily slide shows featuring travel destinations such as Nepal, East Africa, Ireland, China, and Mount Kilimanjaro. Special sale merchandise was featured in every department throughout the store. Following the grand opening week, REI continued the celebration for 4 weeks, featuring different activities, such as camping week, cycling/paddling week, outdoor week, and skiing/climbing week. Special events and merchandise sales were geared to the featured activity.

Celebrity Appearances

The **celebrity appearance**, featuring an individual from inside or outside the fashion industry to promote a new product or designer line, is a common special event. Bill Blass took in $600,000 in orders in 1 year after personally presenting his resort collection at Saks Fifth Avenue in Lake Tahoe, California, ("Blass Shows," 1997). Celebrity appearances are often cooperative events, with designers, retailers, and publishers participating. *Vogue* magazine sponsored a celebrity appearance by Tommy Hilfiger to introduce his women's collection at Bloomingdale's in 1996. He shook hands and signed autographs for more than 500 fans. Figure 14.7 shows how the appearance of Donna Karan at a trunk show added excitement to the presentation of her new designs.

Figure 14.6

REI grand opening in-store flyer

Cosmetic lines often celebrate new fragrances with the designer or celebrity appearing at the product launch. During slower sales periods, malls may invite television stars, particularly soap opera personalities, for 1-day guest appearances to sign autographs and lunch with a special winner to increase traffic for the mall.

Product Launches

Product launches are special events planned to set in motion the promotion and sale of new products such as the new line of sleepwear in Figure 14.4. In 1996, 24,000-plus new products were launched (Hennies, 1997). The special event to kick off a new product is the climax of many months of preparation and planning from the inception of the product to release to the consumer. The goal of a product launch is to make sure every marketing element, advertisement, press release, and direct-mail piece has a cohesive sustained message that enhances the brand equity of the product. While many product launches are conducted at retail stores, the events are planned in cooperation with the producers, manufacturers, or designers of the product. Color Plate 6 shows one medium used in the IMC campaign to launch Pretty Polly hosiery.

Vendor or Category Weeks

Vendor or **category weeks** are special events that feature a merchandise category or brand. The event may be store-specific, such as Levi's week at Joslins, or the event may be sponsored by a producer and involve several competing retailers. For example, the

Figure 14.7

Donna Karan makes a celebrity appearance at a trunk show at Bloomingdale's.

Intimate Apparel Council sponsors Lingerie Week. During the week, in-store events are held at Bloomingdale's, Macy's, and Nordstrom's to increase the sales of intimate apparel. Events have included fashion shows, celebrity appearances, and musical performances by Broadway stars. Bloomingdale's added to the success of the event by sending out its Elegant Essentials catalog prior to the vendor week (Monget, 1997).

Product Demonstrations

Product demonstrations, which illustrate how consumers can use merchandise, are simple yet effective special events orchestrated to promote new or improved products. Demonstrations are common in accessory and cosmetic departments, and in warehouse retailing (where most product demonstrations require minimal space, perhaps a table or counter as the only requirements.) A cosmetic department may offer facials or makeovers for participants who register ahead of time for product demonstrations. The department store may conduct the consultations on the sales floor or have a special room set aside to provide privacy for the customers. Warehouse retailers often have product representatives set up at stations within the store. Food samples or cleaning solutions are often tested before an audience for their reaction. In the case of an environmentally sensitive cleaning product, demonstration of adequate soil removal may cause favorable product evaluation and create increased sales.

Budgeting for the product must be considered when staging a demonstration. In accessory departments, scarves or other items that will be returned to the floor for sale do not have to be purchased prior to the demonstration. Although the merchandise is saleable, expenses may still be incurred for TVs or VCRs rented for the demonstration. Food or other products that will be consumed as part of the demonstration must be accounted for in the budgeting process.

FEASIBILITY STUDY

The most frequent problem in event planning is timing. Event planners often try to stage events before they are ready. They forgo the feasibility study or wait too long before implementing actions to coordinate the event. A **feasibility study** is a survey to determine if the plan has potential to be successful. A professional consultant may be hired to determine feasibility or, minimally, the event planner and management team—including buyers, department managers, vice presidents, CEOs, or others with vested interests—should discuss the feasibility of the event, taking all factors into account. Answers should be based objectively on solid, factual, and timely information. Often event planners already have a particular type of event in mind. Regardless, all options should be considered to determine which type of event will draw the largest audience and, therefore, have the greatest possibility for success.

Determinants, including weather, competition, population, attitudes, facilities and services, community support and reputation, and sponsorships, should be evaluated. People will not drive and/or walk to events in bad weather, nor will they spend time outside if the weather is too windy or hot. Sunny, warm weather will deter plans for winter festivals just as cold weather will hamper warm weather events. As illustrated by the winter of 1997–98, when even professional sporting events were canceled because of blizzards, weather can be a strong deterrent to indoor and outdoor events.

When planning an event, one should study potential competing events to determine if the planned audience will be diverted. Schools and churches, chambers of commerce, and convention and visitors bureaus publish event calendars and are excellent resources about community events. Sometimes events are heightened by competing events; an example is sidewalk sales, when several malls plan the sidewalk sale for the same day. Customers are more willing to make a day of shopping various sales rather than stopping after the first store visit, so everybody wins. In most cases, however, planning for direct competition to other events is not wise. Scheduling of multiple community events on the same weekend will cause attendance to decrease at all events. It will also result in negative opinions by community members who consider the event planners inconsiderate for planning competing events. Holidays, national events, and media events should also be considered when planning events. Although a 3-day holiday weekend may seem ideal for an event, a less-than-desired attendance may prove that family getaways were a greater priority. Unless the event is directly related to the Super Bowl, or planned for a few nonfootball fans, an event planned for the last Sunday in January will generally fail. This is also true of the day after a presidential election. The media is so involved in reporting election results that publicity for any event is likely to be a disappointment.

Event planners need to consider whether there are enough interested people available to support the proposed event. Have such events in the past brought a good turnout? Does the local media give reasonable coverage to events? Demographic research into the community and intended audience are considered in the feasibility study and should tell the event planners the distribution of the intended population. Age, education, income, minority and ethnic groupings, unemployment statistics, and growth predictions are factors to be examined. The total population living within the trading area, along with the percentage of those likely to attend, can be estimated as one determinant to hosting an event. For example, a citywide event will draw attendees who will generally drive up to 2 hours to attend an event. A regional festival over multiple days may draw a crowd from a larger geographical radius area who are willing to drive a bit longer to reach the destination. On the other hand, during holiday sales, when every metropolitan retailer is competing for the same customers, consumers will be less likely to drive very far to shop, creating a smaller marketing radius for the event.

Attitudes of the intended audience may be the greatest asset or detriment to a proposed event. Residents in a community in which too many local dollars have gone to subsidize less-than-successful events may hesitate to attend yet another first-time event. Although an event worked in one community, it may not work in another community due to the attitudes of the residents. Retailers also must find niche events that match the attitudes of their customers. For example, a local T-shirt vendor in a college town may discover that sales are better over Parents' Weekend than during Homecoming. At Homecoming, alumni are so busy with campus events that they do not go shopping off campus, whereas on Parents' Weekend, parent and student leisure time and off-campus shopping is planned into the schedule. Whenever parents visit, the prevailing attitude leads to spending money on their children.

Facilities are the next concern. Does an adequate facility exist, and will the selected location accommodate intended participants in a safe and efficient manner? Pedestrian and vehicular traffic patterns must be controlled efficiently, and law enforcement officials may be needed to handle the demands of increased traffic. Retailers may hire additional security personnel and ask employees to park in remote lots to accommodate increased customers. What services are available to dispose of refuse after the event? Are there adequate volunteer and professional personnel to accommodate the event, and have those costs have been considered? If these questions can be answered in the affirmative, the event is feasible.

A comprehensive feasibility study should include:

- Exact date, time, duration, and location
- Target market
- Name or slogan
- Timeline for the accomplishment of tasks
- Budget
- Marketing plan
- Strategy for obtaining sponsorship
- List of suppliers
- Future of the event projected 1, 5, and 10 years

If the feasibility study determines that the event is likely to be successful, further planning should take place. The following list includes additional planning considerations:

- Objectives of the event
- Concept of the event
- Featured merchandise or service and corresponding departments
- Anticipated attendance
- Sales promotion incentives
- Food and beverage requirements
- Personnel involved
- Equipment needs
- Advertising and publicity needs
- Evaluations of past similar events

The feasibility study should be referred to throughout the planning process. Almost all potential problems in special events planning can be anticipated and avoided if the feasibility study and follow-up planning are complete before execution of the event begins. Before execution, it is important to thoroughly discuss the framework for the event with everyone involved. Prepare a checklist similar to the one on page 428 of everything that needs to be arranged, and then assign responsibilities. Anticipate everything that could go wrong and be prepared with contingencies.

Also important to the process is a formal request to conduct the special event. A civic organization must get permission from the retailer or manufacturer. A division within a retail or manufacturing firm must seek permission from senior management to assure the event is approved through all necessary financial and human resources departments. An event request form used by the Escada firm is shown in Figure 14.8.

PERSONNEL INVOLVED IN SPECIAL EVENTS

Special events planning may be coordinated by a special events director or by a team of associates—buyers, department managers, visual merchandising personnel—within the retail firm. Planning will involve management representatives who approve the objectives, concept, and budget allocations. Execution of the special event is usually left to buyers, department supervisors, and/or the visual merchandising team.

In certain instances, a retail store may have a team of volunteers, such as teen or college boards, who will take on specific responsibilities. Teen or college boards are retail department store fashion advisory boards made up of youth that advise the retailer as fashion authorities for the teen or college segment, helping the retailer establish leadership in teen- or college-related activities. These youthful shoppers also become an important marketing segment as they develop into a mature customer base. Fashion shows, modeling, personal improvement programs, or musical events may be coordinated with emphasis on the echo boomer customer.

One individual or a team of associates may plan a special event, but everyone must know the duties for which they will be responsible. Retailers print planning calendars for distribution to those involved in the process, such as advertising, visual merchandising departments, and department heads, to allow everyone to know which merchandise will be featured during specific time periods.

SIZE AND SCALE OF EVENTS

The size and diversity of a firm's special events program will determine whether a separate department is needed to handle events. Large retailers are more likely than small retailers to separate special events efforts into specific divisions that include promotion; often special events are included in the operations of a publicity department.

Although large retailers have budgets and personnel to coordinate smooth and efficient special event programs, the same ideas they use can work for small independent retailers as well. The current trend among retailers is to plan special events that are community-oriented, such as demonstrations or services. One small event that has been successful in winter climates has been a one-day Patagonia sale. In cooperation with the manufacturer, retailers of cold weather apparel and gear sell Patagonia merchandise at special savings and give a percentage of the sales to a charitable organization. A second trend among sponsors is a higher-quality event with a smaller population rather than

Special Events Planning Checklist

Event:

Location:

Date:

☐ Plan schedule for events during next promotion cycle and personnel and divisions involved with direction from the Management Team for Special Events.

☐ Identify contact person(s) at each location (volunteer, teen board member, branch manager).

☐ Discuss the type of event, the promotion, and personnel who might be involved with contact person.

☐ Determine the date and location for the special event, taking into consideration other local community events and the schedule of personnel who might be involved with the event.

☐ Contact the facility to discuss cost of using facility, food service, equipment, parking, deposits, RSVP, confirmation dates, and other details. Order a catering menu.

☐ Determine costs for use of facility and food service. Determine reasonable charge for guests, if necessary.

☐ Determine guest list.

☐ Determine timeline for mailing invitations, reminders, and RSVP date.

☐ Draft invitation and RSVP.

☐ Inform accounting department of expenses.

☐ Order invitations and RSVPs, with specific quantity and date to be completed.

☐ Check draft from printer. Sign off. Double-check quantity.

☐ Mail invitations.

☐ Inform all necessary personnel of the event, both verbally and with written details so that they can answer questions.

☐ Have contracts signed and send deposit to facility and/or caterer if necessary.

☐ Develop RSVP list. Have information systems input this data into main database.

☐ Confirm RSVPs, meal selection, and equipment needs.

☐ Confirm with facility and caterer, number of RSVPs.

☐ Have checks drafted for payment to caterer/facility/entertainment and other expenses.

☐ Prepare materials for event (gift-with-purchase, name tags, drawing numbers, etc.)

☐ Conduct event.

☐ Submit receipts.

☐ Write thank-yous.

☐ Follow-up payments to vendors.

a lower-quality event with a larger audience. Small events have the potential to attract a targeted market and get customers more intimately involved with the retailer or event sponsor. As the population continues to increase and diversify, the need for individuals to feel part of a smaller, more familiar group will grow.

Storewide events are common among large department store retailers. Nieman Marcus was famous for its 2-week Fortnight promotions each fall. Fortnight was a storewide special event held annually in the downtown Dallas store during a slow selling period.

Figure 14.8

Escada Event Request
Form

ESCADA (USA) Retail Inc.
Event Request Form

Division: ☐ ESCADA ☐ LAUREL

Store Number: _____ Location: _____ Manager: _____

Date of Event: _____ Location: _____

Group, Charity or Organization Having Event
(include background, past events; attach any information):
_____
_____
_____

Contact of Group: _____ Telephone #: _____

Description of Event: _____
_____
_____
_____
_____

Value to the Company: _____
_____
_____

Level of Involvement (marketing support necessary): _____
_____

Approximate Cost (i.e., modeling, catering, staging, invitation): _____
_____

_____   _____
DMM Approval   Date   RMM Approval   Date

In 1984, the celebration grew to 3 weeks and featured *Britain Then and Now.* The large event was sustained over a longer period of time to disperse the cost of the promotion over a longer sales period. As a promotional and institutional event, the entire store had a decidedly British theme celebrating culture, cuisine, and fashion. The third floor was dressed as *Kings Road & Carnaby Street,* complete with merchandise representing the British fashion punk look. Punk look clothing included black leather jackets, stud-decorated jeans, T-shirts, and startling bright colors, such as yellow, orange, pink, green, and purple. The fifth-floor restaurant was turned into a pub. Craftsmen were brought in from Britain for special demonstrations and exhibits. The Fortnight was launched by an invitation-only gala, with proceeds going to the Dallas Public Library.

Fortnights were planned 18 months or more in advance of the event and usually held in cooperation with a featured country. Featured countries were thought to be newsworthy and had a large quantity of available merchandise that could be sold profitably. Shortly after the 1986 Fortnight celebrating Australia, Nieman Marcus announced it would no longer hold the annual events but rather feature occasional celebrations in locations other that the Dallas flagship store. This was done as a cost-saving technique and as an opportunity to promote events to consumers who were more likely to shop at branch stores than at the downtown store. It was reinstated in 1999 with a tribute to Italy.

FINANCIAL CONSIDERATIONS

In Chapter 5, we discussed budgeting. Budgeting for special events is similar to the budget process for other promotional activities. Special events should be allocated within the total sales promotional budget. Events that generate sales will affect volume, sales, and profit margins for the company. These expenses may be weighed against their cost. Events that are image-oriented may not affect sales, but their expenses should still be considered in the annual budgeting process. When considering the feasibility of staging an event, it may be useful to look at past financial records of events and consider charging admission for the event.

All special event expenditures are considered either essential or optional. **Essential expenditures** are expenses that are primary or necessary to produce the event. These expenses are paid for by the sponsoring department or group through fund-raising or operating budgets and may include such items as advertising and rental fees for space or equipment. **Optional expenses** are those that are not necessary to the event. Such optional expenses may include entertainment or food service for invited guests. Optional expenses may be paid by the sponsoring department or by an outside vendor. Common benefits outside vendors may be willing to support financially include signage, corporate hospitality, tickets to a ticketed event, media coverage, product usage, staff support, sampling and sales opportunities, and trade-out possibilities.

The question of whether to charge an admission fee for an event is always a discussion point when planning an event. Some event planners sense that the public will consider a free event inferior. Others contend that paid-admission events may not be worth the ticketed price. Paid attendance may affect attendance negatively.

Ticketed events serve several purposes beyond generating funds. Ticketed events allow for control over the number of people who can attend. If RSVPs are required before distribution of tickets, event planners can secure accurate counts for caterers, chairs, or other logistics of the event. Complementary tickets can be used as incentives for media to cover the event or special fund-raising promotions prior to the event. If tickets are sold, the public must perceive that the price is equitable to what is being offered. In the case of a not-for-profit sponsored event, the ticket price should cover only the actual cost of the event, unless the sponsor or event planner has let the public know prior to the event that part of the purchase price will go to a specified charity. Knowing what the local market will bear for similar events is important. The public must be convinced that the event is well produced, well marketed, and if necessary, well sponsored.

Events free-of-charge to the public can serve as goodwill for the sponsoring business. Free outdoor concerts, parades, and open houses are examples of events that often draw adequate spectators.

EVENT SPONSORSHIP

Event sponsorship has become increasingly popular in recent years. **Event sponsorship** involves a company supporting an event through monetary and/or in-kind contributions as a way to meet one or more of its corporate objectives. Throughout this text, we have mentioned event sponsorship many times. It can be used as a consumer-oriented sales promotion technique to entice consumers to buy certain products. Corporations will sponsor events as part of the public relations strategy to enhance their image, improve customer relations, increase employee morale, or fulfill civic responsibilities. And, event sponsorship should be considered in the planning and budgeting processes of promotion strategy development. Figure 14.9 is a billboard showing Swatch's sponsorship of the Olympics.

Very few successful large-scale events can be sustained without some form of financial support from the corporate community. The growing trend by corporations is to establish event budgets or use foundation money to sponsor special events or projects. Although event planners often play on the emotions of organization personnel to obtain sponsorship, a company will rarely make a significant contribution unless it can expect to obtain a reasonable business return for the investment.

From an event coordinator standpoint, financial support from a commercial sponsor can help cover expenses, keep patron costs to a minimum, or ensure quality and longevity of the event. From a sponsor's point of view the event can create publicity, differentiate the sponsor from its competition, complement marketing programs, sell product or services directly, and fulfill responsibilities as a good corporate citizen. Box 14.2 discusses the corporate goals for sponsorship. By understanding the reasons companies choose to sponsor an event, event planners can be better prepared to approach a potential sponsor.

Many times the content of a special event or project being funded may not be overtly related to the event sponsor, but subtle messages definitely reinforce the idea that the sponsor's products, services, and resources are important to the attendees (Radman, 1997). Ralph Lauren provided an example of the subtle messages that a special event or project can have. (See Fig. 12.3.) In 1998, then First Lady Hillary Rodham

Figure 14.9

Billboard for Swatch, announcing its corporate sponsorship of the Olympics

BOX 14.2

Good Sponsors Know How to Set Their Goals

You cannot tune into a sports event these days without seeing the names of corporate sponsors attached to it. Accurately measuring the effect of corporate sponsorship on a company's bottom line is difficult, especially when millions of dollars are spent. But that has not stopped some companies from trying. A 1994 study tied to Visa's 1994 Olympic sponsorship showed that 68 percent of those consumers who were aware of the company's Olympic participation said it was the best overall credit card, compared with 47 percent of those who were not aware of the sponsorship, according to *BusinessWeek*.

Sometimes the analysis does not have to be scientific. A spokesperson for John Hancock who requested anonymity said that the company noticed a significant increase in the number of individuals who considered John Hancock for their financial needs following the company's sponsorship if the 1994 Winter Olympic Games.

Obviously, the more exposure an event offers, the more a company must spend to gain exposure. With an event like the Olympics or the World Cup, companies can easily spend well into the tens of millions of dollars. But your company does not have to be a big gun to get a shot at a sponsorship that produces results.

Many local community groups, charities, and private organizations desperately need sponsors, and a company's goodwill in helping them achieve their objectives can be fruitful not only for the recipient of the funds but for the company's stature in the community. Whether your company wants to cough up millions of dollars to sponsor an event or would prefer to spend far less in promoting local ventures, ask yourself two key questions: "What opportunity can a sponsorship create for the company?" and "What problem will sponsorship help the company overcome?"

Event sponsorship is nothing more than a tool to help you achieve a specific goal, even if it only means bringing clients, prospective clients, and salespeople to the same venue for an informal get-together. Be careful about tying a sponsorship to the performance of an individual. If he or she falters, it is a blemish on the firm. Think twice, too, about sponsoring a highly visible event only because a senior executive at the company has a strong affinity for the organization. But do not immediately pass on such an opportunity.

Sponsoring an event that benefits a good cause can lead to more business. A study conducted by Roper Starch Worldwide found that 66 percent of those polled said they would switch brands if their purchase helped a cause close to their heart.

Make sure your company is associated with a well-respected event, perhaps one that has been in existence for several years. This is particularly important if your firm relies heavily on a quality image to build business. That image could be cheapened by an event that is poorly managed.

Get the word out about your sponsorship before the event. Depending on the breadth and scope of the event, you can do this in any number of ways, such as ads and direct mail. Failing to spread the word is a key reason companies do not achieve their business goal when sponsoring an event.

If there are other sponsors involved, make sure your company receives the exposure you expect. For example, assume you are sponsoring a race and company logos will appear in locations along the course, find out where your company's logos will appear beforehand.

Having the right attitude is also important in making a sponsorship work. You need to do more than hang signs. You have to become a partner and help the organizer with promotional ideas. By doing so, it becomes a more enjoyable experience for everyone involved.

Realize that success at sponsoring one event is not a one-time occurrence. It often leads the company to sponsor similar events. For example, John Hancock started out sponsoring the Boston Marathon in 1985 and is now a major sponsor at the New York City and Los Angeles marathons.

A final note: Whichever approach you take to sponsorship, do it for the right reasons. People need to know that you are behind the event and that you are not in it purely for business reasons. This will add credibility to what you do and credibility increases the image that you want to portray, regardless of your goal.

Adapted from: Del Prete, D. (1996, September 23). Good sponsors know how to set their goals. Marketing News, 35.

Clinton began a national public awareness campaign to *Save America's Treasures* ("Ralph Lauren," 1998). The campaign was meant to stimulate interest by the public to restore and protect historical treasures such as Thomas Edison's laboratory and George Washington's Revolutionary War Headquarters, among other sites and items. To kickoff the campaign, the Polo Ralph Lauren Corporation gave a $10 million corporate gift to help restore and protect the flag that inspired Francis Scott Key to compose the words to the national anthem. The wool and cotton flag, on display at the Smithsonian's National Museum of American History in Washington, D.C., needed extensive repair. Measuring 34 by 30 feet, it had survived a British bombardment as it flew over Fort McHenry outside Baltimore, Maryland, in 1814, but since then had been damaged by dust and light. In addition to the corporate gift, Ralph Lauren personally contributed another $3 million to pay for an advertising campaign to increase public awareness of the *Save America's Treasures* efforts. While these generous contributions did not overtly generate sales for the Polo Ralph Lauren Corporation, they subtly reinforced his *American label* image to consumers and the industry.

FUTURE TRENDS IN SPECIAL EVENTS

Event planners are looking more and more to websites to assist with the logistics of event planning. More websites are a future trend in special event planning. The Trade Show News Network (TSNN) is one such website. The TSNN site at *http://www.tsnn.com*, allows browsers to locate shows by industry, date, city, and name. There is also an exhibitor database to find specific company shows. This site offers the latest trade show news from leading publications, exhibitor and attendee tips, and travel services. The TSNN event database posts an up-to-date trade show calendar, and allows exhibitors, suppliers, and producers to edit the information ("For the Bookmark," 1998). Figure 14.10 is an example of the apparel and fashion industry trade shows posted on the TSNN website. They include domestic and international trade shows.

A second website of benefit to event planners is the Event Planning Search Engine at *http://www.eventsource.com*. This site is intended for those who are planning meetings, conventions, and trade and public shows, and those who supply the infrastructure, from service companies to convention centers. Event designers can research over 9,000 event sites, destinations and services. Professional event planners can request planning guides and book sites, post event requests or want ads, and transact with suppliers.

Future trends in special events will concentrate on sponsorship. Companies not normally associated with fashion or apparel are becoming interested in sponsoring events in the industry. Examples include Microsoft and General Motors. For the first time, Microsoft set up a booth at the 1997 MAGIC (Men's Apparel Guild in California) show in Las Vegas and sponsored a fashion show for buyers. According to Judy Dulcich, retail industry marketing manager for Microsoft, the company was really interested in educating retailers to help them use technology as a tool (Ellis & Ozzard, 1997). Microsoft sponsored the event to demonstrate to retailers that it was interested in their needs. Small businesses represent 31 percent of the retail industry, and they are hard to service. Microsoft felt that the MAGIC show was a good forum to reach these retailers. General Motors has also entered into fashion industry sponsorship as the corporate sponsor for the annual "7th on Sixth" shows. The 3-year, multimillion-dollar deal has even led to the renaming of the New York collections as "General Motors

Figure 14.10

Trade Show News
Network Homepage

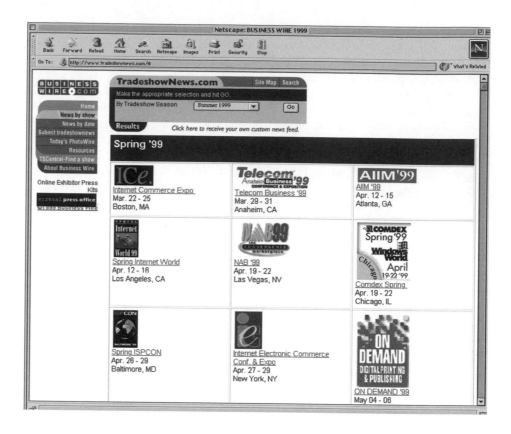

Fashion Week" (Wilson, 1998). The GM name will be included on all the organization's events—two shows for women's and two for men's each year. The reason GM signed on to sponsor the shows was to attract female consumers. The trend is already occurring internationally; for instance, Mercedes Benz hosts shows in Sydney, Australia.

Special events, as compared to the other promotion techniques we have discussed, are not as influenced by technological advances. This is not to say technology is not important to special event planning, but special events are not being replaced or enhanced by the use of technology. Consumers will always enjoy the excitement and personal participation that special events provide.

Special events are planned activities to encourage consumers to come together. A special event may be used to sell merchandise or to promote the image of a brand or a company. Store image is promoted and differentiated through the use of special events. An otherwise ordinary happening is made into a newsworthy milestone when someone plans a special promotion around the happening. Special events are an important ingredient to the promotion mix strategy because of the excitement they create.

SUMMARY

- Special events are planned activities intended to encourage individuals or groups to gather at a specific time and place because of a shared interest.

- Some special events are intended to generate sales by selling large quantities of featured products or services or reaching specifically targeted market segments.
- Special event programs that focus on communicating a positive image of the company have goals such as exhibiting good corporate citizenship, enhancing customer and VIP relations, contributing to community economic development, and promoting a charitable cause.
- Strategically planned short-term and long-term events can build links between a product or brand and the public that can help a firm establish rapport between customers and its product or service.
- Successful special events are those that have been planned in a timely manner.
- While generating increased sales is an important goal behind a special event, other business goals, such as the introduction of a new product, revamping a store image, or offering thanks for continued store loyalty, are additional reasons to stage a special event.
- Special event planners should refer back to the objective of the event and create measurable evaluators to use in judging the success of the event. Intangible factors may be of more importance than the tangible sales figures reflected after the event.
- Adherence to the projected budget is also a measure of success for special events. Adequate preplanning by the event planning team will ultimately decide the success of any special event, large or small.
- Future trends in special events include website assistance and corporate sponsorship from firms not generally associated with the fashion industry.

KEY TERMS

anniversary celebration	gallery exhibit	optional expenditure
category week	institutional events	product demonstration
celebrity appearance	in-store exhibit	product launch
essential expenditure	merchandise events	store opening
event sponsorship	museum exhibit	vendor week
feasibility study	musical performance	

QUESTIONS FOR DISCUSSION

1. What are the primary and secondary reasons companies stage special events?
2. What is the difference between an institutional and a merchandise special event?
3. Who are the personnel responsible for special event planning and implementation?
4. Why do corporations sponsor events?

ADDITIONAL RESOURCES

Devney, D. (1993). *Organizing special events and conferences: A practical guide to busy volunteers and staff.* Sarasota, FL: Pineapple Press.

Freedman, H., and Feldman, K. (1998). *The business of special events.* Sarasota, FL: Pineapple Press.

Goldblatt, J. (1997) *Special events: Best practices in modern event management.* New York: Wiley.

Goldblatt, J., and McKibben, C. (1996). *The dictionary of event management.* New York: Wiley.

Jackson, R. (1997). *Making special events fit in the 21st century.* Champaign, IL: Sagamore.

Reed, M. (1990). *IEG legal guide to sponsorship.* Chicago: International Events Group.

Soares, E. (1991). *Promotional feats: The role of planned events in the marketing communications mix.* Portland, OR: Greenwood Publishing Group.

6th Annual
Y-ME Benefit
Luncheon and Fashion Show

October 18, 1997

Program

Welcome and Introduction
Michelle Muro
Arizona 5 CBS News Anchor

Opening Remarks
Patricia Stewart
President, Y-ME

Why Me?
Jami McFerren
Radio Personality

Woman to Woman
Linda Turley
TV Personality

Live Auction
Diamond Ring
Molina's Jewelers

Fashion Show
Judy Edwards
Dillard's

"Wind Beneath Our Wings"
Y-ME Breast Cancer Survivors

Raffle Drawing
Michelle Muro

Silent Auction
Jami McFerren and Linda Turley

Figure 15.1

Y-ME fashion show program and advertisement in resource book

chapter 15

FASHION SHOWS

Each October the Phoenix, Arizona, chapter of Y-ME hosts an annual luncheon and fashion show as a charity event (Fig. 15.1). Y-ME National Organization for Breast Cancer Information and Support is a nonprofit organization, founded in Chicago, Illinois, to help women live with a diagnosis of breast cancer through education, research, hope, and a resounding affirmation of life. The theme for a recent show was *Wind beneath our wings,* declaring support from breast cancer survivors to others waging the battle against breast cancer. Nine breast cancer survivors, ranging in age from 32 to 72, were featured as models at the benefit. The program, referred to as a resource book, identified participants and advertising sponsors, highlighted early breast cancer detection information, listed support groups for breast and ovarian cancer, and provided an index of emergency hotline numbers. Promotional favors were contributed by Estée Lauder, Dillard's, and major hospitals and medical organizations in Arizona to show their support of the organization. Fashion shows are a major promotion tool used by organizations such as Y-ME to generate contributions for their cause.

After you read this chapter you will be able to:

Discuss the purpose of fashion shows.

Describe fashion shows at trade and retail levels.

List the characteristics of different types of fashion shows.

Discuss personnel responsibilities for producing fashion shows.

Explain fashion show planning details.

Evaluate budget considerations.

List the elements of a fashion show.

This chapter will begin by discussing the role of fashion shows as a promotion tool in the fashion industry and specifically discuss fashion shows created by producers, manufacturers and designers, and retailers. We then look at different types of fashion shows. Many people are involved in fashion shows, and fashion show personnel will be the topic of the next section. Our focus then moves to planning a fashion show and to differentiating all of the elements necessary to rehearse, conduct, and evaluate a fashion show. The chapter concludes with a discussion of future trends in fashion shows.

PURPOSE OF FASHION SHOWS

Of all the promotion activities, fashion shows are the most thrilling. A fashion show is a presentation of apparel, accessories, and other products to enhance personal attractiveness on live models to an audience. It includes all the elements of a theatrical production—music, lighting, staging, and a script as a performance for a live audience. More than other elements of promotion, a fashion show makes the audience feel influential. It is announced in advance, has a theatrical opening, and creates a sense of exclusivity for the invited audience. An effective show generates a sense of being in on the latest news and hottest trends of the fashion world. Additionally, it reinforces the fashion leadership of the designer or retailer producing the show. The excitement of fashion shows is apparent at all market levels, from the haute couture shows in Milan and Paris (Fig.15.2), to the trade shows in major markets, to consumer and charity shows produced in local communities. While the average consumer probably does not buy the fashions shown at a haute couture show, these shows illustrate the pinnacle of fashion-forward design. The trends and inspirations that are forecasted through these shows trickle down to designer ready-to-wear, to bridge, and finally to knock-off merchandise that is available to the mass market.

Although fashion shows are produced for a variety of reasons, the primary one is to sell merchandise. The fashion show helps to make an authoritative visual statement about garments and accessories, thus encouraging a potential customer (manufacturer, designer, retailer, or general public) to buy what has been shown. Shows are also staged for employees and customers to share important fashion information about trends, silhouettes, fabrics, colors, and services. New merchandise, product assortments, special offerings, in-store themes, or sales promotions may be introduced at fashion shows. Firms may also present fashion shows to attract new customers, build traffic, and encourage loyalty from existing customers. This promotion tool enhances a store or brand image and fashion authority, and communicates goodwill to the population.

Fashion shows can play an important role in the overall integrated marketing communications strategy of a firm. For example, a fashion show may be developed with the public relations team as an image-building exercise. As part of the team, the advertising unit suggests the theme for the show as a tie-in to the latest ad campaign. Direct-response mailings inform targeted customers of the show, while the visual merchandis-

Figure 15.2

The most famous fashion shows are those of haute couture and designer ready-to-wear that are used to introduce designer lines each season. A. a Valentino show in Paris and B. a Prada show in Milan

A   B

ing unit creates a comprehensive store image and set design based on the fashions selected for the show. Because fashion shows have the power to influence designers, retailers, buyers, the press, and the public, they are a very important element of promotion.

If you have ever watched the Oscar or Emmy award shows honoring outstanding people in movies and television, you have probably noticed the considerable press coverage given to the clothes worn by the stars. The Oscar ceremony has turned into a fashion show as print and broadcast media report who designed the outfits, accessories, matching bags, diamond earrings, and so on. The day after the show, the focus of many viewers is not so much on who won the major awards, as on who was the best dressed. This is an example of the growing curiosity consumers have for fashion as well as the connection they make between haute couture and the fashions they see in their neighborhood stores. Fashion shows can assist consumers in making this connection.

MARKET LEVEL FASHION SHOWS

Fashion shows are produced by raw materials producers, manufacturers, designers, and retailers. The most consequential reason for staging a show is to sell merchandise to the targeted audience. In Chapter 6, we defined the different market levels within the industry as primary, secondary, and tertiary. Fashion shows are produced at the primary and secondary levels as trade shows and at the tertiary level as retail shows.

Trade Shows

Textile producers, apparel manufacturers and trade associations sponsor trade shows. In Chapter 6, we learned that trade shows were an excellent resource for discovering future trends. Many trends are identified on runways at fashion shows sponsored by producers or manufacturers. The typical audience at a trade show is composed of retail buyers. Fashion shows produced by textile firms attract audiences of fashion designers and manufacturers looking for fabric and color trends because they are ready to buy the latest fabrics or findings. These trade shows demonstrate the use and versatility of the raw materials, trusting that the audience will like what they see and want to include the fabrication, findings, or piece goods in their next collection.

Shows produced by an apparel manufacturer will draw an audience of retail buyers and professional forecasting agents. In Figure 15.3, a model at a bridal trade show carries a card to tell buyers the style number that can be referenced in the show catalog. At trade shows such as MAGIC, fashion shows are presented three or more times daily throughout the trade show to accommodate the many buyers who comprise the audience and whom the manufacturer wants to influence. The press is invited to trade shows to encourage publicity for the fabrics or piece goods being presented in trade publications and in materials produced by forecasting services.

In 1993, 7th on Sixth was created by the Council of Fashion Designers of America to produce and coordinate centralized seasonal runway shows in New York City. Participating designers included Ralph Lauren, Donna Karan, Calvin Klein, and Betsey Johnson among other U.S. designers. Over the years the venue for the shows has changed. The shows first used the Bryant Park area of New York City at 42nd Street. For one year, in 1997, the shows were changed to the Chelsea Piers when several of the staging areas at Bryant Park became unavailable. In addition to hosting 50 to 55 shows, the Chelsea

Figure 15.3

Model at a bridal trade show

Piers facility offered restaurants, stores, a golf range, a health club, an ice skating rink, and other entertainment facilities for the enjoyment of show attendees. Claiming the Piers were too inconveniently located for buyers and press reporters, the shows returned to Bryant Park in 1998. Shows in 1999 were held at the Bryant Park location or at individual showrooms around Manhattan. The 7th on Sixth trade shows showcase ready-to-wear designers collectively through runway presentation of men's and women's designer collections four times a year and exhibit accessories twice a year.

Retail Shows

Retail shows are sponsored by retailers and are directed toward the retail staff and consumer market. Retail shows include in-store shows, consumer shows, community or charity shows, and press shows. An **in-store show** is presented for the benefit of store employees, to inform the staff of new and exciting trends for the upcoming season, and is coordinated with the advertising and visual display departments to create a storewide theme. Thus, it stimulates enthusiasm, and contributes to suggestion selling. Informed sales associates can, in turn, influence customers by sharing expertise on style characteristics, color combinations, and proper accessories for the latest fashions. Through the use of an in-store fashion show, merchandise trends and the store promotion plan can be conveyed to the entire staff and implemented throughout every department within the store.

A consumer show is produced by the retailer to sell ideas and merchandise to the buying public. Consumer shows may feature seasonal, storewide, departmental, designer, private label, or manufacturer-brand merchandise. Manufacturers may cooperatively produce the show or provide elements for the show when their merchandise is shown exclusively or is presented prominently. Sales representatives will be on hand to present the merchandise to customers after the show in special 1-day or preseason trunk show events. Consumer fashion shows are a popular magazine tie-in event. Magazines such as *Harper's Bazaar* (Fig. 15.4) invite readers to attend fashion shows shown throughout the country, which are co-sponsored by local retailers.

A community or charity show is generally produced by one or more retailers to raise money and awareness for national, local, or fund-raising charities. This type of show was highlighted in the opening segment of this chapter. The retailer may be headlined as a co-sponsor or assist behind the scenes by loaning merchandise for the fashion show. In addition to selling merchandise, the retailer is promoting goodwill and building a strong community image. Celebrities, designers, and models often lend their support to these charitable events.

Macy's California has held a charity fashion show, called Passport, to benefit AIDS charities for over 15 years. In 1997, the annual event, which was held in San Francisco and Los Angeles, raised $2 million dollars for charities to benefit HIV/AIDS organizations nationwide ("Macy's," 1997). Over 10,000 guests, over the period of four nights, viewed fashions by Kenneth Cole, Ralph Lauren, and Canadian-designer Lida Baday, among others, worn by such models as Irina, Tyson Beckford, and Matt King, who donated their time on the runway. Elizabeth Taylor, Tina Turner, k.d. lang, and Jasmine

Figure 15.4

An advertisement from *Harper's Bazaar* inviting consumers to attend fall fashion shows around the country

Guy participated in the event to show their support for AIDS research. In this type of show, the designers and retailers get exposure for their brands, while the individuals involved lend support to important causes. Everybody wins.

A **press show** is a special presentation of fashions for the press. A press show is generally presented ahead of the regularly scheduled show to encourage publicity for the event. Press shows are limited to larger trade and retail sponsors who seek substantial publicity for the event or institution.

Lerner's New York and Express launched press shows in the early 1990s. The shows were so successful that the idea has continued ("In the Middle," 1996). At a typical event, Lerner's would host a breakfast show at a top New York restaurant with Richard P. Crystal, president and chief executive officer, on hand to answer questions from the press. Express's press show was part of a cocktail party at a popular SoHo lounge. The show venue was such a success that *Entertainment Tonight* and daytime talk show hosts were regular guests at the press events and covered the story for their television programs.

To "give presence to our first show" (Parr, 1997a), Nick Graham, president and founder of Joe Boxer, a sportswear and intimates manufacturer, arranged for an international press show following his first appearance at the 7th on Sixth trade shows. The press show, *Joe Boxer Goes to Iceland,* was held in a Reykjavik, Iceland, airplane hanger for 157 media members, including fashion editors and writers from *Esquire, GQ, Elle, Cosmopolitan, YM, Mirabella,* and others. Combining theatrics and a great deal of advance planning, Graham presented jeans, women's underwear sets, pajamas, and shorts to a captive audience during 48 hours of sightseeing, partying, eating, and show-watching in Iceland to influence the press reporters to give his line added publicity beyond advertising.

FASHION SHOW TYPES

Fashion shows are defined by their production style, which includes four categories: production, formal runway, informal, and video production. Show types are not specific to market levels and may be used at trade or retail levels.

Production Show

The **production show** is the most elaborate and expensive type of fashion show, loaded with theatrical and dramatic elements. Production shows, also known as *spectaculars,* feature theatrical backdrops and scenery, lighting effects, live or specially produced music, and dancing or specialized choreography to create a highly energized event. Trends are shown in a presentation format lasting approximately an hour with 15 to 50 models, depending on the needs of the sponsoring organization. High-end fashion-forward merchandise, including couture, eveningwear, bridal, or ready-to-wear collections, are usually the highlights of production shows. Production shows require a great deal of organization and advance planning. A professional show produced by a national magazine or charity will send an advance team to the community prior to the event to ensure all details are in place before the arrival of the merchandise and models. Shows produced locally may be coordinated by a team that plans for the show a year in advance of the event.

Production shows are often promoted as special events for fund-raising purposes and include hor d'oeuvres and cocktails followed by a luncheon or dinner. The Macy's

California Passport show discussed earlier in this chapter is an example of a production show. To add to the theatrical aspect of this show, the runway was 120 feet, quite long compared to a typical trade show runway.

Formal Runway Show

The show type most readers are likely to visualize when thinking about fashion shows is the formal runway show. **Formal runway shows** present merchandise as a parade with the audience seated at the perimeter of the runway. Haute couture designers and apparel manufacturers use this traditional method almost exclusively to present lines each season.

Formal runway shows may last from 30 minutes to 1 hour and feature models that parade down the runway sequentially, individually, or in groups to present the merchandise. It is very common to have all models come out onto the runway at the conclusion of the show to present a fashion finale and to acknowledge the designer when he or she is present (Fig. 15.5).

A formal runway show is planned around a merchandise theme and held at a special location, such as an auditorium, hotel, restaurant, or on a retail sales floor. Staging,

Figure 15.5
Ralph Lauren takes a walk down the runway after the showing of his line at the 7th on Sixth shows.

lighting, models, music, and in some cases commentary, are all elements of the runway show. Merchandise is generally seasonal, specialty, or ready-to-wear merchandise. A runway show may be directed toward the general public or a specialty market, such as petites, college students, or career women.

Informal Fashion Show

Informal fashion shows present merchandise on models in a casual environment. Lighting, music, staging, and other special elements are not used. A model walks through a sales floor, manufacturer's showroom, or restaurant showing the merchandise and answering questions about the product. Models may carry a sign or distribute business cards, coupons, or handouts to the audience as a teaser, hoping the audience will visit the retailer after the presentation. Types of informal fashion shows include tea-room modeling, trunk shows, hatbox shows, and mannequin modeling.

Tea-room modeling is a specific type of informal modeling that takes place in a restaurant on a regularly scheduled day. Models walk from table to table showing the merchandise to interested dining guests. Models are discouraged from interrupting the guests unless they are specifically asked about a feature or detail of the merchandise.

Trunk shows feature garments from a single manufacturer or designer and are presented as informal fashion shows in retail stores. A manufacturer or designer ships the complete line to the retail store in "trunks," or sales representative's cases. A sales representative or designer accompanies the fashions and, during an in-store event, answers questions about the products and takes orders from invited guests.

Trunk shows are advantageous to the retailer because the complete line can be presented to the customers without inventory risk to the retailer; rarely will retailers buy an entire line from a manufacturer or designer. Trunk shows also allow the retailer and the manufacturer or designer to gather immediate feedback about the merchandise. By listening to customers, designers and manufacturers can incorporate customers' desires into next season's line. Trunk shows that feature personal appearances by designers also increase the reputation of the retailer as a fashion leader.

Trunk shows are a useful tool in creating preseason sales. One series of trunk shows produced by Mark Badgley and James Mischka brought in over $2 million in fall orders during May and June at such retailers as Nordstrom in South Coast Plaza and Neiman Marcus in San Francisco ("Market Basket," 1996). Ralph Lauren generated $1.27 million in sales during a 4-day spring trunk show at the Madison Avenue flagship store ("Lauren Rings," 1997). Box 15.1 discusses suggestions for generating sales through trunk shows.

Hatbox shows are very informal fashion shows that utilize a small space and a limited budget, *carrying everything needed in a hatbox*. A single person acts as model and commentator, changing outfits behind a screen while at the same time maintaining the commentary. The individual responsible for hatbox shows must have an extensive fashion vocabulary and feel very confident of his or her abilities to conduct this type of fashion show.

In a contemporary twist to the hatbox show, Nova USA presented its 1999 spring men's wear collection as a hatbox show done as a window display in its soon-to-be opened New York City store. The audience included fashion editors and retailers who blocked the street for the unusual show. Inside the window display, a lone model dressed and undressed in 25-or-so knit sportswear pieces.

BOX 15.1

Do Trunk Shows Translate into Sales?

What is the secret behind a successful trunk show? "Give sales people collections they feel they can sell, so that they can make their commissions," explains consultant Peter Dubow. "If you motivate the sales department, the sell will be easy," he says.

For many designer and upscale labels, trunk shows are not only viable . . . they are crucial to business. They actually develop a customer for a label. But that is not all. They can help build a mystique and through it additional business and give both the store and manufacturer a chance to learn what the customer wants in the market so the product can be tailored or refined to fit. Plus, they are a wonderful way to cement a vendor/store relationship.

In many cases, and especially with European designers, a trunk show allows the sales associates to preview the collection before it comes into the stores and gives them advice on how to sell it. "We hold sales meetings in the morning to show how the line should be presented because the more the sales associates are behind a line, the better all of us will do," explains Jean Nuzzi, director of sales, Genny USA.

Actually, way-in-advance planning is essential to the success of a trunk show. Announcement of the show can be through a newspaper ad or an invitational mailing to the store or sales staff's preferred customer list, or both. And the sales and/or personal shopping staff should also call customers who have expressed interest in the designer or already purchased the label, to bring them in and/or set up appointments, especially if the designer him- or herself is making a store appearance.

It is a great draw to have the designer there only if he or she has a good rapport with customers and people skills. Often, however, a charming rep with an excellent knowledge of both the line and customer can be equally effective.

In order for a trunk show to do what it is supposed to do, here are a few suggestions from the experts:

Trunk shows are most successful when they are held mid-week, either before stock is delivered or as delivery begins. Especially with an upscale clientele, Mondays and Fridays tend to be dead days.

While it can stand on its own, you can also treat a trunk show as a special promotion and tie it in with a charity event. Not only will it raise money, but it might also bring in new exposure in the local media. Of course, the charity must be geared to the label's customer. If, for example, the line is very trendy and fashion forward and patrons of the charity are conservative, there is not likely to be a match . . . nor any sales.

Do not schedule a show too far in advance of the season because customers generally cannot plan ahead or can end up changing their minds. Early in the season, or just prior to the season is usually the best time to capture the customer's excitement.

To warrant the promotion and expense, show in stores that place broad orders in styles and sizes. When properly done, the show can help sell up to 20 percent of the order in advance. At the end of the season, it can insure the sell-through of the entire collection. When this happens, the store will usually increase its open-to-buy the following season.

If you are showing in a store that holds continual trunk shows, try not to be at the end of the cycle. Unless you have a very specific customer who is loyal to your label, you may find the response poor because customers have been called so frequently to attend other shows.

Avoid doing a trunk show during sales periods, such as the first and second week of January. The store may not be geared for an exclusive event at that time and the mindset of the customer, even an affluent one, may be to buy off-price.

Try to avoid working only with sample sizes because they are generally not true to size and the customer cannot relate to them or imagine how the style would look in her size.

"When they work, trunk shows are viable business builders, despite the expense. The trend, however, is toward stores paying less," says Jean Nuzzi, who feels that business for European designer trunk shows, where customers order from pictures, is shrinking. "I think people want instant gratification," she says, adding that Ungaro does a fabulous trunk show business because the collection is here.

Adapted from: Sommers, S. (1996, August 26). Do trunk shows translate into sales? The Look On-Line [On-line]. Available: http://www. lookonline.com/htdocs/trunk.html.

Mannequin modeling is a form of informal modeling in which the model acts as a live mannequin in a store window or on a display platform. Live models strike poses similar to a stationary display form. These models must pose in stiffened positions and possess a great discipline and composure to remain perfectly still as the audience inevitably tries to make the models laugh or move.

Video Production Show

Video production shows are specifically produced to be videotaped and distributed to sales representatives or retailers. Common videotaped fashion shows include point-of-purchase, instructional, and documentary videos. Point-of-purchase videos are used as sales promotion tools on the sales floor. Customers are given the opportunity to see the original runway show or an action view of how to wear the presented merchandise. Instructional videos are created for in-store training of sales personnel in place of a formal runway show. The videos demonstrate current information on fashion trends and illustrate special features of the products. A cosmetic line may use a demonstration video to present the new seasonal color palette and show how to creatively apply makeup. Documentary videos focus on the designer or behind-the-scenes activities of a manufacturer. They may be used as training films for company employees, produced for television shows, or used as a point-of-purchase sales promotion item. Immediately following the deaths of Gianni Versace and Diana, Princess of Wales, documentary videos were produced and sold highlighting the lives of both these influential fashion figures.

PERSONNEL INVOLVED

The key person in any fashion show production is the coordinator. In a retail organization, fashion show production is generally the responsibility of the fashion director. The fashion director produces the show or delegates a member of the promotional staff to oversee the production. At the manufacturer's level, a seasoned sales representative or member of the promotion staff will oversee fashion show production or hire an outside production agency.

Leadership qualities of a fashion show coordinator include extensive fashion knowledge, enthusiasm, patience, and good communication skills. The coordinator is ultimately responsible for making sure the show runs smoothly, continually reviewing the progress of the show, meeting deadlines, and staying within the budget.

In most situations a fashion director will have the opportunity to assign staff to assist with the production. An ideal staff will consist of a model coordinator, merchandise coordinator, stage manager, and a publicity and advertising coordinator. The **model coordinator** is responsible for hiring, training, and coordinating all activities that involve the models. A **merchandise coordinator** is responsible for collecting and preparing the merchandise, fitting the merchandise to the models, and returning the merchandise to departments after the show. In some cases the merchandise coordinator will select the merchandise to be used, in other situations the fashion director, or a team of managers, or a manufacturer representative will select the merchandise to be presented in the show. In the case of a magazine tie-in show, the fashion editor of the publication will coordinate the merchandise. A **stage manager** oversees the use of the stage and runway, organizes equipment, and supervises people providing behind-the-scenes services, such as sound and lighting technicians. The **publicity and advertising coordi-**

nator is responsible for all promotion of the event. This person may work in cooperation with the advertising or promotion department.

PLANNING

Planning a fashion show involves all aspects of preliminary preparation necessary to present a well-executed show. Planning involves organizing the show and working out every detail to avoid unexpected problems. Planning details include audience selection, theme development, location selection, timing of the show, and security issues.

Audience Selection

Every fashion show needs an audience (Fig. 15.6). It is necessary to select the right audience if the show is to be successful as a promotion tool. An audience can be based on merchandise or the merchandise can be selected after a target audience has been

Figure 15.6

A model gets an attentive reception, from the audience.

determined. In either case, the audience and merchandise must be properly targeted. A fashion show audience may be guaranteed or created. A **guaranteed audience** is established before the show is planned, and is made up of individuals who will attend regardless of the fashions shown. A **created audience** is established after the show is planned as a result of publicity and advertising. The size of the audience should be considered and a location selected that will allow all members of the audience to view the show comfortably. If the primary reason for the fashion show is to sell merchandise, the income level of the audience should be considered. Retailers know the approximate spending habits of their customers and should review this information before selecting merchandise. Demographic and psychographic characteristics of an audience should also be considered when planning a show. A missed detail about the audience can change the atmosphere of the show and decrease the opportunity for sales.

Theme Development

Fashion shows should have a theme and title, which will tell the audience the nature of the fashion show. The theme may be selected around a targeted audience or a specific merchandise category. Themes may be developed to implement new trends for the season (as discussed in Chapter 6). Theme ideas may come from holidays or seasons, current art or music trends, geographical locations, merchandise categories, or characteristics of the audience. Fashion show themes may also be taken from the fashion theme calendar established by senior management, as discussed in Chapter 4.

Themes should be creative and imaginative for both the staff creating the promotional theme and the audience viewing it. Theme categories include storewide, color, fabrication, lifestyle, and special occasion. The theme should be selected early in the process to allow other details to be coordinated with it. Merchandise selection will be dictated by the theme. Because fashion shows are generally divided into segments, depending on the merchandise selected, each segment or scene can be created to coordinate with the chosen title.

Location Selection

At the retail level, fashion shows can be held in-store or out-of-store at civic locations, auditoriums, restaurants, or hotels. The advantage of an in-store fashion show is obvious; it allows customers to immediately purchase the items they have just seen, fulfilling the promotional objective to sell merchandise. If, on the other hand, the promotional objective is to create goodwill within the community, an out-of-store location may be desirable for charity or spectacular events in which a large audience is expected.

Timing of the Show

Determining the day, date, and time of the fashion show as well as confirming the length of the performance are timing elements necessary in show preparation. It is of great importance for a show coordinator to plan shows so they will not conflict with other events in the store or the community. Conflict will diminish the intended audience.

The ideal length of a fashion show is 45 minutes (Everett and Swanson, 1993). In a well-executed show 50 to 60 garments can be shown in this time frame. Audiences will be hesitant to attend a show if they perceive it will last longer than an hour.

Once the fashion show location, theme, date, and time have been established, they are posted on a fashion show calendar. The fashion show calendar can then be used by the fashion director and staff to plan, delegate, and follow through with elements of the show production.

Security Issues

The security of merchandise, equipment, the audience, and special guests is a concern when producing a fashion show. Merchandise on loan from retailers or departments within a retail store is the responsibility of the show staff. The merchandise must be protected from damage while being worn and from theft or vandalism while on loan. In rare instances, merchandise with an extremely high cost might need the added protection of hired security guards. Show staff also have the responsibility for securing the location and protecting borrowed or leased equipment.

To protect all individuals involved, every transferal of merchandise and equipment should be recorded through written agreements signed by show personnel and the leasing agent. Show staff must ensure the safety of the audience and the participants to protect the retailer or sponsoring organization from legal damages resulting from accidents. Celebrities may need hired security personnel to protect them during the show and transport them to and from the fashion show. Protection of people and materials should be reviewed as the show is finalized.

BUDGET

One of the most crucial elements of planning a fashion show is budget preparation. The budget is the estimate of revenues and expenses necessary to produce the show. The type of show being produced, audience, location, and special features of the show will dictate the projected budget of the show. For example, budgets for Paris couture shows may run from as little as $47,000 to as much as $279,000 depending on the elaborateness of the sets ("Deconstructing," 1998). Fashion show budgets are only one component of the entire promotional budget discussed in Chapter 5.

The following list is a sample of possible show expenses.

Advertising	Overtime
Alterations	Pressing
Commentator fee	Programs
Deposits	Props
Depreciation of merchandise	Public address system
Dry cleaning	Publicity
Electricians	Rent
Insurance	Stage and runway construction
Lights	Taxes
Meals	Tickets
Model fees	Transportation
Music	Wages

Every show will not have the same elements to consider when developing a budget, but it is well to use some sort of checklist to make sure the budget allows for every expense, planned and unexpected.

Physical facilities should also be considered during the budget process. An out-of-store fashion show may require fees to use the property and rental fees for one or more of the following: tables, chairs, runways, stage, lighting, and public address system. Additionally, a caterer may be needed to provide food service and decorations. An in-store show may eliminate the property fee but may still require rented elements and catering to produce the show.

Show personnel require a large proportion of the estimated budget. All but the smallest shows require the expertise of technicians to guarantee the success of a show. Electricians, music, and lighting technicians may be required to assist with the setup and perform safety inspections. Photographers and video production crews may be hired to record the event for the sponsoring organization. Models may require makeup and hair stylists at the performance. In addition to a paid modeling staff, dressers, cue people, transportation staff, hosts, and ushers may need to be hired.

Publicity and advertising are necessary elements for a fashion show and must be considered when establishing the budget. The publicity and advertising budget should be reviewed by the sales promotion division of the organization to determine if cooperative promotions may be beneficial. Publicity costs include the production of press releases, press photographs, or press kits. Elements of sales promotion, such as give-aways, coupons, or samples, have costs associated with them. Invitations, tickets, and programs may be produced. Advertising costs include production fees and the cost of air time or print space needed to promote the event. As part of a public relations effort, the show producer may include hospitality, such as hotel accommodations for celebrity or special guests, transportation, entertainment, and gratuities.

Expenses related to the use of merchandise should also be considered. Merchandise must be cared for to ensure that it is saleable after the show. Models may require garment alterations. After the show, garments may require dry cleaning or removal of alterations to return the merchandise to a saleable condition. When merchandise has been damaged beyond repair, show personnel may have to cover the cost of the item borrowed from the retailer or department.

Other expenses to consider include taxes, which vary from state to state, and liability insurance to cover the audience, show personnel, and merchandise. Additionally, the show coordinator should have an emergency reserve that can be used on a contingency basis to cover any unforeseen problems.

The preceding discussion has centered on fashion show expenses. Many shows are produced as publicity tools with the intent to sell merchandise. Costs of these fashion shows are supposed to be covered by sales generated from the show. Revenues may also be gained to cover some or all of the show expenses. These revenues come from sales or show sponsorship by an organization or corporation.

SHOW ELEMENTS

A fashion show is made up of many elements that, together, make an exciting show that tells the audience what to wear, when to wear it, and how to accessorize it. Box 15.2 takes a lighthearted look at the Chelsea runway shows and discusses several of the elements common to runway shows. Elements of a fashion show include merchandise, models, commentary, set, and music.

BOX 15.2

Do's and Don'ts of Runway Shows

To get to *Day for Night,* a stylish space on fashion's new frontier in the westernmost reaches of Chelsea Piers, you need to take a slow-moving, living-room-size, don't-touch-the-walls-they're-filthy freight elevator up to the 18th floor. Including waiting time, air kisses, and loading-dock chit chat, it takes maybe 10 minutes.

The Nautica show for spring 1999, held there, was over in maybe 8 minutes.

The 32 outfits on display went by in a flash of sleeveless T-shirts and neoprene pants, leaving the audience wanting more—a full-fledged sampling of David Chu's latest collection, perhaps—or less, that is, no show at all. In its brevity, the Nautica show was the soul of folly. All that expense and for what? Cotton jams and a couple of suits.

Nicole Farhi, the British sportswear designer, used the term "focused collection" in her notes for her men's wear show at the New York Public Library. In that phrase, she hit upon the essence of any good fashion show. It cannot be too radical, too somber, or too cute. It must be focused, but fulfilling.

The spring 1999 men's shows in New York—officially known as the General Motors Fashion Week—offered plenty of lessons in how to show fashion and how not to. The proceedings proved that not every designer is up to the task of showing on a runway and that it takes a particular confluence of ingredients to get it right.

What are those ingredients?

Location, location, location. It is one of the unspoken rules of fashion. If a show is held in a convenient place, it does not have to set the world on fire. If it is hard to get to a show, however, it had better be good.

An air of exclusivity is important, too. Marc Jacobs showed his collection in a tiny space on Mercer Street. It felt as if you were in for something, although after the show there was considerable debate on the merits of cashmere fatigues.

Tommy Hilfiger took exclusivity to the extreme at his show. Once his bouncers closed the doors of the Dia Center for the Arts, they didn't want to open them.

Once you get in, a runway full of the right models can do wonders to help you forget the challenge of getting in. A celebrity in the room helps too.

As much as the right models, giveaways are a good thing at a fashion show. Parting gifts cannot make a presentation—usually—but they leave the audience feeling better than it might without them. Believing that only too much is enough, Cynthia Rowley (a designer of Speedo-style bikinis), plied her guests with enough gear for a day at the beach—a striped towel, lip balm, aloe vera gel, and a good book. The folks at Hugo Boss handed out metal-framed sunglasses in black bags, and Marc Jacobs gave away plain white T-shirts with his name written tiny and silk-screened in white on white on the back between the shoulders. There were note pads from Nautica.

Of all fashion show ingredients, cool music is among the most important. It focuses opinion and sometimes explains a designer's impetus. You hear "Planet Claire" by the B-52's, and you imagine John Barlett, in a new wave state of mind. At Kenneth Cole, it was a disco remake of "Dreams" by Fleetwood Mac that lent the collection its hipness. As the audience entered Gene Meyer's show (a designer of colorful neckties and boxer shorts), it heard "It's My Turn," then "I've Never Been to Me." At the finale, it was "Xanadu" by Olivia Newton-John. The cheery schmaltz was irresistible.

And the focus should always be on the clothes. If the clothes are really good, not much more is needed.

Adapted from: DeCaro, F. (1998, July 31). Do's and don'ts of runway shows. New York Times, *1, 5. Reprinted by permission of Frank DeCaro.*

Merchandise

Merchandise selection is the designation of apparel, shoes, and accessories for presentation in a fashion show. The fashion director will discuss with department heads, management teams, or manufacturer representatives the appropriate merchandise to be presented in the show. Merchandise must make a clear fashion statement about current trends to stimulate sales after the show. The merchandise must be appropriate to the demographic and psychographic features of the audience, including age, sex, income, and lifestyle, and be priced according to what the audience is projected to spend on clothing. Trade shows will display the best-selling trends of the current season's line to demonstrate the breadth and depth of merchandise. Consumer shows will display merchandise from a specific retailer or selected retailers within a geographical area.

Only merchandise that will be available immediately after the show should be selected for presentation. Trends that will be out-of-season or out-of-fashion by the time the show is presented should be excluded from the selection process. Additionally, if reorders are tight or the merchandise must be back-ordered, a fashion director should eliminate that item.

Ideal charts are tools a fashion director may use to plan merchandise selection. An **ideal chart** lists all categories of merchandise that will be represented in the show. Within each category, the important trends or looks are listed to ensure they will not be missed when selecting merchandise. The ideal chart may also list the number of garments to be included within each merchandise category. Figure 15.7 is an example of an ideal chart.

Figure 15.7

Ideal Chart

> Good Mornin'—Leisure wear—15 pieces
>   leggings
>   sweatshirts
>   boxer shorts
>   T-shirts
>   tunics
>   2-piece knit coordinates
> Goin' Through the Motions—Lingerie—15 pieces
>   bras
>   panties
>   bustiers
>   teddies
>   slips
>   coordinate sets
> Workin' Overtime—Career wear—25 pieces
>   coordinate separates
>   blouses
>   jumpers
>   trousers
>   suits
>   tailored dresses
> You Can Leave Your Hat On—Casual wear—25 pieces
>   jeans
>   denim dresses
>   denim skirts
>   cargo pants
>   sweaters
>   knit and woven tops
>   jean jackets
>   leather pants and jackets
> Girl Just Want to Have Fun—Evening wear—20 pieces
>   cocktail dresses
>   rayon pants sets
>   sequined tops
>   silk blouses
>   dressy leather

Once the merchandise is selected, it is pulled from the sales floor and kept in reserve for the show. Extra merchandise should be pulled to avoid last minute searches of appropriate merchandise when for some reason the selected item does not fit the model or has sold out before the show. Basic seasonal items should be pulled first, newer looks and trends should be left for decision closer to the show. After the merchandise is pulled it should be grouped or coordinated into specific categories that make a series of fashion statements. The merchandise categories should flow from one statement to another, creating excitement for the audience. The first and last categories should make the strongest statements. After completing the merchandise grouping, a line-up should be created. The **line-up** is a listing, in order of appearance, of models and the outfits they will be wearing. The line-up will be used for many different purposes throughout the show, such as planning dressing area organization and scripting the show.

Models

Models are individuals, hired or volunteer, who wear the merchandise and accessories during the show (Fig. 15.8). Models must be able to present merchandise effectively in a believable manner. While models should be attractive, the beauty of the model should

Figure 15.8

Fashion show models are chosen according to how well they will show off a particular line of fashion merchandise.

Source: J. Estrin/NYT Pictures

not detract from the clothing that they are wearing. The type of show being produced, the targeted audience, and the merchandise selected will determine the type of model to be featured in the show. There are several typical female model types. These include models for sizes 4 to 16 in petite, junior, and misses sizes. Junior models are typically aged 15 to 19. Petite and misses models run the spectrum from young models (teens and 20s) with mature looks, to mature models (aged 55 to 60) with distinguishing gray hair and features, and a young appearance. Male and female models should be appropriate to the audience and merchandise. Gender, age, (or perceived age), and ethnicity are characteristics that should be evaluated during model selection. Figure 15.9 is an example of a voucher or model release form that all models should sign upon being hired or volunteering for a show.

Amateur or professional models may be used. Amateur models are not professionally trained and are selected from such resources as a retail store's fashion advisory board, customers, and employees; members of the sponsoring organization; or students. Professional models are trained in modeling techniques and are hired through modeling agencies or schools.

Ford Models Incorporated is a premier modeling agency headquartered in New York City, with eight offices worldwide. Eileen and Jerry Ford established the agency in 1947. Their daughter Katie took the helm as president and chief executive officer in 1995. Ford prides itself on turning over rocks to find new and fresh models (Nicholson, 1997). It has a legion of scouts who tour the world, and holds open casting calls in the United States and abroad. A search accomplished through a CBS morning television show procured 20,000 applicants, and the agency interviewed a few thousand of them for possible hire. The agency hires both fit and runway models. According to Katie Ford, it takes 6 months to 2 years to get a model's career off the ground, but, she says, it only takes a few weeks to know whether a girl has top model potential.

Attributes of an excellent model include confidence and poise in walking, timing, turning, and posing for the audience and the camera. A model must move with a smooth light pace. Body weight should be forward on a straight but not stiff frame. Arms should be loose but not swinging away from the body. Hands should be used to highlight design details such as pockets or accessories. Runway turns are known as pivots. A model should have the ability to pivot in a smooth, graceful, and continuous motion as an individual or simultaneously within a group of models. Models are responsible for the timing of the show. The speed and pace of a model's walk can prolong or shorten the show as dictated by the merchandise line-up or the body language of the audience.

Models are responsible for attending fittings and rehearsals. They should have hair and makeup appropriately applied to accentuate garments and accessories. Garments should be ready for the models when they arrive, and the models should quickly assist show personnel in making necessary alterations or merchandise substitutions. Models should attend the rehearsal and practice the route they will take as they enter and exit the stage. Ideally, the stage and backstage will be adjacent, but in some locales, such as an auditorium or a restaurant, this may not be possible. Models should take note of stairs, doors, and other obstacles that may interfere with their moving to and from the stage. Each model should be fully informed about the outfits and accessories he or she will be wearing and the order in which the garments will be worn. Fittings will have taken place prior to the show, and models will have a clear idea what they are wearing and what is expected of them.

The fashion office should create a file or record on models who have been used for fashion shows. Information should include name and address, sizing information, and

Voucher–Sample

Voucher/Model Release

Bill to:	Requested by:
Customer ID:	Client:
Invoice #:	Product:
Date of first insertion:	Studio/Location:

PO#	JOB#	EMPLOYER	TERMS

MODEL/TALENT:

DATE	TIME FR.	TIME TO	JOB, REH. OR FITTING	TTL HOURS	1ST RATE	2ND RATE	TTL
TRAVEL RATE							
WARDROBE							
MISC. EXP.							
BUYOUT							
BONUS							
SUBTOTAL							

[ ] Billboard   [ ] National Ad   [ ] Point-of-Purchase   [ ] Product Packaging

Photography to be used for any listed use must be checked and pre-negotiated with and signed-off by talent or release is not valid. By my signature below I warrant that I am signing in the official capacity of my company with the intent to bind the undersigned company and that I have read, understand, and accept all the terms herein. The above information is correct.

_____   _____
Client Signature   Talent Signature

In consideration of the sum stated hereon, inclusive of agent's service fee, and valid only upon receipt of full payment (talent fee and service fee), I hereby sell, assign, and grant to above or those for whom they act as indicated above, the right/permission to copyright and/or use, circulate, reuse, and/or publish photographs or other likeness of me in which I may be, in whole or in part, or composites or reproductions thereof, in color or otherwise, still or moving, without restriction as to changes or alterations from time to time, for commercial or print advertising purposes only through any media, trade, or any other similar lawful purpose, except television, billboards, point-of-purchase displays, phone arcades, bus shelters, poster, subway, bus displays, national ads, or other high exposure usages as these require bonuses through special negotiations. Likenesses of me may be used for a period of 12 months, after which reusage fees must be negotiated or rights to use my photograph terminate.

The buyout fee refers to use as purchased. Please note the blocks to the left for separate bonus negotiations.

I hereby waive my right to inspect and/or approve the finished product or the advertising copy that may be used in connection therewith.

I hereby release and discharge the above, its successors and all persons acting under its permission or authority, or those for whom it is acting from any liability by virtue of any blurring, distortion, alteration, optical illusion, or use in composite form that may occur or be produced in the taking of said picture or in any processing thereof through completion of the finished product.

All payments are due in thirty days from date of booking. Talent will receive payment based on payment from client, unless otherwise negotiated by agency.

FOR ALL NEW YORK JOBS ONLY:
You,_____ , as employer of record for this booking, agree that any professional model(s) used in connection with this agreement are employees of _____ for purposes of New York Labor Law.

(W4 info)

THIS RELEASE NOT VALID UNTIL PAYMENT IN FULL IS MADE TO:

Figure 15.9

Model Release Form

personal attributes of the model. Each model should be evaluated on his or her performance after each show to assist the fashion director or model coordinator in selection of future models.

France, Italy, England, and other European countries have had a modeling industry for many years. A newcomer to the world of fashion models is China. There are about 400 models working in China, and of that number only about 20 are nationally known ("China Backs," 1996). Over 200 of these models work for The New Silk Road Company, a Chinese modeling agency that has clients in Europe and the United States in addition to China. Aware of the need for more models, Beijing's Institute of Clothing and Technology has begun offering classes to teach students how to perform on a runway.

Commentary

Commentary is the oral delivery of information used to identify trends of the season. Commentary should entertain the audience and help interpret clear fashion statements to help sell the merchandise. Good commentary tells something about the merchandise that the audience cannot readily see. Well-executed commentary makes the models and audience feel at ease with one another.

A **commentator** is the individual who is responsible for commentary. Commentary is written from the merchandise line-up, using a detailed fashion vocabulary to highlight important details of the merchandise. Commentary should emphasize trends, feeling, moods, and intrinsic values of the apparel rather than obvious details evident to the audience. As with models, commentary may be used to change the pace of the show.

Commentary is scripted on **commentary cards,** which may include full commentary, partial commentary, or impromptu commentary. Figure 15.10 is a sample of full and partial commentary styles. **Full commentary** involves writing every word on the cards as a script prior to the show. The commentator then reads the rehearsed words that are appropriately timed to the model's appearance. **Partial commentary,** written prior to the show, highlights pertinent details. Partial commentary allows for the commentator to ad-lib about the garments during the show. Oftentimes, tight timelines cause a commenta-

Figure 15.10

Samples of commentary styles.

Full Commentary	
Celina Bechner	Good Mornin' #1

Rise and shine! Time to meet the morning! The morning can be fun when you're wearing this hip-length sweatshirt and matching boxer shorts! It's easy to get up when you know you'll be comfortable in this cotton/polyester fleece sweatshirt with ribbed trim. The shorts are equally comfortable, made of brushed cotton and polyester with an elasticized waist and those all important pockets! Whether it's savoring that first cup of coffee or being pestered by the cat for breakfast, we all want to move in comfort as we start the day! This pigment-dyed set from Victoria's Secret shouts cozy fleece comfort in anticipation for the day.

Partial Commentary	
Celina Bechner	Good Mornin' #1
GARMENT DESCRIPTION:	Hip-length sweatshirt and matching boxer shorts. Pigment-dyed to match.
ACCESSORIES:	White T-shirt under sweatshirt. Tennis shoes and socks. Coffee cup
PROVIDED BY:	Victoria's Secret

tor to prepare only partial commentary before the show begins. **Impromptu commentary** is commentary created spontaneously during the show using cards as brief cues. Impromptu commentary should be used only by highly experienced commentators.

Commentary is the one optional element of a fashion show. Audiences today are stimulated by music, video presentations, and lighting features as a result of TV exposure and are less likely to require a descriptive or analytical narrative of what they are seeing at a fashion show. Fashion particularly lends itself to visual excitement rather than audio explanation of details. Consumer shows are more likely to use commentary. Spectacular productions will substitute music and video in place of commentary.

Set Design

Models, merchandise, and commentary all come together as the stage set design and staging are planned. The set is the physical layout of the facilities, including the stage, runway, backdrops, lighting, and props. The stage is the background where models enter and exit. The runway is an extension of the stage or a freestanding unit that projects into the audience. The stage and/or runway will vary according to the physical location and needs of the show. When planning a runway show the stage manager should consider the time required of models to enter and exit the runway, the walking route and traffic flow on the runway, and the height, size, and shape of the runway as it relates to the room and audience visibility. Runways may be built in a variety of shapes including the T, I, X, H, Y, U or Z. The primary limitation to stage shape is the size of the fashion show location. Good lighting and seating should be considered when designing a set to ensure a positive experience by everyone involved in the show.

Set design should also include a model **dressing area** that is behind the scenes. The dressing area should be large enough to accommodate clothing racks, tables, chairs, full-length mirrors, and all the models and support personnel required for the show. Merchandise should be spaced on racks to prevent wrinkling and allow easy access by the **dressers,** preparation assistants to the models. The dressing room should be organized so that each model has his or her own area. Additionally, model areas should be planned to alternate with busy areas. Models grouped together in the merchandise line-up should be apart in the dressing area to minimize traffic flow problems. Space should also be reserved for hair and makeup. The dressing room should have a clearly defined entrance and exit, preferably through different doors to prevent awkward movements that may be seen by the audience.

Stage backgrounds are used to enhance the show by creating atmosphere, emphasizing fashion trends, or reinforcing the designer or manufacturer's image through use of a logo. The extent of backdrops or scenery is dependent on the type of show, budget, and personal style of the show producer. Stage backgrounds can range from simple to exotic. The winter 1998–99 couture collection for Givenchy opened with a model perched on the back of a haltingly high-stepping horse, amid an Amazonian rain forest and a three-story waterfall (Spindler, 1998). At another show, John Galiano for Dior opened at a Paris railroad station with a model on the front of an engine. Color Plate 5 shows how Alexander McQueen used platforms that could be lowered beneath the stage floor for the 1999 Givenchy haute couture show.

As with backdrops, props can be used to highlight the featured merchandise. Props may be stationary items such as a car, furniture, or a gazebo. Mobile props, such as a briefcase or tennis racket, may also be carried by the model to emphasize a lifestyle characteristic influenced by the fashions. In Figure 15.11 a model uses a prop to accentuate the featured apparel.

Figure 15.11

Props accentuate fashions.

Music

Fashions shows produced with or without the use of commentary rely heavily on music to set the mood of the show and appeal to the emotions of the audience. Music is an aesthetically pleasing or harmonious sound or combination of sounds. The right music can prepare an audience to enjoy the show more than any other element of fashion shows. Music is taped or live, and may be instrumental or vocal in nature. Each music category—blues, contemporary, rock, classical, or jazz—can be influential to the audience, causing the members to leave the show excited to buy merchandise. However, the music must be selected to fit the appropriate target market. Professionals should research preferences and be able to match musicians with the selected audience.

Music is used to set the atmosphere for the audience and set the pace for models. Upbeat, dance-oriented music will cause models to walk at a more rapid speed and may require more outfits to fill the time properly. The music should match the commentary and the merchandise, starting with a strong selection to capture the attention of the audience. Just as the merchandise is presented in a flowing, natural progression, so too should the music. During the middle segments, music should not overpower the merchandise but should keep the audience interested. A finishing selection should be strong, with a driving momentum that leaves the audience remembering the show after the finale.

Music directors, who are in charge of selecting and presenting the audio portion of the show, and other technicians are generally hired for fashion shows. It is the responsibility of the music director or designated technician to obtain permission to use copyrighted music, mix the music at the event, and prepare the sound system at the show location.

STEPS IN PRODUCING A FASHION SHOW

In addition to show elements, it is necessary to discuss the various stages of fashion show production. These steps include the rehearsal, behind-the-scene preparations on show day, and evaluation following the show.

Rehearsal

The rehearsal is a practice performance, held in private, in preparation for a public performance. The rehearsal is an opportunity for the show coordinator to solve any problems prior to viewing by the public. The rehearsal may be a simple run-through or a full-dress rehearsal. A run-through is a rehearsal of the show sequences without the merchandise to show models choreography. A full-dress rehearsal consists of a complete walk through with clothing, music, commentary, and all other technical aspects. The type of show and level of expertise of the participants will dictate the type of rehearsal needed. Dressers, starters, and all other show personnel should be involved with the dress rehearsal to understand the sequence of the show and assist with show timing during the actual performance.

Preshow Preparation and Stage Strike

After hours, days, or months of planning, the show is ready to be presented. However, before the models arrive, behind-the-scene details need to be completed. A complete sound and lighting check should take place to ensure the audio and visual levels are correct for the audience, models, and commentator. The dressing room facilities need to be prepared for the arrival of merchandise. Line-up sheets should be posted at strategic locations and everyone should know the proper entrances, flow of traffic, and exits. Merchandise should be ready for models to wear. Tags are hidden, alterations are finished, and garments are pressed. Programs and/or promotional samples should be placed on audience seats, and hosts should be completely familiar with the seating arrangement for reserved seating.

First impressions by the audience will influence the show's success or failure. All of the preparation will pay off when every element works in concert to present the right fashion to the right audience with all elements correctly executed. As with any performance, it is important to start on time. People grow increasingly impatient when they feel their time is being wasted. Communication between technicians, the fashion director, commentators, and necessary show personnel will influence the smooth running of the show. Show producers should also be aware of the audience's reactions and respond as necessary to make the audience comfortable. Most shows finish with a finale, bringing all models on stage together and acknowledging the designer. When the show is finished, stage strike and cleanup should occur with all participants fulfilling their assigned responsibilities.

Evaluation

The fashion show is not complete until personnel involved in the production have come together one last time to evaluate the performance. Evaluation consists of reviewing all aspects of the show, people, places, and processes. Was it appropriate for the audience? Participants, including models, show personnel, and technicians, should be evaluated for future consideration. Audience reaction to the fashion show should be considered. Was the theme appealing to the audience? Aspects of the in-store or out-of-store location should be considered with respect to the show personnel and the audience. Models, merchandise, and commentary should be evaluated and notes about what went well and what improvements are needed for the next show should be recorded. The success of the advertising and publicity campaign should be reviewed along with the budget. Evaluation is the subject of Chapter 17.

FUTURE TRENDS IN FASHION SHOWS

The glitz and glamour of fashion shows will always make them an enjoyable promotion medium by which to view fashions. However, in an industry that is global, alternatives to runway shows are part of the future. Future directions of fashion shows include the use of the Internet and CD-ROMs to view fashion innovations. The first designer to introduce a collection on the Internet and CD-ROM was Helmet Lang, in 1998. He also accompanied his collection with a 15-minute video "look-book" and offered editors and buyers an opportunity to view the collection on racks in his SoHo showroom (White, 1998b). Lang's idea was a success because the artistry and social elements of fashion overcame the cold, gray world of computers. The multimedia format was not intended to replace live shows every season; it is an added alternative to viewing shows. According to Lang, showing a line via the Internet and CD-ROM saves time and allows for a large number of people to view the show at once, thereby making a small show a big show. However, the disadvantages include not being able to see the fabric close up or in three dimensions.

In another first, the trade show went on-line for the first time in 1998. Instead of traipsing through miles of aisles at a convention center, store buyers were able to click on the Internet to see fashion designers' and manufacturers' offerings through an on-line trade show called Fashion Millennia at *http://www.fashionmention.com* ("On-line Trade Show," 1998). The concept has value to small design houses that do not put on fashion shows, offering them a forum to be seen by buyers unfamiliar with their lines. Figure 15.12 is Fashion Millennia's website.

In yet another first, on February 3, 1999, Victoria's Secret broadcast the world's most watched fashion event to date, a fashion show broadcast live on the Web (Color Plate 1). The 1.5 million viewers who visited the show at *http://www.victoriassecret/fashionshow99* made the audience one of the largest for a single Internet event (Quick, 1999). The cybercast show demonstrated better than any previous event the merging of Internet technology and fashion show promotion.

Not only was this fashion show adapted to the Internet; it was a model for a com-

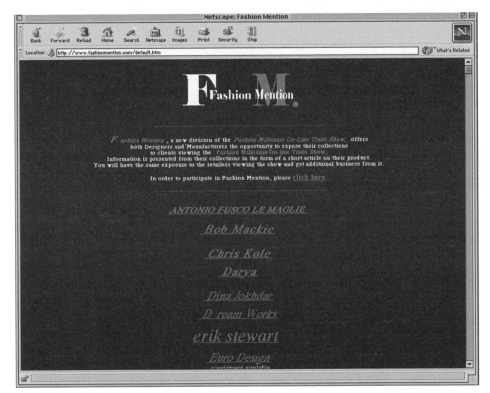

Figure 15.12

Fashion Millennia's website

pletely synthesized promotion using an IMC approach. On the Sunday prior to the show, Victoria's Secret spent $1.5 million on a single television commercial aired during the Superbowl, followed by $4 million for advertising internationally in newspapers (Napoli, 1999). Print ads inviting viewers to tune in were placed in magazines such as *Business Week*. The *Wall Street Journal* was a corporate sponsor, with banner ads linked to the event on its website. According to representatives of Victoria's Secret, the value of the Web was the ability to reach customers in countries where the company does not have stores or does not distribute the 350 million catalogs that it mails annually. The impact of the fashion show broadcast may have best been stated by Allan Mottus, publisher of *The Informationist*, a beauty industry newsletter: "Fashion ain't Paris anymore, and it ain't New York, and it's not Victoria's Secret's 800 stores. Now, every household that has an Internet connection is a fashion store (Napoli, 1999, p. 1)."

Fashion shows are one of the most exciting promotion tools. They create excitement for everyone involved, from the audience to models, designers, and retailers. Understanding its appeal, Intel used this promotion strategy as the theme in a late-1990s campaign to introduce a *new look* in computers. In ads that ran in print and broadcast media, the models were dressed as brightly colored *BunnyPeople*, a take-off on the clean room suits that are standard uniforms in computer chip manufacturing. In Color Plate 4 the flashy colored bunnies display the new computer chip using it as a runway prop.

Live fashion shows are a very traditional form of promotion but are no less important to the integrated marketing communications mix. Although the Internet and CD-ROMs have provided an opportunity to enhance the way buyers and consumers view fashion, promotion via a live model, with music, sets, and grand entertainment, will never be completely dismissed, because the audience likes the theatrical spectacular.

SUMMARY

- A fashion show is a presentation of apparel, accessories, and other products to enhance personal attractiveness on live models to an audience.
- Fashion shows include all the elements of a theatrical production — music, lighting, staging, and a script as a performance for a live audience.
- The primary reason to produce a fashion show is to sell merchandise.
- Trade shows are sponsored by producers of raw materials to demonstrate the utilization and versatility of these products to buyers at the next market level.
- Retail shows are sponsored by retailers and are directed toward the retail staff and consumer market; they include in-store, customer, charity, and press shows.
- The most elaborate and expensive fashion show to produce is the production show or spectacular.
- The most familiar fashion show is the formal runway show in which merchandise is presented on models who parade in front of a seated audience.
- Informal fashion shows present merchandise on models in a casual environment, which includes tea-room modeling, trunk shows, hat box shows, and mannequin modeling.
- Fashion shows may be produced on videotape for use at point-of purchase, to provide instruction, or as a documentary.
- Fashion shows are produced by coordinators or fashion directors. The coordinator or fashion director may delegate responsibilities to staff, including model, merchandise, and publicity coordinators, and a stage manager.
- Fashion shows must be planned. Planning details include audience selection, theme development, location selection, timing, and security.
- Fashion show planning must include budget preparation.
- Merchandise selection is the designation of apparel, shoes, and accessories for presentation in a fashion show.
- A show may include the oral delivery of commentary to identify trends of the season, which are shown through garments and accessories.
- Models and merchandise are displayed on a set that may include a runway, stage, props, background, music, and lighting.
- Steps of fashion show production include a rehearsal and preshow preparation before the event and stage strike and evaluation afterward.

KEY TERMS

commentary	ideal charts	partial commentary
commentary card	impromptu commentary	press show
commentator	informal fashion show	production show
created audience	in-store show	publicity and advertising
dressers	0line-up	coordinator
dressing area	mannequin modeling	retail show
formal runway show	merchandise coordinator	stage manager
full commentary	merchandise selection	tea-room modeling
guaranteed audience	model coordinator	trunk show
hatbox show	music director	video production show

QUESTIONS FOR DISCUSSION

1. What are the differences between fashion shows produced for trade and retail events?
2. In what situations would one use a production show, formal runway show, or video production?
3. What are the primary responsibilities of a model coordinator, merchandise coordinator, stage manager, and advertising and publicity coordinator when planning a fashion show?
4. What should happen during the rehearsal, preparation for the show, and show, and at the conclusion of the show?
5. Compare and contrast live and broadcast fashion shows. What are some advantages and disadvantages of each?

ADDITIONAL RESOURCES

Esch, N., Gayheart, R., and Walker, C. (1996). *The Wilhelmina guide to modeling*. New York: Fireside.

Everett, J., and Swanson, K. (1993). *Guide to producing a fashion show*. New York: Fairchild.

Goschie, S. (1986). *Fashion direction & coordination* (2nd ed.). Mission Hills, CA: Glencoe.

Guerin, P. (1987). *Creative fashion presentations*. New York: Fairchild.

Hamilton, B. (1998). *The art of the walk*. New York: HarperPerennial.

Morris, S. (1996). *Catwalk: Inside the world of supermodels*. New York: Universe.

Rubinstein, D., and Bloom, J. (1998). *The modeling life*. New York: Berkley.

Figure 16.1

Sears de México features brands with youth appeal, such as in this shop-in-shop.

chapter 16

VISUAL MERCHANDISING

Trendy and young are not words generally associated with Sears, but that was the image projected at Sears de México following its youth-oriented renovation of its physical appearance and merchandise mix. Like its U.S. counterpart, Sears de México had been known as the store where a customer could buy both an affordable dress and a washing machine. Under the leadership of Grupo Carso, the Mexican conglomerate that purchased the division from Sears U.S., the first remodeled store opened in 1998 (Ramey, 1998). Market studies revealed that younger Mexicans were in tune with global fashion trends and had more disposable income. Therefore, Sears refocused on shoppers who were 15 to 30 years old, instead of the 25-to-50-year-old group that had been targeted in the past. The rejuvenated Plaza Satelite store, located in a middle-class neighborhood of Mexico City, featured shop-in-shops (Fig. 16.1) where garments were displayed on blonde wood tables and shelves. Junior apparel was highlighted on one side of the main entrance with an emphasis on CK Calvin Klein, Sears' brand—Canyon River Blues—and Furor, a concept shop for jeans and related apparel with a high-tech atmosphere. Stores such as Sears de México use the physical selling space and presentation of merchandise to attract the target consumer as one of the promotion mix elements.

After you have read this chapter you will be able to:

Explain the roles visual merchandising and display play in the promotion mix.

Differentiate among the various types of visual merchandising categories.

Discern the component parts of a display.

Explain the importance of store layout and design as a promotion mix tool.

Schedule display changes and store renovations.

Visual merchandising is the last promotion mix category to be discussed in Part III of this text. We begin this chapter by defining the terms visual merchandising and display. Next, the importance of visual presentation of merchandise at the different market levels is evaluated. Display locations and categories are presented before the elements of a display are defined. Then, store design and layout are considered as an integral part of creating a pleasant shopping environment. We look at changing and updating the look of the store as a part of scheduling display installations and store remodeling. The chapter concludes with a look at future trends in visual merchandising.

Visual merchandising refers to the physical presentation of products in a nonpersonal approach to promote the image of a firm and the sale of merchandise to the consumer. Displays are the physical exhibits of merchandise and support materials. Although the terms display and visual merchandising are regularly used synonymously, visual merchandising encompasses a greater number of practices and responsibilities than simply displaying merchandise. When a retailing or manufacturing organization coordinates its visual merchandise presentations with its advertising, direct marketing, and/or sales promotion programs, it is following an integrated marketing communications approach.

Table 16.1   **Primary Sources for Fashion Ideas**

Rank	Source	Percent Mentioning
1	Store displays	62
2	Friends and peers	51
3	Catalogs	30
4	Commercials and ads	26
5	Family members	24
6	Fashion magazines	23
7	Salespeople	14
8	Celebrities	10

Source: *Show me the clothes: Store displays are the primary source of clothing ideas (1997).* Women's Wear Daily *(From Cotton Incorporated's Lifestyle Monitor), 2.*

In 1949, John Mertes, Chair of Marketing at the University of Oklahoma, defined the responsibilities of visual merchandisers to include store design, planning, store and department identification, customer traffic control, store layout, space-sales analysis, fixturing, window display, interior display, and display research (Marcus, 1978.) It became an occupation that was far more demanding than a window *trimmer,* whose job was generally limited to the creation of window displays in previous decades. Although, the phrase visual merchandising was introduced in the 1940s, the term did not gain widespread acceptance in the industry until the 1970s.

Customers are more likely to respond favorably to merchandise if they are able to view the actual product rather than interpret it from an illustration, photograph, or video. According to research conducted by Cotton Incorporated's Lifestyle Monitor (Table 16.1), over 60 percent of all women get their clothing ideas from store displays ("Show Me," 1997). Thus, visual presentation has an advantage over print and broadcast advertisements, which require consumers to interpret what a product looks like. When a garment is shown with suitable accessories in a perfect setting, the shopper's urge to buy the merchandise is stimulated. Visual merchandising is used to enhance the image of a product, demonstrate how the consumer can use it, and create an enjoyable shopping experience. We begin by looking at the different settings in which merchandise is presented through displays.

FIRMS THAT USE VISUAL MERCHANDISING

Visual merchandising takes place in many different locations both inside and outside of the traditional marketing channel. The most obvious place where physical presentation of merchandise occurs is in a retail store. In addition to retailers, manufacturers present products in their showrooms and at trade shows. Other firms that use visual merchandise presentation are museums, historical societies, trade associations, tourism groups, and educational institutions. First, we examine merchandise presentation in the retail environment, then its use by manufacturers and other types of organizations.

Retailers

In today's complex retailing environment, the merging of retail firms such as Dayton-Hudson, Dillard's, and May Company have produced stores that carry very similar merchandise. Customers often complain that there is little if any difference between merchandise sold by one store and another. What makes a customer choose merchandise in one store and ignore the same merchandise in another is often some intangible factor such as how the merchandise is arranged or how easy the merchandise is to find within the store. The task of visual merchandising is first to make the merchandise desirable and then to make it easy to locate in the store.

The retail visual merchandising professional attempts to bring the customer into the store with creative and interesting displays that incorporate aesthetic principles with basic merchandising techniques to inform and educate potential buyers about the products and/or services carried by the business. Displays utilize products, props, backdrops and fixtures to sell merchandise. An attractive store layout also brings patrons to the selling areas where sales personnel can close the sale.

Consumers in the United States and abroad are spending less time in stores—an estimated 7 to 8 minutes in a store in 1996, compared to 13 to 14 minutes a decade before (Dyches, 1996). Hoping to keep customers in the store for a longer period by making the retailing environment more comfortable, stores began using fragrances. AromaSys, a distributor of fragrance machines that cost $3,000 to $5,000, devised a way to dispense fragrance electromagnetically (Miller, 1993). Retailers using aromatherapy have discovered that people shopping for gym shoes are 84 percent more likely to buy in a room infused with a floral scent than a room without fragrance (Dyches, 1996). Scent, like background music, is part of a store's ambiance. Alan Hirsch, researcher and director of the Smell and Taste Research and Treatment Foundation, said he does not know why one scent works while another one does not, but it is clear that odors have an impact on spending behavior (Miller, 1993).

In addition to creating stimulating and inspiring presentations, retail visual merchandisers use their craft to introduce and explain new products. A display may be the first three-dimensional representation of a new silhouette or feature an electronic gadget that the shopper has previously read about or seen on television. This type of display can be used to educate the consumer about how to wear, accessorize, or use new products.

A window display can promote a store image and entice a shopper to enter the store. Displays featuring the latest fashion trends or lifestyle products can pique the interest of the shopper. Turning a passerby into a *browser* inside the store can greatly increase the possibility of patronage from that person. Displays can show the type of merchandise assortment, stage of fashion leadership, and brand names carried by the store. This enables a store to establish and promote the image and products of the store.

Fashion retailers with limited promotional budgets may use visual merchandising as their only form of nonpersonal promotion. Stores may not have the budget to purchase advertising, launch fashion shows, or distribute direct mail catalogs, but they almost always will use window or interior displays to strengthen sales activities. The article in Box 16.1 reports how Paco Underhill uses store planning to create positive first impressions for his retail clients. Figure 16.2 illustrates population density analysis, which can assist retailers with floor presentation.

BOX 16.1
Making First Impressions Count

One of the dangers in store planning is the romance with presentation drawings. Somehow the art form that is a mix of technical skill and surrealistic vision is seen as the hallmark of a good design and designer. From the standpoint of the consumer or businessman, it is important to recognize that any architectural rendering is a means of getting to a three-dimensional end. One of the first drawings you see in a store planner's presentation is the front view of the store.

The assumption that a front view has anything to do with the customer's first or ongoing perception of a store is hogwash. Generally, the only person that sees a store entrance, from the perspective of most presentation drawings, is the random policeman who happens to be in the middle of the street directing traffic in front of the building.

First impressions for any retail site are critical, particularly for stores that depend on impulse purchases. The front of a store and the first 10 to 20 paces into the stores are the most seminal elements in forming the consumer's perception of that business and setting up the disposition to make a purchase.

A good retailing team is advised to think about the entrancing experience from the consumer's perspective. In setting the stage for that understanding, it is important to start by reviewing some prevailing retail myths.

Myth No. 1, which we hear often in American retailing circles, is the right product, at the right price, at the right location. The truth is that in the 1990s, we can accept all of those conditions as givens.

Myth No. 2 is about competition. Again, we hear retailers comparing themselves to other retailers in their specialty area. The truth is that retailers, from dress shops to electronics stores, are competing with one another in the big scramble for the same piece of the public's discretionary income. The dollar spent on fashion might just as well be spent on almost anything else, from fast food to auto accessories.

In the broad scope of things, most stores can segment their customer base into two groups: those that need portals and those that need doorways.

Portal shoppers are presold or pre-directed and make up a large portion of the business for some lucky retailers. For example, in the word of booksellers, some customers are book lovers. For them the entrance to a bookstore does not have to be enticing or seductive.

Book lovers walk in knowing more than many of the employees. They are comfortable asking questions, and price point may very well make no difference at all. The store can be a mess, with stacks of books in the aisles and dirty windows, and they could not care less—all of those elements are part of the ambiance they are willing to accept. For book lovers, the entrance is not a door but a portal into the world of books.

While portal shoppers may be a strong element of retail business, store owners pay rent to attract the shopper that needs doorways.

Although advertising dollars can build public awareness of a shop and announce a sale, the retailer needs the on-site recognition to close the marketing loop. High consumer awareness does not necessarily translate into customers walking in the door. Advertising only reinforces predisposition—the process of bringing the consumer through the entrance is a design and merchandising issue. That is why store designers and planners exist.

The process of tickling the shopping impulse in the passing consumer is based on time. The longer customers have to think about possibly entering a store, the more likely they will. Our work has shown that often the most important view of the store may be a side or approaching view. The first chance that most shops get to start their impulse tickle may be 25 paces before the customer reaches the doorway. On main streets and in shopping malls, progressive planners have been allowing stores to build out their storefronts to enhance pedestrians' view as they move down the sidewalk or mall concourse. In the same spirit, windows featuring displays that the consumer can recognize or identify with at a 20- to 25-pace distance do a better job of pulling the customer in the door. From our research, we have established a number of general rules concerning windows.

First, it is better to get two messages across positively than five messages possibly—keep it simple. In many retail locations, you can count on the fact that your customer base will pass your window with a certain regularity, be it biweekly, or in some cases, daily. Simple windows that change often may very well be a better use of the display budget than elaborate windows that remain in place for longer periods of time.

Consumer interest is motivated by change. Window spaces that are easy to work with are creative marketing decisions—the small amount of floor space that may be lost is a small trade-off.

When designing a window display, it is important to take into account the way a consumer is going to live with the product and allow passing shoppers to view the product from that distance.

For example, some years ago I saw a window display on New York City's Fifth Avenue, where a small department store had an elegant arrangement of silver flatware on the floor of the window casement. The only shoppers who looked at that section of the window were middle-aged women, who did so from a bent-over position. Their interest was terminated, however, when someone brushed past their protruding rear ends on the busy sidewalk behind them.

Our research also has shown that there is a dominant direction from which people pass almost any storefront. That dominance may be created by the location of the parking lot, a public transportation terminus, or some other physical feature. We have found that displays canted or slanted to that dominant direction of traffic will get more serious attention.

And finally, if graphic information is part of the storefront's message, make sure that it can be read as shoppers walk past; do not expect them to stop to get the message, because they very well may not.

Modern graphics theory has pointed out that people read differently than they did in 1960. Americans and Europeans no longer read letter by letter but have graduated to reading letter clump by letter clump—one reason why typefaces that allow for closer positioning of letters are used much more often than 30 years ago.

One common flaw of store entrances is that they do not take people into account. For many department stores and main street locations, a common flaw is not planning a transition zone. Consider that people have many different walking speeds. The pace at which they move down a rainy street or across a hot parking lot is very different from the pace at which they move through a store. It takes time for people to slow down once they get through the store's entrance.

Directional and promotional signage and displays can be more effective when placed deeper into the store. For one of our clients, we were able to triple the number of customers shopping with in-store circulars by adjusting where, and at what height, the circulars were presented to the customer. Poor placement of information systems not only translates into consumers who may walk out of the store because they do not want to commit to finding their way, but it also means headaches for sales associates, as they are asked the same series of questions over and over.

Aisles and entrances need to be stroller accessible. Even if babies and toddlers are not a store's primary market, the consumers they bring with them are. In reviewing film data for a client, we discovered the comedy of mothers trying to negotiate their baby strollers around a lease-line table. Appearing clumsy becomes one more reason for a customer to leave the store. In this case, almost nothing was sold from the lease-line table—the job of getting around that fixture took precedence.

Good retailers can work magic if they can get people in the door. A good store involves an ongoing dialogue between store designers, merchants, and consumers. Modern retailing history is littered with stores that failed for the most mundane reasons. The difference between stores that work well and look great in the flesh and those that do not often has nothing to do with price points and inventory, and everything to do with a well-executed strategy based on human needs.

Adapted from: Underhill, P. (1999, February). Making first impressions count. Display & Design Ideas *[On-line]. Available: http://www.envirosell.com/articles/dispdes.html. Reprinted with permission from* Display & Design Ideas, *© Shore-Varrone, Inc.*

Population Density Map

Figure 16.2

Envirosell's Population Density Map.

Retail firms are not the only businesses that use visual merchandising as an important promotional strategy. Next, we consider the role of visual merchandising by manufacturers as a promotional strategy.

Manufacturers

Fashion designers and manufacturers use display techniques at their showrooms, which may or may not have window displays. Showrooms in the Chicago Apparel Mart and Dallas Apparel Center have windows inside the marts that serve a function similar to a store window on the street or inside a mall. This type of window display serves to inform the retail buyer about products carried and promote the image of the firm. Once the buyer is inside the showroom, interior displays can help the designer or the manufacturer's sales representative sell the line by making products look coordinated and attractive.

Manufacturers and designers may also develop an assortment of display aids for fashion retailers to use in their stores. These supports, featured in their showrooms or through catalogs, may include signs, props, banners and decals, counter signs, counter racks, and wall and floor fixtures. These items may be provided to retailers free or on a fee basis.

Manufacturers also show merchandise to retailers at trade shows. Vendor exhibits are set up in convention centers and hotels. Events, such as MAGIC, the men's apparel trade show discussed in Chapter 15, and WWDMagic, its counterpart featuring women's apparel that is also held in Las Vegas twice each year, attract retail buyers and manufacturer's representatives from all over the world. Large international firms, such as Levi's, Perry Ellis, and Calvin Klein, set up huge *showrooms* at trade shows, whereas small vendors, such as JNCO set up **exhibit booths,** small exhibit spaces with temporary walls and fixtures, to sell their trendy clothing. Figure 16.3 shows the Sigrid Olsen exhibit space at the WWDMagic show in the fall of 1998. Firms that specialize in building trade show exhibits can create selling spaces for vendors. Exhibit booths are moved

Figure 16.3

This Sigrid Olsen exhibit booth at the fall 1998 WWDMagic show is typical of the space set up to display fashion merchandise at trade shows.

from vendors' headquarters to trade shows, and therefore must be transportable. Channel-Kor, an exhibit manufacturing firm, creates modular systems that may be adjusted in size, so that booths may be used in large or small exhibit spaces and/or updated regularly. The trade publication for such firms is *Exhibit Builder* magazine.

Merchandise Presentation by Other Organizations

Museums, historical societies, trade associations, tourism groups, and educational institutions create displays for enhancing costume knowledge, scholarship, information, fashion details, and trend directions. The Whitney Museum of American Art in New York, the Los Angeles County Museum, London's Victoria and Albert Museum, and the Musée de la Mode et du Costume in Paris are among the international museums that exhibit important historical and contemporary fashion designs. These exhibitions included retrospectives of designers and artists, such as Christian Dior and Gianni Versace, works by Tiffany and Cartier, and themes such as *Wordrobe,* and *Fashion in Film.* Museum curators and assistants use display techniques to feature costumes and accessories for these popular presentations. *The Warhol Look: Glamour, Style, Fashion,* was a traveling exhibit organized by The Andy Warhol Museum in Pittsburgh. The exhibit recreated window displays by Warhol and his display mentor, Gene Moore. Thus, the exhibit featured a display of displays (Fig. 16.4).

The Arizona Office of Tourism established a *Welcome Center* in Lupton near the Arizona and New Mexico border. Representatives from seven geographical regions in Arizona were asked to set up displays featuring products and events relating to their

Figure 16.4

Display for Tiffany's from the late 1950s from *The Warhol Look: Glamour, Style, Fashion.*
Source: *The Archives of The Andy Warhol Museum, Pittsburgh. Founding Collection, Contribution, The Andy Warhol Foundation for the Visual Arts, Inc.*

areas. The Flagstaff Convention and Visitor's Bureau sent representatives to this remote site to create a display depicting the arts and events occurring in that city. Displays featured Native American jewelry, pottery, and rugs in showcases that identified the stores where visitors could purchase similar items when they arrived in Flagstaff.

Educational institutions, such as the Fashion Institute of Technology (FIT), also launch exhibits of historical and contemporary clothing. *Fifty Years of Fashion: New Look to Now, Claire McCardell and the American Look,* and *China Chic: East Meets West,* are among the costume exhibits promoted by FIT in the late 1990s. Exhibits such as these assist designers and manufacturers in reviving fashion trends and creating new ones. Consumer interest in these shows provides an audience for the manufacturer's latest innovations as well as merchandise, such as books, fashion, or home accessories, created exclusively for the exhibit. Educational institutions also set up exhibit booths, similar to trade show booths, designed for use at new student orientations, college recruitment fairs, and exhibitions at academic conferences.

The primary trade publication for the visual merchandising industry is *Visual Merchandising & Store Design (VM+SD).* The articles in the publication cover a wide range of topics related to lighting, store renovations, new store designs, fixtures, and so forth. *VM+SD* selects a store of the year in each of several categories and devotes an issue of the magazine to the winners (see Color Plate 8). The publisher also features a website with highlights from the publication.

DISPLAY CATEGORIES

There are four basic categories of display: window, exterior, interior, and remote. Which type of display category is used, and how, depends upon the architecture of the building in which the business or organization is located. Retailers use all four categories, whereas manufacturers primarily use window, interior, and remote formats.

Window Display

Window displays are used in large cities with downtown shopping districts and in some mall stores that use conventional windows. Although downtown shopping has declined in many cities because consumers prefer to go to suburban malls, window displays continue to be a source of entertainment and information for workers in cities such as New York, Chicago, Kansas City, and San Francisco. Christmas windows at such retailers as Tiffany's, Lord and Taylor, and Saks Fifth Avenue attract numerous consumers who visit the downtown store only once a year to see these elaborate presentations. In November 1997, actor Hal Linden, dressed in Victorian era clothing, appeared at the Lord and Taylor store in New York when the Charles Dickens Christmas Windows were unveiled. This festive occasion brought many shoppers to the Fifth Avenue store.

Windows serve as the eyes to the interior of the retail store. The image of the store is portrayed in the window. Several clues are given to persons walking past the store window. If the display contains wallets, handbags, jewelry, and belts, the consumer is assured that the store sells a range of accessories. The look and fashion image of the merchandise serves as an introduction to the consumer. When the window is used effectively the potential customer is attracted into the selling space. Windows can strengthen a store's traffic and sales volume.

Store windows are either closed-back or open-back. **Closed-back windows** are completely contained display spaces. These windows have walls on three sides. There is a door or sliding panel, which can be moved to bring in merchandise, mannequins, and props. The advantage for the visual merchandiser is that he or she will not have to contend with background distractions. But, this type of window may serve as a barrier to the customer, who might be intimidated and afraid to enter. A smaller store with this type of window may seem insignificant or claustrophobic.

In contrast **open-back windows** do not have a back wall. The customer can see into the store, viewing not only the display but also the store itself. This may be an advantage since the customer can see merchandise other than that on display. The disadvantage of an open-backed window is distraction from store merchandise in the background. Display professionals may use screens, curtains, banners or plants to create a backdrop for this type of window to minimize the problems.

Straight Front Window

The **straight front** store has windows that are parallel to the road or sidewalk. A store with a straight front may have a single window or several windows, called a **bank of windows.** The entrance may be on one side or in the middle of two or more straight front windows (Fig. 16.5A). Large retailers, such as New York-based Bloomingdale's, Chicago-based Carson Pirie Scott, or Boston-based Filene's, in downtown locations frequently use this type of window. Visual merchandisers like to work with this type of window because they are typically working with a closed back, which does not have visual interference from the store interior. The stagelike settings are ideal for elaborate displays.

Angled Front Window

The entrance to an **angled front** store is recessed from the sidewalk, providing more exposure to display space. There are large display windows on one or both sides of the storefront, creating an aisle for the consumer to walk through to the door. The display windows may be on an angle or parallel to the back wall of the display space. The aisle is frequently covered and serves as a lobby, which leads the shopper to the store's entrance (Fig. 16.5B).

Arcade Front Window

The **arcade front window** is a spacious display space with a variety of configurations, normally found in downtown shopping districts. There are several windows with islands or peninsulas made from glass extending out from the sides. Arcade windows may take on unusual shapes from concave or slanted glass. The shopper may have to take a circuitous route to enter the store. This type of window also has a covered entry that serves as a lobby and a transition zone. The arcade front window, like the angled front, requires the entrance to be set back from the sidewalk. This extends the display area, but limits the store's interior selling space (Fig. 16.5C).

Corner Front Window

The **corner front window** is located where the window faces two streets that are perpendicular to each other; as a result it can be viewed from either street (Fig. 16.5D). The corner window may be next to the store entrance or it may be next to a series of straight windows. The floor plan for this type of window is triangular. It offers special problems for the display professional, who may find it difficult to eliminate distractions from the other side. On the other hand, the corner front window can take advantage of passersby from two different directions.

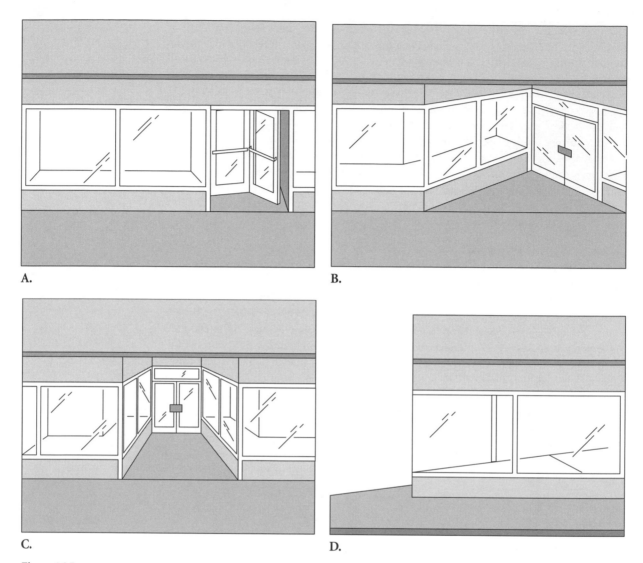

A. B. C. D.

Figure 16.5

Illustrations of A. straight, B. angled, C. arcade, and D. corner windows

Shadow Box Window

The **shadow box** is a small closed-back window, dimensioned on a much smaller scale than the previously discussed window styles (Fig. 16.6A). The shadow box is used for small, yet relatively expensive items. Typically, shadow box windows are used for fine jewelry, cameras, cosmetics, books, or shoes. Tiffany's uses the shadow box window to attract customers into its famous Fifth Avenue store.

Windowless Window

Stores in enclosed shopping malls often choose to construct their stores without conventional windows. Mall retailers use the **windowless window** or no-window concepts as the entrance to their stores (Fig. 16.6B). They believe that wide openings at the front

Figure 16.6
A. a shadow box window
and B. a windowless
storefront in a mall

A.

B.

of the store will bring consumers in to shop for merchandise easily visible to the passerby. Security is the greatest risk with this concept, because shoplifters can easily steal merchandise from stores with wide openings. It is common to see security guards or store greeters at the entrance of mall stores to prevent theft of merchandise.

Exterior Display

Exterior display, also called façade display, is the outside appearance of the storefront. Along with the style of architecture and building location, exterior display has a great impact on the image of a retail business. Exterior display has greatest applicability to main street and downtown stores, which use storefront design to strengthen the store's image. Stores located in enclosed suburban malls may have limited opportunities for exterior display because they have few or no windows; visual merchandising in such locations is focused on interior displays, space planning, and signage, discussed later in this chapter. Exterior display involves such components as signs, seasonal decorative elements, outdoor lights, and awnings.

Exterior Sign

The exterior sign, which consists of words and/or graphic symbols placed on the outside of a store, is often the initial attention grabber seen by a potential customer. It creates the first impression and sets the mood for the store. City and county codes may regulate how signs are used on the exterior of a building. The style and size of lettering can be used as an attention getting device. TOYS "R" US in bright primary colors sets the youthful and playful mood for the international toy store.

The sign can be a plus or a minus for the retailer. A neat and well-kept sign invites customers to enter the store, but a sign with chipped paint and burned out or missing lights in a dirty window shouts another type of message: *Don't shop here!*

The sign should be a store's signature. The logo or graphic symbol used on interior walls and other promotional materials, such as advertising, can be professionally reproduced for the exterior of the store. The exterior sign can be a memorable part of a complete graphic promotional package, which includes shopping bags, sales receipts, and interior signs.

Seasonal Decorative Elements

Seasonal decorative elements include props and symbols to enhance the mood of the time period. Various seasons lend themselves to such time period or theme decorations. An obvious example of seasonal decorations used in exterior display is the Christmas tree. This image creates a feeling of nostalgia and festivity and puts the consumer in a holiday mood, recalling past events. Rotating planters and flower boxes with each season can proclaim other seasonal changes. Tulips set the scene for spring, while pansies and petunias can be used for summer and the Fourth of July. Adding dried corn stalks and colorful leaves to the outdoor planters can show the arrival of fall.

Banners or flags, which are hangings made from paper or cloth with colors and/or symbols that depict nations, states, or other decorative elements, are colorful, eye-catching devices for the store exterior. Flags can depict the store logo, symbol, or a seasonal theme. Using international flags on the outside of the store for a multinational theme helps to promote the global nature of the event. Banners can also convey a special theme, such as *Back to School,* with a crayon package design.

Storewide themes, such as anniversary sales or import fairs, can also suggest exterior decorative elements. During the anniversary sale, a painted plywood sign that represents a cake with candles can be attached to the outside of the store. An Italian import event may utilize Italian flags, a model of the Coliseum, or reproductions of Italian paintings at the store entrance.

Outdoor Lights

Outdoor lights, which illuminate the front of the store, not only serve a decorative function, but also are essential tools because most stores today are open in the evening. As such, outdoor lighting serves a security and safety function. Outdoor lights can fit the historical architectural style of a building or emphasize the contemporary nature of the merchandise carried. Lighting can also be used to call the consumer's attention to seasonal or merchandise themes promoted at the store. For example, a menorah with lightbulbs can be lit during each of the eight days of Hanukkah.

Awnings

Awnings are another element that can serve both a functional and a decorative purpose. The awning is a structure, frequently made from canvas, that extends from a window or entrance, providing protection from rain, snow, or sun. Windows with direct exposure to the sun will fade valuable merchandise; the awning can protect merchandise from deteriorating and cut down on the window glare. Awnings may also be used to emphasize the store name or a seasonal theme. Additionally, awnings may be used to cluster independent stores into a grouping with greater impact in an outdoor setting.

Interior Display

Store **interior display,** practiced by both downtown and mall stores, consists of presenting merchandise attractively on variety of architectural forms, fixtures, and furniture. Although an architect or interior designer created the actual interior design of the store, the visual merchandiser suggests how to best feature the store's merchandise. The style of fixtures, flooring, lighting, mirrors, interior signs, and other decorative elements can reinforce the mood and image of the store.

Architects, interior designers, and visual merchandisers work with **floor plans,** which are scale drawings of the walls, fixtures, and other architectural elements. These floor plans (Fig. 16.7) show the placement of permanent and temporary items. The first consideration with interior space planning is how customers enter and move through a store. If a customer does not have a specific target department to visit, research indicates that most consumers will turn to the right as they enter a store. It is estimated that 80–90 percent of people, or more, will do this (Weishar, 1998). To counteract this behavior, the designer should use aisle and fixture placement to move the customer through the store. A well-planned traffic pattern will bring the customer in contact with as much appropriately placed and attractively presented merchandise as possible.

The selling floor of the store is a functional environment that should also provide a pleasant shopping experience for the consumer. At the same time, visual merchandisers must carefully assess where fixtures will be placed, what merchandise will be put on them, and how to move customer traffic through the store. The components of the store interior display are perimeter walls, trend shops, island displays, fixtures, and interior signs.

Perimeter Walls

The walls that surround the selling area are called perimeter walls. They are among the first merchandising spaces viewed by a potential consumer. This area should be attractively presented, featuring coordinated merchandise. It serves as an invitation for the customer to come into the area to browse. The perimeter wall can be attractively displayed using waterfalls, hanging bars, shelves, and/or pin-up boards. Retailers should avoid using this area as a place to put sale or clearance items, because sale items rarely have the visual impact of a color-coordinated merchandise group.

A **T-wall** is a type of perimeter wall used to separate one department from another. It has a flat end, near an aisle, that is converted to display space by using a panel to cover the end of the unit. The panel is the top of the "T." A platform, a raised stagelike surface, may be used in front of the wall to highlight merchandise.

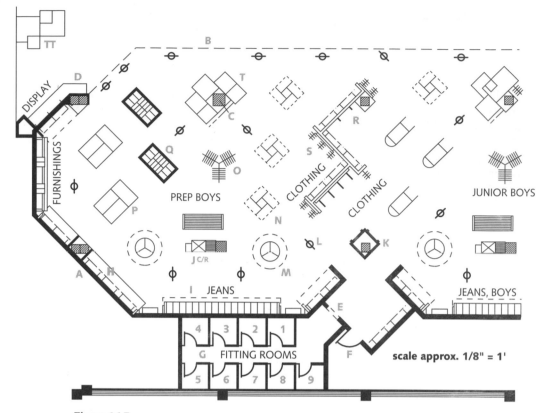

Figure 16.7

Architects, interior designers, and visual merchandisers use floor plans to illustrate how a store layout will appear.

Trend Shop

The **trend shop,** also known as a *highlight shop,* is a merchandising area set apart by special flooring, walls, or ceiling treatments. At a mall store it may be at the retailer's entrance, set apart by a carpeted sales floor. In a traditional downtown department store, it may be an area close to an escalator or elevator. This space is converted into a theme shop based upon whatever merchandise promotions or seasonal events are going on. In April the theme shop might be a *Spring Showers Shop.* This trend shop emphasizes raincoats, boots, umbrellas, and floral accessories. Figure 16.8 illustrates a Trend Shop Request Form that gives all of the pertinent information required to implement a special shop.

Island Display

The **island display** is a three-dimensional display space, frequently located at the mall entrance or in a central location where several aisles come together. The island display may be set off by a raised or multilevel platform. A ceiling crown or special lighting or other details may help to stress the importance of this merchandise. Several showcases pulled together are used to form an island display for cosmetics or accessories. These showcases may be enclosed for security or open to encourage self-service.

Trend Shop Request

Shop Name:
Shop Type
❐ Classification
❐ Fashion Theme
❐ Seasonal

Date of Request:

Parent Department(s):

General Merchandise Description:

Opening Date:

Locations:

General Design Suggestions:

Signs needed:

Planned Stock by Unit and Dollar Amounts:

Planned Advertising:

Staffing:

Approved by:

Figure 16.8

Trend Shop Request Form.

Fixtures

Cabinets covered in green slime? Garbage can-styled endcaps? These fixtures were introduced at Nickelodeon, an in-store concept shop located inside the Chicago Viacom Retail Group's Entertainment Store, as fixtures that supported merchandise and created atmosphere ("Specialty Stores," 1998). The system included several eye-popping pieces, such as a large, orange-colored cash wrap accented with green "slime," and a kidney-shaped tiered table with yellow metal stripping and exposed screw-heads. Fun colors and interesting shapes made the shopping environment fun and entertaining.

Fixtures include a wide variety of furniture and equipment to hold and display merchandise. Fixtures include display tables, cubes, counters, showcases, ledges, and racks. Each type of fixture holds a particular category of merchandise.

Display tables are used as a self-service selling activity. Display tables house a large quantity of apparel, such as sweaters, or nonapparel, such as boxed costume jewelry. Customers are allowed to touch and feel the stock, selecting the size or color they desire. **Cubes** are box-style display fixtures used for self-selection. Cubes are ideal for flat folded apparel, home textile products such as towels and sheets, and children's clothing. Actually ringing up the sale and handing over merchandise takes place at a counter called a **cash wrap.** Money or credit cards are used to purchase products at this space, which may have an all glass or partial glass surface where additional merchandise is displayed. These products include high-impulse items like jewelry, accessories, or hosiery.

Showcases are fixtures used to enclose groupings of similar merchandise. These types of display cases are used in cosmetic, jewelry, and accessory departments. During most of the year, shelves in showcases can be pleasingly presented with seasonal or theme displays. But, in the middle of the busy Christmas holiday season, shelves can be mass merchandised or heavily stocked with coordinated groups of merchandise.

Ledges are located behind islands created by showcases, generally in the cosmetic and accessory departments or behind cash wrap desks. Ledges are traditionally raised about 5 feet above the selling floor. They can be used for back stock, promotional packages, or major theme displays. Some ledges may be large enough to hold standing mannequins, but sitting mannequins or other decorative elements may also be used. Showcases and ledges prevent customers from touching products, making this location ideal for merchandise requiring security.

Racks are wooden or metal fixtures, ranging from simple T-stands for small quantities of merchandise to large round racks, which hold hundreds of garments. T-stands are used for new or color-coordinated merchandise. These racks are often found near an aisle, at the entrance to a department, or near a T-wall display. Four-way racks are also used to hold coordinated merchandise groups, consisting of a collection of skirts, pants, blouses, and jackets from one vendor.

Point-of-purchase (P.O.P) programs use fixtures created by manufacturers for retailers. The trade association, The Point-of-Purchase Advertising Industry (POPAI), represents this industry. Dick Blatt, POPAI president, defines point-of-purchase merchandising as "displays, signs, structures, and devices that are used to identify, advertise and/or merchandise an outlet, service, or product and which serve as an aid to selling" (Diamond and Diamond, 1999). Retailers who use this type of fixturing and signage hope that point-of-purchase promotions and in-store displays developed by manufacturers will motivate shoppers to buy. Point-of-purchase was introduced in Chapter 11 as an example of trade-oriented sales promotion. The cartoon in Figure 16.9 takes a humorous look at the widespread use of POP in the retail setting.

Interior Signs

Company policy determines how signs are used inside stores. One firm might use manufacturer-created signs, while another retailer bans such signs and produces its own signage. A variety of signs are used as interior signs; these include marks that identify the department, type of merchandise, advertised products, special events, sales promotions, storewide themes, prices, guest appearances, and so forth. Interior sign categories include the following:

- **Banners** and **flags** are used inside the store in a manner similar to the way they are used as decorative elements for window and exterior displays.
- **Counter top signs** are placed on top of showcases to highlight merchandise displayed.
- **Easels,** upright artists' frames used to hold a painting, are also used by retailers and manufacturers to hold signs.

Figure 16.9
This cartoon takes a humorous look at the widespread use of POP.
Source: ©The Toos Studio/drewtoos@aol.com

- **Elevator** and **escalator signs** may be attached to the wall as a permanent sign or may be placed as a freestanding unit near an elevator or escalator. These signs are used to help consumers find their way through a store.
- **Fixture toppers** are signs that are placed on top of various fixtures, such as round racks, T-stands, and four-ways. These signs promote a particular category of merchandise, brand, or theme.
- **Hanging signs** are hung from the ceiling. They may be permanent signs that identify a department or provide directions, but they also could be temporary signs signifying a special theme or event, such as a gift-with-purchase promotion.
- **Posters** are placards that offer reinforcement to a merchandising theme or act as an artistic decoration on a wall or in a display.

No matter how attractive or creative an interior display is, effectiveness is lost unless a customer enters the store. This limitation of interior display may be overcome by attracting customers to the store by window displays, advertising, or publicity designed to increase store traffic. In addition to these practices, store designers are asked to renovate and redesign departments or entire stores, to make the shopping experience more desirable.

Renovation

According to "Understanding Your Customer," a study of consumer logistics conducted by Roger Blackwell Associates, consumers tend to categorize specific stores as places where they would or would not typically buy a certain item because of the store's housekeeping and layout more than the merchandise itself (Seckler, 1998). Overall, the study found store choices were most often influenced by convenience, and how a store performed on details, such as well-lit parking lots and cash registers that face the consumer.

With the needs of the consumer in mind, several major global retailers have undertaken major **renovations,** remodeling and refurbishing the interior design and layout of a selling space. Macy's at Herald Square in New York spent at least $150 million on a three-phase remodeling project to create a better store layout with bigger brand name shops (Moin, 1997). Phase one of the project started with an overhaul of cosmetics, shoes, lingerie, large sizes, contemporary sportswear, and the Cellar. Phase two involved rolling out new apparel and cosmetics departments, while phase three remodeled the mezzanine, establishing a food court and expanding the men's department on the lower level. The project was geared to bring razzle-dazzle into the store promoted as the world's largest.

Also in 1997, Bloomingdales completed a 10-month renovation of its 17 departments on the main floor, arcade, balcony, and mid/lower levels at the 59th Street and Lexington Avenue store (Barr, 1998). Phase one of its remodeling project created a brighter and interactive shopping environment. In addition to its updating the flagship store in New York, Bloomingdales opened four stores in California, remodeling sites vacated by the Broadway chain. Among the top priorities for the renovation program were to make it easier for the customer to shop.

European retailers were also following this trend. La Rinacente, Italy's leading department store, launched an extensive renovation program and added high fashion labels to attract customers who had been defecting to shopping malls, hypermarkets, and specialty chains. The renovation at its flagship store near Piazza Duomo in Milan resulted in significant increases in sales (Galbraith, 1997). Several Paris stores also polished their images in the 1990s. Galeries Lafayette celebrated its 100th birthday with a redesigned home department conceived by French architect Yves Taralon, while Printemps spent $40 million to renovate its fashion and accessories floors (Weisman, 1996). Printemps' remodeling (Fig. 16.10) was more like a revolution. The store's in-house design team visited Japan and the United States to integrate ideas for Printemps' new plan. Like Macy's and Bloomingdales, Printemps floor plans were cumbersome and hard to shop, with tall walls that obstructed sight lines. New organization and open floor plans made it easier for customers to navigate through each of these stores.

Remote Display

Remote display is the only category of display where products are featured away from the point-of-purchase. A **remote display** is a physical presentation of merchandise by a retailer or manufacturer placed in such locations as hotel lobbies, exhibit halls, or public transportation terminals. Another type of remote display involves a mall retailer that places a merchandise display in a case at the shopping center entrance, a location that is away from the store, to encourage consumers to visit the store. The display can attract attention and create interest, but in order to purchase the product the customer must travel to the place where the merchandise is sold or make a phone call.

Remote display is effective for products relating to travel. A unique suitcase design may be featured in a display located in the waiting area of an airport. Customers waiting for a flight might view the display, understand advantages of the product, and order it from a cell or pay phone.

Figure 16.10
Renovation at the Paris
department store
Printemps gave the store
a more open and brighter
appearance.

DISPLAY COMPONENTS

Each display, regardless of its location or the type of business that creates it, consists of several common components. Universal to every display is the merchandise being offered for sale, functional and/or decorative props, backgrounds, lighting, signage, and three-dimensional arrangements.

Merchandise

The products selected are the most important component of a display. The merchandise will determine all other elements of the display, from the theme to supporting elements. Merchandise is the focus of the display and the primary purpose for creating the display.

Selection of merchandise and timing of the display are essential to the success of displays. Sometimes unexpected events trigger desires in consumers. For example, a swimwear display featured in a store window immediately after a February snowstorm led to big sales of swimwear to winter-weary customers planning a cruise or a trip to a resort. People passing by the store fantasized about spring and days at the beach.

Props

Props are functional structures used to lean or place merchandise on or decorative elements used symbolically to create a mood. **Functional props** are the physical supports, such as mannequins and furniture, used to hold merchandise. Mannequins are body forms that wear apparel. Because mannequins may cost several thousand dollars, they represent a major investment and are a major portion of a visual merchandiser's budget. Other functional props include such standard fixtures as cubes, steps, and racks that may be used for either interior or window displays.

Decorative props, used to establish a mood or theme for the merchandise, include baskets, plants, flags, banners, and musical instruments. There are almost unlimited styles and items that may be used as decorative props. Furniture can be used to create the illusion of a room or soft-sculpture forms can be used to create the image of a southwestern desert.

Backgrounds

The **background** is the foundation, real or implied, where the display is built. A back wall can serve as the base for a background. If the display space does not have a wall, the illusion of a wall can be created with another material. Banners, screens, partial walls, or seamless paper are examples of elements that can be used to create backdrops. In most cases, it is easier for the visual merchandiser to create a stronger visual merchandise impact if the display has some type of background that prevents the viewer's eye from being distracted by other things.

Lighting

Proper **lighting,** or illumination of the display or selling area is vital to the selling environment. Lighting is used to draw attention to the merchandise or the entire display. Moreover, it can be used to direct consumers through the store. A spotlight or track lighting can be used to draw the eye to the specific merchandise featured. Consumers are attracted toward well-lit areas. Therefore, lighting on a display should be two to five times stronger than the general room lighting (Mills, Paul, and Moorman, 1995).

Lighting designer Bernard Bauer, principal of Integrated Lighting Concepts, planned and implemented the lighting program for Bloomingdales' renovation project. His plan called for an increase of 200 percent over some previously existing lighting (Barr, 1998). Bauer combined energy-efficient resources and effective luminaire design to achieve the brighter appearance. "Lighting has to assume a more important role in communicating information that will assist customers in making buying decisions," Bauer pointed out. "They have less time to shop—a by-product of increased family and social responsibilities" (Barr, 1998). Therefore, lighting plays a significant role in directing consumers through the store and to desired products.

In addition to highlighting the merchandise and directing customers through the store, light can also be used to create a mood. Twinkling Christmas lights can establish a festive holiday spirit, whereas strobe lights, which turn on and off rapidly, can be used to achieve dramatic effects. Color can be introduced into a display by using overlays, called acetate gels, or by using colored, round glass filters. As mentioned in Box 14.1, Henri Bendel used colored gels to flood the front of its store pink to add to the ambiance at a breast cancer awareness event. Using templates projected by a pattern and framing projector can also create special effects. Such images are used to simulate scenery, create atmosphere, or apply additional depth to a display setting.

Signage

Signs used in a display convey information about the merchandise or emphasize the theme. Signs may also be used to provide information for the person walking past a window. Details such as the name of the designer or manufacturer and where to find the merchandise in the store are common informational signs.

Carson Pirie Scott developed a new in-store printing system for its point-of-purchase signs to improve customer service and to save staff time by making sure that all signs are up, on time, with current prices, and appropriate information. The *Find It—Sign It* system delivers signs through the company's data network, making it easy for store employees to find a sign for a specific item or a whole group of signs for a particular promotion or vendor's line (Carroll, 1998). Signs are produced and ordered from a central library of sign records through a Windows PC network, providing individual stores with the capability of retrieving only the signs they need, when they need them. The benefit-oriented system produces signs that feature product information with reasons to buy and prices.

Many European retailers incorporate prices of the merchandise in the window display. This helps to inform the potential customer about the expense and status of the products in the store. The practice of including the price of merchandise is not common in the United States.

Display Arrangements

Because displays are three-dimensional designs incorporating merchandise and props, some commonly used arrangements can help to effectively handle space. These proportional arrangements include the pyramid, step, zigzag, and repetition.

The **pyramid** is a triangular geometric shape, in which the base of the pyramid is the widest space and the sides rise to a center point or peak in the middle. A **step** arrangement is a series of elevations similar to a stair step. This leads to a high end on one side or the other. The pyramid is an example of formal balance, the step arrangement makes use of informal balance. **Zigzag** is based on a reversing step design. It consists of a series of short, sharp angles in alternating directions. This design uses the diagonal lines in reaching its objectives.

Repetition is a type of arrangement that uses the same merchandise and/or props in a style that occurs again. Repetition arranges all items in the same way. Although repetition can be considered monotonous and boring, it can be used to emphasize a particular product. A good example of effective use of repetition involves placing several T-shirts or sweaters in a rainbow of colors. Repetition accentuates the product and the color variation not only adds interest but shows the range of available colors.

PLANNING VISUAL PRESENTATIONS

Ideally, the planning and scheduling of visual presentations are coordinated into the integrated marketing communications planning process. This is appropriate because displays are often created to feature merchandise that is advertised. A visual merchandising calendar identifies what merchandise will be displayed in which locations during each month. Window and interior display changes can be scheduled on a regular basis using the calendar as a guideline.

How frequently to change displays is an important question for the visual merchandising staff. There are several issues relevant to establishing a display schedule that influence display changes.

- Will the displays be tied to other promotional activities such as advertising or special events?
- Will the same people pass by the display area every day?

- Is the merchandise likely to be damaged by sunlight, lamps, or dust if it is left in the display area too long?
- Are there skilled visual merchandise personnel on staff to facilitate change?
- Are the displays in a high traffic area of the store where they should be kept up-to-date?
- Is the budget large enough to change the displays frequently?
- Where is the display area located?

The store should establish a policy regarding display change frequency. Change may occur once a week or once a month, depending upon the needs of the individual store. Department stores tend to schedule display changes every 7 to 14 days. Specialty stores, with limited stock in particular sizes or colors, change display more frequently as determined by customer demand. Once a schedule is set, it should be followed. The biggest problem with changing displays is the failure to make any changes. Because retailers in tourist areas attract out-of-town visitors, they do not need to change their displays as frequently as other stores. However, displays start to look old and merchandise becomes outdated if displays are not changed. One rural retailer became so lazy about display that the windows were not changed in 6 months. Needless to say that retailer is no longer in business.

Some visual merchandising conditions are within the control of the store, while others are not. Planning an audit of the visual spaces for the store will give a retailer guidelines scheduling a visual merchandising program. Tips for performing this activity are given in Box 16.2.

BOX 16.2

Conduct Your Own Internal "Visual Audit"

As retailers, we routinely conduct end-of-the-month assessments of our financial health, usually through month-end bookkeeping procedures. In addition, an annual physical count of inventory is essential to maintain correct internal financial records. You could call this procedure your own internal financial audit.

Obviously, the financial health of your company is extremely important. However, retailers should also conduct an annual "audit" of their store's visual appeal to customers, because the visual image of a store will have significant impact on a customer's buying decisions.

So, what are the important elements of a visual merchandising (VM) audit? First, start by making a list of the different areas of your store—exterior parking, exterior signage, exterior entry, cash wrap, traffic flow/store layout, store fixtures, and more (see checklist). Make sure your list includes every area that impacts the overall "character" of your store.

Next, identify those areas over which you have total control, some control, or no control. A "no-control" area might be the overall exterior visual style of the building or mall in which your store is located. Building managers or landlords may place other restrictions on signage, window displays, and so on.

Defining Your Store's Criteria

Before you actually start your VM audit, you need to define your criteria for what would be acceptable or unacceptable visually. For example, you cannot give yourself low marks on an exterior sign if the lease agreement prohibits you from changing it, no matter what you personally think about the sign.

Also, consider the pricing strategy of your store. A store's price orientation should be reflected in how the store looks. Are there other constraints? Be sure to consider these, too.

Now that you have the basics of your audit form prepared, it is time to get going. As you walk through your store, try to see it through your customers' eyes. Pretend that this is the first time you have ever been inside your store. What makes sense? What does not? You may know why it is reasonable to put a certain fixture in a certain spot, but your customer does not. Make sure the store layout makes sense to your customer first, even if it means it is not quite as convenient for you.

Some retailers actually enlist the help of trusted customers or friends. They walk through the store together, and the owner asks, "What do you see?" "What does this say about the store?"

Gaining an Edge over the Competition

Evaluating your store in this manner provides you with two significant benefits: (1) you identify areas in which you can gain an advantage over competitors; and (2) you get a head start on identifying those aspects of the store that should change the next time you remodel.

If you conduct these evaluations on a regular basis, you can compare them to each other over a period of time. That way you can see the progress you have made in the store's overall design—and see where to go next.

To sum up, make your once-a-year appointment with yourself to complete the visual merchandising audit. After all, a set of well-organized financial records is not likely to affect a customer's impression of your store, but your store's image will certainly have a dramatic impact on your customer—and your bottom line.

VM Audit Form

When conducting an internal visual merchandising audit, consider many aspects of your store's overall look and feel. Below is a list of the major areas that you should consider. Customize this form to fit your store.

Exterior
❐ Parking lot
❐ Lighting
❐ Window display
❐ Signage
❐ Entry
❐ Overall ease of ingress and egress

Interior
❐ Entry
❐ Cash wrap
❐ Traffic flow/store layout
❐ Store fixtures
❐ Lighting
❐ Flooring
❐ Ceiling
❐ Signage
❐ Service areas
❐ Cleanliness
❐ Sensory elements (music, smell, colors)
❐ Focal points
❐ Clarity of definition of departments
❐ Wall displays

Miscellaneous Items
❐ Store packaging
❐ Advertising and public relations
❐ "Entertainment value" (a measure of the level of enjoyment customers experience as they shop)

Adapted from: Dyches, B. (1998, January). Conduct your own internal "visual audit." WWD Specialty Stores: A Special Report, *17–18.*

Brian Dyches is president of Retail Resource Group.

VISUAL MERCHANDISING PERSONNEL

There is a wide variety of career opportunities and working environments for a person interested in careers in visual merchandising. Although the most prominent career path for merchandise presentation personnel is working for retailers, we have seen there are several other types of firms that hire individuals with skill and training in visual merchandising.

Whether a store is a large multibranch operation or a small single proprietor, a business that sells consumer goods is involved in the processes of merchandise layout, presentation, and display. Employees of a small store may be given the task of displaying merchandise as one of many different duties assigned. A sales associate with a flair for fashion and an interest in display may fulfill the needs of a specialty retailer.

In corporate department stores, such as May Company, or specialty retailers, such as Saks Fifth Avenue, the Promotion Division has responsibility for the visual merchandising department. Figure 16.11 shows an organization chart for a visual merchandising department of a large retailer. The department head is a vice-president or director of visual merchandising. This person serves as the administrative manager, overseeing the planning, budgeting, and communication about store layout and merchandise presentation. Much coordination takes place with advertising, publicity, special events, and merchandising departments. This administrative manager must be able to communicate with his or her peers and subordinates about the visual image of the store. This supervisor must also be able to translate merchandising and fashion trends into window and interior displays as well as set up special retailing shops as needed by the merchandising staff.

Multibranch chain stores usually have a display person at each location, whereas larger branches may have more than one visual merchandiser. This person has the responsibility of creating displays according to the corporate visual merchandising plan,

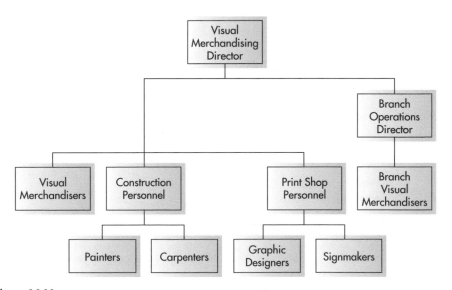

Figure 16.11

An organization chart of a visual merchandising department for a large retail company

delivered to the branches as a planogram. The **planogram** is a detailed plan or map that serves as a guide for setting up window, exterior, and interior displays. It has descriptions about merchandise quantities, fixtures, and placements. This type of planning system provides continuity between the various locations.

J. C. Penney sends each one of its 1,250 stores a photo CD that shows a selection of merchandise with ideas suggested for display ("Show Me," 1997). It provides information about what merchandise will be advertised in 50 million weekly Sunday supplements, so branches may coordinate merchandise displays with ads. Although the corporate office in Plano, Texas, sends detailed recommendations on style, color, and floor and window layouts, each branch is able to interpret and apply those concepts.

A person interested in visual merchandise presentation may work for a store or independently. Individuals who prefer to work alone may find career opportunities as a "freelancer." This person may be hired to complete a specific job on a one-time basis. Some rural or small town freelancers may set up contracts with several retailers to change window or interior displays on a regular schedule.

In addition to creating displays for retailers or manufacturers, visual merchandisers may find work in comparable fields. The visual merchandiser may find work in trade show exhibition, museum exhibit installation, architecture, and interior, fixture, industrial, or point-of-purchase design.

No matter what size or type of firm the visual merchandiser is working for, he or she is expected to be creative, aware of current fashion directions and display trends. And, the visual merchandiser must be able to execute the plans within the assigned budget. The visual merchandiser may be called upon to work with store advertising, public relations, graphic design, and fashion show personnel. He or she will be expected to communicate with other store personnel, management, and customers. Communication skills, both oral and written, are a necessity.

FUTURE TRENDS IN VISUAL MERCHANDISING

In addition to the continual updating of stores through renovation programs, retailers will be depending upon new and emerging technologies to assist with visual merchandising programs. Wal-Mart, led the way by developing computer technology to tailor planograms to individual stores, with software designed by Intactix International of Dallas (Tosh, 1996). The technology made planograms available to all international branches, providing information in all merchandise categories, from apparel and soft lines to hard lines, such as housewares, hardware, and automotive products. The system, licensed exclusively to Wal-Mart, provides store planning analysis and a system for storing and transferring merchandising information between the headquarters and individual stores. Other firms will be looking for ways to communicate this type of information to their stores in the future.

From interactive information displays called kiosks to virtual arcades, retail design will offer a variety of extra-sensory experiences for consumers of all ages. Themed stores and interactivity are limited only by retail designers' imaginations. In an attempt to get consumers to come to the stores and stay longer, a variety of entertainment-oriented formats are being developed for the 21st century. For instance, touch-screen kiosks were introduced at the 150-store Great Mall of the Plains in Olathe, Kansas (Barr, 1997). These interactive promotional tools promote stores and their products as an automated sales representative that can answer a multitude of consumer queries. GameWorks, an AMC 30-plex, an UltraScreen theater, the Virgin MegaStore, and American Wilderness experience were cited as prototypes for the next big wave of entertainment-oriented retail environments created by Viacom, Disney, Warner Brothers, and MGM, among others.

The store as theme park trend was evident as Nike introduced Niketown. Yes, you can buy shoes there, even if the merchandise seems more like an afterthought. Images flash on banks of television sets, larger than life posters of athletes and memorabilia, such as Tiger Woods' golf card and Jerry Rice's cleats, and a live disk jockey playing the hippest music are all a part of the entertaining atmosphere. As shoppers grow bored with malls and advertising messages, entertainment is being developed to bring the consumer back to the store. Because consumers responded, the trend toward creating memorable and enjoyable shopping experiences is anticipated to grow into the 21st century (Fost, 1998).

Hugo Boss, an innovator in the high-tech visual merchandising field, led the way by using digital imaging and three-dimensional interactive technology to introduce its latest line to Neiman Marcus (Zimmermann, 1998a). The interactive system gives buyers a sense of how items in the Hugo Boss collection will look displayed at the retail store. The digital version of the *Hugo Boss Academy,* which is an extensive collection of information about the company and its products, will enable key retail accounts to see how various items will look when they are displayed at the retailer's store. Apparel manufacturers are searching for efficient and cost-effective methods to present and display merchandise. The virtual showroom is expected to be a futuristic method of visual presentation.

Virtual store planner, a product developed by ModaCAD in cooperation with Duck Head Apparel, is an example of a high-tech merchandising, sales tracking, and replenishment system. The software enables a retailer to lay out a floor plan, plan merchan-

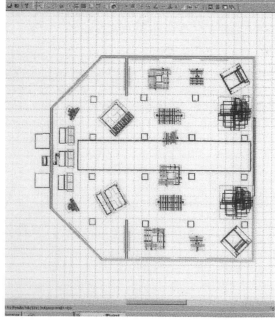

Figure 16.12

ModaCAD's 3D Visual Merchant.

dising strategies, and track point-of-sale information. The system will allow a retailer to design an in-store shop from scratch. Dimensions of the boutique, display fixtures, signs, and point-of-purchase materials can be created and displayed in the virtual shop. "I've always believed that technology will increase efficiency and increase profits if your merchandise is what the customer wants to buy," said Paul Robb, CEO of Duck Head (Hye, 1997).

ModaCAD developed another space and store planning tool. Its 3D Visual Merchant (Fig. 16.12) allows merchandisers to complete three-dimensional walk-throughs of their stores. The program creates a photo-realistic rendering of store plans and layouts, which enable a retail storeowner to use a computer to complete planning, merchandising, and analysis ("Innovative E-Merchandising Software," 1999). This type of computer-assisted visualization will continue to be developed and perfected in the 21st Century.

Visual merchandising involves much more than creating pleasing window and in-store displays. The objective of the visual merchandising staff is to create an attractive, interesting, yet functional merchandising and selling environment. Activities such as store planning and design, traffic flow management, and signage complement the window and interior display projects. The visual merchandising staff typically is part of the retail store's promotion division. Coordination and balance should exist among the advertising, public relations, and fashion offices to produce a cohesive and organized fashion and promotional statement to the public.

SUMMARY

- Visual merchandising refers to the physical presentation of products in a nonpersonal approach to promote the image of the firm and the sale of merchandise to the consumer, whereas displays are the physical exhibits of merchandise and support materials.
- Firms that use visual merchandising techniques include retailers, manufacturers, museums, historical societies, trade associations, tourism groups, and educational institutions.
- The four basic categories of display are window, exterior, interior and remote.
- Universal to every display is the merchandise being offered for sale, functional and/or decorative props, backgrounds, lighting, signage, and three-dimensional arrangements.
- Planning and scheduling of visual presentations are coordinated into the integrated marketing communications planning process, because displays are often created to feature merchandise that is advertised.
- A visual merchandising calendar identifies what merchandise will be displayed in which locations during each month.
- The most prominent career path for visual merchandising personnel is working for retailers, but other types of firms, such as manufacturers, museums, and other firms, hire individuals with skill and training in the field.

KEY TERMS

angled front window	bank of windows	corner front window
arcade front window	cash wrap	cubes
background	closed-back window	decorative props

exhibit booth	open-back window	showcases
exterior display	planogram	step
fixtures	props	straight front window
floor plan	pyramid	trend shop
functional props	racks	T-wall
interior display	remote display	windowless window
island display	renovations	zigzag
ledges	repetition	
lighting	shadow box window	

QUESTIONS FOR DISCUSSION

1. How do the professional responsibilities of a window trimmer differ from those of a visual merchandiser?
2. How does the practice of visual merchandising differ in a retail store, a manufacturer's showroom, a museum, and a trade show?
3. What types of elements can be used to enhance a consumer's shopping experience?
4. What types of firms use visual merchandisers?
5. How does visual merchandising relate to the other promotion mix techniques?

ADDITIONAL RESOURCES

Barr, V., Field, K., and Retail Store Image (Eds.). (1997). *Stores: Retail display and design.* Glen Cove, NY: PBC International.

Colborne, R. (1996). *Visual merchandising: The business of merchandise presentation.* Albany, NY: Delmar.

Diamond, J., and Diamond, E. (1998). *Contemporary visual merchandising.* Upper Saddle River, NJ: Prentice-Hall.

Doonan, S. (1998). *Confessions of a window dresser.* New York: Penguin.

Institute of Store Planners and Editors of VM+SD (Eds.). (1996). *Great store design 2: Winners from the Institute of Store Planners/Visual Merchandising and Store Design Annual Competition.* Gloucester, MA: Rockport.

Lopez, M. J. (1995). *Retail store planning and design manual (The National Retail Federation Series)* (2nd ed.). New York: Wiley.

Mills, K. H., Paul, J. E., and Moormann, K. B. (1994). *Applied visual merchandising* (3rd ed.). Upper Saddle River, NJ: Prentice-Hall.

Pegler, M. M. (Ed.). (1996). *Lifestyle stores.* Glen Cove, NY: PBC International.

Pegler, M. M. (Ed.). (1997). *Stores of the year (annual)* (10th ed.). New York: McGraw-Hill.

Pegler, M. M. (1998). *Visual merchandising and display: The business of presentation* (4th ed.). New York: Fairchild.

Ruderman, L., and Ruderman, A. (1998). *In-store signage and graphics.* Cincinnati, OH: ST Publications.

Underhill, P. (1999). *Why we buy: The science of shopping.* New York: Simon & Schuster.

Evaluation and Accountability

Figure 17.1

JWT's website provides information about awards won for the creativity of its promotional campaigns.

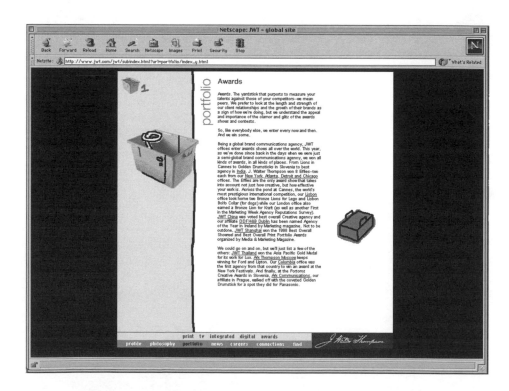

MEASURING PROMOTIONAL EFFECTIVENESS

J. Walter Thompson (JWT), one of the largest global advertising agencies, has offices in 80 countries worldwide with North American branches in Atlanta, Chicago, Detroit, New York, San Francisco, and Toronto. Table 17.1 reveals that JWT was ranked as the third largest agency brand in worldwide gross income by *Advertising Age* in 1997. It has received recognition many times from its professional peers for agency creativity and marketing ability. Information about the amount of business the agency does and the numerous awards the individual branches have received can be found on the JWT Internet website as part of its portfolio (Fig. 17.1).

After you have read this chapter you will be able to:

Explain the reasons why measuring promotional effectiveness is important.

Identify the methods used to measure promotional effectiveness.

Discuss the limitations of measuring promotional effectiveness.

Differentiate the roles of various personnel involved in measuring promotional effectiveness.

Table 17.1   **World's Top 10 Agency Brands**

1997 Rank	Agency	Worldwide Gross Income (1997)[a]	Worldwide Volume (1997)[a]
1	Dentsu	$1,927.1	$14,192.3
2	McCann-Erickson Worldwide	1,451.4	$11,016.1
3	J. Walter Thompson Co.	1,120.9	7,637.3
4	BBDO Worldwide	989.6	8,058.9
5	DDB Needham Worldwide	920.2	6,881.9
6	Grey Advertising	918.3	6,125.4
7	Euro RSCG Worldwide	883.2	6,536.0
8	Leo Burnett	878.0	5,977.1
9	Hakuhodo	848.0	6,475.6
10	Ogilvy & Mather Worldwide	838.4	7,375.0

[a]Figures are in millions of U.S. dollars. Worldwide agency brands are defined as international networks associated with the agency and the agency's U.S. brand, the latter excluding specialty units and independent subsidiaries. Source: World's top 25 agency brands. (1998). Advertising Age *[On-line]. Available: http://www.adage.com. dataplace/archives/dp219.html.*

Chapters 17 and 18, which comprise Part IV of this text, focus on evaluation and accountability. This chapter considers the importance of assessing promotional effectiveness. It discusses why evaluation takes place, defines the conditions necessary for evaluation to take place, and examines contemporary evaluation methods. Because measuring promotional effectiveness is difficult and expensive, some critics think it is a waste of both time and money. But, it is necessary for people involved in the promotion process to assess how to proceed in the future.

Promoting merchandise and services in a global environment is a billion-dollar business. In order to justify these allocations, promotion personnel need to have information about various promotion mix activities and be able to evaluate their effectiveness. From the smallest print ad placed in a local newspaper to the global launch of a designer fragrance, the sponsor needs to know what was effective and what was not.

WHY PROMOTIONAL EVALUATION TAKES PLACE

In the absence of promotional evaluation, the sponsor can only guess at the impact of his or her promotional package. Almost everyone agrees that once a project or activity is performed, some evaluation needs to take place. Evaluation, the process of judging the worth or value of any activity, helps to determine how effective the communication program is by measuring against some standards.

Because more firms are using an integrated marketing communications approach, measuring its effectiveness is an essential component in justifying use of this type of promotional approach. In Chapter 4, we explained that success or failure of each promotional project should be measured and evaluated as the starting point for planning for another project or time period. This evaluation serves as a basis for new activities, making planning and evaluation essential considerations. Research allows the promotional manager to evaluate specific program components and provides input into the next period's situational analysis. Although measurement and evaluation are necessary parts of the planning process, they are often neglected or ignored.

Because billions of dollars are spent on promotional activities each year, avoiding costly mistakes is a very compelling reason to measure promotional effectiveness. Sponsors of promotional programs want to know if their communications packages are achieving objectives. If the objectives are not being met, the manager wants to know so he or she can stop wasting money on ineffective approaches and redirect promotional efforts.

Opportunity, from a marketing perspective, is viewed as an area into which the company could move to enjoy a competitive advantage. Thus, opportunity loss is a missed possibility or a penalty associated with poor communications. There can be losses from ineffective expenditures in addition to potential benefits that are not met. Consequently, evaluating effectiveness of promotion activities may provide an opportunity to make money in addition to saving money.

Measuring promotional effectiveness assists managers in evaluating alternative strategies and making decisions. Typically, promotional executives must make many decisions in developing promotional strategies. They must decide between various creative approaches to determine which message is more effective. Should the cosmetic manufacturer use an emotional or an informational approach? Companies must also decide which media to use for communication placement. Should the furniture retailer place newspaper or television advertisements? Or, the decision-maker might need to decide which of the promotion mix components to implement. Should the manufacturer create magazine advertisements or sponsor a special event? Research techniques and pretesting methods can assist the promotion manager in choosing the most effective creative approach, media, or promotion mix element.

Clients are demanding accountability for the expenses allocated for promotional activities. Has the creative department been too creative, losing site of the promotional objectives? Have the media planners appropriately evaluated the best media alternatives? Conducting research helps companies develop more effective and efficient communications. Appropriate measurement will increase the efficiency of promotional efforts in general.

It is important to note that the research methodology discussed in this chapter is conducted as an evaluative tool, used to measure the effectiveness of advertising and/or promotion mix tools or to assess various strategies prior to implementation. This analysis is different from the research conducted earlier in the promotion planning process to provide input into the creation of the promotional strategy. Evaluative research concentrates primarily on assessing the effects of differing strategies. Although evaluative research is frequently used after the advertising or promotion is implemented, it may be conducted at any stage of the campaign development in order to measure the effectiveness of a message or approach.

CONDITIONS NECESSARY FOR PROMOTIONAL EVALUATION

In order to measure promotional effectiveness, certain conditions or prerequisites must be in place. These conditions must be defined as part of the total promotional planning package prior to implementing a useful evaluation tool. The most significant prerequisite is the establishment of a measurable objective for each element of the promotional mix at the start of the promotional program. In Chapter 4 on planning, we discussed the establishment of goals and objectives for the promotional campaign in detail. Well-defined objectives developed at the beginning of the project give the personnel involved a benchmark against which the actual results of the campaign can be measured. Whether a specific promotion mix element or the total integrated marketing communications package is being considered, the evaluation must be related to the original objectives. As a reminder, let us look at the elements of good communications objectives:

- **Target audience**—the market segments the firm wants to attract considering demographic and psychographic factors; for example, *35-to-49-year old females* or *college-age males.*
- **Product**—the main features, advantages, benefits, uses, and applications of one or more of the company's wares. An example of this objective is, *to communicate the distinctive benefits of 4.7-ounce flannel sheets—more cotton per square yard that provides a soft feel and warmth due to increased ability to trap body warmth.*
- **Brands**—the company's and competitors' brands. This example requires the target audience to associate the product with a particular manufacturer, designer, or retailer, such as, *to communicate that Coming Home with Land's End sells 4.7-ounce flannel sheets that fit.*

- **Behavioral responses**—the responses sought from trial, repurchase, brand switching, or increased usage. The example might be as follows: *to have 20 percent of the target customers purchase 4.7-ounce flannel sheets within 3 weeks of catalog distribution.*

With well-stated objectives such as these, the promotional sponsor and creative staff will be able to implement a program to measure the effectiveness of the campaign.

In addition to developing objectives, a second condition for measuring promotional effectiveness is the willingness to devote time and money toward these researching activities. Marketing research experts have developed a number of techniques and methodologies that can be applied to the questions surrounding promotional effectiveness. These methods require commitment of financial and personnel resources to fulfill the requirements of this task. Next, we look at some of these methods.

CONTEMPORARY RESEARCH METHODS

A variety of scientific and nonscientific techniques have been developed to measure the effectiveness of the promotion mix elements. At first glance, analyzing sales is the simplest method of evaluating the success of any of the promotion mix elements. Yet, if a retail organization merely counts the number of items sold during a 3-day period after the product was advertised in the local newspaper, there are still many unanswered questions. How did each branch display the merchandise? Did the sales associates know the product was advertised? Did the customer come into the store and fail to locate the merchandise? Did the customer find something else to buy? What other variables could affect the success of the advertisement? How does this product advertising fit in with the overall promotional goals of the organization? The following discussion looks at the evaluation of each of the promotion mix elements in detail.

Measuring Advertising, Direct Marketing, and Sales Promotion Effectiveness

Marketing researchers have thoroughly studied print and broadcast advertising effectiveness and developed a variety of inquiry methods. As a result of this extensive commitment, a whole industry of advertising measurement companies has emerged. Direct marketing and sales promotion executives also use their methods. Much of the evaluative advertising research is directed toward investigation of media usage and the creative promotional message.

Media Research
Media research is investigation that attempts to determine the size of advertising outlets and their ability to attract the target audience. As we discussed in Chapters 8 and 9, specific advertising media are evaluated by a number of targeted media measurement organizations. But, there is one important general resource for all media, Competitive Media Reporting (CMR), which combines industry standard resources for competitive monitoring of advertising expenditures, occurrences, creative executions, and broadcast verification data into a single company. CMR incorporates the expertise of recognized industry experts: Leading National Advertisers (LNA), MediaWatch, Multi-Media Service, Radio Expenditure Reports (RER), and Radio TV Reports (RTV). This service provides detailed information pertaining to specific expenditure data for 90,000 brands

and more and than 14 media. Clients are able to access customized reports that can be integrated with other data. The strategic information can be delivered via disk, CD-ROM, or modem to CMR clients.

Each medium has a variety of individual resources for determining the potential audience and for securing information regarding that audience. There are two respected services involved in the measurement of magazines. Simmons Market Research Bureau (SMRB) and MediaMark Research Inc. (MRI) provide information about magazine readership characteristics and size in addition to other media measurements. These companies provide similar and competitive services.

Long-time specialist Nielsen Media Services has started to see some competition in evaluating TV ratings. Statistical Research Inc. (SRI) has been testing a new system, Systems for Measuring and Reporting Television (SMART), in the Philadelphia area since mid-1996. The SMART system started by measuring homes using television, the number of homes that have sets on, the number of persons using television, and how many people are watching them. SRI installed decoders to record what programs people were watching, generating program ratings data. The Committee on Nationwide Television Audience Measurement, which was formed by research directors at ABC, CBS, NBC, and the National Association of Broadcasters in the late 1980s, initiated SMART. Feeling there was erosion in the quality of the Nielsen Service, the group commissioned SRI to begin work on SMART in 1994. In addition to the original sponsors, 14 advertisers plus FOX Network and cable companies—Discovery Networks, ESPN, USA Networks, and Lifetime Television—became sponsors.

Nielsen depends upon meters wired into TVs and VCRs of each sample household. In contrast, SMART uses people meters with sensors that can pick up signals from the air, without wired connections. SMART was programmed to pick up and read new Universal Television Program Codes (UTPC) that are embedded into some program signals. This was developed to create a less intrusive methodology in an environment where it has been difficult to attract survey participants. Participants log in whenever they enter a room with a TV set, making the approach a reflection of the way people use television today.

Arbitron Ratings Company analyzes radio audiences. Arbitron measures between 250 and 13,000 randomly selected individuals, aged 12 or older, in 250 U.S. markets. Participants are compensated for keeping diaries of their listening behavior over a 7-day time frame. Subscribers to Arbitron, including more than 5,000 radio stations, advertisers, and agencies, pay to receive reports detailing participants' listening patterns, station preferences, and demographic characteristics. Advertisers and agencies use this information to profile the audience, making it easier for the advertising sponsor to target the desired market.

AC Nielsen is also one of the best-known international firms engaged in market research, information collection, and analysis for the consumer products and services industries. Besides conducting research on TV usage, Nielsen conducts research about a variety of media in more than 90 countries. In order to participate in the emerging technologies, Nielsen has attempted to measure the audience for Internet advertising. Box 17.1 describes Nielsen Net Ratings, Nielsen's system for analyzing website audiences as well as the efforts of Media Matrix, the leading rater of Internet markets. Measurement of website audiences is one of the biggest concerns facing Internet advertisers, because it is difficult to obtain information about users of this constantly changing and relatively young medium.

The primary method for tracking website usage has been through software that tallies the number of "hits" or the number of visits a website receives. Unfortunately, this

BOX 17.1
Keeping up with the Nielsens

Ever since HotWired served up the first banner ad in 1994, traditional media types have been crying for a Nielsen of the Net—an audience measurement standard that ad buyers and sellers could universally accept and use to demographically dissect how many people are visiting a website. It has finally arrived: the "Nielsen family"—the mythical moms, dads, and kids who have couch-potatoed their way into the pantheon of American advertising—is about to take up residence on the Web.

Nielsen Media Research, the New York-based company that has served as the industry dean of television ratings since 1950, expects to unveil its first Web ratings system in the first quarter of 1999. Gathering data from 5,000 randomly selected Web users, it will project the habits of the estimated 54 million-strong on-line population and gauge traffic to specific sites. Nielsen recently partnered with Milpitas, California-based Net Ratings, which develops sophisticated tools for tracking Internet users.

[Meanwhile, Media Metrix, the industry leader, in business since January 1996, merged in October 1998] with RelevantKnowledge and today has nearly 300 customers.

In essence, Web ratings work similarly to TV ratings. Both Media Metrix and Nielsen NetRatings recruit panels of Web users—selected by randomly dialing homes looking for people with Internet access—using methodologies designed to create a mirror of the on-line population's demographic spread. (The science of random sampling equates a higher participation rate with a more accurate snapshot of the on-line population at large.) Panelists install software that tracks their movements on-line and reports findings to the rating company, which uses the data to project how big a site's audience is and who comprises it (e.g. half are women older than 30, earning $50,000 or more.)

Rankings of the top weekly and monthly Web properties are made public, and more detailed demographic information about a site or its competition is sold to clients. Media Metrix says it sells the data for anywhere from $50,000 into the six figures, but Nielsen will not disclose its sales figures.

While slow to get into Internet ratings, Nielsen has moved quickly to design metering for WebTV to measure Internet usage as it relates to TV watching. In late October 1998, Nielsen closed a 7-year deal with Time Warner to get early access to set-top boxes in order to design meters for them and to jointly test new measurement systems across media. Nielsen has already done *studies* on whether TV-watching patterns change when a home gets Internet access.

Manish Bhatia, Nielsen's vice president of interactive services, admits that the company was late in meeting its on-line goals but says it's serious about the Web. Audience measurement "has a more important role to play on the Web [than TV]. There's commerce, direct advertising campaigns, a lot more activity to measure."

Bhatia also says Nielsen is interested in measuring audiences and advertising effectiveness across both media. "Companies are going to want to know both what is being seen on TV and all these convergence platforms [like WebTV]. We expect to bring two research products [TV and Web ratings] together and provide full service." With client companies such as Disney wanting to measure activity on-line and on the air and wanting to know if a TV campaign drives website visits or vice versa, Nielsen sees combining TV with Web reporting as a core product in the near future.

In its partnership with NetRatings, Nielsen will collect data on metrics similar to those monitored by Media Metrix: the number of visitors to each URL; demographic profiles of visitors; ranking of audiences size and page views; pages per use on a site, etc. The NetRatings technology, however, will give it the unique ability to capture the actual GIF image of each banner as that appears on a Web user's page, to verify exactly which ad ran of a rotating series and to give media planners more information about the response to each ad they run. And Nielsen pledges that its experience in panel recruiting—using live operators, random digit dialing, and persistence to convince participants—will help achieve the greatest accuracy for its Web projections.

IrrelevantKnowledge

Accuracy and consistency have been hard to come by in on-line measurement, and the market has been frustrated by wildly divergent numbers. [In 1998], America Online howled when its website, aol.com, was ranked as both the number-one and number-six site by Media Metrix and RelevantKnowledge respectively. Also [in the same] year, ESPN told Forrester Research analysts that there was a difference of 400 percent between the lowest and highest audience size measured by competing Web rating companies.

"Measurement has been a black box in on-line media," says Rich LeFurgy, chair of the two most influential online advertising organizations, the Internet Advertising

Bureau (IAB) and FAST Forward, a 650-member committee born out of the Future of Advertising Stakeholders Summit hosted by Procter & Gamble [in August 1998]. No one seems to know what happens to information in the measurement process. "Survey data [from measurement companies] does not match server data [from on-line publishers]," says LeFurgy, and buyers and sellers are up in arms about it. Both IAB and FAST Forward are pressing media measurement firms to disclose their methodologies and to come to agreement on what they report.

The problem is easily illustrated by RelevantKnowledge and Media Metrix, which, prior to their merger, used different measurement techniques resulting in vastly different reports, as in the aol.com case. [Jeff] Levy, [chair of Media Metrix] says that his company reported data separately from at-home and at-work survey panels, while RelevantKnowledge combined the two. Both firms also estimated the universe of Web users differently—Media Matrix used a calendar month while RelevantKnowledge chose 4-week cycles. RelevantKnowledge's technology did not properly measure certain users of the AOL browser either, according to Levy.

For media buyers still trying to figure out what the numbers mean, it's been a nightmare. "There are media planners in agencies who do nothing but collate reports. It's very time consuming, costly, and frustrating," says Lee Nadler, director of global marketing at New York-based DoubleClick, an Internet advertising solutions company.

Hip to the criticism, Media Metrix announced in December [1998] that it has not only merged its methods with those of RelevantKnowledge, but it is expanding its offerings to include measuring behavioral data (e.g. how many people who visit a particular site also have a cell phone and do their banking on line) and transactions. Media Metrix is also looking to broaden its measurement internationally. It has set up a panel in Sweden and expects to move into other European, Asian, and Latin American markets "over time."

Many in the industry blame the lack of consistent numbers on the relative dearth of Web ad dollars. The Web generated $907 million in ad revenue in 1997 and was likely to reach over $2 billion in 1998 according to Pricewaterhouse-Coopers, which compiles the IAB numbers, but that leaves it with a paltry 1 percent of the estimated $175 billion to $200 billion spent annually on U.S. advertising across media. Until advertisers know whom they are reaching—something they hope ratings will do with greater accuracy over time—they are going to continue to be cautious in spending their money on-line.

Vintage measurements

Enter Nielsen, which expects to lend credibility to Web ratings. Agencies and advertisers respect the name, and the company believes its TV experience gives it an edge in composing panels and determining the true size of the on-line population.

But Nielsen seems to be fighting battles on two fronts. The major television networks have grown increasingly dissatisfied with the value of Nielsen's TV ratings. Critics say that while the TV market has grown more complex with more networks, cable, and fast-moving channel surfers, Nielsen has not bothered to change its measurement tools since the '50s and, therefore, its data is no longer helpful. Nielsen may soon face a new industry-launched *competitor* as a result. "Nielsen has become progressively less accurate, less reliable, and less useful," says Nicholas Schiavone, senior vice president of research at NBC. Its new Web-ratings model also seems less than impressive at first glance.

Nielsen's model for TV ratings, for example, pulls data from a panel of 5,000 U.S. households (about 13,000 people) to project the viewing habits of a nation of 99 million TV-watching households (or 257 million TV watchers). The company swears by its panel-picking ability for accurate projections and considers the actions of one Nielsen viewer to represent those of about 19,800 people. Apply the same methodology on the Web and that ratio drops: With its initial panel of 5,000, one Nielsen Web user will represent slightly fewer than 11,000 people. Media Metrix, by comparison, already has 40,000 panelists to project the habits of an estimated 55 million U.S. Web users—one for every 1,350 people. Of course even 1-to-1,350 just does not compare to the one-to-one marketing that the Web has long promised. So its not surprising to hear ad salespeople say ratings and audience projections are not as important to the Web as they are to TV.

"Third-party measurement is somewhat of a big security blanket for advertisers on an industry level," says Gina Garrubbo, executive vice president of sales at Women.com, who spent 14 years in television advertising before landing on the Web. Ratings might speak to traditional advertisers in a language they understand, and that can encourage them to come on-line, but once they understand the space, they want more detailed information.

"We are doing pre- and post-buy awareness studies. We hired a research Ph.D. this year. Every day we are proving ROI for our advertisers," says Garrubbo. That powerful data, she says, comes from the Women.com server, not audience measurement firms, and lets her clients measure ad effectiveness not by the site's reach but by purchases made, accounts opened, or the number of visits to specific areas within the site.

There are [also] disagreements as to what counts as an ad impression. Publishers generally count pages served as ads served, but third-party ad servers count only the ads themselves, and no one is sure what to do with cached ads. The IAB hopes to have voluntary guidelines for these issues in the next 6 months; in the meantime, Women.com and other on-line companies must negotiate the definitions of impression on a case-by-case basis.

While the market awaits the new Nielsen ratings, FAST Forward and IAB are steering the industry toward new standards. Meeting as often as weekly (by phone), advertising movers and shakers expect to give shape to some unwieldy concepts this year: They are hammering out guidelines for audience measurement, ad counting, automated media buying and selling, even the development of new ad units—something besides banners and sponsorships.

The goal is "a much more orderly marketplace for the buying and selling of on-line advertising," says LeFurgy. It is still uncertain whether Nielsen can help with that, but it is certain it will have to deliver results to make a name for itself in the new media.

"I don't care if it's Nielsen or Fred's Pharmacy that's doing the measuring," says Garrubbo. "It's accuracy that counts."

Adapted from: Quistgaard, K. (1999, February). Keeping up with the Nielsens. Business 2.0, *p. 63–65, 67. Copyright ©1999 by* Business 2.0, *an Imagine Media, Inc. publication. Reprinted by permission. Kaitlin Quistgaard has written for* Wired, Time, *the Sunday Times of London,* the Miami Herald, *and other publications.*

information cannot give any demographic or psychographic information about that person and does not indicate how long a person looked at the information. It simply records the amount of traffic at the site. The number of hits from site originators was counted even when they accessed their own pages for updates and edits.

Attempts to get more information through site registration have deterred browsers from entering a site. Browsers do not want to provide personal information or take the time to fill out forms. If they do enter a site requiring registration, they frequently provide inaccurate information, which makes the data useless.

Message Research

Message research is inquiry that is done to evaluate effectiveness of the creative message, from copy and ingenuity to the visual impact of the advertisement. This may also be called copy research or copy testing, but these terms are more limiting because they refer to just one component, copy, rather than to a complete package. In order to cultivate better copy testing, a group of executives from 21 different advertising agencies came together in 1982 to set some standards. These resulted in the creation of a set of nine principles, known as PACT (Position Advertising Copy Testing), aimed at improving message testing ("21 Ad Agencies," 1982). These principles, which are still used today, state that a good testing system:

1. Provides measurements that are relevant to the objectives of the advertising.
2. Requires agreement about how the results will be used in advance of each specific test.
3. Provides multiple measurements because single measurements are generally inadequate to assess the performance of an ad.
4. Is based on a model of human response to communication: the reception of a stimulus, the comprehension of the stimulus, and the response to the stimulus.
5. Allows for consideration of whether the advertising stimulus should be exposed more than once.
6. Recognizes that the more finished a piece of copy is, the more soundly it can be eval-

uated and requires, as a minimum, that alternative executions be tested in the same degree of finish.

7. Provides controls to avoid the biasing effects of the exposure context.
8. Takes into account basic considerations of sample definition.
9. Demonstrates reliability and validity empirically.

Pretesting and Posttesting

All testing procedures can be classified corresponding to the time when they are conducted. Tests that are administered prior to the implementation of the advertising campaign are **pretests.** Those measures taken after an advertisement has been placed in the media are known as **posttests.**

Pretests may occur at a number of different times during the development of the advertisement, from idea generation through rough copy to a final version. Concepts may be reviewed prior to creating a rough ad or storyboard. At this point the ad is little more than an idea or positioning proposal. Rough outlines may be reviewed with headlines, rough copy, and preliminary illustrations or art. A final ad can be critiqued prior to publication or broadcast. A variety of methods can be used to provide analysis. A discussion of many of these techniques follows later.

Relatively inexpensive feedback is one of the best advantages of pretesting. Any problems with the concept or message can be detected early in the process. Before huge investments are made in developing final ads or commercials, the concept or artwork can be modified. Also, potential consumers may evaluate more than one concept to determine which approach is more effective. Pretesting allows advertisers to communicate messages better and to reduce the number of unsuccessful presentations.

Posttesting is also a common evaluation tool used by advertisers and agencies. Posttesting allows the sponsor to measure whether or not the objectives for the advertisement were met. At the same time, posttesting provides input into the next time period's situational analysis. It helps supply essential information about what worked and what did not. Survey research methods are used as posttests a majority of the time.

Focus Groups

Focus groups, introduced in Chapter 6, are assemblies of potential consumers, gathered together with a facilitator who conducts a discussion based upon some predetermined questions. Focus group research is considered to be qualitative. The strength of this type of evaluation is through insights consumers can provide regarding consumer motivations, creative content of advertisements, and their reactions to different types of ads. Some advertisers mistakenly believe that focus groups represent the entire population and unfortunately attempt to draw quantitative conclusions from their research. Another weakness is the halo effect, which refers to some focus group members influencing others. The opinion of a few individuals can dominate the reactions of the group, leading to inaccurate data.

Consumer Jury

Advertising researchers can use consumers in another type of analysis, the consumer jury. Similar to a focus group, a **consumer jury** is selected from target customers, but the 50 to 100 participants are interviewed individually or in small groups. Typically 25 or so questions are developed, focusing on aspects of the company, its products, and sample advertisements. Consumers are asked to evaluate ads by answering such questions as:

- Which of these ads would you most likely read if you saw it in a magazine?

- Which of these headlines would interest you the most in reading the ad further?
- Which layout do you think would be most effective in causing you to buy?
- Which ad do you like best?

Effectiveness of advertising can be evaluated through favorable reactions on the predetermined rating scale.

This type of measurement has several advantages: (1) the dimensions of opinions can be isolated, (2) the technique is standardized and can be compared over time, (3) it is reliable and replicable, (4) allowances are made for individual frames of reference, and (5) research problems associated with open-ended questions are reduced (Engel, Warchaw, and Kinnear, 1994). Although consumer juries ease some of the research design problems, they are not without limitations. Some researchers believe the atmosphere of testing introduces bias into the rating system. This could also lead to ratings with questionable validity.

Portfolio Test

The investigation method known as the **portfolio test** involves participants who are exposed to a portfolio of test and control advertisements. **Test ads** are the ads being pretested, the ads being measured for their potential effectiveness. The **control ads** have been evaluated extensively over a period of time and provide a basis for comparing the effectiveness of test ads. Respondents are asked to recall information from the ads; those ads with the highest recall are assumed to be the most effective.

Control ads allow the advertiser to compare the test ad with effectiveness of the control ad. Additionally, the researcher can identify any respondent with scores outside the norm. In other words, if the subject provides responses outside what is expected on the control ads, his or her responses may be eliminated from the analysis of the test ad.

Critics of portfolio tests challenge whether or not recall is the best test to use to measure an advertisement's effectiveness. Factors relating to the ad's creativity and/or presentation may affect recall. Test bias and the simple fact that the respondent is involved in a testing situation may impact the subject's responses.

In an attempt to improve upon the portfolio test, ad agencies or research firms may develop a dummy advertising outlet, which consists of ads and editorial content placed in "dummy" magazines. These magazines are distributed to randomly selected homes within a predetermined geographical region. Participants are told the publisher is interested in their opinions of editorial content and are asked to read the publication as they normally would. Readers are interviewed on their reactions to ads in addition to editorial content. The ads are judged by recall, readership, and interest-generating capabilities.

A more natural environment than that created by the standard portfolio test is the advantage offered by this research technique. Readership takes place in the participant's home, more closely associated with a normal setting. This hopefully provides a more realistic result. However, the testing effect cannot be eliminated and bias may still exist. While this method offers some advantages over the portfolio method, it cannot guarantee an exact measure of the advertising impact.

Readability Test

The **readability test,** which does not require consumer interviews, relies on the forecasting formula developed by Rudolph Flesch (Belch and Belch, 1995). The Flesch formula focuses on the human-interest appeal in the material, the length of sentences, and the familiarity of words. These components are considered and correlated with the educational background of target audiences. Determining the average number of syllables per 100 words assesses readability of copy. Test results are compared to previously established norms for various target audiences. Testing suggests that copy is best understood when sentences are short, words are concrete and well known, and personal references are made.

Although this method overcomes some of the bias associated with consumer input, there are some disadvantages. Copy may become too mechanical and unoriginal. Without consumer input, contributions such as creativity cannot be evaluated. The most beneficial use of this testing method is in combination with another technique for pretesting.

Physiological Profiles

In an attempt to overcome the biases associated with voluntary reactions, some researchers have developed **physiological profile** techniques for measuring the involuntary reactions to ads. Involuntary reactions are responses over which the volunteer has no control. Although these techniques are less commonly used than previously mentioned techniques, involuntary reactions are used to measure physiological responses.

The **eye camera** tracks eye movements with infrared light sensors as a subject reads an advertisement. The beam allows researchers to determine the exact location where the subject focuses. This reading provides data on which elements of the ad attract attention, how long the viewer focuses on them, and the order in which the components are being viewed.

Thus, eye camera tracking furnishes information that can identify strengths and weaknesses of an ad, helping the designer create an ad in which the eye follows the intended path. If the background distracts the viewer's eye from the brand or product, the designer can adjust the distraction prior to finishing the ad.

Although eye tracking has some interesting attributes, the tests are conducted under highly unnatural laboratory conditions. It is questionable whether or not the results would be the same if the subject were not looking into a large device. As the eye lingers on an element of the ad, the meaning is not clear. Is it a lack of comprehension or interest in an attractive detail? Because it is impossible to read the mind of the viewer, this method could lead to unreliable conclusions.

In addition to the eye tracking techniques, galvanic skin response (GSR), pupil dilation response (PDR), and brain wave measurements are used to measure physiological changes. Galvanic skin response, also known as electrodermal response, measures the skin's resistance to or conductance of a small amount of current passed between two electrodes. Researchers assume that an increase in GSR was an indicator of arousal of interest in the advertisement.

Pupil dilation response measures minute differences in pupil size and appears to be a gauge of the amount of information processed in response to an incoming stimulus. Dilation was associated with action, while constriction involved the body's conservation of energy. Thus, it is assumed that if the pupil dilated, there is strong interest in the ad. High costs and methodology problems have led to a declining interest in this type of testing.

Brain wave research involves taking electroencephalographic (EEG) measures from the skull to determine electrical frequencies in the brain. EEG research measures brain activity as alpha waves and hemispheric lateralization. While this research has appealed to the academic community, it has not gained much support from advertising practitioners.

Test Markets

In order to evaluate the potential for advertising success, some manufacturers introduce products and advertising campaigns in special test market cities prior to national launches. These **test markets** are geographical areas that have been selected as representative of the target market. If the demographic, socioeconomic, and psychographic profiles of the test market are similar to the desired target population, the advertising and product will be introduced in that region. The test market might be Portland, Oregon; Buffalo, New York; or Columbus, Ohio, if the profile of the city matches the profile of the target market.

The use of test markets has the added benefit of being a realistic presentation of the product or ad in a real setting. Well-designed research can be conducted with a high degree of control. The primary problem associated with test marketing is the high cost and long time necessary to complete the research. A checklist on page 507 provides criteria for selecting a target market.

Product test marketing generally takes the following steps:

1. The manufacturer places the product in an unlabeled container and makes it available to consumers through a testing company, such as Home Testing Institute.
2. The test marketing company distributes the product samples to panel members with a letter describing how to use the product. The correspondence also indicates that the panel member will be given an opportunity to provide opinions about the product in a specified period of time, such as four weeks.
3. The consumer responds to a set of questions.
4. The responses are analyzed.
5. The results are used to redesign the product or develop creative strategy and position the product in relationship to other brands in the market.

The previous discussion has focused on evaluation methods for measuring advertising, direct marketing, and sales promotion. Next, we focus on assessing publicity and public relations effectiveness.

Measuring Publicity and Public Relations Effectiveness

The methods of evaluating the effectiveness of publicity and of the broader scope of public relations are similar. It is essential for these programs to be evaluated in relationship to the contributions they make toward attaining communications objectives. Regular evaluation of public relations and publicity helps management to recognize what these activities have achieved over a period of time. This provides management with quantitative means of measuring achievements as well as a method to judge the quality of the activities and accomplishments.

A variety of methods, from personal observation to evaluation of objectives, evaluation of public opinion, and audits, are used to assess public relations and publicity. With continued expansion into the global market, public relations professionals are looking at the methods for evaluation that work across international boundaries. The growth of global assessment in public relations is further discussed in Box 17.2. Any or all of the following means may assist in evaluations.

Personal observation, carefully watching the job done by the specialist, can be used for evaluation. A specialist's manager usually provides feedback on the person's contributions. The director reports an annual performance evaluation based upon quantitative and qualitative industry and/or company standards to the practitioner.

Checklist for Selecting Test and Control Markets

☐ **Size Characteristics:** Population areas between 100,000 and 300,000 are normally used. The area must be large enough to support a variety of economic activities, but not so large that it is too expensive to conduct the research.

☐ **Population Characteristics:** The area should have a diverse population with characteristics similar to the target population. An ethnically distinct or unique population usually should be avoided; the bias created would limit the objectivity necessary for a test market.

☐ **Distribution Characteristics:** The product should be readily available in a variety of merchandise outlets. The researchers should not inform members of the distribution channel about the test situation in order to avoid their creating some type of special sales promotion causing a bias in the test.

☐ **Competitive Characteristics:** While it is impossible to control what competitors do during a test period, their actions should be monitored to assess any changes that would make the test invalid.

☐ **Media Characteristics:** Media placement must be accessible and available for use. The media in the test market must be comparable in test and control areas.

As with measuring the effectiveness of advertising, the evaluation of public relations and publicity should be led by objectives. Specific objectives for public relations and publicity programs should be established early in the planning stages by staff and management. An individual's objectives might include such things as placing a feature story in a specific number of media. This is an objective, quantitative, and measurable goal. Goals are used as the standard to measure accomplishments for individuals as well as teams.

Public opinion polls of the beliefs and feelings of the citizens can also be used to measure public relations effectiveness. If a retail store sets a public relations goal of becoming known for fashion leadership, research in the form of public opinion surveys may be used to evaluate the success of the program. Opinions about the store can be determined through pretesting. Surveys conducted after conclusion of the program can be used to evaluate whether or not the goals were attained.

Audits are formal reports of activities. Audits may be performed internally or externally. Personnel, superiors, and peers within the firm conduct an **internal audit** to determine the performance of an employee and his or her programs. Consultants or clients from outside organizations conduct an **external audit.** Audits may focus on such criteria as the percentage of positive and/or negative articles over time, ratios of positive to negative articles, and the percentage of positive and/or negative articles by subject, publication, reporter, or target audience. It is also important to evaluate the effectiveness of professional sales associates.

Measuring Personal Selling Effectiveness

From the sales associate on the retail sales floor to the sales manager of a large manufacturing company, it is important to assess the performance of the sales force. The most important tool for evaluating performance is a **performance appraisal system.** An effective appraisal system starts with goal setting. With participation from the sales person and his or her supervisor, realistic and measurable goals can be set for a specific time

BOX 17.2
PR Evaluation Goes Global

Public relations (PR) evaluation is crossing international boundary lines and growing in importance on a global basis, Walter K. Lindenmann, director of research of Ketchum Public Relations Worldwide, New York, told PR practitioners at two meetings in Germany.

"There is a growing surge of interest on the part of those in my field throughout the world to measure public relations effectiveness from a bottom-line perspective," Lindenmann said at a special workshop in Frankfurt on PR evaluation. The workshop was initiated by Ketchum Public Relations GmbH of Munich.

Lindenmann also spoke at the annual meeting of Gesellschaft Public Relations Agenturen in Schlangenbad/Rheingau. GPRA is an association of German PR consulting firms.

"Within our agency, the number of PR measurement and evaluation projects that we have designed and carried out for our clients during the past 4 to 5 years has more than tripled in volume," he said.

Lindenmann noted that more and more Ketchum clients "are starting to ask us to measure the effectiveness of their PR program and activities, not just in one country, but often in several countries in which they operate."

As part of his presentations, Lindenmann described five research projects that had been designed and carried out in recent years, specifically to measure PR effectiveness at the output, outgrowth, and outcome levels. Two of the studies he cited were international.

One involved a well-known U.S.-based technology company that held simultaneous press conferences in New York City and Paris to announce the introduction of six new products. The company then commissioned a study to examine press coverage in 12 countries in an effort to compare how different media in different sections of the world had handled the story.

A study for a well-known beverage company that sells its products in countries throughout the world involved conducting in-depth interviews with journalists in 15 different countries in Europe, Latin America, and Asia in an effort to determine, both qualitatively and quantitatively, how much attention those in the media were paying to the company's publicity efforts, whether or not reporters and editors were fully aware of the range of the client's various products and services, and whether or not those in the media were retaining key messages that the company was disseminating through its publicity.

Lindenmann described numerous techniques for measuring PR effectiveness, including media measurement through content analysis, simple public opinion polls, intercept interviews with elite groups at trade shows, and quasi-experimental studies that involve before-and-after field work.

"There is no one simplistic method for measuring PR effectiveness," he said. "Depending upon which level of measurement is required, an array of different tool techniques are needed to properly assess PR impact."

Source: PR evaluation goes global. (1996, July 15). Marketing News, 30. *16.*

period. Not every member of the sales team should have exactly the same goals, but comparative standards of performance within the organization should be considered.

Typically, sales goals are expressed in quantitative terms of sales volume, sales expense, or number of customers. For example, a sales goal might state, *The employee will maintain minimum sales of $65 per hour.* In addition to the quantitative goals, most performance appraisal systems include some qualitative measures. Although these characteristics are more subjective in nature, they contribute to the overall success of a sales department. Such characteristics rate the individual on attitude and ability to work well with other associates and customers. Rating scales for the quantitative and qualitative contributions are normally ranked on a three-to-five point scale from a low of *has not met expectations,* to a high of *has exceeded expectations.* Figure 17.2 shows an example of a performance appraisal report.

Figure 17.2

Sample Sales Performance
Appraisal Report Form

Performance Appraisal/Sales Associate

Name:

Branch Location:

Review Period: From   **To**

Wage:

(O) Outstanding. Performance **Far Exceeds** requirements of position and objectives. This level is recognized as excellent and unique in contribution and is rarely achieved.

(CE) Consistently Exceeds. Performance **Consistently Exceeds** requirements of position and objectives.

(E) Exceeds. Performance **Sometimes Exceeds** requirements of position and objectives.

(M) Meets. Performance (on average) **Meets** requirements of position and objectives.

(B) Below Requirements. Performance **Does Not Fully Meet** or consistently maintain requirements of position and objectives. **Improvement Plan Required.**

(U) Unsatisfactory. Performance **Fails to Meet** requirements of the position and objectives and does not meet improvement criteria.

Sales Performance
Actual Sales per Hour:
Selling Center Sales per Hour:
Rating (based upon comparison of actual to selling center sales per hour):
Comments:

Selling Skills (includes approaching guests, determining needs, presenting merchandise, answering questions, using suggestion selling and closing techniques, providing product knowledge, developing clientele relationships)
Comments:

Sales Preparation (includes merchandise presentation, stockwork, housekeeping, etc.)
Comments:

Systems and Procedures (includes POS, exchanges, returns, accuracy of transactions)
Comments:

Shortage Awareness and Prevention (includes price changes, claims, transfers, inventory control, merchandise security):
Comments:

(continued)

Performance appraisal systems set a specific period of time for the evaluation, ranging from 6 months to 1 year. The sales manager should have a good idea of the performance of all salespersons within his or her supervision. If there is a problem with a member of the sales team, the manager should not wait until the formal review to implement corrective action. Remedial action and emphasis of *what is expected* should take place where performance is substandard. Next, we look at evaluating the effectiveness of special events and fashion shows.

Figure 17.2

(cont.)

Professional Conduct (includes attendance, punctuality, dress and appearance, work relationships):

Comments:

Summary of Performance:	O	CE	E	M	B	U
Sales Performance	O	CE	E	M	B	U
Selling Skills	O	CE	E	M	B	U
Sales Preparation	O	CE	E	M	B	U
Systems and Procedures	O	CE	E	M	B	U
Shortage Awareness and Prevention	O	CE	E	M	B	U
Professional Conduct	O	CE	E	M	B	U

Strengths:

Improvement Opportunities:

Evaluator's Comments:

Evaluator Signature _____ Date _____
Employee Signature _____ Date _____

Measuring Special Event and Fashion Show Effectiveness

Evaluation serves important purposes for sponsors, special event planners, and fashion show personnel, and as such should not be perceived as a last step of production. Rather, it should be regarded as an ongoing procedure throughout the production. When evaluating special events and fashion shows, personnel should determine the strengths and weaknesses of the project, including successes and failures of sponsors and opportunities for potential additional sponsors. Most importantly, personnel should secure accurate statistics that will help sell and re-sell future activities. One of the primary tools used by special event planners and fashion show producers is an **event diary** or *show diary*, chronicling all of the planning, budgeting, and implementation processes of the activity.

Both sponsors and production personnel, working as a team, establish benchmarks from which to evaluate the event before the event takes place. Success ascertained by benchmarks can be a tool to measure efficiency and expected outcome of the event before its actual execution. In certain instances an outside firm can be hired to analyze the necessary information for evaluation as an independent third party.

Basic statistical information gathered for evaluation includes attendance, demographic reach, media coverage, and cash intake. Attendance can be controlled through the use of ticketing or established seating capacities. In a noncontrolled situation, estimates by law enforcement agencies or other organizations involved in crowd control are reliable. Broadcast audience reaches may be obtained from the station or network providing coverage. Demographic reach can be measured by surveys or polls conducted over the phone, through direct mail or in person during the event. Surveys are a good instrument for determining the perceptions of the particular event or sponsor by attendees. Publicity can be measured by counting sponsor or event specific mentions and multiplying them by the appropriate circulation or number of viewers or listeners.

The audience and its reaction are the primary concerns of fashion show planners. The audience should be evaluated in terms of its size in relationship to the location of the show, its appropriateness to the merchandise, and how it reacted to the presentation. Although many of these aspects are subjective, the staff should be able to tell whether the audience reacted in a positive or negative manner. A fashion show diary also defines the type of show, location and dates, theme and title, merchandise presented, personnel involved, and notes for improvement. This historical record serves as a planning document for the next show. A sample fashion show diary is provided in Figure 17.3.

Special event planners use similar diaries, which can include customer surveys. Consumers may be asked to rate various components of the event with scores ranging from *strongly like* to *strongly dislike*. The fact that audience members may not be willing to take the time to fill out surveys is the one of the biggest problems for both

Figure 17.3

Sample Fashion Show Diary

Fashion Show Diary

Date of Show:
Location:
Show Participants:
   Sponsoring Organization:
   Models:

   Commentator:
   Production Staff:

   Audience:
Theme of Show:
Merchandise Presented:

Publicity and Advertising Activities:

Budget:
   Planned Expenses vs. Actual Expenses:
   Profit/Loss:
Audience Reaction:

Notes for Improvement:

special event and fashion show planners attempting to document audience reaction. Unless customers are willing to provide positive and negative reactions, planners may have a difficult time assessing the presentation. Our last category of measurement involves assessment of a firm's visual merchandising program.

Measuring Visual Merchandising Effectiveness

All too frequently retailers fail to consider the impact that visual merchandise presentation has on retail sales. Ask any store owner if there is a sales increase on displayed products, and he or she will always answer yes. If the owner is questioned further regarding the magnitude of the increase, he or she likely will not know. Retailers fail to keep accurate statistics about the importance that displaying merchandise has on sales.

Saks Fifth Avenue is one major retailer that recognized the significance of window displays and documented its success or failure through a sales tracking procedure. This company has kept accurate sales records on the merchandise presented in its flagship store windows. These windows, located on Fifth Avenue, 49th Street, and 50th Street in New York City, consist of 310 feet of street level glass. There are 31 window displays, which are duplicated by the company's branches. This coordination provides a nationwide fashion statement. When the company moved the gift department from the high traffic main floor to the store's ninth floor, sales decreases of 15 percent were anticipated. The division head persuaded store management to include a display of giftware in the Fifth Avenue windows during the week the department moved. Instead of the anticipated decrease, sales grew by 20 percent that week. The allocation of window space generally correlated with department sales (Gubernick, 1986).

Simple sales tracking techniques such as this can prove to the retailer the significance of display on sales. It will also help to support the existence of the visual merchandising staff in an era when every expense and cost of doing business must be analyzed.

Since the objective for most retail window display is to attract new customers while retaining current consumers, retailers should consider various methods to evaluate the performance of their window displays. Askins (1987) suggested in *California Apparel News* that the sales staff should be asked to keep track of customer reactions. These still-relevant questions were developed as guidelines for evaluation.

- Are window displays attracting customers into the store?
- Are customers asking for displayed merchandise?
- Are customers buying more when a theme is used?
- Is one display working better than another?
- Are any displays being ignored?

An undeniable feature of a merchandise presentation is its short-term nature. By its very existence and purpose, a display should be short-lived. Unlike other art forms such as sculpture or painting a display lacks permanence. A method of preserving this industry's achievements is through photography. It requires a conscious effort and knowledge of photographic method to record displays in this manner, but it is well worth the energy.

There are several reasons why a display professional should take the time to document his or her work. First, it serves as a historical record of displays completed, providing a detailed account of the department's activities. It can also serve as a historical record of the store. Second, photos serve as a portfolio of the display professional's individual accomplishments. This portfolio can be submitted for job interviews, showing the style and depth of display work. Third, photo documentation may be used to enter various display competitions, such as the *VM+SD* Annual Display Competition, or may be sent to local newspapers for publicity purposes (Toevs, 1994).

Photography may not be able to capture the actual window or in-store display, but it can serve as a useful reference. It can show what has been done in the past and function as a source of inspiration, giving the designer new ideas. Taking time to preserve the images shows admiration and value for the creative and hard work concluded.

WHY PROMOTIONAL EFFECTIVENESS MAY NOT BE MEASURED

Companies and individuals give many reasons why they do not evaluate promotional effectiveness. Many of these reasons are simply excuses as to why a job was not fully executed. After the event was over or the advertisement was printed, the job is not complete until follow-up and feedback occur. Just as we learned in the communications model in Chapter 1, communication is not finished until feedback occurs.

Cost

Perhaps the most reported reason for not completing the measurement process is cost. Development of good evaluation techniques and appropriate research methodologies take resources in terms of both cost and time. When time is critical, some managers believe it is better to spend more money on more media placement, more elaborate production, expensive artwork, or bigger celebrity spokespersons rather than on research.

It is true that hiring skilled researchers is expensive. Nevertheless, the risks of creating an ineffective message or of placing it in inappropriate media, or both, may cause a brand to fail to live up to its potential. Spending more money on media placement will not help if the message is poor.

Here is a case in point. A manufacturer of skin care items decided to launch a new moisturizer for people with sensitive skin. As the product went into test markets, sales did not meet expectations. The manufacturer decided to purchase additional advertising space in the regional newspapers and magazines rather than spend money analyzing the advertising. Sales did not improve and the manufacturer abandoned the product. Further analysis showed the problem was in the message, which did not communicate the benefits of the product. Research could have detected the message problem and perhaps saved the brand.

Time

Many managers cite a lack of time as the reason for ignoring the issues of measurement and evaluation. Promotion and advertising professions are highly stressful and competitive by nature. Everyone seems to be diligently working on tight deadlines. Copy is sent to the printer in just enough time to get the job done. Managers believe that everyone has so much to do that they just cannot get around to testing.

Proper planning and time-management skills can be implemented to help overcome the rushed feelings associated with this profession. Although the highly charged atmosphere will never be completely eliminated, timeliness is critical. Getting the wrong message out or placing the message in the wrong media is of little value and may actually be a waste of time and money. When faced with a decision about whether to immediately implement an advertising program or to test it first, managers must make some important decisions. Even some testing can help to avoid costly mistakes or improve effectiveness. Proper planning and scheduling will build in some time for testing.

Research Design Problems

It is difficult to design tests to evaluate exactly what we want to know. Not only is it difficult to isolate the effects of advertising from other variables, but we may also develop research problems relating to validity and reliability or both. **Validity** refers to the testing procedure being free from both random and systematic error. Validity is concerned with bias and deals with the question, *are we measuring what we think we are measuring?* Research **bias** involves creating an influence or prejudice within the design of the research. **Reliability** means that the procedure is free from random error, and the measure is consistent and accurate. Thus, a reliable test would provide consistent results every time an ad is tested, while a valid test would provide predictive power to the performance of the ad in the market every time it is tested.

Although it is not always possible to determine the exact amount of sales attributed to the influence of promotional elements, research can provide some useful information. This information can be used to *fine-tune* promotion activities in order to help the sponsor improve its chances for meeting objectives.

Disagreements about What to Test

Conflicting views about promotion objectives may occur within different industries, through products at differing stages of the product life cycle, or even with various people within the sponsoring organization. Top management may wish to know how promotion affects the overall image of the corporation, while the sales manager wants to know how sales were affected by promotion activities, and the creative director wants to know how well consumers recall or recognize the promotion. Lack of agreement by the constituencies often results in a failure to complete any type of evaluation.

With proper design of evaluation instruments, many or all of the questions identified above might be measured. Promotion elements are developed after objectives are established. By focusing on what objectives are to be met, the evaluation process can look at the results in relationship to objectives.

Difficulty Measuring Creativity

How do we measure creativity? How does a creative message contribute to the communications package? It is difficult to explain what creativity is, let alone determine how to measure its contribution to promotional effectiveness. A natural barrier exists between personnel involved in the creative processes and personnel involved in the sales management operations. Members of the creative team seek an environment where the creative process is not encumbered by measuring promotional effectiveness, feeling that applying these measures stifle creativity. Those involved in the creative side typically take the attitude that the more creative the promotion, the more successful it will be.

Personnel from both the creative and management staffs need to recognize the importance of working together for the success of the brand or product. Ultimately it is the responsibility of the product manager to know how well a promotional program or a specific ad will perform in the market.

REDIRECTION OF PROMOTIONAL EFFORTS

Evaluation of the individual promotional activities in comparison to the overall communications goals is essential information for the redirection of promotional efforts. What part of the promotional campaign worked? What elements were not beneficial? Should more resources be placed in the sales force or made available for media placement? These are just some of the questions that should be asked prior to developing the promotion plan for the next season.

The planning phase, when goals and objectives are established, is essential. Promotion managers are offered many different choices as to how to spend the promotion budget. In a retail store the fashion show director, advertising manager, visual merchandising director, special events coordinator, and sales manager are all in competition to receive money and resources to implement their programs. Despite an overall goal to improve the fashion leadership and public awareness, the vice president of promotion will have to assess the merits of each project. That might mean that a celebrity designer trunk show would be funded rather than buying more advertising in the local newspaper. Budgets limit the choices, and the executive must direct the reallocation of funds and activities to best meet the promotion objectives.

PROFESSIONALISM

According to *Webster's New World Dictionary*, a professional is engaged in a profession worthy of high standards. Thus, professionalism implies work of the highest quality or standards. The status associated with professional work should not be ignored. Sloppy, incomplete work or a lack of attention to detail cannot be accepted in promotion. Only people who are willing to work with high professional standards should consider careers in this field.

Many individuals, from merchandising or design students to members of charitable organizations, may have had opportunities to participate in a variety of fashion shows. A well-planned and well-organized fashion show is a fun and rewarding experience, but fashion show planners who leave everything to the last minute cause only stress and frustration among all of the participants. The same thing is true for any of the other promotion activities. It is a pleasure to work in an atmosphere of quality and professionalism, but it is frustrating to work with people who do not take such activities seriously.

Promotional work almost always requires participation from a variety of people, making professionalism a necessity. In addition, teamwork is a requirement. From the individuals involved in establishing the objectives, plans, and budgets to the personnel concerned with creative ideas and implementation, each person has strengths necessary to contribute to an effective promotional campaign. A promotion team is only as good as its weakest link. If details are overlooked and contingencies not considered, the professionalism of the strongest team members will be forgotten.

A variety of professional organizations assist in offering educational opportunities through training, workshops, or seminars. These organizations often provide networking opportunities for professionals and encouragement to students preparing to enter the professions. Those organizations may be oriented to the academic or the professional world. Some professional groups require entrance examinations. To participate in other groups, potential members need sponsorship from an active member. Next, we look at a few of the various organizations in which members can obtain professional or academic contacts.

Professional Organizations

The **Fashion Group International** (**FGI**) is a global nonprofit professional organization with more than 6,000 members in the fashion industry and related fields. As introduced in Chapter 4, FGI has a primary goal of advancing professionalism in the field of fashion and related lifestyle industries. This organization provides a variety of networking and educational opportunities through regional chapters. Fashion executives gain membership status only after being sponsored by a current member. Through the **Fashion Group Foundation** (**FGF**), members promote educational programs devoted to fashion and related businesses by creating and awarding scholarships, establishing internship programs, and providing career counseling services, sponsorship of seminars, and other educational activities. This group also supports public service activities, such as career days with design or merchandising competitions for students held by various regional groups, including Dallas, Denver, and New York. Like many professional organizations, FGI has developed an Internet site. Figure 17.4 reproduces the Fashion Group International homepage.

In the closely related field of interior design, the most well-known professional organization is the **American Society of Interior Designers** (**ASID**). With more than 30,000 professionals, students, and manufacturers as members, the organization provides a common identity forum for those who work in interior design-related fields. The mission of the association is to promote design excellence through professional education, market expansion, information sharing, and creation of a favorable environment for the practice of interior design. Professional members must pass the National Council for Interior Design Qualifications (NCIDQ) exam created by members. Students may join collegiate chapters.

The **American Advertising Federation** (**AAF**) is the unifying professional organization that binds the mutual interests of corporate advertisers, agencies, media companies, suppliers, and academia. The AAF has more than 50,000 members, who share a commitment to making advertising a positive force in America's economy and culture. As advocates for the rights of advertisers, members of the group educate policy makers, the news media, and the general public about the value that advertising brings to the well-being of the nation.

With 109 chapters throughout the United States, the **Public Relations Society of America** (**PRSA**) is the world's largest organization for public relations professionals ("Public Relations Society of America," 1998.) PRSA was chartered as a forum for addressing issues affecting the profession, providing resources for promoting the highest professional standards, advancing opportunities for improvement of skills and knowledge, and contributing to an exchange of information and experiences with other public relations specialists. A voluntary accreditation program for members with at least 5 years of professional experience, who were able to pass written and oral examinations, was implemented in 1964. Students are able to join a college chapter as a member of the Public Relations Student Society of America (PRSSA).

The **Association for Women in Communications** (AWC) began as a sorority of seven female journalism students at the University of Washington. It has evolved into an organization with professional and student chapters, representing the following disciplines: print and broadcast journalism, television and radio production, film, advertising, public relations, marketing, graphic design, multimedia design, and photography. The related disciplines continue to expand following newer media trends. Newsletters, a quarterly magazine called *Matrix,* and professional conferences assist members in making international contacts and keeping up-to-date with the constantly changing communications industry.

Several organizations provide professional membership to the graphic design and visual communications industries. Many of these organizations also offer student participation and design competitions for students and/or professional members. These groups include the **American Institute of Graphic Arts** (AIGA), the **Art Director's Club of New York** (ADCNY), and the **Type Directors Club of New York** (TDCNY).

Academic Organizations

Many of the goals and benefits of academic organizations are similar to those of the professional groups previously identified. Networking and improving professionalism for the industry are the primary concerns. Additionally, academic organizations provide members, who are normally teachers and professors, the opportunity to share academic research.

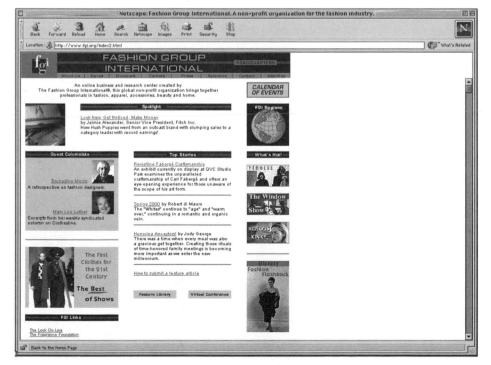

Figure 17.4

Fashion Group International homepage.

The **International Textile and Apparel Association** (ITAA) is an organization of professors of textiles, apparel, merchandising, costume history, cultural aspects of apparel, fashion and textile design, and related disciplines. The group sponsors an annual conference at which members of the organization share information regarding the future of the organization and its disciplines, technology, leadership, networking, teaching, research, and service ideas. The group distributes newsletters, research journals, and conference proceedings each year.

The **American Collegiate Retailing Association** (ACRA) consists of faculty and administrators at 4-year baccalaureate degree-granting accredited colleges or universities. Professors of merchandising and marketing who are interested in furthering educational opportunities in the field of retailing make up the membership. The group sponsors an annual spring conference at which members present current research, network, and visit sites of interest to retailing educators. Each January, ACRA members are invited to participate in the **National Retail Federation** (NRF) Annual Convention and Expo, held in New York City. ACRA holds a business meeting and research presentations during the NRF convention that features internationally known retailing experts making presentations. The Expo also provides industry suppliers an opportunity to present their latest products and innovations.

ACRA is closely related to other academic and professional resources and organizations such as the **European Association of Education and Research in Commercial Distribution (EAERCD)**, the **Academy of Marketing Science** (AMS), the **Canadian and European Institutes of Retailing and Services Studies** (CEIRSS), and the **American Marketing Association** (AMA). Many of the academic and professional organizations have developed Internet websites. Figure 17.5 shows the homepage for the American Marketing Association.

Academic organizations associated with the fields of graphic design and visual communication includes the **International Congress of Graphic Design Associations** (ICGDA), the **National Association of Schools of Art and Design** (NASAD), and the **Graphic Design Education Association** (GDEA). Many of these groups have special conditions that must be met prior to acceptance into membership. A summary of organizations and their webpage addresses are included in the list on the inside covers of the text.

Figure 17.5

American Marketing Association homepage.

AWARDS

One way organizations and associations can provide feedback and recognition for the professionalism, creativity, and hard work associated with developing effective promotional campaigns is through the awards process. A variety of industry trade associations and specialized services establish criteria for acknowledging and honoring outstanding promotional performance. These awards are presented on an international, national, regional, or local level. The awards discussed here give only a sampling of the various tributes paid to promotion executives and their creative messages. They in no way comprise a complete list of all the awards associated with the promotional industry.

The most familiar international prizes given for excellence in the advertising industry are the Clio Awards. For more than 38 years, the Clio Awards have formally recognized accomplishments in advertising and design. With permanent representation in more than 36 countries, this truly is *international* recognition. Clios recognize outstanding performance in print advertising, package design, radio, television/cinema, hall of fame, integrated media, and the World Wide Web categories. Clio Award winners are profiled in a Showcase Reel, containing annual award-winning commercials. In addition to heralding advertising contributions in various traditional media, the Clio Awards have developed a site on the Internet (Fig. 17.6).

In 1968, the New York chapter of the American Marketing Association started presenting Effie Awards, national awards to honor effective advertising. The Effies are based upon creative achievement of advertising campaigns that meet and exceed the advertiser's objectives. Because these awards focus on advertising campaigns that succeeded in reaching their sponsor's objectives, the receipt of an Effie represents

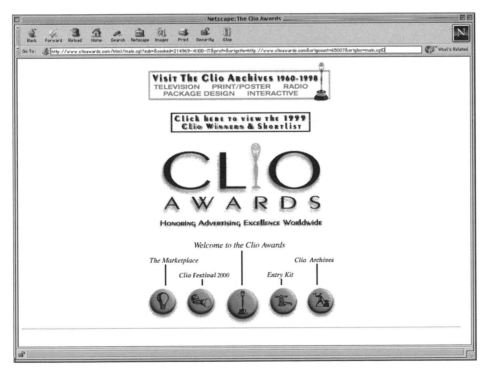

Figure 17.6

Internet homepages for the Clios.

confirmation of advertising effectiveness. Award winners in more than 40 categories are selected by professionals from advertising management, research, media, and other creative fields. The awards have expanded into nine European and Latin American countries with plans to extend to other international markets. The Effie Awards, like the Clios, have created an Internet site.

The Institute of Store Planners and *VM+SD* magazine sponsor an annual International Store Interior Design Competition. With 18 categories, such as traditional department store, shop within an existing hardlines store, jewelry store, or manufacturer showroom, designers or design teams working on retail projects can compete for this award. Winners are featured in a *VM+SD* magazine article and honored for their store design projects. Color Plate 8 features the 1998 store of the year in the category of specialty stores under 2,000 square feet.

VM+SD also sponsors the Visual Image + Identity Competition. Formerly known as the International Visual Merchandising Competition, the event was renamed and expanded in 1997 to include graphics, signage, and fixturing design in addition to visual presentation of merchandise through window or store vignettes. Judges include professionals from media, visual merchandising, and retail industries who examine interiors, window displays, fixtures, signage, and collateral materials and how they work together to present an overall visual image. Eleven different awards are presented.

The fields of visual merchandising and identity are also supported by the Planning and Visual Education Partnership (PAVE), a nonprofit alliance consisting of the National Association of Display Industries (NADI), the Society of Visual Merchandisers (SVM), the Institute of Store Planners (ISP), and *VM+SD* magazine. PAVE sponsors an annual student design competition in addition to other activities to educate and motivate retail management, visual merchandisers, store planners, architects, specifiers, manufacturers, and students. By encouraging interaction among the various constituencies, PAVE sponsors seminars and fundraisers with proceeds targeted to financial aid and student internships. The design competition, open to students enrolled in 2-year or 4-year academic programs, awards cash prizes to winners of first, second, or third place in each category.

FUTURE TRENDS IN EVALUTION

As sponsors of promotional activities demand more results-oriented promotions and accountability for expenses, researchers and agencies will continue to look for better and more sophisticated methods for evaluating promotional performance. Competition to find the best promotional methods and practitioners will continue to grow as more sponsors seek the best methods to meet their objectives.

As we saw earlier in the chapter, Nielsen Media Services had a near monopoly on the TV ratings market. With new technologies and research methodology, that monopoly has been challenged by such organizations as SMART. Television media analysis is not the only measurement strategy that will be questioned in the decades to come.

Competitive Media Reporting uses state-of-the-art technology for monitoring radio and television commercials. Custom-built computer sites in the top 75 media markets support the monitoring system, called MediaWatch. Commercials are digitized, and transported over telephone lines to a location where they are classified. Digital technology speeds the process of obtaining data and increases the accuracy of analysis. Network and cable television stations are monitored 365 days a year, 24 hours a day, while spot TV is observed from 6 A.M. to 2 A.M. Clients are able to view competitive TV commercials on their personal computer screens within 48 hours of the first broadcast ("Competitive Media Reporting," 1997). Researchers will continue to look for solutions to research design problems and ways to improve the accuracy of measuring promotional activities in the future.

Advertisers and other personnel involved in promotion want to know what has been successful and what has not been worthwhile. With so many demands on time, budgets, and the energy of personnel working in this field, the focuses for the future will be on how to justify the expense of promotional activities, and on evaluating which activities contributed the most to the prosperity of the organization.

SUMMARY

- Evaluation is necessary to determine how effective the communications program is by measuring it against standards from the industry and comparing results to the program's objectives.
- In order to create an environment in which promotion effectiveness can be measured, yardsticks for each element of the promotion mix should have been established at the start of the promotional program.
- Advertising, direct marketing, and sales promotion use similar methods to evaluate effectiveness. These methods include pretesting, posttesting, focus groups, consumer juries, portfolio tests, readability tests, physiological profiles, and test markets.
- Evaluation of public relations and publicity depends upon similar strategies, including personal observation, assessing public opinion, and completing internal and/or external audits.
- Performance of the sales force can be accomplished through a performance appraisal system that looks at qualitative as well as quantitative data.
- Special events and fashion shows are documented through event or show diaries, which include all information regarding planning, theme, merchandise, location, timing, audience, and budget.
- Many visual merchandising executives do not keep extremely detailed records of their work. Photographic documentation complemented with sales records could help visual merchandisers scientifically evaluate the effectiveness of their work.
- Reasons why evaluation does not take place include: cost, time, research design problems, disagreements about what to test, and opposition to the testing of creativity.
- Evaluation of performance and promotional effectiveness can help executives to plan for the next time period, and may assist in redirecting resources in the most effective manner.
- Work of the highest professional quality is expected in this highly competitive field. Individuals and companies can benefit from participating in professional organizations related to their specialties. Awards and competitions allow professionals to demonstrate their abilities and receive recognition from others.
- Researchers will continue to work toward improving the methods used to evaluate personnel and programs in the promotional field.

KEY TERMS

audits
bias
consumer jury
control ads
event diary
external audit
eye camera

internal audit
media research
message research
performance appraisal system
physiological profiles
portfolio test
posttests

pretests
readability test
reliability
test ads
test market
validty

KEY ORGANIZATIONS

Academy of Marketing Science (AMS)
American Advertising Federation (AFF)
American Collegiate Retailing Association (ACRA)
American Institute of Graphic Arts (AIGA)
American Marketing Association (AMA)
American Society of Interior Designers (ASID)
Art Director's Club of New York (ADCNY)
Association for Women in Communications (AWC)
Canadian & European Institutes of Retailing and Services Studies (CEIRSS)
European Association of Education and Research in Commercial Distribution (EAERCD)
Fashion Group Foundation (FGF)
Fashion Group International (FGI)
Graphic Design Education Association (GDEA)
International Congress of Graphic Design Associations (ICGDA)
International Textile and Apparel Association (ITAA)
National Association of Schools of Art and Design (NASAD)
National Council for Interior Design Qualifications (NCIDQ)
National Retail Federation (NRF)
Planning and Visual Education Partnership (PAVE)
Public Relations Society of America (PRSA)
Type Directors Club of New York (TDCNY)

QUESTIONS FOR DISCUSSION

1. What are some of the pros and cons of evaluating promotional effectiveness?
2. Why are objectives important in the evaluation of promotional effectiveness?
3. If you were the executive in charge of the promotion division for a retail store, what information would you like to have during the planning process for the upcoming season?
4. What does a professional organization have to offer you as a student? Why do you think it might be important to your career?
5. Suppose you are in charge of promotion for a student-produced fashion show and that an advertising class has developed several different ads. How would you decide which ad to use? How would you know whether you made the right choice?

ADDITIONAL RESOURCES

Burton, P. M., and Purvis, S. C. (Eds.). (1996). *Which ad pulled best? 50 case histories on how to write and design ads that work* (8th ed.). Lincolnwood, IL: NTC Business Books.

Cutlip, S. M., Center, A. H., and Broom, G. M. (1994). *Effective public relations* (4th ed.). Englewood Cliffs, NJ: Prentice-Hall.

Dutka, S., and Colley R. (1995). *Dagmar: Defining advertising goals for measured advertising results* (2nd ed.). Lincolnwood, IL: NTC Business Books.

Hall, R. W. (1991). *Media math: Basic techniques of media evaluation.* Lincolnwood, IL: NTC Business Books.

Kaatz, R. B. (1994) *Advertising and marketing checklists: 107 proven checklists to save time & boost advertising effectiveness.* (2nd ed.) Lincolnwood, IL: NTC Business Books.

Kahle, L. R., and Chiagouris, L. (Eds.). (1997). *Values, lifestyles, and psychographics (Advertising and consumer psychology).* Mahwah, NJ: Lawrence Erlbaum Associates.

Leninson, J. C., and Rubin, C. (1994). *Guerrila advertising: Cost-effective techniques for small-business success.* Boston: Houghton Mifflin.

Levine, M. (1994). *Guerrilla P.R.: How you can wage an effective publicity campaign . . . without going broke.* New York: Harperbusiness.

Wells, W. D. (Ed.) (1997). *Measuring advertising effectiveness.* Mahwah, NJ: Lawrence Erlbaum Associates.

Winters, A. A., and Winters, P. F. (1996) *What works in fashion advertising.* New York: Retail Reporting Corporation.

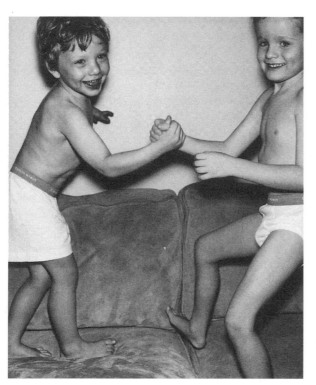

Figure 18.1

The Calvin Klein Company removed this ad from publication after one run because of controversy.

chapter 18

SOCIAL IMPACT
AND ETHICAL CONCERNS

I n 1999, a billboard in Times Square in New York City displayed an image from a Calvin Klein campaign introducing boys' and girls' underwear using young children as models. Print ads in the *New York Times,* the *New York Times Magazine,* and other publications were also part of the campaign (Fig. 18.1). The billboard image was removed after one day, and the *New York Times* removed the ad from its newspaper after controversy arose over what some critics considered the provocative poses of the children.

This was not the first time Calvin Klein's ads had been deemed controversial. In the 1980s, the company dressed a young Brooke Shields in a pair of skintight designer jeans. The tagline read *Nothing comes between me and my Calvins.* Later, the company graced outdoor ads with male models in scanty Calvin Klein underwear. In 1995, a billboard, also in Times Square, displayed an image from a Calvin Klein jeans campaign using young models, and, as with the 1999 campaign, some believed the advertising campaign exploited them in suggestive and tasteless poses hinting at child pornography. The ad stirred such controversy that the Federal Bureau of Investigation became involved ("Making," 1998). The integrated campaign, which included print, broadcast, and out-of-home media, was intended to run through the opening of the downtown Manhattan Calvin Klein store. Although the Calvin Klein Company stood by its work, commenting that the campaign was "quite effective as written," the company halted it 2 months before its scheduled end (Elliott, 1995). According to Ron Galotti, publisher of *Vogue,* "He's always pushing the envelope, and people pay attention to that" ("Making," 1998).

After you have read this chapter you will be able to:

Evaluate the ethical issues and social responsibilities related to promotion.

Discuss self-regulation in advertising and promotion.

Understand some of the laws and government regulations that regulate promotion.

Does the Calvin Klein Company cross the boundaries of acceptability? From the perspective of a marketer—*no.* The company does what needs to be done to sell products. From the perspective of a consumer—*maybe.* Consumers question the ads but they do go out and buy more product. From the perspective of watchdog groups and the government—*yes.* That is why the FBI got involved. While no legal action was taken, the ads were investigated.

Where does society draw the social or moral line when it comes to selling products? Companies, consumers, governments, lawyers, trade associations, and others struggle daily over the ethical issues raised by advertising campaigns that create word-of-mouth publicity and increased sales but disturb some consumers.

This text would not be complete without a discussion of the social and ethical concerns that are raised when advertising and promotion are used. However, a thorough discussion of every social or ethical situation, government regulation, and attempt at self-regulation is beyond the scope of this text. The purpose of this chapter is to create reader awareness about possible unethical or unacceptable situations. It is desired that the reader broadly apply the social and ethical standards from one promotion activity to other promotion activities where ethical standards may also apply.

The chapter begins with a discussion of the ethical and social issues that surface when creating promotion strategies. Then, we discuss self-regulation as a monitor for ethical and social concerns, followed by examination of some of the laws and government regulations affecting advertising and promotion. The chapter concludes by looking at future trends in promotion with respect to social and ethical issues.

ETHICAL ISSUES AND SOCIAL RESPONSIBILITY

We began this book by defining promotion as a comprehensive term for all of the communication activities initiated by the seller to inform, persuade, and remind the consumer about products, services, and/or ideas offered for sale. Through the many different topics related to promotion, and the national and international examples of promotion illustrated in this text, we have demonstrated how big in scope promotion activities are. *Promotion is comprehensive.* We send messages to consumers via advertising, direct marketing, sales promotion, publicity and public relations, personal selling, special events, fashion shows, and visual merchandising. Consumers cannot help but hear or see our communication messages, and they cannot avoid them.

Additionally, we have stated throughout this text that for promotion to be effective, marketers need information about consumers. We have also demonstrated some of the technological advances that provide promotion planners with that information. Professionals can determine where consumers live, what they buy, where they buy it, how much money they make, and what promotions they react to. They can monitor what consumers watch on television, listen to on the radio, or read in magazines, and how they use the Internet. With increasingly sophisticated marketing tools, some voluntary and some not, sponsors can analyze consumers, and consumers cannot avoid being examined.

Therefore, everyone involved in the field of promotion must be careful not to abuse the influence they have over consumers. Professionals must be responsible to the public and consider the social and ethical ramifications of their messages, before they are sent to consumers. In the next section, we introduce a few of the social and ethical considerations that should be evaluated when planning a promotion, including offensive advertising, plagiarism, and social correctness. This is not an all-inclusive list. The topics are presented in hopes of starting discussions about issues of social responsibility and ethical behavior.

Offensive Advertising

Advertising can offend consumers in several ways, including the product itself, a demonstration of the product in use, or the anxiety associated with a product in the mind of the consumer. Certain products, such as personal hygiene products, hemorrhoid medicines, and other medical products and contraceptives, by nature are offensive to some consumers. Although marketers believe educational information can be derived from advertising items such as condoms, certain segments of the population do not believe in the use of contraceptives and are offended by the advertising of these products to the public.

Some product demonstrations may not appeal to certain consumer audiences because of the personal nature of the product. While consumers are not offended by deodorant advertisements, the product is often demonstrated on the hands, lower arms, or mirrors, away from the actual area of application. Diaper ads do not show a baby being diapered. The diaper is shown either away from the baby or already being worn.

Clothing has always pushed the limit in offending some consumers. For example, up through the early 1960s, fashion magazines did not give advertising or editorial space to underwear or swimsuits because the items were too personal in nature and made consumers uncomfortable. However, society has loosened its stance on the discomfort of personal apparel, and swimsuits and underwear are commonly advertised in print and broadcast media.

As in the Calvin Klein examples at the beginning of this chapter, consumers can be offended by advertisements that are perceived as too sexual in nature or show nudity. Sexuality and nudity may be perceived as manipulative if they are used solely to get the attention of the consumer with no relation to the product being promoted. The ad in Figure 18.2 is acceptable because it advertises a line of lingerie. If the same ad, showing an almost nude model were used to advertise cars or liquor, for example, the ad would not be acceptable to some people. Ads may also be criticized as being demeaning to men and women if the individuals are depicted as sex objects. What is your reaction to the bare-chested male model in Figure 18.3? Is he a sex object or an appropriate model for advertising a belt? Sexuality and nudity are treated differently in countries outside the United States. Some countries are more liberal, while others are more conservative in showing the human form unclothed. In the United States, women's breasts are censored out of most advertisements. In other countries, women's hair, hands, and/or legs and men's facial hair may not be allowed in advertisements. Global promotions should be considerate of the values each country puts on certain areas of the body. Box 18.1 highlights some of the difficulties advertisers face when promoting products in other countries. Products that may not be offensive in the United States are considered offensive in other parts of the world.

Consumers also become offended if an advertisement is perceived as too heavyhanded, implying that they are bad people if they do not use the product or purchase it for their family. In recent years, consumers have criticized computer promotions for making parents believe their child will not succeed at school if they do not have a personal computer at home.

Plagiarism

Plagiarism is the act of using or passing off as one's own an idea, writing, or the creative thought of another. In recent years ethical questions have been raised regarding plagiarism in advertising. In several situations companies have been accused of using ideas without recognizing and crediting the individual who initially pitched the idea. In one example, the creation of an Anheuser-Busch television campaign featuring talking frogs has been questioned. The person bringing the suit claims he pitched the idea

Figure 18.2

If this ad were used to advertise items other than lingerie, it would not be acceptable in the United States.

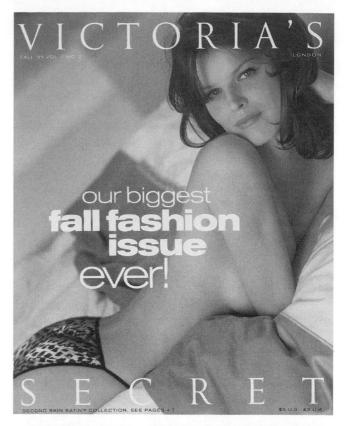

Figure 18.3

Gucci used an attention-getting bare-chested male model to advertise a belt.

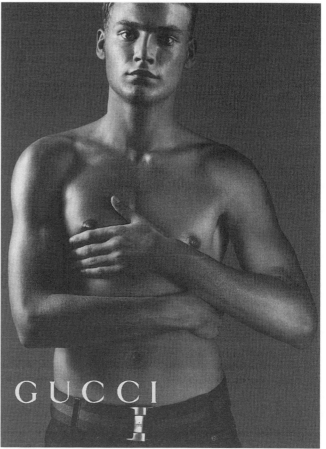

BOX 18.1
Culture Shock: A Mixed Message

Bare backs, spaghetti-thin models and ice-cream cones may be family fare in the West, but in the Middle and Far East, advertisers had better steer clear of such images.

Most of the time, the big international brands are safe sticking to their global advertising strategies. But sometimes, local customers and laws prevent fashion companies from flaunting their racier images. Arab countries are particularly sensitive, especially Kuwait and Saudi Arabia, where nudity is strictly prohibited—not to mention women's faces and flashes of skin in some places. In ads, even a woman's hair, another no-no, must be covered.

Italian companies—often notorious for walking advertising's edge, especially where sex is concerned—adapt their global campaigns to sensitive markets by focusing on accessories or brand image, or by cropping or blacking out potentially offensive images. American firms such as Calvin Klein and Guess, often give different ads to the Mideast. Some play up the logo, or for fragrance, the bottle.

Gianfranco Ferré recently had to crop the naked backs of models from the giant photos, that cover the walls of a new Ferré Jeans store in Abu Dhabi.

"The photo showed the models with their backs to the camera, wearing Ferré jeans. Now the photo just shows the legs in the jeans," said Patrizia Grassini, the head of advertising at Ittierre, which manufactures its own line, Exte, and jeans and sportswear lines for Gianfranco Ferré, Versace, Dolce & Gabbana, and Romeo Gigli under license.

Grassini said Ittierre is used to censoring its Exte catalogs—blacking out certain pages during printing—for Mideastern markets. In Hong Kong and Taiwan, Ittierre's distributors, who direct the local advertising budget, have refused to use photos that feature models that are too skinny or unhealthy looking.

"In those countries, physical and moral health are closely tied, so no one wants to see skinny models," Grassini said.

Giorgio Armani solves the problem by filling the "mupi" boards that line the roads in Kuwait, Saudi Arabia, and the United Arab Emirates with ads for accessories, a company spokeswoman said.

Like Armani, Gucci creates one global ad campaign and then picks still-life and product shots for markets in the Mideast.

Each season, Diesel, known for its outrageous ads—granny grabbing grandpa's crotch, for example—puts together a "side-order" campaign for the Mideast using the same photographer, models, and location as for the global campaign.

"We focus on the product, and try our best to preserve the image and mood of the global campaign," said Maurizio Marchiore, the head of Diesel's advertising division. "Advertising in the Mideast is always a big problem for us because there are so many restrictions. You can't even show a girl eating an ice-cream cone because it's too suggestive."

But the Mideast isn't the only problem; Diesel had to cancel its spring-summer 1998 campaign in Argentina after human rights groups protested ads for the company's stonewashed jeans.

"The campaign showed models chained to stones and floating in water. What we didn't realize was that it was one way the *desaparecidos* were killed. The day after the protests began, we called a press conference, apologized, and pulled the ads. We're always pushing the limits with our campaigns, and when we push limits, sometimes you have to be ready to take a step backward and admit you are wrong," Marchiore said.

Marchiore said the company received more than 300 letters from angry clerics protesting an ad showing denim-clad nuns saying the rosary in front of a Madonna dressed in jeans. The copy read: "Pure, virginal 100 percent cotton. Our jeans are cut from superior denim . . . The finest denim clothing. This is our mission."

"The letters said the ad was in bad taste," Marchiore said, "and we answered saying Diesel's advertising philosophy is to be provocative and ironic. After the whole episode, one nun wrote back saying she'd bought a pair of our jeans at the store in Covent Garden."

A Benetton spokesman—perhaps the most notorious politically incorrect advertiser—said the company's campaigns were the same throughout the world, and that it took a wait-and-see approach. "We don't censor anything," the spokesman said.

"Every culture reacts differently to certain images. In India, people didn't like the newborn baby with the umbilical cord; in parts of the Mideast, they protested against Israeli and Palestinian kids kissing on the cover of our spring-summer 1998 catalog, called 'Enemies.' In Japan, nudity is OK, but they don't want to see any dead naked bodies," he added.

Sometimes the company offends in ways it could not foresee. "In Turkey, we had some trouble with the campaign that showed the white horse and the black horse mating. It turns out there are opposing parties in Turkey, one with the white horse as its symbol, the other with the black horse." The British, known for their advertising creativity, have found it occasionally gets them into hot water—at home and abroad.

Such companies as The Body Shop, French Connection plc, Levi Strauss, Hennes & Mauritz and the department store Harvey Nichols have run afoul of the British Advertising Standards Authority.

But controversy has dogged the Brits even when they didn't expect any problem. Levi's, for instance, recently ran a television ad in Britain showing a hamster happily playing on a treadmill, then dying when the treadmill breaks. The animal-loving British complained to the standards authority in droves, and the ASA banned the campaign—but not until its scheduled run was over.

Harvey Nichols thought its ad to launch a designer shoe department at its London store was witty and fun—a photograph of a woman in labor wearing a pair of high-heeled, strappy sandals. But 11 people complained and the ASA banned the ads—again, when the campaign had ended.

Julie Bowe, the store's marketing director, couldn't understand why the campaign, created by ad agency Harari Page Moon, caused problems. "Everyone uses sex ad nauseum and no one bats an eyelid," she said. "We chose childbirth and get banned; it's ludicrous." But she admitted the ASA ban had its advantages. The action was reported widely in British newspapers, all of which reproduced the image. "Each time it runs, we get even more publicity," Rowe said.

The Body Shop has created a stir in a number of countries with its poster campaign using Ruby, a size 14 doll. The posters were banned in the Hong Kong subway, for example, where authorities claimed they were too much a distraction. The beauty retailer also raised eyebrows in the U.S. recently with in-store posters showing the naked buttocks of three men.

Anita Roddick, the company's founder and chairman, said European consumers thought the posters were funny and witty, "but women in New Hampshire fainted." The Body Shop recently did an article in its magazine, *The Naked Body*, about six of its posters and the uproar they caused.

One poster showed a man in tiny briefs with a bottle of self-tan lotion stuffed into them and the tag line, "Fake It." The poster had to be withdrawn from eight American stores after complaints that the model's pose was immoral. Another showing a mother cuddling her baby and had the headline Mama Toto—which, unfortunately, means something extremely obscene in parts of Mexico.

Of course, some companies want to create controversy. Clothing retailed French Connection has caused double-takes worldwide for the last several seasons with its FCUK ads. The campaign prompted a string of complaints to the ASA, but French connection has done little to alter the ads. The tagline has become so successful that it has used it as a logo on its clothing. "It isn't advertising unless it stops you," said Andrea Hyde, the company's global marketing director.

"You have two seconds to capture the audience. Unless you grab their attention, they'll move on to something else." The campaign is global, Hyde said, but French Connection does adapt for the Mideast and Asia.

"We might change the image or the tag line in those areas, but not in the major markets of the U.S., U.K., and continental Europe," Hyde said. But the company is adapting its message slightly this season, and varying where it displays the ads.

Calvin Klein known for its sexually charged advertising has had to adjust beauty and jeans ads for the Mideast. Saudi Arabia, for example, discourages showing human figures in outdoor advertising, said a Calvin Klein spokesman. In print, one can only show the face, but no body skin. In Israel, advertisers can't show women with bare skin. "Therefore, we provide some options when taking the campaign to these markets," he said. This spring, Klein shot a beach scene for the jeans campaign for Saudi Arabia with only the Calvin Klein logo—and without Kate Moss.

For Calvin Klein cosmetics, "our images are definitely global," said Michael D'Arminio, advertising manager. "We poll each of the markets to get a sense of what's going on." The company will fine-tune the ads only if there are legal restrictions in a market. In a country where no skin is allowed, for example, the company sometimes will run an image of a bottle. Some countries, like Malaysia, require local performers do voiceovers.

Yves Saint Laurent periodically has stirred things up, but more with its fragrance ads than those for apparel. Clara Saint, a spokeswoman for YSL, said the company has never changed an apparel ad. Rive Gauche ads that showed nudity might have caused some flap, she said, but that is as far as it went.

"The one thing I remember being a big scandal was when Mr. Saint Laurent posed nude for the launch of his men's fragrance in 1971," she said, referring to the famous shot of the designer done by photographer Jean-Loup Sieff.

"There was a big noise about that. But otherwise, we haven't changed anything."

Six years later, YSL decided to launch a fragrance named after an addictive drug—Opium. There are still aftershocks from the furor it caused. "Oh, that wasn't just in the Middle East," said Chrystel Abadie-Truchet, international director of marketing for fragrances at YSL's beauty company. "That was a worldwide furor. Everything, from the name to the advertising to the fragrance to the bottle, was controversial. There were demonstrations in New York where some Chinese protested that we were naming a fragrance after a drug that had killed thousands of Chinese people."

Even today, the name Opium cannot be used in ads in certain Mideast countries. In those markets, the scent is sold in a plain wrapper and called simply "Yves Saint Laurent." YSL's Champagne fragrance is called "Champage." "We try to do as little as possible, such as just changing one letter, so that we can keep the graphic design," said Abadie-Truchet. "But we have to respect the laws of the country."

Eurocos, licensee of such fragrance brands as Hugo Boss and Laura Biagiotti, has a single brand approach in the U.S. and Europe. But when religious customs dictate, the company complies, explained Rita Schweighoeser, central sales marketing manager of the Frankfurt-based fine fragrance division of Procter & Gamble.

"Religious symbols and women are the most delicate subjects," said Schweighoeser, "so we develop a version of the campaign oriented to the product or use a landscape as background."

"Dressing of a Man," the company's newest ad for Boss Hugo Boss, shows model Alex Lundqvist getting dressed and then entering a gigantic Hugo boss bottle. In the Mideast print campaign, Lundqvist is shown fully dressed.

Lancaster toned down its Cool Water Woman ad for the U.S. The northern European version shows a naked woman; in the U.S. she's "more discreet."

"Qualitative research shows that the U.S. and Germany are similar in what works in fragrance, but not in advertising," said Patrick Albalodejo, senior vice president of international marketing at the Lancaster Group.

Adapted from: Culture shock: A mixed message. (1999, February 5). Women's Wear Daily, p. 12, 15.

to Budweiser but was not recognized by the company for the idea. This case and others like it have ended in court. Marketers should give proper acknowledgment and financial compensation to the creators of promotional ideas.

Trademark and copyright laws protect products and ideas. A **trademark** is a word or symbol that indicates a source of origin and can be protected based on actual use. Trademarks can be symbols, words, smells, colors, names, sounds, or even shapes as long as they are used to distinguish a particular good or service from other goods and services. A trademark owner can prevent others from using the marks if that use is likely to confuse or deceive the public, provided the trademark's owner is using the trademark. This protection is available whether the trademark is registered or not (Retsky, 1997).

A **copyright** is the legal right granted to an author, a composer, a playwright, a publisher, or a distributor to exclusive publication, production, sale, or distribution of a literary, musical, dramatic, or artistic work. The federal Copyright Act protects original works of authorship in a tangible medium. Outright copying of the protectable elements of an advertisement or product package is a violation of the copyright laws. However, the Copyright Act protects only the expression of an idea, not the idea itself. If a copycat ad uses similar ideas for an advertisement but produces those ideas in a way that is different from the original ad, the Copyright Act will not protect the owner of the original advertisement from such copying. However, if a copycat ad uses identical portions of the original ad or follows the unique structure, sequence, and organization of the original advertisement, the copycat ad would infringe the original advertiser's copyright ("Protecting Your," 1995). Copyright protection is available to copyright owners once the work is fixed in a tangible form. As with trademarks, registration is not required in order to have copyright rights to a work (Retsky, 1997).

Within the fashion business a growing problem is the sale of merchandise with counterfeit trademarks. **Trademark counterfeiting** is the development and sale of imitative products bearing deliberately copied trademarks. The growing popularity of American brands around the world has created a market for fake goods with counterfeit trademarks and logos, including symbols and company names. The most popular counterfeit logos include jeans, athletic footwear, baseball hats, and T-shirts with logos of hot brands. The merchandise is promoted as authentic when in reality a counterfeiter has manufactured the merchandise and is misrepresenting the firm in the sale of the goods. In some cases, the consumer is not aware that the goods are counterfeited (Fig 18.4).

Figure 18.4

Street vendors selling counterfeit merchandise often operate in areas that attract tourists.

The International Anti-Counterfeiting Coalition (IACC), a Washington, D.C.-based nonprofit organization, estimates the worldwide sales of counterfeit athletic apparel to be, at a minimum, $12 billion annually (Ozzard and Feitelberg, 1996). The IACC lobbied for passage of the Anti-Counterfeiting Consumer Protection Act to make the penalties against counterfeiting stiffer, as for an act of racketeering.

Apparel businesses are educating their international partners, explaining the legal boundaries of trademarks in pamphlets printed in several languages. Fila has encouraged consumers to call an 800 number to report suspicious goods, and the IACC has a website and 800 number for consumers to call for information. Figure 18.5 illustrates the seriousness of the Chanel Company's commitment to its logo. Levi Strauss has created a logo with an embedded hologram to protect the mark from being illegally copied. A hologram is a pattern produced on a photosensitive medium that has been exposed by holography and then photographically developed. The hologram is placed on the Levi's so that counterfeit goods that do not have a hologram can be identified.

Trademark infringement has also appeared in cyberspace. Companies are finding the unauthorized use of trademarked names when they try to set up domain names for web-based retailing addresses. **Domain names** are unique names assigned on a first-come, first-served basis by a company called InterNIC. Clairol filed a trademark in-

Figure 18.5

Chanel's commitment to its trademark is illustrated by this ad, placed in a trade publication.

fringement suit against a Texas firm to force the firm to stop using herbalessence.com as a domain name. Clairol owns the Herbal Essence and Herbal Essences trademarks. In earlier suits, both Givenchy and Estée Lauder, obtained permanent injunctions barring defendants from using infringing names (Young, 1997).

Counterfeit trademarks are illegal because they pass off fraudulent goods as authentic. Another problem within the fashion business is illegally copied goods. These goods are not passed off as authentic; rather, they look so similar to the original product that the consumer may not be able to tell the difference. The fashion industry uses the term **trade dress** to refer to the features of a product that comprise its overall look or image; this includes packaging, labeling, display, product design, and configuration. The product can range from a sweatshirt to the store. Trade dress differs from knockoffs. **Knockoffs** are products that copy either the shape or the design created by a well-known company, but do not bear that company's name. Attorneys who specialize in trade dress saw a rise in trade dress disputes at the end of the 20th century. Further, it was not just the low-end manufacturers who were trying to make a quick knockoff from a brand name; it was also the top designers.

At the time of this writing, Calvin Klein's cosmetic company and the Ralph Lauren Corporation, and its licensee Cosmair Incorporated, were scheduled to go to court over Lauren's alleged infringement of a registered trade dress owned by Klein for a perfume bottle. Lauren was charged with copying the distinctive bottle design associated with Klein's Eternity bottle for Lauren's Romance fragrance. In an earlier suit, the Gianni Versace design house obtained a preliminary injunction barring Alfredo Versace, a New York designer, from using the Versace name as a trademark. Alfredo Versace had been using the Versace name on apparel and accessories, including jeans. The federal court judge in the case ruled that use of the name created a likelihood of appreciable customer confusion with the marks of the Milan-based design house. The judge also barred Alfredo Versace from copying the trade dress of Gianni Versace's jeans. He was allowed to use his full name but with restrictions. The aim of such suits is to prevent others from trading on a firm's goodwill, that is, the value of the business in the fashion industry. A company's reputation determines whether customers will continue to buy from it (Young, 1998).

Social Correctness

The example at the beginning of this chapter illustrates a social concern that is evident in some advertisements. While it may not be illegal to show young models in provocative poses, is it socially correct? Advertisers should evaluate promotions for social correctness in terms of age, gender, and cultural diversity.

A major criticism of advertising in the past has been the negative portrayal of women. In addition to showing women as sex objects, advertisements often depicted them in menial jobs or exclusively as housewives, leading to inappropriate stereotyping of women. Women and men should be represented accurately at all occupational levels in a variety of roles. Advertisements should not use them in **decorative roles,** roles in which the man or woman is placed in the advertisement with no purpose other than to look attractive. Likewise, people with disabilities should be represented in integrated promotions that show them actively participating and do not bring attention to their limitations.

In advertisements of the past, it was also considered inappropriate to show pregnant women. Pregnancy was a state that was to be ignored, and pregnant women were

A.

B.

Style is not a size... it's an Attitude! MARINA RINALDI

C.

Figure 18.6

Models in contemporary advertisements may be pregnant (A.) or mature (B.) or any size (C.).

discriminated against. Socially correct advertisements should depict women in all life stages, including pregnancy (Fig. 18.6A).

A third criticism of the images women in past advertisements was that they were always pictured as young and thin. In the early 1980s the fashion and advertising industries were directly accused by the public for increased cases of eating disorders such as bulimia and anorexia. Women of all ages (Fig. 18.6B) and all sizes (Fig. 18.6C) should be represented in advertisements.

Culture is a set of socially acquired behavior patterns of a particular society of people. Culture is a way of life and includes material objects, food, dress, ideas, and values. Society is made up of many different religious and ethnic cultures. Within each culture different segments exist. Black, Hispanic, Jewish, Asian, and all ethnic and religious groups should be equally represented in advertisements. Successful promotions do not stereotype individuals in a manner unbecoming to their culture. They are inclusive of the culture they are targeting and not disparaging toward other cultures or segments within a culture. In many advertising scenarios, a relationship is often depicted in which one side is powerful and one side is weaker. It is important that when it comes to ethnic stereotypes, both the powerful and the weaker side are represented equally.

While the goal of advertising and promotion is to encourage and persuade consumers to purchase goods, services, and/or ideas, the persuading should not be done in a misleading or dishonest fashion. A credible integrated marketing communications plan will include the following social and ethical considerations:

- **Persuasion.** The promotional plan will induce a consumer to take action through reason, not manipulation.
- **Ethics.** A promotional plan will be created using principles of correct conduct based on moral values.
- **Gender.** Men and women will be represented portraying contemporary roles in a nonstereotypical manner.
- **Globalization.** Language, customs, tastes, attitudes, lifestyle, values, and ethical and moral standards of each society will be accurately represented.
- **Children.** A promotional plan will not be directed to or contain material that may exploit children.
- **Cultural diversity.** A promotional plan must accurately reflect the behavior patterns, arts, beliefs, and institutions of all individuals of the country in which it is broadcast or published.

Ethical and social considerations should be reflected throughout an entire promotion, beginning with the public relations image of the company and carried through to every aspect of promotion. Advertising, publicity, direct mail, and electronic media messages should reflect an ethical image to the customer. Events produced and/or sponsored by the company should reflect the ethical code the company stands for. The image presented within a store, including visual merchandise presentations, sales promotions, and the sales personnel hired to sell the merchandise, should have a consistent ethical image.

But how does a firm monitor itself to ensure it is upholding ethical and social standards? Through a set of voluntary and obligatory checks and balances that are discussed in the next section.

CHECKS AND BALANCES

Professionals in the promotion industry have the opportunity to monitor their actions and messages through a series of checks and balances. The checks and balances include a code of ethics and self-regulation. Codes of ethics set standards of conduct for individuals and companies. Self-regulation sets standards for industries.

Code of Ethics

Laws are the body of rules and principles governing the actions of individuals or organizations and enforced by a political authority. They are in place to guard against false or misleading advertising. **Ethics** are the rules or standards governing the conduct of a person or the members of a profession. They are not mandated by law, but rather are directed by moral values. The conduct of an individual or group of individuals may be within the law but outside the social or ethical parameters of a society.

One tool, used to set standards of behavior by professionals and corporations, is a code of ethics. A **code of ethics** is a procedure of conduct the company intends to follow and expects from its employees, clients, vendors, and/or customers. A code of ethics enhances the credibility of a profession, and of companies or individuals working within the profession. In certain industries those who choose not to establish a code of ethics suffer from a lack of respect by clients, employees, and the general public.

Codes of ethics are established through examination of the practices and procedures of an industry or a company and are put in place to protect individuals and the company. A code of ethics may outline how the business expects to treat customers and employees, a policy on fee structures, how advertising and promotion will be handled, and how the company expects to work within a community. A very simple code of ethics for a promotion consultant may include the following statements:

- *I will represent each client fairly and honestly.*
- *I will provide all agreed upon services in a timely and cost-efficient manner.*
- *I will establish reasonable and proper fees for services and provide written estimates to each client.*
- *I will use honest and factual information in all promotions.*
- *I will operate in a manner that is a credit to the community.*

In Chapter 17, we listed some of the professional organizations that can assist in setting standards for evaluating promotions. Many of these organizations also have a code of ethics in place for their members. Figure 18.7 illustrates the principles of professional conduct and ethics the **International Special Events Society (ISES)** expects of its members.

Good corporate mission statements should include company priorities for interaction in the social and political community. Some organizations choose to include a code of ethics to accompany the mission statement. Ethics policies often prohibit employees from accepting gifts or other tokens. For example, the Kmart Corporation has also taken steps to monitor its business efforts by asking managers and vendors to sign an integrity pledge. The **integrity pledge** prohibits employees from accepting any gifts, samples, loans, free travel, and entertainment or other benefits ("Kmart," 1996).

Self-regulation

An industry that voluntarily monitors itself for ethically and socially correct messages participates in a policy of self-regulation. **Self-regulation** means that an entity voluntarily controls or directs itself according to rules, principles, or laws without outside monitoring. Self-regulation is imposed to assure that advertising will not offend, deceive, or exploit individual consumers or groups. Self-regulation begins with the firm and the advertising agency as part of the negotiation process between the client and the

---

Principles of Professional Conduct and Ethics

Each member of ISES shall agree to adhere to the following:

1. Provide to all persons truthful and accurate information with respect to the professional performance of duties.
2. Maintain the highest standards of personal conduct to bring credit to the special events industry.
3. Promote and encourage the highest level of ethics within the profession.
4. Recognize and discharge by responsibility, to uphold all laws and regulations relating to ISES policies and activities.
5. Strive for excellence in all aspects of the industry.
6. Use only legal and ethical means in all industry activities.
7. Protect the public against fraud and unfair practices, and attempt to eliminate from ISES all practices which bring discredit to the profession.
8. Use a written contract clearly stating all charges, services, products, and other essential information.
9. Demonstrate respect for every professional within the industry by clearly stating and consistently performing at or above the standards acceptable to the industry.
10. Make a commitment to increase professional growth and knowledge by attending educational programs recommended, but not limited to, those prescribed by ISES.
11. Contribute knowledge to professional meetings and journals to raise the consciousness of the industry.
12. Maintain the highest standards of safety, sanitation, and any other responsibilities.
13. When providing services or products, maintain in full force adequate or appropriate insurance.
14. Cooperate with professional colleagues, suppliers, and employees to provide the highest quality service.
15. Extend these same professional commitments to all those persons supervised or employed.
16. Subscribe to the ISES Principles of Professional Conduct and Ethics and to abide by the ISES Bylaws.

Figure 18.7

The principles of professional conduct and ethics of the International Special Events Society (ISES).

advertising agency. Firms and agencies set guidelines, policies, and standards that ads must conform to and that the firm and the client must accept. Beyond self-regulation by agency and client, nonprofit organizations within various industries assist with self-regulation of advertising and promotional efforts. Some of these organizations, including the Better Business Bureau, the Direct Marketing Association, and the National Association of Broadcasters are discussed in the following pages.

Better Business Bureau

The **Better Business Bureau** (BBB) self-regulates advertising to assure the consumer of a correct and ethical message. The mission of the BBB is to foster public confidence in truthful advertising. It is not an enforcement agency but does seek to protect the consumer against untruthful or misleading advertising through voluntary cooperation and self-regulation. To this purpose, it has established a set of advertising guidelines for companies to use based on broad principles of truth and accuracy. Local BBBs regularly monitor advertising for adherence to these principles, as well as compliance with local, state, and federal regulations relating to advertising. When the BBB finds questionable advertising, the advertiser is contacted and requested to substantiate the claims that are being made and to voluntarily comply with the guidelines. In certain areas, local BBBs have also put in place an appeals process for the advertiser.

The Better Business Bureau's guidelines are directed by three basic principles:

1. The primary responsibility for truthful and nondeceptive advertising rests with the advertiser. Advertisers should be prepared to substantiate any claims or offers made

before publication or broadcast and, upon request, present such substantiation promptly to the advertising medium or the Better Business Bureau.

2. Advertisements that are untrue, misleading, deceptive, fraudulent, falsely disparaging of competitors, or insincere offers to sell, shall not be used.
3. An advertisement as a whole may be misleading although every sentence separately considered is literally true. Misrepresentation may result not only from direct statements, but also by omitting or obscuring a material fact ("Better Business Bureau," 1996).

Beyond the three driving principles, the BBB has specific regulations directed toward particular elements of advertisements. Specific regulations cover topics such as price, the use of the word *free*, sales, credit, testimonials and endorsements, rebates, contests, and other elements of advertising. The subjects that the BBB covers with regard to advertising and promotion are very complete.

While Better Business Bureaus monitor advertising in local markets, the parent organization, the **Council of Better Business Bureaus** (CBBB), develops advertising codes and standards at a national level. Since 1971, the National Advertising Division (NAD) of the CBBB and the National Advertising Review Board have served as the self-regulation monitoring council for the advertising industry. In 1974, as a division of NAD, the Children's Advertising Review Unit (CARU) was established. CARU promotes responsible advertising to children. CARU has developed six principles that guide advertising directed at children under age 12. The principles are as follows:

1. Advertisers should always take into account the level of knowledge, sophistication, and maturity of the audience to which the message is primarily directed. Younger children have a limited capacity for evaluating the credibility of information they receive and also lack the ability to understand the nature of the information they provide. Advertisers, therefore, have a special responsibility to protect children from their own susceptibilities.
2. Realizing that children are imaginative and that make-believe play constitutes an important part of the growing-up process, advertisers should exercise care not to exploit unfairly the imaginative quality of children. Advertising should not stimulate unreasonable expectations of product quality or performance either directly or indirectly.
3. Recognizing that advertising may play an important part in educating the child, advertisers should communicate information in a truthful and accurate manner and in language understandable to young children in full recognition that the child may learn practices from advertising that can affect his or her health and well-being.
4. Advertisers are urged to capitalize on the potential of advertising to influence behavior by developing advertising that, whenever possible, addresses itself to positive and beneficial social behavior, such as friendship, kindness, honesty, justice, generosity, and respect of others.
5. Care should be taken to incorporate minority and other groups in advertisements in order to present positive and pro-social roles and role models whenever possible. Social stereotyping and appeals to prejudice should be avoided.
6. Although many influences affect a child's personal and social development, it remains the prime responsibility of parents to provide guidance for children. Advertisers should contribute to this parent-child relationship in a constructive manner ("Better Business Bureau," 1996).

Although the above principles are directed toward advertising to children under the age of 12, they have implications for advertising to other target populations and should be considered in the integrated marketing communications plan.

In 1997, in response to a request by the Federal Trade Commission, CARU established guidelines for advertising to children over the World Wide Web. The guidelines include asking advertisers to make "reasonable efforts" to get children to ask their parents' permission before purchasing a product or service through the Internet, or before answering any personal questions about themselves or their families (Mifflin, 1997). Additionally, advertisers are urged to disclose why information is being requested and how it will be used.

Direct Marketing Association

The **Direct Marketing Association** (DMA) has established ethical guidelines for direct response broadcast advertising, mail list practices, marketing by telephone, and interactive marketing. The philosophy of the Direct Marketing Association is also one of self-regulation rather than government mandates. According to the DMA, self-regulatory practices are more readily adaptable to new techniques, economic fluctuations, and changing social conditions. Because the guidelines are voluntary rather than mandated, use is widespread and incorporated into the business plan of many companies as sound business practice. The DMA Committee on Ethical Business Practice is charged with reviewing any complaint by an individual in violation of the DMA guidelines and has the authority to take appropriate action.

The Direct Marketing Association has put in place generally accepted principles of conduct for individuals and organizations involved in direct mail and direct marketing. As discussed in Chapter 10, the purposes of direct marketing are to promote, sell, and deliver goods and services directly from manufacturer to consumer using a maintained or purchased list of potential customers. The DMA has recognized that businesses should protect the personal privacy of individuals and through the use of guidelines has provided safeguards for the proper handling of personal data contained in files. The DMA guidelines for direct mail include the following:

1. Personal data should be collected by fair and lawful means for a direct marketing purpose.
2. Direct marketers should limit the collection of personal data to only data deemed pertinent and necessary for a direct marketing purpose, and the data should only be used accordingly.
3. Personal data used for direct marketing purposes should be accurate and complete, and should be kept up to date to the extent feasible by the direct marketer. Personal data should be retained for no longer than required.
4. An individual shall have the right to request whether personal data about him or her appears on a direct marketer's file and receive a summary of the information within a reasonable time after the request is made. The individual has the right to challenge the accuracy of personal data relating to him or her. Data shown to be incorrect should be corrected.
5. Personal data should be transferred between direct marketers only for direct marketing purposes. Consumers who provide data that may be rented, sold, or exchanged should be informed of this potential. Marketers should offer an opportunity to have a consumer's name deleted or suppressed upon request.
6. Each direct marketer should be responsible for the security of personal data. Strict measures should be taken to assure against unauthorized access (Direct Marketing Association, 1997a).

On-line and Internet marketing opportunities create special circumstances surrounding an individual's privacy and have become the focus of the DMA to ensure ethical marketing practices on the Internet. Because anyone can access the Internet, it is important to limit the disclosure of personal information to only the party that has permission to receive the information. Depending on the circumstances, information collected about a consumer on-line may include contact or locator information such as name; postal and e-mail addresses; billing information, including account and credit card numbers; transaction information, such as the date of purchase; and information that might reveal the consumer's preferences or choices, such as the time of day purchases are made or sites visited. Because the Internet is growing in popularity, it is important for ethical standards to be developed for the privacy of the individual disclosing information.

The Direct Marketing Association guidelines recommend that all marketers operating on-line sites, whether or not they collect personal information, should make available their information practices in a prominent place to consumers. These practices should be easy to find, read, and understand by the consumer. The notice should identify the markets and disclose an e-mail and postal address to which the consumer can direct questions or comments. Marketers sharing personal information collected on-line should furnish individuals with an opportunity to prohibit the disclosure of that information (Direct Marketing Association, 1997b).

National Association of Broadcasters

The **National Association of Broadcasters** (NAB) is the trade association for the radio and television industry. Its priority is to maintain a favorable governmental, legal, and technological climate for free over-the-air broadcasting industry. The NAB represents radio and television broadcasters before the Federal Communications Commission (FCC) and other federal agencies, courts, and legal and regulatory agencies. The NAB practices self-regulation with codes of standards for both radio and television similar to those in place for print advertising. The NAB has voluntarily set TV parental guidelines to offer parents advance cautionary information so that they can better supervise the TV watching of younger children.

The United States is not the only country to establish self-regulation bodies to monitor advertising messages. The concept of advertising self-regulation has developed since the 1960s. It includes 52 countries, 25 of which have well-established systems in place to clear advertising content and handle complaints from industry and consumers about advertising (Ingrassia, 1995). Canada was one of the first countries to establish a self-regulation body to review advertising, with the **Canadian Advertising Foundation** (CAF) founded in 1967. CAF is parent to the Advertising Standards Council, which administers the Canadian Code of Advertising Standards. Only the United Kingdom (1962), the Netherlands (1964), and Italy (1966) preceded Canada with codes of their own (Ingrassia, 1995).

The Canadian self-regulatory body is an organization of media, advertisers, and agencies. It includes public representatives in various positions in consumer associations who review committee work. The Canadian codes have been developed for various product sectors such as cosmetics, feminine hygiene products, nonalcoholic beverages and food, and children's advertising. CAF has been successful in promoting consensus when there is a dispute on advertising content. In traditional Canadian style, meetings rather than fights are held to resolve problems. Such meetings are private, and the nature and results of them are not disclosed to the press or the public.

Occasionally self-regulation has proven so successful that regulations have been retired. Such was the case with the advertising of feminine hygiene products. Advertising adhered to the regulations, and complaints against the ads decreased, so, the CAF retired the specific regulations in 1992 (Ingrassia, 1995).

Mexico and other Latin American countries have also established self-regulation bodies that monitor advertising messages. The **Council for Self-Regulations and Ethical Advertising** (Conar) was established in Mexico in 1995, modeled after similar bodies already in place in Brazil, Argentina, Chile, Venezuela, and Costa Rica (Bedingfield, 1995). Conar is intended to solve disputes out of court, through amicable negotiation by a board of nine directors drawn from advertising and the media. According to the head of Conar, Guther Saupe, it was in Mexico's best interest to self-regulate to avoid establishing more laws. In Brazil, 99 percent of all conflicts have been resolved during the past 20 years in which the self-regulatory board has been in place. Chile has had similar positive results, 90 percent of its conflicts have been resolved without involving the government (Bedingfield, 1995).

Advertisers, advertising agencies, and advertising outlets have recognized that consumer trust and confidence must be maintained. They also realize that if they do not self-regulate, the government will step in and put rigid restrictions in place.

GOVERNMENT REGULATION

Although professionals within the advertising and promotion professions strive to monitor messages through self-regulation, it is sometimes necessary for the government to intervene to protect consumers in the marketplace.

In the early part of the 20th century, advertising and packaging techniques were designed to increase sales of products rather than assisting consumers in selection and evaluation of sound products. Consumerism has emerged as a reaction to consumers' dissatisfaction with the marketplace. It is a movement seeking to protect and inform consumers by requiring such practices as honest packaging and advertising, product guarantees, and improved safety standards. **Consumerism** is the promotion of the consumer's interest and is achieved through a set of activities monitored by government, businesses, and independent organizations designed to protect the rights of consumers.

Consumerism began in 1914 when Congress established the **Federal Trade Commission (FTC)** in response to the need for consumer protection. The FTC at its inception, and through later amendments, has been given authority to monitor deceptive acts and practices concerning the consumer. Many other federal acts have followed, all designed to protect the consumer. They include the Food, Drug, & Cosmetics Act; Wool Products Labeling Act; Fur Products Labeling Act; Flammable Products Act; Cigarette Labeling and Advertising Act; and Fair Packaging and Labeling Act.

As a statement to show how important consumerism was to President John F. Kennedy, in 1962 he established "rights" for consumers. The four consumer rights include:

1. The right to safety
2. The right to be informed
3. The right to be heard
4. The right to choice

These rights have continued to be protected by Congress and are adhered to in all promotion activities publicizing consumer goods. We will now discuss the specific roles of the FTC and the Federal Communications Commission (FCC). There are other agencies that also monitor advertising of specific products.

Federal Trade Commission

In the United States, the FTC is charged with protecting consumers. The **Federal Trade Commission Act** created the commission, which is responsible for controlling and regulating antitrust and consumer protection laws. According to its mission statement, the FTC works to enhance the smooth operation of the marketplace by eliminating acts or practices that are unfair or deceptive and stopping actions that threaten consumers' opportunities to exercise informed choice ("Statutes relating to," 1997).

The FTC has specific regulations regarding advertising. FTC policy mandates that advertisers substantiate claims that make objective assertions about the item or service being advertised. Additionally, the advertiser must have a reasonable basis supporting these claims. A firm's failure to possess and rely upon a reasonable basis for objective claims constitutes an unfair and deceptive act or practice in violation of the Federal Trade Commission Act ("FTC Policy," 1997).

For example, in 1997 the FTC ordered Zales, the nation's largest jewelry retailer, to stop advertising its *Ocean Treasures* line of imitation pearl jewelry as composed of cultured pearls. The settlement required Zales to disclose, clearly and prominently, the nature of the pearl jewelry it sold. The company was required to use words, such as "artificial," "imitation," or "simulated," in close proximity to any representation of an imitated pearl product. It was also required to use the words "cultured" or "cultivated" for representation of a cultured pearl product ("FTC Year," 1997).

In addition to monitoring the substantiation of advertising claims, the FTC also regulates the labeling of products through various congressional acts. The **Robinson–Patman Act** authorizes the FTC to prevent specified practices involving discriminatory pricing and product promotion. The act stipulates that any manufacturer providing promotional allowances or services to retailers must offer the allowance on a proportionally equal basis to all retailers.

The **Wool Products Labeling Act** of 1939 governs the labeling of wool and wool-blended textiles. The Act requires that wool products moving in interstate commerce be labeled. It also has a provision that mandates that mail-order promotional materials clearly and conspicuously state whether a wool product was processed or manufactured in the United States or was imported.

The **Textile Fiber Products Identification Act** of 1960 requires that a tag or label with certain information relating to the fiber content of textile products be attached to the item at the time of sale and delivery to the consumer. The following items must appear on the textile label: fiber content and the percentage by weight of each over 5 percent, the manufacturer's name, country of origin of imported fabrics, and identification of fibers by generic names. The Act also mandates disclosure in the labeling, invoicing, and advertising of textile fiber products and includes a provision that mail-order promotional materials clearly and conspicuously indicate whether a textile fiber product was processed or manufactured in the United States or was imported. Fur products are handled separately under the **Fur Products Labeling Act** of 1951. This act requires that invoices and advertising for fur and fur products specify, among other things, the true English name of the animal from which the fur was taken.

Federal Communications Commission

The **Federal Communications Commission** (FCC) regulates broadcast communications and has authority over telephone, telegraph, television, radio, private radio, cellular telephone, pagers, cable TV, international communications, and satellite communications. The FCC has the authority to license, renew, and/or take away broadcast station licenses and has the authority to monitor advertising on these stations. The FCC may restrict products to be advertised and the content of the advertisement. Profane or obscene language and messages deemed to be in poor taste are not permitted to be broadcast. The FCC also requires television stations to disclose who is paying for infomercials at the beginning or end of the commercial.

In the United States and other countries where advertising is allowed, government regulations restrict the types of products that can be advertised, content and creative approach, language that may be used, and media in which the advertisement is placed. Additionally, countries may regulate the amount of advertising by a single advertiser and regulate the amount of materials created outside the country by international advertising agencies.

International advertising regulations include restrictions on tobacco products, liquor, medicine, pharmaceuticals, travel, food, and other products and services. Argentina, Canada, France, Italy, Norway, Sweden, and Switzerland (along with the United States) restrict cigarette advertising in broadcast media. Guangzhou, a city in South China, banned all cigarette ads and complementary promotional products, including umbrellas, balloons, and lighters that contain tobacco advertising in public places. Additionally, all buses and other public vehicles must refuse to carry cigarette advertisements. Guangzhou has taken this step to build a sanitary, healthy, and modern metropolis ("South China," 1998).

Brazil regulates any message that makes a comparison of one product to another product. France does not allow the advertising of margarine. Germany and France have legally restricted the word *diet* in advertising messages. West Germany regulates sales promotion techniques. Advertisers may not use premiums within packages, mail-in offers, purchase-with-purchase offers, coupons, or sweepstakes; and Italy does not allow cash rebates (Belch and Belch, 1995).

Some countries ban the depiction of certain products in advertisements. For example, French law disallows the exhibition or representation of marijuana leaves. Police seized Body Shop window display posters and in-store displays that promoted its hemp product line because a hemp leaf was shown in the display. According to the Body Shop, the poster displayed industrial grade hemp that was legal. As a result of the seizure of the promotional items, the Body Shop initiated an educational drive to teach the differences between industrial-grade hemp and marijuana. The company developed educational pamphlets to distribute at its stores and continued to sell the legal hemp product line (Weil and Fallon, 1998).

The international aspect of the Internet—instant accessibility throughout the world—also presents challenges for promotion planners. The question arises of whether nations can regulate on-line advertising or promotional material that originates in a foreign country. Box 18.2 explores this question and provides guidelines for promotional planners who are considering promotions over the Internet.

These are just some of the restrictions countries put on promotion. Promotion specialists doing business in foreign countries must be aware of the changing restrictions that apply to the country they are developing promotions for.

BOX 18.2

Internet Marketing: Practical Suggestions for International Advertising and Promotions

The international aspect of the Internet presents an interesting challenge for the promotion marketer. When a marketer places advertising or sales promotion on a server in Chicago, Boston, or New York, that advertising or promotion offer may be accessed throughout the world. From a legal perspective, the question is whether countries other than the United States can exert jurisdiction over advertising or promotional material that is deemed unlawful by that foreign country.

In late 1995, Compuserve, Inc. blocked access by its subscribers around the world to over 200 sexually explicit Usenet discussion groups and picture data bases in response to a charge by a federal prosecutor in Munich that the material violated German pornography and child-protection laws. In effect, the legal and ethical standards of one country's government dictated what the world could access. The Compuserve case illustrates how information uploaded onto the Internet in one country can elicit a negative response in another country and, to the extent the data provider has an interest in obeying that foreign country's laws, the data provider's altered behavior effects the entire audience for the data.

Foreign entities have also felt worldwide effect of Internet advertising. The British carrier, Virgin Atlantic Airways, advertised over the Internet that a 21-day advance purchase ticket fare between Newark and London was $499 on weekdays during certain travel periods. In a separate section of its site, Virgin Atlantic Airways advised consumers to check with reservations or a local travel agent for the latest fare, availability, and any taxes, charges, or restrictions. The U.S. Department of Transportation slapped the British company with a $14,000 fine for failing to disclose clearly that a tax of $38.91 applied to each ticket. Whether or not the advertising met legal standards in Great Britain, and regardless of where Virgin Atlantic Airway's Internet server was located, the U.S. government successfully asserted jurisdiction over advertising that could be downloaded to a personal computer site in the United States.

Even in the face of worldwide exposure, some U.S. advertisers and marketers choose simply to ignore foreign laws, and take the ill-advised position that if the advertising has been cleared in the United States, then it will probably pass muster in other target countries. That may not be true for all foreign countries. Countries such as Ger-

many, which prohibit comparative advertising or may have different standards regarding sexually implicit advertising, could challenge the advertising and could initiate an action to ban the material, as it did with some of Compuserve's discussion groups. Some countries, such as France, have strict language requirements. The rules of a consumer skill contest open to French residents must be in French, for example. Other countries, such as those that have adopted versions of the European International Code of Advertising Practice of the International Chamber of Commerce (the "ICC CODE"), may regulate the "decency" of a particular advertisement much more stringently than any regulatory body in the United States. In 1995, a German court ruled that the Italian clothier, Benetton Group S.p.A., violated German competition law by exploiting intense "feelings of pity." The Benetton print advertising campaign featured an oil-drenched bird, child laborers in Latin America, and a human body stamped with the words "H.I.V. Positive." A French court extracted $32,000 in damages from Benetton for its "H.I.V. Positive" advertisement on the grounds that the advertisement was "a provocative exploitation of suffering." Because every ad and every promotional offer posted on the Internet can be downloaded in virtually every corner of the world, the prudent marketer must be aware of the potential risks.

However, it is the rare marketer who has the resources to conduct a comprehensive, international clearance program for its advertising or promotion. A reasonable approach is to pick the key foreign markets for the brand and clear advertising or promotional material in those countries. The money saved by the use of the Internet rather than broadcast or event print media should go a long way in financing the legal clearance process.

How do you conduct an international clearance? The first task is to make sure your advertising or promotional material (e.g., contest or sweepstakes rules) conforms to U.S. law. Once you have developed your advertising criteria, you must collect the names and fax numbers of counsel in the likely countries for your brand or promotional objective. Sometimes your U.S. advertising counsel can suggest colleagues overseas (especially if your counsel regularly handles foreign clients).

Perhaps the most important step comes next: preparing the instructions to foreign counsel. The package of materials should contain three components: (1) your advertising and promotional criteria; (2) a cover letter discussing timing, fees, and correspondence in case of conflict or inability on the part of the foreign counsel to handle your particular matter; and (3) a questionnaire. The questionnaire should be carefully designed to elicit the precise information you need. For example, every questionnaire must include the ultimate question, "Can Advertiser run this advertisement (referring to the criteria) in your country?" followed by "What changes, if any, to the advertising should be made in order to conform it to your country's laws?" Depending on the type of advertising or promotion involved, you may want to include specific questions dealing with topics such as:

- Comparative advertising—can an advertiser mention a competing product even if no comparison is made?
- Toys and children's advertising
- Lotteries/sweepstakes/contest/gambling
- Privacy and data protection
- Mail-order and direct response promotions
- Premium offers
- Portrayal of women/minorities
- Testimonials/endorsements
- Special products (e.g., alcohol, cars, cosmetics/hygiene products, dietary products and food, nonprescription drugs, and tobacco).
- Language requirements
- Decency
- Denigration
- Intellectual property
- Guarantees

As you develop your questionnaire, keep in mind that many foreign attorneys practice very differently from U.S. lawyers. In countries with traditions of civil law (based on statutes rather than a judge's decision), lawyers tend to view the law restrictively. Thus, if a particular statute does not expressly permit a certain type of advertising or promotion, some foreign counsel may tell you that your advertising is unlawful. The specificity of the questionnaire is crucial. No matter how precise your questionnaire is, sometimes follow-up correspondence is required in order to obtain a full answer.

Disclaimers are increasingly being used in advertising. Disclaimers should work equally well on the international level, even for consumer goods such as cigarettes, food, cars, and alcohol. For example, Zima Beverage Company's website featuring information and promotional material for its ZIMA malt beverage contains a statement indicating that its site is for those 21 years and older. Similarly, advertisers could post statements that their site is addressed only to consumers in certain countries.

Assuming that your advertisement violates the collective morals of a country somewhere in the world with access to the Internet, what are the risks? As we have discussed, if you plan on doing business in that country the risks can be substantial. Penalties, fines, damages, and conceivably a ban on your product or service are all possible. If you do not do business in that country, and you do not have any assets in that country, your risk of being dragged into court there are low. Because many advertisers conceive of the world as a shrinking place and the world economy is becoming increasingly integrated, it probably makes sense to make a reasonable attempt to consider the impact of your advertising and promotional material on a global basis and perhaps make an effort to clear your marketing material in some key countries prior to dissemination on the Internet.

Adapted from: Rose, L., and Feldman, J. (1996, February 24). Internet marketing: Practical suggestions for international advertising and promotions. Arent Fox [On-line]. Available: http://webcom/lewrose/article/intl.html.

FUTURE TRENDS IN SOCIAL AND ETHICAL PROMOTIONAL BEHAVIOR

Because electronic retailing continues to grow, a critical social and ethical issue facing the promotion industry in the 21st century is awareness of what is and is not advertising, and regulation about what can be broadcast over the Internet. Several factors which have an impact on all elements of the promotion mix have caused the growth in electronic retailing (Knowles, 1997).

- As cable television capacity increases, more cable television channels are becoming available.

- The Internet is expanding and becoming more accessible.
- Personal computer-based on-line shopping services are offering more merchandise and expanding their customer base.
- CD-ROM catalogs are being developed and distributed.
- Interactive services are being developed and tested.
- Additional technological developments and new distributions channels will be available in the future.

Presently, advertising within electronic retailing is monitored by the consumers who use the retailing sources; the federal regulatory authorities, including the FCC and FTC; state and local regulatory agencies; and industry associations such as the DMA. Consumers and regulatory agencies have taken great interest in electronic media practices for several reasons. First, electronic media is a high-profile business. Second, a large number of consumers have access to the electronic information via television, telephone, and personal computers. Additionally, subjects related to shopping services and telecommunications receive a high level of media coverage because of strong public interest in them. Last, television, a principal vehicle for electronic retailing, is monitored closely because of subject content related to violence and children's advertising.

Direct-response electronic media, as defined in Chapter 10, includes infomercials. Infomercials are program-length product demonstrations that often look like TV shows but are really another form of promotion. Infomercials are not illegal. However, the FTC will investigate infomercials that do not disclose their true advertising nature or make deceptive claims about products. The FTC has developed the following criteria for consumers to identify infomercials:

- Look for commercials that are similar to the program content. As a general rule, assume that any "program" that provides ordering information for a specific product or contains commercial interruptions to promote products related to the "program's" content is a paid advertisement.
- Be aware that the advertiser often pays celebrities and "experts" who endorse a product. Additionally, consumers from the studio audience are often preselected by the advertiser.
- If, during the program, a sales pitch is made and order information is given to the audience, it is probably a paid advertisement.
- If a consumer decides to purchase a product from an infomercial, on-line computer shopping service, or television shopping channel, the company is required by law to ship the order within the time stated in the advertisement.
- If no time is promised, the company should ship within 30 days after receiving the order.
- If the company cannot ship within the promised time, the company should offer the consumer the choice of agreeing to the delay of the order or canceling the order and receiving a refund (Infomercials, 1996).

Although currently, information exchanged over the computer is not regulated, it is monitored carefully. Consumers on occasion have taken action against sexually explicit materials and alcoholic beverages available to children under age 18 via the Internet, and vendors who send unsolicited e-mail. The computer industry has fought against regulation, stating that regulation of the Internet is a violation of the first amendment right to free speech. The future will require that consumers become more sophisticated in determining the difference between advertising, programming, and entertainment.

As promotion specialists, we must look at the end result of our communications in view of the influence communications have on the public. Planners must balance the responsibility to promote products effectively with the obligation to present them in socially acceptable ways, ethically, and accurately. Industries have the ability to regulate themselves. In those situations where self-regulation is not enough, laws and governing bodies have set policy to regulate advertising and promotion. Ethical evaluation should take place before, during, and at the conclusion of the creative process. An internal team representing the client and agency should monitor the evaluation, and both parties should agree with the message that is presented to the public. In some instances a company may choose to have an external team evaluate the advertisement to assure objectivity in the reporting of the message to the consumer.

In this chapter, we have pointed out that professional promotion specialists must be responsible to the public and consider the social and ethical ramifications of their messages before they are sent to consumers. But we do not want to leave you with the idea that advertising and promotion are harmful. In fact, the opposite is true. Advertising is good for consumers. It conveys important information about benefits, price, quality, and availability. For example, the National Fluid Milk Processor Promotion Board has been successful in informing consumers of the benefits of drinking milk by

Figure 18.8

A socially conscious *Got Milk* campaign featuring Vanessa Williams

using celebrities in a milk mustache campaign (Fig. 18.8). Promotion represents the right of consumers to choose goods and services from competing suppliers, and we are privileged to live in a country that allows promotion to exist.

SUMMARY

- Promotion professionals must be responsible to the public and consider the social and ethical ramifications of their messages before they are sent to consumers.
- Several social and ethical considerations that should be evaluated when planning a promotion include offensive advertising, plagiarism, and social correctness.
- Laws are the body of rules and principles governing the actions of individuals or organizations and are enforced by a political authority.
- Ethics are the rules or standards governing the conduct of a person or the members of a profession and are directed by moral values.
- A code of ethics is the procedure of conduct the company intends to follow and expects from its employees, clients, vendors, and/or customers.
- During the evaluation process, an integrated marketing communications plan should examine ethical considerations related to the following elements: persuasion, ethics, gender, globalization, children, and cultural diversity.
- The advertising industry monitors itself through a policy of voluntary self-regulation.
- The Better Business Bureau (BBB) self-regulates advertising to assure the consumer of the correct and ethical message.
- The Direct Marketing Association (DMA) has established ethical guidelines for direct response broadcast advertising, mailing list practices, marketing by telephone, and interactive marketing.
- The National Association of Broadcasters (NAB) is the trade association for the radio and television industry with the priority to maintain a favorable governmental, legal, and technological climate for the free over-the-air broadcasting industry.
- The Federal Trade Commission (FTC) works to enhance the smooth operation of the marketplace by eliminating acts or practices that are unfair or deceptive and stopping actions that threaten consumers' opportunities to exercise informed choice.
- The FTC investigates infomercials that do not disclose their true advertising nature or make deceptive claims about products.
- The Federal Communications Commission (FCC) regulates broadcast communications.

KEY TERMS

code of ethics	Federal Trade Commission Act	self-regulation
consumerism	Fur Products Labeling Act	Textile Fiber Products
copyright	integrity pledge	Identification Act
culture	knockoffs	trade dress
decorative roles	laws	trademark
domain names	plagiarism	trademark counterfeiting
ethics	Robinson-Patman Act	Wool Products Labeling Act

KEY ORGANIZATIONS

Better Business Bureau
Canadian Advertising Foundation
Council of Better Business Bureaus
Council for Self-Regulations and Ethical Advertising
Direct Marketing Association
Federal Communications Commission
Federal Trade Commission
International Special Events Society
National Association of Broadcasters

QUESTIONS FOR DISCUSSION

1. What social and ethical issues should a promotion planner be aware of as he or she develops advertising, direct marketing pieces, and other promotion tools?
2. How do the issues social and ethical issues raised with advertising and direct marketing affect the other promotional techniques such as sales promotion, publicity and public relations, special events, fashion shows, and visual merchandising?
3. What are the advantages and disadvantages related to self-regulation?
4. What are the benefits and detriments to using infomercials?
5. What are the benefits and detriments associated with electronic retailing.

ADDITIONAL RESOURCES

Boddewyn, J. (1992). *Global perspectives on advertising self-regulation: Principles and practices in thirty-eight countries.* Portland, OR: Greenwood Publishing.

Phillips. M. J. (1997). *Ethics & manipulation in advertising.* New York: Quorum.

Sivulka, J. (1997). *Soap, sex and cigarettes: A cultural history of American advertising.* Belmont, CA: Wadsworth.

Stauber, J., and Rampton, S. (1995). *Toxic sludge is good for you!: Lies, damn lies and the public relations industry.* Portland, OR: Common Courage.

Turow, J. (1997). *Breaking up America: Advertisers and the new media world.* Chicago: University of Chicago Press.

Twitchell, J. (1997). *Adcult USA: The triumph of advertising in American culture.* New York: Columbia University Press.

REFERENCES

About FGI. (1998). New York: Fashion Group International [On-line]. Available: http://www.fgi. org/about.html.

Ads are coming to dry cleaners. (1998, August 26). New York Times [On-line]. Available: http://www.nytimes.com/yr/mo/day/news/financial/addeda.html.

Aktar, A., and Raper, S. (1997, May 2). Paris mags; new faces, new titles. *Women's Wear Daily,* 10–11.

AMA board approves new marketing definition. (1985, March 1). *Marketing News,* 1.

Americans with Disabilities Act Home Page. (1998, May 8). U.S. Department of Justice [On-line]. Available: http://www.usdoj.gov/crt/ada/adahom1.htm.

Askins, C. (1987, January 16). Window displays: Money well spent, *California Apparel News,* 22.

Barr, P. (1996, August 28). It's anniversary time [On-line]. Available: http://www.buzznyc. com/barr.

Barr, V. (1997, November 1) INFeature: Now showing: Themed retail. *Shopping Center World* [On-line]. Available: http://www.elibrary.compuserve.com.

Barr, V. (1998, May 1). Remaking a legend: A brighter Bloomingdales greets customers in Manhattan. *Lighting Dimensions* [On-line]. Available: http://www.elibrary.compuserve.com.

Barringer, F. (1998, May 4). Newspaper circulation increases again. *New York Times Online* [On-line]. Available: http://www.nytimes.com/yr/mo/day/news/financial/newspaper-circulation-media.html.

BBDO acquires stake in Japan's I & S corporation. (1998, July). *Advertising Age International* [On-line]. Available: http://www.adage.com/international/daily/archives/19980702intld 19980702-13.html.

Beck, R. (1996, August 22). The future is now for this fast-forward thinker. *Los Angeles Times,* D-7.

Bedingfield, J. (1995, September 18). Mexico unleashes watchdog to avoid legal ad disputes. *Advertising Age,* I-6.

Belch, G. E., and Belch, M. A. (1995). *Advertising and promotion: An integrated marketing communications perspective* (3rd ed.) Chicago: Irwin.

Bell Atlantic takes yellow pages online. (1997, February 12). *Advertising Age* [On-line]. Available: www.http://adage.com/interactive/daily/archives/19970212/id19970212-5.html.

Berger, D. How much to spend, (Foote, Cone & Belding Internal Report) in M. L. Rothschild. (1987) *Advertising.* Lexington, MA: D.C. Heath.

Better Business Bureau. (1996). [On-line]. Available: http://www.bbb.org.

Blass shows score $600K in Saks event. (1997, August 12). *Women's Wear Daily,* 11.

Born, P. (1998, May 8). Lauder primes dazzling with $20M push. *Women's Wear Daily,* 7, 9.

Brady, J. (1996, October 31). Wall street: bigger is better. *Women's Wear Daily,* section II, 32.

Burnett, J., and Paul, P. (1996, November 18). Reliable data needed to target mobility-disabled consumers. *Marketing News,* 30 (24), 16.

Carlson, D. (1996, October 1). Do you have holes in your campaign? *Advertising and Marketing Review* [On-line]. Available: http://www.elibrary.com.

Carroll, E. (1998, August). Find it, sign it, *Visual Merchandising + Store Design,* 16–20.

Chain Store Age Chicago Apparel Study. (1996, October) *Chain Store Age,* 22B–23B.

China backs a new industry: Fashion modeling. (1996, April 14). *CNN* [On-line]. Available: http://www.cnn.com/STYLE/9604/14/china.models/index.html.

Christopher, A. (1998, August 3). Blink of an ad. *Time,* 51.

Coen, R. (1994, May 2). Ad gain of 5.2% in 93 marks downturn's end, *Advertising Age,* 4.

Coin-op cool. (1999, May) *In Style,* 118.

Competitive Media Reporting. (1997). State of the art technology for speed and accuracy [On-line]. Available: http://www.usadata.com/usadata/cmr/tech.htm.

Competitive Media Reporting. (1998). Top 20 retail companies. *Advertising Age* [On-line]. Available: http://www.adage.com/dataplace/archives/dp203.html.

Conti, S. (1997, May 9). Italy's glossies glam it up. *Women's Wear Daily,* 11.

Conti, S. (1998, June 19). A very moody Milano. *Women's Wear Daily,* 15–16.

Cox, B. (1999, April 16). Report: Web ad revenues grew to 1.5 billion in 1998. [On-line]. Available: http://www.internetnews.com/IAR/article/0,1087,archive_12_99181.00.html.

D'Innocenzio, A. (1998, June 12). The fashion TV boom. *Women's Wear Daily,* 16.

Daly, E. (1998, March 1). How to turn yesterday's giveaway into today's promotional power. *American Salesman, 43* (7)24, [On-line]. Available: http://www.elibrary.com.

Deconstructing Paris. (1998, April). *Vogue,* 148.

Department stores debate sales commission system. (1996, November). *Stores,* 37–38.

Diamond, J., and Diamond, E. (1997). *The world of fashion* (2nd ed.). New York: Fairchild.

Diamond, J., and Diamond, E. (1990). *Contemporary visual merchandising.* Upper Saddle River, NJ: Prentice-Hall.

Dickerson, K. G. (1995). *Textiles and apparel in the global economy* (2nd ed.). Englewood Cliffs, NJ: Merrill.

Direct Marketing Association, Inc. (1997a). *Protect your customers: The DMA's guidelines for personal information protection* [On-line]. Available: http://www.the-dma.org.

Direct Marketing Association, Inc. (1997b). Responsibly conquer a new frontier with the DMA's marketing online privacy principles and guidance. [On-line]. Available: http://www.the-dma.org.

Dowling, G. (1997, June 22). Do customer loyalty programs really work? *Sloan Management Review, 38* (12), 71.

Drakkar's driveaway. (1997, April 4). *Women's Wear Daily,* 10.

Drier, M., and Ozzard, J. (1997, April 24). Donna Karan: Global retailer. *Women's Wear Daily,* 6.

Dryden, J. (1997, March 17). Realising the potential of global electronic commerce, *Economic Co-Operation and Development Observer,* 20–25.

Du, F., Mergenhagen, P., and Lee, M. (1995, November 1). The future of services. *American Demographics, 17,* 30.

Dyches, B. (1996, August). The scent of a sales floor. *WWD Specialty Stores: A Special Report,* 87–88.

E-Commerce retail shopping report. (1998). [On-line]. Available: http://www.emarketer.com/estats.

Edmondson, B. (1998, March 1). In the drivers seat . . . *American Demographics,* (7), 46.

Educational attainment of people 25 year old and older by sex. (1997, March). *Current Population Survey, U.S. Census.* [On-line]. Available: http://www.bls.census.gov/cps/1997/educ_att.htm.

Elliott, S. (1995, August 29). Will Calvin Klein's retreat redraw the lines of taste? *New York Times,* D1, D8.

Elliott, S. (1998a, July 13). Ad giant forms interactive division. *New York Times on the Web* [On-line]. Available: http://www.nytimes.com/library/tech/98/07/biztech/articles/13advertising.html.

Elliott, S. (1998b, January 28). Advertising: Assessing the super bowl ads. *New York Times* [On-line]. Available: http://www.nytimes.com/yr/mo/day/news/financial/superbowl-ad-column.html.

Elliot, S. (1998c, June 24). Advertising: Rosy and getting rosier. *The New York Times on the Web* [On-line]. Available: http://www.nytimes.com/yr/mo/day/news/financial/forecast-ad-column.html.

Elliott, S. (1998d, June 25). Advertising: Study cites 6 categories of consumers worldwide. *New York Times* [On-line]. Available: http://www.nytimes.com/yr/mo/day/news/financial/consumer-research-ad-column.html.

Elliot, S. (1998e, August). Read, and watch, this travelogue. *New York Times* [On-line]. Available: htpp://www.nytimes.com/yr/mo/day/news/financial/travel-ad-column.html.

Elliott, S. (1998f, July 29). Xanax. Just do it. *New York Times* [On-line]. Available: http://www.nytimes.com/yr/mo/day/news/financial/drugs-ad-column.html.

Elliot, S. (1999, March 19). Marketers expect the high price of Oscar time to be worth it, *New York Times.*

Ellis, K., and Ozzard, J. (1997, February 25). WWDMAGIC. *Women's Wear Daily,* 18.

Emarketer Newsletter No. 38. (1998). [On-line]. Available: http://www.emarketer.com.

Emerson, K. (1995, August). How to win customers and influence sales associates. *Women's Wear Daily,* 38.

Engel, J. F., Warchaw, M. R., and Kinnear, T. C. (1994). Promotional strategy: Managing the marketing communications process. Burr Ridge, IL: Irwin.

Ever after Ferragamo. (1998, September). *Harper's Bazaar*, (24), 168.

Everett, J., and Swanson, K. (1993). *Guide to producing a fashion show.* New York: Fairchild.

Field of view marketing. (1998, March). *Marketing Tools, 5* (2), 10.

Fine, J., Dang, K., and Todé, C. (1997, May). Supply-side surge. Supply in demand [WWD supplement]. *Women's Wear Daily,* 20.

For the bookmark. (1998, March). *Marketing Tools, 5* (2), 11.

Fost, D. (1998, June 1). That's entertainment: Ways retailers enhance the shopping experience. *Marketing Tools, 5,* 36–42.

FTC Policy Statement regarding advertising substantiation. (1997, December 13). Federal Trade Commission [On-line]. Available: http://www.ftc.gov/ftc/mission.htm.

FTC Year in review. (1997). [On-line]. Available: http://www.webcom.com/lewrose/article/97ftc.html.

Furchgott, R. (1998, February 9). Mail order: Have I got a catalog for you. *Business Week* [On-line]. Available: http://www.elibrary.com.

Galbraith, R. (1997, February 26). The great redo. *Women's Wear Daily,* 12–13.

Getting data on customers. (1997, June). WWD Specialty Stores [A Special Report]. *Women's Wear Daily,* 20.

Glock, R. E., and Kunz, G. I. (1990). *Apparel manufacturing: Sewn product analysis.* New York: Macmillan.

Gold, A. (1978). *How to sell fashion.* New York: Fairchild.

GraphiCard debuts in U.S. (1997, June). WWD Specialty Stores [A Special Report]. *Women's Wear Daily,* 20.

Greenbaum, T. L. (1997, March 31). Internet focus groups: An oxymoron. *Marketing News, 31,* 35–36.

Greenwood, K. M., and Murphy, M. F. (1978). *Fashion Innovation and Marketing.* New York, NY: Macmillan.

The Ground Crew. (1997). The fashion report [On-line]. Available: users.aol.com/readfr/n4.html.

Gubernick, L. (1986, August 11). Through a glass brightly. *Forbes,* 98–99.

Heath, R. (1997, November, 21). An engraved invitation: Premium incentives and advertising specialties are increasing popular vehicles for getting the message across—and making it stick. *Marketing Tools, 4* (7) 36, [On-line]. Available: http://www.elibrary.com.

Hendron, J. (1997, January 20). Cosmetics firms offer virtual makeovers. *Marketing News, 31* (2), 17.

Hennies, J. (1997, October 1). On time, on target, on budget. *Marketing Tools, 4* (3), 58.

Hessen, W. (1997). Coach ads, logo go contemporary. *Women's Wear Daily,* 16.

Hinds, J. (1994, September 21). What it is: A trend. *Gannett News Service.* [On-Line]. Available: http://www.electriclibrary.com.

Holch, A. (1996, September 24). FIT: Putting its swatches on CD-ROM. *Women's Wear Daily,* 26.

Holusha, J. (1996, September 1). Times Square signs: For the great white way, more glitz. *New York Times* [On-line]. Available: http://www.search.nytimes.com.

Hye, J. (1997, September 10). Duck Head's virtual planning: A tool for expansion. *Women's Wear Daily,* 16.

In the middle. (1996, May 15). *Women's Wear Daily,* 8.

Industry snap shot. (1997, June 28). *Outdoor Advertising Association of America* [On-line]. Available: http://www.oaaa.org/np/ht/shot.htm.

Infomercials—multimedia communications. (1997, September 12). *National Infomercial Marketing Association* [On-line]. Available: http://www.eznet.com/~phillw/infomer.html.

Infomercials (1996, August). *Federal Trade Commission* [On-line]. Available: http://www.ftc.gov/bcp/conline/pubs/products/info.htm.

Ingrassia, J. (1995, September 18). Canada's ad industry self-regulation aids quality. *Advertising Age,* 28.

Innovative E-Merchandising Software. (1999). [On-line]. Available: http://www.modacad.com/products/products_frame.html.

Internet merchants seek new ways to improve on-line customer service. (1998, August). *Stores,* 62–63.

Internet shopping. (1998, January). *Stores* [an Ernst and Young Special Report]. Section 2, 1–28.

Investor relations. (1998, May 1). News release. *Canadian Corporate News* [On-line]. Available: http://192.139.46/scripts/ccn-release.pl?1998/05/01/0501bay1?cp=hbce.

Judy, P. (1996, July 15). Emerging trends to have huge impact on marketing. *Marketing News, 6.*

Kahle, D. (1997, April 1). Your most powerful sales tool. *American Salesman, 42,* (4), 16.

Kameda, N. (1993). 'Englishes' in cross-cultural communication. In S. M. Puffer, *Management across cultures: Insights from fiction and practice.* (119–130). Cambridge, MA: Blackwell.

Kaplan. D. (1997, February 24). What happens when it works? *Women's Wear Daily* (Section II), 9.

Kaufman, L. (1999, February 21). Playing catch-up at the on-line mall, *New York Times,* Section 3, 1, 6.

Kean, R. C. (1987). Definition of merchandising: Is it time for a change? In R. C. Kean (Ed.), *Theory building in apparel merchandising* (8-11). Lincoln: University of Nebraska-Lincoln.

Klepacki, L. (1998, January 9). Milani's multicultural moves. *Women's Wear Daily,* 8.

Kmart sets up new integrity pledge. (1996, April 12). *Women's Wear Daily,* 2.

Kneale, D. (1988, April 25). Zapping of TV ads appears pervasive. *Wall Street Journal,* 27.

Knowles, J. (1997, September 11). The role of advertising in the age of electronic retailing [On-line] Available: http://www.venable.com/govern/roleofad.htm.

Koenenn, C. (1998, March 25). Future-minded companies think she's the living trend. *The Dallas Morning News,* 3C.

Koprowski, G. (1997, August 1). In-house or outsource: When and how to hire (and fire) a marketing services agency. *Marketing Tools, 4,* (6), 42.

Krantz, M. (1996, July 15). Cashing in on tomorrow a generation after the Tofflers' future shock. *Time,* 52.

Krantz, M. (1998, July 20). Click till you drop. *Time,* 34–37, 40–41.

Krueger, R. A. (1988). *Focus groups: A practical guide to applied research.* Newbury Park, CA: Sage.

Kurt Salmon Associates. (1997, February 24). The ABC's of strategic alliances, *Women's Wear Daily* (Section II), 14–15.

L.L. Bean's on-line expansion. (1997, July 2). *Women's Wear Daily,* 11.

Larson, S. (1997, August 15). Treatment sampling follows scent strips onto magazine pages. *Women's Wear Daily,* 1, 4.

Lauren rings up $1.27 million in 4-day spring trunk show. (1997, February 3). *Women's Wear Daily,* 16.

Lauro, P. W. (1999, April 2). Advertising: New agency payments drive stake through heart of old commission. *New York Times on the Web.* [On-line]. Available: http://www.nytimes.com/yr/mo/day/news/financial/payments-ad-column.html.

Lee does L.A. lunch. (1996, August 22). *Women's Wear Daily,* 11.

Leonhardt, D. (1997, March 17). Two-tier marketing. *Business Week,* 82–87, 90.

Leventon, M. (1995, Spring). Professional concerns. *Costume Society of America News, 20* (4), 2–3.

Levere, J. (1999, January 29). Generation shaped by digital media presents fresh marketing challenges. *New York Times* [On-line]. Available: http://www.nytimes/com/yr/mo/day/news/financial/youth-ad-column.html.

Levy, A. (1997, March). Musical marketing. *Working Woman,* 14.

Lewison, D. M. (1997). *Retailing* (6th ed.). Upper Saddle River, NJ: Prentice-Hall.

Lifestyle Monitor. (1997, November 13). Courting and keeping the catalog customer. *Women's Wear Daily,* 2.

Lockwood, L. (1996a, September 27). The high price of fashion fame, *Women's Wear Daily,* 10.

Lockwood, L. (1996b, May 24). What will you read in 2006? *Women's Wear Daily,* 10, 15.

Lockwood, L. (1997a, March 21). The Latin connection. *Women's Wear Daily,* 16.

Lockwood, L. (1997b, May 23). The look of fall: Big budgets, big plans. *Women's Wear Daily,* 10–11.

Lockwood, L. (1998a, August 11). Cosmo's Fuller heading to Glamour. *Women's Wear Daily,* 2, 16.

Lockwood, L. (1998b, May 15). Fashion's deep pockets, *Women's Wear Daily,* section II., 4.

Lockwood, L. (1998c, June 19). New York's packaged deal. *Women's Wear Daily,* 14.

Love stories. (1996). *The Neiman Marcus Group Annual Report.*

Luchsinger, P. B., Mullen, V. S., and Jannuzzo, P. T. (1977). How many advertising dollars are enough? *Media Decisions, 12,* 59.

Macy's Calif. benefits for AIDS charities raised $2M. (1997, October 6). *Women's Wear Daily,* 15.

Maddox, K. (1998. August 3). Online advertising reaches $544.8 mil, a new report says. *Advertising Age* [On-line]. Available: http://www.adage.com/interactive/articles/19980803/article3.html.

Mahaffie, J. (1995, March 1). Why forecasts fail. *American Demographics, 17* (3), 34.

Majority of fortune 500 increasing PR budgets, study says. (1998, March 9). *Inside PR* [On-line]. Available: http://www.prcentral.com/ipr_mar9_98_budgets.htm.

Making the untraditional part of the Calvin Klein tradition. (1998, August 5). *Advertising Age* [On-line]. Available: http://www.adage.com/new_and_features/special_reports/power50-1996/fashion.html.

Malik, O. (1998, September 7). Out of the box. *Forbes* [On-line]. Available: http://www.forbes.com/forbes/98/0907/6205096a.htm.

Mandese, J. (1998, August 3). Media buying and planning. *Advertising Age,* s1, s18.

Marcus, L. (1978). *The American store window.* New York: Watson-Guptill.

Marcus, S. (1974). *Minding the store.* New York: Signet.

Market basket. (1996, July 9). *Women's Wear Daily,* 11.

Marx, W. (1995, October 1). The power of two . . . *Management Review, 84,* 36 [On-line]. Available: http://www.elibrary@infonautics.com.

Marx, W. (1994, November 1). Branding takes the credit. *Management Review, 83,* 33–34. [On-line]. Available: http://www.elibrary@infonatics.com.

Mazur, P. (1927). *Principles of organization applied to modern retailing.* New York: Harper and Brothers.

Mieszkoeski, K. (1998, April/May). The power of public relations. *Fast Company,* 182–188, 190, 192, 194, 196.

Mifflin, L. (1997, April 21). Ad industry to propose guidelines for internet marketing to children. *New York Times* [On-line]. Available: http://www.nytimes.com/library/cyber/week.

Miller, C. (1993, January 18). Scent as a marketing tool: Retailers—and even a casino—seek sweet smell of success. *Marketing News, 27,* 1–2.

Miller, C. (1996a, November 4). U.S. techniques not best for Chinese sales reps. *Marketing News,* 5.

Miller, C. (1996b, December 2). World leaders acknowledge hurdles to uniform market, chasing global dream, *Marketing News,* 1.

Mills, K. H., Paul, J. E., and Moormann, K. B. (1994). *Applied visual merchandising.* (3rd ed.). Upper Saddle River, NJ: Prentice-Hall.

Minzberg, H., and Waters, J. A. (1983). The mind of the strategist(s). In S. Srivastra, *The executive mind: New insights on managerial thought and action.* San Francisco: Josse-Bass Inc.

Moin, D. (1997, November 3). Macy's redo: Big expectations. *Women's Wear Daily,* 12.

Moin, D. (1998, August 5). Doneger's success stories. *Women's Wear Daily,* 27.

Monget, K. (1997, May 5). Promotion and party—It's Lingerie Week. *Women's Wear Daily,* 14.

Montague, C. (1993, March). How viewers feel about TV. *American Demographics.* [On-line]. Available: http://www.marketingtools.com/publications/AD/93_AD/9303_AD/AD138.htm.

Moore, W. S. (1998, February). Store of the Year: Elegance in the balance. *Visual Merchandising + Store Design* [On-line]. Available: http://www.visualstore.com/newstand/98/Holtrenfrew.html.

Multichannel TV trade group comissions global study. (1998, August). *Advertising Age International* [On-line]. Available: http://www.adage.com/international/daily/archives/19980824/intld19980824–11.html.

Munk, N. (1998, August 3). Gap gets it. *Fortune,* 68–82.

Napoli, L. (1999, February 8). Was the Victoria's Secret show a web failure? Hardly. *New York Times* [On-line]. http://www.nytimes.com/library/tech/99/02/biztech/articles/08adco.html.

New trends. (1995, May). WWD Trend Watch '96 [A Special Report]. *Women's Wear Daily,* 4.

New York Times pulls tobacco ads. (1999, April 28). *Advertising Age* [On-line]. Available: http://www.adage.com.

Newspaper Association of America and Audit Bureau of Circulations, ABC FAS-FAX. (1998). Top 20 US daily newspapers by circulation. [On-line]. Available: http://www.naa.org/info/facts/14.html.

Newspaper Association of America and McCann-Erickson. (1998). U.S. advertising expenditures—all media. [On-line]. Available: http://www.naa.org/info/facts/09.html.

Newspaper readership extends beyond the person who purchases the paper. (1996). *1996 Scarborough top 50 market reports, SRDS circulation 97* [On-line] Available: http://www.naa.org/info/whynewspapers/3.html.

Nicholson, K. (1997, October 27). A Ford in their future. *Women's Wear Daily,* 30–31.

1997 Radio marketing guide & fact book for advertisers. (1997). [On-line]. http://www.rab.com/station/radfact/radfact.html.

Norris, E. E. (1975, March 17) Seek out the consumer's problem. *Advertising Age*, 43–44.

Ogilvy, D. (1983). *Ogilvy on advertising*. New York: Crown.

Online classifieds real threat to newspapers. (1996, November 11). *Newsbytes News Network* [On-line]. Available: http://www.elibrary@compuserve.com.

On-line trade show. (1998, August 18). *New York Times*, B.

Optimedia, Prakit Publicis form joint venture in Thailand. (1998, July). *Advertising Age International* [On-line]. Available: http://www.adage.com/international/daily/archives/19980630/intld19980630–13.html.

Ozzard, J., and Feitelberg, R. (1996, June 27). As logos go global, counterfeiters unfurl the welcome mat. *Women's Wear Daily*, 1, 8–9.

Parr, K. (1996, October 31). The image makers. *Women's Wear Daily*, section II, 32.

Parr, K. (1997a, April 15). Joe Boxer: Have an ice day. *Women's Wear Daily*, 8.

Parr, K. (1997b, July 24). New catalogs target Gen Y. *Women's Wear Daily*, 12.

Parr, K. (1997c, October 23). Reviving Esprit's catalog. *Women's Wear Daily*, 11.

Parr, K. (1998, May 15). The global watch, *Women's Wear Daily*. Section II, 10.

Petrecca, L. (1998, July). Global network of the year: DDB Needham Worldwide, *Advertising Age* [On-line]. Available: http://www.adage.com/news_and_features/features19980330/article7.html.

Piirto, R. (1995, June). New markets for cable TV. *American Demographics* [On-line]. Available: http://www.marketingtools.com/AD/95_AD/9506_AD/AD763.HTM

Powerful marketing expands global reach for U.S. designers. (1996, October 28). *Women's Wear Daily*, 1, 22–23.

PR evaluation goes global. (1996, July 15). *Marketing News, 30* (15), 16.

Printemps offers skating cyberclerks. (1999, April 23). *Women's Wear Daily*, 8.

Protecting your intellectual property rights against knockoffs. (1995, September 7). Arent Fox [On-line]. Available: http://www.webcom.com/lewrose/article/interpro.html.

PRSA Facts. (1998). *Public Relations Society of America.* [On-line]. Available: http://www.prsa.org/facts.html.

Quick, R. (1999, February 5). Victoria's Secret 'cybercast' of underwear was hot, but many were left out in the cold. *Wall Street Journal Interactive Edition* [On-line]. http://interactive.wsj.com/articles/SB918146270332265500.htm.

QVC Corporate HQ. (1998, August 5). Corporate facts. *QVC Web site.* [On-line]. Available: http://www.qcv.com/hqfact.html.

Rabin, S. (1994, March). How to sell across cultures. *American Demographics* [On-line]. Available: http://www.demographics.com/publications/ad94_ad/9403_ad/ad545.htm.

Radman, D. (1997, July 1). Show and tell: using special events to communicate with your market. *Marketing Tools*, 4, (3), 58.

Ralph Lauren gives $10M for flag. (1998, July 13). *New York Times* [On-line]. Available: http://www.nytimes.com/aponline/w/AP-Mrs-Clinton-History.html.

Ramey, J. (1998, June 25). Sears: Younger image in Mexico. *Women's Wear Daily*, 14.

Raper, S. (1998, June 19). The French mix it up. *Women's Wear Daily*, 15–16.

Reda, S (1998, March). Reaching the aging boomers. *Stores*, 22–24.

Reeves, R. (1961). *Reality in advertising*. New York: Knopf.

Retsky, M. (1997, September 15). Making sense of intellectual property laws. *Marketing News*, 25.

Ricks, D. A. (1993). *Blunders in international business*. Cambridge, M.A.: Blackwell.

Ritchie, K. (1995, April). Marketing to generation X. *American Demographics* [On-line]. Available: http://www.marketingtools.com/Publications/AD/9504AF02.htm.

Rust, M. (1998, May). Sole man. *Vogue*, 126.

Schmidt, M. (1996, April). Improving sales associate selection with structured interviews. *Stores*, RR1–3.

Schnedler, D. E. (1996, March 22). Use strategic market models to predict customer behavior. *Sloan Management Review, 37*, 85–93.

Schneiderman, I. (1997, July 15). The need for speed at the register. *Women's Wear Daily*, 4.

Schoemaker, P. H. (1995, January 1). Scenario planning: A tool for strategic thinking. *Sloan Management Review, 36*, 26–41.

Schultz, D. (1993, January 18). Integrated marketing communications: Maybe definition is in the point of view, *Marketing News*, 17.

Schultz, D., and Barnes, B. (1995). *Strategic advertising campaigns*. Lincolnwood, IL: NTC Business Books.

Schwartz, E. (1998, August 10). Affiliate networks: Letting other sites do your marketing. *New York Times* [On-line]. Available: http://www.nytimes.com/library/tech/yr/mo/biztech/articles/10view.html.

Scoop du Jour. (1997, January 22). *Women's Wear Daily,* 7.

Sears, Wal-Mart unveil co-branded Mastercards. (1996, October). *Women's Wear Daily,* 12.

Seckler, V. (1997, January 16). Futurist Alvin Toffler: Information explosion to shock retail world, *Women's Wear Daily,* 1, 29.

Seckler, V. (1998, May 26). Consumer study reveals stores' flaws. *Women's Wear Daily,* 9.

Seckler, V., Edelson, S., and Moin, D. (1997, October 6). Retailers: In the front lines. *Women's Wear Daily,* 2, 4.

Seiler, M., and Martinez, J. (1997, July 1). Leads on the line: Using inbound/outbound telemarketing to manage the leads-to-prospects-to-customers cycle. *Marketing Tools, 4* (7), 20–25.

Seo, D. (1998, May 14). Advertising and marketing: Ad agencies sponsor new image. *Los Angeles Times* [On-line]. Available: http://www.elibrary@infonautics.com.

September event at Saks to spotlight British fashion. (1998, August). *Women's Wear Daily/Global,* 12.

Services, service analyses: Advertising. (1997, June 30). *World Trade Press* [On-line]. Available: http://www.electriclibrary.com.

Sheehy, G. (1995). *New passages: Mapping your life across time.* New York: Random House.

Shermach, K. (1997b, June 9). What consumers wish brand managers knew. *Marketing News, 31* (12), 9, 17.

Show me the clothes: Store displays are the primary source of clothing ideas. (1997). *Women's Wear Daily* (From Cotton Incorporated's Lifestyle Monitor), 2.

Simmons study of media & markets for spring 1997. (1998). [On-line]. Available. http://www.amic.com/amic_mem/scoreboard/sm97sa.html.

Simon, J.A., and Arndt, J. (1980). The shape of the advertising response function, *Journal of Advertising Research, 20* (4), 11–28.

Simon, J. L. (1971). *The management of advertising.* Englewood Cliffs, NJ: Prentice-Hall.

Singer, N. (1997, August 29). Once decadent, now de rigueur. *Women's Wear Daily,* 10.

Socha, M. (1997, October 3). Ellen Tracy takes to the tube. *Women's Wear Daily,* 12.

Socha, M. (1998, May 5). Levi's new ads play the name game. *Women's Wear Daily,* 16.

Sorkin, A. (1998, April 30). Advertising: Britain's yellow pages blanket London. *New York Times* [On-line]. Available: http://www.nytimes.com/yr/mo/day/news/financial/yellowpage-ad-column.html.

South China city bans tobacco ads. (1998, August 6). *Advertising Age* [On-line]. Available: http://www.adage.com/international/index.html.

Specialty stores dress up with fixtures. (1998, January). *Chain Store Age,* 86–87.

Spindler, A. (1998, July 21). In Paris couture, the spectacle's the thing. *New York Times* [On-line]. Available: http://www.nytimes.com/yr/mo/day/nws/style/paris-fashion.html.

Statutes relating to consumer protection mission. (1997, December 13). *Federal Trade Commission* [On-line]. Available: http://www.ftc.gov/ftc/mission.htm.

Steinberg, J. (1970). *Customers don't bite.* New York: Fairchild.

Stewart-Allen, A. (1996, November 18). Customer care. *Marketing News,* 17.

Stewart-Allen, A. (1997, January 6). Keys to success in Europe's massive mail-order market. *Marketing News, 31* (1), 17.

The strength of color. (1995). *The Newspaper Society* [On-line]. Available: http://www.naa.org/info/whynewspapers/13.html.

Style gazing: How a fashion forecasting service looks into the future. (1997, February). *The Magic Guide* [Show guide] MAGIC International, 6200 Canoga Ave, Suite 303, Woodland Hills, CA 91367.

Swasy, A. (1990, December 6) How innovation at P&G restored luster to washed-up Pert and made it no. 1. *Wall Street Journal,* B1.

Sykes, J., and Pepe, M. (1998, August 3). Fortune smiles. *Fortune* [On-line]. Available: http://www.pathfinder.com/fortune/pfortune/0803edd.html.

Tate, S. (1989). *Inside fashion design.* New York, NY: Fairchild.

Tedeschi, B. (1998, August 21). A growing ad strategy: "click to win!" *New York Times* [On-line]. Available: http://www.nytimes.com.

Telemarketing cited as chief form of direct marketing. (1996, January 1). *Marketing News,* 9.

Television Bureau of Canada. (1998). *Resources and Video Services.* [On-line]. Available: http://www.tvb.ca/resources.htm.

Tema-Lyn, L. (1997, March 31). All the world's a stage, and the players are marketers. *Marketing News, 31,* 12.

The ten top grossing infomercials for 1997. (1998, January 4). *Business Wire* [On-line]. Available: http://www.elibrary.com.

Think New Ideas goes global. (1998, July). *Advertising Age* [On-line], Available: http://www.adage.com/interactive/daily/archives/19980707/id/19980707-11.html.

Tillotson, K. (1998, January 31). Selling futures. *Star Tribune,* 1E.

Timberland taps Cone for brand values promotion. (1998, August 17). *Inside PR* [On-line]. Available: http://www.prcentral.com/ipr_aug17_98_timberland.htm.

Todé, C. (1998, January 9). Bathroom chic goes mail order. *Women's Wear Daily,* 10.

Toevs, R. (1994, December). Shooter's guide. *Visual Merchandising + Store Design,* 33–40.

Topolnicki, D. M. (1998, July/August). Is retail dying? *Working Woman,* 48–51.

Tosh, M. (1996, April 3). New Wal-Mart software allows tailored planograms. *Women's Wear Daily,* 16.

Tosh, M. (1997, December 31). Federated reprograms sales training. *Women's Wear Daily,* 8.

Tracking U.S. trade. (1998, February 19). *Center for the Study of Western Hemispheric Trade: A Quarterly Trade News Service for the Americas.* [On-line]. Available: http://www.lanic.utexas.edu/cswht/tradeindex.html.

Trout, J. (1995). *The new positioning.* New York: McGraw-Hill.

Trout, J., and Ries, A. (1972, April 24). The positioning era cometh. *Advertising Age,* 35–38.

Turley, L., and Kelley, S. (1997, December 22). A comparison of advertising content: Business to business versus consumer services. *Journal of Advertising, 26,* 39–49.

21 ad agencies endorse copy-testing principles. (1982, February 19). *Marketing News, 17.* p. 1.

Tyre, P. (1997, April 8). TV, Internet giving fashion magazines a run for their money. *Style* [On-line]. Available: http://cnn,com/style/9704/08/fashion.media/index.html.

Uchitelle, L. (1988a, April 30). Globalization has not severed corporations' national links. *New York Times.* [On-line]. Avilable: http://www.nytimes.com/yr/mo/day/news/financial/global-econ.html.

Uchitelle, L. (1998b, April 30). World economy is as interconnected today as is 1913. *New York Times.* [On-line]. Available: http://www.nytimes.com/yr/mo/day/news/financial/global-1913.html.

Updike, E. H., and Schatz, R. D. (1997, October 13). Enterprise: Marketing: Advertising: Shhh-my TV commercial is on. *Business Week, 3548,* ENT4.

Veronis, Suhler and Associates. (1997, July). *Communication industry forecast* (11th ed.) [On-line]. Available: http://www.208.16.54.216/publications/forecast/highlights.html.

Visa Europe account in review. (1998, June). *Advertising Age* [On-line]. Available: http://www.adage.com/news_and_features/dealine/archives/19980630/dd19980630-18.html.

Walker, C. (1996, May 1). Can TV save the planet? *American Demographics, 18.* 42. [On-line]. Available: http://www.elibrary@infonautics.com.

Waldrop, J. (1994, May 1). Advertising that works. *American Demographics, 16,* 48. [On-line]. Available: http://www.elibrary@infonautics.com.

Webb, C. H. (Ed.). (1995). *Handbook for alumni administration.* Phoenix, AZ: Oryx.

Weil, J., and Fallon, J. (1998, September 4). Body Shop's hemp paraphernalia seized in France. *Women's Wear Daily,* 7.

Weishar, J. (1998, December/January). Moving targets: Customer's traffic flow patterns, *Fashion Group International Bulletin.* 1–2.

Weisman, K. (1996a, October 10). Paris polishes its act. *Women's Wear Daily,* 5.

Weisman, K. (1996b, September 24). Prêt-à-porter exhibits a global panache. *Woman's Wear Daily,* 19.

Wells, W., Burnett, J., and Moriarty, S. (1998). *Advertising principles and practice* (4th ed.). Upper Saddle River, NJ: Prentice-Hall.

White, C. (1997a, December 11). At the Met, a golden melting pot. *New York Times* [On-line]. Available: http://www.nytimes.com/yr/mo/day/news/style/versace-opening.html.

White, C. (1997b, August 19). A shoe giveaway. *New York Times* [On-line]. Available: http://www.nytimes.com.

White, C. (1998a). Shift in New York shows. *New York Times* [On-line]. Available: http://www.nytimes.com/yr/mo/day/news/style/patterns-fashion.html.

White, C. (1998b, April 1). The runway via the Internet and CD-ROM. *New York Times* [On-line]. http://www.nytimes.com/library/style/040198ny-fashion.html.

Wilson, E. (1998, March 24). 7th on Sixth signs GM as sponsor. *Women's Wear Daily,* 2, 27.

Wired to spend. (1998, February 19). Echo Boomers: The power of Y [Advertising Supplement]. *Women's Wear Daily,* 4.

Youmans, J. (1997, March 28). What does it mean to be "middle class"? University of Alabama Center for Business and Economic Research [On-line]. Available: http://www.cba.ua.edu/~cber/middle2.html.

Young, J. W. (1975). *A technique for producing ideas* (3rd ed.). Chicago: Crain Books.

Young, V. (1997, November 7). Web wars. *Women's Wear Daily,* 10.

Young, V. (1998, September 14). Copycat suits increase with competition. *Women's Wear Daily,* 20–21.

Zimmerman, D. (1997, August 13). Bloomingdale's video link. *Women's Wear Daily,* 14.

Zimmermann, K. (1997a, July 2). Neiman Marcus seeking expanded loyalty program. *Women's Wear Daily,* 11.

Zimmermann, K. (1997b, August 20). Nordstrom tests loyalty. *Women's Wear Daily,* 20.

Zimmermann, K. (1998a, April 29). Airshop's new data mining. *Women's Wear Daily,* 16.

Zimmermann, K. (1998b, January 21). Carson's database marketing. *Women's Wear Daily,* 14.

Zimmermann, K. A. (1998, August 19). A Hugo Boss CD for sales. *Women's Wear Daily,* 17.

GLOSSARY

Account management division   The division within an agency that works with the client, interpreting the client's needs to agency personnel.

Action research   A one-time study with a very narrow application.

Ad specialties   See *premium.*

Adjacencies   Radio commercials sold at a premium rate, to run just before or after a program.

Advertising   Any nonpersonal information paid for and controlled by the sponsoring organization.

Advertising agencies   Outside organizations hired to assist a company in achieving its promotional goals.

Advertising calendar   A guide that identifies when, where, and what items will be advertised.

Advertising campaign   A series of multiple messages, focused on a central theme or concept, presented in a variety of media.

Advertising department   The department of a company responsible for planning, creating, placing advertising in the media, and evaluating the effectiveness of ads.

Affiliate networks   On-line networks that entice on-line shoppers to click over to another website to make a purchase.

Affiliates   Regional television stations.

All one can afford   A budgeting method in which the portion of the operational budget allocated to promotional activities is the amount the firm can financially manage to spend.

Amplification   Information that fills out the rest of a story following the lead.

Angled front window   A store window that is recessed from the sidewalk, which provides more exposure to display space.

Animation   A production technique that uses illustrated figures, such as cartoon characters or puppets—inanimate objects that come to life.

Anniversary celebration   An occurrence used by companies to bring attention to their longevity in the community.

Appeals   The reasons to buy given by the advertiser.

Applied research   The use of scientific methods to solve a problem that already exists.

Approach   The way an advertiser chooses to present an appeal.

Arbitrary allocation   A budgeting method in which the budget is determined by management solely on the basis of executive judgment.

Arcade front window   A spacious display space with a variety of configurations, normally found in downtown shopping districts.

Assignment editor   An individual who has control over the flow of information and assignments and, as such, is probably the best connection at a broadcast news outlet.

Assistant editor   An individual who is responsible for reading all press releases submitted to a media organization and reporting the newsworthy pieces to the more senior editors.

Associate editor   A reporter who is assigned to cover certain topics and events.

Associate producer   A specialist in a particular subject, working for a producer.

Assortment advertisement   A sponsored message featuring a range of merchandise.

Audits   Formal reports of activities, which may be performed internally or externally.

Baby boomer   A consumer born between the years of 1946 and 1964.

Background   The foundation, real or implied, where a display is built; a back wall can serve as the base for a background.

Bank of windows   Several windows at the front of a store.

Banner advertisements   See *on-line advertisements.*

Behavioristic segmentation   A method of segmenting markets based on consumer usage, loyalty, or buying responses to a product or service.

Best time available (BTA)   See *run-of-schedule.*

Bias   Prejudiced results occurring because of problems with research methodology design.

Bleed pages   A technical feature of a magazine advertisement that allows the dark or colored background to extend to the edge of the page

Blink ads   One-second commercials.

Bonus   A sum of money or the equivalent given to an employee in addition to the employee's usual compensation.

Bonus pack   Extra amounts of a product, given in addition to what is expected.

Bottom-up approaches   Budgeting methods that consider a firm's goals and objectives and assign a portion of the budget to meet those objectives.

Bounce-back coupon   A coupon that is good for redemption of the same product.

Brand   Any name, trademark, logo, or visual symbol that identifies a product or group of products by a specific manufacturer or identifies a specific retailer and helps to differentiate the product(s) or retailer(s) from competitors.

Broadsheet   The large standard size newspaper format, six columns wide.

Brokered list   Customer inventories offered for sale or rent through negotiation of a contract in return for a fee or commission to a list broker.

Buying allowance   A price reduction on merchandise purchased during a limited time period.

Buying and selling process   The method used by a salesperson to encourage a customer to reach a buying decision about a product or service.

Buying signal   A statement or action by which a customer will often signify that he or she is ready to close a sale.

Camera ready   Paste-up that is ready to go to the printer.

Cash wrap   A counter at which transactions such as ringing up the sale and handing over merchandise take place.

Category week   An occurrence that features a merchandise category or brand; also known as a *vendor week*.

Celebrity appearance   The physical presence of a well-known individual from inside or outside the fashion industry to promote a new product or designer line.

Channels   The methods by which a message is translated.

Chat lines   On-line discussions with celebrities from a network's programs.

Classic   A trend that endures over a long period of time, undergoing only minor changes as it progresses through the product life cycle.

Clearance advertising   Sponsored messages promoting end-of-the-month or end-of-the-season stock.

Clients   Persons seeking recognition for their products or service.

Clipping service   A service that cuts out competitors' advertisements from local or national print media to track spending.

Closed-back window   A store window with a completely contained display space.

Co-branding   A cooperative effort in which a card issuer that wants to increase volume combines with a consumer company to develop a credit card.

Code of ethics   A procedure of conduct a company intends to follow and expects from its employees, clients, vendors, and/or customers.

Color story   A collection of fashion, staple, warm, cool, neutral, and dark colors, coordinated for the upcoming season and different from the preceding season.

Co-marketing   Cooperative efforts whereby a manufacturer and retailer join forces to increase the revenue and profits for both parties.

Commentary   The oral delivery of information at a fashion show used to identify trends of the season.

Commentary card   An index card on which commentary is written.

Commentator   The individual who is responsible for commentary.

Commercial advertising   Sponsored messages directed toward the profit-making sector.

Commission   A percentage of money given to an agent who assists in a business transaction.

Communication   A transmission or exchange of information and/or messages.

Competitive parity   A budgeting method in which the amount of money that a competitor spends on promotion is used as a guide to set budgets.

Comprehensive   A realistic impression of a final ad.

Computer based training programs CD-ROM based sales training programs established by Federated Department Stores.

Concentrated marketing A marketing strategy that offers the promotional mix to the target segment with the greatest potential for success, regardless of size.

Consumer behavior The study of consumers' decision-making processes, as they acquire, consume, and dispose of goods and services.

Consumer jury A group of 50 to 100 target customers who are interviewed individually or in small groups to evaluate promotional effectiveness.

Consumerism A set of activities monitored by government, businesses, and independent organizations designed to protect the rights of consumers.

Consumer-oriented sales promotion A sales promotion aimed at the ultimate consumer.

Consumption The process of acquiring, using, and discarding products.

Contests Promotions in which consumers compete for a prize based on skill and ability.

Continuity A scheduling method using a steady placement of advertisements over a designated period of time.

Contract A legal agreement establishing a fee for limited services based upon specific activities.

Control ads Sponsored messages that have been evaluated extensively over a period of time and provide a basis for comparing the effectiveness of test ads.

Cooperative advertising An agreement in which a manufacturer works with a retailer to develop an ad and shares in the cost of running that advertisement.

Cooperative promotion Activities jointly planned and paid for by two members of the distribution channel.

Copy The verbal component of a print advertisement.

Copy platform A document, typically prepared by an account representative or creative manager, that specifies the basic foundation of the creative strategy.

Copyright The legal right granted to an author, a composer, a playwright, a publisher, or a distributor to exclusive publication, production, sale, or distribution of a literary, musical, dramatic, or artistic work.

Corner front window A store window located in such a way that it faces two streets that are perpendicular to each other; as a result it can be viewed from either street.

Cost per point (CPP) See *cost per ratings point.*

Cost per ratings point (CRP) A measurement determined by dividing the cost of commercial time by the program rating.

Cost per thousand (CPM) A measurement determined by dividing the medium's audience into the cost for space or time, that is, the cost of attracting 1,000 readers, viewers, or listeners.

Cost-plus agreement A pay rate based upon cost of the work plus an agreed-on profit margin, normally a percentage of total costs.

Counter top signs Signs that are placed on top of showcases to highlight merchandise displayed.

Coupons Printed forms or vouchers that entitle the bearer to certain benefits, such as a cash refund or a gift when redeemed.

Cover position The first page, the inside back cover, and the back cover of a magazine, which are sold at a premium advertising rate.

Coverage The potential audience that might receive the message through a media outlet.

Covered publicity Situations of interest to the general public, written in the form of a publicity release.

Created audience A group that is established after a fashion show is planned, as a result of publicity and advertising.

Created publicity Situations that may, by themselves, have little news value but are made newsworthy by creating a special event around them.

Creative boutique An agency that provides only creative services, such as innovative layout, logo, or graphic design.

Creative services division The division of a full-service agency responsible for the creation and the execution of advertisements.

Creative strategy A plan for determining what an advertising message will say.

Creative tactics Steps for implementing an advertising message.

Creativity A quality manifested in individuals that enables them to generate clever or imaginative approaches or new solutions to problems.

Cross-ruff coupon   A coupon that is good for redemption of a different product manufactured by the same producer.

Cross-selling   The sale of additional products and services to the same customer.

Cubes   Box-style fixtures used for consumer self-selection of merchandise.

Culture   A set of socially acquired behavior patterns of a particular society of people.

Cumulative audience   The total number of different people who are exposed to a schedule of commercials.

Customer directories   Directories of customer names, addresses, telephone numbers, and important details of a customer's purchases and preferences, compiled by a salesperson.

Database   A collection of data arranged for ease and speed of search and retrieval.

Dayparts   Television or radio time periods used in buying and selling advertisements.

Decode   The process by which a receiver transforms a message back into thought.

Decorative props   Items used to establish a mood or theme for the merchandise, including such things as baskets, plants, flags, banners, and musical instruments.

Decorative roles   Inclusion of a man, woman, or child in an advertisement with no purpose other than to look attractive.

Deferred billing   The opportunity for a consumer to postpone or delay payment of a purchase.

Demographics   The statistics used to study a population.

Departmental advertisements   Sponsored messages presenting merchandise from a specific department.

Departmental stories   Articles written from the viewpoint of a specific section or column of a newspaper, such as fashion, lifestyle, travel, state and local, finance, sports, or entertainment, among others.

Design division   The division of a company, headed by a designer, responsible for designing and producing a minimum of four collections or lines of garments each year.

Differentiated marketing   A marketing strategy that offers a different promotion mix to two or more select target markets.

Digital video effects units   Production units that are able to manipulate graphics, music, and sound.

Diminishing returns model   A model with a concave-downward shape, demonstrating that advertising expenditures will increase sales to a point, after which the benefits of additional advertising expenses will diminish.

Direct marketing   The process by which organizations communicate directly with target customers to generate a response or transaction.

Direct marketing agencies   Agencies that provide services necessary to conduct direct marketing activities, including research, database management, creative assistance, direct mail, media services, and production capabilities.

Direct premium   A gift attached to or placed inside the promoted item and available immediately to the consumer upon purchase.

Direct sellers   Companies that sell directly to the consumer.

Direct-response   The method of distribution in which a sale or solicitation is initiated and completed through advertisements or promotions that require a direct reply.

Direct-response advertising   Sponsored messages offering merchandise through nonstore sales sponsors.

Direct-response media   Mail, telephone, magazine, Internet, radio, or television messages that provide a means of responding directly to the advertiser.

Direct-response driver-consumers   Drivers with cell phones.

Direct-to-consumer   Sales messages aimed at the consumer.

Discretionary income   Personal income available after taxes and necessities have been paid for.

Display   The physical exhibits of merchandise and support materials.

Disposable income   Personal income available after taxes.

Distribution channel   The path through which goods are dispersed from raw materials producers to retailers.

Domain names   Unique Internet names assigned on a first-come, first-served basis by a company called InterNIC.

Dressers   Preparation assistants for the models at a fashion show.

Dressing area The place where models get ready before, and change during, a fashion show.

Drive time The period when radio listenership is the highest, usually between 6:00 A.M. and 9:00 A.M. and 4:00 P.M. and 7:00 P.M..

Early majority Early adopters who purchase during the acceleration phase of a fashion.

Echo boomers Consumers born between the years 1980 and 1987.

Editor The person responsible for maintaining the editorial focus for a news organization.

Editor-in-chief The person in charge of all aspects of reporting the news at a newspaper or magazine.

E-commerce Transactions of business based on the electronic transmission of data over communications networks such as the Internet.

Encoding A combination of words or symbols to be presented orally or in written/visual form by the sender.

Essential expenditure An expense that is primary or necessary to produce an event.

Ethics The rules or standards governing the conduct of a person or the members of a profession.

Event bonus A premium paid above the fixed fee, if the attendance goal for an event is exceeded.

Event diary A document chronicling all of the planning, budgeting, and implementation processes of an activity; also called a *show diary.*

Event sponsorship A company's support of an event through monetary and/or in-kind contributions as a way to meet one or more of its corporate objectives.

Exchange The ambition and interest to give up something in replacement for something else.

Exhibit booth A small exhibit space with temporary walls and fixtures used by manufacturers to sell products at trade shows.

Exterior display The outside appearance of a storefront; also known as the façade display.

External audit An evaluation conducted by a consultant or client from outside the audited organization.

Eye camera A piece of equipment that tracks eye movements with infrared light sensors as a subject reads an advertisement.

Fact sheet A detailed glossary of significant facts contained in a press kit.

Fad A very short-lived trend.

Fashion The prevailing style or expression that is popular at any given period of time.

Fashion count A research method used to survey what people are currently wearing.

Fashion department The department involved in developing the fashion image for a company.

Fashion director The individual at a retail organization responsible for fashion direction and leadership.

Fashion forecaster A professional who works for a fashion forecasting service or the forecasting division within a retail, manufacturing, or advertising firm.

Fashion innovators Early adopters who will adopt a trend at the very earliest opportunity.

Fashion laggers Earlier adopters within the regression stage of the product life cycle.

Fashion show A presentation of apparel, accessories, and other products to enhance personal attractiveness on live models to an audience.

Fashion show planning calendar A guide that identifies locations, themes, dates, and times for planned fashion shows; used by fashion and sales staffs to plan and perform the various steps in fashion show production.

Fashion show production agencies Agencies that provide services necessary to present fashion shows.

Fashion specialists Later adopters who will accept a trend as it begins to rise in popularity.

Fashion theme calendar A guide that indicates fashion trends and creative interpretations of basic categories.

Fashion trend The visible direction in which fashion is moving, such as a color, a fabric, or a style characteristic apparent for the coming season.

Fashion trend portfolio A series of visual boards, slides, videos, or kits, projecting major trends in silhouettes, fabrics, colors, patterns, accessory treatments, catch phrases, and theme ideas.

Feasibility study A survey to determine if a plan has potential to be successful.

Feature story A prominent or lead article in a newspaper or magazine.

Federal Trade Commission Act   1914 act creating the FTC to enforce antitrust and consumer protection laws.

Fee-commission combination   A fee system in which media commissions are credited against a fee.

Feedback   A receiver's response to a sender.

Fiber optics   The technology of light transmission through very fine, flexible glass or plastic fibers.

Financial control division   The division of an organization responsible for administering the budget and handling all of the financial functions, such as payroll, accounts receivable, accounts payable, and inventory control.

Fixed-fee rate   A basic monthly rate charged by an agency for all of its services.

Fixtures   A wide variety of furniture and equipment designed to hold and display merchandise.

Floor plan   A scale drawing of the walls, fixtures, and other architectural elements of a selling space.

Focus group   A carefully planned discussion designed to obtain perceptions on a defined area of interest in a nonthreatening environment.

Font   The complete range of capitals, small capitals, lowercase letters, numerals, punctuation marks, and other characters for a particular typeface and size.

Ford   A best-selling trend with strong customer demand, available at several different price points, and produced by many different manufacturers.

Forecaster   A nonspecific title given to any individual within an organization who is responsible for trend identification and image.

Forecasting   The activity of projecting trends.

Formal runway show   A fashion show that presents merchandise as a parade with the audience seated at the perimeter of the runway.

Frequency   The number of times the receiver is exposed to a media outlet within a specified period of time.

Frequent-buying program   See *reward program.*

Full commentary   A form of commentary in which every word is written on the cards as a script prior to a fashion show.

Full-service agency   A firm that offers a full range of marketing, communications, and promotion services.

Functional props   Physical supports, such as mannequins and furniture, used to hold merchandise.

Fur Products Labeling Act   Legislation (1951) that governs fur product labeling to specify, among other things, the English name of the animal from which the fur was taken.

Futurists   Professionals who make long-range forecasts for many industries.

Gallery exhibit   A presentation of fashion items in an artistic setting at a gallery.

Gatefold   A special kind of magazine insert, created by extra-long paper with the sides folded into the center to match the size of the other pages.

General stories   Articles prepared for the main news section of a newspaper, including changes in a company's policy, administration or personnel, business-related news, and announcements or special events of interest to the general public.

Generation X   The twentysomething generation, aged 20 to 35 years.

Generic brand   Merchandise that is not trademarked or lacks a logo to establish a unique identity.

Geographic segmentation   A differentiated marketing strategy based on geographic breakdowns such as regions, metropolitan statistical area (MSA) size, density of population, and climate.

Gift-with-purchase program   An incentive program in which consumers are offered a special gift if they buy merchandise over a certain dollar amount.

Global advertising   Sponsored messages available throughout the world.

Global brand   A trademarked or brand name product broadly distributed throughout many parts of the world.

Global marketing   International marketing activities.

Global promotion   Promotional programs aimed at consumers in several different countries and implemented by manufacturers and retailers of internationally distributed merchandise.

Globalization   The integration of international trade and foreign investment.

Glocalization   A combination of global branding practices and localized marketing.

Goals   The end results that a business wants to achieve, usually in the long term.

Greeting approach   A pleasant salutation expressing good wishes to the individual.

Grid cards   A multilevel rate card for radio advertising, in which the rates for each time period vary, week to week, depending upon available air time.

Gross ratings points (GRPs)   The sum of all ratings delivered by a commercial schedule.

Guaranteed audience   A group that is established before a fashion show is planned, made up of individuals who will attend regardless of the fashions shown.

Guaranteed audience plan   See *total audience plan.*

Halftone illustration   A drawing using shades or tones created by watercolor, chalk, pencil, markers, or other art medium to illustrate an image with tonal qualities.

Hard sell   The sales approach that pushes customers to buy a product they may not want.

Hatbox show   A very informal fashion show that utilizes a small space and a limited budget.

Headline   The boldest statement of an advertisement.

High-definition television (HDTV)   Crystal-clear television visuals achieved through higher resolution.

Human resources division   The division of an organization responsible for hiring, training, monitoring legal issues and, if necessary, firing personnel.

Ideal charts   Lists of all categories of merchandise that will be represented in a fashion show.

Illustration   Visual matter used to clarify or decorate text in an advertisement.

Image advertising   Sponsored messages that create an identity for a product or service by emphasizing a symbolic association with certain values, lifestyles, or an ideal.

Image consultants   Individuals who sell products to enhance personal attractiveness in a direct sales approach.

IMC objectives   See *integrated marketing (IMC) communications objectives.*

Impromptu commentary   Commentary created spontaneously during a fashion show using cards as brief cues.

Impulse buying   Buying that occurs when no previous need recognition has taken place before the purchase is made.

In-bound call   A phone response initiated by a consumer.

Incentive   Something put in place to induce action or motivate effort.

Incentive program   Motivational tools generally designed to increase the sales productivity of sales associates at the retail level.

Incentive-based compensation   A compensation system that ties payments to performance.

Infomercial   A program-length product demonstration that often looks like a TV show.

Informal fashion show   A fashion show that presents merchandise on models in a casual environment.

In-house list   Customer inventories developed, owned, and maintained by a company participating in direct marketing activities.

Inner-driven consumers   A VALS consumer group comprised of I-am-me's, experimentalists, and socially conscious consumers.

Insert   A newspaper advertisement printed on high-quality paper stock.

Instant coupon   A form placed on the outside of a package to encourage the consumer to immediately redeem the coupon.

Institutional advertising   Sponsored messages geared toward building the reputation of a firm, enhancing civic sponsorship and community involvement, and developing long-term relationships between customers and the firm.

Institutional events   Occurrences produced to enhance the company image, exhibit good corporate citizenship, embellish customer relations, contribute to the community's economic development, or promote a charitable cause.

In-store exhibit   A special presentation of fashion items in a retail setting that are used to entice regular and new customers into a shop.

In-store sampling   Distribution of samples in the retail environment.

In-store show   A fashion show presented for the benefit of store employees, in order to inform the staff of new and exciting trends for the upcoming season.

Integrated consumers   A VALS consumer group comprised of self-actualized consumers.

Integrated marketing communications (IMC)   A concept of marketing communications planning that recognizes the added value of a comprehensive plan that evaluates the strategic roles of a variety of communication disciplines.

Integrated marketing communications (IMC) objectives   Statements about what various aspects of the IMC program will accomplish.

Integrity pledge   A statement that prohibits employees from accepting any gifts, samples, loans, free travel, and entertainment or other benefits.

Interactive television (ITV)   A form of television entertainment in which the signal activates an electronic apparatus in the viewer's home or the viewer uses the apparatus to affect events on the screen, or both, allowing for viewer control.

Internal audit   An evaluation conducted by a firm's human resources personnel, superiors, and peers to determine the performance of an employee and his or her programs.

Interior display   Presentation of merchandise on variety of architectural forms, fixtures, and furniture inside of a store.

Jingle   A catchy verse or song with an easy rhythm that is used to create a verbal link to a product.

Knockoffs   Products that copy either the shape or design created by a well-known company, but do not bear that company's name.

Late majority   Later adopters who purchase items during the general acceptance phase of a trend.

Laws   The body of rules and principles governing the actions of individuals or organizations and enforced by a political authority.

Layout   The arrangement of the physical elements of art, copy, and white space within the boundaries of a print advertisement.

Lead   One or two sentences in a publicity release that summarize the news, including who, what, where, when, and how.

Ledges   Display areas located behind islands created by showcases, generally in the cosmetic and accessory departments or behind cash wrap desks.

Lighting   Illumination of the display or selling area.

Line drawing   An illustration using lines to represent the pictorial image.

Line-up   A list of models in the order in which they will appear and in the outfits they will be wearing.

Live action   A production technique that portrays people, animals, and objects as lifelike in everyday situations.

Local advertising   Sponsored messages developed for an immediate trading area.

Logos   Graphic symbols or distinctive typefaces that represent a company's name, mark, or emblem.

Mail-in premium   A gift that requires the consumer to send in a proof-of-purchase to receive the item.

Management and finance division   The division of a full-service agency that handles commercial operations, including managing the office, billing clients, making payments to the various media, and controlling personnel issues.

Mannequin modeling   A form of informal modeling in which the model acts as a live mannequin in a store window or on a display platform.

Manufacturer's sales representative   A personal sales associate at the wholesale level.

Market research   The process of gathering data on consumers' preferences.

Market research companies   Research organizations that gather information about a firm's clients to enable the advertiser to plan and evaluate its advertising and promotion programs.

Market segmentation   The subdivision of the marketplace into relatively homogeneous subsets of consumers.

Marketing   The process of planning and executing the conception, pricing, promotion, and distribution of ideas, goods, and services to create exchanges that satisfy individual and organizational objectives.

Marketing mix   The coordination of the four P's—product, price, place, and promotion.

Marketing objectives   Statements that specify what is to be accomplished by the overall marketing program within a short time period and that are expressed as part of the planning process.

Maslow's Hierarchy of Needs   A motivation theory based on five levels of needs: basic physiological, safety and security, love and belonging, esteem, and self-actualization.

Mass communication   The channels through which a message is sent to many people at once through a widely viewed broadcast or print media.

Mass market A large group of consumers with similar needs.

Mean income The average value of all incomes within a sample.

Mechanical See *paste-up.*

Media buying services Independent firms that exclusively handle purchasing media time, primarily for radio and television.

Media division The division of a full-service agency that analyzes, selects, and contracts for space or time in the media.

Media mix The combination of media that enables the advertiser to communicate the message in the most effective manner to the largest number of potential customers at the lowest cost.

Media organizations Print, broadcast, or electronic communication sources that provide the mechanism by which communication and advertising messages are distributed to large audiences.

Media representatives Personnel hired to sell space for print and/or electronic communication sources.

Media research An investigation that attempts to determine the size of advertising outlets and their ability to attract the target audience.

Media savings A share of the money saved by one agency over another in media placement.

Median income The middle value in the income distribution with an equal number of incomes above and below the midpoint.

Medium (Plural: **media**) A particular communication category such as newspapers, magazines, television, or radio.

Mega niche brand A trademarked or brand name launched into a broad number of different merchandise categories.

Merchandise approach A sales technique that directly makes reference to the merchandise at hand.

Merchandise coordinator The person who is responsible for collecting and preparing the merchandise, fitting the merchandise to the models, and returning the merchandise to departments after the show.

Merchandise events Occurrences planned to influence the sale of goods.

Merchandise selection The designation of apparel, shoes, and accessories for presentation in a fashion show.

Merchandising Forecasting what customers want to buy, investigating where to find that merchandise, determining the price the customer is willing to pay, and making it available through outlets where the customer is willing to buy the merchandise.

Merchandising division The division of a retail store responsible for locating, buying, and reselling products.

Merchandising environment All of the products and services relating to personal and home surroundings.

Merit pay Extra pay awarded to an employee for outstanding past performance.

Message research An inquiry that is done to evaluate the effectiveness of the creative message, from copy and ingenuity to the visual impact of the advertisement.

Middle class Members of society positioned socioeconomically between the lower working class and the wealthy.

Mission statement The formalization of an organization's mission, which usually has been derived from the strategic analysis of the company's products, services, and target consumers.

Model coordinator The person who is responsible for hiring, training, and coordinating all activities that involve the models for a fashion show.

Motivations The drives within people that stimulate wants and needs.

Multiplexing See *videocompression.*

Museum exhibit A presentation of fashion items in an interpretive setting at a museum.

Music director The person in charge of music selection, permissions, and sound at a fashion show.

Musical performance A music presentation hosted by a retailer or manufacturer.

Narrative dramatization A form of radio commercial with actors portraying individuals in real-life situations.

National advertising Sponsored messages for consumer products or retail stores that are widely available throughout the United States.

National brand Trademarked or brand name products available anywhere in the United States.

National promotion   The planning and execution of promotional activities by primary resources, secondary resources, and national retailers to the ultimate consumer.

Need-driven consumers   A VALS consumer group comprised of survivors and sustainers.

News story   An article written about recent events or happenings.

News/feature story   An article that combines information from a news story with the special emphasis of a feature article.

Newspaper supplement   A targeted special issue of a newspaper.

Newsworthy   A happening of sufficient interest or importance to the public to generate a print or broadcast story.

Niche market   A small group of consumers with characteristics noticeably different from the mass market.

Noise   Outside factors that interfere with the reception of information or lead to some distortion of the message.

Nonprofit advertising   Sponsored messages used by nonprofit organizations.

Objective and task   A budgeting method in which a budget is created based on planning objectives.

Objectives   Outcomes desired by a firm within a short time period, typically 1 year or less.

One-step approach   An appeal that directly obtains an order.

On-line   Data and graphics transmitted from an interactive electronic computer network over telephone or cable lines and displayed on a user's computer-terminal screen.

On-line advertisements   Sponsored messages that appear on websites by third-party vendors.

On-line retailing   The selling of goods to the consumer via an interactive computer network.

On-package sampling   A trial size sample placed on the product or within another product.

On-premises signage   Signage used to promote goods or services offered by businesses on the property where the sign is located.

On-screen entertainment   The slide show that previews before a movie.

Open-back window   A store window without a back wall.

Operations division   The branch of a retailer responsible for sales support functions such as facilities management, security, customer service, merchandise processing, and warehousing.

Optional expenditure   A cost that is not essential to an event.

Organization chart   A flow chart showing the structure of a firm and how responsibilities and authority are delegated within the firm.

Out-bound call   A phone appeal initiated by the vendor.

Outer-driven consumers   A VALS consumer group comprised of belongers, emulators, and achievers.

Out-of-home media   Advertising messages that reach consumers away from their homes.

Page   See *homepage.*

Partial commentary   The script that is written prior to a fashion show, highlighting the pertinent details.

Participations   An arrangement in which advertisers pay for commercial time during one or more programs.

Paste-up   The format of a print advertisement, including art, copy, and logo in its presentation layout.

Payout planning   A budgeting strategy used for the introduction of new products, requiring up to 1.5 to 2 times as much promotional expenditure as an existing product.

Pay-per-view   System by which consumers are allowed to watch shows at predetermined times by the entertainment or sports producer for a specified charge.

Penetration   The total number of persons or households that can physically be exposed to a medium by the nature of that medium's geographical circulation or broadcast signal.

Percentage charges   A method of compensating an agency by adding a markup to costs for work done by outside suppliers.

Percentage of sales   A budgeting method in which the promotion budget is based upon a specific percentage of anticipated annual sales.

Performance appraisal system   A system for measuring an individual's performance that starts with goal setting.

Personal selling The direct interaction between the customer and the seller for the purpose of making a sale.

Personal shoppers Sales associates who assemble items for specific customers prior to or in place of a visit to the retail store.

Persuasion The promotional plan that induces a consumer to take action through reason not manipulation.

Photography A process for visual reproduction of a pictorial image.

Physiological profiles Techniques for measuring involuntary reactions to ads.

Plagiarism The act of using or passing off as one's own, an idea, writing, or the creative thought of another.

Planogram A detailed plan or map that serves as a guide for setting up window, exterior, and interior displays.

Point-of-purchase Merchandise presentations of products at the point where the sale is made, such as a checkout line or a cosmetic or jewelry counter.

Portfolio test An evaluation method in which participants are exposed to a series of test and control advertisements.

Positioning Using advertising to establish the specific product or service in a particular place in the mind of the consumer.

Posttest Measurement taken after an advertisement has been placed in the media.

Premium A gift or merchandise offered free or at a reduced price as an inducement to buy something else.

Press conference A gathering held by a firm seeking publicity for an event or happening for news reporters.

Press kit A collection of publicity materials delivered to the press as a single unit.

Press release The form used to pass information from the sponsoring party to a media outlet; also known as *publicity release.*

Press show A special presentation of fashions for the press.

Prestige advertising Sponsored messages created for a long-term effort to build and maintain a fashionable reputation.

Pretests Test administered prior to the implementation of an advertising campaign.

Price-off deal Price reductions offered on a package of specially marketed items.

Primary market segment The essential target group identified for communication.

Prime time Television programming broadcast between 8 P.M. and 11 P.M.

Private label brand Merchandise manufactured for a specific retailer.

Problem detection A system for finding ideas that could stimulate the formation of creative strategies.

Producer A top manager of a broadcast organization.

Product advertising Sponsored messages promoting specific goods or services.

Product demonstration An occurrence orchestrated to show how new or improved products can be used by consumers.

Product launch An occurrence planned to set in motion the promotion and sales of new products.

Product placement The positioning of a branded product versus an unbranded generic product as a prop in a movie or a television show.

Product positioning The use of the promotion mix to cause consumers to perceive a particular company's product as completely different from other brands of the same product or competing products.

Production division The division responsible for mass-producing merchandise and filling orders placed by retailers.

Production show The most elaborate and expensive type of fashion show, loaded with theatrical and dramatic elements; also called a *spectacular.*

Profit sharing A plan that offers employees a chance to purchase stock in the company and an opportunity to receive shares of any profits earned by the company.

Program rating The audience for a program; an estimate of the total number of homes reached as a percentage of the total population.

Program sponsorship Advertising time sold for a specific radio show that will include an opening mention, commercials during the show, and a closing credit.

Promotion A comprehensive term for all of the communication activities initiated by the seller to inform, persuade, and remind the consumer about products, services, and/or ideas offered for sale.

Promotion calendars A set of calendars that assist manufacturers, retailers, and advertising agencies in achieving their promotional goals.

Promotion vice president The individual in charge of a promotion division for a retailer or manufacturer.

Promotion division The division responsible for promotion mix activities, including advertising, direct marketing, public relations, sales promotion, event coordination, fashion shows, and visual merchandising.

Promotion mix The basic tools used for achieving a firm's communication and marketing goals.

Promotion objectives Common and universally accepted objectives of promotion aimed at the consumer, including informing, arousing interest, persuading, encouraging purchase, and gaining loyalty.

Promotion planning The development of strategies and methods for accomplishing all of the activities necessary to carry out promotional projects.

Promotional allowance An incentive from a manufacturer for performing certain promotional activities to support its brand or product.

Props Functional structures used to lean or place merchandise on or decorative elements used symbolically to create a mood.

Psychographic segmentation A method of profiling markets based on consumer lifestyles, including activities, interests, and opinions.

Public opinion The beliefs and feelings of the citizens.

Public relations The interrelationship between service providers and the public to project a positive image of an organization through all levels of communication.

Public relations department The department of a firm responsible for developing broad-range policies and programs to create a favorable public opinion of the firm.

Public relations director The individual in charge of a firm's public relations; also known as a *publicity director.*

Public relations firm An agency hired to manage a client's public image, the client's re-lationships with consumers, and any other services related to publicity.

Public service announcement A print or broadcast spot that runs free of charge to charitable organizations.

Publicists Individuals who may work for a public relations agency or as freelance consultants to sell a client or client's product through good publicity.

Publicity Nonpaid, unsponsored information initiated by the party seeking to tell others about a product, service, idea, or event and delivered to the public at the discretion of the media.

Publicity and advertising coordinator The person who is responsible for all promotional activities for an event.

Publicity director The individual in charge of a firm's public relations; also known as *public relations director.*

Publicity outlet Any mass communication medium used by a firm or agency to communicate with the public about a product, service, idea, or event.

Publicity photographs Pictures that accompany press releases and are prepared with the format or visual style of the publication in mind.

Publicity release The form used to pass information from the sponsoring party to a media outlet; also known as a *press release.*

Publicity writers Individuals who write press releases to seek recognition for their event or products.

Publisher The individual who coordinates all organizational and functional components of a media organization.

Pulsing A method of scheduling that combines continuity and flighting scheduling.

Purchase cycle The interval of time between acquisition and replacement of the same or a similar product in a routine manner.

Purchase-with-purchase program An incentive program in which consumers are offered a special purchase price for an additional item if they buy merchandise over a certain dollar amount.

Pure research A scientific inquiry conducted to find new knowledge about a subject.

Pyramid A triangular geometrically shaped display arrangement, in which the base is the widest space.

Quantitative mathematical models Techniques involving multiple regression analysis used to analyze the relationship of variables to the relative contributions of promotional activities to sales.

Racks Wooden or metal fixtures, ranging from simple T-stands for small quantities of merchandise to large round racks, which hold hundreds of garments.

Radio frequency The number of radio waves a transmitter produces in a second.

Rate cards Documents that list the costs for space, production (mechanical and copy) requirements, deadlines, and other publication information relating to print advertisements.

Rate of response The potential customers that can be expected to respond to an advertisement.

Reach The percentage of a target audience, homes or individuals, exposed to an advertiser's message at least once in a period of time.

Reach plan See *total audience plan*

Readability test An evaluation technique that depends upon the Flesch formula, which focuses on the human-interest appeal in the material, the length of sentences, and the familiarity of words.

Rebate A deduction from the amount to be paid or a refund of part of an amount paid upon proof-of-purchase.

Refund Money directly given back to the consumer at the point-of-purchase.

Regional advertising Sponsored messages distributed within a limited geographical region.

Regional brand Trademarked or brand name products or distributors located in one region or district in the United States.

Regular price advertising Sponsored messages offering merchandise at the normal price.

Related-items advertisements Sponsored messages featuring merchandise from a store's retailing division, which is not always purchased by the same buyer.

Reliability A characteristic used to describe a research procedure that is free from random error, ensuring a measure that is consistent and accurate.

Remote A live broadcast on location.

Remote display The physical presentation of merchandise by a retailer or manufacturer placed in such locations as hotel lobbies, exhibit halls, or public transportation terminals.

Renovations Remodeling and refurbishing the interior design and layout of a selling space.

Repetition A type of display arrangement that uses the same merchandise and/or props in a style that occurs again.

Research The investigation of a subject in order to understand it in a detailed, accurate manner.

Research division The division of a full-service agency responsible for gathering, analyzing, and interpreting information used to develop promotional activities.

Retail calendar A guide that indicates what merchandise is currently available in a retail store.

Retail product advertising Paid messages sponsored by a retailer.

Retail promotion Store promotion of products and an institutional image to ultimate consumers.

Retail show A fashion show sponsored by retailers and directed toward the retail staff and consumer market.

Return on investment A budgeting method in which advertising and promotion are considered investments that will lead to some type of long-term return.

Reward program An incentive through which frequent buyers are compensated for their purchases.

Robinson–Patman Act Legislation that authorizes the Federal Trade Commission to prevent specified practices involving discriminatory pricing and product promotion.

Rough A workup of the chosen thumbnail, rendered in actual size to represent where the art, headlines, copy, and logos for an advertisement will be placed.

Rough cut Film or video tape edited for review or testing prior to making the final commercial.

Run-of-schedule A radio advertising rate plan that allows a commercial to run at any time between 5:00 A.M. and 1:00 A.M. with no guaranteed distribution by daypart.

Salary enhancements Special bonuses, merit pay, or salary incentives used to motivate employees.

Salary plus commission An incentive used by some retailers or departments in which employees are given a base salary plus an additional percent based on sales generated.

Sales approach   The opening recognition and greeting of a customer.

Sales contests   Competitions between sales associates in a store, against other stores within a chain, or against established goals, used by retailers to increase sales.

Sales division   The division of a firm responsible for selling the line or collection of merchandise.

Sales promotion   Activities that provide extra value or incentives to the sales force, distributors, or ultimate consumer.

Sales promotion agencies   Agencies hired to develop and manage sales promotion programs, such as contests, refunds or rebates, premium or incentive offers, sweepstakes, or sampling programs.

Salesmanship   The ability to sell goods in a fair, sincere, and distinctive manner.

Sampling   A sales promotion technique in which a small quantity of a product is given to a consumer at no charge to coax a trial use.

Scenario planning   A disciplined ten-step process used by companies as a method to imagine possible futures.

Scheduling   Setting the time for advertisements or commercials to run.

Secondary market segment   An auxiliary target group identified for communication.

Self-liquidating premium   A type of premium in which the consumer must pay for the cost of the gift.

Self-regulation   Control or direction exercised voluntarily by an entity according to rules, principles, or laws without outside monitoring.

Selling points   The features and characteristics of the merchandise that make it desirable.

Senior editor   An individual who manages a news section such as business, fashion, or travel for a media organization.

Shadow box window   A small closed-back window, dimensioned on a much smaller scale than other window styles.

Share   The size of an audience for any given time period.

Short-term plan   A plan for a period of 6 months to 1 year.

Showcases   Fixtures used to enclose groupings of similar merchandise.

Silver Streakers   Consumers over age 50.

Simplified selling   Direct contact with merchandise by the consumer, involving no sales personnel.

Single price cards   Radio advertising rates showing single prices for each of the dayparts, time periods, and days of the week.

Single-item advertisement   A sponsored message for one piece of merchandise.

Site   See *homepage.*

Slogan   Repeated selling points or appeals that are primarily associated with a product, brand, or company.

Soft sell   A sales approach that presents merchandise in a discriminating, not forceful way.

Special effects   Production techniques such as moving titles, whirling logos, and dissolve images.

Special events   Planned activities intended to cause individuals or groups to gather at a specific time and place because of a shared interest.

Special events calendar   A guide that identifies guest appearances, product demonstrations, vendor promotions, and other special activities coordinated by the promotion department or fashion office.

Special events coordinator   The individual responsible for directing all special events.

Special price advertising   A sponsored message promoting merchandise that is offered as a special purchase to build store traffic and sales.

Spiffs   Sales incentives that may be given to employees in the form of extra money, additional discounts, or merchandise whenever sales of specific items are made; also called *push money* (PMs).

Split-run advertising   Paid messages that are run in one or more geographical editions of a magazine, depending upon the advertiser's needs.

S-shaped curve model   A model in the shape of an S, demonstrating that initial outlays of advertising will have little or no impact on consumers in the early stages of sales.

Stage manager The person who oversees the use of the stage and runway, organizes equipment, and supervises people, providing behind-the-scenes services, such as sound and lighting technicians, at a fashion show.

Standard advertising unit A measurement used to sell advertising space.

Step A display arrangement that is a series of elevations similar to a stair step.

Store opening A celebration that introduces customers to a new merchant.

Storyboard A graphic presentation, part advertising layout and part script, that describes television commercials of any length.

Straight front window A store window that is parallel to a road or sidewalk.

Strategic alliance A partnership between a manufacturer and a retailer working in a particular supply chain that leverages the core competencies of each firm.

Strategic analysis A statement of the historical events leading to the current condition of an organization.

Strategic market modeling A method of generating and testing alternative business strategies, including choice modeling, cluster analysis, and needs segmentation.

Strategic planning The process of determining what one wants to accomplish, how to accomplish it, and how to implement it that forecasts more than 2 years into the future as a long-term plan.

Subheadline A secondary statement used to further clarify the primary headline.

Suggestion selling Offering related merchandise, such as accessories, larger quantities of the same merchandise in other colors or styles, promotional merchandise, or advertised merchandise.

Suppliers Personnel that assist clients and advertising departments or agencies in preparing promotional materials.

Sweepstakes Promotions in which winners are determined solely by chance and a proof-of-purchase is not required as a condition of entry.

Tabloid Newspaper format, approximately half the size of a broadsheet format, with five columns.

Target ratings points (TRPs) The number of people in the primary target audience the media buy will reach.

Tea-room modeling A specific type of informal modeling that takes place in a restaurant on a regularly scheduled day.

Test ads Advertisements pretested or measured for their potential effectiveness.

Test market A geographical area that has been selected as representative of the target market.

Textile Fiber Products Identification Act Legislation (1960) that requires that a tag or label with certain information relating to the fiber content of textile products be attached to the item at the time of sale and delivery to the consumer.

Theme A reoccurring idea that is seen in color, silhouette, fabric, and other design components.

Theme advertisements Advertisements coordinating groups of products from individual departments, divisions, or an entire store.

Thumbnail A preliminary unpolished design for an advertisement, produced in a small size so several versions can be tried.

Top-down approaches Budgeting methods in which the highest management level of the firm establishes the amount for the entire retail corporation or manufacturing concern.

Total audience plan A radio advertising package rate given for a combination of time periods.

Trade allowance A discount offered to a retailer as an incentive to stock and display merchandise from a specific vendor.

Trade calendar The monthly guide to events occurring at the manufacturing level.

Trade customer Organizational markets composed of governments, industrial firms, or resellers representing the intermediate stage between manufacturers of raw materials and the ultimate consumer.

Trade dress The features of a product that comprise its overall look or image and include the product's packaging, labeling, display, product design, and configuration.

Trade promotion Activities promoting products from one business to another business.

Trademark A word or symbol that indicates a source of origin and can be protected based on actual use.

Trademark counterfeiting The development and sale of imitative products bearing deliberately copied trademarks.

Trade-oriented sales promotion A sales promotion aimed at manufacturers, wholesalers, distributors, and retailers.

Trading area The city, county, state, or region a company services.

Trading up The process of encouraging the purchase of higher-priced merchandise during merchandise presentation.

Traffic department The department of a full-service agency that organizes all phases of production.

Traffic time See *drive time*.

Trend The general direction in which something is moving.

Trend shop A merchandising area set apart by special flooring, walls, or ceiling treatments; also called a *highlight shop*.

Trial purchase A technique by which consumers are encouraged to test a trial-size portion of a new product.

Trunk show A fashion presentation that features garments from a single manufacturer or designer, presented as an informal fashion show in retail stores.

T-wall A type of perimeter wall used to separate one department from another in a retail store.

Two-step approach An appeal that first identifies and/or qualifies potential buyers and then follows up with a second request to generate a response.

Typeface The style of type.

Typography The selection and setting of a typeface.

Undifferentiated marketing A marketing strategy that offers the same promotional mix to the entire population without regard to market segments.

Unique sellixng proposition The most important reason for a consumer to prefer a particular product to all others.

Unit sales incentive A base fee and a bonus for unit sales above the goal or target sales.

Validity A characteristic used to describe a testing procedure that is free from both random and systematic error.

Values and Lifestyle System (VALS) A psychographic segmentation program consisting of four consumer groups: need-driven, outer-driven, inner-drive, and integrated.

Vendor advertisements Sponsored messages featuring merchandise from one single manufacturer or designer.

Vendor week An occurrence that features a merchandise category or brand; also known as a *category week*.

Video news release A publicity piece created by a publicist and delivered to television stations as a news story.

Video production show A presentation that is specifically produced to be videotaped and distributed to sales representatives or retailers.

Videocompression The combination of radio and TV signals to allow more than one channel to beam on a frequency width.

Visual merchandising The physical presentation of products in a nonpersonal approach to promote the image of a firm and the sale of merchandise to the consumer.

Visual merchandising calendar A guide developed to organize visual presentations for a business.

Visual merchandising department The department of a retail organization responsible for the visual presentation of the store image and its merchandise.

Volume advertisements Sponsored messages created for best-selling products.

Windowless window A no-window concept used as the entrance to mall stores.

Wool Products Labeling Act Legislation (1939) that governs the labeling of wool and wool-blended textiles.

Word-of-mouth Direct or face-to-face communication.

Zigzag A display arrangement based on a reversing step design.

Zone editions Newspapers that provide news and advertising focused to an area within a city.

INDEX